W9-CFB-983

10/12/2017

The Environmental Debate

Third Edition

A Documentary History with Timeline,

Glossary, and Appendices

Edited by

Peninah Neimark

and

Peter Rhoades Mott

GREY HOUSE PUBLISHING

PUBLISHER: Leslie Mackenzie
EDITORIAL DIRECTOR: Laura Mars
PRODUCTION MANAGER: Kristen Hayes

MARKETING DIRECTOR: Jessica Moody

Grey House Publishing, Inc.
4919 Route 22
Amenia, NY 12501
518.789.8700
FAX 845.373.6390
www.greyhouse.com
e-mail: books@greyhouse.com

Publisher's Cataloging-In-Publication Data
(Prepared by The Donohue Group, Inc.)

Names: Neimark, Peninah, 1938- editor.
Title: The environmental debate : a documentary history with timeline, glossary, and appendices / edited by Peninah Neimark.
Description: Third edition. | Amenia, NY : Grey House Publishing, [2017] | First edition published: Westport, Conn. : Greenwood Press, 1999. | Includes bibliographical references and index.
Identifiers: ISBN 978-1-68217-550-7 (hardcover)
Subjects: LCSH: Environmentalism--United States--History--Sources. | Environmental protection--United States--History--Sources.
Classification: LCC GE197 .E7 2017 | DDC 363.7/05/0973--dc23

Contents

Foreword

Since the last edition of *The Environmental Debate* was published in 2011, controversy over environmental issues has intensified. Air and water pollution, waste disposal, alternative energy sources, and climate change continue to be debated with urgency. This new edition brings current a wide range of environmental issues, from biotechnology to the environmental impact of the American diet. Most importantly, it addresses those topics that are causing the most controversy – global warming, clean power, and the U.S. withdrawal in 2017 from the Paris Accords on climate change.

Primary Documents

This work contains 185 primary documents arranged chronologically from Biblical times to the present, including 17 new documents, many reprinted in their entirety. All documents include an informative introduction that includes biographical information about the document's author, the evolution of thinking regarding the specific environmental issue being discussed, and relevant historical context crucial to the understanding of the specific environmental challenges the document focuses on. The text is extensively cross-referenced to help compare and contrast opinions and goals from one time to another. Each document includes complete citations, making additional research easy and quick.

Documents include diaries of explorers, letters from politicians, relevant fictional excerpts, speeches of scientists, environmentalists and politicians, court cases, and laws passed, and are arranged in the following eight parts, each with a lengthy introduction that includes the historical context crucial for understanding the specific environmental challenges of the time:

1. Foundations of American Environmental Thought and Action
2. Politicians, Naturalists, and Artists in the New Nations, 1776–1839
3. The Origins of Environmental Activism, 1840–1889
4. The Roots of the Conservation Movement, 1890–1919
5. Rethinking our Relationship to Nature, 1920–1959
6. The Heyday of the Environmental Movement, 1960–1979

7.   Confronting Economic and Social Realities, 1980–1999
8.   Politicizing the Environmental Debate, 2000–2017

Special Features

In addition to 185 carefully selected primary documents, *The Environmental Debate* includes the following useful sections:

- **General Introduction** – a clear, detailed view of the often-complicated environmental issues that are the subject of the primary documents. In 11 pages, it addresses the following major categories:
  - Population
  - Land Use and Property Rights
  - Water Availability and Quality
  - Energy
  - Air Quality, Climate Change, and Atmospherics Issues
  - Waste Production and Disposal
  - Toxic Chemicals and Radioactive Waste and Their Disposal
  - Forests, Wilderness, and Wildlife
  - Fisheries, Oceans, and Aquatic Life
  - The Loss of Biodiversity
  - The Complexity of Environmental Issues

- **Appendix I – Significant Dates in American Environmental History**
  This timeline Includes discoveries, inventions, court cases, legislation, and world events. It starts with the 1626 ordinance passed by the Plymouth Colony regulating the cutting and selling of timber, and ends with the 2017 withdrawal of the United States, by President Trump, from the Paris Accords on climate change.

- **Appendix II – Major International Environmental Organizations**
  This section includes detailed listings of the most significant organizations around the world that are involved with environmental decisions, from Clean Water Network to the World Wildlife Fund. It has been updated for this edition to include worldwide groups.

- **Glossary**
  The Glossary includes 90 terms – scientific, legal, and political. It includes terms that are frequently heard, like Acid Rain and Fracking, as well as those not as common, like Biota and Environmental Justice.

- **Further Reading**
  This list of more than 100 books and articles is designed to deepen the reader's understanding of any given aspect of the environmental debate.

- **Notes, Copyright Acknowledgments, Index**
  These final sections provide sources, citations, and helpful ways for readers to find the exact information they are looking for.

Note: Peninah Neimark and Peter Mott together developed the first two editions of *The Environmental Debate*. Grey House Publishing is grateful to both editors for their combined expertise. Presently retired for many years, Peter Mott did not contribute to this third edition, and we thank Peninnah Neimark for continuing this important work.

Preface

The Environmental Debate is a documentary history of how Americans have thought about environmental issues from the colonial period to the present. The selections, excerpted from legal and congressional documents, letters, newspaper and magazine articles, speeches, and books, offer diverse perspectives on the issues. Among the authors are naturalists, conservationists ranging from forest managers to game hunters, biological as well as physical scientists, philosophers and theologians, lawyers, politicians and grass-roots activists, farmers and industrialists, journalists, historians, sociologists, economists, artists and architects, and poets and novelists.

In choosing material for inclusion, I have sought writings and official documents that indicate very early interest in particular environmental issues or indicate remarkable foresight into problems that would later become serious environmental concerns, writings that had a major impact on the development of environmental concern and policy, and writings that capture the tenor of thinking of a particular period. I have also tried to show the evolution of both popular attitudes and government policy concerning the environment and the use of natural resources.

The documents examine a large number of environmental issues including air and water pollution, food production, waste disposal, endangered species, land development, resource extraction and use, open space, toxic chemicals, wetlands, wilderness and wildlife, genetic engineering, and climate change. In the process, they call attention to the essentials of life—breathable air, clean water, adequate food—together with the fundamentals of human civilization—agriculture, shelter construction, energy, and transportation. They give evidence of the continuing interaction between environmental factors and the course of development in the United States, and they detail the growth of concern about the connections among increasing numbers of people, expanding industrialization, technological change, urbanization, pollution, and resource depletion. Although only a few of the documents deal directly with technological development, several of the more recent documents underline the need to recognize limits to our ability to control nature.

Selections concerned with conservation focus on land and resource use and development and record an overall change from the feeling that America's resources were virtually unlimited to an understanding that particular resources are finite and that how we use one resource can affect the availability of other resources. The documents offer an overview of how Americans have thought about their natural resources and how they have dealt with conflicts stemming from the need to use these resources while ensuring their availability for future generations, as well as conflicts stemming from the desire to exploit resources for economic gain while ignoring competing interests. Selections relating to pollution focus on air and water quality, as well as toxic chemicals and waste disposal and illustrate increasing concern about the effects of pollution. They look at rising demand for people and the government to take action as well as opposition to the costs of regulation in terms of both their economic effect and their limitation on personal freedom. Selections centered on the human-nature relationship deal with the issues of preserving open space and wilderness areas and protecting species from extinction. They discuss the need of an increasingly urbanized population for a connection with nature and the effects of population growth and technological innovation on the natural world.

The documents chronicle how environmental interests have evolved alongside changing social and economic conditions and increasing technological development, and they recount the evolution of environmental movements and environmental organizations. In addition, they depict how shifting political attitudes can result in major reversals of environmental policy. As the selections indicate, while environmental action generally stems from concern about a particular local issue—pollution in Plymouth Colony harbor, smog in Los Angeles, the decline in the osprey population on Long Island, New York—since the nineteenth century, activists have recognized that local remedies frequently are inadequate, and that they must generate state, federal, or even international change to obtain satisfactory solutions. Because environmental issues are complex and intertwined with economic and social issues, resolving them often requires the coming together of groups and governmental entities that have separate and sometimes competing agendas.

This book attempts to show how some of the most important of these clashes have been resolved. It also indicates some areas in which there will be increasing conflict between various communities and between humans and the rest of the natural world in the anthropocene era—the current age when humans are the dominant factor affecting the environment.

The magnitude of the impact of our environmental choices on national security, economic well-being, public health, and social harmony and justice is greatly underappreciated. However, before we can find acceptable solutions to the country's and the planet's complex, much-debated environmental problems, it is necessary for people to become more willing to come together with those whose core interests differ from their own. The current polarized political atmosphere in the United States poses a threat to our ability to examine environmental issues in a rational way and to seek sensible, workable resolutions.

Introduction

The advancement of technological development and scientific knowledge that began 500-600 years ago not only laid the foundation for the great voyages of discovery and the Industrial Revolution, but also enabled the human population to multiply at an accelerating rate and set humans on a path to becoming a dominant element of nature. By the early 1800s, Thomas Malthus and others were predicting that eventually there would be insufficient land to support this massive population growth. Such a dire outcome was staved off in the nineteenth century by among other things, the opening of new lands, including the American West, and in the twentieth century by the Green Revolution. Now, however, environmentalists and scientists are warning that the accelerating pace of recent chemical, biological, and physical transformations of the earth's environment may be triggering uncontrollable and irreversible alterations of our planet, and that these changes will have a profound, unpredictable impact on all forms of life on Earth.[1]

Although the population growth and technological innovations of the past few centuries created some previously unknown environmental problems, many current problems are merely exacerbations of the kinds that have arisen whenever significant numbers of humans have settled in a region for long periods of time. Concern about resource depletion, See notes on page 413 pollution, environmental degradation, and population growth has existed for centuries. Problems stemming from too little water or land to support dense population centers may have contributed to the collapse of various ancient civilizations, including the Anasazi and the Maya. Nearly 2300 years ago Plato wrote about the degradation of land in Greece.[2] In colonial America the damming of waterways to supply energy for mills had to be regulated because it interfered with the spawning of fish, and the dumping of waste into Atlantic coast harbors caused pollution that required control. By the mid-nineteenth century, air pollution, inadequate clean water, and urban sanitation were acknowledged problems in the United States as well as in Europe, and American voices were being raised in opposition to the wanton destruction of wildlife and calling for the preservation of forests and scenic land. It was not until the 1890s, though, when the U.S. western frontier had disappeared and there was no longer open land for Americans to expand into, that conservation became a major issue. However, only after the dropping of the atomic bomb in 1945 and the consequent realization by people that humans had the ability to make the earth uninhabitable did the concept of environmentalism begin to take hold. In the second half of the twentieth century, as the human impact on the Earth's environment became increasingly apparent, the demand for environmental action to sustain life on our planet intensified.

Finding acceptable solutions to environmental issues, though, has rarely been simple because people expect the solutions to satisfy three fundamental human needs and desires: material and economic well-being (including adequate food, clothing, and shelter), physical well-being (including health and safety), and access to open space and other aspects of nature that enhance spiritual well-being. Proposed solutions invariably arouse competing economic, social, and political interests and may bring to the fore conflicting ethical and religious values. In recent decades as some of the most widely opposed types of pollution have been brought under control, the forces demanding greater, unregulated access to resources have been gaining support.

POPULATION

Environmental problems form a web, with the issue of population growth at its center. The larger the number of people, the more land that will be occupied, the more energy that will be used, the more resources that will be consumed, and the more waste that will be produced. How many people there are in a finite area, how they live, and how they use resources not only affect what happens to all living things in that particular area, but may also impinge on living things, including people, elsewhere on the planet.

The rate of human population growth often surprises those unfamiliar with population dynamics. It took from the beginning of human existence until about 1850 for the world population to reach 1 billion people,3 and only another 80 years for it to reach 2 billion. Just 30 years later the earth contained 3 billion people. Between 1960 and 1975 the world's population grew by another billion to 4 billion. Since 1975 it has been increasing by more than 83 million people annually, with the world population reaching 5 billion in 1987, 6 billion in 1999, 7 billion in 2011, and 7.5 billion in 2017. It is projected that by 2050 the world's population will be more than 9.5 billion and by 2100 more than 11 billion.4 While the rate of population growth has slowed in recent years, the actual numerical increase in population is still staggering. The birth rate in several developed countries in Europe, Asia, and North America has stabilized or is even declining, but in some of these countries a major cause of population increase is immigration from developing and underdeveloped countries, where more than 90 percent of the world's population growth is occurring, as well as refugees from war-torn nations. The annual rate of population increase in the United States, which is the highest in the industrial world, has decreased from about 1.10 percent between 1990 and 1995 to about 0.74 percent in 2016.5

Food supply, habitat suitability, disease, and predation limit how many individual members of a particular species can live in a given ecosystem. Humans, however, have developed technologies to manipulate and control these factors, and as their technological abilities have advanced, their population has been able to increase beyond the natural carrying capacity of the local environment. Although there still are places where people die of starvation, at present there actually is sufficient food in the world to feed everyone; today, people starve only because political, social, or economic factors prevent them from obtaining food. While some places on our planet are unsuitable for human habitation, humans can now live almost anywhere on Earth provided they employ sufficient, and sometimes very expensive, technology. As we produce food more efficiently, reduce death from disease and starvation, and improve nutrition and health care, we make it possible for more babies to be born, for more children to grow up, and for the elderly to live longer. Obviously, human population cannot continue to increase indefinitely, and it is predicted that sometime in the future, probably within the next 200 years, economic, political, socio-cultural, and environmental factors will lead to a sufficient decline in the birth rate to bring about a leveling off of the world's population.

LAND USE AND PROPERTY RIGHTS

Housing, agriculture, grazing, forestry, mining, industry, transportation, and recreation all take up land, and the larger the population, the more land each of these purposes usually requires, although modern technology has made it possible to grow more food, feed more livestock, and build higher-rise housing per acre than in previous centuries. Since land that is used for one purpose generally cannot be used simultaneously for another purpose, population growth in a region or community tends to spur disputes between individuals or groups who want to use the available land for different purposes.

The past several decades have witnessed increasing disagreement between those who want to develop land (including those who want to "reclaim" wet or arid land) or extract its mineral and energy riches and those who want to limit development, control urban sprawl, preserve open space and wilderness, and prevent the removal of land from agricultural use. Conflicts have also arisen when runoff from agricultural land has despoiled rivers and lakes and when the reclaiming of wetlands for farming or home sites has interfered with the land's normal ability to absorb waste and water.

As the population increases, there is more need to regulate land use so that the activities of one property owner do not have a negative impact on the property of others. Land use regulation, though, raises objections from libertarians who believe they should be free to use their private property in whatever way they like.

Land use planning and zoning not only affect the allocation of land for farms, homes, and commercial and industrial establishments and impinge on the kind of accommodation that is made for cars, bicycles, and pedestrians, but also have wide-ranging ramifications for the nation. For example, by permitting large swaths of land to be used for roads and highways, public policy has encouraged urban sprawl and led to dependence on automobiles. Urban sprawl and the use of cars, in turn, have led to public spending on new automobile friendly infrastructure and the decline of public transportation.

As humans use land, less of it is available to the organisms that have evolved to inhabit it. In some cases, land can be shared, but only rarely is human intrusion not followed by major disruption, displacement, or elimination of an area's native organisms. Human use frequently also brings with it, wittingly or unwittingly, a host of exotic species, which may prosper in their new habitat and drive out native species.

Because so many social, economic, and environmental issues are intertwined with land-use issues, efforts to find creative solutions to major land-use conflicts have stimulated people to reexamine some of their fundamental ideas about both property rights and the relationship between humans and the natural world.

WATER AVAILABILITY AND QUALITY

People, industry, and agriculture all require an adequate supply of water that is sufficiently clean and salt free. However, since water resources—like land resources—are finite, expanding populations place ever greater stress on the available water both because of the rising need for water and the increased diversion and contamination of the water that results from human activity.

Conflict over water use has long existed in this country, and it will undoubtedly increase as the population grows and cities and towns continue to expand. In arid parts of the country, intense conflicts have already arisen over who should have access to the limited water supply: Should the bulk of it go to individuals, to agriculture, or to industry? Within the state of California there is ongoing competition for water resources between agricultural regions that require water for irrigation and cities that need water for a growing populace. In the Southwest, California and Arizona have been battling for many decades over allocation of Colorado River water, which is also used by five other states. When water in a river is diverted upstream, protests can be heard if communities downstream feel that insufficient water is being left to provide for their water requirements and to protect river fisheries.

Cities and states have placed stringent limits on the property-use rights of landowners in watershed areas where their reservoirs are located. Partly because these restrictions on property use may have a negative impact on land values, there is often conflict between watershed communities and the distant towns and cities that obtain their water supply from those watersheds.

As housing development expands, more sewage tends to be washed into streams and rivers and to be carried by them into reservoirs and lakes. Runoff of fertilizer, pesticides, animal wastes, and petroleum products from farms, yards, and the increasing number of roads and other paved areas are additional sources of contamination.

Another threat to water supplies is the drilling technique known as hydraulic fracturing (fracking), which is used to obtain gas and oil from shale. New York City worries that drilling for gas near its upstate reservoirs will ruin its excellent drinking water, and in 2015 New York State imposed a ban on fracking. In rural Pennsylvania people with gas drilling sites near or on their property are concerned about the contamination of private wells. Elsewhere, the possibility of leakage from oil pipelines that run under major sources of drinking water, such as the Missouri River, is a cause of contention between the local population and the company that needs to transport its oil.

The ever mounting use of appliances that employ water—toilets, bathtubs, showers, washing machines, dishwashers, and waste disposal units—has led to a continually increasing per capita usage of water in the United States, and in arid regions home-building has created escalating demand for very limited water supplies. Eventually, this nation of extravagant water users may have to impose limits on access to this undervalued and misunderstood resource.

ENERGY

Americans account for only about 4.4 percent of the world's population, yet we use approximately 18 percent of the energy consumed in the world each year.[6] Per capita use of energy has remained fairly steady in the United States since the 1970s. Today the United States is the world's second largest consumer of energy after China, whose energy use surpassed that of the United States just a few years ago.

Most of the energy employed for transportation in the United States, as well as a portion of that used for heating and generating electricity, comes from oil. By the end of the twentieth century, much of the easily extractable oil in the lower forty-eight states had been depleted, the country became increasingly dependent on imported oil as well as oil located in hard-to-access sites (e.g., in deep-water offshore locations in the Gulf of Mexico) or in formerly undisturbed wilderness areas (e.g., in Alaska). In recent years, though, new technology has made it possible to mine shale deposits for oil and gas, and the United States has greatly reduced oil importation. However, since much of the oil used in this country is still transported great distances in huge tanker ships, in rail cars, or by lengthy pipelines, there is a constant risk of environmental damage from shipping or train accidents or pipeline leaks.

In the 1950s and 1960s, nuclear power seemed to offer great hope as a source of cheap, clean energy. Aside from large volumes of hot water released into adjacent rivers or other bodies of water, there appeared to be little negative environmental impact. But as the dangers of nuclear accidents became more apparent and as the risks of storing large quantities of radioactive wastes over long periods of time became increasingly evident, atomic power slowly lost its luster. Consequently, no completely new nuclear power plants have been constructed in the United States since the 1970s, although one new reactor came online at Watts Bar in eastern Tennessee in 1996 and another in 2016. Currently four new reactors are under construction, and these are all additions to existing plants. While nuclear energy is a major source of power in many countries, it provides only about 20 percent of U.S. electricity.7

Both water and wind have been used as power sources in America since the colonial period. Today, about 6 percent of the electricity consumed in the United States comes from major hydroelectric facilities such as Glen Canyon Dam and those operated by the Tennessee Valley Authority. However, because many people are beginning to think that the environmental damage caused by such large dams outweighs the benefits, few new large hydroelectric plants are apt to be built and some older ones in need of costly repairs may eventually be dismantled. Since the 1990s, serious considerations has been given to removing dams from small rivers across the country, and dozens of dams from Maine to Washington State have already been breached.

Energy from the sun and wind, which does not create byproduct pollutants (save in the manufacture of the apparatus for collecting it), is now a fundamental part of the U.S. energy mix. The number of large wind farms is growing rapidly, with wind currently producing nearly 5 percent of the country's electricity, but proposals for these projects have run into opposition from homeowners whose views would be interrupted as well as from environmentalists who are concerned about the danger that wind turbines pose for birds and bats. Although at present less than 1 percent of the electricity consumed in this country comes from solar collectors, solar energy production is likely to grow, even without support from the federal government. Other renewable, non-polluting energy sources that show great potential are geothermal and wave energy, but currently they account for merely a fraction of a percent of America's energy.

Biomass—the substance of plants and various kinds of organic waste—is another small but growing source of energy. However, the conversion of corn, soybeans, and sugarcane into biofuels such as ethanol and biodiesel has numerous opponents. One of the major objections to the U.S. subsidies for corn-based ethanol is that by encouraging farmers to replace the production of a food staple for humans and animals with the production of a fuel source for cars and other vehicles, we are inflating food prices around the world. Other opponents claim that the corn to ethanol conversion process itself requires too much energy.

Although environmentalists have called for better public transportation and vehicles that are more fuel efficient, urban sprawl mandates dependence on the automobile. Over the years, cars have become more fuel efficient, but the ever-increasing number of cars on America's, and the world's, roads counteracts the gains in air pollution control achieved through improved fuel efficiency. Furthermore, although there has been talk about electric cars for a long time and successful hybrids have been on the market for years, a truly satisfactory alternative to the gasoline engine has yet to be developed.

AIR QUALITY, CLIMATE CHANGE, AND ATMOSPHERIC ISSUES

When fossil fuels are burned to produce energy, carbon dioxide, sulfur oxides, nitrogen oxides, and other combustion products are released into the atmosphere. The released nitrogen and sulfur oxides react with atmospheric ozone and water to form acids, and the presence of these acids in the air results in acid rain, which causes widespread damage to forests and life in lakes and rivers. Activated by sunlight, the nitrogen oxides also react photochemically with the hydrocarbons produced by vehicle emissions, power plants and factories, and fumes from volatile solvents to cause smog, which is responsible for impaired respiratory function, especially in the very young and the very old. Early efforts, beginning in the 1970s, to control the emission of polluting gases into the atmosphere were relatively successful, and the smog problem in places like Los Angeles was reduced significantly but by no means eliminated.

According to the National Climate Data Center, there is unequivocal scientific evidence that the concentration in the atmosphere of greenhouse gases, primarily carbon dioxide (CO_2), has been increasing as a result of the burning of coal, oil, and gas. Prior to the beginning of the Industrial Revolution, CO_2 levels were about 280 parts per million by volume (ppmv); current levels are about 400 ppmv and increasing at a rate of 2.0 ppmv per year since 2006. The global concentration of CO_2 in our atmosphere CO_2today far exceeds the natural range over the last 650,000 years of 180 to 300 ppmv,8 and climatologists would like to see CO_2 levels reduced to 360 ppmv before mid-century.

Since the late-nineteenth century, there has also been an increase in global surface temperatures of about 0.74°C (plus or minus 0.18°C). This warming trend has not been uniform across the planet however. In fact, some parts of the southeastern United States and some areas of the North Atlantic have cooled slightly during the last century. It should also be noted, though, that 15 of the 16 warmest years on record have all been in the twenty-first century.

Despite the data, some people believe the warming trend that has been recorded in recent decades is merely the result of normal temperature variations. No matter what the cause, the global rise in temperature and the accompanying change in the distribution of rain will have a major effect on agriculture and the way we live. As the amount of CO_2 in the atmosphere increases and the earth warms, glaciers are melting, sea levels are rising, and the oceans are acidifying. Although many of us find it hard to worry about tides a few more inches above sea level, people in coastal communities recognize the devastating potential of this seemingly minor change. Indeed, island nations as well as countries with large areas of lowlands, such as Bangladesh, stand to lose substantial portions of their national territory, a loss that will destroy natural resources and displace human populations. Extreme climate events such as abnormally severe storms, heat waves, droughts, and flooding are having devastating effects around the world, from Louisiana to Pakistan. Environmentalists think that it would be unconscionable for nations to fail to control carbon emissions even if the causal relation between CO_2 emissions and global warming were unproved and only a strong probability.

While some industrialists have concluded that the threat of global warming is real and have responded with efforts to reduce their carbon footprints, others consider it is foolish to expend vast sums of money and possibly undermine economic prosperity in order to address the possibility of environmental danger. In the international arena, more and more countries are questioning the right of other countries to pursue policies that could have a deleterious effect on the environment of their nation.

WASTE PRODUCTION AND DISPOSAL

As the nation's population has grown, and as cities and towns have expanded, the need to find safe and adequate ways to dispose of everincreasing amounts of both organic and inorganic wastes has become an increasingly formidable challenge.

Since organic wastes are routinely digested by microorganisms both on land and in water, waste from the life processes of various organisms, including humans, are generally recycled in the environment without event. However, because bodily wastes have an environmental impact in addition to being potential sources of disease, when these wastes accumulate and cannot be digested fairly rapidly their disposal poses a problem. In waste-contaminated waterways the oxygen levels become depleted as a result of bacterial activity, often to the point where fish and other aquatic organisms suffocate and die.

Many cities still have sewer lines that merge household wastes with rainwater runoff from streets and buildings. Although the systems may be able to manage household wastes, they frequently are overwhelmed by the combination of household sewage and runoff from a heavy rainfall. The result is that whenever there is a storm these systems overflow and untreated sewage flows into waterways, some of which are used for drinking water or are home to shellfish and other aquatic life. To resolve this problem, cities are faced with the prospect of immense capital expenditures to build structures for temporarily storing millions of gallons of runoff mixed with sewage until it can be treated. People have begun to experiment with replacing asphalt roofs with "green" roofs and planting storm-water catchments that make use of rainwater and thereby reduce runoff.

Today, waste management to reduce or eliminate the harmful effects of sewage release in urban and suburban areas is required by federal law. There are, however, many rural and semi-rural parts of the country with industrial-level animal farms that have hundreds or even thousands of animals and where there are housing developments that use simple, unmonitored septic systems and where no or inadequate effort is made to prevent untreated sewage from seeping into groundwater or flowing into nearby waterways.

As the population increases, more garbage is produced and more disposal sites are needed. Since no one wants a dump or incinerator situated in his or her backyard, a disproportionate number of these waste disposal sites have ended up close by the backyards of the people with the least political clout—usually the poor and members of racial and ethnic minorities. Such obvious inequity makes social justice a factor that must be given consideration when seeking solutions to environmental problems.

In the 1990s, many towns and cities began to reduce the amount of waste moving onto disposal sites by recycling bottles, metal, paper and some plastics, and in recent years there have been increasing attempts to recover valuable materials from electronic waste. Although some waste can be recycled, the economic value of recycling fluctuates with commodity prices. Furthermore, the recovery process itself uses energy and not all material can be reused. More and more communities are imposing recycling regulations, encouraging residents to compost landscaping and kitchen waste, and calling for reduced packaging. The ultimate goal is to limit landfill disposal to less than 25 percent of household waste.

TOXIC CHEMICALS AND RADIOACTIVE WASTE AND THEIR DISPOSAL

The world has always contained toxic substances, and toxic elements such as lead, cadmium and mercury as well as poisonous plants and animals have always had the potential to harm living things. However, today, many industrial processes and products concentrate highly toxic materials, and their disposal has resulted in brownfields filled with huge quantities of toxic waste.

Until the imposition of controls in the latter part of the twentieth century, the lead in leaded gasoline and house paint and mercury from industrial processes were at concentrations high enough to induce a variety of illnesses in humans. Numerous toxicity problems have also arisen from the synthesis of chemicals that do not occur in nature. There are tens of thousands of synthetic chemicals and products currently on the market for which no thorough examination of toxicity has ever been undertaken. Some synthetic chemical compounds, unlike most natural substances are not readily biodegradable (i.e., they deteriorate very slowly). Consequently, several man-made toxic substances such as DDT, an insecticide, and polychlorinated biphenyls (PCBs), chemical compounds used to moderate heat in electric transformers, have accumulated in the environment, causing serious problems for wildlife and humans.

In the process of producing and using the materials, machines, and foods that we employ in our everyday lives, industrial plants and individuals generate wastes, ranging from gases (including carbon dioxide, nitrogen dioxide, and sulfur dioxide) to various solid wastes (including such toxic elements as lead, cadmium, and mercury). These wastes may be carried into the water we drink, the air we breathe, or absorbed by the animals and plants we eat. Some of these wastes are dangerous pollutants that can have harmful effects at a variety of levels, from the cellular to an ecosystem. Although the release of pollutants may be the result of ignorance (such as the lead released from leaded gasoline, which was widely used until the 1970s) or accidents (such as chemical and oil spills), some is the result of blatant illegal dumping of known toxic substances. Because of the expense and effort of proper disposal of toxic wastes, toxic substances often have been deliberately disposed of illegally, and the resultant toxic waste sites can be found across the United States. The cost of dealing with contamination from improperly discarded toxic and radioactive substances is enormous compared to that for proper disposal.

Efforts to remedy pollution resulting from what are designated as "hazardous waste sites" have not been entirely successful despite the passage of laws and huge expenditures of funds. Conflicts have arisen between those who claim that a particular hazardous waste site is the cause of a high incidence of an illness in an area and those who dispute the claim and view the costly cleanup as unnecessary.

The difficulty of disposing of radioactive waste is at the core of the nation's reluctance to expand the use of nuclear energy. While the federal government claims that the much studied and discussed Yucca Mountain Repository in Nevada will be a safe site for storing radioactive waste for a million years, many questions remain unanswered.

FORESTS, WILDERNESS, AND WILDLIFE

When the first European settlers arrived, most of North America was covered with trees. A vast deciduous forest stretched from the East Coast to the Mississippi, and another massive forest extended west from the Rocky Mountains to the Pacific Coast. Only the arid Southwest, the desert lands, and the Great Plains were without sizable forests. Although Native Americans had made changes to original growth forests by burning and cutting the forest in some places and clearing the understory in others, much of the original forest was still intact when the colonists arrived. Today, most of the original forest is gone. As the population of the United States increased, large segments of the original forests were cut down to make way for farms and to provide wood for fuel and construction material.

In much of the eastern part of the United States, forests are returning for several reasons. Wood is no longer used for fuel on a substantial level; wood for construction is increasingly coming from managed forests; and the number of farms and farmers has decreased, allowing farmland to lie fallow and return to forest. Although forested lands have increased in recent years, the nature of the forest has changed. Where once there were thousands of acres of uninterrupted forest, now we see acres of forest segmented by roads and fields.

In some sections of the country, timber companies harvest trees from naturally growing forests on lands owned primarily by the federal government. These corporations have tended to harvest the lumber in the most efficient and cheapest way—by cutting all the trees in a given area. In other parts of the country, growing trees to obtain wood for construction or for the production of paper has become much like farming corn or wheat. Landowners, who are often large corporations, plant thousands of acres with a single tree species intended to be harvested all at once. This type of tree farming and harvesting, known as monoculture and clear-cutting, generates a forest that lacks the diversity of forests native to the area.

The complete removal of the forest during clear-cutting not only leaves those few animals that were able to adapt to the monoculture without shelter, but it also leaves the former forest floor vulnerable to erosion and degradation. If all the trees are removed from an area, the land is exposed to direct sunlight, and the heat from the sun is absorbed by the soil. When rain falls on the exposed land, the rainwater is heated by the warm soil and, because there are no tree roots to hold the soil, the warm runoff from the rain carries the topsoil into adjacent rivers and streams. Where forest runoff once provided clear, cool water for the river or stream, the clear-cut area now supplies warm water with suspended soil particles. Since warm water holds less oxygen than cool water, the amount of oxygen available to the aquatic creatures in the stream is reduced and, as a result, much of the aquatic life of that region will die.

Opposition to corporate clear-cutting of federal forests has come from people who are concerned about disappearing wilderness. They cite the giveaway of valuable timber, the loss of habitat for resident species, and the impact of clear-cutting not only on the forests themselves but also on the streams that run through them. Along the Pacific Coast, conservationists, fishermen, and lumbermen have quarreled over the effects of disturbing mature forests where the spotted owl nests in ancient trees and in whose neighborhood salmon are dependent on clear, cool streams for spawning. But there are signs of change, with conservationists and their opponents coming together to try to find workable solutions and corporations evidencing increased interest in sustainable forest management.

FISHERIES, OCEANS, AND AQUATIC LIFE

This nation, with a heritage of rich fishery resources, has wideranging problems in all of its aquatic quarters. Shellfish habitats have been damaged by sewage and other pollutants so that vast beds of oysters and clams have been ruined or are off limits to harvesters because of the potential presence of pathogens. Krill, an important shrimp-like marine crustacean that is near the bottom of the food chain, is being over-fished to provide food for aquaculture.

The great runs of spawning fish, which return from the ocean along both coasts of the United States, have been reduced, and in some places eliminated, by pollution and the damming of rivers. In the Northeast and the Northwest, few rivers where salmon breed remain unimpeded by dams, although several of these dams have been removed in recent years or are in the process of being removed.9 The largest dam removal project in the world, the dismantling of the Glines Canyon Dam and the downstream Elwha Dam, was completed in 2014, allowing the Elwha River in Washington State to run free once again.

Many eastern rivers are only now beginning to recover from the severe industrial pollution that lasted for nearly a century, from the 1880s to the 1980s. In other places, residual toxic waste in river bottoms continue to circulate in the water column and render the fish inedible. The Hudson River, which serves as a major spawning ground and nursery for a huge population of striped bass, was a thriving fishing base until documentation of PCB carcinogens in the tissues of fish caught in the river ended commercial fishing there.

In the oceans, long viewed as inexhaustible sources of fish and other seafood, the problem seems even worse. As fishing technology has "improved", the fish supply has come under tremendous pressure. New fish-finding techniques and harvesting methods have interrupted the life cycles of fish and pushed populations below the level of sustainability in ocean areas where generations of fishermen once supported themselves and their families by fishing from small boats using unsophisticated techniques. In the global marketplace, astronomical prices are bid for large predatory fish, such as blue fin tuna and swordfish, driving these now harder-to-find fish to the brink of extinction. With fishermen harvesting fewer and smaller fish, governments are struggling both to protect the fish and to keep fishermen employed. Conflicts over how best to manage regional fisheries pit biologists who propose catch limits to allow the replenishment of fish stocks against fishermen who need to earn a living.

There is now no question that the growing quantity of CO_2 in the atmosphere has resulted in a huge increase in the acidity of the ocean.[10] While organisms that construct carbonate shells (such as shellfish) and other calcifying species (such as corals) are undoubtedly being affected by this acidification, many of its other consequences for marine life are still unknown.

Also not yet known are the long-term consequences of oil spills and leaks such as the Deepwater Horizon-British Petroleum leak in the Gulf of Mexico.

THE LOSS OF BIODIVERSITY

The earth is populated with billions of different species of living things, ranging from an enormous variety of bacteria to hundreds of species of orchids to a multitude of different kinds of primates, including humans. Where and how each species lives is a product of geologic and climatic factors as well as its interactions with other living things in its habitat.

The biologically diverse organisms in a habitat are dependent on one
another for both food and the well-being of the ecosystem that they share. This complex interdependence of living things results in there being a maximum and a minimum number of each species that can exist within a particular ecosystem without upsetting what has been called the "food chain", the "web of life", and the "balance of nature."

Changes in the populations of member species that live in particular habitats have occurred naturally since the beginning of life on Earth. Climatic factors, such as fluctuations in rainfall and temperature, and geologic upheavals, such as volcanic eruptions and earthquakes, can cause the decline, extinction, or movement of species. The introduction of invasive foreign species, which can be brought as seeds in the feathers, fur, or feces of migrating species or result from animal migrations caused by geological upheavals or climatic changes, may also cause species extinction and result in disruptions in the food chain. Invasive species can also be brought by people, who may carry an organism from a native habitat where it has numerous enemies to a new setting where it has few or no predators.

Humans, by making major alterations in the natural environment and by replacing a varied environment with one that is much more uniform, have been responsible for the extinction of numerous species. Towns and cities replace wild habitat; farmers, seeking to maximize food supply or income, grow only edible or cash crops and may eliminate all other plants from the land; the timber industry clear-cuts whole forests of diverse species of trees and then plants new forests that contain only a single species. As the habitat becomes more homogeneous, the number and variety of species that can be sustained by it grows smaller. The rate of species extinction, which has accelerated as the human population has grown and as human civilization has developed and expanded around the world, is unparalleled in the recent history of the Earth.

There are multiple reasons for concern about species extinction and the resultant loss of biodiversity. First, as diversity is lost, the population balance is disturbed and the resilience of the remaining species in the entire area is reduced. As a result, their population may decrease. Then, if some kind of blight occurs that affects a particular species, the loss of that species is likely to have a much more devastating effect on the whole area. Second, the loss of biodiversity results in the loss within species of individuals that carry varied genetic material. The wild strains of many domesticated plants retain genetic material that has been bred out of the current domesticated varieties but that may be of critical value in rejuvenating domesticated strains in the future (for example, if a domesticated strain became vulnerable to some kind of blight or if there were a need to develop a more heat tolerant strain). As the world becomes more and more dependent on a smaller and smaller variety of plants and animals for food, timber, and natural fibers, there is increasing concern about the loss of genetic diversity. Third, environmentalists and scientists warn that we are losing species that may be of great value to humans and that many of these organisms may not yet even have been discovered.

Because biodiversity reaches its maximum in rainforests, when rainforests are destroyed, incredibly diverse and potentially valuable communities are also lost. In Indonesia, for example, where the rainforest is being cut down to make way for palm plantations to supply the demand for palm oil, the helmeted hornbill is but one of the species in danger of disappearing.[11] Opposition to rainforest destruction is particularly strong among environmentalists, but for loggers, miners, and farmers, who may use the rainforest in ways that damage or destroy it, the long-term effects of forest destruction are not an immediate concern.

THE COMPLEXITY OF ENVIRONMENTAL ISSUES

As long as uninhabited or sparsely inhabited lands existed and the human impact on the environment was confined to small segments of the planet, the consequences of human population growth and technological innovation could be largely ignored. Today, though, there are few frontiers left on earth, and many human activities have global impacts. Pollution, industrial and mining activity, disease and population dislocations can have devastating impacts not only on nearby communities but also on distant countries. Chemicals released into the atmosphere cause acid rain that destroys forests hundreds of miles away from the point of source and may even affect the climate of the whole earth; the fishing and ocean dumping practices of one nation impinge on the availability of seafood to nations around the globe; microbes on food produced in one country result in outbreaks of illness thousands of miles away; people caught in the crossfire of war or facing environmental degradation in their homelands as a result of rising sea levels, encroaching deserts, or vanishing water supplies become refugees seeking entry into other countries.

People throughout the world are being forced to make difficult economic and social choices as they attempt to balance human needs with environmental limitations. They must decide what kinds of technology and infrastructure their nation should invest in (e.g., alternative energy, biotechnology, roads and bridges, coastal barriers), what kinds of limits on individual rights they are willing to accept (e.g., property, healthcare, child-bearing), and on what basis they want to make these decisions (e.g., economic impact, moral values, equity).

Recognition that these decisions will affect how we and future generations of Americans will live has prompted vociferous arguments about where our nation's priorities should lie. On one side are those who argue that we must immediately diminish our impact on the environment and lower our carbon footprint; on the other are those who maintain that we should use all available resources to further human well-being and that human ingenuity will enable us to do this into the foreseeable future. While the most strident of the voices at the two extremes of this debate have often been the most effective in raising people's consciousness, it is only by listening to all the voices in the debate and carefully examining the facts supporting the arguments that we will be able to comprehend and assess the long-term social, economic, and political ramifications of alternative pathways for addressing complex environmental problems.

Part I

Foundations of American Environmental Thought and Action

About twelve to fourteen thousand years ago, when the sea level was substantially lower than it is today and Asia and North America were still connected by a land bridge in the area of the Bering Strait, a few Asian hunters and gatherers crossed this narrow stretch of land between what are now Russia and Alaska and became the first humans to set foot in the Western Hemisphere.[1] Like other people who migrated to the Americas during the ensuing millennia, these prehistoric men and women probably came in pursuit of food or more hospitable surroundings. Possibly, when they ventured into this vast unpeopled land, they were tracking game animals. As word of good hunting in the newly discovered region filtered back into Asia, additional groups of migrants made their way to the Western Hemisphere. Some of these people drifted south along the western coast of the great land mass, and within about a thousand years, a few bands had roamed as far as South America.

By the time Columbus arrived in the "New World" in 1492, the indigenous population had grown to an estimated seven million people, living throughout North and South America and the Caribbean. The approximately one million inhabitants of North America occupied every part of the continent, from the ice-bound north to the dry southwest and the luxuriant lands of the Gulf Coast, from the forests of the northwest to those of the northeast, and from the grassy central plains down to the rich, watery lands of the southeast. In the Great Plains region, it is estimated, there were about 225,000 people, and west of the Rocky Mountains perhaps 350,000 people.[2] Most tribes throughout the continent practiced some form of farming and relied on hunting, fishing, and foraging to satisfy their material and dietary needs. Among the crops they cultivated was maize, which had been developed (beginning about nine thousand years ago in southern Mexico) from wild teosinte.[3] They had no iron for tools, no horses or wheels for transportation, and in the northern regions (in what would become the United States and Canada), no written language or knowledge of higher mathematics.

Contact Between Europe & America

Across the Atlantic Ocean, in Europe, a great renaissance had begun in the fourteenth century. A surge of economic growth and an intellectual blossoming during this period resulted in advances in science and mapmaking. The increased intellectual openness, as well as the spread of knowledge that followed the invention of printing with movable type in about 1450, made possible the technological advances, including key advances in maritime technology, which in turn led to an expansion of maritime trade and the great voyages of discovery of the late fifteenth and sixteenth centuries.

Spanish explorers established bases in the Caribbean region early in the sixteenth century. By the middle of the century, they had sailed up and down the Atlantic and parts of the Pacific coasts of North America, had made forays into much of the territory that eventually became the southern part of the United States, and had set up a permanent colony at St. Augustine, Florida. They had also tried, unsuccessfully, to establish permanent settlements along the Atlantic coast as far north as what is now South Carolina. Other explorers, sailing under the flags of various European states, including England and France, had also explored the Atlantic seaboard. Both the French and the English had attempted to establish colonies along the Atlantic shore during the sixteenth century, but resistance from the native inhabitants, disease, and lack of food proved to be insurmountable obstacles to the survival of these colonies. It was not until 1609 that the English gained a permanent foothold on the western shores of the Atlantic with the establishment of a settlement at Jamestown, Virginia.

During the century that followed the successful colonization of Jamestown, the landscape of North America was transformed by an influx of permanent settlers from western Europe. Colonies were established all along the Atlantic seaboard, and traders, trappers, and missionaries traveled deep into the interior of the continent. By 1700, the territory that would eventually form the thirteen rebellious British colonies had a population approaching 300,000.

The Clash of Cultures

The vast majority of the fifteenth- to eighteenth-century explorers and colonists of North America—whether they came from Spain, England, France, the Netherlands, or elsewhere in Europe—brought with them very similar attitudes about the relationship between humans and the natural world. Predominant among these was a belief that humanity is at the center of creation, that people have a right to use the resources of the land for human benefit, and that it was their divine duty to subdue the land they had discovered and the non-Christians who occupied it. For the most part, the natural world was seen as either a beneficent garden with riches created fundamentally for the use of humans or as a savage, evil wilderness to be conquered and tamed. Those parts of the world that had been occupied and cultivated were viewed as potential gardens, while the uninhabited wilderness was looked on with fear and mistrust.

The European explorers' and colonists' worldview was shaped by the Bible and the classics as well as by their own local customs and traditions. The Bible, a work familiar to all of the early explorers and fundamental to the education of the colonists, was a primary sourcebook [*see* Document 1]. A wide range of other writings had also influenced the mind-set of the Europeans, including classics such as the *Eclogues* of Virgil [*see* Document 2] and scientific and philosophical writings such as the works of Francis Bacon [*see* Document 8] and Isaac Newton. It is doubtful that many of the colonists would have been familiar with the writings of St. Francis of Assisi,[4] whose vision of a bond between all creation closely paralleled the views of some North American Indians but was an anomaly in European thought until recently.

The Europeans considered the Native Americans as either merely another resource created for the use of civilized humans (Europeans) or as savage, uncivilized creatures to be Christianized. However, despite the European interlopers' condescending attitude toward the Indians, the explorers and colonists were clearly dependent on the natives for knowledge about the weather, plants, and animals in the New World [*see* Document 7].

The newcomers were intent on claiming for themselves—both as representatives of their sovereigns and as individuals—as much of the land and its wealth as they could lay their hands on [*see* Documents 3-5]. However, the Native Americans were steadfast in their desire to continue to farm, hunt, and fish on the lands and in the rivers where they had done so traditionally. As the growing white population appropriated more and more of America's land and wildlife, the native tribes found themselves with access to fewer of the resources essential to their well-being and continued existence, and the conflict between the Indians and the Europeans intensified.

The Indians, according to many writers, had no concept of private property rights. They did not consider land and water to be transferable assets and, as long as the land was unoccupied by others, probably assumed that they would continue to have access to its resources, even if it was sold [see Document 32]. They viewed themselves as part of a great whole, as just one of the many inhabitants of the earth, along with the birds and the four-legged animals, and they saw the wilderness as an integral part of the natural order.

Europeans and colonists, on the other hand, had little appreciation of or respect for the wilderness. This was true even of the great naturalists of the eighteenth century, both European- and American-born. Although they may have been impressed with the variety of plants found in the wilderness, they considered the wilderness's major value to lie in its potential as a source of plants that could be cultivated on farms and in gardens or as land that could be transformed into farms and gardens [see Documents 15, 17, and 19].

In spite of their belief that the resources of the land were a God-given gift to humans and their sense of being separate from the natural world, the colonists were forced to recognize, within just a few decades of their arrival in America, that, without planning, some of the resources of their new land might soon become scarce. By the mid-seventeenth century the colonists had begun to institute laws regulating the use of timber, fish, and game animals [see Documents 9, 10, and 13], and even to limit pollution [see Document 12]. In the English colonies, it was standard practice to set aside common land for grazing and timber [see Document 13], but the commons had to be regulated to ensure that no individuals would use more than their allotted share of the common resources.

The Clash of Ecosystems

The arrival of the Europeans in the Americas produced a clash not only of two very distinct cultures but also of two separate ecosystems. In the holds of their ships, the Europeans carried horses, pigs, cattle, sheep, and chickens, as well as crop seeds and fruit trees [see Document 5]. They also brought, on their clothes and boots, the seeds of blue grass, dandelions,

and daisies and, in their bodies, the microorganisms that cause smallpox and measles. When they returned to Europe they took with them beans, maize, potatoes, and tomatoes. In America, the horse (first brought to the "New World" by the Spaniards in 1493) gave the Europeans a huge military advantage and then transformed the lives of the Indians. But it was European diseases as much as the European's military strength that caused the decimation of the Native American population [see Document 6]. Some scholars have estimated that as much as one-half of the precontact population of the Americas had died of smallpox within a few decades of Columbus's landing. In Europe, on the other hand, the introduction of the potato changed the continent's agricultural base and helped to fuel population growth.[5]

The increase in Europe's population created a need for more agricultural and grazing lands, while the expanding maritime industry required increasing amounts of timber. As a consequence, the great forests that had at one time covered much of England and the European continent slowly began to fall to the ax. Simultaneously, European industrial growth produced a need for increasing quantities of raw materials for its factories and mills. The Western Hemisphere provided a haven for Europe's burgeoning and increasingly urban population, a source of raw materials, and a market for its industrial products.

Forging a New Nation

While the immediate cause of the American Revolution was resistance to taxation without representation, the revolutionary spirit had long been fostered by colonial resentment of England's dumping of manufactured goods and unwanted people (including criminals) on American land, imposed limits on manufacturing, and a sense that the exploitation of America was being carried out for the benefit of England with little regard for the colonies' inhabitants.

In spite of their differences with England, the rebellious colonists looked to England, as well as to France, for legal precedents and philosophical values as they prepared to launch a new nation. And when they required a philosophical and legal basis for defining the human relationship with the land, they turned to the writings of Europeans such as Thomas Hobbes [see Document 11], René Descartes, Jean-Jacques Rousseau, John Locke [see Document 14], and William Blackstone [see Document 18].

DOCUMENT 1: Biblical Views of Nature and Humanity

Many believe that a religious foundation for human abuse of the environment lies in the story of creation at the beginning of Genesis, where humans are directed to subdue the earth and exert dominion over it. Although there has been extensive debate about the meaning of "dominion," there is little doubt about the interpretation given to the term by the newcomers to North America. The explorers and colonists aimed to "subdue" the land and exploit its riches and to "replenish" it with increasing numbers of Europeans.

The biblical story of Noah, which describes Noah's management of the flood according to God's instructions, suggests another role for humanity in relation to the natural world. The sort of dominion Noah exercised over the creatures that he took onto the ark indicates respect for the inherent value of nature and a sense of a reciprocal relationship between living things. If this act of saving all living things can be considered "dominion," it surely contrasts with the interpretation given the biblical injunction by the colonists and later Americans.

In Isaiah, as well as elsewhere in the Bible, the contrast between the garden and the wilderness is vivid. The language and concept of this dichotomy, with its preference for cultivated land over "wilderness" and "waste places," and which is also found in the writings of Virgil, Hobbes, Locke, and many of the early naturalists, traveled across the Atlantic and became embedded in the thinking of the colonists.

A. Genesis: The Story of Creation

So God created man in his own image, in the image of God created he him; male and female created he them.

And God blessed them, and God said unto them, Be fruitful, and multiply, and replenish the earth, and subdue it; and have dominion over the fish of the sea, and over the fowl of the air, and over every living thing that moveth upon the earth.

And God said, Behold, I have given you every herb bearing seed, which *is* upon the face of all the earth, and every tree, in the which *is* the fruit of a tree yielding seed; to you it shall be for meat.

B. Genesis: The Story of Noah and the Flood

And behold, I, even I do bring a flood of waters upon the earth, to destroy all flesh, wherein is the breath of life, from under heaven: *and* every thing that *is* in the earth shall die.

But with thee will I establish my covenant: and thou shalt come into the ark, thou, and thy sons, and thy wife, and thy sons wives with thee.

And of every living thing of all flesh, two of every *sort* shalt thou bring into the ark, to keep them alive with thee; they shall be male and female.

. . .

And God remembered Noah, and every living thing, and all the cattle that *was* with him in the ark: and God made a wind to pass over the earth, and the waters asswaged.

. . .

And God spake unto Noah, saying,

Go forth of the ark, thou, and thy wife, and thy sons, and thy sons wives with thee.

Bring forth with thee every living thing that *is* with thee, of all flesh, *both* of fowl, and of cattle, and of every creeping thing that creepeth upon the earth; that they may breed abundantly in the earth, and be fruitful, and multiply upon the earth.

C. Isaiah, c. 725 B.C.E.

Upon the land of my people shall come up thorns and briers, yea, upon all the houses of joy in the joyous city:

Until the spirit be poured upon us from on high, and the wilderness be a fruitful field, and the fruitful field be counted for a forest.

Then judgment shall dwell in the wilderness, and righteousness remain in the fruitful field.

. . .

[The Lord shall comfort Zion: he will comfort all her waste places, and he will make her wilderness like Eden, and her desert like the garden of the Lord; joy and gladness shall be found therein, thanksgiving, and the voice of melody.

Source: Holy Bible, Vol. 1 (Philadelphia: R. Aitken, 1782), Genesis 1: 27-29, 6: 17-19, 8: 1, 15-17; Isaiah 32: 13, 15-16, 51: 3.

DOCUMENT 2: Virgil's Pastoral View of Nature (c. 50 B.C.E.)

From the age of the Greeks and Romans through the Renaissance, nature was considered to be at its most sublime when molded by the human hand and turned into farmland, gardens, or parks—land that provided both serenity and sustenance. This domesticated nature was celebrated in pastoral poetry, such as that of the Roman poet Virgil. Virgil's "Pastorals" or "Eclogues" as they are frequently called, depict the domesticated countryside as a place of joy for those who live there and a place yearned for by those who do not. In this extract, Meliboeus, who has been turned out of his land in a redistribution of property by the Roman emperor Augustus, is speaking to Tityrus, who has been permitted to stay.

The celebration of nature in poetry and other writings is probably as ancient as literature itself. Such writing usually expresses a timeless human sense of wonderment about the beauty or awesomeness of nature; it also reflects a sense of the human relationship with the natural world at a particular time and place. The pastoral ideal may have colored the dreams of some early Americans, but it was inappropriate for the American landscape. Toward the end of the eighteenth century, American writers and painters began to reject this pastoral ideal and turn to untamed nature for inspiration [see Document 22], and by the mid-eighteenth century the romantic appreciation of wilderness had become a dominant influence in American art and literature [see Document 34].

Beneath the shade which beechen boughs diffuse,
You, Tityrus, entertain your silvan muse.
Round the wide world in banishment we roam,
Forc'd from our pleasing fields and native home;
While, stretch'd at ease, you sing your happy loves,
And Amaryllis fills the shady groves.

***

O fortunate old man! Whose farm remains—
For you sufficient—and requites your pains;
Though rushes overspread the neighbouring plains,
Though here the marshy grounds approach your fields,
And there the soil a stony harvest yields.
Your teeming ewes shall no strange meadows try,

Nor fear a rot from tainted company.
Behold! yon bordering fence of sallow trees
Is fraught with flowers, the flowers are fraught with bees:
The busy bees, with a soft murmuring strain,
Invite to gentle sleep the labouring swain.
While, from neighbouring rock, with rural songs,
The pruner's voice the pleasing dream prolongs,
Stock-doves and turtles tell their amorous pain,
And, from the lofty elms, of love complain.

Source: Virgil, "Pastoral I," in *Dryden's Version of Virgil's Pastorals and Georgics; and the First Volume of Aeneis; Vol. 10 of The Works of the Greek and Roman Poets, Translated into English* (London: Suttaby, Evance and Fox, 1813), pp. 37, 39-40.

DOCUMENT 3: Christopher Columbus Inventories the New World's Natural Resources (1493)

In this letter to Luis de Santangel, comptroller of the treasury of King Ferdinand and Queen Isabella of Spain, Columbus describes the riches of the Caribbean islands he has discovered, and extols the opportunities for the exploitation of their abundant resources. To Columbus, Jean Ribaut [see Document 4], and other early explorers, the "New World's" resources appeared to be limitless, and for more than three centuries most Americans believed that this was indeed the case.

I discovered many islands inhabited by people without number, and of which I took possession for their Highnesses by proclamation with the royal banner displayed, no one offering any contradiction. . . . All these countries are of surpassing excellence, and in particular *Juana*, which contains abundance of fine harbours, excelling any in Christendom, as also many large and beautiful rivers. The land is high and exhibits chains of tall mountains which seems to reach to the skies, and surpass beyond comparison the isle of *Cetrefrey*. . . . They are accessible in every part, and covered with a vast variety of lofty trees, which it appears to me, never lose their foliage, as we found them fair and verdant as in May in Spain. Some were covered with blossoms, some with fruit, and others in different stages, according to their nature. The nightingale and a thousand other sorts of birds were singing in the month of November wherever I went. There are palm-trees in these countries, of six or eight sorts, which are surprising to see, on account of their diversity from ours, but indeed, this is the case with respect to the other trees, as well as the fruits and weeds. Beautiful forests of pines are likewise found, and fields of vast extent. Here is also honey, and fruits of a thousand sorts, and birds of every variety. The lands contain mines of metals, and inhabitants without number. The island of Espanola is pre-eminent in beauty and excellence, offering to the sight the most enchanting view of mountains, plains, rich fields for cultivation, and pastures for flocks of all sorts, with situations for towns and settlements. . . . The preference [among the islands discovered] must be given to Espanola, on account of the mines of gold which it possesses, and the facilities it offers for trade with the continent, and countries this side, and beyond that of the Great Cau, which traffic will be great and profitable. . . . At present there are within reach, spices and cotton to as great an amount as they can desire, aloe in as great abundance, and equal store of mastick, a production nowhere else found except in Greece and the island of Scio, where it is sold at such a price as the possessors choose. To these may be added slaves, as numerous as may be wished for. Besides I have as I think, discovered rhubarb and cinnamon, and expect countless other things of value will be found.

Source: Christopher Columbus, *Personal Narrative of the First Voyage of Columbus to America* (Boston: T. B. Wait, 1827), pp. 253, 255-56, 260, and 263.

DOCUMENT 4: Jean Ribaut Discovers the Natural Abundance of Terra Florida (1563)

Like other explorers and colonizers both before and after him, Jean Ribaut, a captain in the French navy who established a colony at what is now Port Royal, South Carolina, sought to claim and exploit as much territory as possible for the nation under whose flag he sailed. Greatly impressed by the riches of the "New World," he depicted it as a paradise abounding in honey and venison and made note of the many plants cultivated by the Indians that were unknown in Europe.

We entered and viewed the countrey thereabouts, which is the fairest, fruitfullest, & pleasantest of all the worlde, abounding in honye, venison, wylde foule, forests, woods of all sorts, Palme trees, Cypres & Cedres, Bayes the highest & greatest, with also the fairest vines in all the world, with Grapes according, which without naturalle arte & without mans helpe or trimming wil growe to toppes of Oks, & other trees that be of wonderfull greatnesse and heyght. And the syght of the fayre Medowes is a pleasure not able to be expressed with tongue: full of Hernes, Curlues, Bitters, Mallardes, Egreyths, Wodkockes, & all other kynde of small byrdes: With Hartes, Hyndes, Buckes, wylde Swine, & all other kyndes wylde brathes, as we perceyved well bothe by theyr footing there, & also afterwardes in other places, by theyr crye & roryng in the nyght.

Also there be Connies & Hares: Silke wormes in mervelous number, a great dell fairer & better then be our silk wormes. To be short, it is a thing unspeakable to consider the thinges that be seene there, & shalbe found more & more in this incomparable lande, whiche never yet broken with ploughe was [but] bryngs forthe all things according to its first nature, wherewith the eternal God endowed it. About theyr houses they [the Indians] labour & tyll the grounde, sowyng theyr fields with a grayne called Mahis, whereof they make theyr meale: & in theyr Gardens they plant beanes, gourdes, cocumbers, citrons, peason & many other fruites & rootes unknown unto us. Their spades: mattocks made of wood, so well & fitly as is possible: which they make wyth certayn stones, oyster shells & muscles, wherewith also they make theyr bowes & small launces: & cutte & polyshe all sortes of Wood, that they imploye aboute theyr buildings, & necessarie use: There groweth also manye Walnut trees, Hasell trees, Cheritrees, very fayre and great.

Source: Jean Ribaut, *The Whole and True Discovereye of Terra Florida*, trans. Thomas Hacket (London: Rouland Hall, 1563), unfolioed.

DOCUMENT 5: Baltasar de Obregon's Account of the Riches of New Mexico (1584)

In the latter part of the sixteenth century, Spaniards who were based in Mexico made several expeditions to the lands of the Pueblo Indians. The Chamuscado-Rodriguez expedition of 1582, mentioned in this document, was one the most important of these ventures. Although the primary object of these forays was to find gold, silver, and copper and to record the locations of mines, the expedition reports also detailed how the Indians interacted with their environment and evaluated the potential for introducing European crops and domesticated animals.

Blankets; salines; mats; pottery; Castile flax and linen

The natives gather quantities of corn, beans, calabashes, cotton, and *piciete*, a very useful herb. They make large numbers of blankets, both heavy and light, beautifully woven and dyed with various bright colors. They possess numerous turkeys. They utilize the feathers, interweaving them in heavy cotton blankets.

They have quantities of salines of rich salt. There are salt deposits that extend over five leagues. They have large numbers of mats made of rushes and reeds, and large and small baskets. They possess good crockery, both heavy and fine, brilliantly decorated with admirable colors. They grow Castile flax without cultivation. It flourishes naturally at Cieneguilla and the Valle de los Valientes [Rio Grande]. Consequently they make Castile cloth.

Number of cattle; wool used for cloth; nature of the land

. . . Thirty or forty leagues away are numerous cattle which they utilize; the meat for food and the hides for many purposes like the hides of the cattle of Spain. They use their wool for clothing, the fat for candles and other things. The hides are good for making shoes and weapons when very well tanned. These provinces and towns mentioned have a fine climate, numerous plains, valleys, mountains, rivers, streams, lakes, springs and riverbanks, suitable for the cultivation of any kind of grain from Spain and for raising all sorts of cattle.

. . . There are many sierras on its confines where I saw and examined rich metals when I was on the expedition with General Francisco de Ibarra. In the ridges of these mountains and near the settlements are the mines discovered and inspected by Francisco Sanchez Chamuscado and his companions.

Source: Baltasar de Obregon, *Obregon's History of 16th Century Explorations in Western America entitled Chronicle, Commentary, or Relation of the Ancient and Modern Discoveries in New Spain and New Mexico,* trans. and ed. George P. Hammond and Agapito Rey (Los Angeles: Wetzel, 1928), pp. 300-301.

DOCUMENT 6: Thomas Hariot on the Death of Indians from a Disease Brought from Europe (1588)

In 1585 the Oxford mathematician Thomas Hariot accompanied Sir Walter Raleigh on his voyage to the "New World" to set up a colony to be named Virginia, in honor of England's virgin queen, Elizabeth. Hariot's main duties were to observe the customs of the Indians and to make an accounting of the natural resources in their lands. Like Ribaut [see Document 4], he was greatly impressed by the abundance of resources. His account details one of the unintended consequences of the European contact with the native Americans; the decimation of a large segment of the indigenous population as a result of "virgin soil epidemics"—the very rapid spread of pathogens among populations encountering them for the first time. Because Hariot provides no description of the disease that brought death to the Indians with whom his expedition came in contact, other than to note that it had an incubation period of a few days, it is impossible to identify the disease. It could have been smallpox, typhus, or any of a number of other ailments.

One other rare and strange accident, leaving others, will I mention before I ende, which mooved the whole country that either knew or hearde of us, to have us in wonderfull admiration.

There was no towne where we had any subtile devise practiced against us, we leaving it unpunished or not revenged (because wee sought by all meanes possible to win them by gentlenesse) but that within a few dayes after our departure from everie such towne, the people began to die very fast, and many in short space; in some townes about twentie, in some fourtie, in some sixtie, & in one six score, which in trueth was very manie in respect of their numbers. This happened in no place that wee could learne but where wee had bene, where they used some practise against us, and after such time; The disease also so strange, that they neither knew what it was, nor how to cure it; the like by report of the oldest men in the countrey never happened before, time out of minde. A thing specially observed by us as also by the naturall inhabitants themselves.

Insomuch that when some of the inhabitants which were our friends & especially the *Wiroans Wingina* had observed such effects in foure or five townes to follow their wicked practises, they were perswaded that it was the worke of our God through our meanes, and that wee by him might kil and slai whom wee would without weapons and not come neere them.

* * *

[S]ome people could not tel whether to think us gods or men, and the rather because that all the space of their sicknesse, there was no man of ours knowne to die, or that was specially sicke.

Source: Thomas Hariot, *Narrative of the First English Plantation* (London: Quaritch, 1893; reprint of 1590 edition), p. 41, 42.

DOCUMENT 7: William Bradford on Life in the Wilderness (1620, 1621)

Together with a group of fellow Pilgrims, William Bradford sailed from England in search of religious freedom and intent on missionizing the Indians. Their destination was the Massachusetts coast, which had been explored by expeditions led by Captain Bartholomew Gosnold, in 1602, and Captain John Smith, in 1614. They reached Cape Cod in November 1620, and by the following April many members of the party were ill. Although disdainful of the natives, the Pilgrims would have died of starvation if they had not obtained food from the Pautuxet Indians to make it through the harsh winter and if, in the spring, the Indians had not provided them with seed that was suitable for the Massachusetts soil and climate as well as advice on how to plant it. In this selection, Bradford expresses the fear and distaste for the wilderness that was prevalent among the Pilgrims.

Sept: 6 [1620]

. . . [A]fter longe beating at sea they [the Pilgrims] fell with that land which is called Cape Cod; the which being made and certainly knowne to be it, they were not a litle joyfull. . . . And the next day they gott into the Cape-harbor wher they ridd in saftie.

. . .

Being thus passed the vast ocean, and a sea of troubles before in their preparation . . ., they had now no freinds to wellcome them, nor inns to entertaine or refresh their weatherbeaten bodys, no houses or much less townes to repaire too, to seeke for succoure. It is recorded in scripture as a mercie to the apostle and his shipwraked company, that the barbarians shewed them no smale kindnes in refreshing them, but these savage barbarians, when they mette with them (as after will appeare) were readier to fill their sids full of arrows than otherwise. And for the season it was winter, and they that know the winters of that cuntrie know them to be sharp and violent, and subjecte to cruell and feirce stormes, deangerous to travill to known places, much more to serch an unknown coast. Besides, what could they see but a hidious and desolate wildernes, full of wild beasts and willd men? and what multitude ther might be of them they knew not. Nether could they, as it were, goe up to the tope of Pisgah, to vew from this wildernes a more goodly cuntrie to feed their hops; for which way soever they turnd their eys (save upward to the heavens) they could have litle solace or content in respecte of any outward objects. For summer being done, all things stand upon them with a wetherbeaten face; and the whole countrie, full of woods and thickets, represented a wild and savage heiw.

* * *

Being thus arrived at Cap-Cod the 11. of November, and necessitie calling them to looke out a place for habitation, (as well as the maisters and mariners importunitie) they having brought a large shalop with them out of England, stowed in quarters in the ship, they now got her out and sett their carpenters to worke to trime her up.

. . .

After . . . the shalop being got ready, they set out againe for the better discovery of this place, and the m^r of the ship desired to goe him selfe, so ther went some 30. Men, but found it to be no harbor for ships but only for boats; ther was allso found 2. of their houses covered with matts, and sundrie of their implements in them, but the people were rune away and could not be seen; also ther was found more of their corne, and of their beans of various collours. The corne and beans they brought away, purposing to give them full satisfaction when they should meete with any of them (as about some 6. months afterward they did, to their good contente). And here is to be noted a spetiall providence of God, and a great mercie to this poore people, that hear they gott seed to plant them corne the next year, or els they might have starved, for they had none, nor any liklyhood to get any till the season had beene past (as the sequell did manyfest). Neither is it lickly they had had this, if the first viage had not been made, for the ground was now all covered with snow, and hard frozen. But the Lord is never wanting unto his in their greatest needs; let his holy name have all the praise.

. . .

Anno. 1691

. . . [T]he 14. of Jan: the house which they had made for a general randevoze by casulty fell afire, and some were faine to retire abord [the ship] for shilter. Then the sickness begane to fall sore amongst them, and the weather so bad as they could not make much sooner any dispatch. . . .

Afterwards they (as many as were able) began to plant ther corne, in which servise [the Indian] Squanto stood them in great stead, showing them both the maner how to set it, and after how to dress and tend it. Also, he tould them excepte they gott fish and set with it (in these old grounds) it would come to nothing, and he showed them that in the middle of Aprill they should have store enough come up the brooke, by which they began to build, and taught them how to take it, and where to get other provisions necessary for them; all which they found true by triall and experience.[6] Some English seed they sew, as wheat and pease, but it came not to good, eather by the badnes of the seed, or latenes of the season, or both, or some other defecte.

Source: William Bradford, *History of Plymouth Plantation 1606-1646*, ed. William T. Davis (New York: Scribner's, 1908), pp. 94-96, 100, 115-16.

DOCUMENT 8: Francis Bacon on Science and Technology (1629)

The English statesman, essayist, and philosopher-scientist Francis Bacon established the concept of scientific rationality. He asserted that nature is a machine with no inherent value and proposed that human knowledge should be used to improve on nature and adapt it to human needs. The advancement of technology, Bacon thought, would bring benefit to humans without any negative impacts. Although faith in human innovation would continue to be wide-spread, the negative effects of technology were already evident during the Industrial Revolution. By the end of World War II, recognition of the destructive potential of technology had forced people to reexamine the relationship of humans, nature, and technology [see Documents 87, 88 and 91].

LXXXI. . . . [T]he real and legitimate goal of the sciences is the endowment of human life with new inventions and riches.

CXXIX. . . . [T]he introduction of great inventions appears one of the most distinguished of human actions, and the ancients so considered it; for they assigned divine honors to the authors of inventions, but only heroic honors to those who displayed civil merit (such as the founders of cities and empires, legislators, the deliverers of the country from lasting misfortunes, the quellers of tyrants, and the like). And if anyone rightly compare them, he will find the judgment of antiquity to be correct;

for the benefits derived from inventions may extend to mankind in general, but civil benefits to particular spots alone; the latter, moreover, last but for a time, the former forever. Civil reformation seldom is carried on without violence and confusion, while inventions are a blessing and a benefit without injuring or afflicting any.

Inventions are also, as it were, new creations and imitations of divine works. . . .

Again, let anyone but consider the immense difference between men's lives in the most polished countries of Europe, and in any wild and barbarous region of the new Indies, he will think it so great, that man may be said to be a god unto man, not only on account of mutual aid and benefits, but from their comparative states—the result of the arts, and not of the soil or climate.

Source: Francis Bacon, *Novum Organum*, ed. Joseph Devey, in *A Library of Universal Literature*, Part I (New York: P. F. Collier, 1901), pp. 58, 104, 105.

DOCUMENT 9: Regulating the Herring Run in the Town of Plymouth (1637, 1638, 1639, 1662)

Less than two decades after the Pilgrims' arrival, it became obvious that millers who altered or controlled the flow of water past their mills were interfering with the natural movements of certain fish, notably herring (or alewives), in the stream and that this interference would be detrimental to the entire community because it disrupted the spawning of the fish. As a result, millers were required to let the water flow freely at certain times of the year. The harvesting of the fish was also regulated. The "ware," or weir, was a fence or dam through which the fish could not pass.

The last day of March 1637

It is concluded upon a Townes meeting that Nicholas [Snow] shall repaire the Hering ware and draw and divide the Hering this yeare and shall have foure and fourty bushells of Indian corne for his paynes but the Town shall pay him for the boards used about the repaire there.

* * *

At a Townes meeting held the VIth day of February 1638. . . .

It is ordered that . . . the Milner shall observe such order in stoping and loosening of the water as shalbe given by the overseers of the hering ware.

John Dunhame and Willm Pontus doe undertake to pcure the hering ware repaired and drawne and what they agree for with any that shall doe the worke shalbe payd by the whole Towne according to eich in pporcon of shares.

* * *

At a Townes meeting held xix March 1639.

It is ordered and agreed upon That Thomas Atkins and John Wood shall repaire the hering ware this yeare and shall draw and deliver the herings to eich man according to his shares due to them and shall have ii^s p thousand [2 shillings per thousand fish] for their paynes of the Towne and after the same rate of the country for those the shalbe allowed to eate and for bayte and to be payd either in money or corne at Harvest at such rate as it doth then passe at from man to man.

It is also agreed upon that whosoever shall take any herings either above or below the ware after the ware is sett or shall robb the ware shall forfaite five for one.

* * *

Att a towne meeting held att the meeting house the 23 of March 1662 It was ordered by the towne that henery Wood and Gorge Bonom with one other whom they shall see meet to be added to them; shall draw or take and devide the herrings to the severall families of the Township of Plymouth whoe shall have theire shares in number according to the number of the psons in theire families and they the saide henery Wood and Gorge Bonum etc are to make meanes for the stopage of the said herrings and takeing of them in theire goeing up att theire owe charge; and they are to lett them goe up on fryday nights [,] on saterday nights and on the Lords daies; and the towne doth prohibite all those that have enterest or shalbee Imployed at the Mill to stopp water when the tide is out of the pond during the time of the herrings; and that they the said pties are hereby authorized to take course for the preventing of Boyes[,] swine and doggs from anoying of them in theire coming up.

Source: Town of Plymouth, *Records of the Town of Plymouth*, Vol. 1 (Plymouth: Avery and Doten, 1889), pp. 3, 5, 6, 52-53.

DOCUMENT 10: Predator Control and Game Hunting Regulation in Rhode Island Colony (1639, 1646)

Game was generally plentiful when the colonists arrived in New England, and the earliest game laws were directed primarily at controlling livestock predators and limiting the access of the Indians to the wildlife that the colonists wanted for themselves.

A. Town of Newport, 1639

[A]ll such who shall kill a Fox shall have six shillings and eight pence, for his paines, duly paid unto him by the Treasurer of ye Towne in which lands it was killed: Provided, that he bring the Head thereof to the said Treasurer; and this order shall be of sufficient authority to the Treasurer to pay and discharge the said summ.

It is further ordered, that all Men who shall kill any Deare (except it be upon his own proper Land), shall bring and deliver half the said Deare into the Tresurie, or pay Forty shillings; and further it is ordered, that the Governour and Deputy Governour shall have authority to give forth a Warrant to some one deputed of each Towne to kill some against the Court times for the Countries use, who shall by his Warrant have Libertie to kill wherever he find; Provided, it be not within any man's enclosure, and to be paid by the Thresurer: Provided, also, that no Indian shall be suffered to kill or destroy at any time or any where.

B. Town of Portsmouth, 1646

At a meeting, February the 4th, 1646.

It is agreed to concur with Newport in an order that there shall be no shooting of deere for the space of two months; and if any shall shoot, he shall forfeit five pounds; halfe to him that sueth, and the other halfe to the Treasurie. The reason of this order is, that the wolves the more readily come to bayte that they may be catched for the general good of the Island.

* * *

It is ordered, that the wolfe catcher shall be payed out of the treasurie, and that he that killeth a wolfe shall come to Mr. Balston and Mr. Sanford for theire pay.

It is further ordered, that Newport shall pay four pounds for the killinge of a wolfe, and Portsmouth twentie shillings

* * *

It is further ordered, that there shall be noe shootinge of deere from the first of May till the first of November; and if any shall shoot a deere within that time he shall forfeit five pounds; one halfe to him that sueth, and the other to the Treasure.

Source: John Russell Bartlett, ed., *Records of the Colony of Rhode Island and Providence Plantations in New England*, Vol. 1: *1636 to 1663* (Providence: A. Crawford Greene, 1856), pp. 84, 85, 113.

DOCUMENT 11: Thomas Hobbes's Social Contract Theory (1651)

In his book Leviathan, *the English philosopher Thomas Hobbes outlined his social contract theory, positing that people must submit to governmental authority in order to have peace. The treatise, written in support of absolute government and in defense of the acquisition of private property by the monarchy, also offered a coherent statement about the human relationship to the natural world and about the use of the commons. Jean-Jacques Rousseau, John Locke [see Document 14], and William Blackstone [see Document 18], whose writings were seminal influences on the authors of the U.S. Constitution, took many of their ideas concerning the rights of man, private property, and social contract from* Leviathan.

The right of nature, which writers commonly call *jus naturale*, is the liberty each man hath, to use his own power, as he will himself, for the preservation of his own nature; that is to say of his own life; and consequently, of doing any thing, which in his own judgment, and reason, he shall conceive to be the aptest means thereunto.

* * *

Whensoever a man transferreth his right or renounceth it; it is either in consideration of some right reciprocally transferred to himself; or for some good he hopeth for thereby. Or it is a voluntary act: and of the voluntary acts of every man, the object is some good to himself. For it is a voluntary act: and of the voluntary acts of every man, the object is some good to himself.

* * *

[S]uch things as cannot be divided, [should] be enjoyed in common, if it can be; and if the equality of the thing permit, without stint; otherwise proportionally to the number of them that have right. For otherwise the distribution is unequal, and contrary to equity.

. . . But some things there be, that can neither be divided nor enjoyed in common. Then, the law of nature, which precribeth equity, requireth, *that the entire right; or else, making the use alternate, the first possession, to be determined by lot.*

* * *

The final cause, end, or design of men, who naturally love liberty, and dominion over others, in the introduction of that restraint upon themselves, in which we see them live in commonwealths, is the foresight of their own preservation, and of a more contented life thereby; that is to say, of getting themselves out from that miserable condition of war, which is necessarily consequent, as hath been shown . . ., to the natural passions of men, when there is no visible power to keep them in awe, and tie them by fear of punishment to the performance of their covenants, and observation of those laws of nature [discussed earlier].

. . . For the laws of nature, as *justice, equity, modesty, mercy*, and, in sum, *doing to others, as we would be done to*, of themselves, without the terror of some power, to cause them to be observed, are contrary to our natural passions.

* * *

As for the plenty of matter, it is a thing limited by nature, to those commodities, which from the two breasts of our common mother, land and sea, God usually either freely giveth, or for labour selleth to mankind.

For the matter of this nutriment, consisting in animals, vegetals, and minerals, God hath freely laid them before us, in or near to the face of the earth; so as there needeth no more but the labour, and industry of receiving them. Insomuch as plenty dependeth, next to God's favour, merely on the labour and industry of men.

* * *

I find the words *lex civilis*, and *jus civile*, that is to say *law* and *right civile*, promiscuously used for the same thing, even in the most learned authors; which nevertheless ought not to be so. For *right* is *liberty*, namely that liberty which the civil law leaves us: but *civil law* is an *obligation*, which takes from us the liberty which the law of nature gave us. Nature gave a right to every man to secure himself by his own strength, and to invade a suspected neighbour, by way of prevention: but the civil law takes away that liberty.

Source: Thomas Hobbes, *Leviathan*, ed. Michael Oakeshott (New York: Macmillan/Collier Books, 1962; original ed. 1651), pp. 103, 105, 121, 129, 185, 214-15.

DOCUMENT 12: Pollution in Plymouth Colony Harbor (1668)

Pollution from waste disposal, especially in harbors and along wharves, was a problem throughout the colonies. In 1675, for example, Governor Edmund Andros of New York issued a decree forbidding people "to cast dung, dirt or refuse of ye city, or anything to fill up ye harbor or among ye neighbors or neighboring shores, under penalty of forty shillings."[7] But it was not until more than two hundred years later that the U.S. government began to address the issue of harbor pollution [see Document 61]. The records of Plymouth colony contain one of the first references to harbor pollution in America and probably one of the earliest mentions of any kind of pollution on the continent.

Whereas great complaint is made of great abuse by reason of fishermen that are strangers who fishing on some of the fishing ground on our coast in catches dresing and splitting theire fish aboard through theire Garbidg overboard to the great annoyance of fish which hath any may prove greatly detrementall to the Country; it is ordered by the Court that something be directed from this Court to the Court of the Massachusetts to request them to take some effectuall course for the restraint of such abuse as much as may bee.

Source: William Brigham, ed., *The Compact with The Charter and Laws of the Colony of New Plymouth: Together with the Charter of the Council at Plymouth* (Boston, Dutton and Wentworth: 1836), p. 153.

DOCUMENT 13: William Penn Contracts to Set Aside Timbered Lands (1681)

Whenever an English colony was established, it was customary for the charter holders to set aside a portion of the land for the common use of the whole community. This frequently included wooded land for timber.

In the American colonies, as in all societies, there were individuals who wanted to use more than their fair share of the common resources [see Document 108] or who wasted common resources through carelessness. Occasionally, when burning timber to clear land for planting, colonists allowed the fires to rage out of control, thereby destroying more woodland than necessary. Others cut an excessive amount of wood. Consequently, just a few years after the establishment of Plymouth Colony, town meetings instituted the first restrictions on the cutting and burning of timber.

As payment for a debt that the king had owed his father, William Penn was granted the territory that is now the state of Pennsylvania. In his contract with the original purchasers and renters of parcels of the land that he received from the English Crown, Penn stipulated that woodland, as well as land to be used for roads, would be set aside prior to the allocation of the individual parcels. Transportation within colonies, between colonies, and to England was deemed essential to the common good, and the provision of wood for shipbuilding was the object of many of the earliest set-asides of timbered land. Sometimes, however, the setting aside of woodland was carried out in order to support unrealistic projects. Penn's scheme to develop mulberry groves as the basis for the establishment of a silk industry proved to be a fanciful notion.

The 11 of July 1681

[1ˢᵗ] That so Soone as it pleaseth God that the abovesaid persons Arrive there, a certaine Quant[ity] of Land or Ground platt shall be laid out for a large Towne or City in the most Convenient pla[ce] upon the River for health & Navigation, and every Purchaser & Adventurer shall by lott have soe much Land therein, as will Answer to the Proportion he hath bought or Taken up upon Rent; but it is to be Noted that the Surveyors shall Consider wha[t] Roades or high wayes will be Necessary to the Cittyes, Townes, or through the Lands. Great Roades from Citty to Citty not to Containe Less then Fourty foot in breadth, shall be first laid Out {& declared to be} for highwayes, before the Divident of Acres be laid out for the purchaser, a[nd the] like Observation to be had for Streets in the Townes & Cittyes, that there may be Conven[ient] Roades & Streets preserved not to be Incroached upon by any planter or Builder, and [that] none may build Iregulerly to the dammage of another, in this Custome guide.

* * *

[18ᵗʰ] That in Clearing the Ground, Care be Taken to Leave One Acree of Trees for every five Acres Cleared, especially to Preserve Oak & Mulberries for Silk & Shipping.

Source: The Papers of William Penn, Vol. 2: 1680-1684, ed. Richard S. Dunn and Mary Maples Dunn (Philadelphia: University of Pennsylvania Press, 1982), pp. 98, 100.

DOCUMENT 14: John Locke on Property and Labor (1690)

The writings of the English philosopher John Locke, who was greatly influenced by the views of Francis Bacon [see Document 8], Thomas Hobbes [see Document 11], and René Descartes, were a major source for the drafters of the U.S. Constitution and the early members of Congress. His thesis that an individual's property should not exceed the amount of property that a laborer could tend was later incorporated into the Homestead Act [see Document 42].

31. [I]f gathering the Acorns, or other Fruits of the Earth, &c. makes a right to them, then any one may *ingross* as much as he will. To which I Answer, Not so. The same Law of Nature, that does by this means give us Property, does also *bound* that *Property* too. *God has given us all things richly*, 1 Tim. vi. 12 is the Voice of Reason confirmed by Inspiration. But how far has he given it us? *To enjoy.* As much as any one can make use of to any advantage of life before it spoils; so much he may by his labour fix a Property in. Whatever is beyond this, is more than his share, and belongs to others. Nothing was made by God for Man to spoil or destroy. And thus considering the plenty of natural Provisions there was a long time in the World, and the few spenders, and to how small a part that provision the industry of one Man could extend it self, and ingross it to the prejudice of others; especially keeping within the *bounds*, set by reason of what might serve for his *use*; there could be then little room for Quarrels or Contentions about Property so establish'd.

32. But the *chief matter of Property* being now not the Fruits of the Earth, and the Beasts that subsist on it, but the *Earth it self*; as that which takes in and carries with it all the rest: I think it is plain, that *Property* in that too is acquired as the former. *As much Land* as a Man

Tills, Plants, Improves, Cultivates, and can use the Product of, so much is his *Property*. He by his Labour does, as it were, enclose it from the Common. . . .

33. Nor was this *appropriation* of any parcel of *Land*, by improving it, any prejudice to any other Man, since there was still enough, and as good left; and more than the yet unprovided could use. . . .

34. God gave the World to Men in Common; but since he gave it them for their benefit, and the greatest Conveniencies of Life they were capable to draw from it, it cannot be supposed he meant it should always remain common and uncultivated. He gave it to the use of the Industrious and Rational. . . .

35. 'Tis true, in *Land* that is *common* in *England*, or any other Country, where there is Plenty of People under Government, who have Money and Commerce, no one can inclose or appropriate any part, without the consent of all his Fellow-Commoners: Because this is left common by Compact, *i.e.* by the Law of the Land, which is not to be violated. And though it be Common, in respect of some Men, it is not so to all Mankind; but is the joint property of this Countrey, or this Parish. Besides, the remainder, after such inclosure, would not be as good to the rest of the Commoners as the whole was, when they could all make use of the whole: whereas in the beginning and first peopling of the great Common of the World, it was quite otherwise.

40. Nor is it so strange, as perhaps before consideration it may appear, that the *Property of labour* should be able to over-balance the Community of Land. For 'tis *Labour* indeed that *puts the difference of value* on everything.

42. Land that is left wholly to Nature, that hath no improvement of Pasturage, Tillage, or Planting, is called, as indeed it is, *wast*; and we shall find the benefit of it amount to little more than nothing. This shews, how much numbers of men are to be preferd to largenesse of dominions, and that the increase of lands and the right imploying of them is the great art of government.

Source: John Locke, *Two Treatises of Government* (London: J. Whiston, 1772), pp. 198-99, 202-3, 207, 209.

DOCUMENT 15: John Ray on Gardens and Wilderness (1691)

The Father of English Natural History, John Ray, associated a cultivated landscape with civilization, and wilderness with barbarism. He also believed that the richness and diversity of nature was a reflection of God's magnificence and that God had provided this great bounty for human use. Most of Ray's writings were devoted to the systematic description of plants and animals.

I perswade my self, that the bountiful and gracious Author of Man's Being and Faculties, and all Things else, delights in the Beauty of his Creation, and is well pleased with the Industry of Man, in adorning the Earth with beautiful Cities and Castles; with pleasant Villages and Country-Houses; with regular Gardens and Orchards, and Plantations of all Sorts of Shurbs, and Herbs, and Fruits, for Meat, Medicine, or moderate Delight; with shady Woods and Groves, and Walks set with Rows of elegant Trees; *with Pastures cloathed with Flocks, and Valleys covered over with Corn,* and Meadows burthened with Grass, and whatever else differenceth a civil and well cultivated Region, from a barren and dissolate Wilderness.

If a Country thus planted and adorn'd, thus polished and civilized, thus improved to the height by all manner of Culture for the Support and Sustenance, and convenient Entertainment of innumerable multitudes of People, be not to be preferred before a barbarous and inhospitable

Scythia, without Houses, without Plantations, without Corn-fields or Vineyards, where the roving *Hords* of the savage and truculent Inhabitants, transfer themselves from place to place in Waggons, as they can find Pasture and Forrage for their Cattle, and live upon Milk, and Flesh roasted in the Sun, at the Pomels of their Saddles; or a rude and unpolished *America,* peopled with slothful and naked *Indians,* instead of well-built Houses, living in pitiful Huts and Cabbins, made of Poles set end-ways; then surely the brute Beasts Condition, and manner of Living, to which, what we have mention'd doth nearly approach, is to be esteem'd better than Man's and Wit and Reason was in vain bestowed on him.

Source: John Ray, *The Wisdom of God Manifested in the Works of the Creation,* 8th ed. (London: William and John Innys, 1722), pp. 164-65.

DOCUMENT 16: Jonathan Edwards on God and Nature (1739)

Like John Ray [see Document 15], the New England theologian Jonathan Edwards attempted to show how nature—the totality of the many aspects of the creation—was a reflection of God's magnificence. Despite his conviction that the whole natural world was created for human use, Edwards believed that people had to live in harmony with the natural world if they were to enjoy its benefits and bask in God's love. According to Edwards, the contemplation of nature helped to turn people away from evil action. Unlike Hobbes [see Document 11], Edwards concluded that people, using reason, could deduce civil and moral precepts from the "nature of things." Edwards' writings and sermons set the groundwork for a Protestant aesthetic spirituality (a belief that the experience of beauty and nature made one sensitive to the presence of God) that was popularized by the transcendentalists in the nineteenth century [see Documents 36 and 44] and found its way into the early writings of John Muir [see Document 47].

The sense I had of divine things, would often of a sudden kindle up, as it were, a sweet burning in my heart; an ardor of soul, that I know not how to express.

Not long after I first began to experience these things . . . I walked abroad alone, in a solitary place in my father's pasture, for contemplation. And as I was walking there, and looking up on the sky and clouds, there came into my mind so sweet a sense of the glorious *majesty* and *grace* of God, that I know not how to express. I seemed to see them both in a sweet conjunction; majesty and meekness joined together; it was a sweet, and gentle, and holy majesty; and also a majestic meekness; an awful sweetness; a high, and great, and holy gentleness.

After this my sense of divine things gradually increased, and became more and more lively, and had more of that inward sweetness. The appearance of every thing was altered; there seemed to be, as it were, a calm, sweet cast, or appearance of divine glory, in almost every thing. God's excellency, his wisdom, his purity and love, seemed to appear in every thing; in the sun, moon, and stars; in the clouds and blue sky; in the grass, flowers, trees; in the water, and all nature.

Source: Jonathan Edwards, "Personal Narrative," in Clarence Faust and Thomas Johnson, eds., *Jonathan Edwards: Representative Selections* (New York: American Book Company, 1935), pp. 60-61.

DOCUMENT 17: Peter Kalm on Land Management (1753)

Peter Kalm was a professor of economy at the University of Aobo in Swedish Finland. His travels in America between 1748 and 1751 were one of a series of voyages sponsored by the Royal Academy at Stockholm "to make . . . such observations and collections of seeds and plants as would improve the Swedish husbandry, gardening, manufactures, arts and sciences. [The great Swedish botanist] Dr. [Carl] Linnaus. . . thought that a voyage through North America would be yet of a more extensive utility, than that through [Siberia and Iceland]; for the plants of America were then little known, and not scientifically described."[8] Here Kalm discusses land use in the colonies.

The rye grows very poorly in most of the fields, which is chiefly owing to the carelessness in agriculture, and to the poorness of the fields, which are seldom or never manured. After the inhabitants have converted a tract of land into a tillable field, which had been a forest for many centuries together, and which consequently had a very fine soil, they use it as such; as long as it will bear any corn; and when it ceases to bear any, they turn it into pasture for the cattle, and take new corn-fields in another place, where a fine soil can be met with and where it has never been made use of for this purpose. This kind of agriculture will do for some time; but it will afterwards have bad consequences, as every one may clearly see. A few of the inhabitants, however, treat their fields a little better: the *English* in general have carried agriculture to a higher degree of perfection than any other nation. But the depth and richness of the soil, which those found here who came over from England (as they were preparing land for plowing, which had been covered with woods from times immemorial) misled them, and made them careless husbandmen. It is well known, that the *Indians* lived in this country for several centuries before the *Europeans* came into it; but it is likewise known, that they lived chiefly by hunting and fishing, and had hardly any fields. They planted maize, and some species of beans and gourds; and at the same time it is certain, that a plantation of such vegetables as serve an *Indian* family during one year, take up no more ground than a farmer in our country takes to plant cabbage for his family upon; at least, a farmer's cabbage and turnep ground, taken together, is always as extensive, if not more so, than the corn-fields and kitchen-gardens of an *Indian* family. Therefore, the *Indians*

could hardly subsist for one month upon the produce of their gardens and fields. Commonly, the little villages of *Indians* are about twelve or eighteen miles distant from each other. From hence one may judge, how little ground was formerly employed for planting corn-fields; and the rest was overgrown with thick and tall trees. And though they cleared (as is yet usual) new ground, as soon as the old one had lost its fertility; yet such little pieces as they made use of were very inconsiderable, when compared to the vast forest which remained. Thus the upper fertile soil increased considerably for centuries together; and the *Europeans* coming to *America* found a rich, fine soil before them, lying as loose between the trees as the best bed in a garden. They had nothing to do but to cut down the wood, put it up in heaps, and to clear the dead leaves away. They could then immediately proceed to plowing, which in such loose ground is very easy; and having sown their corn, they got a most plentiful harvest. This easy method of getting a rich crop has spoiled the *English* and other *European* settlers, and induced them to adopt the same method of agriculture which the *Indians* make use of; that is, to sow uncultivated grounds, as long as they will produce a crop without manuring, but to turn them into pastures as soon as they can bear no more, and to take on new spots of ground, covered since time immemorial with woods, which have been spared by the fire or the hatchet ever since the creation.

Source: Peter Kalm, *Travels into North America; containing Its Natural History, and a Circumstantial Account of Its Plantations and Agriculture in General*, trans. John Reinhold Forster, Vol. 2 (Warrington, England: William Eyres, 1772), pp. 191-94.

DOCUMENT 18: William Blackstone's On the Rights of Things (1765-1769)

William Blackstone's history of the doctrines of English law greatly influenced the development of jurisprudence in the United States, and the roots of American law concerning property rights can be traced to this seminal work. Private property and property rights would become core areas of contention in the ongoing environmental debate.

There is nothing which so generally strikes the imagination, and engages the affections of mankind, as the right of property; or that sole and despotic dominion which one man claims and exercises over the external things of the world, in total exclusion of the right of any other individual in the universe. And yet there are very few, that will give themselves the trouble to consider the original and foundation of this right. . . .

In the beginning of the world, we are informed by holy writ, the all-bountiful creator gave to man, "dominion over all the earth; and over the fish of the sea, and over the fowl of the air, and over every living thing that moveth upon the earth." This is the only true and solid foundation of man's dominion over external things, whatever airy metaphysical notions may have been started by fanciful writers upon this subject. The earth therefore, and all things therein, are the general property of all mankind, exclusive of other beings, from the immediate gift of the creator. And, while the earth continued bare of inhabitants, it is reasonable to suppose, that all was in common among them, and that every one took from the public stock to his own use such things as his immediate necessities required.

These general notions of property were then sufficient to answer all the purposes of human life; and might perhaps still have answered them, had it been possible for mankind to have remained in a state of primaeval simplicity: as may be collected from the manners of many American nations when first discovered by the Europeans; and from the antient method of living among the first Europeans themselves. . . . Not that this communion of goods seems ever to have been applicable, even in the earliest ages, to ought but the *substance* of the thing; nor could it be extended to the *use* of it. For, by the law of nature and reason, he who first

began to use it acquired therein a kind of transient property, that lasted so long as he was using it, and no longer. . . .

But when mankind increased in number, craft, and ambition, it became necessary to entertain conceptions of more permanent dominion; and to appropriate to individuals not the immediate *use* only, but the very *substance* of the thing to be used. Otherwise innumerable tumults must have arisen, and the good order of the world been continually broken and disturbed. . . .

* * *

Property, both in lands and moveables, being thus originally acquired by the first taker, which taking amounts to a declaration that he intends to appropriate the thing to his own use, it remains in him, by the principles of universal law, till such time as he does some other act which shews an intention to abandon it: for then it becomes, naturally speaking, *publici juris* once more, and is liable to be again appropriated by the next occupant. . . .

But this method of one man's abandoning his property, and another seising the vacant possession, however well founded in theory, could not long subsist in fact. It was calculated merely for the rudiments of civil society, and necessarily ceased among the complicated interests and artificial refinements of polite and established governments. In these it was found, that what became inconvenient or useless to one man was highly convenient and useful to another; who was ready to give in exchange for it some equivalent, that was equally desirable to the former proprietor. Thus mutual convenience introduced commercial traffic, and the reciprocal transfer of property by sale, grant, or conveyance.

Source: William Blackstone, *Commentaries on the Laws of England*, Vol. 2 (Philadelphia: Bell, 1771-1772), pp. 2-4, 9.

DOCUMENT 19: John Bartram on Reclaiming Florida's Wetlands (1767)

Traditionally, the marsh was a wild, evil place that was feared and had to be subdued. It was thought to be the home of murderous spirits and dangerous monsters such as Grendel, the huge moor-stalking subject of the tenth-century Anglo-Saxon epic poem "Beowulf" "who held the wasteland, fens, and marshes."[9]

The colonists brought this view of wetlands with them to the new world. In the United States, until the latter part of the twentieth century, marshes and other wetlands were generally regarded as wastelands, evil places, and sources of diseases such as malaria; they were places to be avoided and, if technologically possible, to be done away with.

John Bartram, the first American-born naturalist, was a self-educated farmer. Although he never traveled to Europe, he knew all the major European naturalists of his day either personally—because, like Peter Kalm [see Document 17], they came to visit his acclaimed garden at his home outside Philadelphia—or through written correspondence. Eager to have contact with the greatest thinkers of his time, Bartram urged his friend and fellow Philadelphian Ben Franklin to organize a society of the "most ingenious and curious men"[10] in America, and in 1692 Franklin formed the American Philosophical Society, the first scientific organization in America, to promote useful knowledge and encourage scientific agriculture.

When Bartram was in his sixties, he was appointed botanist to the king of England, and in this capacity he surveyed the newly acquired territory of Florida for the English Crown. Although he remarked upon the richness of the wetlands and recognized their function as a sanctuary for young fish, he nevertheless was the first of many people to recommend the reclamation of Florida's wet-lands.

The pine-lands, as they are here called, contain a variety of soil, according to their different situations. . . . The pine-land, by the help of dung and cultivation, will produce good corn, potatoes, and cotton; the large palmetto declining ground, between the pines and swamps, are moist and seem rich, and perhaps will suit both corn and indigo; but the shelly bluffs seem to be the most fertile spots of high ground, and the Indians chief plantations for corn and pumkins: That which is called hammocky ground is generally full of large evergreens and water-oaks, mixed with red-bay and magnolia, and in many places the great palmetto or cabbagetree: this is generally reckoned proper both for corn, cotton, and indigo: but the marshes and swamps (so extensive upon the river St. John's) are exceedingly rich, the last of which are full of large ash, maple, and elm, being of an unknown depth of rich mud; so are the marshes on the upper part of the river, which are covered with water-canes and reeds, as the lower marshes are with grass and weeds; all of which when they are drained dry, will produce, in all probability, great crops of corn and indigo, and without much or any draining, a fine increase of rice. . . .

St. John's river, by its near affinity to the sea, is well replenished with variety of excellent fish, as bass, sea-trout, sheep-head, drums, mullets, cats, garr, sturgeon, stingrays; and near its mouth, oysters, crabs, and shrimps, sharks and porpoises, which will doubtless continue. . . . Its shores, being generally shoal . . . afford a fine asylum to the young fry against their devouring enemies.

Source: William Stork, A Description of East-Florida, with a Journal, Kept by John Bartram of Philadelphia, Botanist to His Majesty for the Floridas; upon a Journey from St. Augustines up the River St. John, as Far as the Lakes, 4th ed. (London: Faden & Jefferys, 1774), p. 34.

Part II

Politicians, Naturalists, and Artists in the New Nation, 1776–1839

On the eve of the Revolution, the thirteen belligerent British colonies clustered along the Atlantic coast had a population of approximately 2.5 million, including about half a million blacks. Approximately 90 percent of the workforce was engaged in agriculture. By 1790, there were nearly 4 million people in the United States, by 1820 over 9.5 million, and by 1830, close to 13 million. In just sixty-five years the nation's population had more than quintupled. It had also begun to be both more urban and more industrial.

Educated Americans, such as Thomas Jefferson and James Madison who followed trends in Europe and purchased many of their reading materials abroad, were knowledgeable about and interested in the theories of European economists, including Thomas Malthus, concerning the relationship of populousness, land ownership, and poverty [see Documents 21 and 26]. However, these issues did not arouse the passions of most Americans. Although there were poor people in the United States, large pockets of urban poverty comparable to those found in London and Paris were unknown in the United States until well into the nineteenth century. Furthermore,

in late eighteenth- and early nineteenth- century America, there was plenty of unsettled land available for farmers—unlike in western Europe, where much of the arable land had been farmed for generations. Indeed, the U.S. government was anxious to populate the nation's western lands with Europeans and their descendants.

Growth of The Nation

In the Treaty of 1783, Great Britain not only recognized the independence of the thirteen American colonies but also, very generously, established the Mississippi River as the western boundary of the new nation, far beyond the westernmost border of any of the existing colonies. Twenty years later, Thomas Jefferson's purchase of the Louisiana Territory from France moved the young nation's western boundary to the Rocky Mountains and incorporated into the country the Great Plains, a terrain vastly different from the deciduous forest regions of the Northeast.

The territories west of the original thirteen colonies gained new inhabitants during the first half-century of the country's existence. One of the most formidable obstacles to the western movement of the populace was the difficulty of overland transportation. Even within the former colonies, overland travel was slow and arduous because there were virtually no paved roads. Indeed, the nation's earliest cities—Boston, New York, Philadelphia, and Charleston—were on the Atlantic coast, and the first inland areas to develop had easy river access to the Atlantic, since boat transportation was far more efficient than road travel.

The Indians—abetted at times by Britain, France, and Spain—also posed a continuous hindrance to the expansion of the country. In 1829, President Andrew Jackson proposed that the remaining tribes in the eastern United States be bodily moved and resettled west of the Mississippi; this was the beginning of an official U.S. policy of removing Indians from lands that whites coveted. In 1832, Indians, under the leadership of Black Hawk, tried to reoccupy their land in Illinois, but their rebellion was crushed [see Document 32] in a bloody battle. In Florida, which the United States had acquired from Spain in 1819, the Seminole Indians also fiercely resisted eviction and white settlement, but by the end of the 1830s, three-quarters of them had been moved to Oklahoma.

The extensive territorial growth of the country, along with its increasing industrialization, demanded the development of an efficient transportation infrastructure, and by the late 1830s, several hard-surfaced turnpikes had been constructed, steamboats were plying some of the nation's rivers, railroads had begun to radiate out from major cities, and the Erie Canal had been completed, connecting the Hudson River and the East with Lake Erie and the West. Simultaneously, the occupational base of the country was changing, and by the 1830s less than three-quarters of the nation's workforce was employed on farms. It was a trend that had disturbed Americans like Thomas Jefferson when it first became apparent, but as the century progressed, the increasing industrialization and urbanization of the United States was recognized as necessary for national economic development [see Document 20].

Since the end of the seventeenth century, trappers and traders, eager to obtain furs to ship to Europe, had been slowly moving into the interior of the country and encouraging Indians, often against their will, to join them in hunting and trapping in the furtherance of trade rather than for mere subsistence. Miners and, later, loggers and farmers followed the trappers and traders west. In 1720 the first lead mine in the country was opened in Missouri. As roads and trains improved, the trickle of pioneers going west became a flood.

Caring for The Land and its Resources

The abundance of cheap land worked against the development of an attitude of respect for the land and its resources. Early American farmers found it more expedient to deplete the land and move on than to maintain their property [see Document 17]. Even farmers such as George Washington and Thomas Jefferson, who were greatly invested in caring for their land, recognized that the availability of cheap land made it impractical to spend large sums for fertilizer for their fields [see Document 25]. It was only when land values had risen sufficiently to warrant large expenditures on soil improvement that farmers began to devote energy and money to the maintenance of the soil's fertility.

Forests were cleared for farmland with great abandon, and the only serious efforts to preserve woodland stemmed from the desire to maintain stands of trees for the shipbuilding industry or to satisfy local construction and firewood needs [see Document 13]. Dr. Benjamin Rush's call in 1791 for the preservation of the sugar maple [see Document 24] was motivated more by social, economic, and political considerations than by environmental factors.

At the federal level, there was little evidence of concern about resources and their conservation during the first half-century of the nation's existence. The acquisition of new lands, access to Atlantic fisheries, and the availability of timber for shipbuilding were the primary resource issues. The Treaty of 1783, the Treaty of Ghent (which settled the War of 1812 and which John Quincy Adams helped to negotiate), and the Treaty of 1818 all stipulated that Americans would continue to have access to the fisheries off the coast of Newfoundland.

In 1799, Congress, conscious of the need for suitable timber for tall ship masts and also aware that hardwoods were being stolen from public lands along the coast of the Gulf of Mexico, appropriated $200,000 for President John Adams to purchase two heavily forested islands off the Georgia coast, Grover's Island and Blackbeard's Island. The policy of protecting timber resources for the fledgling U.S. Navy was continued under the administrations of James

Monroe and John Quincy Adams, during which time Congress passed three acts—in 1817, 1822, and 1827—to set aside land along the Gulf Coast to provide timber for the navy [*see* Document 28]. In 1828, President John Quincy Adams took over a timbered area of Pensacola, Florida, to establish a naval station, and then set aside 30,000 acres of live-oak forest land, on Santa Rosa Island, near Pensacola, to provide wood for the future shipbuilding needs of the navy.[1]

Not much thought was given to conservation at the state level either. But in 1818, in Massachusetts, the nation's first bird- protection law [*see* Document 29] was passed, because farmers recognized that birds provided not only meat and feathers but also some measure of crop protection.

During these early years of the country, naturalists such as William Bartram [*see* Document 23] and John James Audubon [*see* Document 33] and explorers such as Meriwether Lewis and William Clark [*see* Document 27] traveled through the United States, drawing, painting, and inventorying the nation's flora, fauna, and geological resources. Their reports and journals extolled the beauty and diversity of the land and the creatures that inhabited it. But they also depicted the effects of the human presence on the natural landscape. By the 1830s writers were deploring the destruction of the buffalo, the killing of birds, and the wanton slaughter of many species of wild animals.

Other writers and artists increasingly conveyed a growing appreciation of the wilderness, often accompanied by a fascination with American Indians and their way of life. Probably the earliest expression of this admiration for both wild nature and Native Americans is to be found in the myth of the noble savage, who loves and understands the wilderness and is unhappy when forced to live apart from it. The myth, whose origins date back to the seventeenth century, was in part a reaction to growing industrialization—a look backward to a disappearing way of life—and in part a rejection of the pastoral ideal. It was the springboard for countless poems, stories, and paintings, ranging from Philip Freneau's "Indian Student" [*see* Document 22] to George Catlin's realistic portraits of Indian chiefs. Catlin, who traveled to the West to paint Indians in their natural settings, fell in love with the magnificent western scenery and, realizing that the land would soon be overrun by settlers from the East, suggested that some of the grasslands be set aside for a national park [*see* Document 31]. The novelist James Fenimore Cooper also saw the hand of progress destroying the old way of life. The hero of his Leatherstocking series is an upstate New York frontiersman with a great attachment to the wilderness and disdain for many of the laws and trappings of modern civilization [*see* Document 30].

DOCUMENT 20: Thomas Jefferson on Agrarianism and Industrialization (1785, 1816)

Thomas Jefferson's early agrarianism reflected a conviction that contact with the land improves the human soul and is good for the human spirit, but eventually Jefferson recognized the importance of industrial development for the well-being of the United States. By the end of the century, however, as the Industrial Revolution began to impinge on the lives of most Americans, the Transcendentalists, including Ralph Waldo Emerson and Henry David Thoreau [see Documents 36 and 44], and the Romantics, such as Thomas Cole [see Document 34] would once again raise the banner of agrarianism.

A. From *Notes on the State of Virginia*, 1785

The political oeconomists of Europe have established it as a principle that every state should endeavour to manufacture for itself; and this principle, like many others, we transfer to America, without calculating the difference of circumstance which should often produce a difference of result. In Europe the lands are either cultivated, or locked up against the cultivator. Manufacture must therefore be resorted to of necessity not of choice, to support the surplus of their people. But we have an immensity of land courting the industry of the husbandman. Is it best then that all our citizens should be employed in its improvement, or that one half should be called off from that to exercise manufactures and handicraft arts for the other? Those who labour in the earth are the chosen people of God, if ever He had a chosen people, whose breasts He has made His peculiar deposit for substantial and genuine virtue. It is the focus in which he keeps alive that sacred fire, which otherwise might escape from the face of the earth. Corruption of morals in the mass of cultivators is a phaenomenon of which no age nor nation has furnished an example. . . . While we have land to labour then, let us never wish to see our citizens occupied at a work-bench, or twirling a distaff. Carpenters, masons, smiths, are wanting in husbandry; but, for the general operations of manufacture, let our work-shops remain in Europe.

B. To Benjamin Austin, 1816

We must now place the manufacturer by the side of the agriculturalist. . . . The grand inquiry now is, shall we make our own comforts, or go without them at the will of a foreign nation? He, therefore, who is now against domestic manufacture, must be for reducing us either to dependence on that foreign nation, or to be clothed in skins, and to live like wild beasts in dens and caverns. I am not one of these. Experience has taught me that manufactures are now as necessary to our independence as to our comfort.

Source: **A.** Thomas Jefferson, *Notes on the State of Virginia* (London: Stockdale, 1786), pp. 273-75. **B.** Thomas Jefferson Randolph, ed., *Memoirs, Correspondence, and Private Papers of Thomas Jefferson,* Vol. 4 (London: Colburn and Bentley, 1829), p. 279.

DOCUMENT 21: James Madison on Population and Property (1786, 1787/1788)

One of the drafters of the U.S. Constitution, James Madison, devoted much thought to the issue of private property ownership. Among his concerns were how an increase in the population of the country would affect the equitable distribution of land and the divisions that would develop as a result of ownership of property or the lack thereof.

A. To Thomas Jefferson, June 19, 1786

I have no doubt but that the misery of the lower classes will be found to abate wherever the Government assumes a freer aspect, & the laws favor a subdivision of property, yet I suspect that the difference will not fully account for the comparative comfort of the mass of people in the United States. Our limited population has probably as large a share in producing this effect as the political advantages which distinguish us. A certain degree of misery seems inseparable from a high degree of populousness. If the lands in Europe which are now dedicated to the amusement of the idle rich, were parcelled out among the idle poor, I readily conceive the happy revolution which would be experienced by a certain proportion of the latter. But still would there

not remain a great proportion unrelieved? No problem in political economy has appeared to me more puzzling than that which relates to the most proper distribution of the inhabitants of a country fully peopled. Let the lands be shared among them ever so wisely, & let them be supplied with labourers ever so plentifully; as there must be a great surplus of subsistence, there will also remain a great surplus of inhabitants, a greater by far than will be employed in cloathing both themselves & those who feed them, and in administering to both, every other necessary & even comfort of life. What is to be done with this surplus? Hitherto we have seen them distributed into manufactures of superfluities, idle proprietors of productive lands, domestics, soldiers, merchants, mariners, and a few other less numerous classes. All these classes notwithstanding have been found insufficient to absorb the redundant members of a populous society; and yet a reduction of most of those classes enters into the very reform which appears so necessary & desirable. From a more equal partition of property, must result a greater simplicity of manners, consequently a less consumption of manufactured superfluities, and a less proportion of idle proprietors & domestics.

B. The Federalist, Number 10, 1787/1788

As long as the reason of man continues fallible, and he is at liberty to exercise it, different opinions will be formed. As long as the connection subsists between his reason and self-love, his opinions and his passions will have a reciprocal influence on each other; and the former will be objects to which the latter will attach themselves. The diversity in the faculties of men, from which the rights of property originate, is not less an insuperable obstacle to a uniformity of interests. The protection of these faculties is the first object of government. From the protection of different and unequal faculties of acquiring property, the possession of different degrees and kinds of property immediately results; and from the influence of these on the sentiments and view of the respective proprietors, ensues a division of the society into different interests and parties.

. . . [T]he most common and durable source of factions has been the various and unequal distribution of property. Those who hold and those who are without property have ever formed distinct interests in society.

Source: **A.** Saul K. Padover, ed., *The Complete Madison: His Basic Writings* (New York: Harper, 1953), pp. 317-18. **B.** Alexander Hamilton, James Madison and John Jay, *The Federalist,* ed. Benjamin Fletcher Wright (Cambridge, MA: Harvard University/Belknap Press, 1966), pp. 130-31.

DOCUMENT 22: Philip Freneau's Noble Savage (1788)

The Swiss-born American poet and essayist Philip Freneau used the romantic myth of the noble savage as the basis for his tale of "The Indian Student." By juxtaposing the life of a Harvard student with a life lived closer to nature, Freneau was subtly raising a question about the superiority of Western values, a question that would be posed more vociferously by environmentalists in the latter part of the twentieth century. The student, who yearns for a return to wild nature and lays aside his Virgil, embodies the romantic rejection of the pastoral ideal of the cultivated landscape [see Document 2].

From Susquehanna's utmost springs
Where savage tribes pursue their game,
His blanket tied with yellow strings,
A shepherd of the forest came.

Not long before, a wandering priest
Express'd his wish, with visage sad—
"Ah, why (he cry'd) in Satan's Waste,
"Ah, why detain so fine a lad?

"In Yanky land there stands a town
"Where learning may be purchas'd low—
"Exchange his blanket for a gown,
"And let the lad to college go."—

From long debate the Council rose,
And viewing *Shalum's* tricks with joy,
To *Harvard hall,* o'er wastes of snows,
They sent the copper-colour'd boy.

***

Awhile he writ, awhile he read,
Awhile he learn'd the grammar rules—
An Indian savage so well bred
Great credit promis'd to their schools.

Some thought he would in *law* excel,
Some said in *physic* he would shine;
And one that knew him, passing well,
Beheld, in him, a sound divine.

But those of more discerning eye
Even then could other prospects show,
And saw him lay his *Virgil* by
To wander with his dearer *bow.*

The tedious hours of study spent,
The heavy-moulded lecture done,
He to the woods a hunting went,
But sigh'd to see the setting sun.

No mystic wonders fir'd his mind;
He sought to gain no learn'd degree,
But only sense enough to find
The squirrel in the hollow tree.

***

"And why (he cry'd) did I forsake
"My native wood for gloomy walls;
"The silver stream, the limpid lake
"For musty books and college halls.

"A little could my wants supply—
"Can wealth and honour give me more;
"Or, will the sylvan god deny
"The humble treat he gave before?

***

"Where Nature's ancient forests grow,
"And mingled laurel never fades,
"My heart is fix'd;—and I must go
"To die among my native shades."

He spoke, and to the western springs,
(His gown discharg'd, his money spent)
His blanket tied with yellow strings,
The shepherd of the forest went.

Source: Philip Freneau, "The Indian Student," *The Poems and Miscellaneous Works,* ed. Lewis Leary (Delmar, NY: Scholar, 1975; facsimile of two works printed separately in 1786 and 1788 by F. Bailey), pp. 69-71.

DOCUMENT 23: William Bartram on the Human Impact on the Environment (1791)

Before setting out on his own to explore the southeastern coast of America, the renowned botanical illustrator William Bartram had traveled through much of the area with his father, John Bartram [see Document 19], and had attempted to raise indigo (a plant used to obtain a blue dye) in Florida. In his travels along the St. Johns River, William Bartram took note of the interplay between people—both Indians and whites—and their surroundings, remarking on how people changed the face of the land to suit their own particular needs when they settled in a certain place, and on how humans could turn a beautiful place into a devastated landscape. Many people consider William Bartram to have been the first American environmentalist.

About the middle of May, every thing being in readiness to proceed up the river, we sat sail. . . .

We had a pleasant day, the wind fair and moderate, and ran by Mount Hope, so named by my father John Bartram, when he ascended this river, about fifteen years ago. It is a very high shelly bluff, upon the little lake. It was at that time a fine Orange grove, but now cleared and converted into a large indigo plantation, the property of an English gentleman, under the care of an agent. In the evening we arrived at Mount Royal, where we came and stayed the night. . . .

From this place we enjoyed a most enchanting prospect of the great Lake George, through a grand avenue, if I may so term this narrow reach of the river, which widens gradually for about two miles, towards its entrance into the little lake, so as to elude the exact rules of perspective, and appears of an equal width.

At about fifty yards distance from the landing place, stands a magnificent Indian mount. About fifteen years ago I visited this place, at which time there were no settlements of white people, but all appeared wild and savage; yet in that uncultivated state it possessed an almost inexpressible air of grandeur, which was now entirely changed. At that time there was a very considerable extent of old fields round about the mount; there was also a large orange grove, together with palms and live oaks, extending from near the mount, along the banks, downwards, all of which has since been cleared away to make room for planting ground. But what greatly contributed towards completing the magnificence of the scene, was a noble Indian highway, which led from the great mount, on a straight line, three quarters of a mile, first through a point or wing of the orange grove, and continuing thence through an awful forest of live oaks, it was terminated by palms and laurel magnolias, on the verge of an oblong artificial lake, which was on the edge of an extensive green level savanna. This grand highway was about fifty yards wide, sunk a little below the common level, and the earth thrown up on each side, making a bank of about two feet high. Neither nature nor art could any where present a more striking contrast, as you approached this savanna. The glittering water pond played on the sight, through the dark grove, like a brilliant diamond, on the bosom of the illumined savanna, bordered with various flowery shrubs and plants; and as we advanced into the plain, the sight was agreeably relieved by a distant view of the forests, which partly environed the green expanse on the left hand, whilst the imagination was still flattered and entertained by the far distant misty points of the surrounding forests, which projected into the plain, alternately appearing and disappearing, making a grand sweep round on the right, to the distant banks of the great lake. But that venerable grove is now no more. All has been cleared away and planted with indigo, corn, and cotton, but since deserted: there was now scarcely five acres of ground under fence. It appeared like a desart to a great extent, and terminated, on the land side, by frightful thickets, and open pine forests.

Source: William Bartram, *Travels Through North and South Carolina, Georgia and Florida* (Philadelphia: James and Johnson, 1791), pp. 96-98.

DOCUMENT 24: Benjamin Rush on Saving the Sugar Maple (1791)

The relationship between conservation and political and social issues is evident in this letter by a prominent Revolutionary era physician. Dr. Benjamin Rush's plea for the preservation of the sugar maple, which was combined with a quest for the emancipation of slaves, was probably one of the earliest proposals to save trees that was not concerned with timber for construction or firewood.

Sugar was a luxury commodity in the colonial period and during the early decades of the nation. It was only in the mid-nineteenth century that it became inexpensive enough to come into wide use among the middle class.

The *Acer Sacharinum* of Linnaeus, or Sugar Maple-tree, grows in great quantities in the western counties of all the Middle States of the American Union. Those which grow in New-York and Pennsylvania yield the sugar in a greater quantity than those which grow on the waters of the Ohio.

***

But the profit of the maple tree is not confined to its sugar. It affords a most agreeable molasses, and an excellent vinegar. The sap which is suitable for these purposes is obtained after the sap which affords the sugar has ceased to flow, so that the manufactories of these different products of the maple tree, by *succeeding,* do not interfere with each other. The molasses may be made to compose the basis of a pleasant summer beer. The sap of the maple is moreover capable of affording a spirit, but we hope this precious juice will never be prostituted by our citizens to this ignoble purpose. Should the use of sugar in diet become more general in our country, it may tend to lessen the inclination or supposed necessity for spirits, for I have observed a relish for sugar in diet to be seldom accompanied by a love for strong drink.

***

Cases may occur in which sugar may be required in medicine, or in diet, by persons who refuse to be benefited, even indirectly by the labour of slaves. In such cases, the innocent maple sugar will always be preferred.

It has been said, that sugar injures the teeth, but this opinion now has so few advocates, that it does not deserve a serious refutation.

To transmit to future generations, all the advantages which have been enumerated from the maple tree, it will be necessary to protect it by law, or by a bounty upon the maple sugar, from being destroyed by the settlers in the maple country, or to transplant it from the woods, and cultivate it in the old and improved parts of the United States. An orchard consisting of 200 trees, planted upon a common farm would yield more than the same number of apple trees, at a distance from a market town. A full grown tree in the woods yields five pounds of sugar a year. If a greater exposure of a tree to the action of the sun, has the same effects upon the maple, that it has upon other trees, a larger quantity of sugar might reasonably be expected from each tree planted in an orchard.

***

In contemplating the present opening prospects in human affairs, I am led to expect that a material share of the happiness, which Heaven seems to have prepared for a part of mankind, will be derived from the manufactory and general use of maple sugar, for the benefits which I flatter myself are to result from it, will not be confined to our own country. They will, I hope, extend themselves to the interests of humanity in the West-Indies. With this view of the subject of this letter, I cannot help contemplating a sugar maple tree with a species of affection and even veneration, for I have persuaded myself to behold in it the happy means of rendering the commerce and slavery of our African brethren, in the sugar Islands as unnecessary, as it has always been inhuman and unjust.

Source: Benjamin Rush to Thomas Jefferson, July 10, 1791, in Benjamin Rush, *Essays, Literary, Moral and Philosophical* (Philadelphia: Bradford, 1806), pp. 270, 282, 284-85, 287.

DOCUMENT 25: The Founding Fathers on the Care of the Land (1793, 1818)

Three of the first four U.S. presidents—George Washington, Thomas Jefferson, and James Madison—were Virginia planters who devoted a great deal of thought, study, and effort to the development of techniques for making their land more productive. While they carefully rotated crops and fields, they rejected the use of high-priced fertilizers until rising land prices made such expenditures practical. They were all active members of the American Philosophical Society, one of whose primary goals was the furtherance of scientific agriculture.

A. Thomas Jefferson to George Washington, June 28, 1793

Manure does not enter into this [the making of a good farm] because we can buy an acre of new land cheaper than we can manure an old acre.

B. Thomas Jefferson to Thomas Mann Rudolphe, July 28, 1793

[Dr. George Logan] thinks that the whole improvement in the modern agriculture of Europe consists in the substitution of red clover instead of 3 years of fallow or rest, whether successive or interspersed leaves the land much heartier at the close of the rotation; that there is no doubt of this fact, the difference being palpable.

C. George Washington to Thomas Jefferson, n.d.

I permit no separate inclosures of my fields. their limits are preserved by 2. Rows of peach trees, leaving a road between them. my fields are by this means protected from pasturage as follows

Wheat after 2. years of clover, the clover turned in in autumn by [illegible] ploughing, the wheat sowed on that & buried by a harrow drawn the direction of the furrows. . . . as soon as the wheat is cut I propose (as soon as I can get the winter vetch) to turn in the stubble, sow vetch and cut it for green fodder in Feb. & March. Then turn in the stubble of that as a green . . . dressing, & the ground is ready for [illegible] in alternate rows 41 feet apart. Put into the drills the long dung which has been made from the straw of this field in the preceding winter, in autumn sow vetch again.

D. James Madison on Intelligent Husbandry, 1818

The error first to be noticed [in our husbandry] is that of cultivating land, either naturally poor or impoverished by cultivation. This error, like many others, is the effect of habit, continued after the reason for it has failed. Whilst there was an abundance of fresh and fertile soil, it was the interest of the cultivator to spread his labor over as great a surface as he could. Land being cheap and labor dear, and the land co-operating powerfully with the labor, it was profitable to draw as much as possible from the land. Labor is now comparatively cheaper and land dearer. . . . It might be profitable, therefore, now to contract the surface over which labor is spread, even if the soil retained its freshness and fertility. But this is not the case. Much of the fertile soil is exhausted, and unfertile soils are brought into cultivation.

***

The evil of pressing too hard upon the land, has also been much increased by the bad mode of ploughing it. Shallow ploughing, and ploughing up and down hilly land, have, by exposing the loosened soil to be carried off by rains, hastened more than any thing else, the waste of its fertility.

***

The neglect of manures is another error which claims particular notice. It may be traced to the same cause with our excessive cropping. In the early stages of our agriculture, it was more convenient, and more profitable, to bring new land into cultivation, than to improve exhausted land.

Source: **A-C.** Edwin Morris Betts, ed., *Thomas Jefferson's Farm Book* (Princeton, NJ: Princeton University Press, 1953), pp. 194, 188-89, 314. **D.** "Agricultural Society of Albemarle; Address by Mr. Madison," *Niles' Weekly Register,* Vol. II (New Series), No. 21 (July 18, 1818), in Robert McHenry and Charles Van Doren, eds., *A Documentary History of Conservation in America* (New York: Praeger, 1972), pp. 273-75.

DOCUMENT 26: Thomas Malthus's *Essay on the Principle of Population* (1798)

By the seventeenth century, population pressures in Europe had created an increasing need for farmland and a demand for changes in landownership patterns. Thomas Malthus's apocalyptic essay theorizing that population, if unchecked, multiplies geometrically while the food supply multiplies only arithmetically and that this will eventually result in a food crisis was an outgrowth of an ongoing discussion among economists in France and England about how to deal with population growth and its consequences. At the time that Malthus published his essay, many people in the United States, including James Madison [see Document 21], were familiar with these discussions but did not consider them to have much bearing on the contemporary U.S. situation. Two and a half decades later, in a letter to Edward Everett (a Harvard professor of Greek who later became a congressman, senator, and governor of Massachusetts), Madison complained that Malthus had ignored the effects of political and social policy on population growth.

By the mid-twentieth century, though, the growth of the U.S. population and the increase in poverty had made food supply and land availability relevant issues, and doom-saying American economists and biologists, such as Paul Ehrlich [see Document 107], could be heard repeating the Malthusian arguments, including his law of "diminishing returns," which states that, as time goes by, increasingly greater effort is required to obtain the same yield from a mine, a forest, or a piece of land.

A. Malthus's Essay

I think I may fairly make two postulata.

First, That food is necessary to the existence of man.

Secondly, That the passion between the sexes is necessary and will remain nearly in its present state.

These two laws, ever since we have had any knowledge of mankind, appear to have been fixed laws of our nature, and, as we have not hitherto seen any alteration in them, we have no right to conclude that they will ever cease to be what they now are, without an immediate act of power in that Being who first arranged the system of the universe, and for the advantage of his creatures, still executes, according to fixed laws, all its various operations.

I do not know that any writer has supposed that on this earth man will ultimately be able to live without food. But Mr. [William] Godwin has conjectured that the passion between the sexes may in time be extinguished. As, however, he calls this part of his work a deviation into the land of conjecture, I will not dwell longer upon it at present than to say that the best arguments for the perfectibility of man are drawn from a contemplation of the great progress that he has already made from the savage state and the difficulty of

saying where he is to stop. But towards the extinction of the passion between the sexes, no progress whatever has hitherto been made. It appears to exist in as much force at present as it did two thousand or four thousand years ago. . . .

Assuming then, my postulata as granted, I say that the power of population is indefinitely greater than the power in the earth to produce subsistence for man.

Population, when unchecked, increases in a geometrical ratio. Subsistence increases only in an arithmetical ratio. A slight acquaintance with numbers will shew the immensity of the first power in comparison of the second.

By that law of our nature which makes food necessary to the life of man, the effects of these two unequal powers must be kept equal.

This implies a strong and constantly operating check on population from the difficulty of subsistence. This difficulty must fall some where and must necessarily be severely felt by a large portion of mankind.

Through the animal and vegetable kingdoms, nature has scattered the seeds of life abroad with the most profuse and liberal hand. She has been comparatively sparing in the room and the nourishment necessary to rear them. The germs of existence contained in this spot of earth, with ample food and ample room to expand in, would fill millions of worlds in the course of a few thousand years. Necessity, that imperious all pervading law of nature, restrains them within the prescribed bounds. The race of plants and the race of animals shrink under this great restrictive law. And the race of man cannot, by any efforts of reason, escape from it. Among plants and animals its effects are waste of seed, sickness, and premature death. Among mankind, misery and vice.

B. James Madison to Edward Everett, November 26, 1823

That the rate of increase in the population of the U.S. is influenced at the same time by their political & social condition is proved by the slower increase under the vicious institutions of Spanish America where Nature was not less bountiful. Nor can it be doubted that the actual population of Europe wd be augmented by such reforms in the systems as would enlighten & animate the efforts to render the funds of subsistence more productive. We see everywhere

in that quarter of the Globe, the people increasing in number as the ancient burdens & abuses have yielded to the progress of light & civilization. . . .

Mr. Malthus has certainly shewn much ability in his illustrations & applications of the principle he assumes, however much he may have erred in some of his positions. But he has not all the merit of originality which has been allowed him. The principle was adverted to & reasoned upon, long before him, tho' with views & applications not the same with his. The principle is indeed inherent in all the organized beings on the Globe, as well of the animal as the vegetable classes; all & each of which when left to themselves, multiply till checked by the limited fund of their pabulum, or by the mortality generated by an excess of their numbers.

Source: **A.** Thomas Robert Malthus, *An Essay on the Principle of Population,* ed. Philip Appleman (New York: W. W. Norton, 1976), pp. 18, 19-20. **B.** Saul K. Padover, ed., *The Complete Madison: His Basic Writings* (New York: Harper, 1953), p. 322.

DOCUMENT 27: Meriwether Lewis on the Slaughter of Buffaloes (1804-1806)

In their expedition to find a practical route to the Pacific Ocean (the fabled Northwest Passage) and, simultaneously, to explore the new lands acquired in the Louisiana Purchase, Captain Meriwether Lewis and William Clark traveled up the Missouri River to its source, across the Great Divide in the Rocky Mountains, and then down the Columbia River to the Pacific Ocean. The purposes of this first official U.S. expedition and first official survey of some of the nation's resources were commercial, political, and scientific—to acquire data about the geographic features of the land, Indian life and culture, and the flora and fauna west of the Missouri. One of Lewis's conclusions was that much of the land through which they had passed was unsuitable for intensive farming.

Lewis took note in his journals of the great diversity of Indian cultures and commented on variations in diet, housing, and farming, fishing, and hunting techniques. In this selection, Lewis describes an Indian method of hunting bison without employing a horse, gun, or even a bow and arrow. Use of the buffalo jump technique, which enabled Indians to kill 100 to 200 animals at a time, had little impact on the bison population compared with the massive slaughters that the whites were able to carry out using firearms, horses, and horse-drawn vehicles.

today we passed on the Stard. side the remains of a vast many mangled carcases of Buffalow which had been driven over a precipice of 120 feet by the Indians and perished; the water appeared to have washed away a part

of this immence pile of slaughter and still their remained the fragments of at least a hundred carcases they created a most horrid stench. in this manner the Indians of the Missouri distroy vast herds of buffaloe at a stroke; for this purpose one of the most active and fleet young men is sce-lected and disguised in a robe of buffaloe skin, having also the skin of the buffaloe's head with the years and horns fastened on his head in form of a cap, thus caparisoned he places himself at a convenient distance between a herd of buffaloe and a precipice proper for the purpose, which happens in many places on this river for miles together; the other indians now surround the herd on the back and flanks and at a signal agreed on all shew themselves at the same time moving for-ward towards the buffaloe; the disguised indian or decoy has taken care to place himself sufficiently nigh the buffaloe to be noticed by them when they take to flight and runing before them they follow him in full speede to the precepice, the cat-tle behind driving those in front over and seeing them go do not look or hesitate about following untill the whole are precipitated down the preci-pice forming one common mass of dead an[d] mangled carcases: the decoy in the mean time has taken care to secure himself in some cranney or crivice of the clift which he had previously pre-pared for that purpose. the part of the decoy I am informed is extremely dangerous, if they are not very fleet runers the buffaloe tread them under foot and crush them to death, and sometimes drive them over the precipice also, where they per-ish in common with the buffaloe. we saw a great many wolves in the neighbourhood of these man-gled carcases they were fat and extreemly gentle.

Source: Meriwether Lewis, Journal entry for May 29, 1805, in Reuben Gold Thwaites, ed., *Original Journals of the Lewis and Clark Expedition, 1804-1806*, Vol. 2 (New York: Antiquarian Press, 1959; reprint of edition of 1905), pp. 93-94.

DOCUMENT 28: Act Establishing the First Federal Forest Reserve (1817)

The first national effort to set aside forest lands was undertaken during the administration of James Madison. It was a pragmatic act to ensure the fledgling U.S. Navy of adequate timber supplies for shipbuilding. Madison's secretary of state, John Quincy Adams, who as president would later expand the nation's forest reserves, was undoubtedly a supporter of the act.

Be it enacted . . . That the Secretary of the Navy be authorized, and it shall be his duty, under the direction of the President of the United States, to cause such vacant and unappropriated lands of the United States as produce the live oak and red cedar timbers to be explored, and selection to be made of such tracts or portions thereof, where the principal growth is of either of the said timbers, as in his judgment may be necessary to furnish for the navy a sufficient sup-ply of the said timbers. The said Secretary shall have power to employ such agent or agents and surveyor as he may deem necessary for the afore-said purpose, who shall report to him the tracts by them selected, with the boundaries ascer-tained and accurately designated by actual sur-vey or water courses, which report shall be laid before the President, which he may approve or reject in whole or in part; and the tracts of land thus selected with the approbation of the Presi-dent, shall be reserved unless otherwise directed by law, from any future sale of the public lands, and be appropriated to the sole purpose of sup-plying timber for the navy of the United States.

Source: George P. Sanger, ed., *The Statutes at Large, Treaties, and Proclamations of the United States of America,* 14th Cong., 2nd sess., chap. 22, March 1, 1817, p. 347.

DOCUMENT 29: Act to Protect Useful Birds in Massachusetts (1818)

The earliest law to protect birds in the United States was an act by the Massachusetts legislature designated "An Act to prevent the destruction of certain useful Birds at unseasonable times of the year." It was probably the first law to recognize nature's services.

Whereas there are within the Commonwealth, many birds which are useful and profitable to the citizens, either as articles of food, or as instruments in the hands of Providence to destroy various noxious insects, grubs and caterpillars, which are prejudicial or destructive to vegetation, fruits and grain; and it is desirable to promote the increase and preservation of birds of the above description, and to prevent the wanton destruction of them at improper seasons:

. . . hereafter it shall not be lawful for any person to take, kill or destroy, any of the birds called partridges and quails, at any time from the first day of March, to the first day of September in every year; and no person shall take, kill or destroy, any of the birds called woodcocks,

snipes, larks and robins, at any time from the first day of March to the fourth day of July in each year; and if any person shall take or kill, or shall sell, buy or have in his possession after being killed, or taken, any of the birds aforesaid, within the times limited as aforesaid respectively, he shall forfeit and pay for each and every partridge, quail or woodcock, so taken, killed or in his possession, two dollars; and for each and every snipe, lark or robin, so killed, taken, or in his posession, one dollar.

Source: Laws of the Commonwealth of Massachusetts, Vol.7, chap. 103 (Boston: 1818), in Robert McHenry and Charles Van Doren, eds., A Documentary History of Conservation in America (New York: Praeger, 1972), pp. 272-73.

DOCUMENT 30: James Fenimore Cooper Laments the Disappearance of Unregulated Wilderness (1823)

The woodsman Natty Bumppo (also called Leatherstocking), the main character in the James Fenimore Cooper Leatherstocking series, here laments the loss of open land in New York State. He holds that wild game should belong to whoever kills it, while the judge claims that it belongs to the owner of the property on which it was killed. The difference in viewpoints, as Madison pointed out [see Document 21B], was produced by the difference in the property holdings of the two claimants.

"The legislature have been passing laws," continued [Judge] Marmaduke [Temple], "that the country much required. Among others, there is an act, prohibiting the drawing of seines, at any other than proper seasons, in certain of our streams and small lakes; and another, to prohibit the killing of deer in the teeming months. These are laws that were loudly called for, by judicious men; nor do I despair of getting an act, to make the unlawful felling of timber a criminal offence."

The hunter [Natty Bumppo] listened to this detail with breathless attention, and when the Judge had ended, he laughed in open derision for a moment, before he made this reply:—

"You may make your laws, Judge, but who will you find to watch the mountains through the long summer days, or the lakes at night? Game is game, and he who finds may kill; that has been the law in these mountains for forty years, to my sartain knowledge; and I think one old law is worth two new ones. None but a green-one would wish to kill a doe with a fa'n by its side, unless his moccassins was getting old, or his leggins ragged, for the flesh is lean and coarse. But a rifle rings along them rocks along the lake shore, sometimes, as if fifty pieces were fired at once:—it would be hard to tell where the man stood who pulled the trigger."

"Armed with the dignity of the law, Mr. Bumppo," returned the Judge, gravely, "a vigilant magistrate can prevent much of the evil that has hitherto prevailed, and which is already rendering the game scarce. I hope to live to see the day when a man's right in his game shall be as much respected as his title to his farm."

"Your titles and your farms are all new together," cried Natty; "but laws should be equal, and not more for one than another. I shot a deer, last Wednesday was a fortnight, and it floundered through the snow-banks till it got over a brush fence; I catch'd the lock of my rifle in the twigs, in following, and was kept back, until finally the creater got off. Now I want to know who is to pay me for that deer; and a fine buck it was. If there hadn't been a fence, I should have got another shot into it. . . .—No, no, Judge, it's

the farmers that makes the game scearce, and not the hunters."

"Ter teer is not so plenty as in ter old war, Pumppo," said the Major, who had been an attentive listener, amidst clouds of smoke; "put ter lant is not mate for ter teer to live on, put for Christians."

"Why, Major, I believe you're a friend to justice and the right, though you go so often to the grand house [Temple's house]; but it's a hard case to a man to have his honest calling for a livelihood stopt by sitch laws, and that too when, if right was done, he mought hunt or fish on any day in the week, or on the best flat in the Patent, if he was so minded."

"I unterstant you, Letter-stockint," returned the Major, fixing his black eyes, with a look of peculiar meaning, on the hunter; "put you tidn't use to be so prutent, as to look ahet mit so much care."

"Maybe there wasn't so much 'casion," said the hunter, a little sulkily; when he sunk into a profound silence, from which he was not roused for some time.

Source: James Fenimore Cooper, *The Pioneers* (London: Allman, 1823), pp. 150-51.

DOCUMENT 31: George Catlin's Proposal for a National Park (1832)

George Catlin, who traveled in the West from 1832 to 1839, gathering information about American Indians and painting their portraits in natural settings, was the first American to recognize that, without government protection, the western wilderness would be overrun by settlers and that the buffalo would be wiped out. Unfortunately, the grasslands of the Great Plains did not become objects of government conservation policy until 50 years after Catlin made these observations in his journal while at Fort Pierce, in present day South Dakota.

Many are the rudenesses and wilds in Nature's works, which are destined to fall before the deadly axe and desolating hands of cultivating man; and so amongst her ranks of *living*, of beast and human, we often find noble stamps, or beautiful colours, to which our admiration clings; and even in the overwhelming march of civilised improvements and refinements do we love to cherish their existence, and lend our

efforts to preserve them in their primitive rudeness. Such of Nature's works are always worthy of our preservation and protection; and the further we become separated (and the face of the country) from that pristine wildness and beauty, the more pleasure does the mind of enlightened man feel in recurring to those scenes, when he can have them preserved for his eyes and his mind to dwell upon.

Of such "rudenesses and wilds," Nature has nowhere presented more beautiful and lovely scenes, than those of the vast prairies of the West; and of *man* and *beast*, no nobler specimens than those who inhabit them—the *Indian* and the *buffalo*—joint and original tenants of the soil, and fugitives together from the approach of civilized man.

***

This strip of country, which extends from the province of Mexico to Lake Winnipeg on the North, is almost one entire plain of grass, which is, and ever must be, useless to cultivating man. It is here, and here chiefly, that the buffaloes dwell; and with, and hovering about them, live and flourish the tribes of Indians, whom God made for the enjoyment of that fair land and its luxuries.

It is a melancholy contemplation for one who has travelled as I have, through these realms, and seen this noble animal in all its pride and glory, to contemplate it so rapidly wasting from the world, drawing the irresistible conclusion too, which one must do, that its species is soon to be extinguished, and with it the peace and happiness (if not the actual existence) of the tribes of Indians who are joint tenants with them, in the occupancy of these vast and idle plains.

And what a splendid contemplation too, when one (who has travelled these realms, and can duly appreciate them) imagines them as they *might* in future be seen (by some great protecting policy of government) preserved in their pristine beauty and wildness, in a *magnificent park,* where the world could see for ages to come, the native Indian in his classic attire, galloping his wild horse, with sinewy bow, and shield and lance, amid the fleeting herds of elks and buffaloes. What a beautiful and thrilling specimen for America to preserve and hold up to the view of her refined citizens and the world, in future ages! A *nation's Park,* containing man and beast, in all the wild and freshness of their nature's beauty!

I would ask no other monument to my memory, nor any other enrolment of my name amongst the famous dead, than the reputation of having been the founder of such an institution.

Source: George Catlin, letter to *New York Commercial Advertiser,* in Catlin, *North American Indians: Being Letters and Notes on Their Manners, Customs, and Conditions, Written during Eight Years' Travel amongst the Wildest Tribes in North America, 1832-39,* Vol. 1 (London, 1880), pp. 294-95.

DOCUMENT 32: Black Hawk on the Indians and the Land (1833)

The Sac Indian chief Black Hawk led the Sac and Fox in battle against the whites who came to take their farms. In his memoirs, he described the rich Illinois land that his tribe lost and commented on its place in the lives of his people. Conflict over use of Native Americans lands has continued into the twenty-first century [see Document 173A].

Our village was situated on the north side of Rock River, at the foot of the rapids, on the point of land between Rock River and the Mississippi. In front a prairie extended to the Mississippi, and in the rear a continued bluff ascended from the prairie.

On its highest peak our Watch Tower was situated, from which we had a fine view for many miles up and down Rock River, and in every direction.

On the side of this bluff we had our cornfields, extending about two miles up parallel with the larger river, where they adjoined those of the Foxes, whose village was on the same stream, opposite the lower end of Rock Island, and three miles distant from ours. We had eight hundred acres in cultivation including what we had on the islands in Rock River. The land around our village which remained unbroken was covered with blue grass which furnished excellent pasture for our horses. Several fine springs poured out of the bluff near by, from which we were well supplied with good water. The rapids of Rock River furnished us with an abundance of excellent fish, and the land being very fertile, never failed to produce good crops of corn, beans, pumpkins, and squashes. We always had plenty; our children never cried from hunger, neither were our people in want. Here our village had stood for more than a hundred years, during all of which time we were the undisputed possessors of the Mississippi Valley, from the Wisconsin to the Portage des Sioux, near the mouth of the Missouri, being about seven hundred miles in length.

At this time we had very little intercourse with the whites except those who were traders. Our village was healthy, and there was no place in the country possessing such advantages, nor hunting grounds better than those we had in possession. If a prophet had come to our village in those days and told us that the things were to take place which have since come to pass, none of our people would have believed him. What! To be driven from our village and our hunting grounds, and not even to be permitted to visit the graves of our forefathers and relatives and friends?

**

My reason teaches me that land cannot be sold. The Great Spirit gave it to his children to live upon, and cultivate, as far as is necessary for their subsistence; and so long as they occupy and cultivate it, they have the right to the soil, but if they voluntarily leave it then any other people have a right to settle on it. Nothing can be sold but such things as can be carried away.

In consequence of the improvements of the intruders on our fields, we found considerable difficulty to get ground to plant a little corn. Some of the whites permitted us to plant small patches [of corn] in the fields they had fenced, keeping all the best ground for themselves. Our women had great difficulty in climbing their fences, being unaccustomed to that kind, and were ill-treated if they left a rail down.

One of my old friends thought he was safe. His cornfield was on a small island in Rock River. He planted his corn, it came up well; but the white man saw it, he wanted it [the island], and took his team over, ploughed up the corn, and replanted it for himself. The old man shed tears; not for himself, but on account of the distress his family would be in if they raised no corn.

Source: Black Hawk's Autobiography, interpreted by Antoine LeClaire, ed. J. P. Patterson and James D. Rishell (Rock Island, IL: American Publishing, 1912), pp. 62-63, 84-85.

DOCUMENT 33: John James Audubon on the Senseless Destruction of Fish, Birds, and Quadrupeds (1833)

The Haitian-born naturalist and painter John James Audubon traveled throughout the United States and parts of Canada in search of subjects for his paintings of the birds and quadrupeds of North America. He deplored the senseless destruction of America's wildlife that was obviously taking place all around him.

We are often told rum kills the Indian; I think not; it is oftener the want of food, the loss of hope as he loses sight of all that was once abundant, before the white man intruded on his land and killed off the wild quadrupeds and birds with which he has fed and clothed himself since his creation. Nature herself seems perishing. Labrador must shortly be depeopled, not only of aboriginal man, but of all else having life, owing to man's cupidity. When no more fish, no more game, no more birds exist on her hills, along her coasts, and in her rivers, then she will be abandoned and deserted like a worn-out field.

Source: John James Audubon, *Labrador Journals,* in A. Donald Culross Peattie, ed., *Audubon's America* (Boston: Houghton Mifflin, 1940), p. 245.

Part III

The Origins of Environmental Activism, 1840–1889

The acquisition of the Oregon Territory in 1846 and the Mexican Cession of 1848 expanded the United States' western border to the Pacific Coast, while the annexation of Texas in 1845 and the Gadsden Purchase of 1853, together with the Mexican Cession, defined the country's southern border. By 1867, with the purchase of Alaska from Russia, all the land that was to form the continental United States had become part of the nation.

Industrial and Urban Growth

While the country was in the throes of its great westward expansion, the landscape of the eastern portion of the country was undergoing stupendous change. In 1776 New York and Philadelphia were the only cities with more than 20,000 inhabitants; by 1860 there were forty-three metropolises with populations of at least that size. Not only was the number of cities growing, but the size of those cities was also expanding rapidly. The population of New York City, for example, was estimated to be 75,770 in 1805; by 1850 it had risen to 515,000, and by 1890, in Manhattan alone, it had reached

1,441,216. The 1890 population for the whole city (which by then included Brooklyn) was over 2.5 million.

The growth of the urban population between 1840 and 1890 was in great part the result of a tremendous flood of immigrants from western Europe, which carried nearly 10 million newcomers to America's shores. It also reflected the nation's accelerating industrialization and shifting pattern of employment. In 1861 the United States had nearly 31.5 million people, 19.8 percent residing in large towns and cities, and fewer than half living on farms. By 1880, the population had swelled to more than 50 million people, 28.2 percent of them living in urban areas.

During the Civil War (1861-1865), which pitted the increasingly urban North against the predominantly agrarian South, the need for armaments and other wartime goods spurred the expansion of industry and brought workers into towns and cities to work in the factories. Especially in the larger cities along the eastern seaboard, the vast majority of new urban residents and industrial workers came from among the tens of thousands of immigrants pouring into the United States every year.

The large-scale mining of coal (which had intensified with industrialization in England around the beginning of the nineteenth century) and drilling for oil (initiated when the world's first oil well was drilled in 1859 in Titusville, Pennsylvania, at the site of a natural oil seepage) marked the beginning of the "systematic exploitation of the earth's supply of fossil fuels" and provided people, for the first time in history, with "a huge supply of concentrated energy by means of which the energy commanded by one person could be greatly increased."[1]

Urban Sanitation and Infrastructure Problems

Industrial and urban expansion were accompanied by a host of problems: smoke and soot, noise, garbage, poor sanitation and raw sewage, poor drainage, inadequate and unclean water supplies, and droppings from horses [see Documents 40, 41, and 46]. Doctors and others concerned about human health and well-being pressed for improved garbage collection and sanitation, the regulation of quarantines during epidemics, more widespread vaccination against smallpox, and the collection of accurate data concerning births and deaths. Their efforts marked the beginning of the sanitary movement, which led to the formation of public health regulatory organizations and raised the consciousness of both the public and local governments about the need for better sanitation and health record keeping.

At midcentury, few cities other than Boston, New York and Philadelphia had public sewage systems. (Boston's system actually dated from the seventeenth century.) Except in these few cities, indoor plumbing was to be found mainly in the homes of the wealthy. In cities and towns that lacked sewer systems, drain pipes from indoor plumbing emptied into pits beneath people's homes or yards. Those who were without indoor plumbing also emptied their chamber pots and wastewater pans into pits in their yards or beneath their outhouses. By the 1850s, though, municipalities with booming populations, such as Brooklyn and Chicago, were forced to draw up plans for sewer systems, both to eliminate the stench emanating from the slop holes and for health

reasons.[2] These new sewer systems, however, like the older sewer systems in Boston and New York, were designed simply to dump raw sewage into nearby rivers, streams, or harbors.

Rapidly increasing populations greatly strained city water supplies, while the growth in industrialization placed added demands on municipal water supply systems. Prior to the 1840s, most city residents depended on local communal wells, cisterns, springs, streams, and transported water for their water needs, but by the 1840s, local water supplies were beginning to prove inadequate. Even municipalities that for years had supplemented their well water with local reservoirs found it necessary to draw on more distant water sources. In 1842, for example, New York City built the Croton Aqueduct to carry water from a reservoir in Westchester County, forty-one miles north of the city.[3] As indoor running water and flush toilets became commonplace in urban areas, and as the nation became more industrial, the per capita usage of water increased, placing ever greater demands on municipal water supplies.

Keeping the water supply clean proved very difficult. During periods of heavy rain, there was the constant danger of contamination of municipal wells by runoff from the slop pits and manure-laden streets. Microbial diseases such as typhoid fever spread quickly when wells became contaminated.

Railroads and Westward Expansion

One of the major spurs to industrial development was the spread of the railroads. The completion of the New York—Chicago rail link in 1853 and the first transcontinental rail route in 1869 gave impetus not only to industrialization but also to resource exploitation and the settlement of the West. People and manufactured goods could be transported across the country quickly and easily, and timber, coal, iron, and, later, oil could be carried to mills, factories, and refineries. The discovery of iron near Lake Superior in 1844 and of gold in Sutter's Mill, California, in 1848 and at Pikes Peak, Colorado, in 1859 hastened the westward movement of settlers and entrepreneurs.

To encourage the settlement of the West, Congress passed legislation that enabled settlers to buy land cheaply [*see* Document 42] and have easy access to land with mineral deposits [*see* Document 51] and grazing lands. Low purchase prices and—if the lands were to remain in the public domain—leasing fees became the norm. Vast tracts of land were turned over to the railroad companies as inducements for building additional railroads, and the railroad companies advertised in both Europe and the eastern part of the United States for new settlers to make the westward journey. The expansion of railroads, mining operations, grain fields, and factories was financed by bank loans; when this growth proved too rapid for the country to absorb, many banks failed, resulting in the panic of 1873.

The panic prompted some national soul searching and a questioning of federal policy. Reformers, including the social economist Henry George, attacked national land policies as enormous giveaways designed to enrich speculators and powerful real estate, industrial, mining, and ranching interests. In place of prevailing practices, George advocated a national land development policy that would take into account the public well-being and the interests of ordinary people [*see* Document 53].

Although the growth of the railroads had proved a boon to the expansion of the country and the development of industry, it posed an unforeseen threat to the nation's health. The danger first became evident during the yellow fever epidemic of 1879, which began in Memphis and quickly spread to nearby states as already-infected people traveled by rail to escape the plague. A National Board of Health was formed by Congress to help prevent the further spread of the disease and to study sanitation in Memphis.4

Scientific Innovation

During the late nineteenth century, enormous changes were taking place in science as well as industry. Building on a foundation laid down by John Ray [*see* Document 15] and Carl Linnaeus in the first half of the eighteenth century, naturalists working in both Europe and America in the late eighteenth and early nineteenth centuries had attempted to identify, describe, and classify all the known species of plants and animals. But these natural historians accepted the idea that each species was created by God and had retained a specific, immutable structure from the beginning of time. By the middle of the nineteenth century, however, scores of botanists, zoologists, and natural philosophers in western and central Europe and in the United States, buoyed by a liberal political and social atmosphere, were occupied with comprehending how changes in species occurred and were attempting to understand the relationships among organisms, and between organisms and their environments.

In England, in 1858, the Linnean Society of London published papers by Alfred Russel Wallace and Charles Darwin on the theory of natural selection. The two men had independently developed the same theory—Wallace, based on his eight years of travel through the Malay archipelago, and Darwin, based on his around-the-globe voyage on the H.M.S *Beagle,* during which he spent more than four years doing studies along the coast and the nearby interior of South America, sailed through the Galapagos archipelago, and visited Tahiti and New Zealand. A year after presenting his theory to the Linnean Society, Darwin published *The Origin of Species,* a book that produced controversy on both sides of the Atlantic and sparked the imagination of the public as well as the scientific community. In the United States, in 1864, George Perkins Marsh published his monumental *Man and Nature* [*see* Document 43], the first wide-ranging, scholarly study of how human actions affect the natural world around them. In Moravia in 1865, Gregor Mendel wrote his laws concerning the inheritance of physical characteristics (but they remained unknown outside of Moravia until the twentieth century), and in Germany in 1866, Ernst Haeckel published his *Generelle Morphologie der Organismen,* in which he coined the term *ecology,* defining it as "the comprehensive science of the relationships of the organism to the environment."5 Then, in 1871, Darwin published *The Descent of Man* [*see* Document 49], which theorized that humans are part of the natural system and not a unique creation, separate from all other living things. The idea that humans might have evolved from a common ancestry with apes caused an enormous public uproar, whose echoes can still be heard.

The studies on which these writings were based constituted the beginning of modern scientific investigation and were the hallmarks of an era when scientists and talented amateurs formed a large number of organizations to promote scientific study. While most of these groups—such as the American Ornithologists' Union (AOU), organized in 1883—had a very specific scientific focus, the most prominent of the American societies, the American Association for the Advancement of Science (AAAS), founded in 1848, attempted to reach out to a wide range of professional scientists and to establish a recognized forum for them. Many of the American scientific societies established in the middle of the nineteenth century, including the AAAS and the AOU, continue to play an important role in the furtherance of scientific research today.

The Need for Contact with Nature

As the eastern part of the nation became increasingly urban and industrial, as technology progressively limited people's contact with nature, and as awareness of the natural beauty of the western landscape gradually filtered into the national consciousness, American writers and artists began to idealize the natural world. The Romantic movement, which developed in Europe in the latter part of the eighteenth century partly as a reaction to the Industrial Revolution and its distancing of people from nature, influenced the depiction of the wilderness by both the Hudson River school painters [see Document 34] and the American transcendentalists [see Documents 36 and 44].

Henry David Thoreau [Document 44], John Muir [Document 47], and Frederick Law Olmsted and Calvert Vaux [Document 48] were among the ardent and eloquent advocates of the need for people to get away from urban, industrialized areas and the importance of setting aside space for this purpose. A recognition of the human need for nature as well as a sense that open space was disappearing inspired foresighted individuals to suggest that land be set aside for parks. Among the first of these were the painter George Catlin [see Document 32], the poet and journalist William Cullen Bryant [see Document 37], and journalist and landscape architect Andrew Jackson Downing [see Document 38]. Bryant and Downing, in planting the idea for a large-scale public park in New York City, launched the urban parks movement, the first concerted conservation effort in the United States. Cities, states, and the nation as a whole began to be cognizant of the need to set aside land for human recreation and spiritual restoration, as well as to preserve places of unique natural beauty. Before the end of the century, a host of magnificent urban, state, and national parks were created, including Central and Prospect Parks in New York City [see Document 48], Fairmont Park in Philadelphia, Yosemite Park (originally chartered as a California state park but later to become a national park) [see Document 45], New York State's Adirondack Forest Preserve [see Document 54], and Yellowstone, the first national park [see Document 50].

The Beginning of the Conservation Idea

As the new century approached, increasing numbers of people—primarily wealthy individuals—became aware that not only were America's wilderness areas beginning to disappear, but that the wildlife that inhabited them was also being destroyed. In 1865, fifteen million bison roamed the Great Plains; by 1885 only about three thousand bison remained in the United States.

Organized resistance to the wanton slaughter of birds and mammals and to the destruction of habitats suitable for fish and game coalesced around individuals such as George Bird Grinnell and Theodore Roosevelt who realized that our resources were disappearing and who had the journalistic or political clout to effect change. Grinnell started the Audubon Society in 1886, with one of its goals being to stop the killing of birds to provide feathers for women's hats [see Document 56]. Scientific organizations also actively lobbied at both the state and federal levels for the passage of laws that encouraged conservation. In 1873, the AAAS, in a memo to Congress, requested that laws be passed to protect the nation's natural resources, and Grinnell's bird protection drive was aided by the American Ornithologists' Union, which prepared a model bird protection law [*see* Document 55] and printed and distributed 100,000 copies of it.

Other conservation-minded groups chartered in the last three decades of the nineteenth century included the Appalachian Mountain Club, formed in 1876, and the Sierra Club, organized in 1892 by John Muir—both of which were primarily hiking clubs that advocated the preservation of scenic lands for the enjoyment of the public —and the Boone and Crockett Club, established in 1887 [*see* Document 57], which was primarily a hunting club that promoted the conservation of the habitats of game animals. These use-oriented organizations, together with the scientific societies and the advocacy-oriented state Audubon societies, formed a base of organized public support for the nascent conservation movement.

While these nongovernmental organizations were becoming established, the federal government was starting to look at issues related to the management and conservation of resources. The government's main concerns were the administration of timber, water, minerals, and land. Toward the end of the nineteenth century, a number of people were brought into government service to manage resources and help develop resource management policies. The recommendations and actions of three of these individuals—Carl Schurz, Gifford Pinchot, and John Wesley Powell—greatly affected the course of U.S. environmental policy for more than half a century.

Schurz, who served as Secretary of the Interior from 1877 to 1881, promoted the scientific management of forests and recommended that timberland be set aside [*see* Document 52]. Pinchot, the first professional American forester, served as head of the Division of Forestry (later called the U.S. Forest Service). Powell joined the staff of the U.S. Geological Survey in 1875, and served as its head from 1881 to 1894. After touring the Southwest, Powell began a campaign to "reclaim" the arid lands of that region [*see* Document 58].

Powell's campaign paralleled the efforts of Louisianans and Alabamans to convince the federal government to enact legislation that would allow them to drain wetlands [*see* Document 39]—swamp and overflow land not suited for cultivation—so that they could sell the "reclaimed" land to land-hungry buyers. As a result of these efforts, the large-scale manipulation of the environment to develop agricultural lands, water resources, and hydroelectric power had become established federal policy in both arid regions and wetlands by the beginning of the twentieth century. The environmentally disastrous consequences of this policy would not be widely recognized for another half-century.

DOCUMENT 34: Thomas Cole's Lament of the Forest (1841)

A distinguished member of the Hudson River school of landscape painters, Thomas Cole, along with other adherents of the Romantic movement, viewed the spread of factories across the land not only as a blight on the natural landscape but also as an encroachment on the human spirit. Cole and other Hudson River school artists, such as Asher B. Durand, painted pictures of well-dressed people walking in rustic settings (e.g., Durand's "Kindred Spirits," painted in 1849, depicts William Cullen Bryant and Thomas Cole in a woodland scene), and these pictures helped to make excursions to rustic areas fashionable.

. . . Our doom is near; behold from east to
west The skies are darkened by ascending
smoke; Each hill and every valley is become
An altar unto Mammon, and the gods
Of man's idolatry—the victims we.
Missouri's floods are ruffled as by storm,
And Hudson's rugged hills at midnight
glow By light of man-projected meteors.
We feed ten thousand fires: in our short day
The woodland growth of centuries is consumed.

* * *

A few short years!—these valleys, greenly clad,
These slumbering mountains, resting in our arms,
Shall naked glare beneath the scorching sun,
And all their wimpling rivulets be dry.
No more the deer shall haunt these bosky glens,
Nor the pert squirrel chatter near his store.

Source: Thomas Cole, "Lament of the Forest," *Knickerbocker* 17, no. 6 (June 1841), in Robert McHenry and Charles Van Doren, eds., *A Documentary History of Conservation in America* (New York: Praeger, 1972), p. 175.

DOCUMENT 35: John James Audubon on the Decimation of the Bison Herds (1843)

In the summer of 1843 Audubon traveled to the Great Plains. He was one of the first Americans to become alarmed by the wanton slaughter of bison.

July 21
. . . we could see [the buffalo chase] when nearly a mile distant.

. . .

What a terrible destruction of life, as it were for nothing, or next to it, as the tongues only were brought in, and the flesh of these fine animals was left to beasts and birds of prey, or to rot on the spots where they fell. The prairies are literally *covered* with the skulls of the victims, and the roads the Buffalo make in crossing the prairies have all the appearance of heavy wagon tracks.

August 2
Buffaloes become so very poor during hard winters, when the snows cover the ground to the depth of two or three feet, that they lose their hair, become covered with scabs, on which the Magpies

feed, and the poor beasts die by hundreds. One can hardly conceive how it happens, notwithstanding these many deaths and the immense numbers that are murdered almost daily on these boundless wastes called prairies, besides the hosts that are drowned in the freshets, and the hundreds of young calves who die in early spring, so many are yet to be found. Daily we see so many that we hardly notice them more than the cattle in our pastures about our homes. But this cannot last; even now there is a perceptible difference in the size of the herds, and before many years the Buffalo, like the Great Auk, will have disappeared; surely this should not be permitted.

Source: John James Audubon, "The Missouri River Journals," in Maria R. Audubon, *Audubon and His Journals,* Vol. II (New York: Scribner's, 1899), pp. 107, 131.

DOCUMENT 36: Ralph Waldo Emerson on Nature (1844, 1884)

The leader of a group of New England idealists known as the transcendentalists, Ralph Waldo Emerson called upon people to give heed to the relationship between humanity and nature. The transcendentalists, who were influenced by German idealist philosophers and American Romantic writers and artists, were heirs to a uniquely American Protestant view of nature that was firmly rooted in the writings of eighteenth-century American theologians such as Jonathan Edwards [see Document 16].

A. From *Essay on Nature, 1844*

To speak truly, few adult persons can see nature. Most persons do not see the sun. At least they have a very superficial seeing. The sun illuminates only the eye of the man, but shines into the eye and the heart of the child. The lover of nature is he whose inward and outward senses are still truly adjusted to each other; who has retained the spirit of infancy even into the era of manhood. His intercourse with heaven and earth becomes part of his daily food. In the presence of nature a wild delight runs through the man, in spite of real sorrows. Nature says,—he is my creature and maugre all his impertinent griefs, he shall be glad with me. Not the sun or the summer alone, but every hour and season yields its tribute of delight; for every hour and change corresponds to and authorizes a different state of the mind, from breathless noon to grimmest midnight. Nature is a setting that fits equally well a comic or a mourning piece. In good health, the air is a cordial of incredible virtue. Crossing a bare common, in snow puddles, at twilight, under a clouded sky, without having in my thoughts any occurrence of special good fortune, I have enjoyed a perfect exhilaration. I am glad to the brink of fear. In the woods, too, a man casts off his years, as the snake his slough, and at what period soever of life, is always a child. In the woods is perpetual youth. Within these plantations of God, a decorum and sanctity reign, a perennial festival is dressed, and the guest sees not how he should tire of them in a thousand years. In the woods, we return to reason and faith. There I feel that nothing can befall me in life,—no disgrace, no calamity (leaving me my eyes), which nature cannot repair. Standing on the bare ground,—my head bathed by the blithe air, and uplifted into infinite space,—all mean egotism vanishes. I become a transparent eye-ball; I am nothing; I see all; the currents of the Universal Being circulate through me; I am part or parcel of God. The name of the nearest friend sounds then foreign and accidental: to be brothers, to be acquaintance,—master or servant, is then a trifle and a disturbance. I am the lover of uncontained and immortal beauty. In the wilderness, I find something more dear and connate than in streets or villages. In the tranquil landscape, and especially in the distant line of the horizon, man beholds somewhat as beautiful as his own nature.

The greatest delight which the fields and woods minister is the suggestion of an occult relation between man and the vegetable. I am not alone and unacknowledged. They nod to me, and I to them. The waving of the boughs in the storm is new to me and old. It takes me by surprise, and yet is not unknown. Its effect is like that of a higher thought or a better emotion coming over me, when I deemed I was thinking justly or doing right.

Yet it is certain that the power to produce this delight does not reside in nature, but in man, or in a harmony of both.

B. From *The American Scholar,* 1884

The first in time and the first in importance of the influences upon the mind is that of nature. Every day, the sun; and, after sunset, Night and her stars. Ever the winds blow; ever the grass grows. Every day, men and women, conversing, beholding and beholden. The scholar is he of all men whom this spectacle most engages. He must settle its value in his mind. What is nature to him? There is never a beginning, there is never an end, to the inexplicable continuity of this web of God, but always circular power returning into itself. Therein it resembles his own spirit, whose beginning, whose ending, he never can find,—so entire, so boundless. Far too as her splendors whine, system on system shooting like rays, upward, downward, without centre, without circumference,—in the mass and in particle, Nature hastens to render account of herself to the mind.

Source: Ralph Waldo Emerson, *Nature: Addresses and Lectures* (Boston: Houghton Mifflin, 1884), pp. 86-87, 14-17.

DOCUMENT 37: William Cullen Bryant's Proposal for a Great Municipal Park (1844)

For nearly three-quarters of a century, beginning in 1811 with his poem "Thanatopsis," William Cullen Bryant inspired American nature lovers, artists, and writers by conveying a sense of the wonder and divinity of nature. In 1844, motivated by his knowledge of the great parks of Europe, including Regents Park in London, the noted poet and editor of the influential New York Evening Post *proposed setting aside a very large tract of land for a municipal park. Previously, half a dozen or so acres had been set aside for local parks, such as Madison Square in New York City, but no municipal public park on the scale proposed existed anywhere in the world, for the great European parks were actually private lands that had been opened to the public. Although the site he suggested was not the one finally selected for New York's Central Park, he set in motion a movement to create a rural park in the city.*

If the public authorities, who expend so much of our money in laying out the city, would do what is in their power, they might give our vast population an extensive pleasure ground for shade and recreation in these sultry afternoons, which we might reach without going out of town.

* * *

On the road to Harlem, between Sixty-eighth Street on the south, and Seventy-seventh on the north, and extending from Third Avenue to the East River, is a tract of beautiful woodland, comprising sixty or seventy acres, thickly covered with old trees, intermingled with a variety of shrubs. The surface is varied in a very striking and picturesque manner, with craggy eminences, and hollows, and a little stream runs through the midst. The swift tides of the East River sweep its rocky shores, and the fresh breeze of the bay comes in, on every warm summer afternoon, over the restless waters. The trees are of almost every species that grows in our woods—the different varieties of ash, the birch, the beech, the linden, the mulberry, the tulip tree, and others; the azalea, the kalmia, and other flowering shrubs are in bloom here in their season, and the ground in spring is gay with flowers. There never was a finer situation for the public garden of a great city. Nothing is wanting but to cut winding paths through it, leaving the woods as they now are, and introducing here and there a jet from the Croton aqueduct, the streams from which would make their own waterfalls over the rocks, and keep the brooks running through the place always fresh and full.

Source: William Cullen Bryant, "A New Park," *New York Evening Post,* July 3, 1844, quoted in Allan Nevins, *The Evening Post: A Century of Journalism* (New York: Russell & Russell, 1968; reissue of 1922 edition), p. 194.

DOCUMENT 38: Andrew Jackson Downing Talks about Public Parks and Gardens (1848)

The horticulturalist, nurseryman, and landscape architect Andrew Jackson Downing is frequently given credit for instigating the urban parks movement, but that honor actually belongs to William Cullen Bryant [see Document 37]. Downing, however, was the first to view the building of a great urban park as consonant with American democracy. In this selection Downing discusses the American rural cemeteries that were the precursors of the great municipal parks: Mt. Auburn, opened in Cambridge, Massachusetts, in 1832; Laurel Hill, established on the outskirts of Philadelphia in 1836; and Green-wood, opened in Brooklyn, New York, in 1840. The popularity of these cemeteries—by 1852 100,000 people were visiting Green-wood annually—gave impetus to the urban parks movement.

Traveller. I dare say you will be surprised to hear me say that the French and Germans—difficult as they find it to be republican, in a political sense—are practically far more so, in many of the customs of *social* life, than Americans.

Editor. Such as what, pray?

Trav. Public enjoyments, open to all classes of people, provided at public cost, maintained at public expense, and enjoyed daily and hourly by all classes of persons.

Ed. Picture galleries, libraries, and the like, I suppose you allude to?

Trav. Yes; but more especially at the present moment, I am thinking of PUBLIC PARKS and GARDENS—those salubrious and wholesome breathing places, provided in the midst of, or upon the suburbs of so many towns on the continent— full of really grand and beautiful trees, fresh grass, fountains, and, in many cases, rare plants, shrubs and flowers. Public picture galleries, and even libraries, are intellectual luxuries; and though we must and will have them, as wealth accumulates, yet I look upon public parks and gardens, which are great social enjoyments, as naturally coming first. Man's social nature stands before his intellectual one in the *order* of cultivation.

Ed. But these great public parks are mostly the appendages of royalty, and have been created for purposes of show and magnificence, quite incompatible with our ideas of republican simplicity.

Trav. Not at all. In many places these parks were made for royal enjoyment; but even in these, they are, on the continent, no longer held for royal use, but are the pleasure grounds of the public generally. Look, for example, at the Garden of the Tuileries—spacious, full of flowers, green lawns, orange trees and rare plants, in the very heart of Paris, and all open to the public, without charge.

* * *

Ed. Enough. I am fully satisfied of the benefits of these places of healthful public enjoyment, and of their being most completely adapted to our institutions. But how to achieve them? What do we find among us to warrant a belief that public parks, for instance, are within the means of our people?

Trav. Several things: but most of all, the condition of our public *cemeteries* at the present moment. Why, twenty years ago, such a thing as an embellished, rural cemetery was unheard of in the United States; and at the present moment, we surpass all other nations in these beautiful resting places for the dead. Green-wood, Mount Auburn, and Laurel Hill, are as much superior to the far famed *Père la Chaise* of Paris, in natural beauty, tasteful arrangement, and all that constitutes the charm of such a spot, as St. Peter's is to the Boston State House. Indeed, these cemeteries are the only places in the country that can give an untravelled American any idea of the beauty of many of the public parks and gardens abroad. Judging from the crowds of people in carriages, and on foot, which I find constantly thronging Green-wood and Mount Auburn, I think it is plain enough how much our citizens, of all classes, would enjoy public parks on a similar scale.

Source: Andrew Jackson Downing, "A Talk about Public Parks and Gardens," *Horticulturalist*, III, no. 4 (October 1848): 154, 157.

DOCUMENT 39: Swamp and Overflow Act (1850)

The passage of the Swamp and Overflow Act–An Act to enable the State of Arkansas and other States to Reclaim the "Swamp Lands" within their Limits–reflected both a lack of understanding of the nature and significance of wetlands by Americans and the ever-present desire for more land for farmers and real estate developers. This act made the development of the Florida Everglades possible and also led to some classic land frauds in the 1930s and 1940s. Its passage was followed by a century of profligate wetland draining that dried up more than half of the nation's invaluable flood moderators and biological gold mines. Much of the "reclamation" attitude still persists, and conflict over the protection and restoration of wetland areas like the Everglades continues to this day.

Be it enacted by the Senate and House of Representatives of the United States of America in Congress assembled, That to enable the State of Arkansas to construct the necessary levees and drains to reclaim the swamp and overflowed lands therein, the whole of those swamp and overflowed lands, made unfit thereby for cultivation, which shall remain unsold at the passage of this act, shall be, and the same are hereby granted to said State.

Sec. 2. *And be it further enacted,* That it shall be the duty of the Secretary of the Interior, as soon as may be practicable after the passage of this act, to make out an accurate list and plats of the lands described as aforesaid and transmit the same to the governor of the State of Arkansas, and, at the request of said governor, cause a patent to be issued to the State therefor; and on that patent, the fee simple to said lands shall vest in the State of Arkansas, subject to the disposal of the legislature thereof: *Provided, however,* That

the proceeds of said lands, whether from sale or by direct appropriation in kind, shall be applied, exclusively, as far as necessary, to the purpose of reclaiming said lands by means of the levees and drains aforesaid.

Sec. 3. *And be it further enacted,* That in making out a list and plats of the land aforesaid, the greater part of which is "wet and unfit for cultivation," shall be included in said list and plats; but when the greater part of a subdivision is not of that character, the whole of it shall be excluded therefrom.

Sec. 4. *And be it further enacted,* That the provisions of this act be extended to, and their benefits be conferred upon, each of the other States of the Union in which such swamp and overflowed lands, known as designated as aforesaid, may be situated.

Source: George Minot, ed., *The Statutes at Large and Treaties of the United States of America,* Vol. 9 (Boston: Little, Brown, 1854), 31st Cong., 1st sess., chap. 84, September 28, 1850, p. 519.

DOCUMENT 40: The Shattuck Report's Recommendations for Sanitary Improvement (1850)

The degradation of sanitary conditions and the high death rate among the poor that accompanied the rapid growth of urban populations spurred various state and local organizations to examine the spread of communicable diseases as a result of unsanitary water, milk, food, waste disposal, and living conditions and to make recommendations for change. The Massachusetts Sanitary Commission's Report, prepared under the direction of Lemuel Shattuck, a pioneer in American public health, was one of the most thorough and influential of these studies. The conditions it sought to alleviate were well documented in both the fiction [see Document 41] and the nonfiction [see Document 46] of the period. While many state and local authorities had begun to deal with these problems by the mid-eighteenth century, several of the problems proved overwhelming for local authorities, and as the century progressed, they intensified [see Documents 64, 65, 67, and 72]. The federal government did not start to confront many of the issues raised in the Shattuck Report until well into the twentieth century.

II. We recommend that a GENERAL BOARD OF HEALTH be established, which shall be charged with the general execution of the laws of the State, relating to the enumeration, the vital statistics, and the public health of the inhabitants. . . .

V. We recommend that a LOCAL BOARD OF HEALTH be appointed in every city and town. . . .

XIV. We recommend that the laws relating to the public registration of births, marriages, and deaths be perfected and carried into effect in every city and town of the State. . . .

XVII. We recommend that, in laying out new towns and villages, and in extending those already laid out, ample provision be made for a supply, in purity and abundance of light, air, and water; for drainage and sewerage; for paving and for cleanliness. . . .

XIX. We recommend that, before erecting any new dwelling-house, manufactory, or other building, for personal accommodation, either as a lodging-house or place of business, the owner or builder be required to give notice to the local Board of Health, of his intention and of the sanitary arrangements he proposes to adopt. . . .

XX. We recommend that local Boards of Health endeavor to prevent or mitigate the sanitary evils arising from overcrowded lodging-houses and cellar-dwellings. . . .

XXI. We recommend that open spaces be reserved, in cities and villages, for public walks; that wide streets be laid out; and that both be ornamented with trees. . . .

XXIII. We recommend that local Boards of Health, and other persons interested, endeavor to ascertain, by exact observation, the effect of mill-ponds, and other collections or streams of water, and of their rise and fall, upon the health of the neighboring inhabitants. . . .

XXIV. We recommend that the local Boards of Health provide for periodical house-to-house visitation, for the prevention of epidemic diseases, and for other sanitary purposes. . . .

XXV. We recommend that measures be taken to ascertain the amount of sickness suffered in different localities; and among persons of different classes, professions, and occupations. . . .

XXIX. We recommend that nuisances endangering human life or health, be prevented, destroyed, or mitigated. . . .

XXX. We recommend that measures be taken to prevent or mitigate the sanitary evils arising from the use of intoxicating drinks, and from haunts of dissipation. . . .

XXXV. We recommend that the authority to make regulations for the quarantine of vessels be intrusted to the local Boards of Health. . . .

XXXVI. We recommend that measures be adopted for preventing or mitigating the sanitary evils arising from foreign emigration. . . .

XXXIX. We recommend that public bathing-houses and wash-houses be established in all cities and villages. . . .

XL. We recommend that, whenever practicable, the refuse and sewage of cities and towns be collected, and applied to the purposes of agriculture. . . .

XLI. We recommend that measures be taken to prevent, as far as practicable, the smoke nuisance. . . .

XLII. We recommend that the sanitary effects of patent medicines and other nostrums, and secret remedies, be observed; that physicians in their prescriptions and names of medicines, and apothecaries in their compounds, use great caution and care; and that medical compounds advertised for sale be avoided, unless the material of which they are composed be known, or unless manufactured and sold by a person of known honesty and integrity. . . .

XLIII. We recommend that local Boards of Health, and others interested, endeavor to prevent the sale and use of unwholesome, spurious, and adulterated articles, dangerous to the public health designed for food, drink, or medicine.

Source: Lemuel Shattuck et al., *Report of the Sanitary Commission of Massachusetts* (Cambridge, MA: Harvard University Press, 1948; facsimile of *Report of a General Plan for the Promotion of Public and Personal Health* [Boston: Dutton & Wentworth, 1850]), pp. 111, 115, 135, 153, 164, 166, 168, 171, 183, 200, 209, 212, 218, 220.

DOCUMENT 41: Rebecca Harding Davis on Smoke and Soot in a Mill Town (1861)

This fictional account of life in a mill town is an indictment of air pollution caused by the burning of coal as well as the general squalor of the lives of poor immigrants.

A cloudy day: do you know what that is in a town of iron-works? The sky sank down before dawn, muddy, flat, immovable. The air is thick, clammy with the breath of crowded human beings. It stifles me. I open the window and, looking out, can scarcely see through the rain the grocer's shop opposite, where a crowd of drunken Irishmen are puffing Lynchburg tobacco in their pipes. I can detect the scent through all the foul smells ranging loose in the air.

The idiosyncrasy of this town is smoke. It rolls sullenly in slow folds from the great chimneys of the iron-foundries, and settles down in black, slimy pools on the muddy streets. Smoke on the wharves, smoke on the dingy boats, on the yellow river,—clinging in a coating of greasy soot to the house-front, the two faded poplars, the faces of the passers-by. The long train of mules, dragging masses of pig-iron through the narrow street, have a foul vapor hanging to their reeking sides. Here, inside, is a little broken figure of an angel pointing upward from the mantel-shelf; but even its wings are covered with smoke, clotted and black. Smoke everywhere! A dirty canary chirps desolately in a cage beside me. Its dream of green fields and sunshine is a very old dream,—almost worn out, I think.

Source: Rebecca Harding Davis, "Life in the Iron-Mills," *Atlantic Monthly* 7 (April 1861): 430.

DOCUMENT 42: Homestead Act (1862)

The object of the Homestead Act was to encourage the rapid settlement of the western territories that the United States had acquired since the beginning of the nineteenth century. Although some of these lands were unsuitable for intensive farming, farmers who had exhausted their land in the more settled areas of the United States were lured west by the availability of free land. The intensive cultivation of semiarid lands would eventually create a host of problems for the farmers and for the nation as a whole.

Be it enacted . . . , That any person who is the head of a family, or who has arrived at the age of twenty-one years, and is a citizen of the United States, or who shall have filed his declaration of intention to become such, as required by the naturalization laws of the United States, and who has never borne arms against the United States Government or given aid and comfort to its enemies, shall, from and after the first January, eighteen hundred and sixty-three, be entitled to enter one quarter section or a less quantity of unappropriated public land, upon which said person may have filed a preemption claim, or which may, at the time the application is made, be subject to preemption at one dollar and twenty-five cents, or less, per acre; . . . *Provided,* That any person owning or residing on land may, under the provisions of this act, enter other land lying contiguous to his or her said land, which shall not, with the land so already owned and occupied, exceed in the aggregate one hundred and sixty acres.

Sec. 2. *And be it further enacted,* That the person applying for the benefit of this act shall, upon application to the register of the land office in which he or she is about to make such entry, make affidavit before the said register or receiver that he or she is the head of a family, or is twenty-one years or more of age, or shall have performed service in the army or navy of the United States, and that he has never borne arms against the Government of the United States or given aid and comfort to its enemies, and that said application is made for his or her exclusive use and benefit, and that said entry is made for the purpose of actual settlement and cultivation, and not either directly or indirectly for the use or benefit of any other person or persons whomsoever; and upon filing the said affidavit with the register or receiver, and on payment of ten dollars, he or she shall thereupon be permitted to enter the quantity of land specified.

Source: George P. Sanger, ed., *The Statutes at Large, Treaties, and Proclamations of the United States of America,* Vol. 12, Part 2 (Boston: Little Brown, 1865), 37th Cong., 2nd sess. , chap. 75, March 20, 1862, p. 392.

DOCUMENT 43: George Perkins Marsh's *Man and Nature* (1864)

George Perkins Marsh, a lawyer and philologist who served for a term as a U.S. congressman, was the first to put forth the concept of the "carrying capacity" of the land and to point out that human activity could cause permanent change in the land. His book Man and Nature, *from which this selection is taken, offers a broad view of the impact of human activity on nature and the balance of life. It had a major influence on most of the naturalists (who today would be called ecologists) of the end of the nineteenth and the beginning of the twentieth centuries. Marsh's wide-angle perspective resulted not only from his varied experiences in the United States but also from his many years in Europe, during which he served as ambassador to Turkey and to Italy.*

In the rudest stages of life, man depends upon spontaneous animal and vegetable growth for food and clothing, and his consumption of such products consequently diminishes the numerical abundance of the species which serve his uses. At more advanced periods, he protects and propagates certain esculent vegetables and certain fowls and quadrupeds, and, at the same time, wars upon rival organisms which prey upon these objects of his care or obstruct the increase of their numbers. Hence the action of man upon the organic world tends to subvert the original balance of its species, and while it reduces the numbers of some of them, or even extirpates them altogether, it multiplies other forms of animal and vegetable life.

The extension of agricultural and pastoral industry involves an enlargement of the sphere of man's domain, by encroachment upon the forests which once covered the greater part of the earth's surface otherwise adapted to his occupation. The felling of the woods has been attended with momentous consequences to the drainage of the soil, to the external configuration of its surface, and probably, also, to local climate; and the importance of human life as a transforming power is, perhaps, more clearly demonstrable in the influence man has thus exerted upon superficial geography than in any other result of his material effort.

Lands won from the woods must be both drained and irrigated; river banks and maritime coasts must be secured by means of artificial bulwarks against inundation by inland and by ocean floods; and the needs of commerce require the improvement of natural, and the construction of artificial channels of navigation. Thus man is compelled to extend over the unstable waters the empire he had already founded upon the solid land.

The upheaval of the bed of seas and the movements of water and of wind expose vast deposits of sand, which occupy space required for the convenience of man, and often, by the drifting of their particles, overwhelm the fields of human industry with invasions as disastrous as the incursions of the ocean. On the other hand, on many coasts, sand hills both protect the shores from erosion by the waves and currents, and shelter valuable grounds from blasting sea winds. Man, therefore, must sometimes resist, sometimes, promote, the formation and growth of dunes, and subject the barren and flying sands to the same obedience to his will to which he has reduced other forms of terrestrial surface.

Besides these old and comparatively familiar methods of material improvement, modern ambition aspires to yet grander achievements in the conquest of physical nature, and projects are meditated which quite eclipse the boldest enterprises hitherto undertaken for the modification of geographical surface.

Source: George P. Marsh, *Man and Nature; or, Physical Geography as Modified by Human Action* (New York: Scribner, 1864), pp. iii-v.

DOCUMENT 44: Henry David Thoreau on the Value of Living Things (1864)

Henry David Thoreau, a disciple of Ralph Waldo Emerson [see Document 36] and associated with the transcendentalists, was very much an original thinker. His writings about the importance of leaving nature undisturbed, the need for all humans to have contact with nature, and the relationship between humans and other living things were not fully appreciated until the mid-twentieth century, when environmentalists canonized him as their patron saint. He is best known for his essay "Walden," a record of the two years he spent living in a cabin near Walden Pond in Concord, Massachusetts. In the following passage, taken from the section of The Maine Woods *(a posthumously published book) based on a journal he kept during his 1853 trip to Maine, Thoreau expresses dismay over the human use of other living things. He also offers a prescient model for a U.S. national parks system.*

Strange that so few ever come to the woods to see how the pine lives and grows and spires, lifting its evergreen arms to the light,—to see its perfect success; but most are content to behold it in the shape of many broad boards brought to market, and deem *that* its true success! But the pine is no more lumber than man is, and to be made into boards and houses is no more its true and highest use than the truest use of a man is to be cut down and made into manure. There is a higher law affecting our relation to pines as well as to men. A pine cut down, a dead pine, is no more a pine than a dead human carcass is a man. Can he who has discovered only some of the values of whalebone and whale oil be said to have discovered the true use of the whale? Can he who slays the elephant for his ivory be said to have "seen the elephant"? These are petty and accidental uses; just as if a stronger race were to kill us in order to make buttons and flageolets of our bones; for everything may serve a lower as well as a higher use. Every creature is better alive than dead, men and moose and pine-trees, and he who understands it aright will rather preserve its life than destroy it.

* * *

The kings of England formerly had their forests "to hold the king's game," for sport or food, sometimes destroying villages to create or extend them; and I think that they were impelled by a true instinct. Why should not we, who have renounced the king's authority, have our national preserves, where no villages need be destroyed, in which the bear and panther, and some even of the hunter race, may still exist, and not be "civilized off the face of the earth,"—our forests, not to hold the king's game merely, but to hold and preserve the king himself also, the lord of creation,—not for idle sport or food, but for inspiration and our own true recreation? or shall we, like the villains, grub them all up, poaching on our own national domains?

Source: Henry David Thoreau, *The Maine Woods* (Boston: Houghton, Mifflin, 1893), pp. 163-164, 212-13.

DOCUMENT 45: Act Granting Yo-Semite Valley to California (1864)

As the first large public park in the United States, Yosemite became a model for future parks in the national parks system, which was established a few years later. The federal stipulations regarding the use of the land emphasized the public nature of the park and made clear the intent to establish a permanent park.

Be it enacted . . . , That there shall be, and is hereby, granted to the State of California the "Cleft" or "Gorge" in the granite peak of the Sierra Nevada mountains, situated in the county of Mariposa, in the State aforesaid, and the headwaters of the Merced River, and known as the Yo-Semite valley, with its branches or spurs, in estimated length fifteen miles, and in average width one mile back from the main edge of the precipice, on each side of the valley, with the stipulation, nevertheless, that the said State shall accept this grant upon the express conditions that the premises shall be held for public use, resort, and recreation; shall be inalienable for all time; but leases not exceeding ten years may be granted for portions of said premises. All incomes derived from leases of privileges to be expended in the preservation and improvement of the property, or the roads leading thereto; the boundaries to be established at the cost of said State by the United States surveyor-general of California, whose official plat, when affirmed by the commissioner of the general land-office, shall constitute the evidence of the locus, extent, and limits of the said Cleft or Gorge; the premises to be managed by the governor of the State with eight other commissioners, to be appointed by the executive of California, and who shall receive no compensation for their services.

Source: United States Statutes at Large, Vol. 13 (Boston: Little, Brown, 1866), 38th Cong., 1st sess., chap. 184, June 30, 1864, p. 325.

DOCUMENT 46: The Citizens' Association of New York on Sewage and Disease (1865)

In the latter part of the nineteenth century numerous civic associations were formed to advocate for improvements in the local environment. Their newsletters railed against poor sanitation as well as noise and air pollution. In time, some of these organizations became strong supporters of the urban parks movement.

The unspeakable filthiness and neglect of the privies pertaining to the tenant-houses demand attention. These necessaries of every domicile are so neglected and filthy in all the crowded districts of the city as to have become prolific sources of obstinate and fatal maladies of a diarrhoeal and febrile character, and they must be reckoned among the most active of localizing causes of prevailing diseases among the poor. The miserable economy that has attached to every tenant-house, court, or cellar a series of *midden* sinks, frequently without any sewer connection, and seldom with sufficient drainage of any kind, should be superseded by suitable water-closet arrangements for constant "flushing" and cleanliness. Reform in these matters is vitally important to the health of tenant-houses.

Source: Report of the Council of Hygiene and Public Health of the Citizens' Association of New York upon the Sanitary Condition of the City (New York: Appleton, 1865), p. 91.

DOCUMENT 47: John Muir on the Spirituality of Nature (1866)

John Muir, an amateur naturalist noted for his books and magazine articles on the mountains, valleys, and parks of the West, was an ardent supporter of wilderness preservation in the western states [see Document 68]. He first achieved national attention as a result of a letter about the calypso borealis, a rare white orchid, which was quoted in the Boston Recorder. *The letter recounted the turning point in Muir's life that moved him to become what today would be termed an "advocate of the rights of nature" or biocentrist. His description of the spirituality of the encounter with natural beauty echoes the experiences of Jonathan Edwards [see Document 16] and the New England transcendentalists.*

For several days in June I had been forcing my way through woods that seemed to become more and more dense, and among bogs more and more difficult to cross, when, one warm afternoon, after descending a hillside covered with huge half-dead hemlocks, I crossed an ice cold stream, and espied two specimens of Calypso. There upon an open plat of yellow moss, near an immense rotten log, were these little plants so pure.

They were alone. Not a vine was near, nor a blade of grass, nor a bush. Nor were there any birds or insects, for great blocks of ice lay screened from the summer's sun by deep beds of moss, and chilled the water. They were indeed alone, for the dull ignoble hemlocks were not companions, nor was the nearer arbor-vitae, with its root-like pendulous branches decaying confusedly on the wet, cold ground.

I never before saw a plant so full of life; so perfectly spiritual, it seemed pure enough for the throne of its Creator. I felt as if I were in the presence of superior beings who loved me and beckoned me to come. I sat down beside them and wept for joy. Could angels in their better land show us a more beautiful plant? How good is our Heavenly Father in granting us such friends as are these plant-creatures, filling us wherever we go with pleasure so deep, so pure, so endless.

I cannot understand the nature of the curse, "Thorns and thistles shall it bring forth to thee." Is our world worse for this "thistly curse"? Are not all plants beautiful? or in some way useful? Is our world better for this "thistly curse"? Would not the world suffer by the banishment of a single weed?

Source: John Muir, letter to Mrs. Jeanne Carr, quoted in J. D. Butler, "The Calypso Borealis: Botanical Enthusiasm," *Boston Recorder*, December 21, 1866, p. 1, in Muir Scrapbook I, p. 26 (John Muir Collection at the University of the Pacific, Stockton, CA).

DOCUMENT 48: Frederick Law Olmsted and Calvert Vaux on Creating Parks to Serve the Public (1866, 1872)

Frederick Law Olmsted and Calvert Vaux developed their two great New York City parks, Central Park in Manhattan and Prospect Park in Brooklyn, to fulfill a democratic vision of park space accessible to all classes of people, based in part on a belief that contact with nature has an uplifting effect on the human spirit. Both Olmsted and Vaux had visited Green-wood Cemetery in Brooklyn in 1852 and were very much aware of its popularity among a broad cross-section of the city's population. In the first selection, Olmsted and Vaux justify their approach to park design on the basis of their knowledge of European parks. In the second selection, they detail how they went about translating the European idea of a park into one suitable for a great city in a democratic nation.

A. From a Report to Commissioners of Prospect Park, 1866

The word park has different significations, but that in which we are now interested has grown out of its application centuries ago, simply to hunting grounds; the choicest lands for hunting grounds being those in which the beasts of the chase were most happy, and consequently most abundant, sites were chosen for them, in which it was easy for animals to turn from rich herbage to clear water, from warm sunlight to cool shade; that is to say, by preference, ranges of well-watered dale-land, broken by open groves and dotted with spreading trees, undulating in surface, but not rugged. Gay parties of pleasure occasionally met in these parks, and when these meetings occurred the enjoyment otherwise obtained in them was found to be increased. Hence, instead of mere hunting lodges and hovels for game-keepers, extensive buildings and other accommodations, having frequently a festive character, were after a time provided within their enclosures. Then it was found that people took pleasure in them without regard to the attractions of the chase, or of conversation and this pleasure was perceived to be, in some degree, related to their scenery, and in some degree to the peculiar manner of association which occurred in them; and this was also found to be independent of intellectual gifts, tranquilizing and restorative to the powers most tasked in ordinary social duties, and stimulating only in a healthy and recreative way to the imagination. Hence, after a time, parks began to be regarded and to be maintained with reference, more than any thing else, to the convenient accommodation of numbers of people, desirous of moving for recreation among scenes that should be gratifying to their taste or imagination.

In the present century, not only have the old parks been thus maintained, but many new parks have been formed with these purposes exclusively in view, especially within and adjoining considerable towns and it is upon our knowledge of these latter that our simplest conception of a town park is founded. It is from experience in these that all our ideas of parks must spring.

B. From a Letter to H. G. Stebbins (president of the New York City Department of Parks), 1872

[O]ne of the considerations [affecting the design of Central Park] was suggested by the frightful increase of mortality among very young children which annually occurs in this city about mid-summer; the number of deaths of infants, notwithstanding so many are taken out of town, often being double as many in a day about the middle of July as in any day of several previous months. The causes act in part directly upon the children, but largely, also indirectly, by inducing nervous irritation with nursing mothers.

A visit to the country offers the surest means of escaping the danger, and, in incipient stages, the best means of cure of the special disorders in which the danger lies. To most mothers, however, this is impracticable, and the best that can be done is to spend an occasional day or part of a day on the Park. It has been for some years a growing practice with physicians to advise this course.

The whole Park is, of course, open as much to mothers with children as to any other class; but on a hot day a mother carrying a sick child, and perhaps leading other children, if she follows the throng, is liable to become more heated and feverish through fatigue, anxiety and various slight embarrassments, than if she remained quietly within a close, dark chamber. If she comes with a party of friends, she will be glad to find some quiet nook in which, while others wander, she can be left with her baby. The class of considerations thus suggested had influenced the treatment of several localities, but had been controlling in a larger way than elsewhere at the point in question.

. . . [J]ust here in the midst of the general bleakness, barrenness and filth of this quarter of the Park site, there was a pretty bit of natural scenery, having a somewhat wild and secluded character. It was designed to follow up the natural suggestions of this class, and by thickening and extending the original sylvan defences, secure a more decided effect of rural retirement.

The [natural] advantage for this purpose supplied one ground for the selection of the spot, the proximity of the play-grounds for larger children, another; and that of one of the sunken roads of the Park another; but the main reason for it was the fact that *it was the precise point in the Park which could be reached with the fewest steps* on an average, by visitors coming from the denser parts of the city by seven different lines of railway, and after the Park should be entered, wholly along walks by which the crossing of any carriage road would be avoided.

Source: **A.** Report to Commissioners of Prospect Park, 1866, and **B.** Department of Public Parks, 2nd Annual Report, Appendix B, in Frederick Law Olmsted, Jr., and Theodora Kimball, eds., *Frederic Law Olmsted: Landscape Architect, 1822-1903* (New York: Benjamin Blom, 1970; reissue of Olmsted and Kimball, *Forty Years of Landscape Architecture: Being the Professional Papers of Frederick Law Olmsted, Senior* [1928]), pp. 211-12, 242-43.

DOCUMENT 49: Charles Darwin on the Similarity between Humans and Other Animals (1871)

Charles Darwin, like many other early British naturalists, was educated for the ministry but had been fascinated by nature since childhood. His development of the theory of natural selection was influenced in part by reading Malthus's "Essay on the Principle of Population" [see Document 26], which led him to contemplate the effects of living in an overcrowded world. His carefully documented theoretical work presented in The Origin of Species *launched a continuing debate about whether humans are a special creation distinct from all other living things. The idea that humans are subject to the same "principles of evolution" as other animals was barely alluded to in* The Origin of Species. *It was Thomas Henry Huxley's* Evidence of Man's Place in Nature, *published in 1863, that provided the first detailed discussion of the theory. Darwin himself did not expand on the topic until 1871, when he wrote* The Descent of Man, *from which this selection is taken.*

He who wishes to decide whether man is the modified descendant of some pre-existing form, would probably first inquire whether man varies, however slightly, in bodily structure and in mental faculties; and if so, whether the variations are transmitted to his offspring in accordance with the laws which prevail with the lower animals. Again, are the variations the result, as far as our ignorance permits us to judge, of the same general causes, and are they governed by the same general laws, as in the case of other organisms; for instance, by correlation, the inherited effects of use and disuse, etc.? Is man subject to similar malconformations, the result of arrested development, of reduplication of parts, etc., and does he display in any of his anomalies reversion to some former and ancient type of structure? It might also naturally be inquired whether man, like so many other animals, has given rise to varieties and sub-races, differing but slightly from each other, or to races differing so much that they must be classed as doubtful species? How are such races distributed over the world; and how, when crossed, do they react on each other in the first and succeeding generations? And so with many other points.

The inquirer would next come to the important point, whether man tends to increase at so rapid a rate, as to lead to occasional severe struggles for existence; and consequently to beneficial variations, whether in body or mind, being preserved, and injurious ones eliminated. Do the races or species of men, whichever term may be applied, encroach on and replace one another, so that some finally become extinct? We shall see

that all these questions, as indeed is obvious in respect to most of them, must be answered in the affirmative, in the same manner as with the lower animals. . . .

The Bodily Structure of Man. — It is notorious that man is constructed on the same general type or model as other mammals. All the bones in his skeleton can be compared with corresponding bones in a monkey, bat, or seal. So it is with his muscles, nerves, blood-vessels, and internal viscera. The brain, the most important of all the organs, follows the same law, as shown by [Thomas Henry] Huxley and other anatomists.

Source: Charles Darwin, *The Descent of Man and Selections in Relation to Sex* (New York: A. L. Burt, n.d.; reprinted from the 2nd English ed. rev.), pp. 5-6.

DOCUMENT 50: Act Establishing Yellowstone National Park (1872)

Scouts and trappers who ventured into the Yellowstone River basin in the early nineteenth century spread stories about beautiful waterfalls, splendid canyons, and spectacular geysers to be found near the headwaters of the Yellowstone and Madison Rivers. In 1870 an expedition led by General Henry Washburne, the surveyor-general of Montana, and Lieutenant Gustavus Doane set out to confirm the truth of these tales. When the Washburne-Doane expedition returned, two members of the group, Cornelius Hedges and Nathaniel Langford, spread the word about the natural wonders of this wild region and generated interest in turning the area into a park that could be enjoyed by the general public.[6] In 1872 President Ulysses S. Grant signed legislation setting aside two million acres of federal land, primarily in north-western Wyoming, as a park. This marked the first time that any central government in the world had designated an area of public land as a permanent park.

Be it enacted by the Senate and House of Representatives of the United States of America in Congress assembled, That the tract of land in the Territories of Montana and Wyoming, lying near the head-waters of the Yellowstone river, and described as follows, to wit, commencing at the junction of Gardiner's river with the Yellowstone river, and running east to the meridian passing ten miles to the eastward of the most eastern point of Yellowstone lake; thence south along said meridian to the parallel of latitude passing ten miles south of the most southern point of Yellowstone lake; thence west along said parallel to the meridian passing fifteen miles west of the most western point of Madison lake;

thence north along said meridian to the latitude of the junction of the Yellow-stone and Gardiner's rivers; thence east to the place of beginning, is hereby reserved and withdrawn from settlement, occupancy, or sale under the laws of the United States, and dedicated and set apart as a public park or pleasuring-ground for the benefit and enjoyment of the people; and all persons who shall locate or settle upon or occupy the same, or any part thereof, except as hereinafter provided, shall be considered trespassers and removed therefrom.

SEC. 2. That said public park shall be under the exclusive control of the Secretary of the Interior, whose duty it shall be, as soon as practicable, to make and publish such rules and regulations as he may deem necessary or proper for the care and management of the same. Such regulations shall provide for the preservation, from injury or spoliation, of the timber, mineral deposits, natural curiosities, or wonders within said park and their retention in their natural condition. The secretary may in his discretion, grant leases for building purposes for terms not exceeding ten years, of small parcels of ground, at such places in said park as shall require the erection of buildings for the accommodation of visitors; all of the proceeds of said leases, and all other revenues that may be derived from any source connected with said park, to be expended under his direction in the management of the same, and the construction of roads and bridle-paths therein. He shall provide against the wanton destruction of the fish and game found within said park, and against their capture or destruction for the purposes of merchandise or profit. He shall also cause all persons trespassing upon the same after the passage of this act to be removed therefrom, and generally shall be authorized to take all such measures as shall be necessary or proper to fully carry out the objects and purposes of this act.

Source: United States Statutes at Large, Vol. 17 (Boston: Little, Brown, 1873), 42nd Cong., 2nd sess., chap. 24, May 1, 1872, pp. 32-33.

DOCUMENT 51: Mining Act (1872)

In the 1870s the United States was not only eager to have settlers move into its western territories, it was also anxious to exploit the natural wealth of the region. The giveaway provisions of the Act to Promote the Development of the Mining Resources of the United States, like those of the Homestead Act [see Document 42], were designed to encourage settlement as well as resource development.

The 1872 Mining Act ended the governmental practice, which had been in effect since the colonial period, of charging a royalty for taking minerals from public lands. It allowed prospectors and speculators to stake claims to any public lands containing hard rock minerals (i.e., gold and silver as opposed to oil and gas, which are found in shale), even if the land contained only trace amounts of the minerals. As long as the claim holder made at least $100 worth of improvements on the land annually or obtained a patent for the land, all other individuals were excluded from the land. The Mining Act, with only minor revisions, remains in effect today and continues to govern land use in much of the West. Efforts to truly modernize this law, which would entail reforming the claim-patent system and increasing the fees for mining on public lands, have encountered strong opposition from mining interests.

Be it enacted . . . , That all valuable mineral deposits in lands belonging to the United States, both surveyed and unsurveyed, are hereby declared to be free and open to exploration and purchase, and the lands in which they are found to occupation and purchase, by citizens of the United States and those who have declared their intention to become such, under regulations prescribed by law, and according to the local customs or rules of miners, in the several mining-districts, so far as the same are applicable and not inconsistent with the laws of the United States.

SEC. 2. That mining-claims upon veins or lodes of quartz or other rock in place bearing gold, silver, cinnabar, lead, tin, copper, or other valuable deposits heretofore located, shall be governed as to length along the vein or lode by the customs, regulations, and laws in force at the date of their location. A mining-claim located after the passage of this act, whether located by one or more persons, may equal, but shall not exceed, one thousand five hundred feet in length along the vein or lode; but no location of a mining-claim shall be made until the discovery of the vein or lode within the limits of the claim located. No claim shall extend more than three hundred feet on each side of the middle of the vein at the surface, nor shall any claim be limited by any mining regulation to less than twenty-five feet on each side of the middle of the vein at the surface. . . .

SEC.. 3. That the locators of all mining locations heretofore made, or which shall hereafter be made, on any mineral vein, lode, or ledge, situated on the public domain, their heirs and assigns . . . shall have the exclusive right of possession and enjoyment of all the surface included within the lines of their locations, and of all veins, lodes, and ledges throughout their entire depth. . . .

SEC.. 5. That the miners of each mining district may make rules and regulations not in conflict with the laws of the United States, or with the laws of the State or Territory in which the district is situated, governing the location, manner of recording, amount of work necessary to hold possession of a mining-claim, subject to the following requirements: The location must be distinctly marked on the ground so that its boundaries can be readily traced. . . . On each claim located after the passage of this act, and until a patent shall have been issued therefor, not less than one hundred dollars' worth of labor shall be performed or improvements made during each year. . . .

SEC.. 6. That a patent for any land claimed and located for valuable deposits may be obtained in the following manner: Any person, association, or corporation authorized to locate a claim under this act, having claimed and located a piece of land for such purposes, who has, or have, complied with the terms of this act, may file in the proper land-office an application for a patent . . . and shall thereupon be entitled to a patent for said land in such manner: The register of the land-office, upon the filing of such application, plat, field-notes, notices, and affidavits, shall publish a notice that such application has been made, for the period of sixty days, in a newspaper to be by him designated as published nearest to said claim; and he shall also post such notice in his office for the same period. The claimant at the time of filing this application, or at any time thereafter, within the sixty days of publication, shall file with the register a certificate of the United States surveyor-general that five hundred dollars' worth of labor has been expended or improvements made upon the claim by himself or grantors; that the plat is correct . . . . If no adverse claim shall have been filed with the register and the receiver of the proper land-office at the expiration of the sixty days of publication, it shall be assumed that the applicant is entitled to a patent, upon the payment to the proper officer of five dollars per acre, and that no adverse claim exists.

Source: United States Statutes at Large, Vol. 17 (Boston: Little, Brown, 1873), 42nd Cong., 2nd sess., chap. 152, May 10, 1872, p. 91.

DOCUMENT 52: Carl Schurz on the Need for Federal Forest Conservation (1877)

Carl Schurz brought from his native Germany a love of trees and an understanding of forest management. He was the first federal official to recognize the widespread abuse of timbered lands in the United States. As Secretary of the Interior under President Rutherford B. Hayes, Schurz tried (in vain) to control rampant commercial exploitation of federal forests.

The subject of the extensive depredations committed upon the timber on the public lands of the United States has largely engaged the attention of [the Department of the Interior]. That question presents itself in a twofold aspect: as a question of law and as a question of public economy. As to the first point, little need be said. That the law prohibits the taking of timber by unauthorized persons from the public lands of the United States, is a universally known fact. That the laws are made to be executed, ought to be a universally accepted doctrine. That the government is in duty bound to act upon that doctrine, needs no argument. There may be circumstances under which the rigorous execution of a law may be difficult or inconvenient, or obnoxious to public sentiment, or working particular hardship; in such cases it is the business of the legislative power to adapt the law to such circumstances. It is the business of the Executive to enforce the law as it stands.

As to the second point, the statements made by the Commissioner of the General Land Office, in his report, show the quantity of timber taken from the public lands without authority of law to have been of enormous extent. It probably far exceeds in reality any estimates made upon the data before us. It appears, from authentic information before this department, that in many instances the depredations have been carried on in the way of organized and systematic enterprise, not only to furnish timber, lumber, and fire-wood for the home market, but, on a large scale, for commercial exportation to foreign countries.

The rapidity with which this country is being stripped of its forests must alarm every thinking man. It has been estimated by good authority that, if we go on at the present rate, the supply of timber in the United States will, in less than twenty years, fall considerably short of our home necessities. How disastrously the destruction of the forests of a country affects the regularity of the water supply in its rivers necessary for navigation, increases the frequency of freshets and inundations, dries up springs, and transforms fertile agricultural districts into barren wastes is a matter of universal experience the world over. It is the highest time that we should turn our earnest attention to this subject, which so seriously concerns our national prosperity.

The government cannot prevent the cutting of timber on land owned by private citizens. It is only to be hoped that private owners will grow more careful of their timber as it rises in value. But the government can do two things: 1. It can take determined and, as I think, effectual measures to arrest the stealing of timber from public lands on a large scale, which is always attended with the most reckless waste; and, 2. It can preserve the forests still in its possession by keeping them under its control, and by so regulating the cutting and sale of timber on its lands as to secure the renewal of the forest by natural growth and the careful preservation of the young timber.

Source: Annual Report of the Secretary of the Interior on the Operations of the Department for the Fiscal Year Ended June 30, 1877 (Washington, D.C..: Government Printing Office, 1877), [iii], pp. xv-xx, in Roderick Nash, ed., Readings in the History of Conservation (Reading, MA: Addison-Wesley, 1968), pp. 25-26.

DOCUMENT 53: Henry George on Land Development (1879)

The social reformer and economist Henry George was working in San Francisco as a printer and editor during a period when the expansion of the railroads was stimulating a land boom in California. George vehemently objected to policies for land development being determined by landowners and speculators. His writings helped to spark interest in the need for land use planning.

So far from the recognition of private property in land being necessary to the proper use of land, the contrary is the case. Treating land as private property stands in the way of its proper use. Were land treated as public property it would be used and improved as soon as there was need for its use or improvement, but being treated as private property, the individual owner is permitted to prevent others from using or improving what he cannot or will not use or improve himself. When the title is in dispute, the most valuable land lies unimproved for years; in many parts of England improvement is stopped because, the estates being entailed, no security to improvers can be given; and large tracts of ground which, were they treated as public property, would be covered with buildings and crops, are kept idle to gratify the caprice of the owner. In the thickly settled parts of the United States there is enough land to maintain three or four times our present population, lying unused, because its owners are holding it for higher prices, and immigrants are forced past this unused land to seek homes where their labor will be far less productive. In every city valuable lots may be seen lying vacant for the same reason. If the best use of land be the test, then private property in land is condemned, as it is condemned by every other consideration. It is as wasteful and uncertain a mode of securing the proper use of land as the burning down of houses is of roasting pigs.

Source: Henry George, *Progress and Poverty: An Inquiry into the Cause of Industrial Depressions and of Increase of Want with Increase of Wealth* (New York: Robert Schalkenbach Foundation, 1979), pp. 401-2.

DOCUMENT 54: Act Establishing the Adirondack Forest Preserve Act (1885)

"An act to establish a forest commission, and to define its powers and duties and for the preservation of forests" was passed by the New York State legislature on May 15, 1885. In 1894, the "forever wild" clause of the law, section 8, was incorporated into the New York State Constitution as Article XIV, section 7: "[T]he lands of the State now owned or hereafter acquired constituting the Forest Preserve as now fixed by law, shall be forever kept as wild forest lands. They shall not be leased, sold or exchanged, or be taken by any corporation, public or private, nor shall the timber thereon be sold, removed or destroyed." More then half a century later, in the 1950s, this clause[7] provided the impetus for Howard Zahnizer, then the director of the Wilderness Society, to prepare a legislative draft and for a coalition of environmental groups to run a ten-year campaign [see Document 96] that resulted in the passage of the Federal Wilderness Act of 1964. The "forever wild" clause, however, has always had numerous opponents and has been the focal point of several efforts to amend the New York State Constitution.

George Bird Grinnell, the editor and owner of Forest and Stream, an influential periodical with a broad readership that ranged from outdoorsmen to politicians, was the champion of a variety of conservation causes. He feared that commercial timber interests would be allowed to denude the Adirondacks before the land came under state control.

A. The Act

Sec. 1. There shall be a forest commission which shall consist of three persons who shall be styled forest commissioners. . . .

Sec. 7. All the lands now owned or which may hereafter be acquired by the state of New York, within the counties of Clinton, excepting the towns of Altona and Dannemora, Essex,

Franklin, Fulton, Hamilton, Herkimer, Lewis, Saratoga, St. Lawrence, Warren, Washington, Greene, Ulster and Sullivan, shall constitute and be known as the forest preserve.

Sec. 8. The lands now or hereafter constituting the forest preserve shall be forever kept as wild forest lands. They shall not be sold, nor shall they be leased or taken by any person or corporation, public or private.

Sec. 9. The forest commission shall have the care, custody, control and superintendence of the forest preserve. It shall be the duty of the commission to maintain and protect the forests now on the forest preserve, and to promote as far as practicable the further growth of forests thereon. It shall also have charge of the public interests of the state, with regard to forests and tree planting, and especially with reference to forest fires in every part of the state. . . . The forest commission may, from time to time, prescribe rules or regulations . . . affecting the whole or any part of the forest preserve, and for its use, care and administration; but neither such rules or regulations, nor anything herein contained shall prevent or operate to prevent the free use of any road, stream or water as the same may have been heretofore used or as may be reasonably required in the prosecution of any lawful business.

B. George Bird Grinnell's Commentary on the Proposed Act, January 17, 1884

A bill was introduced at Albany last Tuesday by Senator Lansing, which provides for the protection of the Adirondack forests by the establishment of a State Park, to be fenced in and put in charge of a superintendent. The extent of the territory to be included in this park comprises 1,700,000 acres. Of this land the State now owns 750,000, or less than one-half. The bill . . . provides that the State shall assume immediate active control of the forest land now in its possession, and that the remaining 950,000 acres shall come within the same protecting care as it may be gradually abandoned by the present owners and allowed to revert for unpaid taxes.

The bill is a most excellent one, so far as it goes; but it is not sufficient. If the 1,700,000 acres of forest land should be cared for by the State, that care should be assumed at once, before the land has been denuded of its timber. Protection and conservation, now, prompt, adequate—this is what the Adirondack forests demand, not restoration years hence, after the damage shall have been wrought and ruin has followed.

We hear much ado made lest the proposition to assume State control of those lands shall terminate in a huge job; and again we urge that such a fear is not based on good grounds. The forests ought to be saved, even at great (but not exorbitant) cost, and in this day and generation most surely the man with the big pocket to fill ought not to stand in the way.

Source: **A.** *Laws of New York*, chap. 283, May 15, 1885, pp. 482-83. **B.** "The Adirondacks," *Forest and Stream* 21, no. 25 (January 17, 1884): 489.

DOCUMENT 55: American Ornithologists' Union's Model Law (1886)

In 1883, a group of professional and amateur ornithologists chartered the American Ornithologists' Union (AOU) to further the study of bird biology and economics. However, not long after the founding of the AOU, George Bird Grinnell and other members of the group decided to form the Committee on the Protection of North American Birds to effect social action in contrast to scientific study. The committee's most significant contribution was the writing of the "Model Law," which was widely distributed and used as a prototype for many state bird protection laws.

Section 1.—Any person who shall, within the state of _____, kill any wild bird other than a game-bird, or purchase, offer, or expose for sale any such wild bird, after it has been killed, shall for each offense be subject to a fine of five dollars, or imprisonment for ten days, or both, at the discretion of the court. For the purposes of this act the following only shall be considered game-birds. The Anatidae, commonly known as swans, geese, brant, and river and sea ducks; the Rallidae, commonly known as rails, coots, mud-hens, and gallinules; the Limicolae, commonly known as shore-birds, plovers, surf-birds, snipe, woodcock, sandpipers, tatlers and curlews; the Gallinae, commonly known as wild turkeys, grouse, prairie-chickens, pheasants, partridges, and quails.

Sect. 2.—Any person who shall, within the state of _____, take or needlessly destroy the nest or the eggs of any wild bird, shall be subject for each offense to a fine of five dollars, or imprisonment for ten days, or both, at the discretion of the court.

Sect. 3.—Sections 1 and 2 of this act shall not apply to any person holding a certificate giving the right to take birds, and their nests and eggs, for scientific purposes, as provided for in Section 4 of this act.

Source: American Ornithologists' Union, Committee on Protection of Birds, "An Act for the Protection of Birds and Their Nests and Eggs," *Bulletin of the Committee on Protection of Birds,* reprinted in *Science* 7, no. 160 (February 26, 1886): 204.

DOCUMENT 56: George Bird Grinnell and Celia Thaxter on the Audubon Society Cause (1886)

Continuing to use Forest and Stream *to promote his conservation agenda [see Document 54B], Grinnell suggested the formation of an association for the protection of birds that would further the work he had started with the AOU [see Document 55]. Grinnell's idea was wildly successful, and within three years he had 39,000 members pledged to protect birds. However, the group, named the Audubon Society after the ornithologist John Audubon [see Document 33], on whose subdivided estate Grinnell had grown up and whose widow had provided his education, was disbanded after two years because Grinnell could not manage the fledgling society along with his weekly journal and publishing business. Nevertheless, within eight years, state Audubon societies had been chartered in Massachusetts and Pennsylvania, and by the turn of the century many others had been formed. Championing the cause of the Audubon Society were a large number of women, including the writer and gardener Celia Thaxter, whose family owned a resort on the Isle of Shoals, off the coast of New Hampshire, that was popular with nature lovers.*

A. George Bird Grinnell's Proposal for the Formation of the Audubon Society, February 11, 1886

Very slowly the public are awakening to see that the fashion of wearing the feathers and skins of birds is abominable. There is, we think, no doubt that when the facts about this fashion are known, it will be frowned down and will cease to exist. Legislation of itself can do little against this barbarous practice, but if public sentiment can be aroused against it, it will die a speedy death.

The *Forest and Stream* has been hammering away at this subject for some years, and the result of its blows is seen in the gradual change which has taken place in public sentiment since it began its work. The time has passed for showing that the fashion is an outrageous one, and that it results very disastrously to the largest and most important class of our population—the farmers. These are injured in two ways; by the destruction of the birds, whose food consists chiefly of insects injurious to the growing crops, and of that scarcely less important group the Rapaces, which prey upon the small rodents which devour the crop after it has matured.

The reform in America, as elsewhere, must be inaugurated by women, and if the subject is properly called to their notice, their tender hearts will be quick to respond. In England, this matter has been taken up and a widespread interest in it developed. If the women of America will take hold in the same earnest way, they can accomplish an incalculable amount of good.

While individual effort may accomplish much, it will work but slowly, and the spread of the movement will be but gradual. Something more than this is needed. Men, women and children all over our land should take the matter in hand, and urge its importance upon those with whom they are brought in contact. A general effort of this kind will not fail to awaken public interest, and information given to a right-thinking public will set the ball of reform in motion. Our beautiful birds give to many people a great deal of pleasure and add much to the delights of the country. These birds are slaughtered in vast numbers for gain. If the demand for their skins can be caused to fall off, it will no longer repay the bird butchers to ply their trade and the birds will be saved.

* * *

We propose the formation of an association for the protection of wild birds and their eggs, which shall be called the Audubon Society. Its membership is to be free to every one who is willing to lend a helping hand in forwarding the objects for which it is formed. These objects shall be to prevent, so far as possible (1), the killing of any wild birds not used for food; (2) the destruction of nests or eggs of any wild bird, and (3) the wearing of feathers as ornaments or trimming for dress.

B. Celia Thaxter Attacks Bird-Wearing Women

When the Audubon Society was first organized, it seemed a comparatively simple thing to awaken in the minds of all bird-wearing women a sense of what their "decoration" involved. We flattered ourselves that the tender and compassionate heart of woman would at once respond to the appeal for mercy, but after many months of effort we are obliged to acknowledge ourselves mistaken in our estimate of that universal compassion, that tender heart in which we believed. Not among the ignorant and uncultivated so much as the educated and enlightened do we find the indifference and hardness that baffles and perplexes us. Not always, heaven be praised! But too often,—I think I may say in two-thirds of the cases to which we appeal. One lady said to me, "I think there is a great deal of sentiment wasted on the birds. There are so many of them, they will never be missed any more than mosquitoes. I shall put birds on my new bonnet." . . . and she went her way, a charnel-house of beaks and claws and bones and feathers and glass eyes upon her fatuous head.

Another, mockingly, says, "Why don't you try to save the little fishes in the sea?" and continues to walk the world with dozens of warblers' wings making her headgear hideous. Not one in fifty is found willing to remove at once the birds from her head, even if, languidly, she does acquiesce in the assertion that it is a cruel sin against nature to destroy them. "When these are worn out I am willing to promise not to buy any more," is what we hear, and we are thankful, indeed, for even so much grace; but alas! birds never "wear out."

Source: **A.** George Bird Grinnell, "The Audubon Society," *Forest and Stream* 24, no. 3 (February 11, 1886): 41. **B.** Celia Thaxter, *Woman's Heartlessness* (Boston 1886; reprinted for the Audubon Society of the State of New York, 1899), in the New York Public Library National Audobon Society Collection.

DOCUMENT 57: Constitution of the Boone and Crockett Club (1887)

In the latter part of the nineteenth and early part of the twentieth centuries, a number of outdoor clubs devoted to hiking, fishing, and hunting were organized with constitutions that contained conservation agendas aimed at protecting their interests. Among the most influential of these sportsmen's groups was the Boone and Crockett Club, whose founding members included the painter Albert Bierstadt; George Bird Grinnell; Jay Pierpont; Archibald Rogers, secretary; Theodore Roosevelt, president; and several other Roosevelt family members. William "Buffalo Bill" Cody joined the club soon after its inception.

Article II. The objects of the club shall be—
1. To promote manly sport with the rifle.
2. To promote travel and exploration in the wild and unknown or but partially known portions of the country.
3. To work for the preservation of the large game of this country, and, so far as possible, to further legislation for that purpose, and to assist in enforcing the existing laws.
4. To promote inquiry into, and to record observations on the habits and natural history of the various wild animals.
5. To bring about among the members the interchange of opinions and ideas on hunting, travel and exploration; on the various kinds of hunting rifles; on the haunts of game animals, etc.

Article III. No one shall be eligible for membership who shall not have killed with the rifle in fair chase, by still-hunting or otherwise, at least one individual of one of the various kinds of American large game.

Article IV. Under the head of American large game are included the following animals: Bear, buffalo (bison), mountain sheep, caribou, cougar, musk ox, white goat, elk (wapiti), wolf (not coyote), pronghorn antelope, moose and deer.

Article V. The term "fair chase" shall not be held to include killing bear, wolf, or cougar in traps, nor "fire-hunting," nor "crusting" moose, elk or deer in deep snow, nor killing game from a boat while it is swimming in the water.

Source: "Constitution of the Boone and Crockett Club," in Theodore Roosevelt and George Bird Grinnell, eds., *American Big Game Hunting* (New York: Forest and Stream Publishing, 1893), pp. 337-38.a

DOCUMENT 58: John Wesley Powell on the Lands of the Arid Regions (1890)

John Wesley Powell, who was the first person of European descent to travel by boat through the Grand Canyon, spent many years studying the Great Basin region between the Rocky and Sierra Mountains while serving on the staff of the U.S. Geological Survey. He was an enthusiastic supporter of the idea of scientifically studying and developing the nation's natural resources.

In 1878, Powell published his original report on the arid regions of the West and sent a copy to Carl Schurz [see Document 52]. The report was ignored in government circles. However, Powell spent the next twenty years promoting his ideas in a variety of venues, including popular publications such as Century Magazine, *from which the following selections are taken. Eventually, Powell's writings came to the attention of Theodore Roosevelt, who took much of his 1901 address to Congress [see Document 62] from Powell's report. The Reclamation Act [see Document 63], passed the following year, was an outgrowth of the address.*

Although Powell's writings on the arid lands show him to be a man of his times who believed that nature could be harnessed and controlled, they also reveal him to have been a visionary conservationist who recognized the need to conserve the forests of the West.

A. The Irrigable Lands

[W]ill not the hills of New England, the mountains and plains of the sunny South, and the prairies of the middle region be sufficient for the agricultural industries of the United States? The area is vast, the soil is bountiful, and the heavens kindly give their rains. Why should the naked plains and the desert valleys of the far West be redeemed? Why should our civilization enter into a contest with nature to subdue the rivers of the West when the clouds of the East are ready servants?

Gold is found in the graves of the West; silver abounds in the cliffs; copper is found in the mountains; iron, coal petroleum, and gas are supplied by nature. The mountains and plateaus are covered with stately forest; the climate is salubrious and wonderfully alluring. So the tide of migration rolls westward and the arid region is being carved into States. The people are building cities and towns, erecting factories, and constructing railroads, and great industries of many kinds are already developed. The merchant and his clerk, the banker and his bookkeeper, the superintendent and his operative, the conductor and his brakeman, must be fed; and the men of the West are too enterprising and too industrious to beg bread from the farms of the East. Already they have redeemed more than six million acres of this land; already they are engaged in warfare with the rivers, and have won the first battles. An army of men is enlisted and trained, and they march on a campaign—not for blood, but for bounty; not for plunder, but for prosperity.

But arid lands are not lands of famine, and the sunny sky is not a firmament of devastation. Conquered rivers are better servants than wild clouds. The valleys and plains of the far West have all the elements of fertility that soil can have. As the blood in the body is the stream which supplies the elements of its growth, so the water in the plant is its source of increase. As the body must have more than blood, so the plant must have more than water for its vigorous growth. These conditions of plant growth are light and heat. While the roots of the plant are properly supplied with water and other elements of plant growth, the leaves must be supplied with air and sunshine. The light of a cloudless sky is more invigorating to plants than the gloom of storm. Abundant water and abundant sunshine are the chief conditions for vigorous plant growth, and that agriculture is the most successful which

best secures these twin primal conditions; and they are obtained in the highest degree in lands watered by streams and domed by clear skies. For these reasons arid lands are more productive under high cultivation than humid lands. The wheatfields of the desert, the cornfields, the vineyards, the orchards, and the gardens of the far West, far surpass those of the East in luxuriance and productiveness. In the East the field may pine for delayed rains and the green of prosperity fade into sickly saffron, or the vegetation may be beaten down by storms and be drowned by floods; while in the more favored lands of the arid region there is a constant and perfect supply of water by the hand of man, and a constant and perfect supply of sunshine by the economy of nature. The arid lands of the West, last to be redeemed by methods first discovered in civilization, are the best agricultural lands of the continent. Not only must these lands be redeemed because of the wants of the population of that country, they must be redeemed because they are our best lands.

B. The Non-irrigible Lands

[A]bout one-tenth of the arid region is covered with firewood timber, but this timber is very scant, and often the open spaces are large. It could all stand on one-fiftieth of the entire arid area and not be crowded. The milling timber also covers about another tenth of the ground, but there are many barren places, and usually the trees are widely scattered, so that they could all stand on one-fortieth of the space and still have abundant room. So both classes combined could easily stand on less than one-twentieth of the arid regions.

The merchantable timber is all on the high plateaus and mountains; hence the lands where it grows are not valuable for agricultural purposes. Canyon walls, cliffs, crags, and rocky steeps are not attractive farming-grounds. But more: at these great attributes deep snows fall, ice appears early and lingers long, and frosts come on many a summer night.

The agricultural lands are situated in the valleys where the streams flow. Thus forest and farm are dissevered by dozens and scores of miles. So forest industries are segregated in one region, farming industries in another. It is no small task for the farmer and the villager to haul their wood from distant mountains and to bring poles and logs from the upper region. . . .

The miners are also interested in these forests. As they penetrate their shafts, drifts, and galleries into the hills and mountains, they carry away to the surface the rock in which the gold, silver, copper and lead are found, that the metals may be extracted on the ground above.

* * *

Before the white man came the natives systematically burned over the forest lands with each recurrent year as one of their great hunting economies. By this process little destruction of timber was accomplished; but, protected by civilized men, forests are rapidly disappearing. The needles, cones, and brush, together with the leaves of grass and shrubs below, accumulate when not burned annually. New deposits are made from year to year, until the ground is covered with a thick mantle of inflammable material. Then a spark is dropped, a fire accidentally or purposely kindled, and the flames have abundant food.

There is a practical method by which the forests can be preserved. All of the forest areas that are not dense have some value for pasturage purposes. Grasses grow well in the open grounds, and to some extent among the trees. If herds and flocks crop these grasses, and trample the leaves and cones into the ground, and make many trails through the woods, they destroy the conditions most favorable to the spread of fire. But if the pasturage is crowded, the young growth is destroyed and the forests are not properly replenished by a new generation of trees. The wooded grounds that are too dense for pasturage should be annually burned over at a time when the inflammable materials are not too dry, so that there may be no danger of great conflagrations.

The area of good timber being very small, it has great value, and its rapid destruction is a calamity that cannot well be overestimated. These living forests are always a delight, for in beauty and grandeur they are unexcelled; but dead forests present scenes of desolation that fill the soul with sadness. The vast destruction of values, together with the enormous ravishment of beauty, have for years enlisted the sympathy of intelligent men. Forestry organizations have been formed; conventions have been held; publicists have discussed the subject; and there is a universal sentiment in the West, and a growing opinion in the East, that measures should be taken by the General Government for the protection of the forests.

Source: **A.** John Wesley Powell, "The Irrigable Lands of the Arid Region," *Century Magazine* 39, no. 5 (March 1890): 766-68. **B.** John Wesley Powell, "The Non-irrigable Lands of the Arid Region," *Century Magazine,* 39, no. 6 (April 1890): 917-20.

Part IV

The Roots of the Conservation Movement, 1890–1919

As a major producer of iron and steel, coal and coke, oil, cotton and woolen goods, farm implements, and refined sugar, the United States in the 1890s was a modern industrial powerhouse. It was also the fourth most populous country in the world, with a population of nearly 63 million. The steam engine and steam-powered tractors had begun to transform farm life, especially on the large wheat farms of the Midwest, but, as yet, few people had electricity or owned cars.

Over the next three decades, the nation's population would expand greatly as a result of massive immigration from southern and eastern Europe. Simultaneously, the number of households that possessed electric power and lighting, telephones, and/or automobiles would also increase tremendously. By 1920, immigration and technological innovation had altered the face of America.

Public Health and Sanitation

As a result of scientific discoveries made in the second half of the nineteenth century, several major sanitary and medical advances—including the pasteurization of milk, the chlorination and filtration of water, and the use of antiseptics and other bacteria-destroying agents—were gradually introduced throughout much of the United States. Around the 1850s, many cities had begun building both water supply and sewage systems. By the turn of the century, greater cleanliness of water and food as well as improvements in medical care had increased Americans' life expectancy. While life expectancy in 1850 was only about 38.3 years for men and 40.5 years for women, by 1900 it had reached 46.3 years for men and 48.3 years for women, and by 1920 it had risen to 53.6 years for men and 54.6 years for women.[1]

Nevertheless, pollution and poor sanitation remained problems in both urban and rural areas, in part because local efforts to stop pollution were constantly being challenged by industry. The disposal of garbage and waste, including droppings from horses that pulled carriages, and the general lack of good sanitation continued to endanger public health. Furthermore, the problems of industrial waste and soot that had plagued towns and cities in the nineteenth century [see Document 41] had intensified as industrialization increased and cities grew [see Document 67]. In reaction, a movement to improve health, living, and working conditions, especially in the cities, gained ground. It was spearheaded primarily by women, many of them advocates for the poor and working class (like Jane Addams [see Document 72] and Lillian Wald) and doctors, nurses, and scientists (like Alice Hamilton and Ellen Swallow Richards [see Document 65]).

Because pollution and unsanitary conditions tended to be considered local issues, most social and legislative efforts to ameliorate these problems were initiated by local activists or members of state or local governments. The federal government evinced little interest in pollution and sanitation problems until 1899, when the Rivers and Harbors Act [see Document 61]—the first federal antipollution law—was passed.

While industrial growth and urban expansion fueled many urban sanitation problems, the movement of people away from the sources of food production also created new types of sanitary problems related to food production and packaging that called for federal oversight. The need for greater federal involvement together with a popular demand for improved sanitation helped to spark a pure foods movement. This movement, reinforced by the graphic descriptions of unsanitary conditions in the meat-packing industry in Upton Sinclair's novel *The Jungle* [see Document 64], provided the impetus for the passage of both the Pure Food and Drug Act of 1906 and the Meat Inspection Act of 1907.

The Federal Conservation Effort

The recognition that there was effectively no frontier remaining in which to expand [see Document 60] stimulated increasing numbers of people to be concerned about the careless destruction and plunder of the nation's resources. In 1891 President Benjamin Harrison created a national forest system with a set-aside of 13 million acres of forested land [see Document 59]. During President Grover Cleveland's second term of office (1893-1897), Harrison's forest reserve was augmented by another 21 million acres.

In 1901, twenty years after John Wesley Powell began his campaign to reclaim the arid lands of the West, the cause was embraced by President Teddy Roosevelt [see Document 62]. Then, in 1902, following

the passage of the Reclamation Act [see Document 63], the federal government sold off massive amounts of public lands to provide funds for irrigation projects. Roosevelt Dam, on the Salt River in Arizona, the first of the large dams to be built with these funds, was completed in 1911. Roosevelt also championed Powell's proposal to conserve the woodlands of the arid regions, for it was becoming obvious that the nation's woodlands were fast disappearing. By 1900 all but one-quarter of the virgin timberlands that had existed when the first colonists arrived had been cut down.

By 1907 President Theodore Roosevelt was deeply committed to the cause of resource conservation [see Document 66]. The first real effort of the federal government to develop a conservation policy began that year, when Roosevelt, at the urging of WJ McGee [see Document 71] and Gifford Pinchot [see Document 73], formed the Inland Waterways Commission to prepare a comprehensive national plan regarding flood control, irrigation, water transportation, hydroelectric development, and soil conservation. The commission, which included both McGee and Pinchot, determined that the issue of waterways and forest cover was of concern to the nation as a whole, and recommended that the president convene all the state governors to discuss the problem. Invited guests at the conference, held at the White House on May 13, 1908, included congressmen and other prominent politicians, scientists, and Supreme Court justices in addition to the state governors. During the conference it became evident that very little was known about the extent of available natural resources in the country, although it was obvious that a resource problem did exist. The National Conservation Commission [see Document 70] was created to look into the problem, but Congress failed to appropriate sufficient funds for the planned study.

Roosevelt, an ardent anti-monopolist, attempted to prevent the bleeding of America's resources by instituting antitrust legislation aimed at the huge monopolies that at the turn of the century controlled the railroads and the production of beef, sugar, fertilizers, and farm machinery.

In 1909 Roosevelt invited representatives from Canada, Newfoundland, and Mexico to a North American conservation conference. He also tried to organize a gathering of representatives from countries around the world at The Hague, but the proposal garnered little interest because most of the resource issues on his suggested agenda had already been dealt with by the European nations.

Much of the government's "conservation" effort during the administration of Theodore Roosevelt and for a decade thereafter was focused on land reclamation and the building of dams and reservoirs to supply the growing population of the West, where water was a problem because much of the region was arid or semiarid. A proposal to flood the magnificent Hetch Hetchy Valley led to a fierce battle between preservationists, such as John Muir, and wise-use conservationists, such as Teddy Roosevelt and Pinchot, that underlined a serious rift in the rapidly growing conservation movement [see Document 68]. Although the utilitarians—the wise-use advocates—won, the fight brought the preservationists together and galvanized the conservation movement.

In the ensuing years, Roosevelt's conservation initiatives continued to bear fruit. Discussions at the 1909 North American Conservation Conference had set the groundwork for multilateral agreements on migratory species, and in 1916 the United States and Canada signed a Migratory Bird Treaty.

The Changing Landscape

Since the birth of the nation, human activity and population growth had been changing the natural landscape, but in the twentieth century, as the rate of change increased markedly, many species of plants and animals reached the brink of extinction. By 1914, the passenger pigeon, which had once darkened the sky and provided food for thousands of people, was gone, and local oyster supplies for New York City markets had dried up as result of pollution in the city's harbor.

In 1917, though, the attention of the United States was directed to fighting World War I. Efforts were made to fortify the shipbuilding industry and to develop the infant aviation industry. As a result of wartime demands, large numbers of people found jobs in the industrial sector and moved to the cities.

DOCUMENT 59: Forest Reserve Act (1891)

The clause establishing the U.S. Forest Reserve System was buried, as section 24, in a bill to repeal timber culture laws. Following the passage of the bill by Congress, President Benjamin Harrison set aside 13 million acres of forest land.

[T]he President of the United States may, from time to time, set apart and reserve, in any State or Territory having public land bearing forests, in any part of the public lands wholly or in part covered with timber or undergrowth, whether of commercial value or not, as public reservations, and the President shall, by public proclamation, declare the establishment of such reservations and the limits thereof.

Source: United States Statutes at Large, Vol. 26 (Washington, D.C.: Government Printing Office, 1892), 51st Cong., 2nd sess, chap. 561, March 3, 1891, p. 1103.

DOCUMENT 60: Frederick J. Turner on the Disappearance of the Frontier (1894)

Until the late nineteenth century, the existence of a continuously advancing area that contained free land and undiscovered resources was a primary factor in the development of the United States and the actions of its inhabitants. Once the frontier reached the Pacific Ocean, however, Americans were forced to confront such issues as resource limitations and land availability. The Harvard history professor Fredrick Jackson Turner was prompted to write his definitive essay on the closing of the American frontier by the Census Report of 1890, which stated that the "frontier of settlement" no longer existed and that future census reports would not include data on the frontier. [2]

The exploitation of the beasts took hunter and trader to the west, the exploitation of the grasses took the rancher west, and the exploitation of the virgin soil of the river valleys and prairies attracted the farmer. Good soils have been the most continuous attraction to the farmer's frontier. The land hunger of the Virginians drew them down the rivers into Carolina, in early colonial days; the search for soils took the Massachusetts men to Pennsylvania and to New York. As the eastern lands were taken up migration flowed across them to the west. Daniel Boone, the great backwoodsman, who combined the occupations of hunter, trader, cattle-raiser farmer, and surveyor—learning, probably from the traders, of the fertility of the lands on the upper Yadkin, where the traders were wont to rest as they took their way to the Indians—left his Pennsylvania home with his father, and passed down the Great Valley road to that stream. Learning from a trader whose posts were on the Red River in Kentucky of its game and rich pastures, he pioneered the way for the farmers to that region. Thence he passed to the frontier of Missouri, where his settlement was long a landmark on the frontier. Here again he helped to open the way for civilization, finding salt licks, and trails, and land. His son was among the earliest trappers in the passes of the Rocky Mountains.

***

Obviously the immigrant was attracted by the cheap lands of the frontier, and even the native farmer felt their influence strongly. Year by year the farmers who lived on soil whose returns were diminished by unrotated crops were offered the virgin soil of the frontier at nominal prices. Their growing families demanded more lands, and these were dear. The competition of the unexhausted, cheap, and easily tilled prairie lands compelled the farmer either to go west and continue the exhaustion of the soil on a new frontier, or to adopt intensive culture. . . . Thus the demand for land and the love of wilderness freedom drew the frontier ever onward.

***

The stubborn American environment is there [at the frontier] with its imperious summons to accept its conditions; the inherited ways of doing things are also there; and yet, in spite of environment, and in spite of custom, each frontier did indeed furnish a new field of opportunity, a gate of escape from the bondage of the past; and freshness, and confidence, and scorn of older society, impatience of its restraints and its ideas, and indifference to its lessons, have accompanied the frontier. What the Mediterranean Sea was to the Greeks, breaking the bond of custom, offering new experiences, calling out new institutions and activities, that, and more, the ever retreating frontier has been to the United States directly, and to the nations of Europe more remotely. And now, four centuries from the discovery of America, at the end of a hundred years of life under the Constitution, the frontier has gone, and with its going has closed the first period of American history.

Source: Frederick J. Turner, *The Significance of the Frontier in American History* (Washington, D.C.: Government Printing Office, 1894; Readex Facsimile edition), pp. 213, 215, 227.

DOCUMENT 61: Rivers and Harbors Act (1899)

By the end of the nineteenth century, industrial wastes were beginning to have a deleterious effect on the water quality of rivers around the country. Tucked away in section 13 of the Rivers and Harbors Act of 1899—which was primarily an appropriations bill allocating funds for dozens of river and harbor construction, repair, and preservation projects—was a prohibition against dumping refuse in navigable waters, making it the first federal antipollution law. It is interesting to note that the first colonial antipollution statute also concerned the dumping of garbage in harbors [see Document 12].

[I]t shall not be lawful to throw, discharge, or deposit, or cause, suffer, or procure to be thrown, discharged, or deposited either from or out of any ship, barge, or other floating craft of any kind, or from the shore, wharf, manufacturing establishment, or mill of any kind, any refuse matter of any kind or description whatever other than that flowing from streets and sewers and passing therefrom in a liquid state, into any navigable water of the United States, or into any tributary of any navigable water from which the same shall float or be washed into such navigable water; and it shall not be lawful to deposit, or cause, suffer, or procure to be deposited material of any kind in any place on the bank of any navigable water, or on the bank of any tributary of any navigable water, where the same shall be liable to be washed into such navigable water; either by ordinary or high tides, or by storms or floods, or otherwise, whereby navigation shall or may be impeded or obstructed.

Source: U.S. Statutes at Large, Vol. 30, Part II (Washington, D.C.: Government Printing Office, 1900), 55th Cong., 3rd sess., chap. 425, March 3, 1899, p. 1152.

DOCUMENT 62: Theodore Roosevelt Addresses Congress on Forest Preservation and Land Reclamation (1901)

Teddy Roosevelt knew and loved the wild areas of the country, but at heart he was a pragmatic utilitarian whose conservation policies were driven by a desire to manage the land so that it would produce more game to hunt, more trees for timber, more water for irrigation, and more land for farming. Much of the content of this address, which set the stage for the Reclamation Act [see Document 63], is a reworking of John Wesley Powell's Reports on the Lands of the Arid Region [see Document 58]. Some of Roosevelt's later conservation policies were influenced by John Muir [Document 68A] and other preservationists, who convinced Roosevelt of the value of actually setting aside wilderness areas.

Public opinion throughout the United States has moved steadily toward a just appreciation of the nature of forests, whether of planted or natural growth. The great part played by them in the creation and maintenance of the National wealth is now more fully realized than ever before.

Wise forest protection does not mean the withdrawal of forest resources, whether of wood, water, or grass, from contributing their full share to the welfare of the people, but, on the contrary, gives the assurance of larger and more certain supplies. The fundamental idea of forestry is the perpetuation of forests by use. Forest protection is not an end of itself. It is a means to increase and sustain the resources of our country and the industries which depend upon them. The preservation of our forests is an imperative business necessity. We have come to see clearly that whatsoever destroys the forest, except to make way for agriculture, threatens our well-being.

The practical usefulness of the National forest reserves to the mining, grazing, irrigation, and other interests of the regions in which the reserves lie has led to widespread demand by the people of the West for their protection and extension. The forest reserves will inevitably be of still greater use in the future than in the past. Additions should be made to them whenever practicable, and their usefulness should be increased by a thoroughly businesslike management.

* * *

The wise administration of the forest reserves will be not less useful to the interests which depend on water than to those which depend on wood and grazing. The water supply itself depends upon the forest. In the arid region it is water, not land, which measures production. The western half of the United States would sustain a population greater than that of our whole country today if the waters that now run to waste were saved and used for irrigation. The forest and water problems are perhaps the most vital internal questions of the United States.

* * *

The forest alone cannot, however, fully regulate and conserve the waters of the arid region. Great storage works are necessary to equalize the flow of streams and so save the flood waters. Their construction has been shown to be an undertaking too vast for private effort. Nor can

it be best accomplished by the individual States working alone. Far-reaching inter-State problems are involved and the resources of individual States would often be inadequate. It is properly a National function, at least in some of its features. It is as right for the National Government to make the streams and rivers of the arid region useful by engineering works for water storage as to make useful the rivers and harbors of the humid region by engineering works of another kind. The storing of the floods in reservoirs at the headwaters of our rivers is but an enlargement of our present policy of river control, under which levees are built at the lower reaches of the same streams.

* * *

Our aim should be not simply to reclaim the largest areas of land and provide homes for the largest numbers of people, but to create for this new industry the best possible social and industrial conditions, and this requires that we not only understand the existing situation, but avail ourselves of the best experience of the time.

Source: Theodore Roosevelt, "Address to Congress," December 3, 1901, *New York Times*, December 4, 1901, p. 4.

DOCUMENT 63: Reclamation Act (1902)

In 1902 John Wesley Powell's grand plan for the arid lands of the United States [see Document 58], after languishing for thirty-four years, finally became federal policy. Although in previous centuries industrious farmers had watered their dry lands in various parts of the country, prior to the implementation of the Reclamation Act irrigation had never been carried out on a large scale in the United States. As a result of the Reclamation Act, new lands were opened for settlement and farming, and in the process the precarious ecological balance of vast areas of our country was upset. Three-quarters of a century after the act's passage, people began to question the wisdom of the act and consider undoing some of the follies that stemmed from it [see Documents 122 and 132].

Be it enacted . . . , That all moneys received from the sale and disposal of public lands in Arizona, California, Colorado, Idaho, Kansas, Montana, Nebraska, Nevada, New Mexico, North Dakota, Oklahoma, Oregon, South Dakota, Utah, Washington, and Wyoming, beginning with the fiscal year ending June thirtieth, nineteen hundred and one, including the

surplus of fees and commissions in excess of allowances to registers and receivers, and excepting the five per centum of the proceeds of the sales of public lands in the above States set aside by law for educational and other purposes, shall be, and the same are hereby, reserved, set aside, and appropriated as a special fund in the Treasury to be known as the "reclamation fund," to be used in the examination and survey for and the construction and maintenance of irrigation works for the storage, diversion, and development of waters for the reclamation of arid and semiarid lands in the said States and Territories, and for the payment of all other expenditures provided for in this Act.

Source: United States Statutes at Large, Vol. 32, Part I (Washington, D.C.: Government Printing Office, 1903), 57th Cong., 1st sess., chap. 1093, June 17, 1902, p. 388.

DOCUMENT 64: Upton Sinclair on the Adulteration of Processed Food (1906)

Upton Sinclair's novel The Jungle *was a fictionalized expose of abuses in the meat-packing industry. It raised the public's consciousness about such issues as the lack of quality control in the food industry, the mislabeling of packaged foods and other packaged goods, the deliberate use of adulterated products by the packaged foods industry, and the inhumane treatment of animals by slaughterhouses.*

It was only when the whole ham was spoiled that it came into the department of Elzbieta. Cut up by the two-thousand-revolutions-a-minute flyers, and mixed with half a ton of other meat, no odor that ever was in a ham could make any difference. There was never the least attention paid to what was cut up for sausage; there would come all the way back from Europe old sausage that had been rejected, and that was mouldy and white—it would be dosed with borax and glycerine, and dumped into the hoppers, and made over again for home consumption. There would be meat that had tumbled out on the floor, in the dirt and sawdust, where the workers had tramped and spit uncounted billions of consumption germs. There would be meat stored in great piles in rooms; and the water from leaky roofs would drip over it, and thousands of rats would race about on it. It was too dark in these storage places to see well, but a man could run his hand over these piles of meat and sweep off handfuls of the dried dung of rats. These rats were nuisances, and the packers would put poisoned bread out for them, they would die, and then rats, bread, and meat would go into the hoppers together. . . . There was no place for the men to wash their hands before they ate their dinner, and so they made a practice of washing them in the water that was to be ladled into the sausage. There were the butt-ends of smoked meat, and the scraps of corned beef, and all the odds and ends of the waste of the plants, that would be dumped into old barrels in the cellar and left there. Under the system of rigid economy which the packers enforced, there were some jobs that it only paid to do once in a long time, and among these was the cleaning out of the waste barrels. Every spring they did it; and in the barrels would be dirt and rust and old nails and stale water—and cart load after cart load of it would be taken up and dumped into the hoppers with fresh meat, and sent out to the public's breakfast. Some of it they would make into "smoked" sausage—but as the smoking took time, and was therefore expensive, they would call upon their chemistry department, and preserve it with borax and color it with gelatine to make it brown. All of their sausage came out of the same bowl, but when they came to wrap it they would stamp some of it "special," and for this they would charge two cents more a pound.

Source: Upton Sinclair, *The Jungle* (New York: Doubleday, Page, 1906), pp. 161-62.

DOCUMENT 65: Ellen Swallow Richards on
Sanitation and Human Ecology (1907)

Ellen Swallow Richards, an instructor in sanitary chemistry at Massachusetts Institute of Technology, is credited with introducing the term human ecology and with popularizing the concept of ecology and the idea that people should be concerned about and take responsibility for their environment. She was the first woman to receive a science degree from a U.S. university.

Sanitary Science teaches that mode of life which promotes health and efficiency.

The individual is one of a community influencing and influenced by the common environment.

Human ecology is the study of the surroundings of human beings in the effects they produce on the lives of men. The features of the environment are natural, as climate, and artificial, produced by human activity, as noise, dust, poisonous vapors, vitiated air, dirty water, and unclean food.

The study of this environment is in two chief lines:

First, what is often called municipal housekeeping—the cooperation of the citizens in securing clean streets, the suppression of nuisances, abundant water supply, market inspection, etc.

Second, family housekeeping. The healthful home demands a management of the house which shall promote vigorous life and prevent the physical deterioration so evident under modern conditions.

* * *

To secure and maintain a safe environment there must be inculcated *habits* of using the material things in daily life in such a way as to promote and not to diminish health. Avoid spitting in the streets, avoid throwing refuse on the sidewalk, avoid dust and bad air in the house and sleeping rooms, etc.

It is, however, of the greatest importance that every one should acquire such habits of *belief* in the importance of this material environment as shall lead him to insist upon sanitary regulations, and to see that they are carried out.

What touches my neighbor, touches me. For my sake, and for his, the city inspector and the city garbage cart visit us, and I keep my premises in such a condition as I expect him to strive for.

The first law of sanitation requires quick removal and destruction of all wastes—of things done with.

The second law enjoins such use of the air, water, and food necessary to life that the person may be in a state of health and efficiency.

This right use depends so largely upon habit that a great portion of sanitary teaching must be given to inculcating right and safe ways in daily life.

Source: Ellen Swallow Richards, *Sanitation in Daily Life* (Boston: Whitcomb & Barrows, 1910 [1907]), pp. v-viii, in Carolyn Merchant, ed., *Major Problems in American Environmental History: Documents and Essays* (Lexington, MA: Heath, 1993), pp. 445-47.

DOCUMENT 66: Theodore Roosevelt on the Conservation and Use of Natural Resources (1907)

In his December 3, 1907, annual address to Congress, President Roosevelt focused on the need to use the resources of the nation prudently, and he attacked those who were willing to exhaust the nation's resources in the process of fattening their own pockets. As an arch opponent of the concentration of extensive power in the hands of big business, Roosevelt fought the environmental depredations of business conglomerates as well as of ranching and other special interest groups.

The conservation of our natural resources and their proper use constitute the fundamental problem which underlies almost every other problem of our National life. We must maintain for our civilization the adequate material basis without which that civilization can not exist. We must show foresight, we must look ahead. As a nation we not only enjoy a wonderful measure of present prosperity but if this prosperity is used aright it is an earnest of success such as no other nation will have. The reward of foresight for this Nation is great and easily foretold. But there must be the look ahead, there must be a realization of the fact that to waste, to destroy, our natural resources, to skin and exhaust land instead of using it so as to increase its usefulness, will result in undermining in the days of our children the very prosperity which we ought by right to hand down to them amplified and developed. For the last few years, through several agencies, the Government has been endeavoring to get our people to look ahead and to substitute a planned and orderly development of our resources in place of a haphazard striving for immediate profit. Our great river systems should be developed as national water highways; the Mississippi with its tributaries, standing first in importance, and the Columbia second. . . .

Irrigation should be far more extensively developed than at present, not only in the States of the Great Plains and the Rocky Mountains, but in many others, as, for instance, in large portions of the South Atlantic and Gulf States, where it should go hand in hand with the reclamation of swamp land. The Federal Government should seriously devote itself to this task, realizing that utilization of waterways and water-power, forestry, irrigation, and the reclamation of lands threatened with overflow, are all interdependent parts of the same problem. The work of the Reclamation Service in developing the larger opportunities of the western half of our country for irrigation is more important than almost any other movement. The constant purpose of the Government in connection with the Reclamation Service has been to use the water resources of the public lands for the ultimate greatest good of the greatest number; in other words, to put upon the land permanent home-makers, to use and develop it for themselves and for their children and children's children. There has been, of course, opposition to this work; opposition from some interested men who desire to exhaust the land for their own immediate profit without regard to the welfare of the next generation, and opposition from honest and well-meaning men who did not fully understand the subject or who did not look far enough ahead.

The effort of the Government to deal with the public land has been based upon the same principle as that of the Reclamation Service. The land law system which was designed to meet the needs of the fertile and well-watered regions of the Middle West has largely broken down when applied to the dryer regions. . . .

Some such legislation as that proposed [by the Public Lands Commission] is essential in order to preserve the great stretches of public grazing land. . . . As the West settles the range becomes more and more over-grazed. Much of it can not be used to advantage unless it is fenced, for fencing is the only way by which to keep in check the owners of nomad flock which roam hither and thither, utterly destroying the pastures. . . .

. . . We are prone to speak of the resources of this country as inexhaustible; this is not so. The mineral wealth of the country, the coal, iron, oil, gas, and the like, does not reproduce itself, and therefore is certain to be exhausted ultimately; and wastefulness in dealing with it to-day means that our descendants will feel the exhaustion a generation or two before they otherwise would.

Source: Theodore Roosevelt, Address to Congress, December 3, 1907, in *Congressional Record—Senate* (Washington, D.C.: Government Printing Office, 1907), pp. 74-76.

DOCUMENT 67: Frederick Law Olmsted, Jr., on the Smoke Nuisance (1908)

Frederick Law Olmsted, Jr., whose given name was actually Henry Perkins, was the son of Frederick Law Olmsted, Sr. [see Document 48]. As a young man he worked for his father's landscape architecture firm. Not until nearly seventy-five years after the publication of this article did people begin to comprehend the full range of the impacts of soot (particulate matter) on the health of both humans and their environment.

The dweller in a town burning bituminous coal needs no definition of the smoke nuisance. The great cloud that hangs over the city like a pall can be seen from any neighboring hilltop, and the dweller within is only too well aware of the splotches of soot that settle on every object in the city, bedimming buildings, spoiling curtains, injuring books, and increasing the laundry bill. The direct menace to the public health in fostering tuberculous conditions by loading the air with carbon particles to lodge in the lungs, and by causing housekeepers to keep the windows shut for fear of the soot that floats in when they are open, is equaled only by the mentally and physically depressing effect of the pall which shuts out the life-giving and germ-destroying sunshine. Our city parks have mostly lost their evergreen character, where it existed, as conifers cannot long endure city smoke. Thus one treatment of the most pleasing variations in landscape is made impossible.

* * *

There should be complete understanding of the scientific fact that visible black smoke is made up almost entirely of unconsumed particles of combustible carbon, or coal, wasted into the atmosphere through imperfect combustion.

It is economic waste, in itself; and its emission creates additional waste.

No really intelligent person now denies the imperative economic and sanitary need for abating or suppressing the smoke evil, nor the feasibility and absolute power of existing authorities to do so where the will and proper public sentiment exist.

The tearing down of a dangerous house, the draining of a pestiferous swamp, the cleaning of a filthy street, or of a back yard, are simple remedies for simple nuisances. The abolition of smoke, on the other hand, affects the whole community, since the production of smoke is claimed, especially by the careless or the uninformed, to be completely bound up with the material and industrial welfare of a city. The evil is one that grows with the growth of the community, and its abatement calls for a large, comprehensive and tactful treatment, with thorough cooperation between the different parties to the problem. Education of the public, the factory owners and the firemen to the bad economy and the wrong of smoke emission is of great importance.

* * *

The first step in abating smoke is to pass a law or an ordinance, making the emission of black or dark gray smoke an unlawful act, punishable by fine. Such regulations are already in force in New York, Cleveland, Milwaukee, Toronto, Toledo, Indianapolis, Detroit, the District of Columbia, and numerous other cities. The second step is to get the law enforced.

* * *

In every case, *smoke is a preventable nuisance,* and every smoking plant or locomotive is a sign of wastefulness, and a disregard for the rights of the public. The proprietor should be as interested in abating the nuisance as his neighbors, and it has been the experience of smoke-law officials that men who have bitterly complained at being forced to make improvements have afterward thanked the smoke-abating department for the increased economy of the plant.

Source: Frederick Law Olmsted et al., *The Smoke Nuisance,* American Civic Association (Philadelphia) Series II, no. 1 (March 1908), pp. 4-7.

Document 68: John Muir, James Phelan, and the Battle over the Flooding of the Hetch Hetchy Valley (1908-1913)

John Muir was one of the most influential conservationists in the last decades of the nineteenth century and the first decades of the twentieth century. In 1889 he became a major force advocating the development of Yosemite as a national park, and in 1892 he helped found the Sierra Club, the first western-based hiking society. A three-day camping trip that President Theodore Roosevelt took with Muir in the Sierra Nevada Mountains of eastern California in 1903 made a deep impression on Roosevelt and was influential in shaping government policies concerning wilderness and wildlife. Many believe Roosevelt set aside 148 million acres of forest reserve land, in addition to establishing the first National Wildlife Refuge in 1903 and pioneering the federal role in conservation, partly as a result of his relationship with Muir.

When it was proposed that the Hetch Hetchy Valley be flooded to build a reservoir to supply water for the city of San Francisco, Muir launched a fight to save the valley. Although the federal government gave the Hetch Hetchy to San Francisco in 1913, the Muir-led struggle galvanized the nascent conservation movement.

James Phelan, mayor of San Francisco from 1897 to 1902, minimized the aesthetics of the valley in making his plea for its flooding.

I am anxious that the Yosemite National Park may be saved from all sorts of commercialism and marks of man's work other than the roads, hotels, etc., required to make its wonders and blessings available. For as far as I have seen there is not in all the wonderful Sierra, or indeed in the world, another so grand and wonderful block of Nature's mountain handiwork.

There is now under consideration, as doubtless you well know, an application of San Francisco supervisors for the use of the Hetch-Hetchy Valley and Lake Eleanor as storage reservoirs for a city water supply. This application should, I think, be denied, especially the Hetch-Hetchy part, for this Valley . . . is a counterpart of Yosemite, and one of the most sublime and beautiful and important features of the Park, and to dam and submerge it would be hardly less destructive and deplorable in its effect on the Park in general than would be the damming of Yosemite itself. For its falls and groves and delightful campgrounds are surpassed or equaled only in Yosemite, and furthermore it is the hall of entrance to the grand Tuolumne Canon, which opens a wonderful way to the magnificent Tuolumne Meadows, the focus of pleasure travel in the Park and the grand central camp-ground. If Hetch-Hetchy should be submerged, as proposed, to a depth of one hundred and seventy-five feet, not only would the Meadows be made utterly in accessible along the Tuolumne but this glorious canon way to the High Sierra would be blocked.

I am heartily in favor of a Sierra or even a Tuolumne water supply for San Francisco, but all the water required can be obtained from sources outside the Park, leaving the twin valleys, Hetch-Hetchy and Yosemite, to the use they were intended for when the Park was established.

B. James Phelan, Letter to Outlook 1909

The Hetch-Hetchy is one of a dozen mountain gorges, and, while beautiful, it is not unique. It is accessible over difficult trails about three months during the year, and few ever visit it. The Yosemite Valley satisfies every craving for large numbers of tourists, and the State of California, a few years ago freely ceded this Valley to the Federal Government, and at the same time purchased a great redwood forest in the interest of forest preservation. California would not countenance the desecration of any of her scenery, and yet the State Legislature, now in session, has unanimously petitioned Congress to pass this bill. President Roosevelt, Secretary Garfield, Forester Pinchot, will yield to none in their love of nature; yet they strongly favor this bill. . . . The only question is, after all, the conversion of the Hetch-Hetchy Meadow into a crystal clear Lake—a natural object of indeed rare beauty. For the few hundred acres wanted by San Francisco on the floor or the Valley the city gives the Government the original camping-places taken up by the pioneers and until now held in private ownership. The patrol of the watershed will protect it for beauty and from fire loss and defilement. It will be made accessible by good roads, like the beautiful Lake Katrine— the water supply of Glasgow—and it will be a delight to visitors, while at the same time it serves a great and useful purpose. The people of San Francisco have entered into a solemn agreement, by an overwhelming vote, with the Government, by which Secretary Garfield has protected the public interests. There are eight hundred miles of wild mountain scenery in the Sierras, and, according to John Muir, "There are a dozen Yosemites;" then why deplore the loss of a mosquito meadow? . . . .

By yielding their opposition, sincere lovers of nature will turn the prayers of a million people to praise for the gifts bestowed upon them by the God of Nature, whom they cannot worship in his temple, but must perforce live in the sweltering cities. A reduced death rate is a more vital consideration than the discussion of the relative beauties of a meadow or a lake.

C. From John Muir's *The Yosemite,* *1912*

Hetch Hetchy, they say, is a "low-lying meadow." On the contrary, it is a high-lying natural landscape garden. . . .

"It is a common minor feature, like thousands of others." On the contrary it is a very uncommon feature; after Yosemite, the rarest and in many ways the most important in the National Park.

"Damming and submerging it 175 feet deep would enhance its beauty by forming a crystal-clear lake." Landscape gardens, places of recreation and worship, are never made beautiful by destroying and burying them. The beautiful sham lake, forsooth, would be only an eyesore, a dismal blot on the landscape, like many others to be seen in the Sierra. For, instead of keeping it at the same level all the year, allowing Nature centuries of time to make new shores, it would, of course, be full only a month or two in the spring, when the snow is melting fast; then it would be gradually drained, exposing the slimy sides of the basin and shallower parts of the bottom, with the gathered drift and waste, death and decay of the upper basins, caught here instead of being swept on to decent natural burial along the banks of the river or in the sea. Thus the Hetch Hetchy dam-lake would be only a rough imitation of a natural lake for a few of the spring months, an open sepulcher for the others.

"Hetch Hetchy water is the purest of all to be found in the Sierra, unpolluted, and forever unpollutable." On the contrary, excepting that of the Merced below Yosemite, it is less pure than that of most of the other Sierra streams, because of the sewerage of camp grounds draining into it, especially of the Big Tuolumne Meadows camp ground, occupied by hundreds of tourists and mountaineers, with their animals, for months every summer, soon to be followed by thousands from all the world.

These temple destroyers, devotees of ravaging commercialism, seem to have a perfect contempt for Nature, and, instead of lifting their eyes to the God of the mountains, lift them to the Almighty dollar.

Dam Hetch Hetchy! As well dam for water-tanks the people's cathedrals and churches, for no holier temple has ever been consecrated by the heart of man.

Source: **A.** John Muir to Theodore Roosevelt, in William Frederic Bade, ed., *The Life and Letters of John Muir,* Vol. 2 (Cambridge, MA, 1924), quoted in Robert McHenry and Charles Van Doren, eds., *A Documentary History of Conservation in the United States* (New York: Praeger, 1972), p. 307. **B.** James D. Phelan, "Dam Hetch-Hetchy," letter to *Outlook,* February 13, 1909, in McHenry and Van Doren, *Documentary History,* pp. 309-10. **C.** John Muir, *The Yosemite* (Madison: University of Wisconsin Press, 1986; reprint of 1912 Century ed.), pp. 260-62.

Document 69: Richard Ballinger on the Development of the West (1909)

President William Howard Taft's secretary of the Interior, Richard Ballinger, was a fierce opponent of the proposals made by Powell, Pinchot, and other conservationists for government oversight of the development of publicly owned lands with forest, water, and mineral resources, and newspapers of the period referred to the ongoing debate about how to develop the public domain as "the Ballinger-Pinchot contest." In Ballinger's view, the best way to develop the arid lands was to give a helping hand to the big trusts that controlled the hydroelectric power industry.

Ballinger's advocacy for corporate land and resource development was echoed a little over seventy years later when James Watt became secretary of the Interior under Ronald Reagan and again in the twenty-first century when Donald Trump became president.

A. From a 1909 Interview with John L. Mathews

Mathews: What is your object in giving in to the railroads and letting them destroy this water power [that could be developed by the government along the Deschutes River in Oregon]?

Ballinger: . . . You chaps who are in favor of this conservation program are all wrong. You are hindering the development of the West. These railroads are necessary to the country. And more than that, this whole big [public] domain is a blanket—it is oppressing the people. The thing to do with it—In my opinion, the proper course to take with regard to this domain is to divide it up among the big corporations and the people

who know how to make money out of it and let the people at large get the benefit of the circulation of the money.

B. Address to the National Irrigation Congress, August 12, 1909

While the Government has invested over fifty million dollars in irrigation works, many times that amount has been invested since the passage of the Reclamation Act by private enterprise and it is safe to say that a large portion of these private investments have resulted from Governmental example and encouragement; and let me say here that it has not been and is not the policy of the National Government in the administration of this act to hinder or interfere with the investment of private capital in the construction of irrigation works but rather to lend it encouragement. This is particularly true in reference to irrigation under the Carey Act [of 1894] in the various States.

I am not a believer in the Government entering into competition with legitimate private enterprise. Its functions under the Reclamation Act are not of this character. The Western States should therefore be very jealous of the perpetuity of the Reclamation fund and of its constant increase.

The purpose of the Reclamation Act is to undertake the irrigation of arid and semiarid lands where a considerable portion thereof belongs to the public domain, and by the installation of the storage and diversion of available waters to irrigate the largest possible area within a given territory at the least cost to the entrymen and land owners for construction, maintenance and operation, always keeping in view the matter of the settlement of these lands and rendering them capable of supporting the greatest number of families. While it is a reclamation act, it is also a settlements act, and the public lands which are proposed to be irrigated by means of the contemplated works have been rendered subject to entry only under the homestead laws in small tracts capable of supporting a family. It is declared by the act that only the cost of construction and maintenance shall be repaid to the Government. No consideration of profit or direct advantage to the Government is intended, and in this the statute does not trench upon the rights of private enterprise. The law is a beneficent one. . . . It differs, however, from the simple homestead law in that it holds out inducements only to men of sufficient industry and capacity to carry the added burdens of construction, maintenance and operations, which is the cost of the lands. While it is possible that persons of limited means may successfully enter and acquire irrigated lands, it will generally be found that it is not a poor man's proposition, unless coupled with intelligent industry in agriculture.

The whole scheme of the act is based upon the appropriation of the proceeds of the sales of public lands in certain States and Territories for the construction of irrigation works for the reclamation of arid and semiarid lands therein. No further appropriation by the Government is intended, or can be inferred from the Act, and the responsibility for the disbursement of the funds and the construction of the works is placed upon the Secretary of the Interior.

It must be recognized that the Government is acting in the nature of a trustee for the people in the disbursement of this fund; that it must constrict the works for the settlers and turn them over at cost, and has no right to waste the fund. . . .

* * *

Any one who has visited one or more of the Reclamation projects now in operation and sees on the one hand the desert covered with sage brush and barrenness, and on the other, the water flowing over the fertile soil producing heavy crops of grain, or orchards in fruit, appreciates to the fullest extent the benefits of irrigation

The people of the West, therefore, who are familiar with these wonderful results in irrigation, are highly appreciative of the importance of the Reclamation Service, but the great difficulty which that service encounters is in finishing the projects now undertaken as against the clamor for a diversion of the funds to new fields.

* * *

The danger, which the Government is undertaking to overcome, is the establishment of small irrigation projects in localities where by such establishment the larger opportunities are destroyed, thus preventing enormous areas of lands from ever acquiring the use of water. It is quite true that many small projects capable of being financed by men of limited means can be carved out of larger possibilities, but to encourage them means the loss of the larger possibilities. For lack of funds the Government is at present often required to surrender possibilities in water appropriations which means an enormous loss in future development of irrigation works, and I fear this is not fully appreciated. It is for this reason that at times private enterprises are disposed to contend that the Government is obstructing their interests, while from the larger view their interests are obstructing greater possibilities for larger areas of irrigable land. I may mention here what has frequently occurred to me as a source of advantage both to the States and the Federal Government, and that is the securing from the various States of uniform legislation in the matter of appropriation of water and its beneficial use, and also legislation looking to the control and conservation of all available water-power.

This Congress could accomplish no greater work beyond the stimulation of interest in the development of irrigation than to secure uniform water regulations in the States and also uniform legislation affecting interstate waters.

Source: **A.** Richard Ballinger, interview with John L. Mathews, Washington, D.C., quoted in John L. Mathews, "Mr. Ballinger and the National Grab-Bag," *Hampton's Magazine,* December 1909, in Richard A. Ballinger Papers, Manuscript Collection of the University of Washington, Seattle, microfilm roll 12. **B.** R.A. Ballinger , "Attitude of the Administration toward the Reclamation of the Arid Lands in the West," remarks made at the National Irrigation Congress, Spokane, WA, August 12, 1909, in Richard A. Ballinger papers, microfilm roll 11.

DOCUMENT 70: Report of the National Conservation Commission (1909)

As a result of the Conference of Governors, convened by Roosevelt in 1908 to discuss the conservation and appropriate use of natural resources, a National Conservation Commission was created. Gifford Pinchot [see Document 73], who had encouraged Roosevelt to hold the conference, was appointed chairman of the commission. The commission's report emphasized the development of a program of "wise and beneficial uses" of natural resources.

Unfortunately, Congress had failed to allocate adequate funding for the commission to make a thorough study of the nation's resources. That study had to wait until 1952 and the appointment of the President's Materials Policy Commission on Economic Growth and Resource Policy [see Document 89].

The duty of man to man, on which the integrity of nations must rest, is no higher than the duty of each generation to the next; and the obligation of the nation to each actual citizen is no more sacred than the obligation to the citizen to be, who, in turn must bear the nation's duties and responsibilities.

In this country, blessed with natural resources in unsurpassed profusion, the sense of responsibility to the future has been slow to awaken. Beginning without appreciation of the measure or the value of natural resources other than land with water for commercial uses, our forefathers pushed into the wilderness and, through a spirit of enterprise which is the glory of the nation, developed other great resources. Forests were cleared away as obstacles to the use of the land;

iron and coal were discovered and developed, though for years their presence added nothing to the price of the land; and through the use of native woods and metals and fuels, manufacturing grew beyond all precedent, and the country became a power among the nations of the world.

Gradually the timber growing on the ground and the iron and coal within the ground came to have a market value and were bought and sold as sources of wealth. Meanwhile, vast holdings of these resources were acquired by those of greater foresight than their neighbors before it was generally realized that they possessed value in themselves; and in this way large interests, assuming monopolistic proportions, grew up, with greater enrichment to their holders than the world had seen before, and with the motive of immediate profit, with no concern for the future or thought of the permanent benefit of country and people, a wasteful and profligate use of the resources began and has continued.

The waters, at first recognized only as aids to commerce in supplying transportation routes, were largely neglected. In time this neglect began to be noticed, and along with it the destruction and approaching exhaustion of the forests. This, in turn, directed attention to the rapid depletion of the coal and iron deposits and the misuse of the land.

* * *

In the first stage, the resources received little thought. In the second they were wastefully used. In the stage which we are entering wise and beneficial uses are essential, and the checking of waste is absolutely demanded.

* * *

The wastes which most urgently require checking vary widely in character and amount. The most reprehensible waste is that of destruction, as in forest fires, uncontrolled flow of gas and oil, soil wash, and abandonment of coal in the mines. This is attributable, for the most part, to ignorance, indifference, or false notions of economy, to rectify which is the business of the people collectively.

Nearly as reprehensible is the waste arising from misuse, as in the consumption of fuel in furnaces and engines of low efficiency, the loss of water in floods, the employment of ill-adapted structural materials, the growing of ill-chosen crops, and the perpetuation of inferior stocks of plants and animals, all of which may be remedied.

Source: Report of National Conservation Commission, Vol. I, 60th Cong., 2nd sess., Senate Document 676 (Washington, D.C.: Government Printing Office, 1909), pp. 13-14.

DOCUMENT 71: WJ McGee on Conservation (1909)

William John (always referred to as WJ, without periods, at his insistence) McGee became involved in federal resource work when he joined the United States Geological Survey in 1878, at the invitation of John Wesley Powell [see Document 58]. His interest in managing natural resources to serve the public was sparked at a meeting of the Lakes-to-the-Gulf Deep Waterway Association in 1906. This was several months before Gifford Pinchot became an active conservationist [see Document 73] and joined McGee in his effort to have the Inland Waterways Commission established by President Theodore Roosevelt. The appointment of this commission on March 14, 1907, marked the beginning of a national crusade in support of conservation.

[Gifford] Pinchot and [James R.] Garfield [secretary of the Interior, 1907-1909] especially, and [President Theodore] Roosevelt in his turn, sought to counteract the tendency toward wholesale alienation of the public lands for the benefit of the corporation and the oppression or suppression of the settler; and in the end their efforts resulted in what is now known as the Conservation Movement. . . .

On its face the Conservation Movement is material—ultra-material. . . . Yet in truth there has never been in all human history a popular movement more firmly grounded in ethics, in the eternal equities, in the divinity of human rights!

Whether we rise into the spiritual empyrean or cling more closely to the essence of humanity, we find our loftiest ideals made real in the Cult of Conservation. . . .

. . . What *right* has any citizen of a free country, whatever his foresight and shrewdness, to seize on sources of life for his own behoof that are the common heritage of all; what *right* has legislature or court to help in the seizure; and striking still more deeply, what *right* has any generation to wholly consume, much less to waste, those sources of life without which the children or the children's children must starve or freeze? These are among the questions arising among intelligent minds in every part of this country, and giving form to a national feeling which is gradually rising to a new plane of equity. The questions will not down. . . . How shall they find answer? The ethical doctrine of Conservation answers: by a nobler patriotism, under which citizen-electors will cleave more strongly to their birthright of independence and strive more vigorously for purity of the ballot, for rightness in laws, for cleanness in courts, and for forthrightness in administration; by a higher honesty of purpose between man and man; by a warmer charity, under which the good of all will more fairly merge with the good of each; by a stronger family sense, tending toward a realization of the rights of the unborn; by deeper probity, maturing in the realizing sense that each holder of the sources of life is but a trustee for his nominal possessions, and is responsible to all men and for all time for making the best use of them in common interest; and by a livelier humanity, in which each will feel that he lives not for himself alone but as a part of a common life for a common world and for the common good. . . .

Whatever its material manifestations, every revolution is first and foremost a revolution in thought and in spirit. . . . The American Revolution was fought for Liberty; the Constitution was framed for Equality; yet that third of the trinity of human impulses without which Union is not made perfect—Fraternity—has not been established: full brotherhood among men and generations has not yet come. The duty of the [Founding] Fathers was done well according to their lights; but some new light has come out of the West where their sons have striven against Nature's forces no less fiercely than the Fathers against foreign dominion. So it would seem to remain for Conservation to perfect the concept and the movement started among the Colonists one hundred and forty years ago—to round out the American Revolution by framing a clearer Bill of Rights. Whatever others there may be, surely these are inherent and indefeasible:—

1) The equal Rights of all men to opportunity.
2) The equal Rights of the People in and to resources rendered valuable by their own growth and orderly development.
3) The equal Rights of present and future generations in and to the resources of the country.
4) The equal Rights (and full responsibilities) of all citizens to provide for the perpetuity of families and States and the Union of States.

The keynote of all these is Fraternity. They look to the greatest good for the greatest number and for the longest time; they are essential to perfect union among men and States; and until they are secured to us we may hardly feel assured that government of the People, by the People, and for the People shall not perish from the earth.

Source: WJ McGee, "The Conservation of Natural Resources," in *Proceedings of the Mississippi Valley Historical Association* 3 (1909-1910): 376-79, in Roderick Frazier Nash, ed., *Readings in the History of Conservation* (Reading, MA: Addison-Wesley, 1968), pp. 45-46.

DOCUMENT 72: Jane Addams on Garbage (1910)

The Chicago social worker Jane Addams was one of the leading advocates of improved sanitation in the homes and the neighborhoods of the poor. Here she notes that the problem of garbage in lower-class neighborhoods was greater than in wealthier neighborhoods. More than a hundred years later, the lack of environmental justice continues to be an issue [see Document 136].

One of the striking features of our neighborhood twenty years ago, and one to which we never became reconciled, was the presence of huge wooden garbage boxes fastened to the street pavement in which the undisturbed refuse accumulated day by day. The system of garbage collecting was inadequate throughout the city but it became the greatest menace in a ward such as ours, where the normal amount of waste was much increased by the decayed fruit and vegetables discarded by the Italian and Greek fruit peddlers, and by the residuum left over from the piles of filthy rags which were fished out of the city dumps and brought to the homes of the rag pickers for further sorting and washing.

The children of our neighborhood twenty years ago played their games in and around these huge garbage boxes.

* * *

[My attempt to get a contract to remove garbage from the nineteenth ward] induced the mayor to appoint me the garbage inspector of the ward.

. . . The position was no sinecure whether regarded from the point of view of getting up at six in the morning to see that the men were early at work; or of following the loaded wagons, uneasily dropping their contents at intervals, to their dreary destination at the dump; or of insisting that the contractor must increase the number of his wagons from nine to thirteen and from thirteen to seventeen, although he assured me that he lost money on every one and that the former inspector had let him off with seven; or of taking careless landlords into court because they would not provide the proper garbage receptacles; or of arresting the tenant who tried to make the garbage wagons carry away the contents of his stable.

With the two or three residents who nobly stood by, we set up six of those doleful incinerators which are supposed to burn garbage with the fuel collected in the alley itself. The one factory in town which could utilize old tin cans was a window weight factory, and we deluged that with ten times as many tin cans as it could use—much less pay for.

Source: Jane Addams, *Twenty Years at Hull-House* (New York: Macmillan, 1911), pp. 281, 285-86.

DOCUMENT 73: Gifford Pinchot on Conservation and the National Interest (1911)

Gifford Pinchot, the first professional American forester, was appointed head of the Department of Agriculture's Division of Forestry in 1894. In his early years with the forestry division, he focused his attention on encouraging the "production of the largest amount of the most valuable timber in the shortest time on a given area,"[3] but as he became embroiled with government administrators who gave little thought to the consequences of resource exploitation and waste, he became a fierce conservation advocate.

After he instituted charges against President William Howard Taft's secretary of the Interior, Richard Ballinger [see Document 69], for reversing Theodore Roosevelt's conservation policies, Pinchot was dismissed from the U.S. Forestry Service (which had evolved from the Division of Forestry) by Taft for insubordination. Then, under President Franklin D. Roosevelt, he again served as head of the Forestry Service.

The conservation of our natural resources is a question of primary importance on the economic side. It pays better to conserve our natural resources than to destroy them, and this is especially true when the national interest is considered. But the business reason, weighty and worthy though it be, is not the fundamental reason. In such matters, business is a poor master but a good servant. The law of self-preservation is higher than the law of business, and the duty of preserving the Nation is still higher than either.

The American Revolution had its origin in part in economic causes, and it produced economic results of tremendous reach and weight. The Civil War also arose in large part from economic conditions, and it has had the largest economic consequences. But in each case there was a higher and more compelling reason. So with the third great crisis of our history. It has an economic aspect of the largest and most permanent importance, and the motive for action along that line, once it is recognized, should be more than sufficient. But that is not all. In this case, too, there is a higher and more compelling reason. The question of the conservation of natural resources, or national resources, does not stop with being a question of profit. It is a vital question of profit, but what is still more vital, it is a question of national safety and patriotism also.

We have passed the inevitable stage of pioneer pillage of natural resources. The natural wealth we found upon this continent has made us rich. We have used it, as we had a right to do, but we have not stopped there. We have abused, and wasted, and exhausted it also, so that there is the gravest danger that our prosperity to-day will have been bought at the price of the suffering and poverty of our descendants.

Source: Gifford Pinchot, *The Fight for Conservation* (Garden City, NY: Doubleday, Page, 1911), pp. 126-28.

Part V

Rethinking Our Relationship to Nature, 1920–1959

The end of World War I brought with it a slackening of economic and industrial constraints and a surging demand for consumer goods. Within just a few years, a mass consumption economy emerged. By the 1930s, hundreds of thousands of people had acquired telephones, cars, phonographs, radios, and a host of other products that had come on the market in recent decades. During the Roaring Twenties a get-rich-quick mentality bred scandal and corruption. President Warren Harding's inability to rein in his underlings led to the Teapot Dome scandal of 1921, during which the valuable naval oil reserves in Teapot Dome, California, and Elk Hills, Wyoming, were transferred from the Navy Department to the Interior Department and then leased to two oil men, Harry Sinclair and Edward Doheny, after they paid a $100,000 bribe to Secretary of the Interior Albert Fall.

Urban Growth and Rural Development

By the early 1920s, the U.S. population had reached one million, with more than half of the people living in urban areas. The new urban residents not only provided a huge market for America's expanding industry, but they also pushed the borders of cities into what had once been farmland, making it necessary to transport agricultural produce longer distances and placed increasing demands on metropolitan water supplies and waste disposal systems. As cars replaced horses on city streets, the manure problem disappeared. Eventually, however, that problem would be replaced by a new kind of pollution, auto emissions, but this would not become evident until after World War II. Although consumer buying slowed during the Great Depression, New Deal public works programs, such as the Tennessee Valley Authority (TVA) program, brought electrification to rural areas and in time swelled the demand for electrical appliances.

In the 1930s the dust bowl crisis in the south-central United States awakened America to the wastefulness of current farming practices that resulted in devastating soil erosion. John Steinbeck in his novel *The Grapes of Wrath* [*see* Document 84] decried both the environmental and the human degradation resulting from these practices. In 1935, the Soil Conservation Service was established within the

Department of the Interior to combat soil erosion and water wastage. Then, in 1937, President Franklin D. Roosevelt created the Civilian Conservation Corps. The Corps was both a response to the Great Depression—which began with the stock market crash of 1929 and was exacerbated by the dust bowl crisis—and an attempt to redress the country's prodigal use of its natural resources. Roosevelt had long recognized the relationship between resource protection and national well-being [*see* Document 77].

The Synthetic Environment

Expansion of the chemical and food processing industries in the 1920s and 1930s brought a wide range of new products into existence to satisfy both the agricultural sector and the urban market. While many of these new, man-made substances provided great benefits for farmers and the general public, some of them had serious unanticipated negative consequences, including the endangerment of human health and the destruction of wildlife. New factories, unhampered by any kind of governmental environmental constraints, also made existing air and water pollution problems worse.

As the century progressed, opposition among the public to the government's leniency concerning industrial pollution and waste grew [*see* Document 78], and there was increasing demand for greater government oversight of the quality of manufactured goods and the labeling of processed foods and drugs [*see* Document 79]. The passage of the Food, Drug, and Cosmetics Act of 1938 strengthened the federal government's ability to clamp down on the free-wheeling sales of manufactured products to consumers.

In general, though, inadequate consideration was given to the long-term effects of the many new products that came to market in the 1930s and 1940s, such as pesticides like DDT and the numerous synthetic materials, including nylon and plastics, that were developed for use in World War II. It took many years before the impact of certain pesticides on the food chain and the problem of non-biodegradable waste, became evident.

The Growth of Suburbs

After World War II home building boomed. Many of the new homes were constructed in the suburbs on former farmland, woodland, and open space,

far from convenient shopping and transportation. These suburbs spawned a new way of life based on the automobile. With the disappearance of farmland close to city centers, milk, poultry, and other fresh foods for the metropolitan areas had to be brought in from ever more distant farms. While some visionaries worried about the loss of open space and farmland in the 1950s—the Nature Conservancy was founded in 1951—and there were a few state and local efforts to protect farmland in the 1960s and 1970s [*see* Document 104], urban and suburban sprawl did not become a national issue until the early 1980s.

As population numbers rose, automobile use increased, highways spread across the nation, and suburban areas encroached on once-rural watersheds. In more and more places, the air was unfit to breathe and the water unsafe to drink. In 1955, the federal government began to finance and develop programs to prevent and control air pollution [*see* Document 93]. However, truly effective federal water pollution control and safe drinking water legislation were not passed until 1972 [*see* Document 116] and 1974, respectively.

Reconsidering the Human-Nature Relationship

By the 1920s, recognition of the decline in wildlife and wilderness areas had encouraged hunters, fishermen, and other sportsmen, including members of the Boone and Crockett Club [*see* Document 57], to reexamine their relationship with the wild. In 1925, George Bird Grinnell and Charles Sheldon noted, "The original purpose of the Boone and Crockett Club, to make hunting easier and more successful, has changed with changing conditions, so that now it is devoted chiefly to setting better standards in conservation."[1] The drop in the populations of certain wildlife species [*see* Document 86] and the disappearance of wilderness areas provided impetus for the creation of a host of new conservation organizations, including the Izaak Walton League (1922), the Wilderness Society (1935), Ducks Unlimited (1937), Defenders of Wildlife (1947), and the Conservation Foundation (1947), and by 1959 there was strong support for a Wilderness Act [*see* Document 96].

Shortly after the turn of the century, local governments, in an effort to contain building growth and industrial development, had begun to impose land use zoning regulations. By the 1920s, real estate, mining, and industrial interests were feeling the sting of these regulations and appealed to the courts for a redress of grievances [*see* Documents 74 and 75]. In general, the courts tended to side with the interests of big business, but over time, zoning laws became increasingly stringent and forced individual property owners, as well as businesses of every type, to adjust to communal interests. By the 1930s, local and regional planning [*see* Document 83] had made great strides in bringing order to land development. Nevertheless, even in the 1950s, insufficient thought was given to the consequences of building in areas with inadequate water supplies [*see* Document 92].

Much of the nation looked with favor on the transformation of the natural landscape, as industry expanded, dams were built, wetlands reclaimed, and forests and farmland paved over and turned into roads and housing developments. But a small segment of the population was horrified by the complete lack of regard for the needs of nature. In 1928 Henry Beston [*see* Document 76] proposed that we rethink our relationship to other living things, and in 1933 Luther Standing Bear [*see* Document 80] pointed out that respect for other living things is fundamental to the Native American view of life. Arthur Tansley [*see* Document 81] introduced the idea of the ecosystem in 1935; the following year, H. V. Harlan and M. L. Martini [*see* Document 82] raised concerns about decreasing biodiversity. In 1947 Marjory Stoneman Douglas [*see* Document 85], in an evocative book on the Everglades, called into question the policy of draining wetlands to reclaim land for agriculture and building development. By the time Fairfield Osborn proclaimed that Americans needed to become sensible to the interrelatedness of all living things [*see* Document 87] and Aldo Leopold proposed a new "land ethic"— which called for humans to view themselves as ordinary members of a community whose other members include water, soil, plants, and animals rather than as superior to the other members of the community [*see* Document 88]— the foundations for an environmental movement expanded from the conservation movement of the turn of the century, had been laid.

Technology and Resource Policy in the Nuclear Age

One of the reactions to the devastation caused by the atomic bombs dropped on Hiroshima and Nagasaki in 1945 in the process of bringing World War II to a conclusion was a reconsideration of the uses of technology [*see* Document 91]. As people came to understand that they had the ability to destroy life on earth on an unprecedented scale, a litany of voices arose to plead for the preservation of the earth and the living things that inhabit it. Some of the voices belonged to antinuclear weapons activists, while others were those of individuals and groups protesting the waste and destruction of the America's irreplaceable resources.

Forty years after Teddy Roosevelt had attempted to set up a commission to study the nation's resources and establish a viable resource policy [*see* Document 70], President Harry Truman created the Materials Policy Commission with much the same objective. This time, adequate funding was made available. Although the commission's report commented on the dwindling supplies of many natural resource, it nevertheless recommended that the main goal of a U.S. materials policy should be the development of a sufficient supply of resources to ensure economic growth [*see* Document 89]. There was swift reaction to the report, with conservationists like Samuel Ordway calling for sustainable development [*see* Document 90] and economists like John Kenneth Galbraith questioning the right of the United States to continue to consume resources at an inordinately high rate [*see* Document 95]. At about the same time, mining and drilling companies, recognizing that mineral, coal, oil, and gas deposits are finite, were undertaking their own assessments of not just the United States' stocks of resources, but of whole world's [*see* Document 94]. The findings of both the government and industry clearly indicated that the time had arrived for the United States to develop a coherent, long-term energy and resource policy, but Congress, caught in the vise of partisan interests and short-term economic priorities, has never been able to accomplish the task.

DOCUMENT 74: *Pennsylvania Coal Company v. Mahon et al.* (1922)

In 1878, the Pennsylvania Coal Company, the owner of land containing coal deposits, deeded the surface of some of its property with the express reservation that the company had the right to remove the coal beneath the surface land. However, on May 27, 1921, the Pennsylvania legislature passed the Kohler Act, which prohibited the mining of anthracite coal within city limits in a way that would "cause the . . . subsidence of any dwelling or other structure used as a human habitation, or any factory, store, or other industrial or mercantile establishment in which human labor is employed," as well as the subsidence of any public street.

When the owners of a house constructed on land that had been deeded by the Pennsylvania Coal Company tried to prevent the coal company from mining under their building, citing the Kohler Act, the company sued the building's owners. The case, which eventually reached the Supreme Court, confronted the issue of whether the government had a right to impose regulations that diminished the value of private property, and determined that "if regulation goes too far it will be recognized as a taking for which compensation must be paid." Justice Louis Brandeis, in his dissenting opinion, asserted that regulation in the public interest that placed restrictions on the use of land in order to protect the public but did not "appropriate or make any use of" the land is not a "taking."

The case established the doctrine of "regulatory taking" and determined that the extent of diminution in property value is the major factor in deciding if a regulatory act constitutes a taking requiring compensation. The issue of regulatory taking would continue to be raised by opponents of environmental legislation [see Document 164, for example].

A. The Case and the Court's Ruling

This is a bill in equity brought by the defendants in error to prevent the Pennsylvania Coal Company from mining under their property in such way as to remove the supports and cause a subsidence of the surface and of their house. The bill sets out a deed executed by the Coal Company in 1878, under which the plaintiffs claim. The deed conveys the surface, but in express terms reserves the right to remove all the coal under the same, and the grantee takes the premises with the risk, and waives all claim for damages that may arise from mining out the coal. . . .

[The Kohler Act] forbids the mining of anthracite coal in such way as to cause the subsidence of, among other things, any structure used as a human habitation, with certain exceptions, including among them land where the surface is owned by the owner of the underlying coal and is distant more than one hundred and fifty feet from any improved property belonging to any other person. As applied in this case the statute is admitted to destroy previously existing rights of property and contract. The question is whether the police power can be stretched so far.

Government hardly could go on if to some extent values incident to property could not be diminished without paying for every such change in the general law. As long recognized, some values are enjoyed under an implied limitation and must yield to the police power. But obviously the implied limitation must have its limits, or the contract and due process clauses are gone. One fact for consideration in determining such limits is the extent of the diminution. When it reaches a certain magnitude, in most if not in all cases there must be an exercise of eminent domain and compensation to sustain the act. So the question depends upon the particular facts. The greatest weight is given to the judgement of the legislature, but it always is open to interested parties to contend that the legislature has gone beyond its constitutional power. . . .

This is the case of a single private house. . . . A source of damage to such a house is not a public nuisance even if similar damage is inflicted on others in different places. The damage is not common or public.

* * *

The rights of the public in a street purchased or laid out by eminent domain are those that it has paid for. If in any case its representatives have been so short sighted as to acquire only surface rights without the right of support, we see no more authority for supplying the latter without compensation than there was for taking the right of way in the first place and refusing to pay for it because the public wanted it very much. The protection of private property in the Fifth Amendment presupposes that it is wanted for public use, but provides that it shall not be taken for such use without compensation.

B. Justice Louis Brandeis's Dissenting Opinion

Coal in place is land; and the right of the owner to use his land is not absolute. He may not so use it as to create a public nuisance; and uses, once harmless, may, owing to changed conditions, seriously threaten the public welfare. Whenever they do, the legislature has power to prohibit such uses without paying compensation; and the power to prohibit extends alike to the manner, the character and the purpose of the use. . . .

Every restriction upon the use of property imposed in the exercise of the police power deprives the owner of some right theretofore enjoyed, and is, in that sense, an abridgment by the State of rights in property without making compensation. But restriction imposed to protect the public health, safety or morals from dangers threatened is not a taking. The restriction here in question is merely the prohibition of a noxious use. The property so restricted remains in the possession of its owner. The State does not appropriate it or make any use of it. The State merely prevents the owner from making a use which interferes with the paramount rights of the public. Whenever the use prohibited ceases to be noxious,—as it may because of further change in local or social conditions,—the restriction will have to be removed and the owner will again be free to enjoy his property as heretofore.

The restriction upon the use of this property can not, of course, be lawfully imposed, unless its purpose is to protect the public.

Source: United States Reports, Vol. 260 (Washington, D.C.: Government Printing Office, 1923), pp. 412, 413, 415, 417.

DOCUMENT 75: *Village of Euclid et al. v. Ambler Realty Company* (1926)

The earliest zoning laws were instituted at the beginning of the twentieth century by local governments attempting to limit the use of land in ways that were detrimental to the interests of the local community. In recent years, zoning laws have been used as an important means of containing growth near and preventing the development of wetlands and other environmentally sensitive or ecologically important areas. The Euclid (Ohio) case established that communities have the right to enact zoning laws in the public interest even if they cause the property of certain individuals to be devalued.

Appeal from a decree of the District Court enjoining the Village and its Building Inspector from enforcing a zoning ordinance. The suit was brought by an owner of unimproved land within the corporate limits of the village, who sought the relief upon the ground that, because of the building restrictions imposed, the ordinance operated to reduce the normal value of his property,

and to deprive him of liberty and property without due process of law.

* * *

A motion was made in the court below to dismiss the bill on the ground that, because complainant [appellee] had made no effort to obtain a building permit or apply to the zoning board of appeals for relief as it might have done under the terms of the ordinance, the suit was premature. The motion was properly overruled. The effect of the allegations of the bill is that the ordinance of its own force operates greatly to reduce the value of appellee's lands and destroy their marketability for industrial, commercial and residential uses; and the attack is directed, not against any specific provision or provisions, but against the ordinance as an entirety. Assuming the premises, the existence and maintenance of the ordinance, in effect, constitutes a present invasion of appellee's property rights and a threat to continue it. . . .

It is not necessary to set forth the provisions of the Ohio Constitution which are thought to be infringed. The question is the same under both Constitutions, namely, as granted by the appellee: Is the ordinance invalid in that it violates the constitutional protection "to the right of property in the appellee by attempted regulations under the guise of the police power, which are unreasonable and confiscatory?"

Building zone laws are of modern origin. They began in this country about twenty-five years ago. Until recent years, urban life was comparatively simple; but with the great increase and concentration of population, problems have developed, and constantly are developing, which require, and will continue to require, additional restrictions in respect of the use and occupation of private lands in urban communities. Regulations, the wisdom, necessity and validity of which, as applied to existing conditions, are so apparent that they are now uniformly sustained, a century ago, or even half a century ago, probably would have been rejected as arbitrary and oppressive. . . .

The ordinance now under review, and all similar laws and regulations, must find their justification, in some aspect of the police power, asserted for the public welfare. The line which in this field separates the legitimate from the illegitimate assumption of power is not capable of precise delimitation. It varies with circumstances and conditions. A regulatory zoning ordinance, which would be clearly valid as applied to the great cities, might be clearly invalid as applied to rural communities. In solving doubts, the maxim *sic utere tuo ut alienum non laedas* [use what is yours in such a way as not to cause harm to others], which lies at the foundation of so much of the common law of nuisances, ordinarily will furnish a fairly helpful clew. And the law of nuisances, likewise may be consulted, not for the purpose of controlling, but for the helpful aid of its analogies in the process of ascertaining the scope of, the power. Thus the question whether the power exists to forbid the erection of a building of a particular kind or for a particular use, like the question whether a particular thing is a nuisance, is to be determined, not by an abstract consideration of the building or of the thing considered apart, but by considering it in connection with the circumstances and the locality. . . . A nuisance may be merely a right thing in the wrong place, —like a pig in a parlor instead of a barnyard. If the validity of the legislative classification for zoning purposes be fairly debatable, the legislative judgement must be allowed to control. . . .

There is no serious difference of opinion in respect of the validity of laws and regulations fixing the height of buildings within reasonable limits, the character of materials and methods of construction, and the adjoining area which must be left open, in order to minimize the danger of fire or collapse, the evils of over-crowding, and the like, and excluding from residential sections offensive trades, industries and structures likely to create nuisances. . . .

Here, however, the exclusion is in general terms of all industrial establishments, and it may thereby happen that not only offensive or dangerous industries will be excluded, but those which are neither offensive nor dangerous will share the same fate. . . .

It is said that the Village of Euclid is a mere suburb of the City of Cleveland; that the industrial development of that city has now reached and in some degree extended into the village and, in the obvious course of things, will soon absorb the entire area for industrial enterprises; that the effect of the ordinance is to divert this natural development elsewhere with the consequent loss of increased values to the owners of the lands within the village borders. But the village, though physically a suburb of Cleveland, is politically a separate municipality, with powers of its own and authority to govern itself as it sees fit within the limits of the organic law of its creation and the State and Federal Constitutions. Its governing authorities, presumably representing a majority of its inhabitants and voicing their will, have determined, not that industrial development shall cease at its boundaries, but that the course of such development

shall proceed within definitely fixed lines. If it be a proper exercise of the police power to relegate industrial establishments to localities separated from residential sections, it is not easy to find a sufficient reason for denying the power because the effect of its exercise is to divert an industrial flow from the course which it would follow, to the injury of the residential public if left alone, to another course where such injury will be obviated. It is not meant by this, however, to exclude the possibility of cases where the general public interest would so far outweigh the interest of the municipality that the municipality would not be allowed to stand in the way.

Source: United States Reports, Vol. 272 (Washington, D.C.: Government Printing Office, 1927), pp. 367, 386-90.

DOCUMENT 76: Henry Beston on the Human Relationship with Nature (1928)

Henry Beston, like Henry Thoreau and John Muir before him, sought isolation and nearness to nature. Having bought fifty acres and built a two-room cottage among the dunes of Nauset Beach on the eastern shore of Cape Cod, facing the open Atlantic, he planned to spend two weeks there in the fall of 1926, but captivated by "the beauty and mystery of this earth and outer sea,"[2] he stayed for a year and wrote The Outermost House. *In the book, which tells about his year on the beach, Beston proposed that humans need to develop a new relationship with their environment. Rachel Carson [see Document 100] cited* The Outermost House *as the book that most profoundly influenced her writing, and federal officials noted the book's role in inspiring the creation of the Cape Cod National Seashore.*

We need another and a wiser and perhaps a more mystical concept of animals. Remote from universal nature, and living by complicated artifice, man in civilization surveys the creatures through the glass of his knowledge and sees thereby a feather magnified and the whole image in distortion. We patronize them for their incompleteness, for their tragic fate of having taken form so far below ourselves. And therein we err, and greatly err. For the animal shall not be measured by man. In a world older and more complete than ours they move finished and complete, gifted with extensions of the senses we have lost or never attained, living by voices we shall never hear. They

are not brethren, they are not underlings; they are other nations, caught with ourselves in the net of life and time, fellow prisoners of the splendour and travail of the earth.

. . .

As well expect Nature to answer to your human values as to come into your house and sit in a chair. The economy of nature, its checks and balances, its measurements of competing life— all this is this is a great marvel and has an ethic of its own.

Source: Henry Beston, *The Outermost House* (New York: Henry Holt, 1992), p. 25, 217.

DOCUMENT 77: Franklin D. Roosevelt on the Destruction of America's Forests (1930)

Franklin Delano Roosevelt, Theodore Roosevelt's second cousin, grew up in a family that venerated the outdoors and was sensitive to concerns about conservation. In the New York State legislature, FDR served as chairman of the Senate Committee on Forest, Fish, and Game; and as governor of the state he endorsed conservationist efforts. FDR's conviction that the government should take a leadership role in encouraging beneficial social change was probably responsible for his greatest contributions to the conservation movement, the creation of the Civilian Conservation Corps and the Soil Conservation Service.

Stones, steel, concrete and asphalt, bricks and glass meet the eye at every turn in the cities of America. Yet the products of the forest continue indispensable to the structure of our civilization.

A still heavier stake in intelligent conservation of this country's forest resources is held by the people of rural America. Agriculture uses more wood than any other industry. The people in the country benefit most from the prevention of floods. They own the lowlands where crops and property are destroyed. They own the highlands from which erosion sweeps away the fertility.

The small cities and towns, either as municipalities or through civic organizations, can make a notable contribution to progress in forest conservation. . . .

Back in 1911, as a greenhorn member of the New York State Senate, I happened to become chairman of the Committee on Forest, Fish, and Game. Anxious to stir up interest in my committee's work I arranged to have Gifford Pinchot [*see* Document 73] deliver a lecture in Albany. What he said I have probably forgotten but two pictures that he displayed are still vividly remembered.

He threw on the screen first the reproduction of a painting made in meticulous detail about the year 1400 by a Chinese artist. The scene was a beautiful valley in China, peopled with a city of a half million. Luxuriant crops in the carefully cultivated fields of the valley floor indicated a rich and well-tilled soil. A quiet river wound along, with indications on the bank that this was a stream of steady flow, free from periodic floods. A deep and dense forest of pine trees covered the mountains at either side of the valley. The whole scene was one of peace, prosperity and plenty.

Down the mountain at one side had been slashed a strip in which was a wooden trough, or flume, such as is used for sliding logs down a declivity. This was evidence that lumbering operations had been started.

Then Mr. Pinchot flashed on the screen a photograph of the same valley, made in 1900 from the identical spot occupied by the artist who five centuries before had painted the scene in photographic detail.

The mountain slopes had been completely denuded of their forests. Not a tree remained. Jutting rocks, deep gullies and barren spaces were there instead.

The whole valley floor was covered with a wilderness of rocks and bowlders that had been swept down by floods. No crops were growing, because no soil was left in which a seed might sprout. There was no river—only a dry stream bed where in season violent floods added to the destruction of what little was left to be damaged.

A poverty-stricken village of 5,000 remained within the still standing walls of the once prosperous city of a half million.

One need not be an alarmist to foresee that, without intelligent conservation measures, long before half a millennium passes some such contrasting pictures might be possible in our own United States. Even now we are consuming five times as much timber as is being grown. We plant in a year an area about equal to what is cut over in less than five days. Fortunately the federal government and many of the states are planning and working constructively to conserve the nation's timber resources.

A certain amount of sentiment clusters about trees and the forests and this I would not disparage, for I share it. We can however, put that entirely aside, for the dollars and cents argument is powerful enough if we have the slightest consideration for future generations.

If no other fact were available to support this statement one would need only to point out that in eighty-five years lumber prices have increased three and a half time as rapidly as average prices of other common necessities. In consequence, in part at least, of this rise in price our per capita consumption of wood has declined by about forty per cent. Thirty-three of our states are now sending to other states for their lumber supplies.

We pay two hundred and fifty million dollars a year of freight because the remaining forests are so distant from the centers of consumption. The steel rails of our Northern transportation system are being laid on ties shipped from the far Northwest. Our newsprint supplies are coming from long distances. We use eight million tons of paper a year. It takes five million trees annually to support our telephone and telegraph wires. Wood is a staple necessity of everyday life.

Source: Franklin D. Roosevelt, "A Debt We Owe," *Country Home* 54 (June 1930): 12-13.

DOCUMENT 78: Stuart Chase on Waste in the Machine Age (1931)

An author of popular books on economic problems in the United States, Stuart Chase urged that the country develop an industrial order in which production and distribution would be aimed at satisfying the needs of consumers—in the present and future—rather than of profit makers.

[One of the four] main channel[s] of waste is measured not in man-power, but in tonnage and horse-power. It is the measure of the gutting of the continent of North America. For every barrel of oil which has reached the pipe line, three barrels have been lost under ground; for every ton of coal which has come out of the pit, another ton has been left forever unreclaimable in the mine. We are cutting our forests four times faster than they are growing, which gives them—at this rate of exploitation—only another generation, while our effects at reforestation progress at a rate that will require 900 years to plant the land now idle and needing planting. Having cut the wood, we lose two-thirds of it in process of manufacture. Having made the paper, we use such wasteful sizes and grades that ninety-one business organizations taken at random have been found to throw $1,000,000 a year into the wastebasket.

In soils, fisheries, minerals, bird life, the neglect of waterpower—the story of ruthless pioneering, with no provision for the future, is repeated. . . . Meanwhile a single Sunday edition of the *New York Times*—75 per cent of which is advertising matter—consumes in wood pulp about 14 acres of forest land.

* * *

Modern industry, it is universally conceded, is operated on the basis of production for profit. The usefulness of the thing produced is a by-product. Realistic defenders of the present order admit this, but go on to explain that the profit motive provides so strong an incentive for production that more by way of consumable goods is thrown off—even as a by product—than could possibly be attained under any system founded on production for use only. In short, it is claimed that the wayfaring man secures a greater net benefit from the profit system—despite its left-handed regard for his interests—than he could from any system designed directly to serve him.

Source: Stuart Chase, *Waste and the Machine Age* (New York: League for Industrial Democracy, 1931), pp. 34, 36.

DOCUMENT 79: Arthur Kallet and F. J. Schlink on the Dangers of Manufactured Products (1932)

One of the early alarmist books about the dangers of commercial products, Arthur Kallet and F.J. Schlink's 100,000,000 Guinea Pigs *created a public outcry that led to the passage of the Food, Drug, and Cosmetics Act of 1938 and resulted in major changes in food and drug policies.*

In the magazines, in the newspapers, over the radio, a terrific verbal barrage has been laid down on a hundred million Americans, first, to set in motion a host of fears about their health, their stomachs, their bowels, their teeth, their throats, their looks; second, to persuade them that only be eating, drinking, gargling, brushing, or smearing with Smith's Whole Vitamin Breakfast Food, Jones' Yeast Cubes, Blue Giant Apples, Prussian Salts, Listroboris Mouthwash, Grandpa's Wonder Toothpaste, and a thousand and one other foods, drinks, gargles and pastes, can they either postpone the onset of disease, of social ostracism, of business failure, or recover from ailments, physical or social, already contracted.

If these foods and medicines were—to most of the people who use them—merely worthless; if there were no other charge to be made than that the manufacturers', sales managers', and advertising agents' claims for them were false, *[100,000,000 Guinea Pigs]* would not have been written. But many of them, including some of the most widely advertised and sold, are not only worthless, but are actually dangerous. That *All-Bran* you eat every morning—do you know that it may cause serious and perhaps irreparable intestinal trouble? That big, juicy apple you have at lunch—do you know that indifferent Government officials let it come to your table coated with arsenic, one of the deadliest of poisons? The *Pebeco* Toothpaste with which you brush your teeth twice every day—do you know that a tube of it contains enough poison, if eaten, to kill three people; that, in fact a German army officer committed suicide by eating a tubeful of this particular tooth paste? The *Bromo-Seltzer* that you take for headaches—do you know that it contains a poisonous drug which has been responsible for many deaths and, the American Medical Association says, at least one case of sexual impotence?

Using the feeble and ineffective pure food and drug laws as a smoke-screen, the food and drug industries have been systematically bombarding us with falsehoods about the purity, healthfulness, and safety of their products, while they have been making profits by experimenting on us with poisons, irritants, harmful chemical preservatives, and dangerous drugs.

. . . [W]e consumers are being forced into the role of laboratory guinea pigs through huge loopholes in obviously weak and ineffective laws.

Source: Arthur Kallet and F. J. Schlink 100,000,000 Guinea Pigs: Dangers in Everyday Foods, Drugs, and Cosmetics *(New York: Vanguard Press, 1932), pp. 3-4.*

DOCUMENT 80: Luther Standing Bear on Native Americans and the Rights of Other Living Things (1933)

A Sioux chieftain and staunch advocate of Native American rights, Luther Standing Bear offers us a view of Native Americans as conservationists. Although his statement that the Indian "destroyed nothing" is not completely accurate [see, for example, Document 27], Standing Bear's analysis of the Indians' perception of their relationship to other living things vividly depicts a mind-set at variance with the ideas of most other Americans of his time.

The Indian was a natural conservationist. He destroyed nothing, great or small. Destruction was not a part of Indian thought and action; if it had been, and had the man been the ruthless savage he has been accredited with being, he would have long ago preceded the European in the labor of destroying the natural life of this continent. The Indian was frugal in the midst of plenty. When the buffalo roamed the plains in multitudes he slaughtered only what he could eat and these he used to the hair and bones. Early one spring the Lakotas were camped on the Missouri river when the ice was beginning to break up. One day a buffalo floated by and it was hauled ashore. The animal proved to have been freshly killed and in good condition, a welcome occurrence at the time since the meat supply was getting low. Soon another came floating downstream, and it was no more than ashore when others came into view. Everybody was busy saving meat and hides, but in a short while the buffalo were so thick on the water that they were allowed to float away. Just why so many buffalo had been drowned was never known, but I relate the instance as a boyhood memory.

I know of no species of plant, bird, or animal that were exterminated until the coming of the white man. For some years after the buffalo disappeared there still remained huge herds of antelope, but the hunter's work was no sooner done in the destruction of the buffalo than his attention was attracted toward the deer. They are plentiful now only where protected. The white man considered natural animal life just as he did the natural man life upon this continent, as "pests." Plants which the Indian found beneficial were also "pests." There is no word in the Lakota vocabulary with the English meaning of this word.

There was a great difference in the attitude taken by the Indian and the Caucasian toward nature, and this difference made of one a conservationist and of the other a non-conservationist of life. The Indian, as well as all other creatures that were given birth and grew, were sustained by the common mother—earth. He was therefore kin to all living things and he gave to all creatures equal rights with himself. Everything of earth was loved and reverenced.

* * *

From Wakan Tanka there came a great unifying life force that flowed in and through all things—the flowers of the plains, blowing winds, rocks, trees, birds, animals—and was the same force that had been breathed into the first man. Thus all things were kindred and brought together by the same Great Mystery.

Kinship with all creatures of the earth, sky, and water was a real and active principle. For the animal and bird world there existed a brother feeling that kept the Lakota safe among them. And so close did some of the Lakotas come to their feathered and furred friends that in true brotherhood they spoke a common tongue.

The animal had rights—the right of man's protection, the right to live, the right to multiply, the right to freedom, and the right to man's indebtedness—and in recognition of these rights the Lakota never enslaved the animal, and spared all life that was not needed for food and clothing.

Source: Luther Standing Bear, *Land of the Spotted Eagle* (Boston: Houghton Mifflin, 1933), pp. 165-66, 193.

DOCUMENT 81: Arthur Tansley on the Concept of the Ecosystem (1935)

Arthur Tansley, a plant ecologist and one of the founders of the British Ecological Society (established in 1913), introduced the concept of the natural world as a set of complex, interacting communities. This selection from an article by Tansley appeared in the journal of the Ecological Society of America, which begun publication in 1920, five years after the organization of the society.

[T]he more fundamental conception [than the plant biologist Frederic Clements' application of the term *biome* to "the whole complex of organisms inhabiting a given region"] is, as it seems to me, the whole *system* (in the sense of physics), including not only the organism-complex, but also the whole complex of physical factors forming what we call the environment of the biome—the habitat factors in the widest sense. Though the organisms may claim our primary interest, when we are trying to think fundamentally we cannot separate them from their special environment, with which they form one physical system.

It is the systems so formed which, from the point of view of the ecologist, are the basic units of nature on the face of the earth. Our natural human prejudices force us to consider the organisms (in the sense of the biologist) as the most important parts of these systems, but certainly the inorganic "factors" are also parts—there could be no systems without them, and there is constant interchange of the most various kinds within each system, not only between the organisms but between the organic and the inorganic. These *ecosystems*, as we may call them, are of the most various kinds and sizes. They form one category of the multitudinous physical systems of the universe, which range from the universe down to the atom.

Source: "The Use and Abuse of Vegetational Concepts and Terms," *Ecology* 16 (1935): pp. 295-99, in Carolyn Merchant, *Major Problems in American Environmental History* (Lexington, MA: Heath, 1992), p. 451.

DOCUMENT 82: H. V. Harlan and M. L. Martini on the Loss of Genetic Diversity (1936)

Plant and animal breeding and selection has been practiced for thousands of years. While this was done on a limited scale, there continued to be tremendous variation between crops grown in disparate communities in far-flung places. However, as international trade and communications increased, a worldwide preference for a small number of grain species developed and some local species began to disappear.

H. V. Harlan, an agronomist, and M. L. Martini, a botanist, were working in the Department of Agriculture's Bureau of Plant Industry when they recognized that the widespread use of certain popular varieties of cereal grains posed a threat to genetic diversity. Harlan and Martini had many concerns about the loss of genetic resources and ancient, local plant varieties, including the effect of this loss on the development of new species.

Within the next few decades, as scientists began to understand the relationship between biodiversity and ecosystem functioning, the wider ramifications of this loss of biodiversity became evident. Toward the end of the twentieth century, a contentious global debate arose over the benefits versus the drawbacks of the widespread use of genetically modified seed for a handful of strains of corn, rice and other crops that had been developed by a few large agribusinesses [see Documents 151 and 155].

In the great laboratory of Asia, Europe, and Africa, unguided barley breeding has been going on for thousands of years. Types without number have arisen over an enormous area. The better ones have survived. Many of the surviving types are old. Spikes from Egyptian ruins can often be matched with ones still growing in the basins along the Nile. The Egypt of the Pyramids, however, is probably recent in the history of barley.... In the hinterlands of Asia there were probably barley fields when man was young.

The progenies of these fields with all their surviving variations constitute the world's priceless reservoir of germ plasm. It has waited through long centuries. Unfortunately, from the breeder's standpoint, it is now being imperiled. Historically, the tribes of Asia have not been overfriendly. Trade and commerce of a sort have always existed. They have existed, however, on a scale so small that agriculture has been little affected. Modern communication is a real threat. A hundred years ago, when the grain crop of north Africa failed, the natives starved. Today, in years of shortage, the French supply their dependent populations with seed from California. Arab farmers in Mariout sometimes sell short to European buyers and import seed grains from Palestine. In a similar way changes are slowly taking place in more remote places. When new barleys replace those grown by the farmers of Ethiopia or Tibet, the world will have lost something irreplaceable.

Source: H. V. Harlan and M. L. Martini, "Problems and Results in Barley Breeding," in *U.S. Department of Agriculture Yearbook of Agriculture, 1936* (Washington, D.C.: Government Printing Office, 1936), p. 317.

DOCUMENT 83: Lewis Mumford on Regional Planning (1938)

The cultural historian Lewis Mumford advocated strict zoning regulations, regional planning, and communal land ownership as means to prevent inappropriate land development. He believed that a primary goal of the design of buildings, cities, communities, and public and private space should be to tailor an appropriate fit between humankind and the natural world. A generation later, Ian McHarg [see Document 110], a disciple of Mumford, developed the concept of environmental impact.

Regional planning is essentially the effort to apply scientific knowledge and stable standards of judgment, justified by rational human values, to the exploitation of the earth. Such knowledge was deliberately flouted in the opening up of the dry lands which have become the dust-bowl of America, and the commonwealth has paid dearly for that sacrifice to the demands of the individual farmer and speculator. No community can afford such luxuries of ignorance: the function of science is to reduce the area of such costly mistakes and finally wipe them out. Without the decisive control that rests with collective ownership, in the hands of responsible public administrators, working for the common good, regional planning is an all but impossible task: at best it must confine itself to weak admonitions, partial prohibitions, various forms of negative action: at most it can say what shall not be done, but it has little power to command the forces of positive action.

The common ownership of land would put the division and supervision of the land in the hands of the appropriate local and regional authorities, who would map out areas of cultivation, areas of mining, areas of urban settlement, as they now map out areas for public parks. On this basis, a stable social adjustment could be worked out for every part of the region, and for every type of resource and activity. This common ownership is not an objective in itself: it is merely a means toward creating a system of dressing and keeping the land as it must be dressed and kept for an advanced civilization. Something can indeed be done by education and public regulation where the obsolete system of private ownership and control is preserved; but infinitely more can and must be done by active authorities, capable not merely of suggestion but decisive action, capable of looking ahead over half a century or more, and borrowing funds on the basis of such long term action. A useful step toward this system of common ownership consists in a broadly applied scheme of land zoning: such as that provided in the current English law which "sterilizes" against change of use without public permission all existing rural areas, or like that worked out... in the Ruhr district before 1933. A partial step in the same direction—restricting marginal lands against inappropriate uses—has been made in Wisconsin.

Source: Lewis Mumford, *The Culture of Cities* (New York: Harcourt Brace, 1938), p. 329.

DOCUMENT 84: John Steinbeck's *The Grapes of Wrath* (1939)

Like Jonathan Edwards, Thomas Jefferson, and the nineteenth-century transcendentalists, John Steinbeck believed that communion with the land was necessary for the well-being of the human spirit. He saw the dust bowl crisis of the 1930s, which wrought havoc on the lives of the small farmers of the prairie states, as a product of the rape of the land by agribusiness working hand in hand with the government.

His novel The Grapes of Wrath *was a scathing attack on the destructive practices of agribusiness as well as on government land and water policies. In the book, Steinbeck paralleled the degradation of the lives of the Okies with the degradation of the prairie sod and depicted the tragic, systematic destruction of a fragile ecosystem.*

The owner men sat in the cars and explained. You know the land is poor. You've scrabbled at it long enough, God knows.

The squatting tenant men nodded and wondered and drew figures in the dust, and yes, they knew, God knows. If the dust only wouldn't fly. If the top would only stay on the soil, it might not be so bad.

The owner men went on leading to their point: You know the land's getting poorer. You know what cotton does to the land; robs it, sucks all the blood out of it.

The squatters nodded—they knew, God knew. If they could only rotate the crops they might pump blood back into the land.

Well, it's too late. And the owner men explained the workings and the thinkings of the monster that was stronger than they were. A man can hold land if he can just eat and pay taxes; he can do that.

Yes, he can do that until his crops fail one day and he has to borrow money from the bank.

But—you see, a bank or a company can't do that, because those creatures don't breathe air, don't eat side-meat. They breathe profits; they eat the interest on money.

* * *

The squatting men looked down again. What do you want us to do? We can't take less share of the crop—we're half starved now. The kids are hungry all the time. We got no clothes, torn an' ragged. If all the neighbors weren't the same, we'd be ashamed to go to meeting.

And at last the owner men came to the point. The tenant system won't work any more. One man on a tractor can take the place of twelve or fourteen families. Pay him a wage and take all the crop. We have to do it. We don't like to do it. But the monster's sick. Something's happened to the monster.

But you'll kill the land with cotton.

We know. We've got to take cotton quick before the land dies. Then we'll sell the land. Lots of families in the East would like to own a piece of land.

The tenant men looked up alarmed. But what'll happen to us? How'll we eat?

You'll have to get off the land. The plows'll go through the dooryard.

Source: John Steinbeck, *The Grapes of Wrath* (New York: Viking/Penguin, 1939), pp. 43, 44.

DOCUMENT 85: Marjory Stoneman Douglas on the Everglades (1947)

The Florida Everglades, so eloquently described by the writer Marjory Stoneman Douglas as a "river of grass," are a unique area. This 1,700-square-mile wetland is part a of a 9,000-square-mile ecosystem that includes the Kissimmee River basin and Lake Okeechobee and provides the biologic and hydrologic foundation for south Florida's economic prosperity.

Douglas posited that the draining, diking, channeling, and manipulation of the waters of this system to make way for agricultural lands, homes, and roads—which had been official state policy since the late 1800s—was a recipe for destroying the ecosystem. Although she felt that the newly designated Everglades National Park would inhibit further changes to the southern part of the system, she feared the power of special interests. Her warnings were largely ignored until the 1980s [see Document 132].

There are no other Everglades in the world.

They are, they have always been, one of the unique regions of the earth, remote, never wholly known. Nothing anywhere else is like them: their vast glittering openness, wider than the enormous visible round of the horizon, the racing free saltness and sweetness of their massive winds, under the dazzling blue heights of space. They are unique also in the simplicity, the diversity, the related harmony of the forms of life they enclose. The miracle of the light pours over the green and brown expanse of saw grass and of water, shining and slow-moving below, the grass and water that is the meaning and the central fact of the Everglades of Florida. It is a river of grass.

* * *

[H]istory, the recorded time of the earth and of man, is in itself something like a river. To try to present it whole is to find oneself lost in the sense of continuing change. The source can be only the beginning in time and space, and the end is the future and the unknown. . . .

So it is with the Everglades, which have that quality of long existence in their own nature. They were changeless. They are changed.

They were complete before man came to them, and for centuries afterward, when he was only one of those forms which shared, in a finely balanced harmony, the forces and the ancient nature of the place.

* * *

The most important single recommendation of the Everglades Project Reports [issued in 1946] was for a single plan of development and water control for the whole area, under the direction of a single engineer and his board. Only in that way could the conflicting demands of local areas be equalized, so that the soil fit for high cultivation could be used and maintained without detriment to the water supply of the lower areas. It would maintain areas for water conservation. It would control salt intrusion. A well-planned system of canals that would discharge excess lake water into the open Glades would permit the river of grass to flow again with sweet water.

The report was . . . studied by the thoughtful men in the growing cities. Its recommendations received wide attention and support, although there was opposition by local interests with political power. The growers about the lake were still afraid of floods, and they felt that water control would endanger the lands already under production. The cattlemen of the west were still resentful of an over-all control. Many owners of great areas of mucklands, draining and diking and pumping their irrigation ditches full from the seaward-flowing canals, refused to consider anything more important than their own immediate profits and would fight more fiercely than any others a co-ordinated control.

It was too soon to expect that that all these people would see that the destruction of the Everglades was the destruction of all.

Source: Marjory Stoneman Douglas, *The Everglades: River of Grass* (New York: Rinehart, 1947), pp. 5-6, 8-9, 383.

DOCUMENT 86: Roger Tory Peterson on Bird Population (1948)

The noted ornithologist and author of the popular Field Guides Roger Tory Peterson raised people's awareness of how human activity, including the changes that people make in their environment, affect wildlife populations, forcing some species to dwindle and enabling others to multiply. His books offered an innovative means of identifying birds—one that eliminated the need to shoot and collect them in order to be certain of their identity. His books also moved interest in bird-watching— or "birding," as it is popularly referred to— from the pastime of a few hundred to the passion of 47 million Americans.[3] For many people, birding proved to be but the first step in the development of environmental consciousness.

Every ornithologist I know would give his soul to step back into time and walk the [North American] continent in the historic year of 1492. It was all virgin country then, with trees centuries old and the native grass waist high on the prairies. The broad distributional concepts—the life zones or the biomes—probably would have been much more satisfactory in those days when most environments were in relatively stable "climaxes," as the old mature plant associations are called. But that was before man set in motion the constant chain of changes that take place wherever he goes. For civilized man is the great disturber. Some would call him a destroyer, but that I think is a harsh term. Certainly he brings change.

* * *

Let us look briefly at the score sheet and see which way our birds are going.

Most of the waterfowl and the native upland game birds are below par. There has been some restoration in places, but there were many more of them in primitive America. Even twentieth-century America could support more than it does. Hunting often exacts a greater toll than the traffic will bear.

Today all marsh birds, not waterfowl alone, are in the red. The records show that close to 100,000,000 acres of land have been drained in the United States for agriculture alone. Other millions of acres have been ditched to control mosquitoes. Considering that a marsh or swamp habitat harbors nine or ten nesting birds per acre and most farming country an average of fewer than three, this means that at least half a billion birds may have been eliminated from the face of the continent by the simple process of digging ditches.

The birds of prey—the hawks and the owls—are much reduced. . . . [T]he gunner often blamed the growing scarcity of game not on himself but on the natural predators, which had lived in satisfactory adjustment to their prey for thousands of years. He called all hawks "vermin," competitors to be shot and destroyed. And the skies over most of America today are still not empty enough of hawks to satisfy him.

The vultures, on the other hand, seem to be spreading.

Source: Roger Tory Peterson, *Birds over America* (New York: Dodd, Mead, 1948), pp. 71-73.

DOCUMENT 87: Fairfield Osborn on the Interrelatedness of All Living Things (1948)

Fairfield Osborn, who founded the Conservation Foundation in 1947 to raise public consciousness about ecological problems, contended that the idea that humans could replace the fundamental functioning of natural systems was a dangerous illusion. He warned of a "silent spring" more than a dozen years before Rachel Carson wrote her popular book Silent Spring *[see Document 100].*

There is no risk in making the flat statement that in a world devoid of other living creatures, man himself would die. This fact—call it a theory if you will—is far more provable than the accepted theory of relativity. Involved in it is, in truth, another kind of principle of relativity—the relatedness of all living things.

As a somewhat extreme illustration, among many others, take that form of life that man likes the least—of which the unthinking person would at once say, "Kill them all." Insects. Of the extraordinary number of kinds of insects on the earth—about three quarters of a million different species have already been identified—a small minority are harmful to man, such as the anopheles mosquito, lice, the tsetse fly, and crop-destroying insects. On the other hand, innumerable kinds are beneficent and useful. Fruit trees and many crops are dependent upon insect life for pollination or fertilization; soils are cultured and gain their productive qualities largely because of insect life. Human subsistence would, in fact, be imperiled were there no insects. On the other hand, insects, capable of incredibly rapid reproduction, have been freed by man himself of many natural controls such as those once provided by birds, now so diminished in numbers, or by fish, once a potent factor in insect control, no longer existing in countless lakes, rivers and streams now so polluted that aquatic life has disappeared. In attempting to find substitutes for natural controls man has resorted to the use of chemicals of increasing power. A few years ago arsenicals came into style—widely used in freeing fruit orchards of pests. So promising this method has seemed—but insidiously it sometimes results in destroying insect-eating birds; and after several seasons the ground itself, in many orchards, has become so impregnated with the poison that the trees are affected and their fruit-bearing capacity dwindles. More recently a powerful chemical known as D.D.T. seems the cure-all. Some of the initial experiments with this insect killer have been withering to bird life as a result of birds eating the insects that have been impregnated with the chemical. The careless use of D.D.T. can also result in destroying fishes, frogs and toads, all of which live on insects. This new chemical is deadly to many kinds of insects—no doubt of that. But what of the ultimate and net result to the life scheme of the earth? On another front man is blindly in conflict with nature, too often overlooking the fact that the animal life of the earth, its interrelationships, its preservation, are wrapped up directly with his own well-being. Will the day come when this is generally realized?

Source: Fairfield Osborn, *Our Plundered Planet* (Boston: Little, Brown, 1948), pp. 60-62.

DOCUMENT 88: Aldo Leopold's Land Ethic (1949)

Beginning his professional career as a U.S. forester in the Southwest, Aldo Leopold helped develop a national forest policy that included setting aside forested lands as permanently protected areas. After moving to Wisconsin, he became involved with wildlife management. Initially accepting the conventional wisdom of the period, Leopold considered predator control to be the primary object of his work. Eventually, though, he came to see good game management as a much more complex problem and became a champion of the concept of ecology. In A Sand County Almanac, *from which the following selection is taken, Leopold provides us not only with a better understanding of the interrelatedness of all living things, but also with a new set of rules, a new ethic, to govern human behavior toward the environment.*

The first ethics dealt with the relation between individuals; the Mosaic Decalogue is an example. Later accretions dealt with the relation between the individual and society. The Golden Rule tries to integrate the individual to society; democracy to integrate social organization to the individual.

There is as yet no ethic dealing with man's relation to land and to the animals and plants which grow upon it. Land, like Odysseus' slave-girls, is still property. The land-relation is still strictly economic, entailing privileges but not obligations.

The extension of ethics to this third element in human environment is, if I read the evidence correctly, an evolutionary possibility and an ecological necessity. It is the third step in a sequence. The first two have already been taken. Individual thinkers since the days of Ezekiel and Isaiah have asserted that the despoliation of land is not only inexpedient but wrong. Society, however, has not yet affirmed their belief. I regard the present conservation movement as the embryo of such an affirmation.

An ethic may be regarded as a mode of guidance for meeting ecological situations so new or intricate, or involving such deferred reactions, that the path of social expediency is not discernible to the average individual. Animal instincts are modes of guidance for the individual in meeting such situations. Ethics are possibly a kind of community instinct in-the-making.

All ethics so far evolved rest upon a single premise: that the individual is a member of a community of interdependent parts. His instincts prompt him to compete for his place in that community, but his ethics prompt him also to co-operate (perhaps in order that there may be a place to compete for).

The land ethic simply enlarges the boundaries of the community to include soils, waters, plants, and animals, or collectively: the land.

This sounds simple: do we not already sing our love for and obligation to the land of the free and the home of the brave? Yes, but just what and whom do we love? Certainly not the soil, which we are sending helter-skelter downriver. Certainly not the waters, which we assume have no function except to turn turbines, float barges, and carry off sewage. Certainly not the plants, of which we exterminate whole communities without batting an eye. Certainly not the animals, of which we have already extirpated many of the largest and most beautiful species. A land ethic of course cannot prevent the alteration, management, and use of these "resources," but it does affirm their right to continued existence, and, at least in spots, their continued existence in a natural state.

In short, a land ethic changes the role of *Homo sapiens* from conqueror of the land-community to plain member and citizen of it. It implies respect for his fellow-members, and also respect for the community as such.

Source: Aldo Leopold, *Sand County Almanac* (New York: Oxford University Press, 1949), pp. 201-4.

DOCUMENT 89: Harry Truman's Materials Policy Commission on Economic Growth and Resource Policy (1952)

In recommending economic growth as the highest priority in the making of U.S. resource policy, despite the recognition of limitations on the availability of resources, President Harry Truman's Materials Policy Commission revealed an unwillingness to upset the status quo. The report provoked the indignation of both conservationists and economists [see Documents 90 and 95]. One of the outgrowths of this consternation was the formation in 1955 of Resources for the Future, a nonprofit think tank that studies environmental and natural resource economics.[4]

A hundred years ago, resources seemed limitless and the struggle upward from meager conditions of life was the struggle to create the means and methods of getting these materials into use. In this struggle we have succeeded so well that today, in thinking of expansion programs, full employment, new plants, or the design of a radical new turbine blade, too many of us blankly forget to look back to the mine, the land, the forest: the sources upon which we absolutely depend. So well have we built our high-output factories, so efficiently have we opened the lines of distribution to our remotest consumers that our sources are weakening under the constantly increasing strain of demand. As a Nation, we have always been more interested in sawmills than seedlings. We have put much more engineering thought into the layout of factories to cut up metals than into mining processes to produce them. We think about materials resources last, not first.

* * *

The actions we as a Nation take or fail to take in meeting the materials problems in the period immediately ahead will affect profoundly the state of affairs many years hence. Upon our own generation lies the responsibility for passing on to the next generation the prospects of continued well-being.

* * *

[The members of the President's Materials Policy Commission] share the belief of the American people in the principle of Growth. Granting that we cannot find any absolute reason for this belief we admit that to our Western minds it seems preferable to any opposite, which to us implies stagnation and decay. Where there may be any unbreakable upper limits to the continuing growth of our economy we do not pretend to know, but it must be part of our task to examine such apparent limits as present themselves.

. . . [W]e believe in private enterprise as the most efficacious way of performing industrial tasks in the United States. With this belief, a belief in the spur of the profit motive and what is called "the price system" obviously goes hand in hand.

* * *

The over-all objective of a national materials policy for the United States should be to insure an adequate and dependable flow of materials at the lowest cost consistent with national security and with the welfare of friendly nations.

* * *

As a Nation we have long lived and prospered mightily without serious concern for our material resources. Our sensational progress in production and consumption has been attributable not only to the freedom of our institutions and the enterprise of our people, but also to our spendthrift use of our rich heritage of natural resources. We have become the supreme advocates of the idea that man and his labor are the most valuable of all, and that inanimate materials are to be used as fully as possible to give men the greatest amount of return for the effort they put forth.

This still is and should be our goal, but the time has clearly passed when we can afford the luxury of viewing our resources as unlimited and hence taking them for granted. In the United States the supplies of the evident, the cheap, and the accessible (chemically and geologically) are running out. The plain fact seems to be that we have skimmed the cream of our resources as we now understand them; there must not be, at this decisive point in history, too long a pause before our understanding catches up with our needs. . . .

Growth of demand is at the core of the materials problem we face; it is the probability of continued growth, even more than the incursions of past growth and two world wars, that present us now with our long-range problems. It is mainly our unwillingness to stand still, to accept the status of a "mature economy," that challenges the adequacy of our resources.

Source: President's Materials Policy Commission, *Resources for Freedom*, Vol. 1: *Foundations for Growth and Security* (Washington, D.C.: President's Material's Policy Commission, June 1952), pp. 1, 2, 3, 5.

DOCUMENT 90: Samuel H. Ordway, Jr., on Limits to Growth (1953)

Samuel Ordway, a lawyer and proactive member of the boards of several conservation organizations, including the Conservation Foundation, the Natural Resources Council of America, and the American Conservation Association, was one of the first environmental analysts to discuss limits to industrial growth. In the 1970s, Ordway's ideas on growth limitation were expanded on by a number of economists such as Donella Meadows, who asserted that, if civilization is to survive, limits must be placed on industrial investment as well as population growth.[5] By the 1980s the concept of limits to industrial growth had become part of the basic philosophy of such radical environmentalists as Mark Sagoff [see Document 125] and Arne Naess [see Document 129].

The end of expansion, if unexpected and involuntary, would mean the reversal of a major facet of our faith; it would impose a forced revision of ideology; it would mean mass discouragement and unemployment—it could mean revolution and dictatorship. It would not mean a return to pioneering—for there is no new land to pioneer. It would not mean a return from the city to the farm. There are too many people, trained in too many white and blue collar skills, to support themselves in the future by farming individually our remaining productive land. It might even force displaced segments of the American people to set to work clearing needed land of unused factories, roads, and airports and concentrate all our resources on restoring that land to productivity. It is difficult to believe that any such adjustment would be possible without conscription, work relief, and substantial loss of freedom and independence.

The industrial pattern of today has brought us health, wealth and leisure in unprecedented degree. It has made us reliant on machines and government—less reliant on ourselves. Success has led us to believe that the earth is a cornucopia, and the machine a god. It has led us to a false faith in man's omnipotence.

Malthus [*see Document 26*], were he living today, would have to modify his contention that it is [the] increasing number of mouths to feed that will exhaust the earth's food supplies and cause ultimate misery. He would probably say now, in the light of experience, that if the total of popular and industrial consumption of the produce of the earth exceeds reproduction over a long enough period, misery will be inevitable.

Our problem today is to be sure that in the long run we limit consumption to continuing supply. This can be done on a voluntary basis if we begin soon enough to distinguish needs from wants. Indeed, consumption can well continue to increase as the margin of supply increases. It is fundamental, however, that the continued betterment of man's level of living will depend on adjusting supply and demand. That is the new concept of conservation. Consumption cannot run beyond supply for long.

How to limit consumption to supply and maintain free enterprise is a matter of land-use planning, distribution of raw materials and rationing by industry, government and technology cooperating.

Source: Samuel H. Ordway, Jr., *Resources and the American Dream: Including a Theory of the Limit of Growth* (New York: Ronald Press, 1953), pp. 46-48.

DOCUMENT 91: J. Robert Oppenheimer on the Use of Science (1953)

J. Robert Oppenheimer, one of the early advocates of international control of atomic energy, led the Manhattan Project that developed the atomic bomb in 1945. In the late 1940s, however, when President Harry Truman wanted to develop a hydrogen bomb, Oppenheimer objected, and as a result of this opposition, Oppenhimer lost his security clearance during the McCarthy era.

Three hundred years after Francis Bacon had looked to science and technology to solve humanity's problems [see Document 8], Oppenheimer recognized that technology could be a force for evil as well as for good. This change in attitude toward science and technology reflected a growing awareness that humans cannot control nature and that some of our attempts to harness the forces of nature may prove disastrous in the long run.

We are today anxiously aware that the power to change is not always necessarily good.

As new instruments of war, of newly massive terror, add to the ferocity and totality of warfare, we understand that it is a special mark and problem of our age that man's ever-present preoccupation with improving his lot, with alleviating hunger and poverty and exploitation, must be brought into harmony with the overriding need to limit and largely to eliminate resort to organized violence between nation and nation. The increasingly expert destruction of man's spirit by the power of police, more wicked if not more awful than the ravages of nature's own hand, is another such power, good only if never to be used.

We regard it as proper and just that the patronage of science by society is in large measure based on the increased power which knowledge gives. If we are anxious that the power so given and so obtained be used with wisdom and with love of humanity, that is an anxiety we share with almost everyone. But we also know how little of the deep new knowledge which has altered the face of the world, which has changed—and increasingly and ever more profoundly must change—man's views of the world, resulted from a quest for practical ends or an interest in exercising the power that knowledge gives. For most of us, in most of those moments when we were free of corruption, it has been the beauty of the world of nature and the strange and compelling harmonies of its order, that has sustained, inspirited, and led us.

Source: J. Robert Oppenheimer, "The Sciences and Man's Community," in *Science and the Common Understanding* (New York: Simon and Schuster, 1954), pp. 97-98.

DOCUMENT 92: Bernard Frank on Land Development and Water Availability (1955)

Americans have often considered water—whether for drinking, for industry, or for farm use—as an unlimited resource owed to us, almost as a constitutional right. Bernard Frank, who worked in the Watershed Management Research Division of the Forest Service, warns that we must give greater attention to water resource limitations.

The impact of new inventions and new developments and growth in population and industry has not commonly been given the attention it has merited.

Many critical local water shortages therefore occurred that could have been forestalled. For example, rural electrification has brought about such heavy increases in the use of water for household and production purposes that the limited well-water supplies of many farms have been severely strained.

Similarly, factories have been built without prior studies to determine whether water would be available to operate the factories and to provide for the communities around them.

Towns, cities, industries, and farms have kept expanding beyond the safe limits of available water. Often makeshift efforts have been necessary to meet emergencies, especially in years of low rainfall. Such efforts have often hastened the depletion of the limited reserves in underground reservoirs, generated disputes with other cities or industries drawing on the same sources of water, introduced conflicts with the use of water for recreation, and threatened the permanent flooding of lands valuable for farming, forestry, wilderness, or wildlife.

Use continues to rise; advancing standards of health and comfort, the application of more intensive farming practices, and the development of new products all impose demands.

Source: Bernard Frank, "Our Need for Water," in *Water: Agricultural Yearbook of 1955* (Washington, D.C.: U.S. Department of Agriculture, 1955), pp. 4-5.

DOCUMENT 93: Clean Air Act (1955)

Air pollution and air quality have been a problem in the Western world since the beginning of the Industrial Revolution, and Americans have been concerned about these issues since the mid-nineteenth century [see Documents 41 and 67]. Until 1955, however, responsibility for clean air in the United States rested with states and local communities, which frequently ignored the problem. In 1955, the federal government, having recognized that the smoke produced in the Midwest moved with the air as it flowed from west to east, ultimately causing pollution problems in the East, took its first, tentative steps to encourage a nationwide advance toward clean air by funding state and local air pollution prevention and control programs.

A. Congressional Findings and Declaration of Purpose

The Congress finds—

(1) that the predominant part of the Nation's population is located in its rapidly expanding metropolitan and other urban areas, which generally cross the boundary lines of local jurisdictions and often extend into two or more States;

(2) that the growth in the amount and complexity of air pollution brought about by urbanization, industrial development, and the increasing use of motor vehicles, has resulted in mounting dangers to the public health and welfare, including injury to agricultural crops and livestock, damage to and the deterioration of property, and hazards to air and ground transportation;

(3) that air pollution prevention (that is, the reduction or elimination, through any measures, of the amount of pollutants produced or created at the source) and air pollution control at its source is the primary responsibility of States and local governments; and

(4) that Federal financial assistance and leadership is essential for the development of cooperative Federal, State, regional, and local programs to prevent and control air pollution.

The purposes of this Act are—

(1) to protect and enhance the quality of the Nation's air resources so as to promote the public health and welfare and the productive capacity of its population;

(2) to initiate and accelerate a national research and development program to achieve the prevention and control of air pollution;

(3) to provide technical and financial assistance to State and local governments in connection with the development and execution of their air pollution prevention and control programs; and

(4) to encourage and assist the development and operation of regional air pollution prevention and control programs.

B. The Act

Be it enacted . . . That . . . it is hereby declared to be the policy of Congress to preserve and protect the primary responsibilities and rights of the States and local governments in controlling air pollution, to support and aid technical research to devise and develop methods of abating such pollution, and to provide Federal technical services and financial aid to State and local government air pollution control agencies and other public or private agencies and institutions in the formulation and execution of their air pollution abatement research programs. To this end, the Secretary of Health, Education, and Welfare and the Surgeon General of the Public Health Service (under the supervision and direction of the Secretary of Health, Education, and Welfare) shall have the authority relating to air pollution control vested in them respectively by this Act.

SEC. 2. (a) The Surgeon General is authorized, after careful investigation and in cooperation with other Federal agencies, with State and local government air pollution control agencies, with other public and private agencies and institutions, and with the industries involved, to prepare or recommend research programs for devising and developing methods for eliminating or reducing air pollution. For the purpose of this subsection the Surgeon General is authorized to make joint investigations with any such agencies or institutions.

(b) The Surgeon General may (1) encourage cooperative activities by State and local governments for the prevention and abatement of air pollution; (2) collect and disseminate information relating to air pollution and the prevention and abatement thereof; (3) conduct in the Public Health Service, and support and aid the conduct by State and local government air pollution control agencies, and other public and private agencies and institutions of, technical research to devise and develop methods of preventing and abating air pollution; and (4) make available to State and local government air pollution control agencies, other public and private agencies and institutions, and industries, the results of surveys, studies, investigations, research, and experiments relating to air pollution and the prevention and abatement thereof.

SEC. 3. The Surgeon General may, upon request of any State or local government air pollution control agency, conduct investigations and research and make surveys concerning any specific problem of air pollution confronting such State or local government air pollution control agency with a view to recommending a solution of such problem.

SEC. 4. The Surgeon General shall prepare and publish from time to time reports of such surveys, studies, investigations, research, and experiments. . . .

Sec 5. (a) There is hereby authorized to be appropriated to the Department of Health, Education, and Welfare for each of the five fiscal years during the period beginning July 1, 1955, and ending June 30, 1960, not to exceed $5,000,000 to enable it to carry out its functions under this Act and, in furtherance of the policy declared in the first section of this Act, to (1) make grants-in-aid to State and local government air pollution control agencies, and other public and private agencies and institutions, and to individual, for research, training, and demonstration projects, and (2) enter into contracts with public and private agencies and institutions and individuals for research, training, and demonstration projects.

Source: **A.** *United States Annotated Code,* Title 42: *The Public Health and Welfare* (St. Paul, MN: West Publishing, 1995), SS7401, July 14, 1955, pp. 27-28. **B.** Public Law 159, *United States Statutes at Large,* Vol. 69 (Washington, D.C.: Government Printing Office, 1955), 84th Cong. 1st sess. chap. 360, July 14, 1955, pp. 322-23.

DOCUMENT 94: M. King Hubbert on Fossil Fuels and Nuclear Energy (1956)

At about the same time that the federal government was assessing the extent of U.S. natural resources [see Document 89], M. King Hubbert, a Shell oil geologist, was studying the known fossil fuel fields in the United States and elsewhere. Although his predictions that U.S. oil production would peak at the beginning of the 1970s, if not sooner, and that world production would peak in the early twenty-first century were initially pooh-poohed by many, by the 1990s, the overall accuracy of his predictions about U.S. oil production were widely accepted, and his methods for determining the production peak of mined resources were being used to develop up-to-date estimates of world oil supplies.[6] Then, in the first decade of the twenty-first century, the drilling technique known as hydraulic fracturing (fracking) began to be used, and previously inaccessible deposits of oil and gas, whose presence Hubbert acknowledged, became available, disrupting half a century of concern about the impending effect of oil depletion on national security and domestic well-being.

Hubbert expected that nuclear energy would eventually replace fossil fuels, but he viewed oil as an essential resource for the near future.

In the present review an attempt has been made to obtain an approximate idea of the world situation with respect to the requirements and supply of fossil fuels, and of whether nuclear energy from uranium and thorium will be able to replace that from the fossil fuels as the latter approach their inevitable exhaustion The initial supply of fossil fuels, reduced to a common unit of energy, consisted of about 70 percent coal, 14 percent petroleum and natural gas, and about 16 percent oil shale and tar sands. Should the world continue to be dependent upon its fossil fuels for its energy requirements, the peak of coal production would probably be reached with the next 200 years, and that of oil in about 50 years.

Of these initial fuel reserves, the United States had about a third of the world's coal, and about half of its oil shale, but only about an eighth of the initial supply of oil. Of this last, one third has already been consumed. The reserves of coal and oil shale in the United States are sufficient for a few centuries, but the production peaks for both oil and gas will probably occur in the comparatively near future. With regard to uranium and thorium, the heat obtainable from 1 gram of either of these elements, by means of the breeder reaction, is equal to the heat of combustion of 3 tons of coal, or 13 bbl [barrels] of petroleum. The uranium equivalent of all the fossil fuels in the United States is only about a third of a million tons. The so-called high-grade ores of the Colorado Plateau will yield possibly 100,000 tons of uranium, but the large reserves are contained in the low-grade deposits of phosphate rocks and black shales which contain several hundred million tons of uranium. The energy content of these low-grade deposits, occurring at a concentration equivalent to 250 tons of coal, or 1,000 bbl of oil per ton of rock, amounts to several hundred times that of all the fossil fuels combined. It appears, therefore, provided we can refrain from destroying ourselves with nuclear weapons, and provided also that the growth of the human population (which is now doubling in less than a century) can somehow be controlled, that the world at last has discovered a source of energy adequate for its needs for at least the next few centuries of the "foreseeable future."

* * *

[T]here is shown in Figure 21 a graph of the production [of crude oil in the United States] up to the present, and two extrapolations into the future. The unit rectangle in this case represents 25 billion barrels so that if the ultimate potential production is 150 billion barrels, then the graph can encompass but six rectangles before returning to zero. Since the cumulative production is already a little more than 50 billion barrels, then only four more rectangles are available for future production. Also, since the production rate is still increasing, the ultimate production peak must be greater than the present rate of production and must occur sometime in the future. At the same time it is impossible to delay the peak for more than a few years and still allow time for

the unavoidable prolonged period of decline due to the slowing rates of extraction from depleting reservoirs.

With due regard for these considerations, it is almost impossible to draw the production curve based upon an assumed ultimate production of 150 billion barrels in any manner differing significantly from that shown in Figure 21, according to which the curve must culminate at about 1965 and then must decline at a rate comparable to its earlier rate of growth.

If we suppose the figure of 150 billion barrels to be 50 billion barrels too low—an amount equal to eight East Texas oil fields—then the ultimate potential reserve would be 200 billion barrels. The second of the two extrapolations shown in Figure 21 is based upon this assumption; but it is interesting to note that even then the date of culmination is retarded only until about 1970.

One other contingency merits comment. By means of present production techniques, only about a third of the oil underground is being recovered. The reserve figures cited are for oil capable of being extracted by present techniques. However, secondary recovery techniques are gradually being improved so that ultimately a somewhat larger but still unknown fraction of the oil underground should be extracted than is now the case. Because of the slowness of the secondary recovery process, however, it appears unlikely that any improvement that can be made within the next

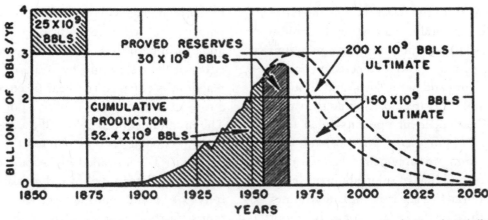

Figure 21 – Ultimate United States crude-oil production based on assumed initial reserves of 150 and 200 billion barrels.

10 or 15 years can have any significant effect upon the date of culmination. A more probable effect of improved recovery will be to reduce the rate of decline after the culmination with respect to the rates shown in Figure 21.

. . .

The Outlook for Fossil Fuels

From this inventory of the energy supplies represented by the fossil fuels, it appears that about three-quarters of the reserves of the fossil fuels of the world are represented by coal and the remaining one-quarter is equally divided between liquid and gaseous hydrocarbons, and oil shales and tar sands. Production of the world's coal has already consumed about 3.7 percent of the minable reserves initially present, that of oil and gas about 7 percent, while the production from shale and tar sands has barely been started.

However, because of the versatility and usefulness of the liquid and gaseous hydrocarbons, and also because of their relative ease of extraction, the rate of exploitation of the latter has increased disproportionately to their magnitude as compared with coal.

. . . On the basis of the present estimates of the ultimate reserves of petroleum and natural gas, it appears that . . . the culmination for petroleum and natural gas in both the United States and the state of Texas should occur within the next few decades.

This does not necessarily imply that the United States or other parts of the industrial world will soon become destitute of liquid and gaseous fuels, because these can be produced from other fossil fuels which occur in much greater abundance. But it does pose as a national problem of primary importance, the necessity, both with regard to requirements for domestic purposes and those for national defense, of gradually having to compensate for an increasing disparity between the nation's demands for these fuels and its ability to produce them from naturally occurring accumulations of petroleum and natural gas.

Source: M. King Hubbert, "Nuclear Energy and the Fossil Fuels," in American Petroleum Institute Drilling and Petroleum Practice, *Proceedings of the Spring Meeting,* San Antonio, TX, 1956, abstract, p. 7, and Shell Development Company Publication No. 95 (Houston, TX: Shell Development Company, Exploration and Production Research Division, 1956), pp. 23-24, 26-27

DOCUMENT 95: John Kenneth Galbraith Asks, "How Much Should a Country Consume?" (1958)

A professor of economics at Harvard who worked in the State Department Office of Economic Security Policy in the 1940s and served as ambassador to India during the Kennedy administration, John Kenneth Galbraith here lays out the dilemma confronting the United States in its attempt to be both a consumer society and a sustainable society.

What should be our policy toward consumption?

First, of course, we should begin to talk about it—and in the context of all its implications. It is silly for grown men to concern themselves mightily with supplying an appetite and close their eyes to the obvious and obtrusive question of whether the appetite is excessive.

If the appetite presents no problems—if resource discovery and the technology of use and substitution promise automatically to remain abreast of consumption and at moderate cost—then we need press matters no further. At least on conservation grounds there is no need to curb our appetite.

But to say this, and assuming that it applies comprehensively to both renewable and nonrenewable resources, is to say that there is no materials problem. It is to say that, except for some activities that by definition are noncritical, the conservationists are not much needed.

But if conservation is an issue, then we have no honest and logical course but to measure the means for restraining use against the means for insuring a continuing sufficiency of supply and taking the appropriate action. There is no justification for ruling consumption levels out of the calculation.

What would be the practical consequences of this calculation—taken honestly and without the frequent contemporary preoccupation not with solution but with plausible escape—I do not pretend to say. . . . I am impressed by the opportunities for resource substitution and by the contribution of technology in facilitating it. But the problem here is less one of theory than of technical calculation and projection.

* * *

[I]t would seem to me that any concern for materials use should be general. It should have as its aim the shifting of consumption patterns from those which have a high materials requirement to those which have a much lower requirement. The opportunities are considerable. Education, health services, sanitary services, good parks and playgrounds, orchestras, effective local government, a clean countryside, all have rather small materials requirements. I have elsewhere argued [in *The Affluent Society*] that the present tendency of our economy is to discriminate sharply against such production. A variety of forces, among them the massed pressures of modern merchandising, have forced an inordinate concentration of our consumption on what may loosely be termed consumer hardware. This distortion has been underwritten by economic attitudes which have made but slight accommodation to the transition of our world from one of privation to one of opulence. A rationalization of our present consumption patterns—a rationalization which would more accurately reflect free and unmanaged consumer choice—might also be an important step in materials conservation.

Source: John Kenneth Galbraith, "How Much Should a Country Consume?" in Henry Jarrett, ed., *Perspectives on Conservation: Essays on America's Natural Resources* (Baltimore: Johns Hopkins Press, 1958), pp. 98-99.

DOCUMENT 96: David Brower Demands Support for the Wilderness Act (1959)

David Brower, who was part of a group that reinvigorated the Sierra Club and moved it to the forefront of environmental activism, raised our sensitivity to the importance of wilderness for the health of our civilization. After leaving the Sierra Club in 1969, Brower founded Friends of the Earth and the Earth Island Institute.

The Wilderness Act was a great victory for the preservationist school of environmentalists, but by the time it was passed in 1964, the original text of the act had been changed in order to delay prohibitions on mining in wilderness areas. In the final version, the proposed wilderness council, which was to publish public reports on the status of the wilderness system, was also eliminated.

The most important source of the vital organic forms constituting the chain of life is the gene bank that exists in wilderness, where the life force has gone on since the beginning uninterrupted by man and his technology. For this reason alone, it is important that the remnants of wilderness which we still have on our public lands be preserved by the best methods our form of government can find. The proposed National Wilderness Preservation System (now before the Congress) provides an excellent route to that goal, and especially dynamic leadership in the Congress and the administration will be required during the next decade to achieve the goal of wilderness preservation which the system would make possible. There will be important subsidiary benefits to recreation, to watershed protection, and to the beauty of the land.

A growing economy will have availed us nothing if it extinguishes our all-important wilderness. A gross misunderstanding of wilderness, in which it is evaluated according to the number of hikers who get into it, has been fostered for the past several years, to the great detriment of all the future. There must be no more needless, careless losses. There is no substitute for wilderness. What we now have is all that we shall ever have.

Source: David Brower, "The Meaning of Wilderness to Science," in Brower, *For Earth's Sake* (Salt Lake City: Peregrine Smith, 1990), pp. 271-72.

Part VI

The Heyday of the Environmental Movement, 1960-1979

The generation that came of age in the 1960s was the first generation of Americans to grow up watching television and escaping from the summer heat in air-conditioned stores, offices, theaters, houses, and cars. It was a generation imbued with a sense of idealism, sparked by the short-lived Kennedy administration and Lyndon Johnson's dream of creating a "Great Society" without poverty or hunger. It was a generation inspired by the endless possibilities made visible by the dawn of the space age. It was also the first generation whose members had lived all their lives with the possibility of nuclear war looming over them like a dark cloud.

The sixties generation was predominantly urban and suburban (the 1960 U.S. population of 180 million was 70 percent urban) and the product of an era of affluence and consumerism. It questioned not only its parents' wholehearted faith in technology and industrialization, but also their attitudes toward other human beings and other living things. Economically secure yet dissatisfied with the status quo, these youthful rebels launched a massive push for social change that took a variety of forms, ranging from the civil rights movement, the anti-Vietnam War protests, and the large counterculture movement of the 1960s to the environmental movement that reached a peak in the 1970s.

The launching of *Sputnik* in 1957, the first manned space flight in 1961, and the first walk on the moon in 1969 provided the world with a whole new perspective on the place of the earth and humans in the universe. Commercial air travel had become commonplace in the 1950s, but by the early 1960s, jets were replacing propeller planes on long-distance routes and changing relationships among people and businesses throughout the world. Computers were just starting to have an effect on the workplace, biotechnology was barely in the gestational stage, and the promises of science and technology had captured the public's imagination and loosened the government's purse strings.

Industrial and agricultural production was at an all-time high. Between 1950 and 1970, the increase in the production of goods and services matched the increase that had occurred between 1620, when the Pilgrims landed, and 1950.[1] The downside of this tremendous growth spurt was an enormous demand for energy and the subsequent increase in oil imports, the consumption of huge quantities of natural resources, and widespread industrial pollution. By the 1970s, concern about the negative impacts of this growth had pushed environmental issues high on the national agenda.

The Environmental Movement

Although for decades writers had expounded on the problems of dwindling resources and increasing pollution, they had left the general population unmoved and, in fact, uneducated. Then, in 1962, Rachel Carson, who had a substantial following from her works about the sea, produced *Silent Spring* [*see* Document 100] and raised public consciousness about environmental degradation. The core message of Carson, Murray Bookchin [*see* Document 99], Paul Ehrlich [*see* Document 107], and other writers in them 1960s—that there is a connection between societal progress and environmental degradation, that human well-being is dependent on the well-being of the natural world, that the use of modern technology and chemicals may have serious negative as well as positive consequences, and that we as a nation cannot continue to destroy or consume our natural resources at an ever increasing rate—was not new. For the past century, knowledgeable Americans had been discussing these issues. However, by stating their ideas in unambiguous and frequently alarmist terms, Carson and other environmentalists were able to arouse a very receptive public to grassroots activism. As a legion of authors wrote elaborations on the silent spring theme, an environmental tsunami slowly built up into the modern environmental movement.

Whereas the conservation movement at the turn of the century was initiated by a wealthy intelligentsia concerned about the nation's future well-being, the new environmental movement was led and supported by ordinary people together with segments of the scientific community, who recognized pollution as a source of immediate danger to their own health and well-being. In addition to being worried about the long-term effects of pesticides like DDT, people were also anxious about the imminent possibility of nuclear war. Despite the signing of the Nuclear Test Ban Treaty in 1963 [*see* Document 102], ocean and underground nuclear testing by signatory nations and

other countries persisted into the 1970s and beyond (the last U.S. nuclear test was conducted in 1992), and the United States and the Soviet Union still have huge numbers of nuclear weapons. In the twenty-first century nuclear tests have been carried out by nations that did not have nuclear capability in 1963, including North Korea, India, and Pakistan, and some American hawks are calling for a resumption of testing by the United States.

Both the Union of Concerned Scientists (organized in 1969) and Greenpeace (founded in Canada in 1971, with an American branch organized the same year) were formed to confront the nuclear threat. As time passed, the two organizations broadened their focus from advocacy for nuclear weapon stockpile destruction and the monitoring of nuclear testing to the control of radioactive and other toxic waste and to efforts to protect the quality of the environment.

Although the concept of environmentalism had entered the federal government's vocabulary toward the end of the Eisenhower administration [*see* Document 97], it was not until Richard Nixon's presidency that the federal government committed itself to environmental action. Nixon devoted a large part of his first State of the Union Address, in January 1970, to the need for an effective, and costly, environmental program [*see* Document 112A]. The impact of the environmental wave became evident in 1970, with Nixon's signing of the National Environmental Policy Act (NEPA) [*see* Document 111] and the first Earth Day celebration. Earth Day, April 22, 1970, marked a high point in popular concern about environment issues and the beginning of a populist push for government regulation of activities and products that had a negative effect on the environment, and it served as a catalyst for a decade of environmental action on the local, national, and international levels. NEPA, probably the most far-reaching piece of federal environmental legislation ever enacted, opened the way for Nixon's creation of the Environmental Protection Agency (EPA), which became the backbone of federal environmental action. During the next decade, strong environmental legislation was passed at every level of government. There were acts to ensure clean air [*see* Document 113] and clean water [*see* Document 116], to protect wetlands, scenic areas, wildlife habitats, forests, marine mammals, endangered species [*see* Document 120], and human health, and to control the effects of agricultural chemicals and radioactive and other toxic wastes. In 1972 Oregon passed the first state bottle recycling law, marking the beginning of a nationwide effort to deal with the accumulating mounds of trash resulting from the mass distribution of packaged consumer goods and foods (including bottled soda, canned foods and drinks, and boxed cereals, whose availability had multiplied exponentially since the beginning of the century) and from the superabundance of printed matter (including newspapers, magazines, and tons of advertising matter).

Meanwhile, new environmental groups were forming and old conservation organizations, such as the Sierra Club, were refocusing and gaining new strength. Two of the most effective new organizations—the Natural Resources Defense Council and the Environmental Defense Fund [*see* Document 114]—took shape to support the causes of environmentalists in the courts. Both were outgrowths of local environmental groups with a much narrower mandate.

The post-Carson generation of writers sought to do more than just promote the enactment of more effective environmental legislation. They wanted to change human attitudes as well as human behavior. In 1972 Justice William O. Douglas [*see* Document 118B] attempted to institutionalize Christopher Stone's advocacy of the rights of nature [*see* Document 117]. Stone's view of the relationship between humans and nature was a rethinking of a concept that had been stated over the centuries in various ways by such diverse writers as St. Francis, Thoreau, Muir, and Osborn [*see* Documents 44, 47, and 87], and by Native Americans [*see* Document 80], but in the Western world this had clearly been a minority viewpoint. However, in the 1970s, for the first time, large numbers of people began to question the idea that humans had a right or even the ability to dominate nature. The time had come to reexamine some of the country's core religious and philosophical values [*see* Document 106].

People also began to be worried about the destabilization of ecosystems that had attained a balance over the course of thousands of years [*see* Documents 98, 109, and 115]. Increasingly, they recognized that whenever someone or something upset this balance, there would be unforeseen and unpredictable consequences as the natural world reacted to the imbalance. Economic considerations alone were no longer sufficient justification for upsetting the balance [*see* Document 103].

The country's land development policies, to which there had been vocal opposition since the 1870s [*see* Document 53], were increasingly attacked as a major cause of ecosystem destabilization. In the mid-1960s, as suburbs, shopping malls, and multilane highways spread across the country, concern mounted that too much open space was being paved over and that much of the construction was being done without any consideration for its impact on the environment. By 1965 California had passed a farmland conservation bill [*see* Document 104], and by 1970 the environment impact statement [*see* Documents 110 and 111] had become part of the approval process for all new projects involving the federal government that might affect environmental quality.

The Beginning of Global Environmental Concern

In the 1960s and 1970s, demographers and economists were again debating the old Malthusian arguments concerning the rate of population growth and the ability of the earth to feed increasing numbers of people [*see* Documents 107 and 108]. However, these new discussions focused on the global nature of the problem and on how world population growth could undermine the social, economic, and political stability of the United States, as well as of other countries. Furthermore, it was also becoming obvious that people in Third World countries wanted to emulate the lifestyle depicted in American movies and television programs—a lifestyle based on high energy use and high material consumption.

The calling of the United Nations Conference on the Human Environment and the organization of the United Nations Environmental Programme (UNEP) in 1972 marked the beginning of a truly global approach to complex environmental issues [*see* Document 119].

The Search for New Solutions

The inflation and unemployment that affected the country in the mid-1970s was sparked in part by the Organization of Petroleum Exporting Countries' (OPEC) oil embargo in 1973. The war in Vietnam had come to an end and so had the era of protest.

Although the oil crisis had brought home to millions of Americans the dangers of dependence on imported oil and had created interest in smaller cars and energy-saving technologies—President Jimmy Carter even had solar panels placed on the White House roof—the popular environmental focus was shifting from utopian solutions [see Document 121] to economically viable approaches that would enable Americans to maintain their way of life. While the general public was turning away from the idealists and from doomsayers such as Paul Ehrlich [see Document 107], some of the more radical environmental groups were borrowing from the tactics of the protest movements of the 1960s to develop new tactics, ranging from civil disobedience to sabotage, to promote their political, ethical, and philosophical views and to effect changes in environmental policies [see Documents 122 and 123].

DOCUMENT 97: The Surgeon General's Report on Environmental Health (1960)

By the end of the 1950s the effect on people's health and well-being of the post-World War II expansion of urbanization, industrialization, and population size was obvious. In its April 1959 report on appropriations for fiscal year 1960, the House of Representatives' Committee on Appropriations noted that "environmental factors affecting health have become increasingly significant" and recommended that "the Public Health Service make a thorough study of the environmental health problems and the most efficient organization of our facilities to meet these needs." The Surgeon General's report on "Environmental Health" was produced in response to that request. It underscored "the multiplying and far-reaching effects of new and complex problems in the field of environmental heath, and the immediate need for their identification and control." Consequently, in the 1961 budget of the Department of Health, Education, and Welfare, "environmental health activities" appeared as a separate line item for the first time.

It is not being overdramatic to suggest that threats from our environment, actual and potential, cannot only generate wholly undesirable effects on the health and well-being of isolated individuals, but under certain circumstances could affect large segments of our population and conceivably threaten the very existence of our Nation.

* * *

[O]ver the past several decades significant and growing nonbiological health hazards in the environment have arisen. Our increased use of materials and products is attended by increasing quantities of potentially toxic substances in our environment of limited physical dimensions. The uses of energy, accompanied by mechanization of processes and services, produce additional hazards of noise, other physical forces, and accidents. The diverse and growing beneficial uses of nuclear energy, potentially of enormous benefit, are producing a whole new spectrum of hazards to health for present and succeeding generations.

While the biological health hazard normally assaults the individual in discrete and separate instances, the chemical and physical hazards come more often in intermittent or continuous doses, which reach him in a variety of ways. It is the total and cumulative exposure of the individual to ionizing radiations which is now recognized to be important, no matter how the separate components reach him. Of no less concern is the total exposure to chemical toxicants, portions of which reach the individual separately through air, water, and food.

Social factors in the environment are contributing to the newer environmental health hazards. Increasing urbanization, the growth and coalescence of large metropolitan complexes, and new patterns of living compound the sources of environmental hazards and concentrate the people affected by them. Reactions between hazards and people are thus multiplied, and controls, to be effective, must be correspondingly more efficient.

The magnitude of our newer environmental health hazards is expanding at more than a linear rate. Acceleration arises from both population growth and technological advance. One of the most significant new elements in man's economic thinking is that the rate of economic growth can be accelerated by planned research and development. Accordingly, our expenditures for industrial research and development have been expanding impressively over the past decade. By comparison, expansion in research activities on the attendant health hazards has been substantially less.

Growing public concern about air and water pollution, food additives, and toxic residues and radiation exposure has, in some cases, led to pressures or demands for control actions for which rational scientific and technological procedures do not now exist.

To a large extent, the programs and activities for dealing with recognized environmental health problems have been developed and carried out each somewhat independent of the other, in response to a specific urgency. . . . Too often the important interrelated biological and social implications have not been given adequate attention.

. . .A unifying concept is needed if the approach to specific problems is to be most effective.

* * *

New chemicals, many of them with toxic properties or capabilities, are being produced and marketed, and put into use at a rapid rate. These include plastics, plasticizers, additives to fuels and foods, pesticides, detergents, abrasives. It is estimated that 400-500 totally new chemicals are put into use each year. With many of these products, new waste byproducts are created which must be disposed of.

Although many commonly used chemicals are checked for toxicity, much is still unknown about their long-term potential hazards. The total dose of chemicals absorbed by man through numerous channels in minute and diluted amounts over his lifetime may be damaging his health.

* * *

Water and air, food and milk, solid wastes, insects and rodents, and shelter are among the channels through which man's health may be endangered. Controls directed at these vehicles may eliminate or reduce not only known hazards, but unknown or little understood ones as well.

* * *

Today, the modern supermarket and frozen food locker permit the use of a wide variety of foods, with resulting nutritional benefits. But modern methods of growing and processing foods introduce new hazards of pesticide spray residuals, preservatives and other food additives, and even contaminants related to packaging, which require attention for control.

Source: Surgeon General, "Environmental Health," Report to the House Committee on Appropriations (Washington, D.C.: Public Health Service, Department of Health, Education, and Welfare, January 1960), in *Departments of Labor and Health, Education, and Welfare Appropriations for 1961, Hearings before the Subcommittee on Appropriations,* House of Representatives, 86th Cong., 2nd sess. (Washington, D.C.: Government Printing Office, 1960), pp. 4-5, 6, 7-8, 9, 10.

DOCUMENT 98: Lorus J. Milne and Margery Milne on the Balance of Nature (1961)

The zoologists Lorus and Margery Milne were disturbed by largescale efforts to eliminate pestiferous animals, insects, and plants. They recognized that even nuisance species often prove useful and that their wholesale destruction would upset nature's precarious balance. The Milnes' review in the New York Times *of Rachel Carson's* Silent Spring *[see Document 100] helped to draw attention to another writer who was also concerned about the consequences of efforts to eliminate pests.*

Often we forget the contrast between man's one-crop fields and nature's endless variety. One crop is the ultimate in imbalance, and must be defended constantly. We overlook, too, how many animals do both good and bad to man. The prairie dog's taste for foliage conflicts with ou[r] interests, but its liking for grasshoppers is a help. Nor is it easy to realize how small an area is home to many native animals. If man removes as weeds all except his crop plants, creatures with no special liking for the economic vegetation may eat it rather than travel to remote supplies of more palatable kinds. Other animals are driven off, upsetting still more the complex balance of undisturbed prairie.

Perhaps we tend to overlook our natural allies through unfamiliarity with modern situations where a true balance can be found. One of these was discovered recently, not on a prairie but in California's avocado orchards. So perfect is biological control in this cropland that each year less than one per cent of the total avocado acreage needs pest-control treatment. Yet insect enemies are present, unnoticed although ready to attack. An experiment tried near San Diego proved how quickly they can respond to opportunity.

For a period of eighty-four days, entomologists removed by hand every helpful parasitic and predatory animal they could find in one portion of a single tree. Within this trial period, caterpillars of one kind multiplied so rapidly that, to save the leaves, it was necessary to destroy the insects one by one. Two other avocado enemies throve until it seemed that similar action might have to be taken against them. But all of this change occurred only in the experimental portion of the tree. Other branches of the same avocado and other trees in the same grove presented no pest problem. Man's natural allies there continued their efficient control—at no cost to the growers.

On prairie ranch land, a balance can be reached if livestock are managed carefully. Prairie dogs cease to be a menace if a good cover of grass is present—neither too much nor too little. Too much grass is a sign of failure to utilize the land economically for cattle, although underuse of this kind can displace prairie dogs entirely. Too little grass leads to more prairie dogs, and often they are blamed unfairly for the barren ground produced by overgrazing by man's animals.

Fortunately, the ranchers are coming to understand the land they supervise. Some of them now recognize an obligation both to leave it in better condition than they found it, and to retain for the future the aesthetic values to be seen in native plants and animals. As this philosophy spreads, so too will a place for a few bison and prairie dogs. With the land once more in balance, man's own economy will also be in order.

Source: Lorus J. Milne and Margery Milne, *The Balance of Nature* (New York: Knopf, 1961), pp. 19-21.

DOCUMENT 99: Murray Bookchin on the
Synthetic Environment (1962)

Murray Bookchin was the author of numerous books on environmental and urban issues. Writing under the pen name Louis Herber, he warned that the use of technological innovations could have unanticipated consequences and create new and unexpected environmental problems, often more serious than the problems the technology was intended to solve. Bookchin's book Our Synthetic Environment, *published a few months earlier than Rachel Carson's* Silent Spring, *contained much the same message, but it failed to capture a wide audience.*

The problems of our synthetic environment can be summed up by saying that nonhuman interests are superseding many of our responsibilities to human biological welfare. To a large extent, man is no longer working for himself. Many fields of knowledge and many practical endeavors that were once oriented toward the satisfaction of basic human wants have become ends in themselves, and to an ever-greater degree these new ends are conflicting with the requirements for human health. The needs of industrial plants are being placed before man's need for clean air; the disposal of industrial wastes has gained priority over the community's need for clean water. The most pernicious laws of the market place are given precedence over the most compelling laws of biology.

* * *

The problems created by our conflict with nature are dramatically exemplified by our chemical war against the insect world. During the past two decades, a large number of insecticides have been developed for general use on farms and in the home. The best-known and most widely used preparations are the chlorinated hydrocarbons, such as DDT, methoxychlor, dieldrin, and chlordane. The chlorinated hydrocarbons are sprayed over vast acres of forest land, range land, crop land, and even semi-urban land on which there are heavy infestations of insects. . . . Aside from the hazards that insecticides create for public health, many conservationists claim that extensive use of the new insecticides is impairing the ability of wildlife and beneficial insects to exercise control over pests. They point out that the insecticides are taking a heavy toll of life among fish, birds, small mammals, and useful insects. There is a great deal of evidence that the new chemicals are self-defeating. Not only have they failed to eradicate most of the pests against which they are employed; in some cases, new pests and greater infestations have been created as a result of the damage inflicted on predators of species formerly under control.

Source: Lewis Herber, *Our Synthetic Environment* (New York: Knopf, 1962), pp. 26, 53-54.

DOCUMENT 100: Rachel Carson's *Silent Spring* (1962)

Rachel Carson, a marine biologist and author of three popular books about the sea (including The Sea Around Us, *which was on the bestseller list for eighty-six weeks), was probably the one individual most responsible for igniting public interest in pollution and other environmental issues.* Silent Spring, *which many consider the most important book about the environment written in the twentieth century, caught the attention and the emotions of large numbers of people in the United States and the rest of the world and alerted them to the dangers of man-made poisons in the environment. The publication of the book marked the beginning of popular concern about pollution and served as the starting point for the environmental movement.*

Carson became interested in the issue of pesticide spraying in the mid-1940s. A neo-Malthusian, she worried that the need for increased agricultural productivity—which would demand an increased use of pesticides—would lead to a catastrophe. She was concerned that the long-term use of synthetic pesticides could result in an accumulation of toxins in part of the food chain and in the elimination of useful insects. Carson never called for a complete ban on pesticides, but rather appealed for their responsible use.

There was once a town in the heart of America where all life seemed to live in harmony with its surroundings. The town lay in the midst of a checkerboard of prosperous farms, with fields of grain and hillsides of orchards where, in spring, white clouds of bloom drifted above the green fields. In autumn, oak and maple and birch set up a blaze of color that flamed and flickered across a backdrop of pines. Then foxes barked in the hills and deer silently crossed the fields, half hidden in the mists of the fall mornings.

Along the roads, laurel, viburnum and alder, great ferns and wildflowers delighted the traveler's eye through much of the year. Even in winter the roadsides were places of beauty, where countless birds came to feed on the berries and on the seed heads of the dried weeds rising above the snow. The countryside was, in fact, famous for the abundance and variety of its bird life, and when the flood of migrants was pouring through in spring and fall people traveled from great distances to observe them. Others came to fish the streams, which flowed clear and cold out of the hills and contained shady pools where trout lay. So it had been from the days many years ago when the first settlers raised their houses, sank their wells, and built their barns.

Then a strange blight crept over the area and everything began to change. Some evil spell had settled on the community: mysterious maladies swept the flocks of chickens; the cattle and sheep sickened and died. Everywhere was a shadow of death. The farmers spoke of much illness among their families. In the town the doctors had become more and more puzzled by new kinds of sickness appearing among their patients. There had been several sudden and unexplained deaths, not only among adults but even among children, who would be stricken suddenly while at play and die within a few hours.

There was a strange stillness. The birds, for example—where had they gone? Many people spoke of them, puzzled and disturbed. The feeding stations in the backyards were deserted. The few birds seen anywhere were moribund; they trembled violently and could not fly. It was a spring without voices. On the mornings that had once throbbed with the dawn chorus of robins, catbirds, doves, jays, wrens, and scores of other bird voices there was now no sound; only silence lay over the fields and woods and marsh.

* * *

As man proceeds toward his announced goal of the conquest of nature, he has written a depressing record of destruction, directed not only against the earth he inhabits but against the life that shares it with him. The history of the recent centuries has its black passages—the slaughter of the buffalo on the western plains, the massacre of the shore-birds by the market gunners, the near-extinction of the egrets for their plumage. Now, to these and others like them, we are adding a new chapter and a new kind of havoc—the direct killing of birds, mammals, fishes, and indeed practically every form of wildlife by chemical insecticides indiscriminately sprayed on the land.

* * *

The questions is whether any civilization can wage [such] relentless war on life without destroying itself, and without losing the right to be called civilized.

Source: Rachel Carson, *Silent Spring* (Boston: Houghton Mifflin, 1962), pp. 1-2, 85, 99.

DOCUMENT 101: Stewart L. Udall on the Land Ethic (1963)

Stewart Udall came onto the national scene as a congressman from Arizona and later served as secretary of the Interior in the Kennedy and Johnson administrations. In the mid-1970s, Udall worked valiantly to guide the Surface Mining Act (the strip-mining bill), which had twice been vetoed by President Gerald Ford, through the House of Representatives. The bill, finally passed in 1977, reclaimed several million acres of coal lands. In this selection he reminds readers of modern America's need for a land ethic like that proposed by Aldo Leopold in the 1940s [see Document 88].

Beyond all plans and programs, true conservation is ultimately something of the mind—an ideal of men who cherish their past and believe in their future. Our civilization will be measured by its fidelity to this ideal as surely as by its art and poetry and system of justice. In our perpetual search for abundance, beauty, and order we manifest both our love for the land and our sense of responsibility toward future generations.

Most Americans find it difficult to conceive a land ethic for tomorrow. The pastoral American of a century ago, whose conservation insights were undeveloped, has been succeeded by the asphalt American of the 1960's, who is shortsighted in other ways. Our sense of stewardship is uncertain partly because too many of us lack roots in the soil and the respect for resources that goes with such roots. Too many of us have mistaken material ease and comfort for the good life. Our growing dependence on machines has tended to mechanize our response to the world around us and has blunted our appreciation of the higher values.

* * *

One of the paradoxes of American society is that while our economic standard of living has become the envy of the world, our environmental standard has steadily declined. We are better housed, better nourished, and better entertained, but we are not better prepared to inherit the earth or to carry on the pursuit of happiness.

A century ago we were a land-conscious, outdoor people: the American face was weather-beaten, our skills were muscular, and each family drew sustenance directly from the land. Now marvelous machines make our lives easier, but we are falling prey to the weaknesses of an indoor nation and the flabbiness of a sedentary society.

A land ethic for tomorrow should be as honest as Thoreau's Walden, and as comprehensive as the sensitive science of ecology. It should stress the oneness of our resources and the live-and-help-live logic of the great chain of life. If, in our haste to "progress," the economics of ecology are disregarded by citizens and policy makers alike, the result will be an ugly America. We cannot afford an America where expedience tramples upon esthetics and development decisions are made with an eye only on the present.

Source: Stewart Udall, *The Quiet Crisis* (New York: Holt, Rinehart and Winston, 1963), pp. vii-viii, 188-90.

DOCUMENT 102: John F. Kennedy on the Nuclear Test Ban Treaty (1963)

During the early years of the cold war, the race between the United States and the Soviet Union to develop and build up their nuclear arsenals resulted in numerous nuclear weapons tests. From the start there was concern about the effects of radiation from nuclear testing, but it was not until 1959, when the relative nuclear position of the United States seemed sufficiently strong, that President Dwight Eisenhower proposed a treaty to limit nuclear testing. Four years of negotiations were required before President John F. Kennedy was able to transmit the treaty to the Senate. The Nuclear Test Ban Treaty of 1963, among the United States, the Soviet Union, and the United Kingdom, banned nuclear testing in the atmosphere, in outer space, and in water.

Concern about radioactive fallout from nuclear weapons testing was a driving force behind the development of the environmental movement, providing the impetus for the formation of such organizations as the Union of Concerned Scientists and Green-peace.

This treaty advances, though it does not assure, world peace; and it will inhibit, though it does not prohibit, the nuclear arms race.

- While it does not prohibit the United States and the Soviet Union from engaging in all nuclear tests, it will radically limit the testing in which both nations would otherwise engage.

- While it will not halt the production or reduce the existing stockpiles of nuclear weapons, it is a first step toward limiting the nuclear arms race.

- While it will not end the threat of nuclear war or outlaw the use of nuclear weapons, it can reduce world tensions, open a way to further agreements and thereby help to ease the threat of war.

- While it cannot wholly prevent the spread of nuclear arms to nations not now possessing them, it prohibits assistance to testing in these environments by others; it will be signed by many other potential testers; and it is thus an important opening wedge in our effort to "get the genie back in the bottle."

...The treaty will curb the pollution of our atmosphere. While it does not assure the world that it will be forever free from the fears and dangers of radioactive fallout from atmospheric tests, it will greatly reduce the numbers and dangers of such tests.

Source: "Special Message to the Senate on the Nuclear Test Ban Treaty. August 8, 1963," in *Public Papers of the Presidents of the United States: John F. Kennedy, 1963* (Washington, D.C:. Government Printing Office, 1964, pp. 622-23.

DOCUMENT 103: *Scenic Hudson Preservation Conference v. Federal Power Commission (1965)*

In the early 1960s, Consolidated Edison, the power company for New York City and Westchester County (just north of the city), proposed the creation of a huge reservoir a thousand feet above the Hudson River on Storm King Mountain. When the water in the reservoir was released down into the river, it could turn a turbine and generate energy. According to the proposal, river water would be pumped into the reservoir and stored there until power was needed to deal with peak energy demands.

After the Federal Power Commission (FPC) granted a license for this substantial project, the Scenic Hudson Preservation Conference (a group formed in opposition to the project and consisting of several conservation organizations and representatives of three Westchester towns) asked the court to require the FPC to reconsider approval of the license application and examine alternatives to the project, as well as other evidence that had been available before the project was approved but had been ignored.

The circuit court of appeal's decision broke new ground and is seen by many as the inauguration of modern environmental law. The decision was significant for four reasons: it was the first case to elevate environment factors to a position of equal consideration with economic factors; it was the first to require the government to consider alternatives in evaluating proposals for projects with negative environmental impact (a requirement established as law in the National Environmental Policy Act of 1969 [see Document 111]); it was among the first to require federal agencies to develop evidence relevant to the public interest, not simply weigh evidence presented by the applicant for license; and it was the first modern case to allow environmental groups with no economic interest in the issue to sue based on environmental issues.

The Court of Appeals, Hays, Circuit Judge, held, inter alia, that Federal Power Commission licensing order and subsequent related orders would be set aside for failure of commission to compile record sufficient to support its decision and because it ignored certain relevant factors and failed to make thorough study of possible alternatives, and matter would be remanded for its new proceedings which were required to include study of preservation of natural beauty and historic shrines and fisheries questions.

Order ["of the Federal Power Commission granting an intervener a license to construct a pumped storage hydroelectric project"] set aside and case remanded with directions.

* * *

To be licensed by the [Federal Power] Commission a prospective project must meet the statutory test of being "best adapted to a comprehensive plan for developing a waterway." . . .

If the Commission is properly to discharge its duty in this regard, the record on which it bases its determination must be complete. The petitioners and the public at large have a right to demand this completeness. It is our view, and we find, that the Commission has failed to compile a record which is sufficient to support its decision. The Commission has ignored certain relevant factors and failed to make a thorough study of the possible alternatives to the Storm King project. While the courts have no authority to concern themselves with the policies of the Commission, it is their duty to see to it that the Commission's decisions receive that careful consideration which the statute [Federal Power Act] contemplates.

* * *

The Storm King project is to be located in an area of unique beauty and major historical significance. The highlands and gorge of the Hudson offer one of the finest pieces of river scenery in the world. The great German traveler Baedeker called it "finer than the Rhine." Petitioners' complaint that the Commission must take these factors into consideration in evaluating the Storm King project is justified by the history of the Federal Power Act.

* * *

Respondent argues that "petitioners do not have standing to obtain review" because they "make no claim of any personal economic injury resulting from the Commission's action."

* * *

In order to insure that the Federal Power Commission will adequately protect the public interest in the aesthetic, conservational and recreational aspects of power development, those who by their activities and conduct have exhibited a special interest in such areas, must be held to be included in the class of "aggrieved" parties.

* * *

The "case: or "controversy" requirement of Article III section 2 of the Constitution does not require that an "aggrieved" or "adversely affected" party have a personal economic interest.

* * *

In this case, as in many others, the Commission has claimed to be the representative of the public interest. This role does not permit it to act as an umpire blandly calling balls and strikes for adversaries appearing before it; the right of the public must receive active and affirmative protection at the hands of the Commission.

Source: Scenic Hudson Preservation Conference, Town of Cortland, Town of Putnam Valley and Town of Yorktown, Petitioners v. Federal Power Commission, Respondent, and Consolidated Edison Company of New York, Inc., Intervener, Docket 29853, United States Court of Appeals, Second Circuit, 354 *Federal Reporter*, 2nd series, No. 106 (1965), pp. 608-9, 612, 613, 615, 620.

Document 104: California Land Conservation Act (1966) and Article XXVIII of the California Constitution (1967)

In the post-World War II years, farmland and open space began to disappear rapidly as a result of pressures from population growth, commercial expansion, and property tax increases. The California Land Conservation Act of 1965, usually referred to as the Williamson Act, was one of the first legislative attempts to address the loss of open space to development. The implementation of the Williamson Act was made possible by the addition, in November 1966, of Article XXVIII to the California Constitution. Article XXVIII (now section 8 of Article XIII) provided tax incentives to discourage farmers and landowners from selling their land to developers because of financial pressures. As townships, counties, and states across the nation established their own land conservation programs, they followed California's lead in using financial incentives (which in time came to include such things as tax abatements and easements as well as the sale of development rights) as a major method of controlling suburban sprawl and encouraging the continuance of family farms.

A. California Land Conservation Act

The Legislature finds:

(a) That the preservation of a maximum amount of the limited supply of agricultural land is necessary to the conservation of the state's economic resources, and is necessary not only to the maintenance of the agricultural economy of the state, but also for the assurance of adequate, healthful and nutritious food for future residents of this state and nation.

(b) That the discouragement of premature and unnecessary conversion of prime agricultural land to urban uses is a matter of public interest and will be of benefit to urban dwellers themselves in that it will discourage discontiguous urban development patterns which unnecessarily increase the costs of community services to community residents.

(c) That in a rapidly urbanizing society agricultural lands have a definite public value as open space, and the preservation in agricultural production of such lands, the use of which may be limited under the provisions of this chapter, constitutes an important physical, social, esthetic and economic asset to existing or pending urban or metropolitan developments.

B. California Constitution, Article XXVIII

SECTION 1. The people hereby declare that it is in the best interest of the state to maintain, preserve, conserve and otherwise continue in existence open space land for the production of food and fiber and to assure the use and enjoyment of natural resources and scenic beauty for the economic and social well-being of the state and its citizens. The people further declare that assessment practices must be so designed as to permit the continued availability of open space lands for these purposes, and it is the intent of this article to so provide.

SEC. 2. . . . . [T]he Legislature may define open space lands and provide that when such lands are subject to enforceable restriction, as specified by the Legislature, to the use thereof solely for recreation, for the enjoyment of scenic beauty, for the use of natural resources, or for production of food or fiber, such lands shall be valued for assessment purposes on such basis as is consistent with such restriction and use.

Source: **A.** *Sessions Laws of American States and Territories: California 1960-1969* (Ann Arbor, MI: Xerox University Microfilms, n.d.), *1965 Regular Session,* p. 3378. **B.** California Constitution, in *Sessions Laws . . . : California 1960-1969,* fiche 273, *1967,* p. A111.

DOCUMENT 105: Kenneth E. Boulding on the Spaceship Economy (1966)

Economist Kenneth Boulding believed that the United States needed to develop economic policies for the future based on minimizing both consumption and production, and that the object of its economic policies should be to maintain its stock of resources as much as possible. It was his contention that there were thermodynamic limits to resource utilization no matter the technological efficiencies.

The closed earth of the future requires economic principles which are somewhat different from those of the open earth of the past. For the sake of picturesqueness, I am tempted to call the open economy the "cowboy economy," the cowboy being symbolic of the illimitable plains and also associated with reckless, exploitative, romantic, and violent behavior, which is characteristic of open societies. The closed economy of the future might similarly be called the "spaceman" economy, in which the earth has become a single spaceship, without unlimited reservoirs of anything, either for extraction or for pollution, and in which, therefore, man must find his place in a cyclical ecological system which is capable of continuous reproduction of material form even though it cannot escape having inputs of energy. The difference between the two types of economy becomes most apparent in the attitude towards consumption. In the cowboy economy, consumption is regarded as a good thing and production likewise; and the success of the economy is measured by the amount of the throughput from the "factors of production," a part of which, at any rate, is extracted from the reservoirs of raw materials and non-economic objects, and another part of which is output into the reservoirs of pollution. If there are infinite reservoirs from which material can be obtained and into which effluvia can be deposited, then the throughput is at least a plausible measure of the success of the economy. The gross national product is a rough measure of this total throughput. It should be possible, however, to distinguish that part of the GNP which is derived from exhaustible and that which is derived from reproducible resources, as well as that part of consumption which represents effluvia and that which represents input into the productive system again. . . .

By contrast, in the spaceman economy, throughput is by no means a desideratum, and is indeed to be regarded as something to be minimized rather than maximized. The essential measure of the success of the economy is not production and consumption at all, but the nature, extent, quality, and complexity of the total capital stock, including in this the state of the human bodies and minds included in the system. In the spaceman economy, what we are primarily concerned with is stock maintenance, and any technological change which results in the maintenance of a given total stock with a lessened throughput (that is, less production and consumption) is clearly a gain. This idea that both production and consumption are bad things rather than good things is very strange to economists, who have been obsessed with the incomeflow concepts to the exclusion, almost, of capital-stock concepts.

Source: Kenneth E. Boulding, "The Economics of the Coming Spaceship Earth," in Henry Jarrett, ed., *Environmental Quality in a Growing Economy* (Baltimore: Johns Hopkins Press, 1966), pp. 9-10.

DOCUMENT 106: Lynn White, Jr., on Western Religions and the Environmental Crisis (1967)

In a speech presented to the American Association for the Advancement of Science (AAAS) in 1966, Lynn White, Jr., a historian and expert on the development of technology, examined some of the human abuses of the environment and suggested that no solution to the ecological crisis could be achieved until people were willing to abandon their belief that nature exists only to serve humans. He directed Americans to reexamine their fundamental beliefs and the attitudes underlying their relationship to the environment, saying that Westerners should "find a new religion or abandon the old one."[2] More than anyone else, White has been responsible for the "greening" of Judeo-Christian thinking and for the development of ecotheology.

Since both *science* and *technology* are blessed words in our contemporary vocabulary, some may be happy at the notions first, that, viewed historically, modern science is an extrapolation of natural theology and, second, that modern technology is at least partly to be explained as an Occidental, voluntarist realization of the Christian dogma of man's transcendence of, and rightful mastery over, nature. But, as we now recognize, somewhat over a century ago science and technology—hitherto quite separate activities—joined to give mankind powers which, to judge by many of the ecologic effects, are out of control. If so, Christianity bears a huge burden of guilt.

I personally doubt that disastrous ecologic backlash can be avoided simply by applying to our problems more science and more technology. Our science and technology have grown out of Christian attitudes toward man's relation to nature which are almost universally held not only by Christians and neo-Christians but also by those who fondly regard themselves as post-Christians. Despite Copernicus, all the cosmos rotates around our little globe. Despite Darwin, we are not, in our hearts, part of the natural process.

We are superior to nature, contemptuous of it, willing to use it for our slightest whim.

* * *

The greatest spiritual revolutionary in Western history, Saint Francis proposed what he thought was an alternative Christian view of nature and man's relation to it: he tried to substitute the idea of the equality of all creatures, including man, for the idea of man's limitless rule of creation. He failed. Both our present science and our present technology are so tinctured with orthodox Christian arrogance toward nature that no solution for our ecologic crisis can be expected from them alone. Since the roots of our trouble are so largely religious, the remedy must also be essentially religious, whether we call it that or not. We must rethink and refeel our nature and destiny. The profoundly religious, but heretical, sense of the primitive Franciscans for the spiritual autonomy of all parts of nature may point a direction. I propose Francis as a patron saint for ecologists.

Source: Lynn White, Jr., "The Historical Roots of Our Environmental Crisis," *Science* 155, no. 3767 (March 10, 1967): 1206, 1207.

DOCUMENT 107: Paul Ehrlich's *The Population Bomb* (1968)

Paul Ehrlich, who was an instructor in entomology when he wrote The Population Bomb, *is now a professor of population studies at Stanford University. Like Malthus in the nineteenth century, he uses the concept of population doubling time to awaken people to the threat of an impending population crisis. Although* The Population Bomb *proved effective in raising people's consciousness of the relationship between population growth, resource depletion, and environmental degradation, several of the most dire short-term predictions that Ehrlich made turned out to be wrong. It now seems likely that the doubling time for the population to reach 8 billion will be closer to 50 years rather than 35 years as Ehrlich predicted.*

Americans are beginning to realize that the underdeveloped countries of the world face an inevitable population-food crisis. Each year food production in these countries falls a bit further behind burgeoning population growth, and people go to bed a little bit hungrier. While there are temporary or local reversals of this trend, it now seems inevitable that it will continue to its logical conclusion: mass starvation. The rich may continue to get richer, but the more numerous poor are going to get poorer. Of these poor, a minimum of ten million people, most of them children, will starve to death during each year of the 1970s. But this is a mere handful compared to the numbers that will be starving before the end of the century. And it is now too late to take action to save many of those people.

However, most Americans are not aware that the U.S. and other developed countries also have a problem with overpopulation. Rather than suffering from food shortages, these countries show symptoms in the form of environmental deterioration and increased difficulty in obtaining resources to support their affluence.

. . . Perhaps the best way to impress you with numbers is to tell you about "doubling time"—the time necessary for the population to double in size.

It has been estimated that the human population of 8000 B.C. was about five million people,

taking perhaps one million years to get there from two and a half million. The population did not reach 500 million until almost 10,000 years later—about 1650 A.D. This means it doubled roughly once every thousand years or so. It reached a billion people around 1850, doubling in some 200 years. It took only 80 years or so for the next doubling, as the population reached two billion around 1930. We have not completed the next doubling to four billion yet, but we now have well over three and a half billion people. The doubling time at present seems to be about 35 years. Quite a reduction in doubling times: 1,000,000 years, 1,000 years, 200 years, 80 years, 35 years. Perhaps the meaning of a doubling time of around 35 years is best brought home by a theoretical exercise. Let's examine what might happen on the absurd assumption that the population continued to double every 35 years into the indefinite future.

If growth continued at that rate for about 900 years, there would be some 60,000,000,000,000,000,000 people on the face of the earth. Sixty million billion people. This is about 100 persons for each square yard of the Earth's surface, land and sea.

Source: Paul R. Ehrlich, *The Population Bomb*, rev. ed. (Rivercity, MA: Rivercity Press, 1975; reprint of 1968 Ballantine Books ed.), pp. 3-4.

DOCUMENT 108: Garrett Hardin on Controlling Access to the Commons (1968)

Every community has commons—resources such as parks, fresh air, waste disposal sites, water, and waterways to which all members of the community have equal access or right. As a community's population increases, the demand for these commons also increases. It is inevitable that, if the population continues to increase, eventually the demand for the common resources will exceed the supply.

According to the human ecologist Garrett Hardin, the time has come to do away with unfettered human access to the commons in four areas: (1) food gathering, (2) waste disposal and pollution, (3) use of open space for pleasure and free expression (limits must be placed on the right to make noise, set up billboards, etc.), and (4) procreation at will. Limits on liberty, he believes, are better than total environmental ruin. Hardin has no faith in the ability of humans to prevent environmental degradation without the imposition of strict controls on human activity.

The tragedy of the commons develops in this way. Picture a pasture open to all. It is to be expected that each herdsman will try to keep as many cattle as possible on the commons. Such an arrangement may work reasonably satisfactorily for centuries because tribal wars, poaching, and disease keep the numbers of both man and beast well below the carrying capacity of the land. Finally, however, comes the day of reckoning, that is, the day when the long-desired goal of social stability becomes a reality. At this point, the inherent logic of the commons remorselessly generates tragedy.

As a rational being, each herdsman seeks to maximize his gain. Explicitly or implicitly, more or less consciously, he asks, "What is the utility to me of adding one more animal to my herd?" This utility has one negative and one positive component.

1) The positive component is a function of the increment of one animal. Since the herdsman receives all the proceeds from the sale of the additional animal, the positive utility is nearly +1.

2) The negative component is a function of the additional overgrazing created by one more animal. Since, however, the effects of overgrazing are shared by all the herdsmen, the negative utility for any particular decision-making herdsman is only a fraction of -1.

Adding together the component partial utilities, the rational herdsman concludes that the only sensible course for him to pursue is to add another animal to his herd. And another; and another. . . . But this is the conclusion reached by each and every rational herdsman sharing a commons. Therein is the tragedy. Each man is locked into a system that compels him to increase his herd without limit—in a world that is limited. Ruin is the destination toward which all men rush, each pursuing his own best interest in a society that believes in the freedom of the commons. Freedom in a commons brings ruin to all.

. . . [N]atural selection favors the forces of psychological denial. The individual benefits as an individual from his ability to deny the truth even though society as a whole, of which he is a part, suffers.

* * *

The tragedy of the commons as a food basket is averted by private property, or something formally like it. But the air and waters surrounding us cannot readily be fenced, and so the tragedy of the commons as a cesspool must be prevented by different means, by coercive laws or taxing devices that make it cheaper for the polluter to treat his pollutants than to discharge them untreated. We have not progressed as far with the solution of this problem as we have with the first. Indeed, our particular concept of private property, which deters us from exhausting the positive resources of the earth, favors pollution.

[M]an is involved in exactly the same type of activity as the chambered nautilus, the bee and the coral, and subject to exactly the same tests of survival and evolution. Form is not the preoccupation of dilettantes but a central and indissoluble concern for all life.

Certainly we can dispose of the old canard, "form follows function." Form follows nothing—it is integral with all processes. Then form is indivisibly meaningful form, but it can reveal ill fit, misfit, unfit, fit and most fitting. There seems to be no good reason to change these criteria for human adaptations. Is the environment fit for man? Is the adaptation that is accomplished fit for the environment? Is the fit expressed in form?

Source: Ian McHarg, *Design with Nature* (Garden City, NY: Natural History Press/Doubleday, 1969), pp. 169-70, 173.

DOCUMENT 111: National Environmental Policy Act of 1969 (1970)

The National Environmental Policy Act (NEPA), signed into law by President Richard Nixon on January 1, 1970, set the stage for much of the environmental legislation passed in the 1970s. Its impact on economic and technological development in the United States has been broader than that of any other environmental legislation. Under this law, all federal agencies and departments are required to "monitor, evaluate, and control" their activities to protect and enhance the quality of the environment. The agencies must inform the public of their actions, review alternate courses of action, and allow the public to comment on those actions.

The law generated new power for the public and for organizations concerned with environmental issues. It also caused the creation of new divisions of law firms and corporations dealing in areas of the environment in which conflict might occur.

The environmental impact statement, the public document required by NEPA for any significant development involving a federal agency, became the focal point for many environmental battles.

SEC. 101. (a) The Congress, recognizing the profound impact of man's activity on the interrelations of all components of the natural environment, particularly the profound influences of population growth, high-density urbanization, industrial expansion, resource exploitation, and new and expanding technological advances and recognizing further the critical importance of restoring and maintaining environmental quality to the overall welfare and development of man, declares that it is the continuing policy of the Federal Government, in cooperation with State and local governments, and other concerned public and private organizations, to use all practicable means and measures, including financial and technical assistance, in a manner calculated to foster and promote the general welfare, to create and maintain conditions under which man and nature can exist in productive harmony, and fulfill the social, economic, and other requirements of present and future generations of Americans.

(b) In order to carry out the policy set forth in this Act, it is the continuing responsibility of the Federal Government to use all practicable means, consistent with other essential considerations of national policy, to improve and coordinate Federal plans, functions, programs, and resources to the end that the Nation may—

(1) fulfill the responsibilities of each generation as trustee of the environment for succeeding generations;

(2) assure for all Americans safe, healthful, productive, and esthetically and culturally pleasing surroundings;

(3) attain the widest range of beneficial uses of the environment without degradation, risk to health or safety, or other undesirable and unintended consequences;

(4) preserve important historic, cultural, and natural aspects of our national heritage, and maintain, wherever possible, an environment which supports diversity and variety of individual choice;

(5) achieve a balance between population and resource use which will permit high

standards of living and a wide sharing of life's amenities; and

(6) enhance the quality of renewable resources and approach the maximum attainable recycling of depletable resources.

(c) The Congress recognizes that each person should enjoy a healthful environment and that each person has a responsibility to contribute to the preservation and enhancement of the environment.

SEC. 102. The Congress authorizes and directs that, to the fullest extent possible: (1) the policies, regulations, and public laws of the United States shall be interpreted and administered in accordance with the policies set forth in this Act, and (2) all agencies of the Federal Government shall—

(A) utilize a systematic, interdisciplinary approach which will insure the integrated use of the natural and social sciences and the environmental design arts in planning and in decisionmaking which may have an impact on man's environment;

(B) identify and develop methods and procedures, in consultation with the Council on Environmental Quality established by subchapter II of this Act, which will insure that presently unquantified environmental amenities and values may be given appropriate consideration in decisionmaking along with economic and technical considerations;

(C) include in every recommendation or report on proposals for legislation and other major Federal actions significantly affecting the quality of the human environment, a detailed statement by the responsible official on—

(i) the environmental impact of the proposed action,

(ii) any adverse environmental effects which cannot be avoided should the proposal be implemented,

(iii) alternatives to the proposed action,

(iv) the relationship between local short-term uses of man's environment and the maintenance and enhancement of long-term productivity, and

(v) any irreversible and irretrievable commitments of resources which would be involved in the proposed action should it be implemented.

Prior to making any detailed statement, the responsible Federal official shall consult with and obtain the comments of any Federal agency which has jurisdiction by law or special expertise with respect to any environmental impact involved. Copies of such statement and the comments and views of the appropriate Federal, State, and local agencies, which are authorized to develop and enforce environmental standards, shall be made available to the President, the Council on Environmental Quality and to the public. . . .

(D) study, develop, and describe appropriate alternatives to recommended courses of action in any proposal which involves unresolved conflicts concerning alternative uses of available resources;

(E) recognize the worldwide and long-range character of environmental problems and, where consistent with the foreign policy of the United States, lend appropriate support to initiatives, resolutions, and programs designed to maximize international cooperation in anticipating and preventing a decline in the quality of mankind's world environment.

(F) make available to States, counties, municipalities, institutions, and individuals, advice and information useful in restoring maintaining, and enhancing the quality of the environment;

(G) initiate and utilize ecological information in the planning and development of resource-oriented projects; and

(H) assist the Council on Environmental Quality.

Source: Public Law 91-190, *United States Statutes at Large,* Vol. 83 (Washington, D.C.: Government Printing Office, 1970), 91st Cong., 1st Sess., January 1, 1970, pp. 852-54.

DOCUMENT 112: Richard Nixon on the Need for Environmental Regulation (1970)

Although few people think of Richard Nixon as an environmentalist, he signed into law—albeit with reluctance on occasion—some of the most important environmental legislation of the century and supported the ratification of several major international environmental agreements. Much of his first State of the Union Address was devoted to a discussion of environmental issues.

Impetus for the amendments to strengthen the 1954 international Convention for the Prevention of the Pollution of the Sea by Oil, and for Nixon's and the general public's support of these amendments, came from a series of high-profile oil spill accidents, including the collision of the tanker Torrey Canyon in 1967 and the massive oil spill off the coast of Santa Barbara, California, in 1969.

A. From the State of the Union Address, January 22, 1970

In the next 10 years we shall increase our wealth by 50 percent. The profound question is: Does this mean we will be 50 percent richer in a real sense, 50 percent better off, 50 percent happier?

Or does it mean that in the year 1980 the President standing in this place will look back on a decade in which 70 percent of our people lived in metropolitan areas choked by traffic, suffocated by smog, poisoned by water, deafened by noise, and terrorized by crime?

These are not the great questions that concern world leaders at summit conferences. But people do not live at the summit. They live in the foothills of everyday experience, and it is time for all of us to concern ourselves with the way real people live in real life.

The great question of the seventies is, shall we surrender to our surroundings, or shall we make our peace with nature and begin to make reparations for the damage we have done to our air, to our land, and to our water?

Restoring nature to its natural state is a cause beyond party and beyond factions. It has become a common cause of all the people of this country. It is a cause of particular concern to young Americans, because they more than we will reap the grim consequences of our failure to act on programs which are needed now if we are to prevent disaster later.

Clean air, clean water, open spaces—these should once again be the birthright of every American. If we act now, they can be.

We still think of air as free. But clean air is not free, and neither is clean water. The price tag on pollution control is high. Through our years of past carelessness we incurred a debt to nature, and now that debt is being called.

The program I shall propose to Congress will be the most comprehensive and costly program in this field in America's history.

* * *

I shall propose to this Congress a $10 billion nationwide clean waters program to put modern municipal waste treatment plants everywhere in America where they are needed to make our waters clean again. . . .

As our cities and suburbs relentlessly expand, those priceless open spaces needed for recreation areas accessible to their people are swallowed up—often forever. Unless we preserve these spaces while they are still available, we shall have none to preserve. . . .

The automobile is our worst polluter of the air. Adequate control requires further advances in engine design and fuel composition. We shall intensify our research, set increasingly strict standards, and strengthen enforcement standards—and we shall do it now.

We can no longer afford to consider air and water common property, free to be abused by anyone without regard to the consequences. Instead, we should begin now to treat them as scarce resources, which we are no more free to contaminate than we are free to throw garbage into our neighbor's yard.

This requires comprehensive new regulations. It also requires that, to the extent possible, the price of goods should be made to include the costs of producing and disposing of them without damage to the environment.

Now, I realize that the argument is often made that there is a fundamental contradiction between economic growth and the quality of life, so that to have one we must forsake the other.

The answer is not to abandon growth, but to redirect it. For example, we should turn toward ending congestion and eliminating smog the same reservoir of inventive genius that created them in the first place.

B. From a Special Message to Congress on Marine Pollution from Oil Spills, May 20, 1970

The oil that fuels our industrial civilization can also foul our natural environment.

The threat of oil pollution from ships—both at sea and in our harbors—represents a growing danger to our marine environment. With the expansion of world trade over the past three decades, seaborne oil transport has multiplied tenfold and presently constitutes more than 60 percent of the world's ocean commerce.

This increase in shipping has increased the oil pollution hazard. Within the past ten years, there have been over 550 tanker collisions, four-fifths of which have involved ships entering or leaving ports. The routine discharge by tankers and other ships of oil and oily wastes as a part of their regular operation is also a major contributor to the oil pollution problem.

. . . The growing threat from oil spills can be contained—not by stopping industrial progress—but through a careful combination of international cooperation and national initiatives.

Source: Public Papers of the Presidents of the United States: Richard Nixon, 1970 (Washington, DC: U.S. Government Printing Office, 1971), pp. 12-13, 443.

DOCUMENT 113: Clean Air Act Amendments (1970)

The Clean Air Act of 1963, building on the Clean Air Act of 1955 [see Document 93], authorized the Department of Health, Education, and Welfare to establish clean air criteria, but it left enforcement of these regulations to the states. A 1967 law required the states to develop implementation plans for the air quality goals they set.

In 1970 Congress took the next, very large step. The Clean Air Act Amendments of 1970 provided for the establishment of national air quality standards and required the states to develop implementation plans and set deadlines for meeting these standards. The law allowed the federal government to regulate, through the Environmental Protection Agency, emissions from automobiles and the composition of automobile fuels and additives. The Clean Air Act Amendments of 1970, together with the Clean Air Act Amendments passed in 1990, had enormous implications for industry, especially the automobile industry, and have had and will continue to have a huge effect on both the health and the economy of Americans.

The first corporate average fuel economy (CAFE) standards were set in 1975, and since then there have been constant efforts to avoid, and even lower, these targets. Early in the twenty-first century several states brought a suit against the EPA for its failure to regulate greenhouse gases [see Document164].

National Ambient Air Quality Standards
Sec. 109. (a) (1) The Administrator [the Environmental ProtectionAgency]—

(A) within 30 days after the enactment of the Clean Air Amendments of 1970, shall publish proposed regulations prescribing a national primary ambient air quality standard and a national secondary ambient air quality standard for each air pollutant for which air quality criteria have been issued prior to such date of enactment; and

(B) after a reasonable time for interested persons to submit written comments thereon (but no later than 90 days after the initial publication of such proposed standards) shall by regulation promulgate such proposed national primary and secondary ambient air quality standards with such modifications as he deems appropriate.

(2) With respect to any air pollutant for which air quality criteria are issued after the date of enactment of the Clean Air Amendments of 1970, the Administrator shall publish, simultaneously with the issuance of such criteria and information, proposed national primary and secondary ambient air quality standards for any such pollutant. . . .

(b) (1) National primary ambient air quality standards, prescribed under subsection (a) shall be ambient air quality standards the attainment and maintenance of which in the judgment of the Administrator, based on such criteria and allowing an adequate margin of safety, are requisite to protect the public health. . . .

(2) Any national secondary ambient air quality standard prescribed under subsection (a) shall specify a level of air quality the attainment and maintenance of which in the judgment of the Administrator, based on such criteria, is requisite to protect the public welfare from any known or anticipated adverse effects associated with the presence of such air pollutant in the ambient air. . . .

Implementation Plans
Sec. 110. Each State shall, after reasonable notice and public hearings, adopt and submit to the Administrator, within nine months after the promulgation of a national primary ambient air quality standard (or any revision thereof) under section 109 for any air pollutant, a plan which provides for implementation, maintenance, and enforcement of such primary standard in each air quality control region (or portion thereof) within such State.

Motor Vehicles Emission Standards.. .: Establishment of Standards Sec 202. (a). . .

(1) The administrator shall by regulation prescribe (and from time to time revise) in accordance with the provisions of this section, standards applicable to the mission of any air pollutant from any class or classes of new motor vehicles or new motor vehicle engines, which in his judgment causes or contributes to, or is likely to cause or to contribute to, air pollution which endangers the public health or welfare. . . . Such standards shall be applicable to such vehicles and engines for their useful life . . . , whether such vehicles and engines are designed as complete systems or incorporated devices to prevent or control such pollution.

Source: Public Law 91-604, *U.S. Statutes at Large,* Vol. 84 (Washington, D.C.: Government Printing Office, 1971), 91st Cong., 2nd Sess., Dec. 31, 1970, pp. 1679-80, 1690.

DOCUMENT 114: Dennis Puleston on the Founding of the Environmental Defense Fund (1971)

Dennis Puleston, who for many years served as chairman of the board of trustees of the Environmental Defense Fund, became an active environmentalist when he realized that the osprey were disappearing from Long Island, New York, where he lived. As often happens, concern about a local environmental problem led to involvement with much broader environmental issues.

Coal miners working deep in the earth learned long ago that one of their most treacherous enemies was the colorless, odorless gas methane. They also found that certain living creatures were more sensitive to this gas than they were, and thus could serve as an early warning system. So they took a canary down with them, and as long as the bird sang cheerfully they knew all was well. But if it became silent they watched it carefully, and if it rolled over dead the alarm rang out and they made a dash for the safety of the pit head.

In recent years many of us who are concerned with the condition of our environment have developed our own canaries. Mine happens to be a large, regal looking brown and white bird with strong, hooked talons and raptorial beak. . . . I can well recall my first visit to Gardiner's Island in 1948, when there were more than 300 active [osprey] nests, producing an average of more than two fledglings per nest. . . . [S]ubsequent frequent visits there convinced me that numbers were declining. By the mid-fifties the number of active nests and also the number of young per active nest were dropping steadily, and by the early sixties the drop had reached collapse proportion. On the mainland [of Long Island] the situation was even more serious; the osprey became a rare sight in places where formerly they had been abundant, and few nestings could be recorded. . . . [O]ne fact is sure; the osprey is an endangered species in the Northeast. . . . And whether we care for the osprey or not, surely its tragic situation is a warning of something that is of concern to our own health and welfare. Perhaps the canary is not yet dead, but it has definitely stopped singing.

Naturally, I wished to determine the reason for this decline. Factors such as human and animal disturbances and shortage of food did not apply here; something else was causing the lack of reproductive success. Then, in the early sixties, Rachel Carson's powerful and eloquent indictment of the chlorinated hydrocarbon pesticides burst into print [*see* Document 100], a book that some critics claim will be recorded as having a greater dramatic effect than almost any other literary work of the century. Several unhatched eggs that I brought back from osprey nests on Gardiner's Island confirmed her findings. Gas chromatography revealed the presence of high concentrations of DDT and its metabolites; certainly >13 parts per million (ppm) was sufficient to kill an embryo.

* * *

Although some of the environmental problems resulting from the widespread use of DDT were not yet known to us by the mid-sixties, we had sufficient evidence to convince us that we must act to bring about a curtailment in its use. Not only the reproductive failure of ospreys, but the almost total disappearance of the blueclaw crab in our bays, the diminished populations of reptiles, amphibians, many species of birds, butterflies, and honeybees—all were sounding the alarm. The canary was far from well.

It was not difficult to point a finger at the chief culprit. For the past 20 years, the Suffolk County Mosquito Control Commission had been aerially spraying DDT in its largely unsuccessful efforts to reduce mosquito populations. From a salt marsh at the mouth of the Carmans River in Brookhaven, mud samples were found with concentrations as high as 32 lbs/acre—this in an area far from any agricultural spraying. Appeals to the Commission had no effect; their job, they claimed, was to kill mosquitoes, and DDT was the best way to do it. Effects on other wildlife forms were not their concern. Besides, they insisted, wasn't DDT "harmless to animals"?

Thus the idea of court action was born. A local lawyer was anxious to try his mettle, and there was plenty of scientific testimony to support his case. This was provided by a small group of life scientists and conservationists, members of the local Brookhaven Town Natural Resources Committee. Affidavits, charts, photographs, and a substantial technical appendix were prepared and in early 1966 an Order to Show Cause, together with a plaintiff's affidavit, summons, and verified complaint were filed with the Supreme Court of the State of New York in Riverhead, Suffolk County. . . . In August the Court determined that ". . . upon all the facts before the Court . . . sufficient grounds exist for the discretion vested in the Court to stay a practice injurious to the County and its residents."

In November 1966, the action was heard. This was a "class action," whereby the plaintiff, instead of seeking personal damages, seeks to persuade the Court that, as a matter of equity and constitutional privilege, the citizenry has a right to the cleanest possible environment consistent with the general welfare. While such a right is not specifically mentioned in the Constitution, it can readily be inferred. This doctrine holds that those who pollute and disturb the environment adversely

in the name of progress and economic necessity should be required to show that their actions are in the public interest. Thus, the suit heard in the Riverhead courtroom was a pioneering effort to establish vital precedents in future conservation law.

The six-day trial was taken up largely with the testimony of scientists and other expert witnesses presented by the plaintiff's legal counsel. The counsel for the defense was hard put to summon any valid scientific support for the necessity of using DDT for mosquito control or to show that it was harmless to nontarget organisms. In fact, any economic arguments in favor of DDT were nonexistent.

The court-imposed temporary ban on DDT use by the defendant held for about a year, at which time the judge ruled that, although it had been proven that DDT was contaminating the environment, action for a permanent ban must come from the state legislature. Victory, however, was snatched from an ultimate defeat, for orders from the County administration came in time to make the ban permanent.

* * *

Emboldened by the small but significant victory in Suffolk, the original group decided to follow their courtroom tactics on a broader scale. . . .

Accordingly, in the fall of 1967, the Environmental Defense Fund (EDF) was formed.

Source: Dennis Puleston, "Defending the Environment: A Case History," *Brookhaven Lecture Series,* Number 104, September 15, 1971 (Springfield, VA: National Technical Information Service, U.S. Department of Commerce, December 1971), pp. 1, 3, 4, 5.

DOCUMENT 115: Barry Commoner on the Ecosphere (1971)

Barry Commoner's concern with the environment began with his alarm about nuclear proliferation but broadened into an understanding of the need for a new view of the human role in the environment. One of the first U.S. scientists to comprehend the relationship between political activism and social change, Commoner played a role in the formation of the Union of Concerned Scientists. As a public advocate and articulate spokesperson for a wide-ranging environmental, social, and political agenda, Commoner moved from an early career as a lecturer and then professor of biology at Washington University to a presidential candidate in 1980, when he campaigned on a ticket calling for public control of the energy industry.

The environment has just been rediscovered by the people who live in it. In the United States the event was celebrated in April 1970, during Earth Week. It was a sudden, noisy awakening.

. . .

Earth Week and the accompanying outburst of publicity, preaching, and prognostication surprised most people, including those of us who had worked for years to generate public recognition of the environmental crisis. What surprised me most were the numerous, confident explanations of the cause and cure of the crisis. For having spent some years in the effort simply to detect and describe the growing list of environmental problems—radioactive fallout, air and water pollution, the deterioration of the soil—and in tracing some of their links to social and political processes, the identification of a single cause and cure seemed a rather bold step. During Earth Week, I discovered that such reticence was far behind the times.

After the excitement of Earth Week, I tried to find some meaning in the welter of contradictory advice that it produced. It seemed to me that the confusion of Earth Week was a sign that the situation was so complex and ambiguous that people could read into it what ever conclusion their own beliefs—about human nature, economics, and politics—suggested.

. . .

Earth Week convinced me of the urgency of a deeper public understanding of the origins of the environmental crisis and its possible cures. . . .

Such an understanding must begin at the source of life itself: the earth's thin skin of air, water, and soil, and the radiant solar fire that bathes it. Here, several billion years ago, life appeared and was nourished by the earth's substance. As it grew, life evolved, its old forms transforming the earth's skin and new ones adapting to these changes. Living things multiplied in number, variety, and habitat until they formed a global network, becoming deftly enmeshed in the surroundings they had themselves created. This is the *ecosphere*, the home that life has built for itself on the planet's outer surface.

Any living thing that hopes to live on the earth must fit into the ecosphere or perish. The environmental crisis is a sign that the finely sculpted fit between life and its surroundings has begun to corrode. As the links between one living thing and another, and between all of them and their surroundings, begin to break down, the dynamic interactions that sustain the whole have begun to falter and, in some places, stop.

. . .

Understanding the ecosphere comes hard because, to the modern mind, it is a curiously foreign place. We have become accustomed to think of separate, singular events, each dependent upon a unique, singular cause. But in the ecosphere every effect is also a cause: an animal's waste becomes food for soil bacteria; what bacteria excrete nourishes plants; animals eat the plants. Such ecological cycles are hard to fit into human experience in the age of technology, where machine A always yields product B, and product B, once used, is cast away, having no further meaning for the machine, the product, or the user.

Here is the first great fault in the life of man in the ecosphere. We have broken out of the circle of life, converting its endless cycles into man-made, linear events: oil is taken from the ground, distilled into fuel, burned in an engine, converted thereby into noxious fumes, which are emitted into the air. At the end of the line is smog. Other man-made breaks in the ecosphere's cycles spew out toxic chemicals, sewage, heaps of rubbish—testimony to our power to tear the ecological fabric that has, for millions of years, sustained the planet's life.

Suddenly we have discovered what we should have known long before: that the ecosphere sustains people and everything that they do; that anything that fails to fit into the ecosphere is a threat to its finely balanced cycles; that wastes are not only unpleasant, not only toxic, but, more meaningfully, evidence that the ecosphere is being driven towards collapse.

Source: Barry Commoner, *The Closing Circle: Nature, Man, and Technology* (New York: Knopf, 1971), pp. 10-12.

DOCUMENT 116: Clean Water Act (1972)

The Clean Water Act of 1972, amending the Federal Water Pollution Control Act of 1948, gave teeth to earlier legislation aimed at preventing or reducing water pollution and laid the groundwork for future efforts to preserve the nation's wetlands. However, in 2001, a Supreme Court decision [see Document152] limited the reach of section 404 and put a roadblock in the way of effective wetlands preservation.

SEC. 101.(a) The objective of this Act is to restore and maintain the chemical, physical, and biological integrity of the Nation's waters. In order to achieve this objective it is hereby declared that, consistent with the provisions of this Act—

(1) it is the national goal that the discharge of pollutants into navigable waters be eliminated by 1985;

(2) it is the national goal that wherever attainable, an interim goal of water quality which provides for the protection and propagation of fish, shellfish, and wildlife and provides recreation in and on the water be achieved by July 1, 1983;

(3) it is national policy that the discharge of toxic pollutants in toxic amounts be prohibited;

(4) it is the national policy that Federal financial assistance be provided to construct publicly owned waste treatment works;

(5) it is the national policy that areawide waste treatment management planning processes be developed and implemented

to assure adequate control of sources of pollution in each State; and

(6) it is the national policy that a major research and demonstration effort be made to develop technology necessary to eliminate the discharge of pollutants into the navigable waters, waters of the contiguous zone, and the oceans.

SEC. 404. (a) The Secretary of the Amy, acting through the Chief of Engineers, may issue permits, after notice and opportunity for public hearings for the discharge of dredged or fill material into the navigable waters at specified disposal sites.

(b) Subject to subsection (c) of this section, each such disposal site shall be specified for each such permit by the Secretary of the Army (1) through the application of guidelines developed by the Administrator, in conjunction with the Secretary of the Army... and (2) in any case where such guidelines under clause (1) alone would prohibit the specification of a site, through the application additionally of the economic impact of the site on navigation and anchorage.

(c) The Administrator is authorized to prohibit the specification (including the withdrawal of specification) of any defined area as a disposal site, and he is authorized to deny or restrict the use of any defined area for specification (including the withdrawal of specification) as a disposal site, whenever he determines, after notice and opportunity for public hearings, that the discharge of such materials into such area will have an unacceptable adverse effect on municipal water supplies, shellfish beds, and fishery areas (including spawning and breeding areas), wildlife, or recreational areas.

Source: Public Law 92-500, *United States Statutes at Large,* Vol. 86 (Washington, D.C.: Government Printing Office, 1973), 92nd Cong., 2nd Sess., Oct. 18, 1972, pp. 816, 884.

DOCUMENT 117: Christopher Stone Proposes Legal Rights for Natural Objects (1972)

Henry David Thoreau suggested that all living things have inherent rights that humans ought to recognize [see Document 44]. John Muir, in his early musings, revealed an inclination to the same line of thought [see Document 47] but later, recognizing political realities, turned to the usefulness of the wilderness to man as the basis for arguing for its preservation. In his essay "Should Trees Have Standing," Christopher Stone, a lawyer, explored a similar but, in a way, more practical approach to acknowleding the rights of natural objects, He suggested that trees or forests or rivers or ecosystems that are about to be or have been damaged should be represented—as children, incompetent adults, corporations, and nations are—by concerned and appropriate guardians.

It is not inevitable, nor is it wise, that natural objects should have no rights to seek redress in their own behalf. It is no answer to say that streams and forests cannot have standing because streams and forests cannot speak. Corporations cannot speak either; nor can states, estates, infants, incompetents, municipalities or universities. Lawyers speak for them. . . . One ought, I think, to handle the legal problems of natural objects as one does the problems of legal incompetents—human beings who have become vegetables. . . .

On a parity of reasoning, we should have a system in which, when a friend of a natural object perceives it to be endangered, he can apply to a court for the creation of a guardianship. . . .

. . . If, for example, the Environmental Defense Fund should have reason to believe that some company's strip mining operations might be irreparably destroying the ecological balance of large tracts of land, it could, under this procedure, apply to the court in which the lands were situated to be appointed guardian. As guardian, it might be given rights of inspection (or visitation) to determine and bring to the court's attention a fuller finding on the land's condition. If there were indications that under the substantive law some redress might be available on the land's behalf, then the guardian would be entitled to raise the land's rights in the land's name, i.e., without having to make the roundabout and often unavailing demonstration . . . that the "rights" of the club's members were being invaded. . . .

As far as adjudicating the merits of a controversy is concerned, there is also a good case to be made for taking into account harm to the environment—in its own right. . . . [T]he traditional way of deciding whether to issue injunctions in law suits affecting the environment, at least where communal property is involved, has been to strike some sort of balance regarding the economic hardships *on human beings.* . . .

The argument for "personifying" the environment, from the point of damage calculations, can best be demonstrated from the welfare economics position. Every well-working legal-economic system should be so structured as to confront each of us with the full costs that our activities are imposing on society. Ideally, a paper-mill, in deciding what to produce—and where, and by what methods—ought to be forced to take into account not only the lumber, acid and labor that its production "takes" from other uses in the society, but also what costs alternative production plans will impose on society through pollution.

Source: Christopher Stone, "Should Trees Have Standing? Toward Legal Rights for Natural Objects," *Southern California Law Review* 45, no. 450 (1972): 33-35.

DOCUMENT 118: *Sierra Club v. Morton* (1972)

Not long after Christopher Stone published his essay on the legal rights of natural objects see [Document 117], William O. Douglas reinforced the idea in a dissenting opinion in the U.S. Supreme Court case Sierra Club v. Morton. *Douglas, who served as an associate justice on the highest court for more than thirty-five years, was an avid naturalist and aggressive advocate for wilderness preservation. The defendant was Rogers Morton, secretary of Interior in the Nixon administration.*

A. The Supreme Court Decision

Action by membership corporation [Sierra Club] for declaratory judgment that construction of proposed ski resort and recreation area in national game refuge and forest would contravene federal laws and for preliminary and permanent injunctions restraining federal officials from approving or issuing permits for the project. . . . The Supreme Court, Mr. Justice Stewart [author of the affirming opinion], held that, in absence of allegation that corporation or its members would be affected in any of their activities or pastimes by the proposed project, the corporation, which claimed special interest in conservation of natural game refuges and forests, lacked standing under Administrative Procedure Act to maintain the action.

B. William O. Douglas's Minority Opinion

The critical question of "standing" would be simplified and also put neatly in focus if we fashioned a federal rule that allowed environmental issues to be litigated before federal agencies or federal courts in the name of the inanimate object about to be despoiled, defaced, or invaded by roads and bulldozers and where injury is the subject of public outrage. Contemporary public concern for protecting nature's ecological equilibrium should lead to the conferral of standing upon environmental objects to sue for their own preservation. See Stone, Should Trees Have Standing?—Toward Legal Rights for Natural Objects [*see* Document 117]. This suit would therefore be more properly labeled as Mineral King v. Morton.

Inanimate objects are sometimes parties in litigation. . . . The ordinary corporation is a "person" for purposes of the adjudicatory processes, whether it represents proprietary, spiritual, aesthetic or charitable causes.

* * *

Mineral King is doubtless like other wonders of the Sierra Nevada such as Tuolumne Meadows and the John Muir Trail. Those who hike it, fish it, hunt it, camp in it, frequent it, or visit it merely to sit in solitude and wonderment are legitimate spokesmen for it, whether they may be few or many. Those who have that intimate relation with the inanimate object about to be injured, polluted, or otherwise despoiled are its legitimate spokesmen.

. . . [T]he problem is to make certain that the inanimate objects, which are the very core of America's beauty, have spokesmen before they are destroyed. It is, of course, true that most of them are under the control of a federal or state agency. The standards given those agencies are usually expressed in terms of the "public interest." Yet "public interest" has so many differing shades of meaning as to be quite meaningless on the environmental front. Congress accordingly has adopted ecological standards in the National Environmental Policy Act of 1969 [*see* Document 111] . . . and guidelines for agency action have been provided by the Council on Environmental Quality. . . .

Yet the pressures on agencies for favorable action one way or the other are enormous. The suggestion that Congress can stop action which is undesirable is true in theory; yet even Congress is too remote to give meaningful direction and its machinery is too ponderous to use very often. The federal agencies of which I speak are not venal or corrupt. But they are notoriously under the control of powerful interests who manipulate them through advisory committees, or friendly working relations, or who have that natural affinity with the agency which in time develops between the regulator and the regulated. As early as 1894, Attorney General [Richard] Olney predicted that regulatory agencies might become "industry-minded." . . .

Years later a court of appeals observed "the recurring question which has plagued public regulation of industry [is] whether the regulatory agency is unduly oriented toward the interests of the industry it is designed to regulate, rather than the public interest it is designed to protect." . . .

The Forest Service—one of the federal agencies behind the scheme to despoil Mineral King—has been notorious for its alignment with lumber companies, although its mandate from Congress directs it to consider the various aspects of multiple use in its supervision of the national forests.

The voice of the inanimate object, therefore, should not be stilled. That does not mean that the judiciary takes over the managerial functions from the federal agency. It merely means that before these priceless bits of Americana (such as a valley, an alpine meadow, a river, or a lake) are forever lost or are so transformed as to be reduced to the eventual rubble of our urban environment, the voice of the existing beneficiaries of these environmental wonders should be heard.

Perhaps they will not win. Perhaps the bulldozers of "progress" will plow under all the aesthetic wonders of this beautiful land. That is not the present question. The sole question is who has standing to be heard?

Those who hike the Appalachian Trail into Sunfish Pond, New Jersey, and camp or sleep there, or run the Allagash in Maine, or climb the Guadalupes in West Texas, or who canoe and portage the Quetico Superior in Minnesota, certainly should have standing to defend those natural wonders before courts or agencies, though they live 3,000 miles away. Those who merely are caught up in environmental news or propaganda and flock to defend these waters or areas may be treated differently. That is why these environmental issues should be tendered by the inanimate object itself. Then there will be assurances that all of the forms of life which it represents will stand before the court—the pileated woodpecker as well as the coyote and bear, the lemmings as well as the trout in the streams. Those inarticulate members of the ecological group cannot speak. But those people who have so frequented the place as to know its values and wonders will be able to speak for the entire ecological community.

Source: Supreme Court Reporter, 768; 92 Supreme Court 1361 (1972), pp. 1361, 1369-71, 1374-75.

DOCUMENT 119: Stockholm Declaration on the Human Environment (1972)

The United States was not alone in its awakening to environmental threats. In June 1972, in response to expanding international environmental consciousness, the United Nations sponsored a Conference on the Human Environment in Stockholm. The declaration produced by the conference took note of the "dangerous levels of pollution in water, air, earth and living beings; major and undesirable disturbances to the ecological balance of the biosphere; destruction and depletion of irreplaceable resources; and gross deficiencies harmful to the physical, mental and social health of man, in the man-made environment."

The conference, which marked the beginning of the United Nations Environmental Programme (UNEP), recognized both the increasing demand by Third World countries for a Western-style standard of living and the desire of the industrialized nations for continued economic growth. The declaration that it produced underscored the fact that international environmental policy is clearly subordinate to the economic interests of individual states, as noted in principles 21 and 24. Nevertheless, during the nearly half century since its founding, UNEP has succeeded in encouraging the nations of the world to take major steps to decrease sea and air pollution. Indeed, many of the UNEP-sponsored protocols and conventions relating to the environment have been incorporated into U.S. law, although the U.S. Senate has balked at ratifying international environmental agreements that it views as detrimental to U.S. strategic or economic interests [see, for example, Documents 130 and 143B].

The Stockholm Declaration also committed the U.N. to the concept of sustainable development—the idea that, with suitable resource management, the resource base of nations, including soil, fisheries, water supplies, and forests, could be maintained, and that at the same time both underdeveloped and developed countries could continue to grow their economies.

The Declaration . . . States the common conviction that:

Principle 1 Man has the fundamental right of freedom, equality and adequate conditions of life, in an environment of a quality that permits a life of dignity and well-being, and he bears a solemn responsibility to protect and improve the environment for present and future generation. . . .

Principle 2 The natural resources of the earth including the air, water, land flora and fauna and especially representative samples of natural ecosystems must be safeguarded for the benefit of present and future generations through careful planning or management, as appropriate.

Principle 3 The capacity of the earth to produce vital resources must be maintained and, wherever practicable, restored or improved.

Principle 4 Man has a special responsibility to safeguard and wisely manage the heritage of wildlife and its habitat which are now greatly imperiled by a combination of adverse factors. Nature conservation including wildlife must

therefore receive importance for planning in economic development.

Principle 5 The non-renewable resources of the earth must be employed in such a way as to guard against the danger of their future exhaustion and to ensure that benefits from such employment are shared by all mankind.

Principle 6 The discharge of toxic substances or of other substances and the release of heat, in such quantities or concentrations as to exceed the capacity of the environment to render them harmless, must be halted in order to ensure that serious or irreversible damage is not inflicted upon ecosystems. . . .

Principle 7 States shall take all possible steps to prevent pollution of the seas by substances that are liable to create hazards to human health, to harm living resources and marine life, to damage amenities or to interfere with other legitimate uses of the sea.

Principle 21 States have, in accordance with the Charter of the United Nations and the principles of international law, the sovereign right to exploit their own resources pursuant to their own environmental policies, and the responsibility to ensure that activities within their jurisdiction or control do not cause damage to the environment of other States or of areas beyond the limits of national jurisdiction.

Principle 24 International matters concerning the protection and improvement of the environment should be handled in a cooperative spirit by all countries, big or small, on an equal footing. Cooperation through multilateral or bilateral arrangements or other appropriate means is essential to effectively control, prevent, reduce and eliminated adverse environmental effects resulting from activities conducted in all spheres, in such a way that due account is taken of sovereignty and interests of all States.

Source: Stockholm Declaration on the Human Environment (New York: United Nations Environmental Programme, 1972), pp. 1-4.

DOCUMENT 120: Endangered Species Act (1973)

The Endangered Species Act, in its original form, came close to acknowledging the rights of species to exist. In the framing of the law, no references were made to the utility of the species; the task was only to identify and list them and to find a way to develop a plan, when necessary, to encourage their recovery.

The history of the act and its enforcement is filled with conflicts in which the rights of property owners and other financially interested parties are pitted against spokespeople for the preservation of endangered species. The conflict over the Tennessee Valley Authority's Teleco Dam, situated on the Little Tennessee River, and the endangered snail darter (a rare species of perch) has been cited for many years as the exemplification of the absurdity of some of these conflicts.[3] In the 1980s and 1990s the controversy surrounding the preservation of the spotted owl in the ancient forests of the Northwest produced a similar exchange of invectives. Over the years, compromises had to be made to enable the country to live with the act, and consequently the law has been substantially altered from the original version presented here.

The act has had its share of both successes and failures. Ospreys, brown pelicans, bald eagles, and peregrine falcons have moved from the brink of extinction to a certainty of survival if current environmental conditions continue, but spotted owls have not.

Sec. 2 (a) FINDINGS.—The Congress finds and declares that—

(1) various species of fish, wildlife, and plants in the United States have been rendered extinct as a consequence of economic growth and development untempered by adequate concern and conservation;

(2) other species of fish, wildlife, and plants have been so depleted in numbers that they are in danger of or threatened with extinction;

(3) these species of fish, wildlife, and plants are of esthetic, ecological, educational, historical, recreational, and scientific value to the Nation and its people;

(4) the United States has pledged itself as a sovereign state in the international community to conserve to the extent practicable the various species of fish or wildlife and plants facing extinction, pursuant to—

(A) migratory bird treaties with Canada and Mexico;

(B) the Migratory and Endangered Bird Treaty with Japan;

(C) the Convention on Nature Protection and Wildlife Preservation in the Western Hemisphere;

(D) the International Convention for the Northwest Atlantic Fisheries;

(E) the International Convention for the High Seas Fisheries of the North Pacific Ocean;

(F) the Convention on International Trade in Endangered Species of Wild Fauna and Flora; and

(G) other international agreements.

(5) encouraging the states and other interested parties, through Federal financial assistance and a system of incentives, to develop and maintain conservation programs which meet national and international standards is a key to meeting the Nation's international commitments and to better safeguarding, for the benefit of all citizens, the Nation's heritage in fish, wildlife, and plants.

(b) PURPOSES.—The purposes of this Act are to provide a means whereby the ecosystems upon which endangered species and threatened species depend may be conserved, to provide a program for the conservation of such endangered species and threatened species, and to take such steps as may be appropriate to achieve the purposes of the treaties and conventions set forth in subsection (a) of this section.

(c) POLICY.— It is further declared to be the policy of Congress that all Federal departments and agencies shall seek to conserve endangered species and threatened species and shall utilize their authorities in furtherance of the purposes of this Act.

Source: Public Law 93-205, *United States Statutes at Large,* Vol. 87 (Washington, D.C.: Government Printing Office, 1973), 93rd Cong., 2nd sess., December 28, 1973, pp. 884-85.

DOCUMENT 121: Ernest Callenbach's *Ecotopia* (1975)

In Ernest Callenbach's novel Ecotopia, *a skeptical American reporter describes the application of utopian environmental ideas in a secessionist Northwest of the future. It brings to mind the many utopian environmental communes that were formed in the 1960s and 1970s, most of which did not survive more than a decade or two. It also reflects the interest in organic farming and sustainable development that took hold during that era.*

Wood is a major factor in the topsy-turvy Ecotopian economy, as the source not only of lumber and paper but also of some of the remarkable plastics that Ecotopian scientists have developed. Ecotopians in the city and country alike take a deep and lasting interest in wood. They love to smell it, feel it, carve it, polish it. Inquiries about why they persist in using such an outdated material (which of course has been entirely obsoleted by aluminum and plastics in the United States) receive heated replies. To ensure a stable long-term supply of wood, the Ecotopians early reforested enormous areas that had been cut over by logging companies before Independence. They also planted trees on many hundreds of thousands of acres that had once been cleared for orchards or fields, but had gone wild or lay unused because of the exodus of people from the country into the cities.

I have now been able to visit one of the forest camps that carry out lumbering and tree-planting, and have observed how far the Ecotopians carry their love of trees. They do no clear-cutting at all, and their forests contain not only mixed ages but also mixed species of trees. They argue that the costs of mature-tree cutting are actually less per board foot than clear-cutting—but that even if they weren't it would still be desirable because of less insect damage, less erosion, and more rapid growth of timber. But such arguments are probably only a sophisticated rationale for attitudes that can almost be called tree worship.

* * *

Our economists would surely find the Ecotopian lumber industry a labyrinth of contradictions. An observer like myself can come only to general conclusions. Certainly Ecotopians regard trees as being alive in almost a human sense— once I saw a quite ordinary-looking young man, not visibly drugged, lean against a large oak and mutter "Brother Tree!" And equally certainly, lumber in Ecotopia is cheap and plentiful, whatever the unorthodox means used to produce it. Wood therefore takes the place that aluminum, bituminous facings, and many other modern materials occupy with us.

An important by-product of the Ecotopian forestry policies is that extensive areas, too steep or rugged to be lumbered without causing erosion, have been assigned wilderness status. There all logging and fire roads have been eradicated. Such areas are now used only for camping and as wildlife preserves, and a higher risk of forest fire is apparently accepted.

Source: Ernest Callenbach, *Ecotopia* (Berkeley, CA: Banyan Tree Books, 1975), pp. 55, 57-58.

DOCUMENT 122: Edward Abbey's *The Monkey Wrench Gang* (1975)

The more radical environmental groups, inspired by Thoreau and borrowing their tactics from the civil rights and anti-Vietnam War protesters, engaged in civil disobedience and even sabotage to bring their environmental message to government and the public and to urge industry to stop its environmentally destructive behavior.

Edward Abbey's fact-based novel The Monkey Wrench Gang, *which describes the acts of sabotage committed by a group of eco-warriors, acquired a cult following and has served as a handbook for some of the most radical environmental activists. In October 1998 a group of activists, in an effort to stem the expansion of the ski resort at Vail Mountain in Colorado, set fire to buildings and lifts, causing an estimated $12 million in damages. Earth First!, whose members elsewhere have chained themselves to trees to prevent logging activity, condoned the sabotage.[4]*

In this selection from Abbey's novel, Glen Canyon Dam's intrusive presence in the landscape offers sufficient justification for one of the gang members to make plans to blow it up. In 1997 some less radical Americans, in a House Resources Committee hearing about Lake Powell, actually proposed that Congress take action to restore Glen Canyon by draining the lake.[5]

They passed the Wahweap Marina turnoff. Miles away down the long slope of sand, slickrock, blackbrush, Indian ricegrass and prickly pear they could see a cluster of buildings, a house-trailer compound, roads, docks and clusters of boats on the blue bay of the lake. Lake Powell, Jewel of the Colorado, 180 miles of reservoir walled in by bare rock.

The blue death, Smith called it. Like Hayduke his heart was full of a healthy hatred. Because Smith remembered something different. He remembered the golden river flowing to the sea. He remembered canyons called Hidden Passage and Salvation and Last Chance and Forbidden and Twilight and many many more, some that never had a name. He remembered the strange great amphitheaters called Music Temple and Cathedral in the Desert. All these things now lay beneath the dead water of the reservoir, slowly disappearing under layers of descending silt. How could he forget? He had seen too much.

Now they came, amidst an increasing flow of automobile and truck traffic, to the bridge and Glen Canyon Dam. Smith parked his truck in front of the Senator Carl Hayden Memorial Building. He and his friend got out and walked along the rail to the center of the bridge.

Seven hundred feet below streamed what was left of the original river, the greenish waters that emerged, through intake, pen-stock, turbine and tunnel, from the powerhouse at the base of the dam. Thickets of power cables, each strand as big around as a man's arm, climbed the canyon walls on steel towers, merged in a maze of transformer stations, then splayed out toward the south and west—toward Albuquerque, Babylon, Phoenix, Gomorrah, Los Angeles, Sodom, Las Vegas, Nineveh, Tucson, the cities of the plain.

Upriver from the bridge stood the dam, a glissade of featureless concrete sweeping seven hundred feet down in a concave facade from the dam's rim to the green-grass lawn on the roof of the power plant below.

They stared at it. The dam demanded attention. It was a magnificent mass of cement. Vital statistics: 792,00 tons of concrete aggregate; cost

$750 million and the lives of sixteen (16) work-men. Four years in the making, prime contrac-tor Morrison-Knudsen, Inc., sponsored by U.S. Bureau of Reclamation, courtesy U.S. taxpayers.

It's too big," she said.

"That's right, honey," he said. "And that's why."

"You can't.

"There's a way."

Source: Edward Abbey, *The Monkey Wrench Gang* (Philadelphia: Lippincott, 1975), pp. 36-37.

DOCUMENT 123: Greenpeace's Declaration of Interdependence (1976)

Greenpeace's "Declaration of Interdependence" explains why Greenpeace—which has employed innovative but always nonviolent tactics to effect environmental change—believed radical activism was necessary. Today, Greenpeace, like many other onceradical groups, maintains an office in Washington, D.C., and works closely with the Washington establishment.

We have arrived at a place in history where decisive action must be taken to avoid a general environmental disaster. With nuclear reactors proliferating and over 900 species on the endangered list, there can be no further delay or our children will be denied their future.

The Greenpeace Foundation hopes to stimulate practical, intelligent actions to stem the tide of planetary destruction. We are "rainbow people" representing every race, every nation, every living creature. We are patriots, not of any one nation, state or military alliance, but of the entire earth.

It must be understood that the innocent word "ecology" contains a concept that is as revolutionary as anything since the Copernican breakthrough, when it was discovered that the earth was not the center of the entire universe. Through ecology, science has embarked on a quest for the great systems of order that underlie the complex flow of life on our planet. This quest has taken us far beyond the realm of traditional scientific thought. Like religion, ecology seeks to answer the infinite mysteries of life itself. Harnessing the tools of logic, deduction, analysis, and empiricism, ecology may prove to be the first true science-religion.

As suddenly as Copernicus taught us that the earth was not the center of the universe, ecology teaches us that mankind is not the center of life on this planet. Each species has its function

in the scheme of life. Each has a role, however obscure that role may be.

Ecology has taught us that the entire earth is part of our "body" and that we must learn to respect it as much as we respect ourselves. As we love ourselves, we must also love all forms of life in the planetary system—the whales, the seals, the forests and the seas. The tremendous beauty of ecological thought is that it shows us a pathway back to an understanding of the natural world—an understanding that is imperative if we are to avoid a total collapse of the global ecosystem.

Ecology has provided us with many insights. These may be grouped into three basic "Laws of Ecology" which hold true for all forms of life—fish, plants, insects, plankton, whales, and man. These laws may be stated as follows:

The First Law of Ecology states that all forms of life are interdependent. The prey is as dependent on the predator for the control of its population as the predator is on the prey for a supply of food. . . .

The Second Law of Ecology states that the stability (unity, security, harmony, togetherness) of ecosystems is dependent on their diversity (complexity). An ecosystem that contains 100 different species is more stable than an ecosystem that has only three species. Thus the complex tropical rain-forest is more stable than the fragile arctic tundra. . . .

The Third Law of Ecology states that all resources (food, water, air, minerals, energy) are finite and there are limits to the growth of all living systems. These limits are finally dictated by the finite size of the earth and the finite input of energy from the sun. . . .

If we ignore the logical implications of these "Laws of Ecology" we will continue to be guilty of crimes against the earth. We will not be judged by men for these crimes, but with a justice meted out by the earth itself. The destruction of the earth will lead, inevitably, to the destruction of ourselves.

So let us work together to put an end to the destruction of the earth by the forces of human greed and ignorance. Through an understanding of the principles of ecology we must find new directions for the evolution of human values and human institutions. *Short-term economics* must be replaced with actions based on the need for conservation and preservation of the entire global ecosystem. We must learn to live in harmony, not only with our fellow man, but with all the beautiful creatures on this planet.

Source: Greenpeace, "Declaration of Interdependence," in Peter C. List, ed., *Radical Environmentalism: Philosophy and Tactics* (Belmont, CA: Wadsworth, 1993), pp. 134-35.

Part VII

Confronting Economic and Social Realities, 1980–1999

In the 1980s the Reagan administration, partly due to its pro- corporate and anti-big-government stance, attempted to eviscerate the Environmental Protection Agency (EPA), first, by drastically cutting its funding and, second, by taking the teeth out of much of the environmental legislation passed in the 1970s. Ronald Reagan brought into the government a number of anti-environmentalists, including James Watt as secretary of the Interior and Anne Gorsuch (Buford) as head of the EPA. Vehemently opposed to the regulation of business and focused on the need to develop and use resources, they encouraged groups in industries such as ranching, mining, and logging to be advocates for the "wise use" of resources. In 1981 Watt stated, "We will mine more, drill more, cut more timber to use our resources rather than simply keep them locked up."[1]

The Reagan administration's pro-corporate position reflected concern about the nation's ability to remain a strong contender in the increasingly competitive global marketplace. For nearly forty years following World II, Germany and Japan had been demilitarized and were busy building modern factories to replace their war-damaged industrial infrastructures, while the United States was still spending large sums to maintain its military power. In the Northeast and Midwest, factory towns were abandoned and inner cities decayed, as factories moved south or overseas in search of cheap labor and freedom from the constraints of labor laws and environmental regulation.

It was not until the disintegration of the Soviet Union at the end of the 1980s that the United States was willing to turn its attention to its own aging infrastructure and the shift to a services-based economy. However, by the 1980s newly industrialized countries in Southeast Asia and the Pacific Rim, including Singapore, Malaysia, and South Korea, and in Latin America, including Brazil, had joined Germany and Japan in competing with the United States for manufacturing jobs, and the nation's blue-collar jobs continued to disappear into foreign factories, some owned by American corporations or their subsidiaries and others by entrepreneurs in the newly industrialized countries.

After World War II, many farm jobs also disappeared, as farmers sold off their land to real estate developers and small farms found it more and more difficult to compete with giant agribusinesses. Slowly, an increasing portion of the country's food supply was imported, and by 1996, 16.4 percent of the produce consumed by Americans was imported.[2]

During the same period, however, the service and high-tech sectors of the American economy were expanding and creating new jobs. As computers found their way into offices and then homes and as computerized machines took over simple factory jobs, the whole structure of the workplace began to change.

Despite the decrease in manufacturing and farm jobs, the possibility of employment continued to attract tens of thousands of foreign immigrants to the United States every year. While the population of most developed countries and much of eastern Europe had stabilized or was even declining, the U.S. population continued to increase as a result of immigration pressures from Latin American and Asia, where populations were still burgeoning. Although the rate of U.S. population growth had begun to decline, the actual numbers of people continued to rise rapidly. In 1990 there were 249 million people in the United States—70 million more than in 1960, and nearly double the nation's population in 1940. The proportion of elderly people in the U.S. population was also increasing as the nation's already high life-expectancy rate (71.8 years for men and 78.8 years for women in 1990) continued to rise.

The Environmental Debate Heats Up

An expanding population required more water, more energy, and more land for home construction and also created more waste and more pollution. By the 1980s, the negative impact of population growth on environmental quality had become evident to most Americans, although individual rights advocates and business interests adversely affected by specific legislative or judicial actions objected to the imposition of environmental controls. While such arch opponents of stringent environmental controls as Dixy Lee Ray [see Document 138] comprehended that a profligate use of natural resources could have unhealthy consequences for the nation, they questioned whether pollution from human activities such as automobile emissions, nuclear energy use, and waste disposal had as much negative impact as environmentalists claimed. How individuals view the potential risk of a

particular environmental hazard is frequently based on how the hazard or its elimination will affect their lives: Is there a chance that it could affect them economically, in a positive or a negative way? Is there a chance that it could affect their health or the health of their children? Is there a chance that it will impinge on their freedom—to use their land, to drive, or to smoke, for example? People's attitudes about environmental hazards and how to deal with them are also colored by socio-economic status, political affiliation, and preconceived notions [see Document 146].

Some economists, including Julian Simon [see Document 127], were convinced that there is no need to panic about the effect of population growth on resource use and degradation, and have asserted that human technological innovation will enable us to overcome, at least in the near future, expanding demand for food and other resources. Simon's vision has been supported by "wise use" advocates, who have long been committed to the continued exploitation and development of America's natural resources for the benefit of its human inhabitants.

In contrast, environmentalists such as Lester Brown [see Document 126] insist that we give greater value to nature's services; we must adjust our appetites to fit in with the functioning of natural processes and the limits of the natural world. Edward Wilson has proposed the development of a new conservation ethic based on a biocentric approach to living on earth, whereby people look at themselves as biological as well as cultural beings [see Document 133].

Environmentalists like Mark Sagoff [see Document 125], Arne Naess [see Document 129], and Barry Lopez [see 143] hold that the country needs to refocus its priorities away from a narrow emphasis on economic efficiency and give greater consideration to social values such as justice, equity, and spirituality when making government policy.

The most radical ecologists and environmentalists have advocated a vast change in the American lifestyle. They claim that the human race must quickly take account of the needs of the natural world and turn from being ignorant predators into thoughtful custodians of other living things on this planet. Whether because we are destroying the only environment suitable for human habitation or because the environment we are creating is not one they would want to live in [*see* Documents 123], they advocate immediate and sometimes radical action.

Intensifying these arguments, which were extensions of the Malthusian debate that had been ongoing since the eighteenth century, was the new issue of global warming. On one side were those, like Dixie Lee Ray [*see* Document 138], who viewed recent warming trends as a product of natural climate variability, and those, like James Hansen [*see* Document 137], who believed that the trend was the result of the greenhouse gases produce by human activity.

The Complexity of Environmental Issues

As the millennium approached, apocalyptic voices predicting devastating global warming, uncontrollable global epidemics, the dwindling of adequate and safe water supplies, and the disappearance of fish [*see* Document 147] were heard with increasing frequency. For half a century, U.S. environmental regulations and internationally adopted conventions had resulted in substantial improvements in the quality of life of large numbers of people. However, by the end of the twentieth century, it had become obvious that many of the environmental problems facing the United States and the world did not have simple solutions, because the problems themselves were very complex and because, especially on the national and international levels, the solutions had to satisfy widely diverse constituencies.

Environmental issues are intertwined with such seemingly disparate issues as health, the economy, social justice, and national security. Resolving such complex problems entails finding acceptable balances among individual rights, societal needs, economic priorities, ethical values, and the constraints of the natural environment.

One pressing problem is how to satisfy an exponentially growing demand for energy. Because the quantity of energy used correlates with how industrially developed a country is, as more countries advanced industrially, it became increasingly clear that not only would energy use increase, but so would the accompanying pollution and environmental degradation—unless the world as a whole grew less dependent on fossil fuels. Compounding this is the disproportionately high per capita use of energy in the United States compared to other industrially advanced nations.

From the 1950s to the 1970s, nuclear energy was widely viewed as a possible solution to increased energy demand [*see* Document 94]. However, the partial meltdown at Three Mile Island and the nuclear plant disaster in Chernobyl, Ukraine, increased American anxiety about the risks posed by nuclear energy use and provided a basis for strenuous opposition to the construction of new nuclear power plants [*see* Document 131]. In 2003 no new nuclear power plant had been built in this country for thirty years.3 Despite calls for the development of renewable energy and clean fuels [*see* Document 142], high cost and low efficiency were impediments to the widespread adoption of alternative fuels.

California, whose severe air pollution problems were exacerbated by a life-style dependent on cars, passed some of the strictest auto emissions regulations in the country in 1990. But in 1996 the state had to roll back plans to attain the agreed on emission reductions [*see* Document 141] because automobiles that met those standards proved too expensive or did not otherwise appeal to consumers and also because the federal government refused to support such stringent CAFE (Corporate Average Fuel Economy) standards. American automakers may have been willing to put effort into the development of fuel-efficient cars [*see* Document 140], but as long as sales of gas-guzzling vehicles—such as sport utility vehicles and pickup trucks—were more profitable, that was where the companies focused their attention. While auto fuel efficiency and emissions quality have steadily improved, the number of vehicles on American roads as well as the number of vehicle miles traveled have continued to climb (between 1980 and 1995 the total number of cars and trucks in use increased by 53.6 million vehicles), thereby reducing air quality gains.

Land use is another complex issue. As the nation's population increases, there is a constant demand for land on which to build homes. But the building of homes on former farmland pushes agricultural regions farther and farther from population centers, and the construction of homes in wilderness areas endangers wildlife habitats and shrinks the nation's open space. Building homes in coastal regions and wetlands areas not only endangers precarious ecosystems, but also poses the issue of the insurability of waterfront property due to shifting water courses and changing land profiles [*see* Document 128].

Using arid lands for home construction, agriculture, or grazing creates a host of new problems, from the urgent need for an adequate water supply to unanticipated consequences of destabilizing a fragile landscape.

The 1980s and 1990s saw a growing movement to protect farmland and open space, as more and more people in suburban and rural areas began to realize that development was eating away at their cherished way of life, and the places with which they had a bond. In November 1998, there were more than two hundred different questions on ballots across the nation on issues relating to open space and farmland conservation programs.

A third complex problem is that of waste disposal. The need to dispose of increasing amounts of household wastes (including tons of packaging); a wide and growing range of toxic chemicals employed in industry, agriculture, and the home; and accumulating radioactive wastes pose problems of where to put the wastes, how to dispose safely of dangerous wastes, and how to deal with pollution from the improper disposal of toxic materials [*see* Documents 124 and 136].

In the 1980s, as localities began to run out of acceptable locations for dumping trash, attention turned to the development of recycling programs, since recycling would certainly help to reduce the space needed for waste disposal. While some people were beginning to think about trash as a valuable source of energy and others were looking at recycling as a useful tool for conserving natural resources, many questioned the economics and physical efficiency of recycling.

The not-in-my-backyard (NIMBY) objections to the siting of garbage dumps as well as of unsightly and polluting industrial development exemplify the social aspect of environmental issues. Those with money and power insist on having clean water, clean air and unpolluted land in their backyards, while the poor and minorities are the most likely to end up living in environmentally degraded neighborhoods [*see* Document 136].

Powerful industries often require a financial inducement to encourage them to undertake environmentally beneficial action. One novel approach to dealing with resistance to pollution regulation is a system of emissions trading known as "cap-and-trade" [*see* Document 139] that was championed by a lawyer working in the Reagan administration, C. Boyden

Gray. While it proved effective in controlling acid rain, attempts to extend the mechanism to other types of pollution were halted by political opposition.

Dealing With Innovations' Unintended Consequences

The introduction of new technologies and products and the alteration of the landscape not infrequently has produced unforeseen changes in the environment. By the late twentieth century numerous efforts were being made to undo some of the unintended consequences of new products and environmental alterations. In Marin County in northern California, whole forests of introduced eucalyptus trees (an invasive species in the California environment) were cut down and replaced with native oaks. In south Florida, efforts have been underway since the early 1980s to undo some of the channelization of the waters flowing into and out of the Kissimmee River, Lake Okeechobee, and the Everglades system that had been instituted over the past century [*see* Document 132]. Both large and small dams on rivers that impeded the movement of fish and interfered with their spawning have been dismantled, and in the 1990s there was even serious talk of undoing such monumental projects as Glen Canyon Dam on the Colorado River in northern Arizona. These kinds of restoration projects, however, may never be able to return the sites to their original condition. Over time the presence of foreign species of plants and animals or of man-made structures may themselves have affected changes that impact the restoration projects.

While many technological advances and scientific innovations—from great dams to wonder drugs—have provided immediate benefits to large numbers of people, we are discovering that some of these "improvements" have merely shifted the nature of the environmental problems with which we have to cope [*see* Document 148]. The biotechnology revolution offers the possibility of creating ever more productive food plants and animals and eliminating genetic diseases, but some of these new organisms and gene changes involve the manipulation of nature at the most fundamental level, and this revolution is sure to be followed by a host of unplanned environmental consequences [*see* Document 150].

As the marine ecologist Jane Lubchenco noted in 1997, "during the last few decades humans have emerged as a new force of nature. We are modifying physical, chemical, and biological systems in new ways, at faster rates, and over larger spatial scales than ever recorded on Earth. Humans have unwittingly embarked upon a grand experiment with our planet. The outcome of this experiment is unknown, but has profound implications for all of life on Earth." [4]

Global Environmental Effects of Local Human Activity

The global environmental effects of many local and national activities complicate the task of balancing competing priorities. Population expansion, energy use, hunting and fishing of migratory species,

wetlands use, waste disposal, and industrial pollution can all have international repercussions.

The recognition that environmental degradation is a global concern has resulted in a multiplicity of international declarations, protocols, and treaties on such issues as acid rain, climate change, marine pollution, the use of marine resources, and ozone protection [see Documents 130, 134, 135, and 143]. But as Jurgen Schmandt et al. point out, such agreements are meaningless unless all the parties to the agreement impose national rulings to enforce the agreement [see Document 134]. Obviously, nations will not undertake such action if the agreement appears to be detrimental to their own economic or political interests [see Documents 130 and 149].

DOCUMENT 124: Comprehensive Environmental Response, Compensation, and Liability Act (1980)

In 1978 the community of Love Canal near Niagara Falls, New York, had to be evacuated when toxic wastes dumped in the region created a serious health hazard. Partly in response to this disaster, Congress passed the Comprehensive Environmental Response, Compensation, and Liability Act, better known as the Superfund Act. In the decades since this law came in effect, a few notorious waste sites have been at least partially cleaned up, but because of the difficulty and cost of toxic waste removal, both industry and government have frequently sought ways to circumvent the law.

Sec. 104. (a) (1) Whenever (A) any hazardous substance is released or there is a substantial threat of such a release into the environment, or (B) there is a release or substantial threat of release into the environment of any pollutant or contaminant which may present an imminent and substantial danger to the public health or welfare, the President is authorized to act, consistent with the national contingency plan, to remove or arrange for the removal of, and provide for remedial action relating to such hazardous substance, pollutant or contaminant at any time (including its removal from any contaminated natural resource), or take any other response measure consistent with the national contingency plan which the President deems necessary to protect the public health or welfare or the environment, unless the President determines that such removal and remedial action will be done properly by the owner or operator of the vessel or facility from which the release or threat of release emanates, or by any other responsible party.

(2) For the purposes of this section, "pollutant or contaminant" shall include, but not be limited to, any element, substance, compound, or mixture, including disease-causing agents, which after release into the environment and upon exposure, ingestion, inhalation, or assimilation into any organism, either directly from the environment or indirectly by ingestion through food chains, will or may reasonably be anticipated to cause death, disease, behavioral abnormalities, cancer, genetic mutation, physiological malfunctions (including malfunctions in reproduction) or physical deformations, in such organisms or their offspring. The term does not include petrochemicals, including crude oil and any fraction thereof which is not otherwise specifically listed or designated as hazardous substances under section 101 . . . of this title, nor does it include natural gas, liquified natural gas, or synthetic gas of pipeline quality. . . .

Sec. 105. Within one hundred and eighty days after the enactment of this Act, the President shall, after notice and opportunity for public comments, revise the national contingency plan for the removal of oil and hazardous substances, originally prepared and published pursuant to section 311 of the Federal Water Pollution Control Act, to reflect and effectuate the responsibilities and powers created by this Act. . . . Such revision shall include a section of the plan to be known as the national hazardous substance response plan which shall establish procedures and standards for responding to releases of hazardous substances, pollutants, and contaminants, which shall include at a minimum:

(1) methods for discovering and investigating facilities at which hazardous substances have been disposed of or otherwise come to be located;

(2) methods for evaluating, including analyses of relative cost, and remedying any releases or threats of releases from facilities which pose substantial danger to the public health or the environment;

(3) methods and criteria for determining the appropriate extent of removal, remedy, and other measures authorized by this Act;

(4) appropriate roles and responsibilities for the Federal, State, and local governments, and for interstate and nongovernmental entities in effectuating the plan;

(5) provision for identification, procurement, maintenance, and storage of response equipment and supplies;

(6) a method for and assignment of responsibility for reporting the existence of such facilities which may be located on federally owned or controlled properties and any releases of hazardous substances from such facilities;

(7) means of assuring that remedial action measures are cost-effective over the period of potential exposure to the hazardous substances or contaminated materials;

(8) (A) criteria for determining priorities among releases or threatened releases throughout the United States for the purpose of taking remedial action, and, to the extent practicable taking into account the potential urgency of such action, for the purpose of taking removal action. Criteria and priorities under this paragraph shall be based upon relative risk or danger to public health or welfare or the environment, in the judgment of the President, taking into account to the extent possible the population at risk, the hazard potential of the hazardous substances at such facilities, the potential for contamination of drinking water supplies, the potential for direct human contact, the potential for destruction of sensitive ecosystems, State preparedness to assume State costs and responsibilities, and other appropriate factors.

(B) based upon the criteria set forth in subparagraph (A) of this paragraph, the President shall list as part of the plan national priorities among the known releases or threatened releases throughout the United States and shall revise the list no less often than annually. Within one year after the date of enactment of this Act, and annually thereafter, each State shall establish and submit for consideration by the President priorities for remedial action among known releases and potential releases in that State. . . .

(9) specific roles for private organizations and entities in preparation for response and in responding to releases of hazardous substances.

Source: Public Law 96-510, *United States Statutes at Large,* Vol. 94, Part 3 (Washington, D.C.: Government Printing Office, 1981), 96th Cong., December 11, 1980, pp. 2774-75, 2779–80.

DOCUMENT 125: Mark Sagoff on the Public Interest (1981)

The political philosopher Mark Sagoff objects to economic efficiency being the sole criterion for determining government policy. Economic efficiency, Sagoff notes, does not distinguish between public and private interests. It takes into account only private, self-serving interests (typically to be satisfied in markets), and ignores morality, justice, and spirituality, which are fundamental public values that should be determined through a deliberative political process.

Writing in the June 1997 issue of the Atlantic Monthly, *he posited that "the world has the wealth and the resources to provide everyone the opportunity to live a decent life. We consume too much when market relationships displace the bonds of community, compassion, culture, and place. We consume too much when consumption becomes an end in itself and makes us lose affection and reverence for the natural world."*[5]

Many economists take the view that environmental problems are economic problems. They believe that market failure causes these problems: private and social costs diverge; profit-maximizing decisions, therefore, are socially inefficient. Economists would correct this market failure by requiring private decision-makers to internalize externalities, that is, to make the price of goods reflect all the economic and social costs of producing them, including the pollution costs. When this is done, they argue, pollution will be controlled, endangered species will be saved, and pristine areas will be preserved, but only to the extent that the benefits exceed the costs. Any increase in environmental protection from an "optimal" level "would cost more than it is worth," while any decrease would "reduce benefits more than it would save in costs."

Although this economic approach purports to allow us to choose the best among available policies, in fact it makes economic efficiency our only goal. Economic efficiency has traditionally been understood to require the maximum satisfaction of the preferences that markets reveal. These are typically self-regarding or self-interested preferences, that is, preferences that reflect a person's idea of his or her individual welfare. Preferences of this sort may be contrasted with preferences that express what the individual believes is in the public interest or in the interest of a group or community to which he or she belongs. Political activity is supposed, in theory at least, to provide a vehicle for airing, criticizing, and settling upon interests or opinions of this group-regarding kind.

The search for economic efficiency might take us to the best public policies if we were a nation of individualists competing each for his or her own welfare with no regard for or conception of the collective good.

. . . But we are not simply a group of consumers, nor are we bent on satisfying only self-regarding preferences. Many of us advocate ideas and have a vision of what we should do or be like as a nation. And we would sacrifice some of our private interests for those public ends.

. . . Why should we believe that the right policy goal is the one that satisfies only the self-interested preferences of consumers? Why should we not take into account the community-regarding values that individuals seek through the political process as well?

* * *

Anyone who believes that government ought to be primarily interested in correcting market failure must find puzzling much of our environmental legislation. Environmentalist groups, not famous for their economic "common sense," successfully backed much of this legislation in the 1970s. It is not surprising, therefore, that environmental protection goes beyond the mere correction of market deficiencies. Congress designed the Clear Air and Clean Water Acts to improve the quality of our air and water. It passed the Endangered Species Act to protect threatened species, even if the economic costs of protection outweigh the benefits. Similarly, the Occupational Safety and Health Act seeks to make the workplace safe and healthful, a goal that is not always consistent with market efficiency.

* * *

Although economic approaches to public policy may purport to weigh both consumer and citizen values, we may, as citizens, believe that certain public values or collective goals (*e.g.*, that an innocent person not be convicted) supersede the values that we pursue as self-seeking individuals (*e.g.*, security from crime). Moreover, we might decide to sacrifice economic optimality for cleaner air and water. Once legislatures, responding to political pressure, have made this choice, is it defensible for economists to insist that our policymaking process include the very consumer values that we have decided to sacrifice?

* * *

When an environmentalist argues that we ought to preserve wilderness areas because of their cultural importance and symbolic meaning, he or she states a *conviction* and not a *desire*. When an economist asserts that we ought to attain efficient levels of pollution, he or she, too, states a belief. Both beliefs are supported by arguments, not money.

* * *

What many economists do not understand is that efficiency is one value among many and is not a meta-value that comprehends all others. Economists as a rule do recognize one other value, namely, justice or equality, and they speak, therefore, of a "trade-off" between efficiency and equality. They do not speak, as they should, however, about the trade-off between efficiency and our aesthetic and moral values. What about the trade-off between efficiency and dignity, efficiency and self-respect, efficiency and the magnificence of our natural heritage, efficiency and the quality of life? These are the trade-offs that are important in setting environmental policy.

Source: Mark Sagoff, "Economic Theory and Environmental Law," *Michigan Law Review* 79 (1981): 1393, 1395-96, 1399, 1416, 1419.

DOCUMENT 126: Lester R. Brown on Building a Sustainable Society (1981)

In 1974 Lester Brown, who holds a degree in agriculture and at one time worked for the U.S. Department of Agriculture, founded the Worldwatch Institute, an organization devoted to worldwide environmental issues relating to sustainability and global interdependency. The institute's influential annual report on the environment, State of the World, became a sourcebook for corporate leaders and government policymakers around the world.

The concept of sustainable development is an outgrowth of ideas developed by conservationist-minded land and forest managers such as John Wesley Powell and Gifford Pinchot who, at the end of the nineteenth century, began calling for the wise use of America's resources [see Documents 58 and 73]. Interest in sustainable development gained momentum in the 1970s, but the focus of the new breed of conservationists who supported this concept was on international economic, energy, and resource policies and on activities that would make sustainability possible.

The international community's commitment to sustainable development was made evident in the Stockholm Declaration [see Document 119] and was clearly enunciated in both the 1987 Brundtland Report (the United Nations World Commission on Environment and Development's plan for nations to find areas of agreement on environmental issues that involve the interplay of environmental and economic factors, which extended the concept of sustainable development to the entire globe).[6] and the 1992 United Nations Conference on Environment and Development (UNCED) "Programme of Action for Sustainable Development," also known as the Rio Declaration [see Document 144].

A sustainable society will differ from the one we now know in several respects. Population size will more or less be stationary, energy will be used far more efficiently, and the economy will be fueled largely with renewable sources of energy. As a result, people and industrial activity will be more widely dispersed, far less concentrated in urban agglomerations than they are in a petroleum-fueled society.

The transition to renewable energy will endow the global economy with a permanence that coal and oil-based societies lack. More than that, it could lead us out of an inequitable, inherently unstable international energy regime since, unlike coal and oil, solar energy is diffuse, available in many forms, and accessible to all countries.

As the switch from fossil energy to solar energy progresses, the geographic distribution of economic activity is destined to change, conforming to the location of the new energy sources. The transition to a sustainable society promises to reshape diets, the distribution of population, and modes of transportation. It seems likely to alter rural- urban relationships within countries and the competitive position of national economies in the world market. Then too, a sustainable society will require labor force skills markedly different from those of the current oil-based economy.

* * *

Before us now is the opportunity to adjust our values according to our changing perceptions of our world and our place in it. Of necessity, the path to sustainability will be littered with cast-off values. Materialism, planned obsolescence, and a desire for large families will not survive the transition. But they will not leave a void. Frugality, a desire for a harmonious relationship with nature, and other values compatible with a sustainable society will take their place.

Source: Lester R. Brown, *Building a Sustainable Society* (New York: Norton, 1981), pp. 247-48, 350.

DOCUMENT 127: Julian L. Simon on Population Growth (1981)

Many people disagree with the apocalyptic environmentalists such as Paul Ehrlich [see Document 107] and the radical environmentalists such as Arne Naess [see Document 129], who argue that we must take immediate action to constrain the human impact on the environment. One of the most strident opponents of their ideas was Julian Simon, a professor of economics and business administration at the University of Illinois at the time that he wrote The Ultimate Resource, *from which this selection is taken, as a popularization of his earlier book about population growth. Simon later moved to the Heritage Foundation, a conservative think-tank in Washington, D.C.*

In 1980, Simon made a now famous wager with Paul Ehrlich[see Document 107] about the future cost of five metals (copper, chromium, nickel, tin, and tungsten), with Ehrlich betting their prices would go up and Simon betting they would go down as a result of improved technology. In 1997, when the wager was settled, Ehrlich was the loser.

Food. Contrary to popular impression, the per capita food situation has been improving for the three decades since World War II, the only decades for which we have acceptable data. We also know that famine has progressively diminished for at least the past century. And there is strong reason to believe that human nutrition will continue to improve into the indefinite future, even with continued population growth.

Land. Agricultural land is not a fixed resource, as Malthus [*see* Document 26] and many since Malthus have thought. Rather, the amount of agricultural land has been, and still is, increasing substantially, and it is likely to continue to increase where needed. Paradoxically, in the countries that are best supplied with food, such as the U.S., the quantity of land under cultivation has been decreasing because it is more economical to raise larger yields on less land than to increase the total amount of farmland. For this reason, among others, land for recreation and for wildlife has been increasing rapidly in the U.S. All this may be hard to believe, but solid data substantiate these statements beyond a doubt.

Natural resources. Hold your hat—our supplies of natural resources are not finite in any economic sense. Nor does past experience give reason to expect natural resources to become more scarce. Rather, if the past is any guide, natural resources will progressively become less scarce, and less costly, and will constitute a smaller proportion of our expenses in future years. And population growth is likely to have a long-run *beneficial* impact on the natural-resource situation.

Energy. Grab your hat again—the long-run future of our energy supply is at least as bright as that of other natural resources, though political maneuvering can temporarily boost prices from time to time. Finiteness is no problem here either. And the long-run impact of additional people is likely to speed the development of a cheap energy supply that is almost inexhaustible.

Pollution. This set of issues is as complicated as you wish to make it. But even many ecologists, as well as the bulk of economists, agree that population growth is not the villain in the creation and reduction of pollution. And the key trend is that life expectancy, which is the best over-all index of pollution level, has improved markedly as the world's population has grown.

* * *

There is no physical or economic reason why human resourcefulness and enterprise cannot forever continue to respond to impending shortages and existing problems with new expedients that, after an adjustment period, leave us better off than before the problem arose. Adding more people will cause us more such problems, but at the same time there will be more people to solve these problems and leave us with the bonus of lower costs and less scarcity in the long run. The bonus applies to such desirable resources as better health, more wilderness, cheaper energy, and a cleaner environment.

Source: Julian L. Simon, *The Ultimate Resource* (Princeton, NJ: Princeton University Press,1981), pp. 5-6, 345-46.

DOCUMENT 128: Coastal Barrier Resources Act (1981)

Much of the energy of the environmental movement that gained ground in the 1960s was concentrated on promoting legislation to protect oceanfront beaches and the salt marshes behind them. In 1972, the same year that the Clean Water Act was passed, Congress approved the Coastal Zone Management Act, a measure designed to convince states to develop broad management plans for their coastal regions and help them pay for the planning process. However, the bill did not directly address any major problems associated with the development of the barrier islands, including the risks to wildlife or the enormous federal expenses that would stem from development. These issues were left for the Coastal Barrier Resources Act, passed in 1981.

The bill clearly affected how private property along the coast would be used. Although it did not restrict land use, it did remove some federal support for the development of coastal lands, and therefore real estate interests opposed it. Environmentalists favored the Coastal Barrier Resources Act because it promoted the conservation of island and salt marsh habitats. Others supported the bill because they believed it would reduce catastrophic property damage and loss of life due to hurricanes. Still others saw the Coastal Barrier Resources Act as a way to reduce federal spending by eliminating federal insurance protection for residences and businesses built in high-risk areas (where, it was estimated, payments for damages in 1980 exceeded premium payments by three to one).

At the hearings preceding the vote on the bill, two of the key speakers were James W. Pulliam, Jr., deputy associate director of the U.S. Fish and Wildlife Service's National Wildlife Refuge System, who favored the bill; and Lawrence Young, representing the National Association of Realtors, who opposed it. Their statements highlight the fundamental conflict between wildlife managers and conservationists on one side and land developers on the other.

A. The Bill

Sec. 2. Findings and Purpose

(a) Findings. The Congress finds that—

(1) coastal barriers along the Atlantic and gulf coasts of the United States and the adjacent wetlands, marshes, estuaries, inlets, and nearshore waters provide—

(A) habitats for migratory birds and other wildlife; and

(B) habitats which are essential spawning, nursery, nesting, and feeding areas for commercially and recreationally important species of fin-fish and shellfish, as well as other aquatic organisms such as sea turtles;

(2) coastal barriers contain resources of extraordinary scenic, scientific, recreational, natural, historic, archeological, cultural, and economic importance, which are being irretrievable damaged and lost due to development on, among, and adjacent to such barriers;

(3) coastal barriers serve as natural storm protective buffers and are generally unsuitable for development because they are vulnerable to hurricane and other storm damage and because natural shoreline recession and the movement of unstable sediments undermine manmade structures;

(4) certain actions and programs of the Federal Government have subsidized and encouraged development on coastal barriers and the result has been the loss of barrier resources, threats to human life, health, and property, and the recurring expenditure of millions of tax dollars; and

(5) a program of coordinated action by Federal, State, and local governments is critical to the more appropriate use and conservation of coastal barrier resources.

(b) Purpose. The Congress declares that it is the purpose of this Act to minimize the loss of human life, wasteful expenditure of Federal revenues, and damage to fish and wildlife and other resources associated with the coastal barriers along the Atlantic and gulf coasts by establishing a Coastal Barrier Resources System, by restricting future Federal expenditures and financial assistance which have the effect of encouraging development of coastal barriers, and by considering the means and measures by which the long-term conservation of these coastal barrier resources may be achieved.

B. Excerpts from Key Testimony

Statement of James W. Pulliam, Jr.

The great concentrations and diversity of fish and wildlife associated with the relatively limited area of coastal barriers can, in part, be attributed to the role of these landforms as the terrestrial buffer between protected estuaries and lagoons and the more turbulent nearshore ocean waters. These waters, including estuarine and lagoon marshes, intertidal beaches and tidal flats, are among the most fertile and productive known. . . . Up to 90 percent of all commercially important fin and shellfish caught on the Atlantic and gulf coasts are dependent during some stage of their life cycle on estuarine habitat largely created by coastal barriers. Many of these species, as well as others, constitute the base of a large recreational fishery along the Atlantic and gulf coasts. . . .

These primary consumers in the estuarine ecosystem in turn attract and support secondary consumers of the food web, including shorebirds, wading birds, waterfowl, raptors, and mammals.

Migratory waterfowl are winter inhabitants of coastal barriers and the waters which lie behind them. Species which rely on these ecosystems include whistling swans, snow and Canada geese, widgeon, gadwall and mallards. . . .

Barriers along the Atlantic and gulf coast are also a key migration route for several raptors. The peregrine falcon and, in particular, the arctic peregrine, use the coastal barriers, feeding primarily on sanderlings, killdeer, flickers, and other medium-sized birds. Other species utilizing these landforms include the bald eagle, merlin, osprey, kestrel, and marsh hawk.

* * *

Over 20 vertebrate species associated with coastal barrier islands have been listed pursuant to the Endangered Species Act of 1973 [*see* Document 120]. These include such endangered birds as the whooping crane, bald eagle, eastern brown pelican, as well as other wildlife species like the manatee, American crocodile, and the green loggerhead, Ridley, and hawksbill sea turtles.

Statement of Lawrence Young

[T]he position of the National Association of Realtors is that it is opposed to the enactment of the Coastal Barrier Resources Act. . . . This legislationwill deny reasonable use of private property and is a de facto Federal land-use bill masquerading as a fiscally conservative measure. The chief aim of this bill is to halt coastal development and Congress should address this legislation on that basis.

Source: Barrier Islands: Hearings Before the Subcommittee on Fisheries and Wildlife Conservation and the Environment and the Subcommittee on Oceanography of the Committee on Merchant Marine and Fisheries, House of Representatives, 97th Cong., 1st sess., on H.R. 3252, April 27, 1981, June 23, 1981, June 22, 1982 (Washington, D.C.: Government Printing Office, n.d.), Serial no. 97-37, pp. 9-10; Statements: pp. 24-26, 346.

DOCUMENT 129: Arne Naess on Deep Ecology (1982, 1984)

The deep ecologist Arne Naess, a Norwegian philosopher who has taught in the United States, developed a radical, very personal approach to environmental issues. In his 1973 essay "The Shallow and the Deep, Long-Range Ecology Movements," Naess dismisses the "fight against pollution and resource depletion" as a "Shallow Ecology movement" with only "the health and affluence of people in the developed countries" as its "central objective."[7] He proposes that people who are seriously concerned about the environment should reconsider some of their basic assumptions and values. Naess's ideas were little known in the United States until the 1980s, when they were promoted and developed by the philosopher George Sessions and the sociologist Bill Devall. His basic principles of deep ecology—the deep ecology platform—were refined on a camping trip to Death Valley, California, with Sessions in April 1984.

A. Arne Naess Explains Deep Ecology, 1982

The essence of deep ecology is to ask deeper questions. The adjective "deep" stresses that we ask why and how, where others do not. For instance, ecology as a science does not ask what kind of a society would be the best for maintaining a particular ecosystem—that is considered a question for value theory, for politics, for ethics. As long as ecologists keep narrowly to their science, they do not ask such questions. What we need today is a tremendous expansion of ecological thinking in what I call ecosophy. *Sophy* comes from the Greek term *sophia,* "wisdom," which relates to ethics, norms, rules, and practice. Ecosophy, or deep ecology, then, involves a shift from science to wisdom.

For example, we need to ask questions like, Why do we think that economic growth and high levels of consumption are so important? The conventional answer would be to point to the economic consequences of not having economic growth. But in deep ecology, we ask whether the present society fulfills basic human needs like love and security and access to nature, and, in so doing, we question our society's underlying assumptions. We ask which society, which education, which form of religion, is beneficial for all life on the planet as a whole, and then we ask further what we need to do in order to make the necessary changes. We are not limited to a scientific approach; we have an obligation to verbalize a total view.

B. The Deep Ecology Platform, 1984

1. The flourishing of human and non-human living beings has value in itself. The value of non-human beings is independent of their usefulness to humans.

2. Richness of kinds of living beings has value in itself.

3. Humans have no right to reduce this richness except to satisfy vital human needs.

4. The flourishing of human life is compatible with a substantial decrease of the human population. The flourishing of non- human life requires such a decrease.

5. Present human interference with the non-human world is excessive, and the situation is worsening.

6. Policies must be changed in view of points (1)-(5). These policies affect basic economic, technological, and ideological structures. The resulting state of human affairs will be greatly different from the present.

7. The appreciation of a high quality of life will supersede that of a high standard of life.

8. Those who accept the foregoing points have an obligation to try to contribute directly to the implementation of necessary changes.

Source: A. Stephen Bodian, "Simple in Means, Rich in Ends: A Conversation with Arne Naess," *Ten Directions* (Zen Center of Los Angeles), Summer-Fall 1982, in Bill Devall and George Sessions, eds., *Deep Ecology: Living as if Nature Mattered* (Salt Lake City: Peregrine Smith Books, 1985), p. 75. B. Arne Naess, "Sustainable Development and Deep Ecology," in J. Ronald Engel and Joan Gibb Engel, eds., *Ethics of Environmental Development: Global Challenge, International Response* (London: John Wiley, 1992), p. 88.

DOCUMENT 130: United Nations Convention on the Law of the Sea (1983)

The Law of the Sea is probably the most far reaching of the United Nations environmental agreements. It sets forth the limits of national sovereignty and demands that parties to the agreement abide by international regulation of activity in non-territorial waters. It marked the end of the days when the high seas could be viewed as a commons in which nations could freely dump garbage and harvest resources.

Although the United States is a signatory to the convention—meaning that it agrees to adhere fundamentally to the convention—and even though several amendments that addressed America's strategic concerns about it were later added to the convention, the United States Senate has never ratified it.

Article 2

The sovereignty of a coastal State extends, beyond its land territory and internal waters and, in the case of an archipelagic State, its archipelagic waters, to an adjacent belt of sea, described as the territorial sea.

This sovereignty extends to the air space over the territorial sea as well as to its bed and subsoil.

Article 3

Every State has the right to establish the breadth of its territorial sea up to a limit not exceeding 12 nautical miles, measured from baselines determined in accordance with this Convention.

Article 33

In a zone contiguous to its territorial sea, described as the contiguous zone, the coastal State may exercise the control necessary to:

(a) prevent infringement of its customs, fiscal, immigration or sanitary laws and regulations within its territory or territorial sea;

(b) punish infringement of . . . laws and regulations committed within its territory or territorial sea.

The contiguous zone may not extend beyond 24 nautical miles from the baselines from which the breadth of the territorial sea is measured.

Article 55

The exclusive economic zone is an area beyond and adjacent to the territorial sea, subject to the specific legal regime established in this Part, under which the rights and jurisdiction of the coastal State and the rights and freedoms of other States are governed by the relevant provisions of this Convention.

Article 56

In the exclusive economic zone, the coastal State has

(a) sovereign rights for the purpose of exploring and exploiting, conserving and managing the natural resources, whether living or non-living, of the waters superjacent to the sea-bed and of the sea-bed and its subsoil and with regard to other activities for the economic exploitation and exploration of the zone, such as the production of energy from the water, currents and winds;

(b) jurisdiction as provided for in the relevant provisions of the Convention with regard to:

(i) the establishment and use of artificial islands, installations and structures;

(ii) marine scientific research;

(iii) the protection and preservation of the marine environment.

Source: The Law of the Sea: Official Text of the United Nations Convention on the Law of the Sea with Annexes and Index (New York: United Nations, 1983), pp. 3, 11, 18.

DOCUMENT 131: Bernard Cohen on Nuclear Energy and Risk Assessment (1983)

Sensible evaluation of environmental issues frequently requires an understanding of complex scientific data in order to assess environmental risk. Alarmists on all sides of complex issues have always been very ready to distort facts by providing one-sided information to the public. In his book Before It's Too Late, *published four years after the partial meltdown of a nuclear reactor at Three Mile Island in Pennsylvania had stifled further discussion of nuclear expansion in the United States, the physicist Bernard Cohen questioned the ability of the public to evaluate the hazardousness of nuclear energy.*

How well does the American public understand the hazards of nuclear power? A poll of radiation health scientists shows that 82% of them feel that the public's fear of radiation is "substantially" or "grossly" exaggerated. Another poll shows that 89% of all scientists, and 95% of scientists involved in energy-related fields, favor proceeding with the development of nuclear power; among the public there is only a slight majority in favor.

In a recent study in Oregon, groups of college students and members of the League of Women Voters were asked to rank thirty technologies and activities according to the "present risk of death" they pose to the average American. Both groups ranked nuclear power No. 1, well ahead of motor vehicles, which kill about 50,000 Americans each year, cigarette smoking, which kills 150,000, and eleven others that each kill over 1,000. How many can be expected to die annually from generation of nuclear power including the risk of accidents, radioactive waste, and all of the other dangers we hear so much about? According to estimates developed by government-sponsored research programs, about *ten* per year. If you don't trust "the Establishment," you might trust the leading anti-nuclear activist organization in the United States, the Union of Concerned Scientists (USC), which estimates an average of 120 deaths per year from nuclear power. In either case, nuclear power is perceived to be *thousands of times* more dangerous than it actuality is . . . Clearly the American public is grossly misinformed about the hazards of nuclear power.

* * *

[T]wo of the most serious environmental problems we face are air pollution and acid rain. Air pollution is doing billions of dollars worth of damage each year, spreading filth and ugliness, and destroying a wide variety of property ranging from women's stockings to granite statues. Acid rain is rendering lakes lifeless, damaging the forestry and fishing industries, and creating international tensions between the United States and Canada. Both the air pollution and acid rain problems could be largely eliminated by large-scale use of nuclear power. The tragedy of the misunderstanding deepens.

As we project into the future, the tragedy multiplies. Burning coal, oil, and gas is causing earthshaking climatic changes that could eventually turn our Midwestern grain belt into a desert, and flood out our coastal cities—New York, Miami, New Orleans, Houston, Los Angeles, and a host of others. Nuclear power could prevent this if the misunderstandings about its dangers could be eliminated.

The most important problem for our distant progeny will be a shortage of materials that we now obtain by mining. We are now consuming the world's scarce mineral resources at a voracious rate; indeed our era has been called "the age of mining," because within less than a century there will be very little left to mine—no copper, no tin, no lead, no mercury, no zinc, and so on. In the desperate search for substitutes, the most fruitful source would be plastics and organic chemicals. But these are made from coal, oil, and gas, which we are now simply burning up at a rate of millions of tons each [and] every day. Wouldn't it be much better if we instead burned uranium, which has no other important uses, leaving the coal, oil, and gas for future generations to use as a source of materials they will so sorely need?

Source: Bernard L. Cohen, *Before It's Too Late: A Scientist's Case for Nuclear Energy* (New York: Plenum, 1983), pp. 1-2, 4-5.

DOCUMENT 132: Bob Graham on Restoring the Kissimmee River—Lake Okeechobee—Everglades Ecosystem (1983)

For more than a hundred years, south Florida wetlands have been subject to draining, channelization, and other manipulations that severely stress the region's entire ecosystem and disrupt the natural quantity and timing of the flow of water into the system. Agricultural runoff further compromises water quality. In August 1983 Florida's governor, Bob Graham, proposed a long-term restoration program to save the Everglades, and in November he issued an executive order to move the program forward. Graham's program, which took into account the needs of the whole south Florida ecosystem, was the kind of wide-ranging program for the area advocated by Marjory Stoneman Douglas in the 1940s [see Document 85] but which had failed to gain adequate public support.

Since the issuing of Graham's executive order, progress in restoring the Kissimmee River—Lake Okeechobee—Everglades ecosystem has often been stymied by political opposition and bureaucratic inertia. On the bright side, all lands needed (102,061 acres) for the restoration of the river have been acquired; continuous flow has been established in the project area; much of the planned back-filling has been completed; more than forty square miles of the river-flood plain ecosystem has been restored, including almost 20,000 acres of wetlands and forty-six miles of the historic river channel;[8] and long-absent wildlife has returned to the Kissimmee Basin.

In the Everglades, the restoration task has been more difficult and progress slower. Following a federal lawsuit, the state of Florida built 45,000 acres of water treatment areas to improve the quality of agricultural runoff, and the Corps of Engineers developed a new plan to improve water flow into Everglades National Park. In 2008 Gov. Charlie Crist implemented a much-compromised proposal with the purchase of 27,000 acres for water treatment.

The Kissimmee River—Lake Okeechobee—Everglades plan is but one of several environmental restoration projects undertaken around the country to undo carefully planned and frequently government sanctioned manipulations of ecosystems.

A. "Save Our Everglades" Issue Paper

The Kissimmee River, once gently meandering for 90 miles from Lake Kissimmee to Lake Okeechobee, was channelized in the 1960['s] by the U.S. Army Corps of Engineers at the request of the State. This one-time paradise of fish and wildlife is now a 48-mile canal, 30 feet deep and 200 feet wide, commonly known as the "Kissimmeem Ditch."

Channelization of the Kissimmee directly destroyed 40,000 acres of river marsh and allowed drainage of more than 100,000 acres of associated wetlands. A once-serpentine river of pristine quality has become a discharge canal into Lake Okeechobee.

B. Executive Order

WHEREAS, it is the policy of the State of Florida to protect and manage the unique Central and Southern Florida natural resources of the Kissimmee River—Lake Okeechobee—Everglades ecosystems, in order to enhance existing ecological, recreational, scientific, economic, water supply, and flood control values for present and future Floridians, and WHEREAS, the future of both the systems of man and nature in Southern Florida depend upon the restoration and enhancement of the functioning Kissimmee River—Lake Okeechobee—Everglades ecosystems, and Whereas, the water resources and ecological health of these systems are extremely vulnerable to development and sensitive to management activities, and

WHEREAS, in their natural condition, these ecosystems perform critical water resource services—and provide natural and free and renewable benefits—in terms of flood control, water treatment, water storage and supply, and aquifer recharge, and

WHEREAS, many species of Florida wildlife, including endangered species, depend upon the Kissimmee River—Lake Okeechobee—Everglades ecosystem for habitat, and

WHEREAS, these ecosystems provide a unique source of natural beauty, wilderness refuge, and recreational enjoyment for millions of residents and visitors, and

WHEREAS, much of the past utilization of lands and waters within these ecosystems has been destructive to ecologically sensitive resources, and

WHEREAS, certain federal, state and regional and local activities, programs and management policies have historically subsidized and encouraged development within these ecosystems resulting in significant destruction of wetlands and other valuable natural resources, and

WHEREAS, various federal, state, regional and local agencies of government are presently involved in a wide range of resource planning and management activities aimed at the protection, restoration and enhancement of the natural values of the Kissimmee River—Lake Okeechobee—Everglades ecosystems.

Now, therefore, I, Bob Graham . . . do hereby promulgate the following Executive Order effective immediately:

The Kissimmee River—Lake Okeechobee—Everglades Coordinating Council (KOECC) is hereby created.

* * *

The KOECC is created for the purpose of coordination and promotion of restoration efforts in the Kissimmee River—Lake Okeechobee—Everglades ecosystems. The purpose shall encompass the following objectives . . . :

- Avoid further destruction or degradation of these natural systems.

- Reestablish the ecological functions of these natural systems in areas where these functions have been damaged.

- Improve the overall management of water, fish and wildlife and recreation.

- Successfully restore and preserve these unique areas.

Source: A. *Save Our Everglades*, Issue Paper (Tallahassee: Governor's Office, August 9, 1983); B. Executive Order 83-178 (Tallahassee: Governor's Office, November 1983).

DOCUMENT 133: Edward O. Wilson on the Need for a Conservation Ethic (1984, 1998)

Edward O. Wilson, one of the world's leading spokesmen for biodiversity and an emeritus professor of entomology at Harvard University, decries "the folly our descendants are least likely to forgive us"—the devastation of the earth's resources. A neo-Malthusian, Wilson believes that the maintenance of the earth's biological diversity is essential for human physical and emotional well-being. He has predicted that the twenty-first century will be "the century of the environment," when humans will be forced to look at themselves "closely as a biological as well as a cultural species."[9]

A. From *Biophilia*, 1984

The future of the conservation movement depends on... an advance in moral reasoning. Its maturation is linked to that of biology and a new hybrid field, bioethics, that deals with the many technological advances recently made possible by biology. Philosophers and scientists are

applying a more formal analysis to such complex problems as the allocations of scarce organ transplants, heroic but extremely expensive efforts to prolong life, and the possible use of genetic engineering to alter human heredity. They have only begun to consider the relationships between human beings and organisms with the same rigor. It is clear that the key to precision lies in the understanding of motivation, the ultimate reasons why people care about one thing but not another—why, say they prefer a city with a park to a city alone. The goal is to join emotion with the rational analysis of emotion in order to create a deeper and more enduring conservation ethic.

* * *

[A] healthful environment, the warmth of kinship, right-sounding moral strictures, sure-bet economic gain, and a stirring of nostalgia and sentiment are the chief components of the surface ethic. Together they are enough to make a compelling case to most people most of the time for the preservation of organic diversity. But this is not nearly enough: every pause, every species allowed to go extinct, is a slide down the ratchet, an irreversible loss for all. It is time to invent moral reasoning of a new and more

powerful kind, to look to the very roots of motivation and understand why, in what circumstances and on which occasions, we cherish and protect life. The elements from which a deep conservation ethic might be constructed include the impulses and biased forms of learning loosely classified as biophilia. Ranging from awe of the serpent to the idealization of the savanna and the hunter's mystique, and undoubtedly including others yet to be explored, they are the poles toward which the developing mind most comfortably moves. And as the mind moves, picking its way through the vast number of choices made during a lifetime, it grows into a form true to its long, unique evolutionary history.

B. From *Consilience*, 1998

[T]he global population is precariously large, will grow another third by 2020, and climb still more before peaking sometime after 2050. Humanity is improving per capita production, health, and longevity. But it is doing so by eating up the planet's capital, including irreplaceable natural resources. Humankind is approaching the limit of its food and water supply. As many as a billion people, moreover, remain in absolute poverty, with inadequate food from one day to the next and little or no medical care. Unlike any species that lived before, *Homo sapiens* is also changing the world's atmosphere and climate, lowering and polluting water tables, shrinking forests, and spreading deserts. It is extinguishing a large fraction of plant and animal species, an irreplaceable loss that will be viewed as catastrophic by future generations. Most of the stress originates directly or indirectly from a handful of industrialized countries. Their proven formulas are being eagerly adopted by the rest of the world. The emulation cannot be sustained, not with the same levels of consumption and waste. Even if the industrialization of developing countries is only partly successful, the environmental after shock will dwarf the population explosion that preceded it.

Source: A. Edward O. Wilson, *Biophilia* (Cambridge, MA: Harvard University Press, 1984), pp. 119, 138-41. B. Edward O. Wilson, *Consilience: The Unity of Knowledge* (New York: Knopf, 1998), p. 280.

DOCUMENT 134: Jurgen Schmandt, Hilliard Roderick and Andrew Morriss on Acid Rain and Friendly Neighbors (1985)

The earliest efforts to control industrial waste gases in order to reduce their negative impact involved building taller smokestacks on factories. These tall stacks did nothing to reduce the amount of waste gases emitted; they simply spread the pollution farther afield. In the 1950s, scientists began to suspect that certain waste gases produced by industrial activity, including sulfur and nitrogen oxides, not only harmed the human respiratory system, but also caused damage to crops and the natural environment when they precipitated out of the air and settled on people, trees, and other living things. Federal efforts to control the production of the noxious gases that caused acid precipitation were initiated with the Clean Air Act of 1955 [see Document 93], but at the time the chemistry and mechanics of acid rain were not well understood. The National Acid Precipitation Assessment Program (NAPAP) was created in 1980 to provide data about the processes leading to acid precipitation and to evaluate its impact.

During these years, Canada began to complain that acid rain resulting from industrial activity in the central United States was destroying forests in Canada. Eventually it became clear that bilateral cooperation would be necessary if measures to reduce acid rain were to prove effective.

Jurgen Schmandt, an environmental policy analyst, and his colleagues offered a model for dealing with complex multinational environmental problems like acid rain, emphasizing that appropriate action must be taken on the national level in order for international environmental agreements to produce desired changes. In the United States the Clean Air Act Amendments of 1990, with their cap-and-trade approach to emissions [see Document 143], proved a very effective way of fulfilling its agreement with Canada to control acid rain.

All current initiatives [concerning acid rain]—in the United States, Canada, and Europe—have in common that they focus on one or two major pollutants (SO_2 and NOx) and attempt to control acid rain under existing air pollution statutes. The existing policies were designed to control local air pollution. The proposed controls thus do not consider the fact that much of the danger of acid rain (for example, the damage to soils or drinking water) may result from the interaction of SO_2 and NOx with toxic pollutants, and from complex chemical processes that occur during the long-range transport of the pollutants. All governments, in our view, need to broaden their view of acid rain and recognize the issue for what it is: a problem of unprecedented complexity, with many aspects that are not yet understood, with little precedent to guide action, and with powerful economic interests that see their livelihoods threatened. If that much is agreed upon, it becomes clear that what is needed is more than an expanded version of the current Clean Air Acts in Canada and the United States.

In the process of developing policy, it will help to increase the dialogue between policymakers and representatives of different interests. Canada and the United States share their environment. National policy in each country affects the other. Informal dialogue offers the opportunity for each nation to make its ideas and concerns known without the constraints of formal negotiations. But whatever will be achieved between the nations will have to be based on policy choices made at home. Without a sound acid rain policy at the domestic level, little can be accomplished internationally.

Past experience in addressing environmental disputes between Canada and the United States suggests that bilateral actions will play a useful but limited role; they are likely to supplement domestic initiatives but are unlikely to become the driving force for resolving the acid rain issue. We make the assumption, therefore, that no full-fledged international control policy will emerge, and that domestic-policy initiatives will have to lead the way. But within the framework of enlarged national policies, cooperation between the two countries (and eventually Mexico) must be agreed upon and implemented that far exceeds current political will, experience, and institutional capabilities. Specific measures include joint research, monitoring, control experiments affecting large areas, and harmonization of national policies.

Given the differences between Canada and the United States in size of population and gross national product, it is likely that decisions by the United States will determine the outcome of the acid rain issue. We expect that decisive domestic action will be delayed until the perceived damage is serious enough to generate broad support for another major initiative in environmental policy. Although such support seems to exist in Canada, the same is not yet the case in the United States. The fear of serious damage observed elsewhere has been the prime motivation for protection of environment and public health in the past, and this pattern is likely to continue in the case of acid rain. Once people become genuinely concerned about the effects of acid rain on wildlife, vegetation and human health, political momentum will build up fast.

Source: Jurgen Schmandt, Hilliard Roderick, and Andrew Morriss, "Acid Rain Is Different," in Jurgen Schmandt and Hilliard Roderick, eds., *Acid Rain and Friendly Neighbors: The Policy Dispute Between Canada and the United States* (Durham, NC: Duke University Press, 1985), pp. 19-20.

DOCUMENT 135: Montreal Protocol on Substances Ozone That Deplete the Ozone Layer (1987)

Chlorofluorocarbon (CFCs)—gaseous and liquid compounds of chlorine, fluorine, and carbon—were originally synthesized in the 1890s. Then, beginning in 1928, variants of these compounds, marketed under the trade name Freon, were developed to replace dangerous chemicals being employed as commercial refrigerants. The invention of Freons led to the widespread household use of refrigeration and the introduction of aerosol sprays. However, in 1974 the chemists Mario Molina and F. Sherwood Rowland reported that ultraviolet radiation from the sun causes the halogens chlorine and bromine to be released from halocarbons (compounds of carbon with halogens) and that these gases then combine with ozone in the stratosphere, resulting in a degradation of the ozone layer, which protects life on earth from ultraviolet radiation from the sun.

   Initially people scoffed at the suggestion that the halocarbons used in refrigerators, car air conditioners, and aerosol cans threatened the earth's ozone shield. Nevertheless, by 1978 chlorofluorocarbons had been banned from use in spray cans in the United States and by 1983 there was a multinational call for a worldwide ban.

   The 1985 Vienna Convention for the Protection of the Ozone Layer provided a framework for dealing with ozone depletion on an international basis, and the 1987 Montreal Protocol spelled out precisely how the goals of the convention—the global banning of the production and use of ozone-depleting chemicals—were to be achieved. The Montreal Protocol marked "the beginning of a new era of environmental statesmanship"[10] in which scientists, governmental leaders, and industrialists from around the world increasingly would work together to address complex issues posed by environmental threats and to formulate restrictions on industrial activity and economic development. The Protocol, which was eventually signed by all 197 members of the United Nations, is one of the most effective environmental treaties ever negotiated and has resulted in an over 98 percent elimination of the use of CFCs and a slow repairing of the ozone layer.

Over the years, as the science of ozone depletion became more accurate, the Montreal Protocol was amended numerous times. The 2016 Kigali Amendments phase out the use of hydrofluorocarbons (HFCs), which were created in the 1980s to replace CFCs but which have proved to be super greenhouse gases, many times more toxic than carbon dioxide.

Preamble

The Parties to this Protocol,

Being Parties to the Vienna Convention for the protection of the Ozone Layer,

Mindful of their obligation under that Convention to take appropriate measures to protect human health and the environment against adverse effects resulting or likely to result from human activities which modify or are likely to modify the ozone layer,

Recognizing the world-wide emissions of certain substances can significantly deplete and otherwise modify the ozone layer in a manner that is likely to result in adverse effects on human health and the environment,

Conscious of the potential climatic effects of emission of these substances,

Aware that measures taken to protect the ozone layer from depletion be based on relevant scientific knowledge, taking into account technical and economic considerations,

Determined to protect the ozone layer by taking precautionary measures to control equitable total global emissions of substances that deplete it, with the ultimate objective of their elimination on the basis of developments in scientific knowledge, taking into account technical and economic considerations,

Acknowledging that special provision is required to meet the needs of developing countries for these substances,

Noting the precautionary measures for controlling emissions of certain chlorofluorocarbons that have already been taken at national and regional level,

Considering the importance of promoting international co-operation in the research and development of science and technology relating to the control and reduction of emissions of substances that deplete the ozone layer,

HAVE AGREED AS FOLLOWS:

Article 2: Control Measures

1. Each Party shall ensure that for the twelve-month period commencing on the first day of the Seventh month following the date of entry into force of this Protocol, and in each twelve-month period thereafter, its calculated level of consumption of the controlled substances in Group I of Annex A does not exceed its calculated level of consumption in 1986. By the end of the same period, each Party producing one or more of these substances shall ensure that its calculated level of production of the substances does not exceed its calculated level of production in 1986, except that such level may have increased by no more than ten per cent based on the 1986 level. Such increase shall be permitted only so as to satisfy the basic domestic needs of the Parties operating under Article 5 and for the purposes of industrial rationalization between Parties.

2. Each Party shall ensure that for the twelve-month period commencing on the first day of the thirty-seventh month following the date of entry into force of this Protocol, and in each twelve-month period thereafter, its calculated level of consumption of the controlled substances listed in Group II of Annex A does not exceed its calculated level of consumption in 1986. Each Party producing one or more of these substances shall ensure that its calculated level of production of the substances does not exceed its calculated level of production in 1986, except that such levels may have increased by no more than ten per cent based on the 1986 level. Such increase shall be permitted only so as to satisfy the basic domestic needs of the Parties operating under Article 5 and for the purposes of industrial

rationalization between Parties. The mechanisms for implementing these measures shall be decided by the Parties at their first meeting following the first scientific review.

3. Each Party shall ensure that for the period I July 1993 to 30 June 1994, and in each twelve-month period thereafter, its calculated level of consumption of the controlled substances in Group I of Annex A does not exceed, annually, eighty per cent of its calculated level of consumption in 1986. Each Party producing one or more of these substances shall, for the same periods, ensure that its calculated level of production of the substances does not exceed, annually, eighty per cent of its calculated level of production in 1986. However, in order to satisfy the basic domestic needs of the Parties operating under paragraph 1 of Article 5 and for the purposes of industrial rationalization between Parties, its calculated level of production may exceed that limit by up to ten per cent of its calculated level of production in 1986.

4. Each Party shall ensure that for the period I July 1998 to 30 June 1999, and in each twelve-month period thereafter, its calculated level of consumption of the controlled substances in Group I of Annex A does not exceed, annually, fifty per cent of its calculated level of consumption in 1986. Each Party producing one or more of these substances shall, for the same periods, ensure that its calculated level of production of the substances does not exceed, annually, fifty per cent of its calculated level of production in 1986. However, in order to satisfy the basic domestic needs of the Parties operating under paragraph 1 of Article 5 and for the purposes of industrial rationalization between Parties, its calculated level of production may exceed that limit by up to fifteen per cent of its calculated level of production in 1986. This paragraph will apply unless the Parties decide otherwise at a meeting by a two-thirds majority of Parties present and voting, representing at least two-thirds of the total calculated level of consumption of these substances of the Parties. This decision

shall be considered and made in the light of the assessments referred to in Article 6.

5. Any Party whose calculated level of production in 1986 of the controlled substances in Group I of Annex A was less than twenty-five kilotonnes may, for the purposes of industrial rationalization, transfer to or receive from any other Party, production in excess of the limits set out in paragraphs 1, 3 and 4 provided that the total combined calculated levels of production of the Parties concerned does not exceed the production limits set out in this Article. Any transfer of such production shall be notified to the secretariat, no later than the time of the transfer.

6. Any Party not operating under Article 5, that has facilities for the production of controlled substances under construction, or contracted for, prior to 16 September 1987, and provided for in national legislation prior to 1 January 1987, may add the production from such facilities to its 1986 production of such substances for the purposes of determining its calculated level of production for 1986, provided that such facilities are completed by 31 December 1990 and that such production does not raise that Party's annual calculated level of consumption of the controlled substances above 0.5 kilograms per capita.

Article 4: Control of trade with non-Parties

1. Within one year of the entry into force of this Protocol, each Party shall ban the import of controlled substances from any State not party to this Protocol.

2. Beginning on 1 January 1993, no Party operating under paragraph 1 of Article 5 may export any controlled substance to any State not party to this Protocol. . . .

Article 5: Special situation of developing countries

1. Any Party that is a developing country and whose annual calculated level of consumption

of the controlled substances is less than 0.3 kilograms per capita on the date of the entry into force of the Protocol for it, or any time thereafter within ten years of the date of entry into force of the Protocol shall, in order to meet its basic domestic needs, be entitled to delay its compliance with the control measures set out in paragraphs 1 to 4 of Article 2 by ten years after that specified in those paragraphs. However, such Party shall not exceed an annual calculated level of consumption of 0.3 kilograms per capita. Any such Party shall be entitled to use either the average of its annual calculated level of consumption for the period of 1995 to 1997 inclusive or a calculated level of consumption of 0.3 kilograms per capita, whichever is the lower, as the basis for its compliance with the control measures.

2. The Parties undertake to facilitate access to environmentally safe alternative substances and technology for Parties that are developing countries and assist them to make expeditious use of such alternatives.

3. The Parties undertake to facilitate bilaterally or multilaterally the provision of subsidies, aid, credits, guarantees or insurance programmes to Parties that are developing countries for the use of alternative technology and for substitute products.

Article 6: Assessment and review of control measures

Beginning in 1990, and at least every four years thereafter, the Parties shall assess the control measures provided for in Article 2 on the basis of available scientific, environmental, technical and economic information. At least one year before each assessment, the Parties shall convene appropriate panels of experts qualified in the fields mentioned and determine the composition and terms of reference of any such panels. Within one year of being convened, the panels will report their conclusions, through the Secretariat, to the Parties.

Annex A Controlled substances

Group	Substance	Ozone-Depleting Potential*
Group I		
$CFCl_3$	(CFC–11)	1.0
CF_2Cl_2	(CFC–12)	1.0
$C_2F_3Cl_3$	(CFC–113)	0.8
$C_2F_4Cl_2$	(CFC–114)	1.0
C_2F_5Cl	(CFC–115)	0.6
Group II		
CF_2BrCl	(halon–1211)	3.0
CF_3Br	(halon–1301)	10.0
$C_2F_4Br_2$	(halon–2402)	6.0

* These ozone depleting potentials are estimates based on existing knowledge and will be reviewed and revised periodically.

Source: unep.org/ozone secretariat/Montreal Protocol on Substances That Deplete the Ozone Layer (Nairobi: UNEP, September 1987).

DOCUMENT 136: United Church of Christ Commission for Racial Justice's Report on Toxic Waste and Race (1987)

The United Church of Christ's report on the siting of hazardous waste facilities was the first comprehensive analysis of the relationship between hazardous waste sites and the racial, socioeconomic, and ethnic makeup of the communities in which they were located. The report was based on two studies, one an analysis of the location of commercial hazardous waste facilities and the other a descriptive study of the racial composition of communities with uncontrolled toxic waste sites. By providing verifiable statistical evidence of the inequitable distribution of hazardous waste sites, it raised awareness of environmental injustice.

Until the late 1970's, most hazardous wastes were discarded without consideration of the dangers they posed. Moreover, proper care was lacking when hazardous chemicals were produced, stored and transported. The glaring lack of hazardous waste management regulations created a permissive atmosphere for discarding wastes in the cheapest possible ways. The EPA recognized that, up to this time, 80 to 90 percent of hazardous wastes were disposed of without adequate safeguards for human health and the environment.

* * *

The descriptive study... found that more than half of the population in the United States lived in residential ZIP code areas with one or more uncontrolled toxic waste sites. The study also found that three out of every five Black and Hispanic Americans lived in communities with uncontrolled toxic waste sites.

* * *

The results of the study suggest that the disproportionate numbers of racial and ethnic persons residing in communities with commercial hazardous waste facilities is not a random occurrence, but rather a consistent pattern. Statistical associations between race and the location of these facilities were stronger than any other association tested. The probability that this association occurred purely by chance is less than 1 in 10,000.

It is significant that race was consistently a more prominent factor in the location of commercial hazardous waste facilities than any other factor examined. This was clearly the case with respect to socio-economic status. The most striking relationship between socio-economic status and the location of commercial hazardous waste facilities was revealed after the study controlled for regional differences and urbanization. Household incomes and home values were substantially lower when communities with hazardous waste facilities were compared to communities in the surrounding area without such facilities. Mean household income was $2,745 less and the mean value of owner-occupied homes was $17,301 less.

* * *

It is clear from these studies that as the number of a community's racial and ethnic residents increases, the probability that some form of hazardous waste activity will occur also increases. The implications of that conclusion are serious. The Heckler Report11 has detailed the excess deaths of Blacks and other racial and ethnic persons in this country; the presence of hazardous waste sites only serves to compound this problem. Since many facilities and uncontrolled sites tend to be located in those urban areas where large numbers of racial and ethnic Americans reside, the potential risk caused by transportation spills, explosions, toxic emissions, and groundwater contamination strikes hardest at racial and ethnic Americans who have been documented to be the most "at risk" when it comes to health and well-being.

Source: Commission for Racial Justice, United Church of Christ, *Toxic Wastes and Race in the United States: A National Report on the Racial and Socio-Economic Characteristics of Communities with Hazardous Waste Sites* (New York: Public Data Access, 1987), pp. 3, 13,15-16, 17.

DOCUMENT 137: James Hansen Makes the Case for Climate Change (1988)

In June 1988 the U.S. Senate Committee on Energy and Natural Resources conducted hearings to examine the global warming trend attributed to increased atmospheric concentrations of carbon dioxide and other heat-retaining gases produced by the burning of fossil fuels and to consider its energy and environmental implications. James Hansen, who was then the director of the National Aeronautics and Space Administration (NASA) Goddard Institute for Space Studies, the premier climate research center in the United States, was among a number of scientists, economists, and others invited to testify at the hearings before the committee, one of whose members was Al Gore [see Document 155]. Hansen's testimony, which presented three model scenarios for possible future emissions of greenhouse gases, raised the hackles of many people both in and out of government, including Dixy Lee Ray [see Document 138], who insisted that there was no proof of a connection between global warming and human activity. The hearings sparked an ongoing debate about global warming and a continuing controversy over the accuracy of Hansen's models. Hansen is considered the father of climate change awareness.

I would like to draw three main conclusions. Number one, the earth is warmer in 1988 than at any time in the history of instrumental measurements. Number two, the global warming is now large enough that we can ascribe with a high degree of confidence a cause and effect relationship to the greenhouse effect. And number three, our computer climate simulations indicate that the greenhouse effect is already large enough to begin to effect the probability of extreme events such as summer heat waves.

My first viewgraph [Fig. 1] . . . shows the global temperature over the period of instrumental records, which is about 100 years. The present temperature is the highest in the period of record. The rate of warming in the past 25 years, as you can see on the right, is the highest on record. The four warmest years . . . have all been in the 1980s. And 1988 so far is so much warmer than 1987, that barring a remarkable and improbable cooling, 1988 will be the warmest year on the record.

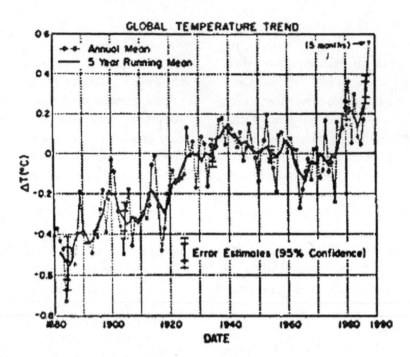

Fig. 1. Global surface air temperature change for the past century, with the zero point defined as the 1951-1980 mean. Uncertainty bars (95% confidence limits) are based on an error analysis . . . ; inner bars refer to the 5-year mean and outer bars to the annual mean. The analyzed uncertainty is a result of incomplete spatial coverage by measurement stations, primarily in ocean areas. The 1988 point compares the January-May 1988 temperature to the mean for the same 5 months in 1951-1980.

Now let me turn to my second point, which is causal association of the greenhouse effect and global warming. Causal association requires first that the warming be larger than natural climate variability and, second, that the magnitude and nature of the warming be consistent with the greenhouse mechanism. These points are both addressed on my second viewgraph [Fig. 2]. The observed warming during the past 30 years, which is the period when we have accurate measurements of atmospheric composition, is shown by the heavy black line in this graph. The warming is almost 0.4 degrees Centigrade by 1987 relative to climatology, which is defined as the 30 year mean, 1950 to 1980 and, in fact, the warming is more than 0.4 degrees in 1988. The probability of a chance warming of that magnitude is about 1 percent. So, with 99 percent confidence we can state that the warming during this time period is a real warming trend.

The other curves in this figure are the results of global climate model calculations for three scenarios of atmospheric trace gas growth. We have considered several scenarios because there are uncertainties in the exact trace gas growth in the past and especially in the future. We have considered cases ranging from business as usual, which is scenario A, to draconian emission cuts, scenario C, which would totally eliminate net trace gas growth by year 2000.

The main point to be made here is that the expected global warming is of the same magnitude as the observed warming. Since there is only a 1 percent chance of an accidental warming of this magnitude, the agreement with the expected greenhouse effect is of considerable significance. Moreover, if you look at the next level of detail in the global temperature change, there are clear signs of the greenhouse effect. Observational data suggests a cooling in the stratosphere while

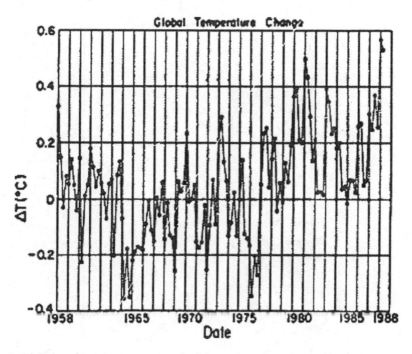

Fig. 2. Global surface air temperature change at seasonal resolution for the past 30 years.

the ground is warming. The data suggest somewhat more warming over land and sea ice regions than over open ocean, more warming at high latitudes than at low latitudes, and more warming in the winter than in the summer. In all of these cases, the signal is at best just beginning to emerge, and we need more data. Some of these details, such as the northern hemisphere high latitude temperature trends, do not look exactly like the greenhouse effect, but that is expected. There are certainly other climate change factors involved in addition to the greenhouse effect.

Altogether the evidence that the earth is warming by an amount which is too large to be a chance fluctuation and similarity of the warming to that expected from the greenhouse effect represents a very strong case, [i]n my opinion, that the greenhouse effect has been detected, and it is changing our climate now.

Then, my third point. Finally I would like to address the question of whether the greenhouse effect is already large enough to affect the probability of extreme events, such as summer heat

waves. As shown in my next viewgraph [Fig. 3], we have used the temperature changes computed in our global climate model to estimate that impact of the greenhouse effect on the frequency of hot summers in Washington, D.C. and Omaha, Nebraska. A hot summer is defined as the hottest one-third of the summers in the 1950 to 1980 period, which is the period the Weather Bureau uses for defining climatology. So, in that period the probability of having a hot summer was 33 percent, but by the 1990s you can see that the greenhouse effect has increased the probability of a hot summer to somewhere between 55 and 70 percent in Washington according to our climate model simulations. [In] the late 1980s, the probability of a hot summer would be somewhat less than that. You can interpolate to a value of something like 40 to 60 percent.

I believe that this change in the frequency of hot summers is large enough to be noticeable to the average person. So, we have already reached a point that the greenhouse effect is important. It may also have important implications other than for creature comfort.

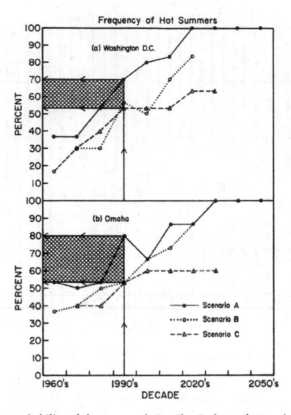

Fig. 3. Estimate of the probability of the summer being "hot", shown for two locations for scenarios A, B, and C. A "hot" summer is one in which the mean temperature exceeds a value which was chosen such that one third of the summers were "hot" in 1950-1979 observations. The estimated probability for hot summers in the 1990s is shown by the shaded region for the range of scenarios.

My last viewgraph [Fig. 4] shows global maps of temperature anomalies for a particular month, July for several different years between 1986 and [2019], as computed with our global climate model for the intermediate trace gas scenario B. As shown by the graphs on the left, where yellow and red colors represent areas that are warmer than climatology and blue areas represent areas that are colder than climatology, at the present time in the 1980s the greenhouse warming is smaller than the natural variability of the local temperature. So, in any given month, there is almost as much area that is cooler than normal as there is area warmer than is normal. A few decades in the future, as shown on the right, it is warm almost everywhere.

However, the point that I would like to make is that in the late 1980s and 1990s we notice a clear tendency in our model for greater than average warming in the southeast United States and the midwest. In our model this result seems to arise because the Atlantic Ocean off the coast of the United States warms more slowly than the land. This leads to high pressure along the east coast and circulation of warm air north into the midwest or the southeast. There is only a tendency for this phenomenon. It is certainly not going to happen every year, and climate models are certainly an imperfect tool at this time. However, we conclude that there is evidence that the greenhouse effect increases the likelihood of heat wave drought situations in the southeast and Midwest United States even though we cannot blame a specific drought on the greenhouse effect.

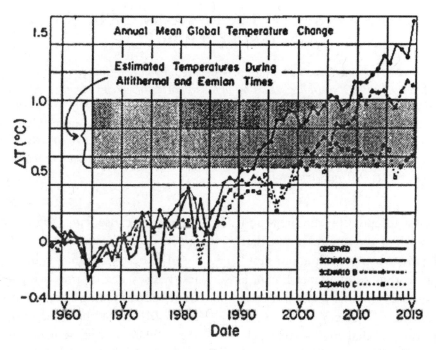

Fig. 4. Annual mean global surface air temperature computed for trace gas scenarios A, B, and C described in reference 1. [Scenario A assumes continued growth rates of trace gas emissions typical of the past 20 years, i.e., about 1.5% yr-1 emission growth; scenario B has emission rates approximately fixed at current rates; scenario C drastically reduces trace gas emissions between 1990 and 2000.]. . . The shaded range is an estimate of global temperature during the peak of the current and previous interglacial periods, about 6,000 and 120,000 years before present, respectively. The zero point for observations is the 1951-1980 mean (reference 6); the zero point for the model is the control run mean.

Therefore, I believe that it is not a good idea to use the period 1950 to 1980 for which climatology is normally defined as an indication of how frequently drought will occur in the future.

Source: Transcript of oral version of statement of Dr. James Hansen, "Greenhouse Effect and Global Climate Change," U.S. Senate, Committee on Energy and Natural Resources, 100th Congress, 1st session, Senate Hearing 100-461, pt. 2, pp. 39-41. http://image.guardian.co.uk/sys-files/Environment/documents/2008/06/23/ClimateChangeHearing1988.pdf. Fig. 3, missing from transcript, from James Hansen et al., "Global Climate Changes as Forecast by Goddard Institute for Space Studies Three-Dimensional Model," *Journal of Geophysical Research,* Vol. 93, D8 (Aug. 20, 1988), p. 9357, Fig. 6.

DOCUMENT 138: Dixy Lee Ray Asks, "Who Speaks for SCIENCE?" (1990)

Dixy Lee Ray, the idiosyncratic former governor of Washington and one-time chairman of the Atomic Energy Commission who had a Ph.D. in biology, was an avid supporter of nuclear energy. Although recognizing a need to curtail the rapid depletion of natural resources and prevent pollution, she questioned the primacy of human activity as the cause of global warming and objected to the placing of stringent environmental limitations on industrial development. Like Bernard Cohen [see Document 131], Ray was concerned about how the environmental riskiness of various activities, including industrial activities, is determined and how the perception of risk affects U.S. industrial policy.

It is now widely accepted by the press and consequently by much of the general public that man's industrial activities are "fouling our nest" and pose a threat to the life of planet Earth, a threat that grows more ominous year by year. Is this conventional wisdom correct?

The risk one runs in challenging so widely held a belief is the risk of being judged an apologist for industry, or worse, to be accused of favoring pollution. Now my disclaimer: I am not in the pay of nor am I employed by any industry and I am as much opposed to pollution as anyone. But I do part company with alarmists who misuse science to foment fear and who clamor with increasing stridency that industrial progress must stop or be redirected into uneconomic alternatives because the world is going to pot. Is it?

* * *

What are our real environmental concerns? Cancer-causing chemicals? Radiation, including radon? Carbon dioxide, ozone, the "greenhouse effect"? . . .

First, the cancer-causing chemicals. With the exception of childhood leukemia—always tragic, but relatively rare—cancer is a malady that afflicts predominantly older adults and the aged. For most cancers, and there are many different kinds, the causes are complex, interactive, and often include genetic factors. If we look at the fatality records, the facts show that the total of carcinogenic substances targeted by the EPA—including chemicals in the work place, environment, food additives, and industrial

products—cause *fewer than eight percent of all cancer deaths in America.*

The best scientific evidence points to genetics, viruses, sexual practices, diet, alcohol, and more than anything else, tobacco, as accounting for nearly all of the remaining 92 percent. Yet, the public, through constantly reported innuendo against industrial chemicals and radiation, is encouraged to believe otherwise. Moreover, a proper look at cancer statistics shows that, aside from a sharp increase in lung cancer caused by cigarette smoking, there have been no significant increases in the rate at which people die from any of the common forms of cancer over the last 50 years. In fact, there have been significant decreases in some types of cancer—for example, stomach cancer—during these decades of rapid industrialization and the introduction of many new man-made chemicals.

But most people believe cancer is caused by toxic substances created by industry. Why? Because they listen to the wrong spokesmen, and that is all they hear. National television has elevated sob-sister journalism to a new dramatic high, with emotional, heart-rending stories about cases of childhood leukemia and other individual or family tragedies as if they were epidemic. These stories capture public attention and play on natural sympathy, and these reactions, in turn, affect the decisions and budgets of governmental scientific agencies. In an internal memo, the Environmental Protection Agency (EPA) admits, with remarkable candor, "Our priorities [in regulating carcinogens] appear [to be] more closely aligned with public opinion than with our estimated risks." And with scientific evidence, too, I hasten to add!

Now as to the second example, radiation exposure, including radon, the simple fact is that we live in a radioactive world. We always have and we always will. Yet now a few scientists have made the unsubstantiated claim that any amount of radon is harmful . . . and many have come to believe it.

* * *

As to the "greenhouse effect," it's true that the concentration of carbon dioxide in the atmosphere has been increasing. It is also true that the *rate* of the carbon dioxide increase—and methane, hydrocarbons, sulfur and nitrogen oxides, and a few other substances—is now approximately one percent a year. Since increases of carbon dioxide have also occurred in the geological past, without the help of human industry, it is unclear whether the burning of fossil fuel is the preeminent or only cause of the present increase, however much it may be adding to the current totals. Moreover, it is not known what the consequences may be, if any, of this increase, nor how long it may last. But this does not stop the doomsayers from hypothesizing radical transformations and other adverse effects in the future.

We do *not* know what caused severe climatic changes in the geological past, but we can be sure they were *not* due to human industrial activity. Most likely, the causes were and still are colossal cosmic forces, quite outside human ability to control. Now that we live in an industrial, high technology society, there is no reason to believe that such cosmic forces have ceased to exist.

* * *

The course of public events, especially in nuclear science and now increasingly in the chemical industry as well, has demonstrated over the last 10 to 15 years that scientists and engineers who speak on behalf of nuclear power and the chemical industry are not trusted. The public does not distinguish the Natural Resources Defense Council from the National Academy of Sciences and is far more likely to believe the opponents of science and technology than the supporters.

Source: Dixy Lee Ray with Lou Guzzo, *Trashing the Planet: How Science Can Help Us Deal with Acid Rain, Depletion of the Ozone, and Nuclear Waste (Among Other Things)* (New York: HarperPerennial, 1992), pp. 3, 5-7.

DOCUMENT 139: Clean Air Act Amendments Create a Cap-and-Trade Mechanism to Reduce Acid Rain (1990)

By the 1980s technology made it possible to determine the point of source—the specific mill or industrial plant—of emissions that had fallen in a particular place as well as to measure the exact amounts of the major components of that deposition. Title IV of the 1990 Clean Air Act Amendments, the acid deposition segment of the amendments, created a financial mechanism called cap and trade to induce companies to meet target acid deposition goals. Each company whose existing and new equipment was known to be a source of acid raid was assigned a maximum allowance for sulfur and nitrogen oxides emissions beginning in 1993, with the allowances decreasing in the following years. This allowance was the "cap." Companies that exceeded their caps could sell their excess emissions to a company whose emissions were below their caps, with price of a unit of emissions being determined through an auction. This was the "trade."

The cap-and-trade process proved highly successful in reducing acid rain. However, efforts to apply this mechanism as a means of reducing other types of pollution ran into fierce opposition. Indeed, this bill, signed into law by President George H.W. Bush, was the last major piece of environmental legislation passed at the federal level.

Sec. 401. Findings and Purposes

(a) FINDINGS.-The Congress finds that-

(1) the presence of acidic compounds and their precursors in the atmosphere and in deposition from the atmosphere represents a threat to natural resources, ecosystems, materials, visibility, and public health;

(2) the principal sources of the acidic compounds and their precursors in the atmosphere are emissions of sulfur and nitrogen oxides from the combustion of fossil fuels;

(3) the problem of acid deposition is of national and international significance;

(4) strategies and technologies for the control of precursors to acid deposition exist now that are economically feasible, and improved methods are expected to become increasingly available over the next decade;

(5) current and future generations of Americans will be adversely affected by delaying measure to remedy the problem;

(6) reduction of total atmospheric loading of sulfur dioxide and nitrogen oxides will enhance protection of the public health and welfare and the environment; and

(7) control measures to reduce precursor emissions from steam-electric generating units should be initiated without delay.

(b) PURPOSES.-The purpose of this title is to reduce the adverse effects of acid deposition through reductions in annual emissions of sulfur dioxide of ten million tons from 1980 emission levels, and, in combination with other provisions of this Act, of nitrogen oxides emissions of approximately two million tons from 1980 emission levels, in the forty-eight contiguous States and the District of Columbia. It is the intent of this title to effectuate such reductions by requiring compliance by affected sources with prescribed emission limitations by specified deadlines, which limitations may be met through alternative methods of compliance provided by an emission allocation and transfer system. It is also the purpose of this title to encourage energy conservation, use of renewable and clean alternative technologies, and pollution prevention as a long-range strategy, consistent with the provisions of this title, for reducing air pollution and other adverse impacts of energy production and use.

Sec. 403. Sulfur Dioxide Allowance Program for Existing and New Units

(a) ALLOCATIONS OF ANNUAL ALLOWANCES FOR EXISTING AND NEW UNITS.-(1) For the emission limitation programs under this title, the Administrator shall allocate annual allowances for the unit, to be held or distributed by the designated representative of the owner or operator of each affected unit at an affected source in accordance with this title, in an amount equal to the annual tonnage emission limitation calculated under section 404 [Phase I sulfur dioxide requirements], 405 [Phase II Sulphur dioxide requirements], 406[Allowances for States with emissions rates at or below 0.80 lbs/mmBtu], 409 [Repowered sources], or 410 [Election for additional sources]except as otherwise specifically provided elsewhere in this title. Except as provided in sections 405(a)(2), 405(a)(3), 409 and 410, beginning January 1, 2000, the Administrator shall not allocate annual allowances to emit sulfur dioxide pursuant to section 405 in such an amount as would result in total annual emissions of sulfur dioxide from utility units in excess of 8.90 million tons except that the Administrator shall not take into account unused allowances carried forward by owners and operators of affected units or by other persons holding such allowances, following the year for which they were allocated. If necessary to meeting the restrictions imposed in the preceding sentence, the Administrator shall reduce, pro rata, the basic Phase II allowance allocations for each unit subject to the requirements of section 405. Subject to the provisions of section 416, the Administrator shall allocate allowances for each affected unit at an affected source annually, as provided in paragraphs (2) and (3) and section 408 [Permits and compliance plans]. Except as provided in sections 409 and 410, the removal of an existing affected unit or source from commercial operation at any time after the date of the enactment of the Clean Air Act Amendments of 1990 (whether before or after January 1, 1995, or January 1, 2000) shall not terminate or otherwise affect the allocation of allowances pursuant to section 404 or 405 to which the unit is entitled. . . .

Sec. 404. Phase I Sulfur Dioxide Requirements

(a) EMISSION LIMITATIONS.-(1) After January 1, 1995, each source that includes one or more affected units listed in table A is an affected source under this section. After January 1, 1995, it shall be unlawful for any affected unit (other than an eligible phase I unit under section 404(d)(2)) to emit sulfur dioxide in excess of the tonnage limitation stated as a total number of allowances in table A for phase I, unless (A) the emissions reduction requirements applicable to such unit have been achieved pursuant to subsection (b) or (d), or (B) the owner or operator of such unit holds allowances to emit not less than the unit's total annual emissions, except that, after January 1, 2000, the emissions limitations established in this section shall be superseded by those established in section 405. The owner or operator of any unit in violation of this section shall be fully liable for such violation including, but not limited to, liability for fulfilling the obligations specified in section 411 [Excess emissions penalty]. . . .

Sec. 416. Contingency Guarantee; Auctions, Reserve

(a) DEFINITIONS.-For purposes of this section-

(1) The term 'independent power producer' means any person who owns or operates, in whole or in part, one or more new independent power production facilities.

(2) The term 'new independent power production facility' means a facility that-

(A) is used for the generation of electric energy, 80 percent or more of which is sold at wholesale;

(B) is nonrecourse project-financed (as such term is defined by the Secretary of Energy within 3 months of the date of the enactment of the Clean Air Act Amendments of 1990);

(C) does not generate electric energy sold to any affiliate (as defined in section 2(a) (11) of the Public Utility Holding Company Act of 1935) of the facility's owner or operator unless the owner or operator of the facility demonstrates that it cannot obtain allowances from the affiliate; and

(D) is a new unit required to hold allowances under this title.

(3) The term 'required allowances' means the allowances required to operate such unit for so much of the unit's useful life as occurs after January 1, 2000.

(b) SPECIAL RESERVE OF ALLOWANCES.- Within 36 months after the date of the enactment of the Clean Air Act Amendments of 1990, the Administrator shall promulgate regulations establishing a Special Allowance Reserve containing allowances to be sold under this section. For purposes of establishing the Special Allowance Reserve, the Administrator shall withhold-

(1) 2.8 percent of the allocation of allowances for each year from 1995 through 1999 inclusive; and

(2) 2.8 percent of the basic Phase II allowance allocation of allowances for each year beginning in the year2000 which would (but for this subsection) be issued for each affected unit at an affected source. The Administrator shall record such withholding for purposes of transferring the proceeds of the allowance sales under this subsection. The allowances so withheld shall be deposited in the Reserve under this section.

(c) DIRECT SALE AT $1,500 PER TON.-

(1) SUBACCOUNT FOR DIRECT SALES.- In accordance with regulations under this section, the Administrator shall establish a Direct Sale Subaccount in the Special Allowance Reserve established under this section. The Direct Sale Subaccount shall contain allowances in the amount of 50,000 tons per year for each year beginning in the year 2000.

(2) SALES.-Allowances in the subaccount shall be offered for direct sale to any person at the times and in the amounts specified in table 1 at a price of $1,500 per allowance, adjusted by the Consumer Price Index in the same manner as provided in paragraph (3). Requests to purchase allowances from the Direct Sale Subaccount established under paragraph (1) shall be approved in the order of receipt until no allowances remain in such subaccount, except that an opportunity to purchase such allowances shall be provided to the independent power producers referred to in this subsection before such allowances are offered to any other person. Each applicant shall be required to pay 50 percent of the total purchase price of the allowances within 6 months after the approval of the request to purchase. The remainder shall be paid on or before the transfer of the allowances. . . .

Table 1 NUMBER OF ALLOWANCES AVAILABLE FOR SALE AT $1,500 PER TON

Year of Sale	Spot Sale (same year)	Advance Sale
1993-1999		25,000
2000 and after	25,000	25,000

Allowances sold in the spot sale in any year are allowances which may only be used in that year (unless banked for use in a later year). Allowances sold in the advance sale in any year are allowances which may only be used in the 7th year after the year in which they are first offered for sale (unless banked for use in a later year).

(d) AUCTION SALES.-

(1) SUBACCOUNT FOR AUCTIONS.-The Administrator shall establish an Auction Subaccount in the Special Reserve established under this section. The Auction Subaccount shall contain allowances to be sold at auction under this section in the amount of 150,000 tons per year for each year from 1995 through 1999, inclusive and 250,000 tons per year for each year beginning in the calendar year 2000.

(2) ANNUAL AUCTIONS.-Commencing in 1993 and in each year thereafter, the Administrator shall conduct auctions at which the allowances referred to in paragraph (1) shall be offered for sale in accordance with regulations promulgated by the Administrator, in consultation with the Secretary of the Treasury, within 12 months of enactment of the Clean Air Act Amendments of 1990. The allowances referred to in paragraph (1) shall be offered for sale at auction in the amounts specified in table 2. The auction shall be open to any person. A person wishing to bid for such allowances shall submit (by a date set by the Administrator) to the Administrator (on a sealed bid schedule provided by the Administrator) offers to purchase specified numbers of allowances at specified prices. Such regulations shall specify that the auctioned allowances shall be allocated and sold on the basis of bid price, starting with the highest-priced bid and continuing until all allowances for sale

at such auction have been allocated. The regulations shall not permit that a minimum price be set for the purchase of withheld allowances. Allowances purchased at the auction may be used for any purpose and at any time after the auction, subject to the provisions of this title.

(3) PROCEEDS.-(A) Notwithstanding section 3302 of title 31 of the United States Code or any other provision of law, within 90 days of receipt, the Administrator shall transfer the proceeds from the auction under this section, on a pro rata basis, to the owners or operators of the affected units at an affected source from whom allowances were withheld under subsection (b). No funds transferred from a purchaser to a seller of allowances under this paragraph shall be held by any officer or employee of the United States or treated for any purpose as revenue to the United States or the Administrator.

(B) At the end of each year, any allowances offered for sale but not sold at the auction shall be returned without charge, on a pro rata basis, to the owner or operator of the affected units from whose allocation the allowances were withheld.

(4) ADDITIONAL AUCTION PARTICIPANTS.-Any person holding allowances or to whom allowances are allocated by the Administrator may submit those allowances to the Administrator to be offered for sale at auction under this subsection. The proceeds of any such sale shall be transferred at the time of sale by the

Table 2 NUMBER OF ALLOWANCES AVAILABLE FOR AUCTION

Year of Sale	Spot Auction (same year)	Advance Auction
1993	50,000*	100,000
1994	50,000*	100,000
1995	50,000*	100,000
1996	150,000	100,000
1997	150,000	100,000
1998	150,000	100,000
1999	150,000	100,000
2000 and after...	100,000	100,000

Allowances sold in the spot sale in any year are allowances which may only be used in that year (unless banked for use in a later year), except as otherwise noted. Allowances sold in the advance auction in any year are allowances which may only be used in the 7th year after the year in which they are first offered for sale (unless banked for use in a later year).

*Available for use only in 1995 (unless banked for use in a later year).

purchaser to the person submitting such allowances for sale. The holder of allowances offered for sale under this paragraph may specify a minimum sale price. Any person may purchase allowances offered for auction under this paragraph. Such allowances shall be allocated and sold to purchasers on the basis of bid price after the auction under paragraph (2) is complete. No funds transferred from a purchaser to a seller of allowances under this paragraph shall be held by any officer or employee of the United States or treated for any purpose as revenue to the United States or the Administrator.

Sec. 407. Sense of The Congress on Emission Reductions Costs

It is the sense of the Congress that the Clean Air Act Amendments of 1990, through the allowance program, allocates the costs of achieving the required reductions in emissions of sulfur dioxide and oxides of nitrogen among sources in the United States. Broad based taxes and emissions fees that would provide for payment of the costs of achieving required emissions reductions by any party or parties other than the sources required to achieve the reductions are undesirable.

Source: epa.gov/airmakets/title-iv-clean-air-act-acid-deposition-control. Sec/ 401, 403, 404, 416, and 407.

DOCUMENT 140: Roger Smith on Industry and the Environment (1990)

Research engineers at General Motors and other car and electronics companies have been working to develop a viable electric car for years. Public reception of a prototype GM electric car displayed at the January 1990 Automobile Show in Los Angeles encouraged Roger Smith, GM's president from 1981 to 1990, to commit GM to producing a commercial electric car. The immediate impact of his commitment was more substantial than he might have expected, not only affecting GM, but also helping prompt the California Air Resources Board to issue stringent vehicle emissions standards [see Document 141A]. While the GM electric vehicle, eventually named the EV-1, was being developed, other automobile manufacturers and oil companies were lobbying to weaken the California regulations mandating Zero Emission Vehicles (which also had been adopted by other states, including several in New England). By the time the EV-1 got on the road in 1996, the change in the California emissions standards [see Document 141B] had virtually eliminated a guaranteed market for the car,[12] which was very expensive and had a limited battery capacity. Furthermore, GM's corporate culture proved inimical to Roger's vision of a future-oriented car company.

In 1997, Toyota put on the market an electric car, the Prius, with an on-board gasoline engine to charge its battery. By June of 2010, Toyota had sold 1.8 million Priuses, more than half of them in the United States. In the 2011 model year, the Prius was joined by at least ten other electric hybrids, including the GM Volt. Although there is ongoing interest in developing alternatives to the standard gasoline engine, whenever the price of gas is low, as it has been since 2012, the market for fuel efficient and clean energy vehicles dips and the incentives for car makers to produce them evaporate.

[E]nvironmental consciousness has moved from a fringe phenomenon . . . into the mainstream value system of people everywhere in the developed world.

. . . [T]his, of course, is of keen interest to us in the auto industry because it focuses attention directly on us and our products. And it bears directly on our two tasks—being successful in the marketplace *and* fulfilling society's expectations. And really, the two are interrelated—because we can't be successful in the marketplace unless.

We fulfill society's expectations, and we won't have the resources to benefit society unless we're successful in the marketplace. What it all comes down to is, we have to market products that consumers want *and* that are environmentally sound. . . .

The first half of the title of my remarks is "Industry and the Environment." What's the relationship between the two? Let me be very explicit about this: our job is to provide goods and services, which, along with their intrinsic purpose, do everything possible to promote cleaner air, water, and earth. You know, it's a little ironic that we've been accused of not understanding the environmental implications of what we do. The truth is that no one understands the importance of the environment *better* than we. Our factories and our products are intimately related to the planet and all its vast resources; they depend on it in order to keep running. We've got to keep that in mind, if we're to preserve the jobs and livelihoods of our people, the health of our businesses—and ultimately, the benefits that customers derive from our products. And we *do* keep it in mind. Lots of companies have a long history of environmental consciousness and involvement—and General Motors is proud to be among them. As far back as 1955, we were conducting research on the atmosphere. Back in 1959, before there was an EPA, we discovered that crankcase emissions contribute to air pollution, and we proposed control measures that are in use on most vehicles today. I'm pleased to tell you—unequivocally—that over the years, GM has done more for automotive emissions control—we've come up with more patents, more publications, more research, more technical contributions—than any other auto company, anywhere.

In emissions and fuel-efficiency, our factories and our vehicles have made enormous strides—here and around the world. Just compare today's cars and trucks with those of 1970, the year of the first Earth Day. Today's vehicles have been downsized and built with lighter-weight materials—so their average weight is down by 27%. We've converted most of them to front-wheel-drive, improved their aerodynamic efficiency by one-third, and set new specifications that cut the rolling resistance of our tires by half. We've reduced friction between parts, and put in more efficient transmissions and air-conditioning, as well as electronically-controlled, fuel-efficient engines. All of this—and more—has increased the fuel economy of GM cars, since the mid-70's, by 130%. And since clean air became a national goal, we've made big reductions in the exhaust emissions from our cars and trucks: nitrogen oxides are down by 76%, and hydrocarbons and carbon monoxide are down by 96%. That's due in large part to the catalytic converter—a GM invention that *The Washington Post* recently called "the nation's most powerful weapon against urban smog." We started putting them into our 1975 cars, and just a few days ago we marked the manufacture of 100 million of them.

* * *

Another promising approach is the electric-powered car, which, I'm convinced, will play an important role in meeting our country's transportation needs and environmental goals. At the beginning of this year, General Motors introduced the Impact, a prototype electric car, to the public. It's the latest step in our continuing program to develop electric cars for personal transportation. . . . [O]ur goal is to be the first automobile company to mass-produce a modern, electric car. And not just *any* electric car, but one that's as safe as any vehicle on the road today, that has a range and cost that consumers will find appealing, and that performs as well as current internal combustion engine vehicles.

Source: Roger B. Smith, "Industry and the Environment: New Directions for the 90s," address to the National Press Club, Washington, D.C., April 18, 1990. GM Business Research Library, Detroit, MI.

DOCUMENT 141: California Air Resources Board Lowers its Vehicle Emissions Standards (1990, 1996)

The California Air Resources Board (CARB) was created in 1968 by Governor Ronald Reagan as an independent state agency to establish pollution emission standards for air polluters in California, including automobiles and oil refineries. In the 1980s, however, as president of the United States, Reagan headed what many view as the most anti-environmental administration of the latter half of the twentieth century.

For years California's air pollution problem had been substantial, in part because the state's climate and geography work together to help produce what the Environmental Protection Agency (EPA) calls "nonattainment" conditions (meaning that the EPA standards for air quality are not met). Cities in California may average as many as 109 nonattainment days per year, while cities and areas of high pollution situated on the other side of the Rocky Mountains in generally have fewer than fifty nonattainment days per year.

The CARB vehicle emissions standards set in September1990, whose strength may have been encouraged by GM president Roger Smith's pronouncements earlier in the year [see Document 140], proved difficult to meet, however, and in 1996, weaker standards replaced them. This was but one of many instances around the nation in which environmental goals set by federal, state, and local agencies and legislatures have been downgraded or ignored. Retreat from strict environmental standards has often occurred when the public or industry has deemed the cost of needed technology too high or the change in business activity or lifestyle too great.

A. Original CARB Proposal for Vehicle Emissions Standards, September 1990

More than three-fourths of California's residents live in areas that do not meet at least one state or federal ambient air quality standard. Many areas of the state, including the South Coast, Bay Area, and Central Coast are non-attainment areas for the state ozone standard. Mobile sources are the largest contributors of precursors that react in the atmosphere to form ozone. These ozone precursors include hydrocarbons (or organic gases) and oxides of nitrogen (NOX). Atmospheric ozone and other pollutants emitted directly by vehicles, including carbon monoxide (CO) and particulate matter (PM), are associated with respiratory irritation and illness. Motor vehicles also emit a substantial portion of both known and potential toxic air contaminants. Vehicle-related toxics include benzene, a known human carcinogen, as well as potential carcinogens such as 1,3 butadiene, formaldehyde, acetaldehyde and diesel particulate.

* * *

Implementation of the proposed regulations would benefit air quality by reducing vehicle emissions throughout the state. The staff estimates that by 2010, the regulations would:

- reduce vehicular emissions of non-methane organic gases (NMOG) by 28 percent and NO_x by 18 percent;
- reduce vehicular emissions of CO by 8 percent and PM by about 2 percent;
- reduce vehicular toxics (benzene, 1,3-butadiene, formaldehyde, acetaldehyde, and diesel particulates) associated with reactive organic gases and the associated potential cancer burden by about 20 to 40 potential cases per year statewide by 2010; and
- possibly reduce emissions of compounds identified as green- house gases that may contribute to global warming.

Beginning in the mid-1990's, vehicle manufacturers would be required to produce vehicles that meet TLEV [transitional limited emission vehicle], LEV [limited emission vehicle], ULEV [ultra-low emission vehicle], or ZEV [zero emission vehicle] exhaust emission standards. The emission standards for these vehicle categories differ in stringency, ranging from a 50 percent reduction in hydrocarbon emissions for TLEVs (compared to conventional gasoline-fueled vehicles sold in the same period) to allowing no emissions of any pollutants for ZEVs.

Table 1 Implementation Rates for Conventional Vehicles, TLEVs, LEVs, ULEVs, and ZEVs Used to Calculate Fleet Average Standards for Passenger Cars

MODEL YEAR	0.39	0.25	TLEV 0.125	LEV 0.075	ULEV 0.04	ZEV* 0	FLEET AVG. STANDARD
1994	10%	80%	10%				0.250
1995		85%	15%				0.231
1996		80%	20%				0.225
1997		73%		25%	2%		0.202
1998		48%		48%	2%	2%	0.157
1999		23%		73%	2%	2%	0.113
2000				96%	2%	2%	0.073
2001				90%	5%	5%	0.070
2002				85%	10%	5%	0.068
2003				75%	15%	10%	0.062

*The percentage requirements for ZEV sare mandatory.

[The schedule for implementation of vehicle quotas (Table 1) shows the percentage of the total vehicles sold each year that will be required to meet the new standards and the level of pollution reduction they will need to reach, as measured by the grams per mile of nonmethane organic gases released by the vehicles.]

B. Proposed Changes to the CARB Vehicle Emission Standards, January 1996

Based on information gathered through [a series of] public forums and [a] Battery [Technical Advisory] Panel, the staff [of CARB] is proposing to amend the LEV regulations to eliminate the percentage ZEV requirements for model years 1998 through 2002. The ten percent requirement for the 2003 model year would remain unchanged. This modification would allow auto manufacturers more time to develop and demonstrate ZEVs powered by advanced batteries and flexibility to determine the best time to introduce this new technology to the market. To encourage the early production of advanced ZEVs, the staff is also proposing to add a provision to allow multiple credits for longer-range ZEVs produced prior to the 2003 model year. These ZEV credits could be applied to a manufacturer's 2003 and subsequent model year requirements.

* * *

Under Title II of the Federal Clean Air Act (FCAA), the U.S. Environmental Protection Agency has promulgated comprehensive regulations to control emissions from new motor vehicles. . . . While both the federal and California automotive emissions standards are similar in purpose and scope, California has adopted standards that are generally more stringent and effective in order to address the severity of California's air pollution problem.

Source: A. State of California Air Resources Board, "Proposed Regulations for Low-emission Vehicles and Clean Fuels," State of California Air Resources Boards staff report, August 13,1990, pp. 3, 4, 24. **B.** California Air Resources Board, "Notice of Public Hearing to Consider Amendments to the Zero-Emission Vehicle Requirements for Passenger Cars and Light-duty Trucks," January 30, 1996, p. 2.

DOCUMENT 142: John P. Holdren on Energy and Human Well-Being (1990)

John P. Holdren, a professor of environmental policy at Harvard, served as a science advisor in both the Clinton and Obama administrations and was involved in preparations for the Kyoto Protocol [Document 145B] and the Paris Climate Agreement of 2016. He is concerned about the failure of the United States to establish an energy policy that adequately encourages the development of clean, safe fuels to satisfy the nation's long-term energy needs. Foreseeing negative social, political, economic, and environmental consequences from the continued absence of such a policy, he worries about its effect on America's position as a world leader.

[C]ivilization is not running out of energy resources in an absolute sense, nor is it running out of technological options for transforming these resources into the particular forms that our patterns of energy use require. We are, however, running out of the cheap oil and natural gas that powered much of the growth of modern industrialized societies, out of environmental capacity to absorb the impacts of burning coal, and out of public tolerance for the risks of nuclear fission. We seem to be lacking as well the commitment to make coal cleaner and fission safer, the money and endurance needed to develop long-term alternatives, the astuteness to embrace energy efficiency on the scale demanded and the consensus needed to fashion any coherent strategy at all.

These deficiencies suggest that civilization has entered a fundamental transition in the nature of the energy-society interaction without any collective recognition of the transition's character or its implications for human well-being. The transition is from convenient but ultimately scarce energy resources to less convenient but more abundant ones, from a direct and positive connection between energy and economic well-being to a complicated and multidimensional one, and from localized pockets of pollution and hazard to impacts that are regional and even global in scope.

The subject is also being transformed from one of limited political interest within nations to a focus of major political contention between them, from an issue dominated by decisions and concerns of the Western world to one in which the problems and prospects of all regions are inextricably linked, and from one of concern to only a small group of technologists and managers to one where the values and actions of every citizen matter.

Understanding this transition requires a look at the two-sided connection between energy and human well-being. Energy contributes positively to well-being by providing such consumer services as heating, lighting and cooking as well as serving as a necessary input to economic production. But the costs of energy—including not only the money and other resources devoted to obtaining and exploiting it but also the environmental and sociopolitical impacts—detract from well-being.

Source: John P. Holdren, "Energy in Transition," *Scientific American* 263, no. 3 (September 1990): 157.

DOCUMENT 143: Barry Lopez on a Sense of Place (1990)

Like John Steinbeck, Edward Abbey, and many native Americans [see Documents 32, 80, 84, 122, 173A] Barry Lopez, who writes about nature and human society, decries the greed that has been the root of the plunder of America's resources since the time of Columbus's landing and whose end result has been the destruction of the places to which its inhabitants are spiritually bound.

A sense of place must include, at the very least, knowledge of what is inviolate about the relationship between a people and the place they occupy, and certainly, too, how the destruction of this relationship, or the failure to attend to it, wounds people. . . .

If, in a philosophy of place, we examine our love of the land—I do not mean a romantic love, but the love Edward Wilson calls biophilia [*see* Document 133A], love of what is alive, and the physical context in which it lives, which we call "the hollow" or "the cane brake" or "the woody draw" or "the canyon"—if, in measuring our love, we feel anger, I think we have a further obligation. It is to develop a hard and focused anger at what continues to be done to the land not so that people can survive, but so that a relatively few people can amass wealth.

* * *

One of our deepest frustrations as a culture, I think, must be that we have made so extreme an investment in mining the continent, created such an infrastructure of nearly endless jobs predicated on the removal and distribution of trees, water, minerals, fish, plants, and oil, that we cannot imagine stopping. In the part of the country where I live [the Pacific Northwest], thousands of men are now asking themselves what jobs they will have—for they can see the handwriting on the wall—when they are told they cannot cut down the last few trees and that what little replanting they've done—if it actually works—will not produce enough timber soon enough to ensure their jobs.

The frustration of these men, who are my neighbors, is a frustration I am not deeply sympathetic to—their employers have behaved like wastrels, and they have known for years that this was coming. But in another way I am sympathetic, for these men are trying to live out an American nightmare which our system of schools and our voices of government never told them was ill-founded. There is not the raw material in the woods, or beyond, to make all of us rich. And in striving for it, we will only make ourselves, all of us, poor.

Source: Barry Lopez, *The Rediscovery of North America* (New York: Vintage Books/Random House, 1992), pp. 40-42, 44-46.

DOCUMENT 144: Rio Declaration on Environment and Development (1992)

The United Nations Rio Declaration focuses on the importance of international cooperation in dealing with environmental issues and on the interrelatedness of environmental and development, embracing the concept of sustainable development originally set forth twenty years earlier in the Stockholm Declaration [Document 119] Principle 15 expands on the precautionary principle, first enunciated in the Montreal Protocol [see Document 135]: when there is the possibility of a serious threat to human life action should be taken despite the lack of scientific certainty. The declaration embraces the concept of sustainable development originally enunciated in the Stockholm Declaration [see Document 119].

The United Nations Conference on Environment and Development . . .

With the goal of establishing a new and equitable global partnership through the creation of new levels of cooperation among States, key sectors of societies and people,

Working towards international agreements which respect the interests of all and protect the integrity of the global environmental and developmental system,

Recognizing the integral and interdependent nature of the Earth, our home,

Proclaims that:

Principle 2: States have, in accordance with the Charter of the United Nations and the principles of international law, the sovereign right to exploit their own resources pursuant to their own environmental and developmental policies, and the responsibility to ensure that activities within their jurisdiction or control do not cause damage to the environment of other States or of areas beyond the limits of national jurisdiction.

Principle 3: The right to development must be fulfilled so as to equitably meet developmental and environmental needs of present and future generations.

Principle 4: In order to achieve sustainable development, environmental protection shall constitute an integral part of the development process and cannot be considered in isolation from it.

Principle 5: All States and all people shall cooperate in the essential task of eradicating poverty as an indispensable requirement for sustainable development, in order to decrease the disparities in standards of living and better meet the needs of the majority of the people of the world.

Principle 6: The special situation and needs of developing countries, particularly the

least developed and those most environmentally vulnerable, shall be given special priority. International actions in the field of environment and development should also address the interests and needs of all countries.

Principle 7: States shall cooperate in a spirit of global partnership to conserve, protect and restore the health and integrity of the Earth's ecosystem. In view of the different contributions to global environmental degradation, States have common but differentiated responsibilities. The developed countries acknowledge the responsibility that they bear in the international pursuit of sustainable development in view of the pressures their societies place on the global environment and of the technologies and financial resources they command.

Principle 8: To achieve sustainable development and a higher quality of life for all people, States should reduce and eliminate unsustainable patterns of production and consumption and promote appropriate demographic policies.

Principle 9: States should cooperate to strengthen endogenous capacity-building for sustainable development by improving scientific understanding through exchanges of scientific and technological knowledge. . . .

Principle 12: States should cooperate to promote a supportive and open international economic system that would lead to economic growth and sustainable development in all countries, to better address the problems of environmental degradation. Trade policy measures for environmental purposes should not constitute a means of arbitrary or unjustifiable discrimination or a disguised restriction on international trade. Unilateral actions to deal with environmental challenges outside the jurisdiction of the importing country should be avoided. Environmental measures addressing transboundary or global environmental problems should, as far as possible, be based on an international consensus.

Principle 13: States shall develop national law regarding liability and compensation for the victims of pollution and other environmental damage. States shall also cooperate in an expeditious and more determined manner to develop further international law regarding liability and compensation for adverse effects of environmental damage caused by activities within their jurisdiction or control to areas beyond their jurisdiction.

Principle 14: States should effectively cooperate to discourage or prevent the relocation and transfer to other States of any activities and substances that cause severe environmental degradation or are found to be harmful to human health.

Principle 15: In order to protect the environment, the precautionary approach shall be widely applied by States according to their capabilities. Where there are threats of serious or irreversible damage, lack of full scientific certainty shall not be used as a reason for postponing cost-effective measures to prevent environmental degradation.

Principle 18: States shall immediately notify other States of any natural disasters or other emergencies that are likely to produce sudden harmful effects on the environment of those States. Every effort shall be made by the international community to help States so afflicted.

Principle 19: States shall provide prior and timely notification and relevant information to potentially affected States on activities that may have a significant adverse transboundary environmental effect and shall consult with those States at an early stage and in good faith

Principle 22: Indigenous people and their communities and other local communities have a vital role in environmental management and development because of their knowledge and traditional practices. States should recognize and duly support their identity, culture and interests and enable their effective participation in the achievement of sustainable development.

Principle 23: The environment and natural resources of people under oppression, domination and occupation shall be protected.

Principle 24: Warfare is inherently destructive of sustainable development. States shall therefore respect international law providing protection for the environment in times of armed conflict and cooperate in its further development, as necessary.

Source: UNEP.org/documents. Report of the United Nations Conference on the Human Environment, Stockholm, 5-16 June 1972 (United Nations publication, Sales No. E.73. II.A.14 and corrigendum), chap. I.

DOCUMENT 145: United Nations Convention (1992) and Protocol (1997) on Climate Change

By the mid-1980s, many scientists suspected that heat-trapping gases such as carbon dioxide, emitted during the burning of fossil fuels, and methane were not only causing acid rain and thinning the ozone layer, but were also rendering a change in the earth's climate [see Document 137]. They proposed that just as the windows of a greenhouse allow heat from the sun to pass through them and then hold that heat inside, thereby raising the interior temperature, so too do heat-trapping gases permit some of the sun's radiant energy to penetrate the atmosphere all the way to the earth's surface, and then prevent the resulting heat from escaping the earth's atmosphere, thereby causing a warming of the earth.

In order to evaluate the scientific basis of this theory, consider the potential impact of global warming, and examine possible policy responses to climate change, the Intergovernmental Panel on Climate Change (IPCC), an international panel of scientists, government representatives, and policymakers working in three groups, was established in 1988. The 1990 report of the IPCC's scientific group[13] concluded that the concentration of greenhouse gases in the earth's atmosphere was increasing and that this might be contributing to a change in the earth's climate.

Bill McKibben, whose 1989 book The End of Nature *was the first popular book on climate change, was among the cadres of environmentalists and scientists who worried that as a result of human activity "the Antarctic ice sheet could fail more quickly than previously believed" and that we are headed for disaster unless we act immediately to stop the warming trend,[14] even if there was as yet no absolute proof that global warming was occurring or that greenhouse gases caused the apparent warming trend. Indeed, some people still insist that higher temperatures recorded around the world in recent years merely reflect normal long-term fluctuations in the global climate. However, by the 1990s most scientists and environmentalists as well as many policymakers felt that the nations of the world would be derelict if they did not take action to forestall a highly probable imminent catastrophe.*

The United Nations Framework Convention on Climate Change, adopted in May 1992, was the international community's response to these concerns. Its goal was to address all the greenhouse gas issues not covered by the Montreal Protocol [Document 135]. The details of how the Climate Change Convention was to be implemented were set forth in the Kyoto Protocol. This historic agreement imposed legally binding limits on the production by developed countries of man-made greenhouse gases. Although the United States was one of the first countries to sign the Climate Change Convention, it was one of the last to sign the Kyoto Protocol, and because of strong opposition by industry [see Document 149] the U.S. Senate never ratified the agreement.

A. United Nations Framework Convention on Climate Change

The parties to this Convention,

Acknowledging that change in the Earth's climate and its adverse effects are a common concern of humankind,

Concerned that human activities have been substantially increasing the atmospheric concentrations of greenhouse gases, that these increases enhance the natural greenhouse effect, and that this will result on average in an additional warming of the Earth's surface and atmosphere and may adversely affect natural ecosystems and humankind,

Noting that the largest share of historical and current global emissions of greenhouse gases has originated in developed countries, that per capita emissions in developing countries are still relatively low and that the share of global emissions originating in developing countries will grow to meet their social and development needs,

Aware of the role and importance in terrestrial and marine ecosystems of sinks and reservoirs of greenhouse gases,

Noting that there are many uncertainties in predictions of climate change, particularly with regard to the timing, magnitude and regional patterns thereof,

Acknowledging that the global nature of climate change calls for the widest possible cooperation by all countries and their participation in an effective and appropriate international response, in accordance with their common but differentiated responsibilities and respective capabilities and their social and economic conditions . . .

Affirming that responses to climate change should be coordinated with social and economic development in an integrated manner with a view to avoiding adverse impacts on the latter, taking into full account the legitimate priority needs of developing countries for the achievement of sustained economic growth and the eradication of poverty . . .

Have agreed as follow:

* * *

The ultimate objective of this Convention and any related legal instruments that the Conference of the Parties may adopt is to achieve . . . stabilization of greenhouse gas concentrations in the atmosphere at a level that would prevent dangerous anthropogenic interference with the climate system. Such a level should be achieved within a time-frame sufficient to allow ecosystems to adapt naturally to climate change, to ensure that food production is not threatened and to enable economic development to proceed in a sustainable manner.

B. The Kyoto Protocol

Article 3

1. The Parties included in Annex I [all the countries of Western Europe and most of the countries of Eastern Europe, as well as the United States, Canada, Japan, Australia, and New Zealand] shall, individually or jointly, ensure that their aggregate anthropogenic carbon dioxide equivalent emissions of the greenhouse gases listed in Annex A [carbon dioxide, methane, nitrous oxide, hydrofluorocarbons, perfluorocarbons, and sulphur hexafluoride] do not exceed their assigned amounts, calculated pursuant to their quantified emission limitation and reduction commitments . . . , with a view to reducing their overall emissions of such gases by at least 5 percent below 1990 levels in the commitment period 2008 to 2012.

2. Each Party included in Annex I shall, by 2005 have made demonstrable progress in achieving its commitments under this Protocol.

6. [A] certain degree of flexibility shall be allowed by the Conference of the Parties . . . to the Parties included in Annex I undergoing the process of transition to a market economy.

Article 6

1. For the purpose of meeting its commitments under Article 3, any Party included in Annex I may transfer to, or acquire from, any other such Party emission reduction units resulting from projects aimed at reducing anthropogenic emissions by sources or enhancing anthropogenic removals by sinks of greenhouse gases in any sector of the economy.

Article 12

3. Under the clean development mechanism:

(a) Parties not included in Annex I will benefit from project activities resulting in certified emission reductions; and

(b) Parties included in Annex I may use the certified emission reductions accruing from such project activities to contribute to compliance with part of their quantified emission limitation and reduction commitments under Article 3.

Source: A. *United Nations Framework Convention on Climate Change,* U.N. document A/AC.237/18, Part II/Add.1 and Corr.1, New York, May 9, 1992, pp.1, 3, 4. B. *Kyoto Protocol to the United Nations Framework Convention on Climate Change,* U.N. document FCCC/CP/1997/L.7/Add. 1, Kyoto, December 1997, pp. 3, 4, 7, 12.

DOCUMENT 146: Donella Meadows on the Complexity of the Malthusian Debate (1993)

Donella Meadows became a prominent voice in the Malthusian debate with the 1972 publication of her book Limits to Growth. *Writing in* The Economist *in 1993, she pointed out that "If a debate persists with passion for nearly two centuries, it must be true not only that the evidence is complex enough to support both sides, but also that each side is actively sifting the evidence, accumulating only that which supports preconceived notions." Meadows warned that it is time to stop arguing and start to take action.*

[I am] a person who has been active in the Malthusian debate but who has become less interested in winning than in understanding the intransigent nature of the discussion. I assume the argument resists resolution partly because the issues it raises are so complex and partly because they are so emotional. What I wonder is, what would we see if we were willing to approach the question of human population growth and planetary limits purely scientifically? What if we could divest ourselves of hopes, fears, and ideologies long enough to entertain all arguments and judge them fairly?

What we would see, I think, is that all sides are partly right and mostly incomplete. Each is focusing on one piece of a very complex system. Each is seeing its piece correctly. But because no side is seeing the whole, no side is coming to wholly supportable conclusions.

In short, to resolve the Malthusian conundrum and to find a way of thinking and acting that can guide a growing population to a sufficient and supportable standard of living within the earth's limits, we need all points of view. We need to treat them all with respect. We need to integrate them.

There are more than two points of view....I will describe four sides of the debate here, with the understanding that many people put elements of these four together in their own unique combination, and that there are other points of view as well.

* * *

The Blues

The Blue view of the Malthusian question focuses on the possibility of keeping capital growing faster than population, so everyone can be better off. Progress, as defined by this view, comes from the accumulation of productive capital, from the building of infrastructure (roads, dams, ports) to make that capital more effective, and from the education of humans to make them more skilled and inventive in producing output from capital.

An important part of the Blue model is the assumption that capital grows most efficiently in a market system, where it is privately owned, where those who make it grow are directly rewarded, and where government interferes minimally.

* * *

The Reds

. . . What the Reds see more clearly than anyone else is the way societies systematically enrich those who already are rich, leaving the poor behind.

Reds do not assume that the enriched ones reap just rewards of superior productivity, while the left-behind ones fail because they are unwilling to work or invest. They point out many social processes, from interest payments to differential education to the distribution of political power, that reward those who already have won and condemn many to lives of continuous losing.

Reds want to fix these inequities and oppressions. They envision a community of people working together to control resources and produce goods. . . .

In the Red view, labor—not capital and not natural resources—is the most critical factor of production.

* * *

The Greens

If Blues turn their attention to the growth of capital and technology and Reds are especially conscious of labor and patterns of distribution, Greens keep their eyes on resource depletion and pollution. They see not capital, not labor, but materials and energy as the most critical factors of production. They are worried about the size of the economic system relative to the size that nature can support. Whereas both Blues and Reds strive to make economies grow bigger, those who see the world through Green lenses fear that economies and population can grow too big to be sustainable.

Progress, according to Greens, should bring people to a state of sufficiency, not one of constant material growth. The key word is *enough*— enough food, clothing, shelter, education, and health care, and also enough clean water, green trees, and unspoiled natural beauty. The major threats to achieving this vision are production methods that waste resources and populations and economies that stress ecosystems.

* * *

The Whites

The White view combines some aspects of all the previously mentioned colors . . . , but it rejects their centralist, we-will-tell-you-how- to-behave tone. Whites see any policy as worthwhile only if it comes out of the wisdom and efforts of the people. . . . They care less about what should be done and more about who decides.

This model sees progress as local self-reliance. An important concept to the Whites is appropriate technology—technology that uses tools that can be manufactured and maintained at the local level, that uses nearby resources and skills, and that yields products needed close at hand.

* * *

The Clash of Models; The Consolidation of Models

I have simplified each of these views greatly, but not as much as they simplify each other. Each side has a tendency to define itself by its own more moderate beliefs and to see the other sides at their extremes.

* * *

In the final analysis, if we were to admit the relevance of all points of view, we would see that we need to pay as close attention to the earth's energy and material flows as we do to our economy's money flows. We need to keep resource accounts, like bank accounts, and never commit the foolishness of spending down our capital while calling it income. If we did that, we would discover that our planet is enormously bountiful but not infinite. We would see how to achieve or human dreams without destroying either the resources or the natural magnificence that will allow future generations to achieve their dreams.

The scarcest resource is not oil, metals, clean air, capital, labor, or technology. It is our willingness to listen to each other and learn from each other and to seek the truth rather than seek to be right. Because we have not done that, another resource has become critically scarce: time. With the world population growing now by 95 million a year, 90 percent of whom are born in poor nations; with forests, soil, water, and ecosystems being degraded around the world; with people to educate and factories to build and new technologies to develop, there is no time to continue the Malthusian argument fruitlessly for another two hundred years.

Source: Donella H. Meadows, "Seeing the Population Issue Whole," *The Economist,* June 1993, in Laurie Ann Mazur, ed., *Beyond the Numbers* (Washington, D.C.: Island Press, 1994), pp. 24-32.

DOCUMENT 147: Carl Safina on the Decline of Fishes (1995)

Carl Safina, the founder of National Audubon's Living Oceans Program and author of Song for the Blue Ocean *(1997), sees a connection between high technology and the decline in the world's fish populations. In 1992 the United Nations banned large drift nets because they frequently trapped a wide range of marine life in addition to the sought-after fish; nevertheless, as Safina notes, they continue to be used by fisherman from several nations.*

Agribusiness also poses a threat to the fishing industry. Nitrogen-rich runoff from land that has been heavily fertilized or contains large amounts of animal wastes has caused red tides—huge growths of small organisms on the surface of near- shore waters—that have resulted in dead zones because oxygen cannot penetrate them.

Because wild fish regenerate at rates determined by nature, attempts to increase their supply to the marketplace must eventually run into limits. That threshold seems to have been passed in all parts of the Atlantic, Mediterranean and Pacific. . . . Worldwide, the extraction of wild fish peaked at 82 million metric tons in 1989. Since then, the long-term growth trend has been replaced by stagnation or decline.

In some areas where the catches peaked as long ago as the early 1970s, current landings have decreased by more than 50 percent. Even more disturbingly, some of the world's greatest fishing grounds, including the Grand Banks and Georges Bank of eastern North America, are now essentially closed following their collapse—the formerly dominant fauna have been reduced to a tiny fraction of their previous abundance and are considered commercially extinct.

Recognizing that a basic shift has occurred, the members of the United Nations's Food and Agriculture Organization (a body that encouraged the expansion of large-scale industrial fishing only a decade ago) recently concluded that the operation of the world's fisheries cannot be sustained. They now acknowledge that substantial damage has already been done to the marine environment and to the many economies that depend on this natural resource.

* * *

How did this collapse happen? An explosion of fishing technologies occurred during the 1950s and 1960s. During that time, fishers adapted various military technologies to hunting on the high seas. Radar allowed boats to navigate in total fog, and sonar made it possible to detect schools of fish deep under the oceans' opaque blanket. Electronic navigation aids such as LORAN (Long-Range Navigation) and satellite positioning systems turned the trackless sea into a grid so that vessels could return to within 50 feet of a chosen location, such as sites where fish gathered and bred. Ships can now receive satellite weather maps of water-temperature fronts, indicating where fish will be traveling. Some vessels work in concert with aircraft used to spot fish.

Many industrial fishing vessels are floating factories deploying gear of enormous proportions: 80 miles of submerged longlines with thousands of baited hooks, bag-shaped trawl nets large enough to engulf 12 jumbo jetliners and 40-mile-long drift nets (still in use by some countries). Pressure from industrial fishing is so intense that 80 to 90 percent of the fish in some populations are removed every year.

. . . Fishers have countered loss of preferred fish by switching to species of lesser value, usually those positioned lower in the food web—a practice that robs larger fishes, marine mammals and seabirds of food. During the 1980s, five of the less desirable species made up nearly 30 percent of the world fish catch but accounted for only 6 percent of its monetary value.

* * *

[T]he development of aquaculture has not reduced the pressure on wild populations. Strangely it may do the opposite. Shrimp farming has created a demand for otherwise worthless catch because it can be used as feed. In some countries, shrimp farmers are now investing in trawl nets with fine mesh to catch everything they can for shrimp food, a practice known as biomass fishing. Much of the catch are juveniles of valuable species, and so these fish never have the opportunity to reproduce.

Fish farms can hurt wild populations because the construction of pens along the coast often requires cutting down mangroves—the submerged roots of these salt-tolerant trees provide a natural nursery for shrimp and fish.

Source: Carl Safina, "The World's Imperiled Fish," *Scientific American* 273 (November(1995): 48-49.

DOCUMENT 148: Edward Tenner on Shifting Liability (1996)

Surely the scientists who developed DDT did not anticipate that the pesticide would drive the bald eagle and several other prized species to the brink of extinction. Neither did the builders of the electric power stations in the Ohio Valley anticipate that acid rain would result from the construction of the tall smokestacks that rid the region between Pittsburgh and Cincinnati of much of its pollution.

Edward Tenner, a historian who writes and lectures about the history of science and technology, questions whether many so-called scientific, technological, and medical advances of the twentieth and twenty-first centuries are not merely shifting the nature of environmental liability. While sixteenth-century scientists and philosophers such as Francis Bacon [see Document 8] believed that technology would give humans control over nature, in the late twentieth century it became increasingly evident to more and more people that it is impossible to foresee all the consequences of a technological innovation[15] or to predict precisely how an ecosystem will respond to its manipulation.

Classic disasters were deterministic. Cause and effect were linked. An exploding boiler killed those it killed, and spared those it spared. Late-twentieth-century disasters are expressed as deviations from a baseline of "normal" background tragedy. The truth is not in immediate view. It emerges from the statistical inferences of trained professionals.

. . .

The old disasters were localized and sudden. New ones may be global and gradual, from radioactive isotopes in milk in the 1950s to climate change in the 1990s.

Our control of the acute has indirectly promoted chronic problems. Medical researchers have recognized this trend for years and have been shifting their efforts to chronic diseases—though so far not with the same results they have had with injury, infection, and acute illness. Our ability to transport animals and plants among continents, deliberately and accidentally, has on balance been decreasing rather than promoting species diversity. But the

invaders have also failed to be as catastrophic to trees and crops as some had feared. Like many chronic illnesses, they have become manageable nuisances, neither conquerable nor fatal, but demanding time-consuming vigilance. Our efforts to modify our environment have also produced chronic problems: the comforts of home have helped produce the annoyances of allergies, suppressing forest fires has helped make them a greater threat, and protecting the shoreline is helping to erode it.

* * *

By intensifying our protection against some forms of natural danger, we have sometimes only shifted greater liability to the future: a rearranging effect. We have traded acute problems for gradual but accumulating ones. This is especially true of the environmental disasters affecting energy.

Source: Edward Tenner, *Why Things Bite Back: Technology and the Revenge of Unintended Consequences* (New York: Knopf, 1996), pp. 24-25, 72.

DOCUMENT 149: The Business Roundtable Objects to the Kyoto Protocol (1998)

The business community—represented here by The Business Roundtable, which includes the chief executives of more than two hundred of the largest corporations in the United States—objected to many of the details of the Kyoto Protocol and opposed its ratification. Following are the Roundtable's "Key Issues of Concern about the Kyoto Protocol."

- **The targets and timetables would require the U.S. to make significant and immediate cuts in energy use.** The Protocol would require the U.S. to reduce emissions 7% below 1990 levels by 2009-2012, an unprecedented 41% reduction in projected emission levels. The process of Senate ratification and the subsequent lengthy domestic implementation process postratification would leave the U.S. very little time to make the painful choices regarding energy use that will be necessary to achieve these reductions. In addition, because the Protocol sets different targets for each industrialized country and the target is based on what is now an eight-year-old baseline, the U.S. in effect will shoulder a disproportionate level of reduction and may be placed at a competitive disadvantage.

- **Unless the Developing Countries also commit to emission reductions, the Protocol is incomplete and will not work.** The Byrd-Hagel Resolution, unanimously adopted by the U.S. Senate in July 1997, states that the U.S. should not be a signatory to any protocol unless it mandates "new specific scheduled commitments to limit or reduce greenhouse gas emissions for the Developing Country Parties within the same compliance period." Many Developing Countries are rapidly growing their economies and will become the largest emitters of greenhouse gases in the next 15-20 years. *Greenhouse gases know no boundaries, and stabilization of greenhouse gas concentrations cannot be achieved without global participation in a limitation-reduction effort.* Moreover, regulating the emissions of only a handful of countries could lead to the migration of energy-intensive production—such as the chemicals, steel, petroleum refining, aluminum and mining industries—from the industrialized countries to the growing Developing Countries.

- **Certain carbon "sinks" may be used to offset emission reductions, but the Protocol does not establish how sinks will be calculated.** Carbon sinks, a natural system that absorbs carbon dioxide, have tremendous potential as a means of reducing emissions, but too much is currently unknown to make a fair determination. *It is unclear how sinks might help the U.S. reach its emission-reduction commitment.* It is understood that the rules for sinks will be addressed at the Fourth Conference of the Parties (COP4) in Buenos Aires, but until they are fully fleshed out their potential impact cannot be evaluated.

- **The Protocol contains no mechanisms for compliance and enforcement.** Simply put, it would be inappropriate for any country to ratify a legally binding international agreement that lacks compliance guidelines and enforcement mechanisms. The Protocol outlines a system of domestic monitoring with over- sight by international review teams, but what constitutes compliance and who judges it will not be determined until after the Protocol enters into force. *The means of enforcement—also unknown—is equally critical, since a country's noncompliance could give it a competitive advantage over the U.S. and eviscerate the agreement's environmental goals.*

- **The Protocol includes flexible, market-based mechanisms to achieve emission reductions, but it does not establish how these mechanisms would work and to what extent they could be used.** The U.S. intends to rely heavily on market-based mechanisms to find the most efficient and cost-effective ways to reduce emissions. But until the rules and regulations are established it is uncertain how effective these mechanisms will be and to what extent they can be used by companies. Many countries are resisting these market-based mechanisms and their reluctance may hinder the development of adequate free-market guidelines. *The absence of many countries from the market- place, and the possible limitations and restrictions on the marketplace, could render these mechanisms useless or of little value.*

- **The Protocol leaves the door open for the imposition of mandatory policies and measures to meet commitments.** Just as the U.S. favors flexible market mechanisms, the European Union and many Developing Countries favor harmonized, mandatory "command-and-control" policies and measures— such as carbon taxes and CAFÉ standards—to meet commitments, and they will have numerous

opportunities to seek adoption of these policies.

- **Finally, the procedures for ratification of, and amendment to, the Kyoto Protocol make it difficult to remedy before it enters into force.** The Protocol may not be amended, nor can rules and guidelines be adopted, until after the Protocol enters into force. The Clinton Administration is now considering the negotiation of a separate or supplemental protocol to attain necessary additional commitments, but this approach would open all issues to further negotiation.

The Business Roundtable believes that the Congress and the American people cannot evaluate the Kyoto Protocol until the Administration sets out a plan as to how it intends to meet the targets of the Protocol. To place the magnitude of the U.S. reduction commitments in perspective, it is the equivalent of having to eliminate all current emissions from either the U.S. transportation sector, or the utilities sector (residential and commercial sources), or industry. The Administration needs to detail how targets in the Protocol will be met, and how the burden will be distributed among the various sectors of the economy.

The Business Roundtable feels that a public dialogue must take place on the major issues highlighted in our Gap Analysis before the Protocol becomes that law of the land and government agencies begin to write regulations.

Source: The Business Roundtable Environmental Task Force, The Kyoto Protocol: A Gap Analysis (Washington, D.C.: The Business Roundtable, June 1998), pp. 1-3.

DOCUMENT 150: Jeremy Rifkin on Biotechnology and the Environment (1998)

Jeremy Rifkin, the president of the Washington, D.C.-based Foundation on Economic Trends, is an economist and political advisor who writes about developments in science and technology and their influence on economic and social trends. His book The Biotech Century *explores some of the possible effects on the environment of manipulating nature to produce overnight the kinds of changes that in the past required tens of thousands of years.*

While the biotech revolution will reshape the global economy and remake our society, it is likely to have an equally significant impact on the Earth's environment. The new technologies of the Genetic Age allow scientists, corporations, and governments to manipulate the natural world at the most fundamental level—the genetic components that help orchestrate the developmental processes in all forms of life. In this regard, it is probably not overstating the case to suggest that the growing arsenal of biotechnologies is providing us with powerful new tools to engage in what will surely be the most radical experiment on the Earth's life forms and ecosystems in history. Imagine the wholesale transfer of genes between totally unrelated species and across all biological boundaries—plant, animal and human—creating thousands of novel life forms in a brief moment of evolutionary time. Then, with clonal propagation, mass-producing countless replicas of these new creations, releasing them into the biosphere to propagate, mutate, proliferate, and migrate, colonizing the land, water, and air.

* * *

Genetically engineered organisms differ from petrochemical products in several important ways. Because they are alive, genetically engineered organisms are inherently more unpredictable than petrochemicals in the way they interact with other living things in the environment. Consequently, it is much more difficult to assess all of the potential impacts that a genetically engineered organism might have on the Earth's ecosystems.

Genetically engineered products also reproduce. They grow and they migrate. Unlike many petrochemical products, it is difficult to constrain them within a given geographical locale. Once released, it is virtually impossible to recall genetically engineered organisms back to the laboratory, especially those organisms that are microscopic in nature. For all these reasons, genetically engineered organisms may pose far greater long-term potential risks to the environment than petrochemicals.

The risks in releasing novel genetically engineered organisms into the biosphere are similar to those we've encountered in introducing exotic organisms into the North American habitat. Over the past several hundred years, thousands of non-native organisms have been brought to America from other regions of the world. While many of these organisms have adapted to the North American ecosystems without severe dislocations, a small percentage of them have run wild, wreaking havoc on the flora and fauna of the continent. Gypsy moth, Kudzu vine, Dutch elm disease, chestnut blight, starlings, and Mediterranean fruit flies come easily to mind. . . . Each year the American continent is ravaged by these non-native organisms, with destruction to plant and animal life running into the billions of dollars.

Whenever a genetically engineered organism is released, there is always a small chance that it too will run amok because, like non-indigenous species, it has been artificially introduced into a complex environment that has developed a web of highly integrated relationships over long periods of evolutionary history. Each new synthetic introduction is tantamount to playing ecological roulette. That is, while there is only a small chance of it triggering an environmental explosion, if it does, the consequences could be significant and irreversible.

Global life-sciences companies are expected to introduce thousands of new genetically engineered organisms into the environment in the coming century, just as industrial companies introduced thousands of petrochemical products into the environment over the course of the past two centuries.

* * *

The reseeding of the planet with a laboratory-conceived second Genesis is likely to enjoy some enviable short-term market successes, only to ultimately fail at the hands of an unpredictable and noncompliant nature. While the genetic technologies we've invented to recolonize the biology of the planet are formidable, our utter lack of knowledge of the intricate workings of the biosphere we're experimenting on poses an even more formidable constraint. The introduction of new genetic-engineering tools and the opening up of global commerce allow an emerging "life industry" to "reinvent" nature and manage it on a worldwide scale. The new colonization, however is without a compass. There is no predictive ecology to help guide this journey and likely never will be, as nature is far too alive, complex, and variable to ever be predictably modeled by scientists. We may, in the end, find ourselves lost and cast adrift in this artificial new world we're creating for ourselves in the Biotech Century.

Source: Jeremy Rifkin, *The Biotech Century: Harnessing the Gene and Remaking the World*(New York: Jeremy P. Tarcher/Putnam, 1998), pp. 67, 72-74, 115.

Part VIII

Politicizing the Environmental Debate, 2000–2017

People born in the last decade of the twentieth century arrived into a digitized world with globalized communication and trade. The first generation for whom the internet and cell phones were commonplace, they came of age with ready access to social and other media that made it easy to find information to support their own preconceived notions of the truth.

While by the beginning of the twenty-first century most climate scientists agreed that global climate change was occurring and that escalating greenhouse gas emissions were the main cause, there were large numbers of Americans, including many consumers of right-leaning media, who continued to declare that climate change was a result of naturally occurring climate fluctuations. However, there was indisputable evidence that the temperature was going up (every decade beginning with the 1980s has been the warmest on record since records started being kept in 1850), ocean acidification was increasing, glaciers were melting, and seas were rising.

Today, while the majority of Americans believe that global warming is occurring and that this warming is caused primarily by human activity, most are not concerned that it might affect them directly, and very few feel compelled to take immediate action to slow the trend. Although in many circles it is fashionable to be eco-conscious and people happily purchase products with a recycled, organic, or other environmental imprimatur--ranging from greeting cards, food, clothing, and furniture to such expensive items as cars and even houses–few people are convinced that they need to make major lifestyle changes. Americans believe that they have a right to a clean, safe environment, including breathable air, drinkable water, and uncontaminated land on which to grow food and let their children play, but many oppose environmental restrictions that limit the way they can use their private property and object to paying for environmental regulation. Most recognize that the world's resources are finite, but large numbers still refuse to consider limits to personal consumption or economic development. An increasing number of people worry that a U.S. failure to reduce greenhouse gas emissions will inhibit the country's ability to maintain economic and societal well-being at home and to continue to play an influential role on a planet capable of sustaining human life, but others view such an idea as alarmist and insufficiently supported by facts.

Political Polarization and Federal Inaction

"During the 1980s and early 1990s, party activists—and not grassroots sentiment, which was still broadly supportive of the environmental agenda—drove the GOP to the right and introduced a fierce anti-environmentalism as a marker of party identity."[1] As a consequence, no major environmental legislation has been passed at the federal level in more than a quarter of a century. Motivated by an economic philosophy that favored limited regulation, the national government during the George W. Bush presidency put the brakes on, and in some cases even reversed, policies and programs designed to improve air and water quality and increase protection of wildlife and natural resources [see Document 152]. Even as evidence of climate change accumulated [see Documents 137, and 160], concern about the dangers of oil, gas, and coal extractions increased [see Documents 167, 172, and 173], recognition of the depletion of the nation's fisheries became more widespread [see Document 147], and worry about contaminants in water grew [see Documents 159 and 170], politicians, especially at the national level, were unwilling to impose new environmental regulations. The Obama administration attempted to create policies that would resolve some of the competing demands on America's resources [see Document 173] and make the United States a leader in the effort to slow climate change [see Document 182], but the Trump administration is intent on undoing much of Obama's environmental legacy and is creating policies favorable to business interests and to oil, gas, coal, and timber companies

The political divisiveness, fed by a pandering to extremists on the left as well as the right, has impeded the development of solutions to a variety of pressing problems, including climate change. On the extreme right you have those who claim that climate change caused by human activity is a debatable theory [see Document 181] or even a hoax and those who oppose federal regulation of private property and federal control of public lands.[2] On the extreme left are anti-capitalists who are anti-growth and anti-big-business [see Document 176] and demand a complete shut-down

of shale fracking operations [see Documents 172 and 173B] and the banning of genetically modified organisms (GMOs) [see Document 155].

Despite resistance at the national level, state and local governments have labored on [see Documents 155, 161, 162, and 163]. In addition, a host of non-governmental organizations (NGOs) [see Document 166] as well as regional consortiums comprised of various governmental entities and environmental and other NGOs [see Documents 159 and 166] have developed effective and forward-looking programs to lead the nation toward sustainability goals yet to be addressed by national policy.

California, long a leader in establishing forward-looking environmental policies, created the first statewide green building standards. New York and Los Angeles as well as a number of much smaller cities, including Seattle, Oakland, and Boulder, have set in motion some of the most innovative programs to deal with such problems as how to expand mass transportation and encourage cycling [see Document 162] and how to decrease the amount of waste going to landfills [see Document 161].

Feeding a Growing Population

In mid-2017 the population of the United States was over 325 million, with 85 percent living in urban areas, and it is projected to grow to nearly 390 million by 2050. Ten U.S. cities had more than a million inhabitants (New York, Los Angeles, Chicago, Houston, Philadelphia, Phoenix, San Antonio, San Diego, Dallas, and San Jose) and two, New York and Los Angeles, were among the world's 31 megacities.—urban agglomerations with more than 10 million people. Twenty-four others had more than 500,000 inhabitants.

While cities and inner suburbs with walkable neighborhoods and good public transportation have become increasingly attractive [see Document 171], the outer suburbs that provide few local jobs and little or no mass transportation have begun to lose their appeal and have seen sharp declines in real estate values in recent years. On the other hand, there are sections of America where the rural population and the number of small farms, after declining for more than half a century, is now increasing.

Part of the impetus for the growth of small farms has been increasing interest in eating local, organic food, an interest that was sparked by people like the

California chef, restaurateur, and food activist Alice Waters, who waged war on the tasteless produce and highly processed foods so readily available on supermarket shelves. By the end of the 1990s, urban green markets were becoming popular, and chefs, food writers, nutritionists, and environmentalists were suggesting that Americans change their eating habits both for environmental and health reasons [see Document 168]. During the past twenty-five years, the expansion of community- supported agriculture groups (CSAs), which sell shares in the annual produce of local farms, have helped to make small organic farms more viable by providing them with an assured income. In 2009, Michele Obama, the president's wife, had a kitchen garden planted on the grounds of the White House, partly to supply greens for the White House table, but mainly to promote healthy eating habits among the nation's schoolchildren.

While locavores and slow food proponents were seeking out heirloom tomatoes and wild rice and objecting to the use of pesticides, genetically modified seed, and cloned animals, many farmers in the developing world and elsewhere were glad to be able to take advantage of the Green Revolution that was made possible by the development of new plant varieties. Their increased crop yield continues to ensure an adequate food supply for most of the world's 7.5 billion people [see Document 151].

In the United States, the owners of huge farms, made possible by technological advances and encouraged by government policy, are happy to use GM seed and work closely with powerful agribusinesses. However, the massive narrowing of the food plant varieties marketed and grown in the United States and abroad poses a potential serious long-term threat to the global food supply.

Another consequence of U.S. policy has been the steady rise in the importation of fresh produce. In 2003-05 about 44 percent of fresh fruit and 16 percent of fresh vegetables consumed in the United States were imported, compared with only 31 percent of fresh fruit and 9 percent of fresh vegetables in 1983-85.[3]

Fueling a Twenty-First Century America

A major issue for the twenty-first century is how to provide sufficient energy for industry, transportation, and buildings without causing irreparable damage to the environment. As the 2010 BP-Horizon oil rig explosion in the Gulf of Mexico made evident, we are drilling and mining for fossil fuels, including oil, gas, and coal, in places that not only are environmentally sensitive and require risky, complex technology [see Documents 172] but also make it necessary to transport the fuel huge distances [see Document 174].

Government subsidies, offered as an antidote to the Great Recession that began in December 2007, created renewed interest in fuel-efficient vehicles and non-fossil fuels. However, by 2015, as gasoline prices declined and fracking reduced the need for imported oil, Americans went back to buying gas-guzzling sport utility vehicles and the marked for small cars dissipated.

Meanwhile, countries such as China, India, and Brazil, with their huge populations and growing importance in the marketplace, have been flexing their economic muscles. With hundreds of millions of people aspiring to live Western-style lives [see Document 175]—hoping to buy cars, or at least motorbikes, and add increased quantities of beef and pork to their diets—these countries are competing to obtain a greater share of the world's finite supply of oil and other resources [see Document 175].

Americans continue to be hesitant to build new nuclear plants, and low gas prices have recently made some nuclear power plants uncompetitive. The economic and environmental viability of ethanol, despite being encouraged by congressional subsidies, remains questionable [see Document 183].[4]

Wind turbines currently produce nearly five percent of the county's energy, and solar panels, the cost of which have decreased markedly during the past decade, now account for nearly one percent of U.S. energy generation. The production of carbon-free electricity throughout the United States is within the realm of possibility [see Document 169]. Potential energy in waste materials and in garbage buried in landfills across the country remains underutilized. But determining what kinds of alternative fuels and fuel sources make the most economic sense and will create the least environmental damage requires careful scientific and technological analysis, and developing new clean energy sources demands substantial economic investment. During the Obama years Congress more than doubled funding for alternative energy research, but this funding is expected to be decreased in the 2018 budget.

Seeking a New Approach to Environmental Issues

The political polarization of the country has forced those interested in advancing an environmental agenda to look for new ways to address complex environmental issues. While it has long been recognized that most so-called environmental issues are intertwined with economic and social issues [*see* Document 146], environmentalists have often taken a very narrow view of environmental issues and failed to consider the benefits and importance of economic growth. Bjorn Lomborg [*see* Document 153] maintains that many environmentalists have the wrong priorities and underestimate the value of human activities that impact the natural world. Michael Schallenberger and Ted Nordhaus, who have proclaimed the death of environmentalism [*see* Document 156], have proposed, with others, an "eco-modernist" alternative that foresees the possibility of "decoupling human development from environmental impacts" [*see* Document 180]. On the other hand, Christine MacDonald questions the whole concept of "sustainable development" [*see* Document 164] and is troubled by the close ties between big environmental groups and the business world.

Because per capita consumption in the United States is 32 times that of the poorest developing countries of the world [*see* Document 168], it is incumbent on us to reconsider not only how we use resources but also how we dispose of them. Some commodities, such as beach quality sand [*see* Document 178], which are in high demand around the world, are often put to questionable uses or too readily discarded. Waste, some of it toxic [*see* Documents 154, 170], often ends up polluting the sea or the most impoverished nations of the world.

Will we achieve change rationally and incrementally through consumption taxes, rationing, a cap-and-trade system, or some other economic control? Will we wait until a financial or environmental crisis forces change upon our country? Or will we wait until we face a military confrontation stemming from competition for one or more of the earth's finite resources, be it water, fossil fuels, habitable and arable land, or strategic minerals?

We can never predict the future with complete accuracy or foresee the consequences of newly introduced technology [*see* Document 179]. As a precaution, though, we need to lower our carbon footprint, prevent the extinction of species, and build resilient coastal communities.

DOCUMENT 151: Norman E. Borlaug on Biotechnology and Antiscience (2000)

There is an ongoing debate about the benefits and dangers of the widespread use of genetically modified seed for corn, wheat, rice and other crops whose patents are held by the agribusinesses, such as Monsanto, that developed them. On the one hand, this type of seed enables the production of more nutritious food, in increasing quantities, to feed the burgeoning population of the world. On the other hand, a position paper posted by the American Academy of Environmental Medicine (an organization whose bona fides have been questioned) claims that "[t]here is more than a casual association between GM foods and adverse health effects."[5] Furthermore, the planting of huge fields resistant to weed-killers such as Roundup Ready may encourage the natural development of super-weeds and also increases the likelihood that agribusiness-owned seed will cross-pollinate with the crops of farmers who prefer to use their own saved seed. In Europe, several countries have banned the planting and importation of genetically modified organisms (GMOs). In the United States, resistance to GMOs has given added impetus to the organic and locavore food movements and has led to the banning of GMOs in Mendocino County, California [see Document 155].

Norman Borlaug, the winner of the 1970 Nobel Peace Prize for his work in reducing world hunger and a professor of international agriculture at Texas A&M University, is considered the father of the Green Revolution.

During the 20th century, conventional breeding produced a vast number of varieties and hybrids that contributed immensely to higher grain yield, stability of harvests, and farm income. Despite the successes of the Green Revolution, the battle to ensure food security for hundreds of millions miserably poor people is far from won. Mushrooming populations, changing demographics, and inadequate poverty intervention programs have eroded many of the gains of the Green Revolution. This is not to say that the Green Revolution is over. Increases in crop management productivity can be made all along the line: in tillage, water use, fertilization, weed and pest control, and harvesting. However, for the genetic improvement of food crops to continue at a pace sufficient to meet the needs of the 8.3 billion people projected to be on this planet at the end of the quarter century, both conventional technology and biotechnology are needed.

What can we Expect from Biotechnology

The majority of agricultural scientists, including myself, anticipate great benefits from biotechnology in the coming decades to help meet our future needs for food and fiber. The commercial adoption by farmers of transgenic crops has been one of the most rapid cases of technology diffusion in the history of agriculture. Between 1996 and 1999, the area planted commercially with transgenic crops has increased from 1.7 to 39 million ha [hectares]. . . . So far, biotechnology has had the greatest impact in medicine and public health. However, there are a number of fascinating developments that are approaching commercial applications in agriculture.

Transgenic varieties and hybrids of cotton, maize, and potatoes, containing genes from *Bacillus thuringiensis* that effectively control a number of serious insect pests, are now being successfully introduced commercially in the United States. The use of such varieties will greatly reduce the need for insecticides. Considerable progress also has been made in the development of transgenic plants of cotton, maize, oilseed rape, soybeans, sugar beet, and wheat, with tolerance to a number of herbicides. . . .

Good progress has been made in developing cereal varieties with greater tolerance for soil alkalinity, free aluminum, and iron toxicities.

These varieties will help to ameliorate the soil degradation problems that have developed in many existing irrigation systems. These varieties will also allow agriculture to succeed in acidic soil areas, thus adding more arable land to the global production base. Greater tolerance of abiotic extremes, such as drought, heat, and cold, will benefit irrigated areas in several ways. We will be able to achieve more crop per drop by designing plants with reduced water requirements and adopting between-crop/water management systems. Recombinant DNA techniques can speed up the development process.

There are also hopeful signs that we will be able to improve fertilizer-use efficiency by genetically engineering wheat and other crops to have high levels of Glu dehydrogenase. Transgenic wheats with high Glu dehydrogenase, for example, yielded up to 39% more crop with the same amount of fertilizer than did normal crop.

Transgenic plants that can control viral and fungal diseases are not nearly as developed. Nevertheless, there are some promising examples of specific virus coat genes in transgenic varieties of potatoes and rice that confer considerable protection. Other promising genes for disease resistance are being incorporated into other crop species through transgenic manipulations.

I would like to share one dream that I hope scientists will achieve in the not-too-distant future. Rice is the only cereal that has immunity to the *Puccinia* sp. of rust. Imagine the benefits if the genes for rust immunity in rice could be transferred into wheat, barley, oats, maize, millet, and sorghum. The world could finally be free of the scourge of the rusts, which have led to so many famines over human history.

The power of genetic engineering to improve the nutritional quality of our food crop species is also immense. Scientists have long had an interest in improving maize protein quality. . . .

Scientists . . . have recently succeeded in transferring genes into rice to increase the quantities of vitamin A, iron, and other micronutrients. This work could eventually have profound impact for millions of people with deficiencies of vitamin A and iron, causes of blindness and anemia, respectively.

Because most of the genetic engineering research is being done by the private sector, which patents its inventions, agricultural policy makers must face a potentially serious problem. How will these resource-poor farmers of the world be able to gain access to the products of biotechnology research? How long, and under what terms, should patents be granted for bio-engineered products? Furthermore, the high cost of biotechnology research is leading to a rapid consolidation in the ownership of agricultural life science companies. Is this consolidation desirable? . . .

National governments need to be prepared to work with and benefit from the new break-throughs in biotechnology. First and foremost, governments must establish regulatory frameworks to guide the testing and use of genetically modified crops. These rules and regulations should be reasonable in terms of risk aversion and implementation costs. Science must not be hobbled by excessively restrictive regulations. Since much of the biotechnology research is under way in the private sector, the issue of intellectual property rights must be addressed and accorded adequate safeguards by national governments.

Standing up to the Antiscience Crowd

The world has or will soon have the agricultural technology available to feed the 8.3 billion people anticipated in the next quarter of a century. The more pertinent question today is whether farmers and ranchers will be permitted to use that technology. Extremists in the environmental movement, largely from rich nations and/or the privileged strata of society in poor nations, seem to be doing everything they can to stop scientific progress in its tracks. It is sad that some scientists, many of whom should or do know better, have also jumped on the extremist environmental bandwagon in search of research

funds. When scientists align themselves with antiscience political movements or lend their name to unscientific propositions, what are we to think? Is it any wonder that science is losing its constituency? We must be on guard against politically opportunistic pseudo-scientists like the late Trofim D. Lysenko, whose bizarre ideas and vicious persecution of his detractors contributed greatly to the collapse of the former USSR.

We all owe a debt of gratitude to the environmental movement that has taken place over the past 40 years. This movement has led to legislation to improve air and water quality, protect wildlife, control the disposal of toxic wastes, protect the soils, and reduce the loss of biodiversity. It is ironic, therefore, that the platform of the antibiotechnology extremists, if it were to be adopted, would have grievous consequences for both the environment and humanity. I often ask the critics of modern agricultural technology: What would the world have been like without the technological advances that have occurred? For those who profess a concern for protecting the environment, consider the positive impact resulting from the application of science-based technology. Had 1961 average world cereal yields (1,531 kg/ha) still prevailed, nearly 850 million ha of additional land of the same quality would have been needed to equal the 1999 cereal harvest (2.06 billion gross metric tons). It is obvious that such a surplus of land was not available, and certainly not in populous Asia. Moreover, even if it were available, think of the soil erosion and the loss of forests, grasslands, and wildlife that would have resulted had we tried to produce these larger harvests with the older, low-input technology! Nevertheless, the antibiotechnology zealots continue to wage their campaigns of propaganda and vandalism.

* * *

Genetically modified organisms and genetically modified foods are imprecise terms that refer to the use of transgenic crops (i.e. those grown from seeds that contain the genes of different species). The fact is that genetic modification started long before humankind started altering crops by artificial selection. Mother Nature did it, and often in a big way. For example. the wheat groups that we rely on for much of our food supply are the result of unusual (but natural) crosses between different species of grasses. . . . Neolithic humans domesticated virtually all of our food and livestock species over a relatively short period 10,000 to 15,000 years ago. Several hundred generations of farmer descendants were subsequently responsible for making enormous genetic modification in all our major crop and animal species. . . .

Genetic modification of crops is not some kind of witchcraft; rather, it is the progressive harnessing of the forces of nature to the benefit of feeding the human race. The genetic engineering of plants at the molecular level is just another step in humankind's deepening scientific journey into living genomes. Genetic engineering is not a replacement of conventional breeding but rather a complementary research tool to identify desirable genes from remotely related taxonomic groups and transfer these genes more quickly and precisely into high-yield, high-quality crop varieties. To date, there has been no credible scientific evidence to suggest that the ingestion of transgenic products is injurious to human health or the environment. Scientists have debated the possible benefits of transgenic products versus the risks society is willing to take. Certainly, zero risk is unrealistic and probably unattainable. Scientific advances always involve some risk that unintended outcomes could occur. So far, the most prestigious national academies of science, and now even the Vatican, have come out in support of genetic engineering to improve the quantity, quality, and availability of food supplies. The more important matters of concern by civil societies should be equity issues related to genetic ownership, control, and access to transgenic agricultural products.

One of the great challenges facing society in the 21st century will be a renewal and broadening of scientific education all age levels. . . . [W]e need to close the biological science knowledge gap in the affluent societies now thoroughly urban and removed from any tangible relationship to the land. The needless confrontation of consumers against the use of transgenic crop technology in Europe and elsewhere might have been avoided had more people received a better education about genetic diversity and variation. Privileged societies have the luxury of adopting a very low-risk position on the genetically modified crop issue, even if this action later turns out to be unnecessary. But the vast majority of humankind, including the hungry victims of wars, natural disasters, and economic crises who are served by the WFP [World Food Program], does not have such a luxury. . . . [E]soteric arguments about the genetic make-up of a bag of grain mean little to those for whom food aid is a matter of life or death. . . .

We cannot turn back the clock on agriculture and only use methods that were developed to feed a much smaller population. It took some 10,000 years to expand food production to the current level of about 5 billion tons per year. By 2025, we will have to nearly double current production again. This increase cannot be accomplished unless farmers across the world have access to current high-yielding crop production methods as well as new biotechnological breakthroughs that can increase the yields, dependability, and nutritional quality of our basic food crops. . . .

Conclusions

Thirty years ago, in my acceptance speech for the Nobel Peace Prize, I said that the Green Revolution had won a temporary success in man's war against hunger, which if fully implemented, could provide sufficient food for humankind through the end of the 20th century. But I warned that unless the frightening power of human reproduction was curbed, the success of the Green Revolution would only be ephemeral.

I now say that the world has the technology that is either available or well advanced in the research pipeline to feed a population of 10 billion people. The more pertinent question today is: Will farmers and ranchers be permitted to use this new technology?

Extreme environmental elitists seem to be doing everything they can to derail scientific progress. Small, well-financed, vociferous, and antiscience groups are threatening the development and application of new technology, whether it is developed from biotechnology or more conventional methods of agricultural science.

. . . [N]o food products, whether produced with recombinant DNA techniques or more traditional methods, are totally without risk. The risks posed by foods are a function of the biological characteristics of those foods and the specific genes that have been used, not of the processes employed in their development.

The affluent nations can afford to adopt elitist positions and pay more for food produced by the so-called natural methods; the 1 billion chronically poor and hungry people of this world cannot.

Source: Norman Borlaug, "Ending World Hunger: The Promise of Biotechnology and the Threat of Antiscience," *Plant Physiology,* Vol. 134 (October 2000), pp. 487-490.

DOCUMENT 152: *Solid Waste Agency of Northern Cook County* v. *United States Army Corps of Engineers et al.* (2001)

Since 1972, when the Clean Water Act was enacted, environmentalists have used this legislation, especially section 404a [see Document 116], to expand protection of the nation's wetlands, which today are diminished by half from what existed a century ago.

In one of the first important environmental cases to come before the Supreme Court in the twenty-first century, the Supreme Court overturned a circuit court ruling and constricted the application of the Clean Water Act. During the following eight years the regulatory agencies and congress would follow suit and go on to narrowly interpret environmental laws and restrict their application, often by withholding funds.

A. The Case

Petitioner, a consortium of suburban Chicago municipalities, selected as a solid waste disposal site an abandoned sand and gravel pit with excavation trenches that had evolved into permanent and seasonal ponds. Because the operation called for filling in some of the ponds, petitioner contacted federal respondents, including the Army Corps of Engineers (Corps), to determine if a landfill permit was required under §404(a) of the Clean Water Act (CWA), which authorizes the Corps to issue permits allowing the discharge of dredged or fill material into "navigable waters." The CWA defines "navigable waters" as "the waters of the United States," and the Corps' regulations define such waters to include intrastate waters, "the use, degradation

or destruction of which could affect interstate or foreign commerce." In 1986, the Corps attempted to clarify its jurisdiction, stating, in what has been dubbed the "Migratory Bird Rule," that §404(a) extends to intrastate waters that, *inter alia*, provide habitat for migratory birds. Asserting jurisdiction over the instant site pursuant to that Rule, the Corps refused to issue a §404(a) permit. . . . The Seventh Circuit held that Congress has authority under the Commerce Clause to regulate intrastate waters and that the Migratory Bird Rule is a reasonable interpretation of the CWA.

B. The Majority Opinion, Delivered by Justice William Rehnquist

Congress passed the CWA for the stated purpose of "restor[ing] and maintain[ing] the chemical, physical, and biological integrity of the Nation's waters." 33 U. S. C. §1251(a). In so doing, Congress chose to "recognize, preserve, and protect the primary responsibilities and rights of States to prevent, reduce, and eliminate pollution, to plan the development and use (including restoration, preservation, and enhancement) of land and water resources, and to consult with the Administrator in the exercise of his authority under this chapter." §1251(b). Relevant here, §404(a) authorizes respondents to regulate the discharge of fill material into "navigable waters," 33 U. S. C. §1344(a), which the statute defines as "the waters of the United States, including the territorial seas," §1362(7). Respondents have interpreted these words to cover the abandoned gravel pit at issue here because it is used as habitat for migratory birds. We conclude that the "Migratory Bird Rule" is not fairly supported by the CWA.

This is not the first time we have been called upon to evaluate the meaning of §404(a). In *United States* v. *Riverside Bayview Homes, Inc.,* (1985), we held that the Corps had §404(a) jurisdiction over wetlands that actually abutted on a navigable waterway. In so doing, we noted that the term "navigable" is of "limited import" and that Congress evidenced its intent to "regulate at least some waters that would not be deemed 'navigable' under the classical understanding of that term."

* * *

We conclude that respondents have failed to make the necessary showing that the failure of the 1977 House bill demonstrates Congress' acquiescence to the Corps' regulations or the "Migratory Bird Rule," which, of course, did not first appear until 1986. Although respondents cite some legislative history showing Congress' recognition of the Corps' assertion of jurisdiction over "isolated waters," as we explained in

Riverside Bayview Homes, "[i]n both Chambers, debate on the proposals to narrow the definition of navigable waters centered largely on the issue of wetlands preservation." Beyond Congress' desire to regulate wetlands adjacent to "navigable waters," respondents point us to no persuasive evidence that the House bill was proposed in response to the Corps' claim of jurisdiction over non-navigable, isolated, intrastate waters or that its failure indicated congressional acquiescence to such jurisdiction.

* * *

We thus decline respondents' invitation to take what they see as the next ineluctable step after *Riverside Bayview Homes*: holding that isolated ponds, some only seasonal, wholly located within two Illinois counties, fall under §404(a)'s definition of "navigable waters," because they serve as habitat for migratory birds.

* * *

Permitting respondents to claim federal jurisdiction over ponds and mudflats falling within the "Migratory Bird Rule" would result in a significant impingement of the States' traditional and primary power over land and water use. Rather than expressing a desire to readjust the federal-state balance in this manner, Congress chose to "recognize, preserve, and protect the primary responsibilities and rights of States . . . to plan the development and use . . . of land and water resources . . . ." We thus read the statute as written to avoid the significant constitutional and federalism questions raised by respondents' interpretation, and therefore reject the request for administrative deference.

Source: "Solid Waste Agency of Northern Cook County *v.* United States Army Corps of Engineers *et al. (2001),*". *United States Reports,* Vol. 531, October Term 2000 (Washington, D.C.: U.S. Government Printing Office, 2002), pp. 159, 166-67, 170-71,174.

Document 153: Bjorn Lomborg Questions the Prioritization of Environmental Issues (2001)

Bjorn Lomborg, an associate professor in the Department of Political Science at the University of Aarhus in Denmark is an internationally respected opponent of the doomsday approach to environmental thinking. He takes issue with environmental alarmists such as Lester Brown [see Document 126] and Julian Simon [see Document 127], and he lauds developers and innovators such as Norman Borlaug [see Document 151], whose work has improved the lives of millions of people.

The State of the World . . . has been published every year since 1984 by the Worldwatch Institute and its leader Lester Brown, and it has sold more than a million copies. The series attempts to identify the world's most significant challenges professionally and veraciously. Unfortunately, . . . it is frequently unable to live up to its objectives. In many ways, though, *The State of the World* is one of the best-researched and academically most ambitious environmental policy publications, and therefore it is also an essential participant in the discussion on the State of the World.

On a higher level this book plays to our general understanding of the environment: the Litany of our ever deteriorating environment. This is the view of the environment that is shaped by the images and messages that confront us each day on television, in the newspapers, in political statements and in conversations at work and at the kitchen table. This is why Time magazine can start an article in 2000, stating as entirely obvious how "everyone knows the planet is in bad shape."

Even children are told the Litany, here from Oxford University Press' *Young Oxford Books:* "The balance of nature is delicate but essential for life. Humans have upset that balance, stripping the land of its green cover, choking the air, and poisoning the seas."

. . .

[Many of our deeply ingrained beliefs from the Litany are not supported by the facts. Conditions in the world are not getting worse and worse. . . . [We have more leisure time, greater security and fewer accidents, better education, more amenities, higher incomes, fewer starving, more food, and healthier and longer lives. There is no ecological catastrophe looming around the corner to punish us.

Consequently, we must stop giving our environmental thinking a Doomsday perspective. It is imperative for us to see the environment as an important—but only *one* important—part of the many challenges we must handle to create an even better world and the most progress for the rest of the century.

Prioritization is absolutely essential if we are to achieve the best possible distribution of resources in society. The environment must participate in the social prioritization on equal terms with all other areas. Environmental initiatives must present sound arguments and be evaluated on the basis of their advantages and disadvantages, in precisely the same way as proposals to boost Medicaid, increase funding to the arts or cut taxes.

However, this necessitates that the precautionary principle be strictly circumscribed. This principle has become enshrined in many different international treaties, as in the 1992 Rio Declaration [*see* Document 144], where it is pointed out: "Where there are threats of serious or irreversible damage, lack of full scientific certainty shall not be used as a reason for postponing cost-effective measures to prevent environmental degradation."

In this formulation, the principle merely informs us that since we can never prove anything absolutely, scientific uncertainty ought not to be used merely as a political strategy to avoid environmental action. The most obvious example is global warming, where the mere fact of scientific uncertainty is not in itself an argument against (or for that matter, for) action. Rather . . . we need to look at the level of uncertainty, the direction of that uncertainty, and then particularly at the likely costs and benefits of different levels of action.

However, this understanding of the precautionary principle is very Anglo-Saxon, whereas a much more radical interpretation comes from the German version (the so-called *Vorsorgeprinzip*), the more common interpretation on the Continent. This principle in essence suggests building "a margin of safety into all decision making." In the Danish interpretation it becomes "giving nature and the environment the benefit of the doubt."

But this is a rather problematic argument. In essence it argues "better safe than sorry," which of course sounds eminently agreeable. However, such an approach ignores the fundamental insight from [a] Harvard study, namely that if we try to become more safe in some areas, we spend resources that cannot be used doing good in other areas. Thus, saving extra lives at great cost—just to be sure—quite possibly means forgoing the chance to save many more lives more cheaply in other areas.

. . .

[A]ny significant prioritization in our society is evaluated against a background of uncertain knowledge and our propensity to be risk averse, and with the realization that the decision will be hard to reverse, and have momentous consequences, both for many people and far into the future. This still makes the environmental proposals just one example among many.

That the environmental area has been able to monopolize the precautionary principle is in essence due to the Litany and our fear of doomsday. Of course, if large-scale ecological catastrophes were looming on the horizon we might be more inclined to afford the extra margin of safety for the environment. But . . . such a general conception is built on a myth.

The whole point of prioritization is to use our resources as well as possible, on the basis of all the information available. For this reason, the precautionary principle should not be used to tip the scales a bit more in favor of the environment, because the distribution would by definition no longer be the best possible. In this way, the precautionary principle is actually all about making worse decisions than we need to.

. . .

When we fear for our environment, we seem easily to fall victim to a short-term feel-good solution which spends money on relatively trifling issues and thus hold back resources from far more important ones. We need to be rational and make well-considered decisions in our use of resources when it comes to the aquatic environment, pesticides and global warming. This does not mean that rational environmental management and environmental investment is not often a good idea—only that we should compare the costs and benefits of such investments to similar investments in all the other important areas of human endeavor.

On the whole I believe it is important to emphasize that being overly optimistic is not without cost, *but that being too pessimistic also carries a hefty price tag.*

Source: Bjorn Lomborg: *The Skeptical Environmentalist: Measuring the Real State of the World* (New York: Cambridge University Press), pp. 3. 348-50.

Document 154: Charles W. Schmidt on Electronic Waste (2002)

The electronics revolution has created a constantly expanding mountain of e-waste, with electronic equipment becoming obsolete at an ever more rapid rate. Although there are federal laws pertaining to the disposal and export of toxic chemicals, for the most part it is left to states, cities, and individual communities to regulate the recycling and disposal of e-waste, only a small percentage of which is recycled. For years much of the recycled e-waste was exported to places like China, India, and countries in Africa that had few environmental restrictions in place.

Do you have an old computer in your closet at home? Odds are the answer is yes. Of course, it's covered in dust, the keyboard is grimy, and you haven't even turned it on for years. You'd like to get rid of it, but you don't know how or where. But rest assured — you're not alone. Obsolete computers and other kinds of electronic junk are piling up everywhere, creating what some experts predict will be the largest toxic waste problem of the 21st century. If that sounds excessive, consider the following: the glass cathode ray tubes (CRTs) found in televisions and computer display monitors each contain an average of 4 pounds of lead. Multiply that by the 315 million computers expected to become obsolete in the United States by 2004, and there is 1.2 billion pounds of lead to worry about. The color monitors of most computers contain a CRT that fails federal toxicity criteria for lead and is classified as hazardous waste by the U.S. Environmental Protection Agency (EPA). Circuit boards and batteries are also full of lead, in addition to smaller amounts of mercury and hexavalent chromium. Plastics used in electronic equipment pose a hazard because they may contain polyvinyl chloride, which produces dioxins when burned. Many other plastics and some circuit boards contain brominated flame retardants (BFRs), several of which are suspected endocrine disruptors that also bioaccumlate in animal and fish tissues. A recent study by the California Department of Health published in the February 2002 issue of Chemosphere found very high levels of BFRs in the blubber of Harbor Seals as well as in the breast milk of nursing mothers in California's bay area.

Most experts believe the full environmental impact of e-waste is just beginning to be fully realized. Thanks to Moore's Law— the 1965 observation of Intel cofounder Gordon Moore that computer processing power was doubling every 18 months and could continue into the foreseeable future— the shiny new computer bought today is virtually obsolete by the time it's plugged into the wall at home. Most of the now-obsolete machines tossed out in the relentless push towards the technologic future are still in storage, according to the Silicon Valley Toxics Coalition (SVTC), an environmental group based in San Jose, California. But as consumers upgrade their computers for the third and fourth time, these older relics are increasingly finding their way into municipal waste streams. And the problem goes way beyond computers. Other obsolete electronic products are also adding to the growing waste problem. With the emergence of DVD players, high-resolution television, and digital flat-screen monitors, traditional television sets and VHS players are also beginning to clutter up landfills, contaminating incinerator feedstocks and adding to waste exports to developing countries, where environmental recycling and disposal standards are often non-existent or ignored. Sales of consumer electronics goods from manufacturers to dealers are expected to surpass $95.7 billion in 2002, according to the Consumer Electronics Association. That figure represents a vast amount of technology—technology that will undoubtedly some day become obsolete. The question is, when it does, what will we do with it all?

Clogging the Waste Stream

e-Waste is the fastest growing component of municipal trash by a factor of three, according to the European Commission. According to the SVTC, consumer electronics in the United States already account for 70% of the heavy metals, including 40% of the lead, found in landfills. Getting all this toxic e-junk out of the waste stream is an environmental priority. "I wouldn't say we're facing a crisis now," says James Doucett, deputy director of the Massachusetts Bureau of Waste Prevention's Business Compliance Division. "But we're expecting a major problem, driven largely by new television technology and high turnover in computer equipment."

The goal for Massachusetts officials— indeed for stakeholders everywhere—is to reuse or safely recycle as much electronic waste as possible. But in the United States, the electronics recycling industry is ill-equipped for the task. "The birth of electronic recycling in this country only dates back to around 1994," says Lauren Roman, vice president for marketing at United Recycling Industries, an electronics recycler based in West Chicago, Illinois. "The volume is still low. We only recycle a small percentage of what's out there." According to the National Safety Council's (NSC) May 1999 *Electronic Product Recovery and Recycling Baseline Report: Recycling of Selected Electronic Products in the United States*, the most widely referenced (and most current) source of e-waste statistics, only 11% of the 20 million computers that became obsolete in the United States in 1998 were recycled. (There are no comparable figures for other types of electronic equipment.) Roman suspects that even this number is overstated. A large percentage of the computers described as recycled by the NSC were probably exported overseas, she says. "There aren't any definitive standards for recyclers in the United States," says Roman. "You could call yourself a recycler when in reality you're a broker who fills containers with electronic waste and ships them to China."

The fate of most of the e-waste produced in the United States remains a mystery. Experts assume the majority is landfilled, incinerated, exported, or just abandoned in storage. Even the recycled minority is hard to track. This is partly because the recycling industry is composed of a veritable jungle of overlapping specialists: primary recyclers that refurbish products for resale; secondary recyclers that "demanufacture" equipment to extract raw materials such as metals, plastic and glass; smelters that use CRT glass as inputs to produce raw metals; and so-called "third party" resellers—typically non-profit organizations—that sort and repair obsolete products for resale or donation.

. . .

Regulating e-Waste

In the United States, reactions to the problems of e-waste are varied, creating a patchwork of inconsistent regulations that suggest the need for a unified strategy, experts say. Nebraska, for instance, has introduced legislation that would impose an advance disposal fee on the sale of CRTs, whereas Massachusetts and California have banned them from disposal altogether. Within 2 years, the European Union nations will adopt the Directive on Waste Electrical and Electronic Equipment, a controversial piece of legislation that saddles electronics manufacturers with financial responsibility for product disposal. A companion measure called the Restriction on Hazardous Substances (ROHS) also bans the use of certain hazardous chemicals in electronics production.

Much of the answer to the question of how to regulate e-waste in the United States hinges on the debate over the extent to which environmental releases occur at disposal facilities. Linking environmental levels of toxic contaminants to e-waste in landfills or incinerators is a nearly impossible task. For policy makers, the issue boils down to whether disposal facilities can capture the chemicals before they're released to the environment, a question that often degenerates into bitter scientific debate. Industry sources insist that pollution controls in both landfills and waste-to-energy incinerators are sufficiently protective. Environmental activists, on the other hand, insist the opposite is true.

. . .

[I]t's perfectly legal under U.S. law to export all forms of electronic waste, including color CRTs which are listed as hazardous waste by the EPA, as long as recycling, and not disposal, is the objective. The legality of these waste exports is somewhat murky in the context of an international agreement called the Basel Convention, whose aim is to limit the international spread of hazardous waste, particularly to the developing world. The convention was brokered by the United Nations Environment Program in Basel, Switzerland, in 1989.... Of the countries that originally signed the convention indicating their intent to ratify, only the United States, Haiti, and Afghanistan have failed to do so. Parties to the convention agree to manage those wastes defined by the Basel Convention that are transferred among themselves using a set of evolving criteria that constitute "environmentally sound management." (The Basel Convention has its own list of hazardous wastes, some of which overlap RCRA [Resource Conservation and Recovery Act], and some of which do not.) Nonparties have no such legally binding obligation. This means that the United States is free to export color CRTs to China—which has banned imports of such items—without incurring liability for the environmental management of its exports. . . ."Our only responsibility is to remind [parties to the convention] of their Basel obligations," says [Robert] Tonetti, [senior environmental scientist with the EPA's Office of Solid Waste]. "But these are sovereign nations and they will do with the waste what they want." As the controversy over electronics recycling heats up, stakeholders across the various sectors are diligently looking for solutions. Currently, a number of different paradigms including local, state, and federally funded recycling programs, as well as manufacturer buyback programs and point-of-sale disposal taxes, are being considered to fund electronics recycling in the United. But a coherent strategy has yet to emerge. In the meantime, as the world remains ever poised to latch onto the "next big thing" in electronics technology, basements, attics, and developing countries will remain the repositories of the last next big thing.

Source: Charles W. Schmidt, "E-Junk Explosion," *Environmental Health Perspectives,* Vol. 110, No. 4 (April 2002), pp. 185-92.

DOCUMENT 155: Mendocino County Ordinance Prohibiting the Propagation, Cultivation, Raising, and Growing of Genetically Modified Organisms (2004)

The biotechnology and the green revolutions have brought with them an ongoing discussion about the kinds of genetically modified plants and animals farmers should be allowed to utilize and that consumers can purchase [see Document 151]. Mendocino, California was the first county in the nation to ban the agricultural use of GMOs. The ordinance establishing the ban does not regulate the use of GMO bacteria or byproducts, nor does it regulate the sale or labeling of GMO food and feed.

Frequently, objection to GMOs in the United States stems from opposition to the big agribusiness companies that control the seed market rather than to concern about the environmental or health effects of genetically modified plants.

A. The Ordinance

Section 1. Finding. The people of Mendocino County wish to protect the county's agriculture, environment, economy, and private property from genetic pollution by genetically modified organisms.

Section 2. Prohibition. It shall be unlawful for any person, firm, or corporation to propagate, cultivate, raise, or grow genetically modified organisms in Mendocino County.

Section 3. Definitions. (a) Genetically modified organisms means specific organisms whose native intrinsic DNA has been intentionally altered or amended with non species specific DNA. For purposes of this ordinance, genetic modification does not include organisms created by traditional breeding or hybridization, or to microorganisms created by moving genes or gene segments between unrelated bacteria.

(b) DNA or deoxyribonucleic acid means a complex protein that is present in every cell of an organism and is the 'blueprint' for the organism's development.

B. Ballot Statement Supporting Passage of the Ordinance

Genetically Modified Organisms (GMOs) threaten county agriculture and commerce in several ways. First, Pollen and seed from GMOs travel great distances, contaminating non-GMO crops. Second, wind-and insect-borne GMO pollen can cross-pollinate with commercial and native grapevines, threatening the economic viability of organic and conventional wineries. Third, GMO-polluted wine is unmarketable in Europe and Japan. Fourth, Mendocino County has 150 organic farmers and wineries; if organic crops become contaminated by GMOs, the organic farmers and wineries will lose organic certification and their products will not be marketable as organic. Over one third of Mendocino County's wine grapes are organic and are an important source of county revenue. Fifth, banning GMO crops will make Mendocino crops attractive in markets where there is a demand for food that is organic and pure.

Through cross-pollination, GMOs will irreversibly contaminate native plants and trees, may create new super-weeds, and may disrupt important ecosystems.

Because of wind-and insect-borne GMO pollen drift and transport of GMO seeds by birds, animals and humans, without passage of the ordinance, property owners who wish to keep their land GMO-free, will be unable to do so.

Source: "Prohibition on the Propagation, Cultivation, Raising and Growing of Genetically Modified Organisms in Mendocino County," mindfully.org/GE/2004/Mendocino-CountyMeasure-H.

Document 156: Michael Schallenberger and Ted Nordhaus Proclaim the Death of Environmentalism (2004)

Michael Schallenberger and Ted Nordhaus co-founded the Breakthrough Institute in 2003 with the aim of developing new approaches to energy, environmental, and economic policy. According to their thinking, while it was suitable for the environmental movement of the 1960s and 1970s to be laser focused on such issues as clean water, clean air, and endangered species, a twenty-first century movement to promote sustainable development calls for a more wide-ranging, global approach that takes into account health, social, and economic policies and values.

Environmentalism as a Special Interest

Those of us who were children during the birth of the modern environmental movement have no idea what it feels like to really win big.

Our parents and elders experienced something during the 1960s and 70s that today seems like a dream: the passage of a series of powerful environmental laws too numerous to list, from the Endangered Species Act to the Clean Air and Clean Water Acts to the National Environmental Policy Act.

Experiencing such epic victories had a searing impact on the minds of the movement's founders. It established a way of thinking about the environment and politics that has lasted until today.

It was also then, at the height of the movement's success, that the seeds of failure were planted. The environmental community's success created a strong confidence – and in some cases bald arrogance – that the environmental protection frame was enough to succeed at a policy level. The environmental community's belief that their power derives from defining themselves as defenders of "the environment" has prevented us from winning major legislation on global warming at the national level.

We believe that the environmental movement's foundational concepts, its method for framing legislative proposals, and its very institutions are outmoded. Today environmentalism is just another special interest. Evidence for this can be found in its concepts, its proposals, and its reasoning. What stands out is how arbitrary environmental leaders are about what gets counted and what doesn't as "environmental." Most of the movement's leading thinkers, funders and advocates do not question their most basic assumptions about who we are, what we stand for, and what it is that we should be doing.

Environmentalism is today more about protecting a supposed "thing" – "the environment" – than advancing the worldview articulated by Sierra Club founder John Muir, who nearly a century ago observed, "When we try to pick out anything by itself, we find it hitched to everything else in the Universe."

Thinking of the environment as a "thing" has had enormous implications for how environmentalists conduct their politics. The three-part strategic framework for environmental policymaking hasn't changed in 40 years: first, define a problem (e.g. global warming) as "environmental." Second, craft a technical remedy (e.g., cap-and-trade). Third, sell the technical proposal to legislators through a variety of tactics, such as lobbying, third-party allies, research reports, advertising, and public relations.

When we asked environmental leaders how we could accelerate our efforts against global warming,

most pointed to this or that tactic – more analysis, more grassroots organizing, more PR.

Few things epitomize the environmental community's tactical orientation to politics more than its search for better words and imagery to "reframe" global warming. Lately the advice has included: a) don't call it "climate change" because Americans like change; b) don't call it "global warming" because the word "warming" sounds nice; c) refer to global warming as a "heat trapping blanket" so people can understand it; d) focus attention on technological solutions — like fluorescent light bulbs and hybrid cars.

What each of these recommendations has in common is the shared assumption that a) the problem should be framed as "environmental" and b) our legislative proposals should be technical.

Even the question of alliances, which goes to the core of political strategy, is treated within environmental circles as a tactical question — an opportunity to get this or that constituency — religious leaders! business leaders! celebrities! youth! Latinos! — to take up the fight against global warming. The implication is that if only X group were involved in the global warming fight *then things would really start to happen.*

The arrogance here is that environmentalists ask not what we can do for non-environmental constituencies but what non-environmental constituencies can do for environmentalists. As a result, while public support for action on global warming is wide it is also frighteningly shallow.

The environmental movement's incuriosity about the interests of potential allies depends on it never challenging the most basic assumptions about what does and doesn't get counted as "environmental." Because we define environmental problems so narrowly, environmental leaders come up with equally narrow solutions. In the face of perhaps the greatest calamity in modern history, environmental leaders are sanguine that selling technical solutions like florescent light bulbs, more efficient appliances, and hybrid cars will be sufficient to muster the necessary political strength to overcome the alliance of neoconservative ideologues and industry interests in Washington, D.C.

The entire landscape in which politics plays out has changed radically in the last 30 years, yet the environmental movement acts as though proposals based on "sound science" will be sufficient to overcome ideological and industry opposition. Environmentalists are in a culture war whether we like it or not. It's a war over our core values as Americans and over our vision for the future, and it won't be won by appealing to the rational consideration of our collective self-interest. We have become convinced that modern environmentalism, with all of its unexamined assumptions, outdated concepts and exhausted strategies, must die so that something new can live. Those of us who pay so much attention to nature's cycles know better than to fear death, which is inseparable from life. In the words of the Tao Ti Ching, "If you aren't afraid of dying there is nothing you can't achieve."

Environmental Group Think

One of the reasons environmental leaders can whistle past the graveyard of global warming politics is that the membership rolls and the income of the big environmental organizations have grown enormously over the past 30 years — especially since the election of George W. Bush in 2000.

. . .

Part of what's behind America's political turn to the right is the skill with which conservative think tanks, intellectuals and political leaders have crafted proposals that build their power through setting the terms of the debate. Their work has paid off. According to a survey of 1,500 Americans by the market research firm Environics, the number of Americans who agree with the statement, "To preserve people's jobs in this country, we must accept higher levels of pollution in the future," increased from 17 percent in 1996 to 26 percent in 2000. The number of Americans who agreed that, "Most of the people actively involved in environmental groups are extremists, not reasonable people," leapt from 32 percent in 1996 to 41 percent in 2000.

The truth is that for the vast majority of Americans, the environment never makes it into their top ten list of things to worry about. Protecting the environment is indeed supported by a large majority — it's just not supported very strongly. Once you understand this, it's much easier to understand why it's been so easy for anti-environmental interests to gut 30 years of environmental protections.

. . .

As individuals, environmental leaders are anything but stupid. Many hold multiple advanced degrees in science, engineering, and law from the best schools in the country. But as a community, environmentalists suffer from a bad case of group think, starting with shared assumptions about what we mean by "the environment" – a category that reinforces the notions that a) the environment is a separate "thing" and b) human beings are separate from and superior to the "natural world."

The concepts of "nature" and "environment" have been thoroughly deconstructed. Yet they retain their mythic and debilitating power within the environmental movement and the public at large. If one understands the notion of the "environment" to include humans, then the way the environmental community designates certain problems as environmental and others as not is completely arbitrary.

Why, for instance, is a human-made phenomenon like global warming — which may kill hundreds of millions of human beings over the next century — considered "environmental"? Why are poverty and war not considered environmental problems while global warming is? What are the implications of framing global warming as an environmental problem – and handing off the responsibility for dealing with it to "environmentalists"?

. . .

Most environmentalists don't think of "the environment" as a mental category at all — they think of it as a real "thing" to be protected and defended. They think of themselves, literally, as representatives and defenders of this thing. Environmentalists do their work as though these are literal rather than figurative truths. They tend to see language in general as representative rather than constitutive of reality. This is typical of liberals who are, at their core, children of the enlightenment who believe that they arrived at their identity and politics through a rational and considered process. They expect others in politics should do the same and are constantly surprised and disappointed when they don't.

The effect of this orientation is a certain literal-sclerosis2 — the belief that social change happens only when people speak a literal "truth to power." Literal-sclerosis can be seen in the assumption that to win action on global warming one must talk about global warming instead of, say, the economy, industrial policy, or health care. "If you want people to act on global warming" stressed Becker, "you need to convince them that action is needed on global warming and not on some ulterior goal."

What we Worry About When we Worry About Global Warming

What do we worry about when we worry about global warming?

Is it the refugee crisis that will be caused when Caribbean nations are flooded? If so, shouldn't our focus be on building bigger sea walls and disaster preparedness?

Is it the food shortages that will result from reduced agricultural production? If so, shouldn't our focus be on increasing food production?

Is it the potential collapse of the Gulf Stream, which could freeze upper North America and northern Europe and trigger, as a recent Pentagon scenario suggests, world war?

Most environmental leaders would scoff at such framings of the problem and retort, "Disaster preparedness is not an environmental problem." It is a hallmark of environmental rationality to believe that we environmentalists search for "root causes" not "symptoms."

. . .

A Path for the Crossing

While it's obvious that conservatives control all three branches of government and the terms of most political debates, it's not obvious why. This is because environmentalists and other liberals have convinced themselves that, in politics, "the issues" matter and that the public is with us on categories such as "the environment" and "jobs" and "heath care." What explains how we can simultaneously be "winning on the issues" and losing so badly politically?

. . .

Conservative foundations and think tanks have spent 40 years getting clear about what they want (their vision) and what they stand for (their values). The values of smaller government, fewer taxes, a large military, traditional families, and more power for big business are only today, after 40 years of being stitched together by conservative intellectuals and strategists, coherent enough to be listed in a "contract with America." After they got clearer about their vision and values, conservatives started crafting proposals that would activate conservative values among their base and swing voters.

Once in power, conservatives govern on all of their issues – no matter whether their solutions have majority support. Liberals tend to approach politics with an eye toward winning one issue campaign at a time – a Sisyphean task that has contributed to today's neoconservative hegemony.

Environmental groups have spent the last 40 years defining themselves against conservative values like cost-benefit accounting, smaller government, fewer regulations, and free trade, without ever articulating a coherent morality we can call our own. Most of the intellectuals who staff environmental groups are so repelled by the right's values that we have assiduously avoided examining our own in a serious way. Environmentalists and other liberals tend to see values as a distraction from "the real issues" – environmental problems like global warming.

If environmentalists hope to become more than a special interest we must start framing our proposals around core American values and start seeing our own values as central to what motivates and guides our politics. Doing so is crucial if we are to build the political momentum – a sustaining movement – to pass and implement the legislation that will achieve action on global warming and other issues.

. . .

Above all else, we need to take a hard look at the institutions the movement has built over the last 30 years. Are existing environmental institutions up to the task of imagining the post-global warming world? Or do we now need a set of new institutions founded around a more expansive vision and set of values?

Source: Michael Schallenberger and Ted Nordhaus, "The Death of Environmentalism: Global Warming in a Post-Environmental World." www.Breakthrough.org./pdf

DOCUMENT 157: Bruce Babbitt Proposes a New Approach to Federal Land-Use Planning (2005)

The federal government owns approximately one-eighth (253 million acres) of the landmass of the fifty states. In addition to the national parks and forests, the government controls a vast number of both large and small tracts of land. Bruce Babbitt, who was secretary of the Interior during the Clinton administration, here offers some advice about how the federal government, working together with local, state, and regional entities can make better use of those lands.

It may come as something of a surprise to learn there is such a thing as "federal land use planning." The notion that land use is a local matter has come to dominate the political rhetoric of our age, obscuring the historical reality that the national government has been involved in land use planning since the early days of the republic. In fact, there is, by whatever name, a considerable body of law that can and, in my view, should be used toward enhanced federal leadership in land use planning and preservation.

The case for federal leadership in land use planning must begin with a consideration of exactly what the national interest consists of. No one, for example, suggests that Congress should be concerned with street patterns in a suburban development or the location of schools or public facilities in your community. But most of us would agree that the national government should be concerned with protecting disappearing species, the integrity of rivers that cross state line, our coastlines, our forests, and regions of special significance for their scenic, ecological, or historical values. Yet with few exceptions we have not engaged in a national discussion of how to define the interest, where to draw the lines and how to involve the states in the process.

* * *

The Florida Everglades represents our most notorious example of a great national park nearly destroyed by highways, water diversions, encroaching development, and agricultural conversion. The area has now become the subject of the largest restoration project ever authorized by Congress, and at the heart of this effort is a comprehensive land use planning initiative for the entire Everglades watershed extending down the Florida peninsula from Lake Okeechobee to the waters of Florida Bay.

* * *

[T]he Endangered Species Act, which, although not usually characterized as a land use planning statute, has become one of the most effective federal laws affecting land use. It has been most successful in California, in large measure because that state government, through both Republican and Democratic administrations has worked out a partnership with the federal government for regional open space planning.

. . . [A] conflict occasioned by the listing of an endangered bird, the California gnatcatcher[,] . . . in turn triggered a land development moratorium and led eventually to a pattern of cooperation on land use that has been extended to other regions of California. . . .

. . . The farmlands of [the Midwest], planted fencerow to fencerow, have obliterated the tallgrass prairie, which lives on only in memory and in small patches in old cemeteries. The vast fields of corn and soybeans have so completely preempted and replaced the old prairie that the natural world seems to have vanished beyond any realistic hope of retrieval.

Ironically, the historical emergence of this region of all-consuming industrial agriculture is due in large measure to federal land use policies. Farm country is one place where no one disputes either the reality or the necessity of federal leadership in land use, even though it goes by the name of "farm policy." Federal farm policy has influenced use of the land since the beginning of the Republic, nearly always directed toward expanding production through the draining, clearing, and planting of more land.

Now, however, farm policy is nearing the threshold of a revolutionary change, made necessary by the globalization of the agricultural economy and emergence of the World Trade organization as the arbiter of agricultural policies that subsidize prices and encourage overproduction. In coming years, the United States will be required to begin dismantling production subsidies, which reach as high as fifteen billion dollars or more per year. As these production subsidies are withdrawn, there will be

an unprecedented opportunity to redirect this money to permanent retirement of marginal farmlands and to restore a network of forested riparian corridors across the land, and even to bring back extensive tracts of the old tallgrass prairie, all in a manner designed to continue providing income and support to farmers.

In farming regions and in urban areas, land use is reflected in the waters. Improper management of the land has seriously degraded our rivers and lakes and estuaries. . . . Chesapeake Bay [is] a large estuary that collects the waters running off the land from six states. The streams and rivers that drain this watershed are contaminated from farmland fertilizers, pesticides, animal waste, the destruction of forests, and residues from urban streets. In consequence that bay in nearing ecological collapse. The once abundant oyster reefs are crumbling, and the once extensive beds of sea grass that shelter and nourish spawning blue crabs are dying, smothered by sediments that accumulate as soils erode, having been exposed by deforestation and excessive tillage. Oyster and crab catches have declined to less than 1 percent of historic levels. Similar declines in fisheries are occurring in every region of the country.

The Clean Water Act, which mandates the restoration of our waters to a "fishable and swimmable" standard, has proven inadequate to the task, in large measure because after thirty years of effort federal administrators and the courts have been unable to bring the states forward as effective partners in the regulation of land use to restore the nation's waters. . . . [T]he Clean Water Act should be revised to promote stronger federal-state partnerships in managing the use of water resources and in regulating the effects of land use on our rivers and lakes.

. . . [O]ur public lands, . . . the flamboyant red-rock landscapes of Arizona and Utah, the distinctive life forms of the Sonoran and Mojave deserts, the towering forests of the Rockies and the Pacific Northwest, the lands of Alaska, are a unique and enduring part of our heritage. They are also a perpetual battleground, where the gun smoke of endless political fights obscures both the meaning of the past and the prospects for the future. For a hundred years, ranchers, miners, and loggers have fought with conservationists, one side seeking to throw the lands open to oil drilling, logging, livestock grazing, and strip mining while the other would have extractive uses excluded, with all the lands protected as the equivalent of national parks.

After eight years of intense participation in these battles as secretary of the interior and subsequent years of observing from the sidelines, I believe the time has come for an armistice followed by a peace conference to which not just westerners, but all Americans, are invited. The outcome should be a new constitution for public lands, in the form of federal legislation that subordinates (but does not eliminate) mining, grazing, and logging to an overriding public mandate for long-term biological diversity, abundant wildlife and fisheries, and the ecological integrity of our streams and waterways.

Source: Bruce Babbitt, *Cities in the Wilderness* (Washington, D.C.: Island Press, 2005), pp. 5-10.

Document 158: Myron Ebell on the Endangered Species Act and Private Property Rights (2005)

Myron Ebell is Director of Global Warming and International Environmental Policy at the Competitive Enterprise Institute, a libertarian think tank, and an advisor to Donald Trump on environmental policy personnel. Ebell is a strong supporter of the private property rights movement, which believes that environmental legislation that places limits on how people can use private property is an illegal taking unless the owner is compensated. Part of the objection to the Endangered Species Act stems from objections to the limits that it places on the use of private property as well as public lands.

The ESA [Endangered Species Act of 1973] is the most sacred of the environmental movement's sacred cows. I use the word "sacred" literally. In the mid-1990s, then-Interior Secretary Bruce Babbitt gave a number of speeches and interviews in which he said that the ESA was the translation into public policy of God's commandment in the Book of Genesis to Noah to save two of every species in the Ark. Anyone who wanted to reform the ESA, said Babbitt, was refusing to hear "the command of our Creator."

The intensity of this faith-based commitment to the ESA may explain why the decade-long efforts to reform the ESA have been completely unsuccessful so far, but it is nonetheless puzzling. The ESA has inspired such fanatical devotion despite the fact that it is a colossal failure. The ESA has done very little to help recover populations of more than a handful of the 1200-plus animal and plant species listed as endangered or threatened, while at the same time it has done an immense amount of harm.

There is one fundamental reason why the ESA does a lot more harm than good. The ESA penalizes people for being good stewards of their land. Landowners whose management practices create and preserve habitat for an endangered plant or animal open their land to being regulated under ESA. And contrary to what many environmental pressure groups claim, ESA regulation does not simply prevent development or changes in land use. Customary land uses and practices, such as farming, livestock grazing, and timber production, have regularly been prohibited, even when such practices help to maintain the species' habitat.

Naturally, faced with the regulatory taking of their property, people sought compensation under the Fifth Amendment to the Constitution. Unfortunately, although compensation is due whenever government physically seizes even an inch of private property, the Supreme Court has ruled that compensation is not required for a regulatory taking as long as the property retains any possible use and any value. An ESA listing can destroy 90 percent or more of the value of a piece of property and prohibit its traditional use without triggering the Fifth Amendment's just compensation clause.

The ESA thus encourages landowners to take the steps necessary to ensure that their land does not contain suitable habitat for any endangered or potentially endangered species. Since around 80 percent of listed species depend largely on private land for their habitat, the effects of this perverse incentive clearly continue to be catastrophic for endangered animals and plants. Given the logic underlying the ESA, it is not entirely fanciful to imagine that rural America will eventually be paved over.

The fact that the ESA is bad for wildlife because it is bad for people suggests some obvious, if politically difficult, solutions. It is the political difficulties that have dominated the past fifteen years.

Calls to reform the ESA began soon after the 1990 listing of the northern spotted owl began to shut down the Northwest's timber industry. (The most productive forests in the world are now off limits to harvesting and active timber management. Between one hundred and two hundred mills have closed as a result. And instead of being harvested and replanted, the great Douglas Fir forests will succumb to disease and insects and eventually catastrophic fires. How this outcome will be good for spotted owls or any other wildlife has not yet been explained.) The spotted owl train wreck sparked significant opposition to the ESA throughout rural America. People could see that their local industry and consequently their livelihood could be the next target.

So when the Republicans took control of Congress in 1995, they moved quickly to take advantage of this growing public dissatisfaction

with the damage the ESA was doing and threatened to do. These efforts took three forms.

First, the House passed a bill to provide for compensation for regulatory takings under the ESA and several other land-use laws, such as the Clean Water Act's section 404 wetlands regulations. Takings compensation would not provide positive incentives to landowners to provide habitat, but it would at least take away most of the perverse incentive to avoid regulation by destroying habitat. Although the House passed takings compensation bills twice more, its backers have never been able to force a vote on it in the Senate.

The second approach taken by the then-Chairman of the House Resources Committee, Representative Don Young (R-Ak.), was comprehensive reform. Young and Rep. Richard Pombo put together a bill that weakened every provision of the ESA that had been identified as being a problem for people. Despite 127 co-sponsors, the Young-Pombo bill never came to the House floor for a vote, largely because then-House Speaker Newt Gingrich was a Sierra Clubber before he was a Republican. Its prospects were doubtful in any case. Environmental pressure groups had convinced the public that the Young-Pombo bill would gut the ESA.

The third approach to fixing the ESA was simply to replace it with a non-regulatory, incentive-based conservation program. Instead of fearing being regulated by the ESA, landowners would be encouraged to preserve and create critical habitat by a variety of incentive programs. This idea was developed by the Grassroots ESA Coalition and found legislative form in a bill introduced by Representative John Shadegg (R-Az.). The Shadegg bill never attracted much attention, but to my mind it remains by far the best as well as politically most feasible solution to the ESA's failure to put the interests of landowners to work to serve the interests of saving species. . . .

The reality that all of these fixes for the ESA have been stymied for a decade is bad enough. But In 1997 and '98, the situation grew much worse. Senator Dirk Kempthorne (R-Id.) came close to gaining Senate passage of a bill to re-authorize the ESA that he described as a reform bill. In fact, Kempthorne's bill would have helped big timber and development companies make deals to escape ESA regulation and left small landowners to bear the full brunt of the law's limitless regulatory reach. The bill was so moderate that even then-Interior Secretary Babbitt gave it an enthusiastic thumbs up. The Grassroots ESA Coalition rallied opposition to Kempthorne's bill, Rep. Pombo opposed it, and it died in the Senate.

Since 1998 the Congress has mostly tried to avoid looking at the ESA. There are three good reasons for this, in addition to a glaring lack of congressional leadership on the issue.

First, Babbitt managed to deflate pressure for reform by cutting deals with many big corporate landowners. Although a federal court has ruled that these "safe harbor" agreements are not legally binding on the federal government and therefore that the federal government can demand more acres be set aside as habitat whenever it wishes, these deals have not yet been overturned in reality.

Second, there have not been any more train wrecks of a magnitude similar to the spotted owl. The Bush Administration is trying to keep it that way by administering the ESA so as to minimize damage to people's economic interests and property rights.

Third and finally, much of rural America has experienced significant economic decline during the past fifteen years (some of it, especially in the West, caused by federal lands policies). Consequently, rural victims of the ESA have fewer resources with which to wage the political fight for reform.

. . .

Some members [of the 109th Congress] are talking about incremental reform. Get some small reforms passed this Congress and thereby build momentum for further reform in future Congresses. Two incremental reform bills are left over in the House from last year. Representative Greg Walden's (R-Oreg.) bill would raise requirements for the quality of scientific procedures and information used during the listing and recovery planning processes. Representative Dennis Cardoza's (D-Calif.) bill would require that recovery planning involve consultation with local people affected and consideration of the economic impact.

Governor Bill Owens (R-Colo.), Chairman of the Western Governors' Association, has also actively advocated some sensible reforms that would concentrate much more effort on recovering endangered species populations and less on listing species. Owens has also tried to put his State in a leadership role in the recovery process. It may be that these two bills and Governor Owens's proposals form the starting point for modest incremental reforms that can be enacted by this Congress. My own view is that such an approach is well worth pursuing, but only if it can be done without provoking a knockdown fight with environmental pressure groups. Perhaps [Senators Lincoln] Chafee and [Mike] Crapo can talk some environmental groups into not strenuously opposing some minor modifications to the ESA, although past experience suggests that proposing to change a comma provokes charges of trying to gut the ESA.

At the same time that these incremental reforms are being pursued, I think that leaders need to step forward to promote takings compensation and to resurrect the non-regulatory, incentive-based habitat conservation approach of the Shadegg bill. The idea that people should be paid whenever the use of their property is taken by government does resonate with voters. Last November, 61 percent of Oregonians voted in favor of an initiative, Measure 37, to compensate property owners when state zoning regulations reduce the value of their property if they owned it before the regulation took effect. And it is likely that majorities in both the House and the Senate would support takings compensation if it were proposed this year.

Enacting a replacement for the ESA that would work by putting the interests of people and endangered wildlife on the same side will require a long-term effort

Source: Myron Ebell, "An Update on Endangered Species Act Reform," in American Legislative Exchange Council, *Issues Analysis*, April 2005. www.cei.org/pdf.

DOCUMENT 159: Great Lakes–St. Lawrence River Basin Sustainable Water Resources Agreement (2005)

The Great Lakes, which contain one-fifth of the world's freshwater, account for 84 percent of North America's surface freshwater and supply 42 million people with their daily water needs. Potable water is a scarce commodity in many parts of the world, including some sections of the United States. In recent decades there have been objections to allowing commercial entities that sell water to distant communities to remove freshwater from public water sources. Some communities in Maine, for example, have tried to prevent Poland Spring Water and its parent company, Nestle, from extracting water from water sources within their jurisdiction.

The alleged motivation for the bi-national Great Lakes—St. Lawrence River sustainable water resources agreement was a 1998 attempt by a Canadian company to ship 156 million gallons of water annually to Asia. This agreement is built on the foundation of numerous earlier national and bi-national agreements, including the Great Lakes Compact and the Great Lakes Charter, that provided a cooperative approach to complex regional and transnational environmental and resource issues. It offers a comprehensive management framework for sustainable water use and resource protection.

The State of Illinois, The State of Indiana, The State of Michigan, The State of Minnesota, The State of New York, The State of Ohio, The Province of Ontario, The Commonwealth of Pennsylvania, The Government of Québec, The State of Wisconsin,

Recognizing that,

The Waters of the Basin are a shared public treasure and the States and Provinces as stewards have a shared duty to protect, conserve and manage these renewable but finite Waters;

These Waters are interconnected and form a single hydrologic system;

Protecting, conserving, restoring, and improving these Waters is the foundation of Water resource management in the Basin and essential to maintaining the integrity of the Basin Ecosystem;

Managing to conserve and restore these Waters will improve them as well as the Water Dependent Natural Resources of the Basin;

Continued sustainable, accessible and adequate Water supplies for the people and economy of the Basin are of vital importance;

The States and Provinces must balance economic development, social development and environmental protection as interdependent and mutually reinforcing pillars of sustainable development;

Even though there has been significant progress in restoring and improving the health of the Basin Ecosystem, the Waters and Water Dependent Natural Resources of the Basin remain at risk;

In light of possible variations in climate conditions and the potential cumulative effects of demands that may be placed on the Waters of the Basin, the States and Provinces must act to ensure the protection and conservation of the Waters and Water Dependent Natural Resources of the Basin for future generations;

Where there are threats of serious or irreversible damage, lack of full scientific certainty should not be used as a reason for postponing measures to prevent environmental degradation;

Sustainable development and harmony with nature and among neighbours require cooperative arrangements for the development and implementation of watershed protection approaches in the Basin;

Reaffirming,

The principles and findings of the Great Lakes Charter and the commitments and directives of the Great Lakes Charter Annex 2001.

. . .

Agree as follows:

Chapter 1: General Provisions
Article 100: Objectives
1. The objectives of this Agreement are:
    a. To act together to protect, conserve and restore the Waters of the Great Lakes–St. Lawrence River Basin because current lack of scientific certainty should not be used as a reason for postponing measures to protect the Basin Ecosystem;
    b. To facilitate collaborative approaches to Water management across the Basin to protect, conserve, restore, improve and efficiently and effectively manage the Waters and Water Dependent Natural Resources of the Basin;
    c. To promote co-operation among the Parties by providing common and regional mechanisms to evaluate Proposals to Withdraw Water;
    d. To create a co-operative arrangement regarding Water management that provides tools for shared future challenges;
    e. To retain State and Provincial authority within the Basin under appropriate arrangements for intergovernmental cooperation and consultation;
    f. To facilitate the exchange of data, strengthen the scientific information

upon which decisions are made, and engage in consultation on the potential effects of Withdrawals and losses on the Waters and Water Dependent Natural Resources of the Basin;
    g. To prevent significant impacts of Withdrawals and losses on the Basin Ecosystem and its watersheds; and,
    h. To promote and Adaptive Management approach to the conservation and managements of Basin Water resources, which recognizes, considers and provides adjustments for the uncertainties in, and evolution of, scientific knowledge concerning the Basin's Waters and Water Dependent Natural Resources.
2. The Parties shall interpret and apply the provisions of this Agreement to achieve these objectives.

Chapter 2: Prohibition of Diversions, Exceptions and Management and Regulation of Withdrawals
Article 200: Prohibition of Diversions and Management and Regulation of Withdrawals
1. The Parties shall adopt and implement Measures to prohibit New or Increased Diversions, except as provided for in this Agreement.
2. The Parties shall adopt and implement Measures to manage and regulate Exceptions in accordance with this Agreement.
3. The Parties shall adopt and implement Measures to manage and regulate Withdrawals and Consumptive Uses in accordance with this Agreement.

Article 201: Exceptions to the Prohibition of Diversions Straddling Communities
1. A Proposal to transfer Water to an area within a Straddling Community but outside the Basin or outside the source Great Lake Watershed shall be excepted from the prohibition against Diversions and be managed and regulated by the Originating Party

provided that, regardless of the volume of Water transferred, all the Water so transferred shall be used solely for Public Water Supply Purposes within the Straddling Community.

* * *

Straddling Counties

3. A Proposal to transfer Water to a Community within a Straddling County that would be considered a Diversion under this Agreement shall be excepted from the prohibition against Diversions, provided that it satisfies all of the following conditions:

   a. The Water shall be used solely for the Public Water Supply Purposes of the Community within a Straddling County that is without adequate supplies of potable water.

   b. The Proposal meets the Exception Standard, with particular emphasis upon ensuring that:

      i. All Water Withdrawn from the Basin shall be returned, either naturally or after use, to the Source Watershed less an allowance for Consumptive Use;

      ii. No surface water or groundwater from outside the Basin is used to satisfy any portion of subparagraph (i) above except if it:

         (a) Is part of a water supply and/or wastewater treatment system that combines water from inside and outside of the Basin;

         (b) Is treated to meet applicable water quality discharge standards and to prevent the introduction of invasive species into the Basin;

         (c) Maximizes the portion of water returned to the Source Watershed as Basin Water, and minimizes the surface water or groundwater from outside the Basin;

      iii. All such Water returned meets all applicable water quality standards.

   c. The Proposal shall be subject to management and regulation by the Originating Party, regardless of its size.

Source: www.cglg.org/projects/compactimplementation/ Great Lake-St. Lawrence River Basin Sustainable Water Resources Agreement.

DOCUMENT 160: Al Gore on the Politicization of Global Warming (2006)

Since losing a highly contested election for president against George W. Bush in 2000, former vice president Al Gore has galvanized public interest in the issue of global warming by means of his slide shows and his heavily illustrated book and documentary film titled An Inconvenient Truth. *Gore, who has long been interested in environmental issues, published his first book on the subject,* Earth in the Balance, *in 1992 when he was a senator.*

As I've traveled around the world giving my slide show, there are two questions I most often get—particularly in the United States—from people who already know how serious the crisis has become . . . :

(1) "Why do so many people still believe this crisis isn't real?" and

(2) "Why is this a political issue at all?"

My response to the first question has been to try to make my slide show—and now this book—as clear and compelling as I can. As for why so many people still resist what the facts clearly show, I think, in part, the reason is that the truth about the climate crisis is an inconvenient one that means we are going to have to change the way we live our lives. Most of these changes will turn out to be for the better—things we really should do for other reasons anyway—but they are inconvenient nonetheless. Whether these changes involve something as minor as adjusting the thermostat and using different light bulbs, or as major as switching from oil and coal to renewable fuels, they will require effort.

But the answer to the first question is also linked to the second question. The truth about global warming is especially inconvenient and unwelcome to some powerful people and companies making enormous sums of money from activities they know full well have to change dramatically in order to ensure the planet's livability.

These people—especially those at a few multinational companies with the most at stake—have been spending many millions of dollars every year in figuring out ways of sowing public confusion about global warming. They've been particularly effective in building a coalition with other groups who agree to support each other's interests, and that coalition has thus far managed to paralyze America's ability to respond to global warming. The Bush/Cheney administration has received strong support from this coalition and seems to be doing everything it can to satisfy their concerns.

For example, many *scientists* working on global-warming research throughout the government have been ordered to watch what they *say* about the climate crisis and instructed not to talk to the news media. More important, all of America's policies related to global warming have been changed to reflect the unscientific view—the administration's view—that global warming is not a problem. Our negotiators in international forums dealing with global warming have been advised to try and stop any movement toward action that would inconvenience oil or coal companies, even if this means disrupting the diplomatic machinery in order to do it.

In addition, President Bush appointed the person in charge of the oil company disinformation campaign on global warming to head up all environmental policy in the White House. Even though this lawyer/lobbyist had no scientific training whatsoever, he was empowered by the president to edit and censor all warnings from the EPA and other government agencies about global warming.

Political leaders—especially the president—can have a major effect not only on public policy (especially when Congress is controlled by the president's party, is compliant, and does whatever the president wants it to) but also on public opinion, especially among those who count themselves followers of the president.

Consider this fact: Even as Americans in general have become increasingly concerned about global warming, opinion polls show members of the president's own party becoming less concerned, probably because they're naturally more inclined to give the president the benefit of the doubt.

The rationale offered by the so-called skeptics for opposing any action to solve the climate crisis has changed several times over the years. At first, opponents argued that global warming was not occurring at all; they said it was a myth. A few of them still say that today, but now there is so much undeniable evidence demolishing that assertion that, most naysayers have decided they need to change tactics. They now acknowledge that the globe is indeed warming, but in the very next breath, they claim it is just due to "natural causes."

* * *

Another related argument used by the deniers is that yes, global warming does seem to be happening, but it will probably be good for us. Certainly any effort to stop it, they continue, would no doubt be bad for the economy.

But the latest—and in my opinion, most disgraceful argument put forth by opponents of change is: Yes it's happening, but there's nothing we can really do about it, so we might as well not even try. This faction favors the continued dumping of global-warming pollution into the atmosphere, even though they acknowledge that the crisis it's causing is real and harmful.

* * *

Part of the problem has to do with a long-term structural change in the way America's marketplace of ideas now operates. The one-way nature of our dominant communications medium, television, has combined with the increasing concentration of ownership over the vast majority of media outlets by a smaller and smaller number of large conglomerates that mix entertainment values with journalism to seriously damage the role of objectivity in America's public forum.

* * *

We have lost a lot of time that could have been spent solving the crisis, because the opponents of action have thus far successfully politicized the issue in the minds of many Americans.

We can't afford inaction any longer, and, frankly, there's no excuse for it. We all want the same thing: for our children and the generations after them to inherit a clean and beautiful planet capable of supporting a healthy human civilization. That goal should transcend politics.

Source: Al Gore, *An Inconvenient Truth* (Emmaus, PA: Rodale, 2006), pp. 285-87.

DOCUMENT 161: Oakland's Zero Waste Resolution (2006)

As the concept of recycling takes hold around the country, waste materials that once would have been sent to the local dump without a thought are now being reused, recycled, or composted. While recognizing that 25 percent or more of their municipal solid waste will probably continue to end up as landfill in the foreseeable future, numerous cities in California as well as Seattle, Washington; Boulder, Colorado; and Austin, Texas, have passed resolutions promoting zero waste. The passage of these resolutions is driven in part by a growing environmental consciousness and in part by the cost and difficulty of finding new dumpsites for the ever-increasing mounds of waste produced by American consumers and industry.

The term "zero waste" was first used in the name of a company, Zero Waste Systems Inc. (ZWS), which was started in Oakland, California, in the mid 1970s by the chemist Paul Palmer to find new uses for many chemicals being excessed by the nascent California electronics industry.

RESOLUTION ADOPTING A ZERO WASTE GOAL BY 2020 FOR THE CITY OF OAKLAND AND DIRECTING THE PUBLIC WORKS AGENCY, IN CONCERT WITH THE MAYOR'S OFFICE, TO DEVELOP A ZERO WASTE STRATEGIC PLAN TO ACHIEVE THE CITY'S ZERO WASTE GOAL

WHEREAS, the California Integrated Waste Management Act of 1989 (AB 939) required that all California jurisdictions achieve a landfill diversion rate of 50% by the year 2000, and reduce, reuse, recycle, and compost all discarded materials to the maximum extent feasible before any landfilling or other destructive disposal method is used; and

WHEREAS, in 1990 Alameda County's voters passed ballot Measure D (The Alameda County Waste Reduction and Recycling Initiative Charter

Amendment), setting a requirement for the County to reduce land filling by 75% by 2010; and

WHEREAS, in 1990 the City Council adopted Resolution #66253 C.M.S establishing solid waste reduction goals, including returning discarded materials to the local economy through reuse and recycling; applying the waste management hierarchy in priority order (reduce, reuse, recycle and compost) to the maximum extent; and promoting recycling market development; and

WHEREAS, in 2002 the City Council adopted Resolution #77500 C.M.S. establishing the goal of 75% reduction of waste disposal landfills by 2010 for the City of Oakland in alliance with the countywide 75% waste reduction requirement; and

WHEREAS, in 2001 the California Integrated Waste Management Board set a goal of Zero Waste in its strategic plan for the state; and cities, councils, counties, and states worldwide have adopted a goal of achieving zero waste, including the counties of San Francisco, Santa Cruz, San Luis Obispo and Del Norte in California; the cities of Palo Alto and Berkeley in California, Seattle in Washington, Toronto in Canada, and Canberra in Australia; and the state of New South Wales in Australia; and 45% of New Zealand's local government councils; and

WHEREAS, strategies to reach zero waste can help to promote the over-arching goal of each generation leaving less and less of an ecological footprint on the earth thus allowing more and more of nature to restore; and

WHEREAS, Zero Waste principles promote the highest and best use of materials to eliminate waste and pollution, emphasizing a closed-loop system of production and consumption, moving in logical increments toward the goal of zero waste through the core principles of:

- Improving "downstream" reuse/recycling of end-of-life products and materials to ensure their highest and best use;
- Pursuing "upstream" re-design strategies to reduce the volume and toxicity of discarded products and materials, and promote low-impact or reduced consumption lifestyles;
- Fostering and supporting use of discarded products and materials to stimulate and drive local economic and workforce development; and

WHEREAS, in 1992 the City Council adopted Resolution #68780 C.M.S. authorizing establishment of a City staff supported Recycling Market Development Zone; and recycling continues to be a significant local industry, whose long-term viability is a key component to Oakland's current and future waste reduction achievements, economic development, and workforce development of "green collar" jobs; and

WHEREAS, in 1998 the City Council adopted the Sustainable Development Initiative (Resolution #74678 C.M.S) embracing the concept of meeting people's current economic, social, cultural, and environmental needs in ways that enhance the ability of future generations to meet their needs; and

WHEREAS, Oakland's FY 2005-07 Mayor and City Council Goals include: Develop A Sustainable City through maximizing socially and environmentally sustainable economic growth, including conserving natural resources; and

WHEREAS, in alliance with the Oakland's Sustainable Development Initiative and Sustainable City goal, in June 2005 Oakland Mayor Jerry Brown joined mayors of 50 of the world's largest and most visionary cities as an original signer of the United Nations World Environment Day Urban Environmental Accords, pledging that Oakland would implement 21 action steps toward sustainable cities in the areas of energy, waste reduction, urban design, transportation, environmental health, and water including: Establish a policy to achieve zero waste; and

WHEREAS, adopting a goal of zero waste disposal and pursuing Zero Waste principles is consistent with, and an explicit validation of Oakland's Sustainable Development Initiative and Sustainable City Goal; now, therefore, be it

RESOLVED, that the Mayor and City Council hereby adopt a Zero Waste Goal by 2020 for the City of Oakland and direct the Public Works Agency, in concert with the Mayor's Office, to develop a Zero Waste Strategic Plan to achieve the City's Zero Waste Goal; and be it

FURTHER RESOLVED, that Public Works Agency, in conjunction with the Mayor's Office, will convene a Zero Waste working group to develop a Zero Waste Strategic Plan that will provide guidance in the planning and decision-making process to achieve the City's Zero Waste Goal; and be it

FURTHER RESOLVED, Oakland will assume a leadership role, partnering with other Zero Waste local, regional and international communities and sustainability advocates to actively pursue and advocate for strategies and incentives to advance Zero Waste principles for materials management, system re-design, highest and best use of discarded products and materials, and a closed-loop sustainable production and consumption society.

Source: Oakland City Council Resolution 79774, www.zerowasteoakland.com/zero waste/zero waste goal by 2020 resolution.

DOCUMENT 162: New York City's PlaNYC 2030 (2007)

New York City, along with several other large, medium-size, and small U.S. cities—including Los Angeles, Chicago, San Francisco, and Oakland—has taken numerous steps in recent years to make itself both more livable and more environmentally sustainable.

On Earth Day 2007, Mayor Michael R. Bloomberg released a comprehensive twenty-five-year plan for the city's future. The plan offered a strategy for reducing the city's greenhouse gas footprint while also accommodating population growth and improving the city's infrastructure and environment. One of its aims was to reduce citywide carbon emissions by 2030 to 30% below 2005 levels. An annual Greenhouse Gas Emissions (GHG) Inventory was designed to track progress toward the plan's carbon reduction goal. By 2017 the city was about two-thirds of the way toward its GHG emissions reduction goal, helped along by a Carbon Challenge for commercial buildings put in place by Mayor Bill de Blasio in 2014.

Within ten years of the inauguration of PlaNYC, the city had initiated major changes in traffic patterns, providing for more and safer space for bicycles and pedestrians, and enabling people to "take back" large sections of asphalt in places with a lot of foot traffic; a new subway line was operating; and, nearly a century after it had been discontinued, there was once again regular ferry service from Brooklyn and Queens to Manhattan. While some segments of the plan were implemented quickly, others, such as a proposal for traffic congestion pricing in midtown Manhattan, almost immediately ran into opposition.

Focusing on the five key dimensions of the city's environment—land, air, water, energy, and transportation—we have developed a plan that can become a model for cities in the 21st century. The combined impact of this plan will not only help ensure a higher quality of life for generations of New Yorkers to come; it will also contribute to a 30% reduction in global warming emissions.

Land

Housing: Create homes for almost a million more New Yorkers, while making housing more affordable and sustainable

Open Space: Ensure that all New Yorkers live within a 10-minute walk of a park

Brownfields: Clean up all contaminated land in New York

Water

Water Quality: Open 90% of our waterways for recreation by reducing water pollution and preserving our natural areas

Water Network: Develop critical back-up systems for our aging water network to ensure long-term reliability

Transportation

Congestion: Improve travel times by adding transit capacity for millions more residents

State of Good Repair: Reach a full "state of good repair" on New York City's roads, subways, and rails for the first time in history

Energy

Energy: Provide cleaner, more reliable power for every New Yorker by upgrading our energy infrastructure

Air

Air Quality: Achieve the cleanest air of any big city in America

Climate Change

Climate Change: Reduce global warming emissions by more than 30%

TRANSPORTATION INITIATIVES

1. Increase capacity on key congested routes
   - Seek to fund five projects that eliminate capacity constraints
2. Provide a new commuter rail access to Manhattan
   - Seek to expand options for rail commuters
3. Expand transit access to underserved areas
   - Seek to provide transit to new neighborhoods
4. Improve and expand bus service
   - Initiate and expand Bus Rapid Transit
   - Dedicate Bus/High Occupancy Vehicle (HOV) lanes on the East River Bridges
   - Explore other improvements to bus service
5. Improve local commuter rail service
   - Seek to make better local use of Metro-North and Long Island Rail Road (LIRR) stations
6. Improve access to existing transit
   - Facilitate access to subways and bus stops citywide
7. Address congested areas around the city
   - Develop congestion management plans for outer-borough growth corridors

8. Expand ferry service
   - Seek to expand service and better integrate it with the city's existing mass transit system
9. Promote cycling
   - Complete the City's 1,800-mile bike master plan
   - Facilitate cycling
10. Pilot congestion pricing
    - Seek to use pricing to manage traffic in the Central Business District (CBD)
11. Manage roads more efficiently
    - Expand the use of Muni Meters
    - Create an integrated traffic management system
12. Strengthen enforcement of traffic violations
    - Expand the force of Traffic Enforcement Agents (TEAs)
    - Enable all TEAs to issue blocking-the-box tickets
    - Expand the use of traffic enforcement cameras
13. Facilitate freight movement
    - Improve access to John F. Kennedy International Airport (JFK)
    - Explore High Occupancy Truck Toll (HOTT) Lanes
14. Close the Metropolitan Transit Authority's state of good repair gap
    - Seek a grant from the SMART Authority to cover the MTA's funding gap
15. Establish a new regional transit financing authority
    - Seek a grant from the SMART authority to cover the City Department of Transportation funding gap
    - Invest in bridge and tunnel upgrades
16. Establish a new regional transit financing authority
    - Seek to create a Sustainable Mobility and Regional Transportation (SMART) Financing Authority to advance new projects and achieve a state of good repair

Source: PlaNYC 2030. www.nyc.gov/html/planyc.org.

DOCUMENT 163: *Massachusetts et al. v. Environmental Protection Agency et al. (2007)*

In 2003, the EPA determined that it lacked authority under the Clean Air Act to regulate carbon dioxide and other greenhouse gases (GHGs). Furthermore, the EPA declined to set GHG standards for vehicles. Massachusetts, together with several other states, cities, and environmental organizations that objected to the EPA's refusal to take action, brought a suit against the agency. The court was called upon to answer two questions: 1) "Whether the EPA Administrator may decline to issue emission standards for motor vehicles based on policy considerations not enumerated in section 202(a)(1)" of the Clean Air Act [see Document 113]; and 2) "Whether the EPA Administrator has authority to regulate carbon dioxide and other air pollutants associated with climate change under section 202(a)(1)."

A. The Case

Based on respected scientific opinion that a well-documented rise in global temperatures and attendant climatological and environmental changes have resulted from a significant increase in the atmospheric concentration of "greenhouse gases," a group of private organizations petitioned the Environmental Protection Agency (EPA) to begin regulating the emissions of four such gases, including carbon dioxide, under §202(a)(1) of the Clean Air Act, which requires that the EPA "shall by regulation prescribe . . . standards applicable to the emission of any air pollutant from any class . . . of new motor vehicles . . . which in [the EPA Administrator's] judgment cause[s], or contribute[s] to, air pollution . . . reasonably . . . anticipated to endanger public health or welfare," 42 U. S. C. §7521(a)(1). The Act defines "air pollutant" to include "any air pollution agent . . . , including any physical, chemical . . . substance . . . emitted into . . . the ambient air." §7602(g). EPA ultimately denied the petition, reasoning that (1) the Act does not authorize it to issue mandatory regulations to address global climate change, and (2) even if it had the authority to set greenhouse gas emission standards, it would have been unwise to do so at that time because a causal link between greenhouse gases and the increase in global surface air temperatures was not unequivocally established. The agency further characterized any EPA regulation of motor-vehicle emissions as a piecemeal approach to climate change that would conflict

with the President's comprehensive approach involving additional support for technological innovation, the creation of non-regulatory programs to encourage voluntary private-sector reductions in greenhouse gas emissions, and further research on climate change, and might hamper the President's ability to persuade key developing nations to reduce emissions.

Petitioners, now joined by intervenor Massachusetts and other state and local governments, sought review in the D. C. Circuit. Although each of the three judges on the panel wrote separately, two of them agreed that the EPA Administrator properly exercised his discretion in denying the rulemaking petition. One judge concluded that the Administrator's exercise of "judgment" as to whether a pollutant could "reasonably be anticipated to endanger public health or welfare," §7521(a)(1), could be based on scientific uncertainty as well as other factors, including the concern that unilateral U. S. regulation of motor-vehicle emissions could weaken efforts to reduce other countries' greenhouse gas emissions. The second judge opined that petitioners had failed to demonstrate the particularized injury to them that is necessary to establish standing under Article III, but accepted the contrary view as the law of the case and joined the judgment on the merits as the closest to that which he preferred. The court therefore denied review.

Held: 1. Petitioners have standing to challenge the EPA's denial of their rulemaking petition.

B. Opinion of the Court Delivered by Justice John Paul Stevens

VI

On the merits, the first question is whether §202(a)(1) of the Clean Air Act authorizes EPA to regulate greenhouse gas emissions from new motor vehicles in the event that it forms a "judgment" that such emissions contribute to climate change. We have little trouble concluding that it does.

* * *

While the Congresses that drafted §202(a)(1) might not have appreciated the possibility that burning fossil fuels could lead to global warming, they did understand that without regulatory flexibility, changing circumstances and scientific developments would soon render the Clean Air Act obsolete. The broad language of §202(a)(1) reflects an intentional effort to confer the flexibility necessary to forestall such obsolescence. See *Pennsylvania Dept. of Corrections v. Yeskey*, 524 U. S. 206, 212 (1998) ("[T]he fact that a statute can be applied in situations not expressly anticipated by Congress does not demonstrate ambiguity. It demonstrates breadth" (internal quotation marks omitted)). Because greenhouse gases fit well within the Clean Air Act's capacious definition of "air pollutant," we hold that EPA has the statutory authority to regulate the emission of such gases from new motor vehicles.

VII

The alternative basis for EPA's decision—that even if it does have statutory authority to regulate greenhouse gases, it would be unwise to do so at this time—rests on reasoning divorced from the statutory text. While the statute does condition the exercise of EPA's authority on its formation of a "judgment," 42 U. S. C. §7521(a)(1), that judgment must relate to whether an air pollutant "cause[s], or contribute[s] to, air pollution which may reasonably be anticipated to endanger public health or welfare," *ibid*. Put

another way, the use of the word "judgment" is not a roving license to ignore the statutory text. It is but a direction to exercise discretion within defined statutory limits.

If EPA makes a finding of endangerment, the Clean Air Act requires the agency to regulate emissions of the deleterious pollutant from new motor vehicles. *Ibid*. (stating that "[EPA] shall by regulation prescribe . . . standards applicable to the emission of any air pollutant from any class of new motor vehicles"). EPA no doubt has significant latitude as to the manner, timing, content, and coordination of its regulations with those of other agencies. But once EPA has responded to a petition for rulemaking, its reasons for action or inaction must conform to the authorizing statute. Under the clear terms of the Clean Air Act, EPA can avoid taking further action only if it determines that greenhouse gases do not contribute to climate change or if it provides some reasonable explanation as to why it cannot or will not exercise its discretion to determine whether they do. *Ibid*. To the extent that this constrains agency discretion to pursue other priorities of the Administrator or the President, this is the congressional design.

* * *

Nor can EPA avoid its statutory obligation by noting the uncertainty surrounding various features of climate change and concluding that it would therefore be better not to regulate at this time. . . . If the scientific uncertainty is so profound that it precludes EPA from making a reasoned judgment as to whether greenhouse gases contribute to global warming, EPA must say so. That EPA would prefer not to regulate greenhouse gases because of some residual uncertainty—which, contrary to *Justice [Antonin] Scalia*'s apparent belief, *post*, at 5-8, is in fact all that it said, see 68 Fed. Reg. 52929 ("We do not believe . . . that it would be either effective or appropriate for EPA *to establish [greenhouse gas] standards for motor vehicles* at this time" (emphasis added))—is irrelevant. The statutory question is whether sufficient information exists to make an endangerment finding.

In short, EPA has offered no reasoned explanation for its refusal to decide whether greenhouse gases cause or contribute to climate change.

Its action was therefore "arbitrary, capricious . . . or otherwise not in accordance with law." . . . We hold only that EPA must ground its reasons for action or inaction in the statute.

VIII

The judgment of the Court of Appeals is reversed, and the case is remanded for further proceedings consistent with this opinion.

Source: "Massachusetts *et al.* v. Environmental Protection Agency *et al.* (2007)," *United States Reports,* October Term 2006, Vol. 497 (Washington, D.C. Government Printing Office, 2010), pp. 497-98, 528, 532-35

DOCUMENT 164: Jared Diamond on Consumption, Population, and Sustainability (2008)

Jared Diamond, a professor of geography at the University of California, Los Angeles and the author of Guns, Germs and Steel *and* Collapse, *has written about the failure of societies to anticipate, recognize, and resolve environmental problems. He contends that a failure to address global environmental issues in a timely manner will result in a decline in the standard of living for much of the world.*

To mathematicians, 32 is an interesting number: it's 2 raised to the fifth power, 2 times 2 times 2 times 2 times 2. To economists, 32 is even more special, because it measures the difference in lifestyles between the first world and the developing world. The average rates at which people consume resources like oil and metals, and produce wastes like plastics and greenhouse gases, are about 32 times higher in North America, Western Europe, Japan and Australia than they are in the developing world. That factor of 32 has big consequences.

To understand them, consider our concern with world population. Today, there are more than 6.5 billion people, and that number may grow to around 9 billion within this half-century. Several decades ago, many people considered rising population to be the main challenge facing humanity. Now we realize that it matters only insofar as people consume and produce.

If most of the world's 6.5 billion people were in cold storage and not metabolizing or consuming, they would create no resource problem. What really matters is total world consumption, the sum of all local consumptions, which is the product of local population times the local per capita consumption rate.

The estimated one billion people who live in developed countries have a relative per capita consumption rate of 32. Most of the world's other 5.5 billion people constitute the developing world, with relative per capita consumption rates below 32, mostly down toward 1.

The population especially of the developing world is growing, and some people remain fixated on this. They note that populations of countries like Kenya are growing rapidly, and they say that's a big problem. Yes, it is a problem for Kenya's more than 30 million people, but it's not a burden on the whole world, because Kenyans consume so little. (Their relative per capita rate is 1.) A real problem for the world is that each of us 300 million Americans consumes as much as 32 Kenyans. With 10 times the population, the United States consumes 320 times more resources than Kenya does.

People in the third world are aware of this difference in per capita consumption, although most of them couldn't specify that it's by a factor of 32. When they believe their chances of catching up to be hopeless, they sometimes get frustrated and angry, and some become terrorists, or tolerate or support terrorists. Since Sept. 11, 2001, it has become clear that the oceans that once protected the United States no longer do so. There will be more terrorist attacks against us and Europe, and perhaps against Japan and Australia, as long as that factorial difference of 32 in consumption rates persists.

People who consume little want to enjoy the high-consumption lifestyle. Governments of developing countries make an increase in living standards a primary goal of national policy. And tens of millions of people in the developing world seek the first-world lifestyle on their own, by emigrating, especially to the United States and Western Europe, Japan and Australia. Each such transfer of a person to a high-consumption country raises world consumption rates, even though most immigrants don't succeed immediately in multiplying their consumption by 32.

Among the developing countries that are seeking to increase per capita consumption rates at home, China stands out. It has the world's fastest growing economy, and there are 1.3 billion Chinese, four times the United States population. The world is already running out of resources, and it will do so even sooner if China achieves American-level consumption rates. Already, China is competing with us for oil and metals on world markets.

Per capita consumption rates in China are still about 11 times below ours, but let's suppose they rise to our level. Let's also make things easy by imagining that nothing else happens to increase world consumption — that is, no other country increases its consumption, all national populations (including China's) remain unchanged and immigration ceases. China's catching up alone would roughly double world consumption rates. Oil consumption would increase by 106 percent, for instance, and world metal consumption by 94 percent.

If India as well as China were to catch up, world consumption rates would triple. If the whole developing world were suddenly to catch up, world rates would increase elevenfold. It would be as if the world population ballooned to 72 billion people (retaining present consumption rates).

* * *

The only approach that China and other developing countries will accept is to aim to make consumption rates and living standards more equal around the world. But the world doesn't have enough resources to allow for raising China's consumption rates, let alone those of the rest of the world, to our levels. Does this mean we're headed for disaster?

No, we could have a stable outcome in which all countries converge on consumption rates considerably below the current highest levels. Americans might object: there is no way we would sacrifice our living standards for the benefit of people in the rest of the world. Nevertheless, whether we get there willingly or not, we shall soon have lower consumption rates, because our present rates are unsustainable.

* * *

Just as it is certain that within most of our lifetimes we'll be consuming less than we do now, it is also certain that per capita consumption rates in many developing countries will one day be more nearly equal to ours. These are desirable trends, not horrible prospects. In fact, we already know how to encourage the trends; the main thing lacking has been political will.

Fortunately, in the last year there have been encouraging signs. Australia held a recent election in which a large majority of voters reversed the head-in-the-sand political course their government had followed for a decade; the new government immediately supported the Kyoto Protocol on cutting greenhouse gas emissions.

Also in the last year, concern about climate change has increased greatly in the United States. Even in China, vigorous arguments about environmental policy are taking place, and public protests recently halted construction of a huge chemical plant near the center of Xiamen. Hence I am cautiously optimistic. The world has serious consumption problems, but we can solve them if we choose to do so.

Source: Jared Diamond, "What's Your Consumption Rate?," *New York Times,* June 2, 2008, Section A, op ed page. www.nytimes.com/jared diamond what's your consumption rate.

DOCUMENT 165: Christine MacDonald on Sustainable Development and Corporate Policy (2008)

As interest in environmental issues has increased, businesspeople have discovered that selling "natural" and "green" can be very profitable. From organically grown food to sustainably produced lumber, green products have become very popular. But buyers need to read labels carefully and know the organizations that stand behind the labels. Christine MacDonald, a writer who at one time was employed by the Global Communications Division of Conservation International, an international arm of The Nature Conservancy, takes the position that close ties between environmental groups and the producers of many environmentally certified products make some eco-labels suspect, and this leads her to question the whole concept of sustainable development.

While it may just be the inevitable conclusion of age and growth, one important factor propelling the transformation of the environmental movement into something like an industry has been an uncritical acceptance of "sustainable development." The concept has been kicking around for decades, supplying the philosophical underpinning for today's corporate-conservationist embrace. It emerged from the confrontational politics of the 1960s and 1970s environmental movement that generally left business communities and environmentalists with no common ground. The idea that development could be environmentally sustainable opened the door to dialogue and innovation aimed at merging two of society's biggest concerns.

In recent years, corporate America has embraced the idea as its own, propelled by consumers who are increasingly informed about the consequences of environmental degradation and climate change. According to a global survey by the business consulting firm McKinsey & Company, corporate executives are more concerned than ever about how environmental problems will affect their companies' bottom-line performance. The report concluded that corporate leaders are now more worried about climate change than the public at large. Nine in ten executives fret over global warming while only 3 percent said they don't believe it is happening. The vast majority said they understand the public expects them to improve their handling of sociopolitical issues. They expect the environment, including climate change, to influence

shareholder value "far more than any other societal issue during the next five years."

As a result of shifting mind-sets, companies have rushed to come up with green marketing campaigns and lavish cash on environmental groups. Lengthy sustainability reports have become commonplace among the world's leading corporations today. These reports chronicle good works that include reducing waste and pollution, developing environmentally friendly products, combating poverty and other social ills.

This is undoubtedly a positive development. However, several social corporate-responsibility studies note a wide gap between the rhetoric and the reality. One study published by the Boston College Center for Corporate Citizenship found that three-quarters of high-level executives polled agreed corporate citizenship needs to be a priority but far fewer had incorporated concrete action into their operations. Their concern hadn't prompted them to start making environmentally sustainable products or rethinking their relationships with employees and suppliers.

While the emerging socially responsible discourse among business leaders is encouraging, it is important to remember executives are not motivated by purely altruistic goals. Corporate social responsibility holds attraction with many business leaders for its utility as a defensive posture in the face of possible new government regulations on carbon emissions and increasingly savvy and interconnected watchdog groups around the globe. Corporate leaders, who run businesses with interests in many far-flung places, have found a proactive sustainability stance can help avoid costly environmental accidents, avert PR messes when they occur, and mute protests, particularly in developing countries, where the bulk of the world's raw materials and finished goods come from these days.

But some ask whether sustainability makes any sense in nature conservation, where ancient forests, oceans, fresh water, and other natural resources have been taken to the brink of collapse after human exploitation dating back millennia. How to harvest these resources sustainably is a concept that has eluded humankind for centuries.

Two projects that illustrate the dilemma of how to strike a truly "sustainable" balance are the Forest Stewardship Council, or FCS, and the Marine Stewardship Council, or, MSC. The product certification programs were launched separately by consortiums made up of corporations and environmental groups. As such, they are the product of compromise, deal-making, and behind-the-scenes wheeling and dealing that critics say have done a disservice to the very nature they set out to protect. While both labels have prominent environmental supporters, their detractors say the FSC and the MSC are half-measures that mislead the public but won't head off extinctions.

Source: Christine MacDonald, *Green, Inc.: An Environmental Insider Reveals How a Good Cause Has Gone Bad* (Guilford, CT: Lyons Press, 2008), pp. 54-56.

DOCUMENT 166: LEED and the Green Building Revolution (2008, 2010)

Buildings consume vast amounts of energy in both their construction and operation. According to some estimates, they generate close to half the carbon emissions of the United States, as well as 12 percent of all freshwater use, 30 percent of all raw materials use, 45-65 percent of waste output to land fills, and 74 percent of electricity consumption. In the 1990s, as concern about global warming and the need to conserve energy became widespread, communities began adding green building standards to their building codes, and in 2008 California became the first state to pass a statewide green building code.

The U.S. Green Building Council was founded by architects S. Richard Fedrizzi, David Gottfried, and Mike Italiano as a nonprofit trade organization whose purpose was to encourage a reduction in the construction and operation costs of new buildings. The retrofitting of old buildings was quickly added to its agenda.

A. Richard Fedrizzi on the Founding of the Green Building Council and its LEED Certification Program (2008)

A revolution is going on all over this land, and it's about time! It is transforming the marketplace for buildings, homes and communities, and it is part of a larger sustainability revolution that will transform just about everything we know, do, and experience over the next few decades. This revolution is about green building, and its aim is nothing less than to fundamentally change the built environment by creating energy-efficient, healthy, productive buildings that reduce or minimize the significant impacts of buildings on urban life and on local, regional and global environments.

In 1993 the U.S. Green Building Council (USGBC) was founded to drive this change, and in 2000 we launched the LEED (Leadership in Energy and Environmental Design) Green Building Rating System to provide a common definition and way to measure green buildings. A point-based system LEED rates buildings according to key environmental attributes such as site impacts, energy and water use, materials and resource conservation, and indoor air quality.

To our delight and somewhat to our surprise, by 2006 LEED had taken the country by storm. As of early 2007, 18 states and 59 cities, along with some of the biggest and most prestigious names in the building industry—including the developer of the "Ground Zero" World Trade Center Site, Larry Silverstein—had all made serious commitments to using the LEED rating system for their projects (the first new building built and occupied at "Ground Zero," Seven World Trade Center, was Gold-certified). In 2006 the U.S. General Services Administration, the country's biggest landlord, along with 10 other federal agencies, endorsed LEED as its rating tool of choice. This is not surprising, because LEED provides a rigorous road map to building green. Projected resource savings from the first 200 LEED-certified projects show that well-designed, fully documented and third-party verified projects get results: an average of 30 percent water-use reduction and 30 to 55 percent energy savings, depending on the level of certification.

B. The LEED Certification System (2010)

LEED is a voluntary certification program that can be applied to any building type and any building lifecycle phase. It promotes a whole-building approach to sustainability by recognizing performance in key areas:

Sustainable Sites

Choosing a building's site and managing that site during construction are important considerations for a project's sustainability. The Sustainable Sites category discourages development on previously undeveloped land; minimizes a building's impact on ecosystems and waterways; encourages regionally appropriate landscaping; rewards smart transportation choices; controls stormwater runoff; and reduces erosion, light pollution, heat island effect and construction-related pollution.

Water Efficiency

Buildings are major users of our potable water supply. The goal of the Water Efficiency credit category is to encourage smarter use of water, inside and out. Water reduction is typically achieved through more efficient appliances, fixtures and fittings inside and water-wise landscaping outside

Energy & Atmosphere

According to the U.S. Department of Energy, buildings use 39% of the energy and 74% of the electricity produced each year in the United States. The Energy & Atmosphere category encourages a wide variety of energy strategies: commissioning; energy use monitoring; efficient design and construction; efficient appliances, systems and lighting; the use of renewable and clean sources of energy, generated on-site or off-site; and other innovative strategies.

Materials & Resources

During both the construction and operations phases, buildings generate a lot of waste and use a lot of materials and resources. This credit category encourages the selection of sustainably grown, harvested, produced and transported products and materials. It promotes the reduction of waste as well as reuse and recycling, and it takes into account the reduction of waste at a product's source.

Indoor Environmental Quality

The U.S. Environmental Protection Agency estimates that Americans spend about 90% of their day indoors, where the air quality can be significantly worse than outside. The Indoor Environmental Quality credit category promotes strategies that can improve indoor air as well as providing access to natural daylight and views and improving acoustics.

Locations & Linkages

The LEED for Homes rating system recognizes that much of a home's impact on the environment comes from where it is located and how it fits into its community. The Locations & Linkages credits encourage homes being built away from environmentally sensitive places and instead being built in infill, previously developed and other preferable sites. It rewards homes that are built near already-existing infrastructure, community resources and transit, and it encourages access to open space for walking, physical activity and time spent outdoors.

Source: A. S. Richard Fedrizzi, Foreword to Jerry Yudelson, *The Green Building Revolution* (Washington, D.C.: Island Press, 2008), p. xv. B. Usgbc.org/LEED.

DOCUMENT 167: Jeff Biggers Questions the Concept of "Clean Coal" (2008)

Jeff Biggers, who writes about Appalachia and the coal industry, insists that the mining and burning of coal will always be dirty and dangerous. He quotes a former EPA official saying, "The industry's indiscriminate attempts to market 'clean coal' are starting to look like the tobacco industry's effort to sell 'safe cigarettes.'"[6]

Although the Trump administration has vowed to bring back coal industry jobs, it is now not only cleaner but also cheaper to build and operate new wind and solar plants than coal plants.

Every time I hear our political leaders talk about "clean coal," I think about Burl, an irascible old coal miner in West Virginia. After 35 years underground, he struggled to conjure enough breath to match his storytelling verve, as if the iron hoops of a whiskey barrel had been strapped around his lungs. In 1983, during my first visit to Appalachia as a young man, Burl rolled up his pants and showed me the leg that had been mangled in a mining accident. The scars snaked down to his ankles.

"My grandpa barely survived an accident in the mines in southern Illinois," I told him. "He had these blue marks and bits of coal buried in his face."

"Coal tattoo," Burl wheezed. "Don't let anyone ever tell you that coal is clean."

Clean coal: Never was there an oxymoron more insidious, or more dangerous to our public health. Invoked as often by the Democratic presidential candidates as by the Republicans and by liberals and conservatives alike, this slogan has blindsided any meaningful progress toward a sustainable energy policy.

Democrats excoriated President Bush last month when he released a budget calling for more — billions more — in funds to reduce carbon emissions from coal-burning power plants to create "clean coal." But hardly a hoot could be heard about his proposed cuts to more practical investments in solar energy, hydrogen fuel and home energy efficiency.

Meanwhile, leading Democrats were up in arms over the Energy Department's recent decision to abandon the $1.8 billion FutureGen project in eastern Illinois, planned as the first coal-fired plant to capture and store harmful carbon dioxide emissions. Energy Department officials, unlike politicians, had to confront the spiraling costs of this fantasy.

Orwellian language has led to Orwellian politics. With the imaginary vocabulary of "clean coal," too many Democrats and Republicans, as well as a surprising number of environmentalists, have forgotten the dirty realities of extracting coal from the earth. Pummeled by warnings that global warming is triggering the apocalypse, Americans have fallen for the ruse of futuristic science that is clean coal. And in the meantime, swaths of the country are being destroyed before our eyes.

Here's the hog-killing reality that a coal miner like Burl or my grandfather knew firsthand: No matter how "cap 'n trade" schemes pan out in the distant future for coal-fired plants, strip mining and underground coal mining remain the dirtiest and most destructive ways of making energy.

Coal ain't clean. Coal is deadly.

More than 104,000 miners in America have died in coal mines since 1900. Twice as many have died from black lung disease. Dangerous pollutants, including mercury, filter into our air and water. The injuries and deaths caused by overburdened coal trucks are innumerable. Yet even on the heels of a recent report revealing that in the last six years the Mine Safety and Health Administration decided not to assess fines for more than 4,000 violations, Bush administration officials have called for cutting mine-safety funds by 6.5 percent. Have they already forgotten the coal miners who were entombed underground in Utah last summer?

Above ground, millions of acres across 36 states have been dynamited, torn and churned into bits by strip mining in the last 150 years. More than 60 percent of all coal mined in the United States today, in fact, comes from strip mines.

In the "United States of Coal," Appalachia has become the poster child for strip mining's worst depravations, which come in the form of mountaintop removal. An estimated 750,000 to 1 million acres of hardwood forests, a thousand miles of waterways and more than 470 mountains and their surrounding communities — an area the size of Delaware — have been erased from the southeastern mountain range in the last two decades. Thousands of tons of explosives — the equivalent of several Hiroshima atomic bombs — are set off in Appalachian communities every year.

How can anyone call this clean?

When the Bush administration announced a plan last year to do away with a poorly enforced 1983 regulation that protected streams from being buried by strip-mining waste — one of the last ramparts protecting some of the nation's oldest forests and communities — tens of thousands of people wrote to the Office of Surface Mining in outrage. Citizens' groups also effectively halted the proposed construction of 59 coal-fired plants in the past year. Yet at last weekend's meeting of the National Governors Association, Democratic and Republican governors once again joined forces, ignored the disastrous reality of mining and championed the chimera of clean coal. Pennsylvania Gov. Ed Rendell even declared that coal states will be "back in business big time."

How much more death and destruction will it take to strip coal of this bright, shining "clean" lie?

As Burl might have said, if our country can rally to save Arctic polar bears from global warming, perhaps Congress can pass the Endangered Appalachians Act to save American miners, their children and their communities from ruin by a reckless industry.

Or at least stop talking about "clean coal."

Source: Jeff Biggers, "Clean Coal? Don't Try to Shovel That," *Washington Post,* March 2, 2008, p. B2.

DOCUMENT 168: Mark Bittman on the Environmental Impact of the American Diet (2009)

Shoppers' demand for low cost food and high variety combined with the need for produce to resist the effects of long-distance shipping resulted in a decline in the nutritive value and sometimes even the taste of the products available on supermarket shelves. Furthermore, large-scale farms and meat producers routinely ignored the effects of their production techniques on the environment or their workers.

In recent decades, however, organic farming, the locivore movement, the slow food movement, and the green markets that have become increasingly common in urban areas have created a widespread change in American attitudes about food, food production, and diet. According to Bill McKibben [see Document 174], "local farmers' markets are the fastest-growing part of the food economy, with sales up by 10 to 15 percent a year, and the number of markets doubling and then doubling again in the last decade" McKibben has also noted that "local land trusts, which used to concentrate on preserving unspoiled scenic views, increasingly save land precisely to turn it over to small farmers"[7]

Mark Bittman, a cookbook author and popular food writer, is among a growing contingent of advocates for a diet that features more fresh fruits and vegetables and less red meat.

Even the most conscientious agriculture has some environmental impact, and though much food production yields greenhouse gases, raising livestock has a much higher potential for global warming than crop farming. For example: To produce one calorie of corn takes 2.2 calories of fossil fuel. For beef the number is 40: *it requires 40 calories to produce one calorie of beef protein.*

In other words, if you grow corn and eat it, you expend 2.2 calories of energy in order to eat one of protein. But if you process that corn, and feed it to a steer, and take into account all the other needs that steer has through its lifetime — land use, chemical fertilizers (largely petroleum based), pesticides, machinery, transport, drugs, water, and so—you're responsible for 40 calories of energy to get that same calorie of protein. According to one estimate, a typical steer consumes the equivalent of 135 gallons of gasoline in his lifetime, enough for even some gas guzzlers to drive more than halfway from New York to Los Angeles, or for an energy efficient car to make the drive back and forth twice. Or try to imagine each cow on the planet consuming almost seven barrels of oil.

Another way to put it is that eating a typical family-of-four steak dinner is the rough equivalent, energy wise, to driving in an SUV for three hours while leaving all the lights on at home. In all, the average American meat eater is responsible for one and a half tons more CO^2-equivalent greenhouse gas —-enough to fill a large house—-than someone who eats no meat. If we each ate the equivalent of three fewer cheeseburgers a week, we'd cancel out the effects of all the SUV's in the country. Not bad.

Yet thanks to agricultural subsidies and the lack of regulation about how meat is raised, it is far less expensive than it actually should be.

Source: Mark Bittman, Food Matters: A Guide to Conscious Eating with More than 75 Recipes (New York: Simon & Schuster, 2009), pp. 16-17.

DOCUMENT 169: Mark Z. Jacobson and Mark A. Delucchi's Plan for Carbon-Free Electricity by 2030 (2009)

Stanford professor Mark Jacobson and Mark Delucchi, who is now at the University of California, Berkeley, Transportation Sustainability Research Center, were challenged by Al Gore's 2008 proposition that a way should be found to power America with 100 percent carbon-free electricity within a decade. They came up with the following plan showing that it might be feasible to supply "100 percent of the world's energy for all purposes (using wind, water and solar resources) as early as 2030."[8] In 2015, together with other researchers at Stanford, they created a state-by-state plan for 100% carbon-free energy. Their work, which influenced both Obama's Clean Power Plan and the United States' goals set forth in the Paris Accords, emphasizes that although this change in powering the world is economically and technologically possible, it requires social, political and industrial support in order to be carried out.

Scientists have been building to this moment for at least a decade, analyzing various pieces of the challenge. Most recently, a 2009 Stanford University study ranked energy systems according to their impacts on global warming, pollution, water supply, land use, wildlife and other concerns. The very best options were wind, solar, geothermal, tidal and hydroelectric power—all of which are driven by wind, water or sunlight (referred to as WWS). Nuclear power, coal with carbon capture, and ethanol were all poorer options, as were oil and natural gas. The study also found that battery-electric vehicles and hydrogen fuel-cell vehicles recharged by WWS options would largely eliminate pollution from the transportation sector.

Our plan calls for millions of wind turbines, water machines and solar installations. The numbers are large, but the scale is not an insurmountable hurdle; society has achieved massive) transformations before. During World War II, the U.S. retooled automobile factories to produce 300,000 aircraft, and other countries produced 486,000 more. In 1956 the U.S. began building the Interstate Highway System, which after 35 years extended for 47,000 miles, changing commerce and society.

Is it feasible to transform the world's energy systems? Could it be accomplished in two decades? The answers depend on the technologies chosen, the availability of critical materials, and economic and political factors.

Clean Technologies Only

Renewable energy comes from enticing sources: wind, which also produces waves; water, which includes hydroelectric, tidal and geothermal energy (water heated by hot underground rock); and sun, which includes photovoltaics and solar power plants that focus sunlight to heat a fluid that drives a turbine to generate electricity. Our plan includes only technologies that work or are close to working today on a large scale, rather than those that may exist 20 or 30 years from now.

To ensure that our system remains clean, we consider only technologies that have near-zero emissions of greenhouse gases and air pollutants over their entire life cycle, including construction, operation and decommissioning. For example, when burned in vehicles, even the most ecologically acceptable sources of ethanol create air pollution that will cause the same mortality level as when gasoline is burned. Nuclear power results in up to 25 times more carbon emissions than wind energy, when reactor construction and uranium refining and transport are considered. Carbon capture and sequestration technology can reduce carbon dioxide emissions from coal-fired power plants but will increase air pollutants and will extend all the other deleterious effects of coal mining, transport and processing, because more coal must be burned to power the capture and storage steps. Similarly, we consider only technologies that do not present significant waste disposal or terrorism risks.

In our plan, WWS will supply electric power for heating and transportation—industries that will have to revamp if the world has any hope of slowing climate change. We have assumed that most fossil-fuel heating (as well as ovens and stoves) can be replaced by electric systems and that most fossil-fuel transportation can be replaced by battery and fuel-cell vehicles. Hydrogen, produced by using WWS electricity to split water (electrolysis), would power fuel cells and be burned in airplanes and by industry.

Plenty of Supply

Today the maximum power consumed worldwide at any given moment is about 12.5 trillion watts (terawatts, or TW), according to the U.S. Energy Information Administration. The agency projects that in 2030 the world will require 16.9 TW of power as global population and living standards rise, with about 2.8 TW in the U.S. The mix of sources is similar to today's, heavily dependent on fossil fuels. If, however, the planet were powered entirely by WWS, with no fossil-fuel or biomass combustion, an intriguing savings would occur. Global power demand would be only 11.5 TW, and U.S. demand would be 1.8 TW. That decline occurs because, in most cases, electrification is a more efficient way to use energy. For example, only 17 to 20 percent of the energy in gasoline is used to move a vehicle (the rest is wasted as heat), whereas 75 to 86 percent of the electricity delivered to an electric vehicle goes into motion.

Even if demand did rise to 16.9 TW, WWS sources could provide far more power. Detailed studies by us and others indicate that energy from the wind, worldwide, is about 1,700 TW. Solar, alone, offers 6,500 TW. . . .

The other WWS technologies will help create a flexible range of options. Although all the sources can expand greatly, for practical reasons, wave power can be extracted only near coastal areas. Many geothermal sources are too deep to be tapped economically. And even though hydroelectric power now exceeds all other WWS sources, most of the suitable large reservoirs are already in use.

The Plan: Power Plants Required

Clearly, enough renewable energy exists. How, then, would we transition to a new infrastructure to provide the world with 11.5 TW? We have chosen a mix of technologies emphasizing wind and solar, with about 9 percent of demand met by mature water-related methods. (Other combinations of wind and solar could be as successful.)

Wind supplies 51 percent of the demand, provided by 3.8 million large wind turbines (each rated at five megawatts) worldwide. Although that quantity may sound enormous, it is interesting to note that the world manufactures 73 million cars and light trucks *every year*. Another 40 percent of the power comes from photovoltaics and concentrated solar plants, with about 30 percent of the photovoltaic output from rooftop panels on homes and commercial buildings. About 89,000 photovoltaic and concentrated solar power plants, averaging 300 megawatts apiece, would be needed. Our mix also includes 900 hydroelectric stations worldwide, 70 percent of which are already in place.

Only about 0.8 percent of the wind base is installed today. The worldwide footprint of the 3.8 million turbines would be less than 50 square kilometers (smaller than Manhattan). . . .

The Materials Hurdle

The scale of the WWS infrastructure is not a barrier. But a few materials needed to build it could be scarce or subject to price manipulation.

. . .

Smart Mix for Reliability

A new infrastructure must provide energy on demand at least as reliably as the existing infrastructure. WWS technologies generally suffer less downtime than traditional sources. The average U.S. coal plant is offline 12.5 percent of the year for scheduled and unscheduled maintenance. Modern wind turbines have a down time of less than 2 percent on land and less than 5 percent at sea. Photovoltaic systems are also at less than 2 percent. Moreover, when an individual wind, solar or wave device is down, only a small fraction of production is affected; when a coal, nuclear or natural gas plant goes offline, a large chunk of generation is lost.

The main WWS challenge is that the wind does not always blow and the sun does not always shine in a given location. Intermittency problems can be mitigated by a smart balance of sources, such as generating a base supply from steady geothermal or tidal power, relying on wind at night when it is often plentiful, using solar by day and turning to a reliable source such as hydroelectric that can be turned on and off quickly to smooth out supply or meet peak demand. . . .

Because the wind often blows during stormy conditions when the sun does not shine and the sun often shines on calm days with little wind, combining wind and solar can go a long way toward meeting demand, especially when geothermal provides a steady base and hydroelectric can be called on to fill in the gaps.

As Cheap as Coal

The mix of WWS sources in our plan can reliably supply the residential, commercial, industrial and transportation sectors. The logical next question is whether the power would be affordable. . . .

For comparison, the average cost in the U.S. in 2007 of conventional power generation and transmission was about 7¢/kWh, and it is projected to be 8¢/kWh in 2020. Power from wind turbines, for example, already costs about the same or less than it does from a new coal or natural gas plant, and in the future wind power is expected to be the least costly of all options. The competitive cost of wind has made it the second-largest source of new electric power generation in the U.S. for the past three years, behind natural gas and ahead of coal.

Solar power is relatively expensive now but should be competitive as early as 2020. . . .

Transportation in a WWS world will be driven by batteries or fuel cells, so we should compare the economics of these electric vehicles with that of internal-combustion-engine vehicles. Detailed analyses by one of us (Delucchi) and Tim Lipman of the University of California, Berkeley, have indicated that mass-produced electric vehicles with advanced lithium-ion or nickel metal-hydride batteries could have a full lifetime cost per mile (including battery replacements) that is comparable with that of a gasoline vehicle, when gasoline sells for more than $2 a gallon.

When the so-called externality costs (the monetary value of damages to human health, the environment and climate) of fossil-fuel generation are taken into account, WWS technologies become even more cost-competitive.

Overall construction cost for a WWS system might be on the order of $100 trillion worldwide, over 20 years, not including transmission. But this is not money handed out by governments or consumers. It is investment that is paid back through the sale of electricity and energy. . . .

Political Will

Our analyses strongly suggest that the costs of WWS will become competitive with traditional sources. In the interim, however, certain forms of WWS power will be significantly more costly than fossil power. Some combination of WWS subsidies and carbon taxes would thus be needed for a time. . . .

Taxing fossil fuels or their use to reflect their environmental damages also makes sense. But at a minimum, existing subsidies for fossil energy, such as tax benefits for exploration and extraction, should be eliminated to level the playing field. Misguided promotion of alternatives that are less desirable than WWS power, such as farm and production subsidies for biofuels, should also be ended, because it delays deployment of cleaner systems. For their part, legislators crafting policy must find ways to resist lobbying by the entrenched energy industries.

Finally, each nation needs to be willing to invest in a robust, long-distance transmission system that can carry large quantities of WWS power from remote regions where it is often greatest—such as the Great Plains for wind and the desert Southwest for solar in the U.S.—to centers of consumption, typically cities. Reducing consumer demand during peak usage periods also requires a smart grid that gives generators and consumers much more control over electricity usage hour by hour.

A large-scale wind, water and solar energy system can reliably supply the world's needs, significantly benefiting climate, air quality, water quality, ecology and energy security. As we have shown, the obstacles are primarily political, not technical. A combination of feed-in tariffs plus incentives for providers to reduce costs, elimination of fossil subsidies and an intelligently expanded grid could be enough to ensure rapid deployment. Of course, changes in the real-world power and transportation industries will have to overcome sunk investments in existing infrastructure. But with sensible policies, nations could set a goal of generating 25 percent of their new energy supply with WWS sources in 10 to 15 years and almost 100 percent of new supply in 20 to 30 years. With extremely aggressive policies, all existing fossil-fuel capacity could theoretically be retired and replaced in the same period, but with more modest and likely policies full replacement may take 40 to 50 years. Either way, clear leadership is needed, or else nations will keep trying technologies promoted by industries rather than vetted by scientists.

Source: Mark Z Jacobson and Mark A. Delucchi, "A Path to Sustainable Energy by 2030," *Scientific American*, Nov. 2009, pp 58-65.

Document 170: John Wargo on Our Chemical Environment (2009)

John Wargo, a professor at the Yale University School of Forestry and Environmental studies, specializes in environmental law with a focus on human health. In this selection he discusses how and why federal law fails to protect us from the possible dangers of many of the chemicals in our environment. Because both the federal and local governments tend to be reactive to chemical contamination, rather than proactive, disasters like the lead contamination of Flint, Michigan's water supply will continue to occur.

One unexpected side effect of twentieth-century prosperity has been a change in the chemistry of the human body. Each day most people are exposed to thousands of chemicals in mixtures that were never experienced by previous generations, Many of these substances are recognized by the governments of the United States and European Union to be carcinogens, neurotoxins, reproductive and developmental toxins, or endocrine disruptors that mimic or block human hormones. In 1999, the U.S. Centers for Disease Control and Prevention (CDC) began testing human tissue among populations across the country to detect the presence of environmental contaminants, and reported that most individuals carry in their bodies a mixture of metals, pesticides, solvents, fire retardants, waterproofing agents, and by-products of fuel combustion. Children often carry higher concentrations than adults, with the amounts of contaminants also varying according to gender and ethnicity.

Our petroleum-and chemical-dependent economy is the primary cause of these exposures. Every year hundreds of billions of pounds of chemicals are release into the environment as commercial products while trillions of additional pounds of pollutions are discharged into the atmosphere, surface and groundwater, oceans, and land as by-products of fuel combustion or as wastes. Often the distinction between commercial chemicals and pollutants is only a matter of time as once sought-after products lose their utility, are discarded, and slowly degrade, releasing their ingredients into the surrounding areas. Our global economy concentrates raw chemicals, mixes them in millions of products that are distributed through markets, and reconcentrates remaining wastes in landfills or incinerators, where once again they are dispersed unpredictably into the air, soil, and water. The human exposures that occur at every step along the way are often unrecognized or ignored by individuals, corporations, and governments. And most in society have little comprehension of the chemical mixtures they experience in everyday life and the dangers posed to their health.

During the last half-century, society's growing chemical imprint has been accompanied by an increase in the prevalence of many illnesses. These include respiratory diseases such as childhood asthma, neurological impairments, declining sperm counts, fertility failure, immune dysfunction, breast and prostate cancer, and developmental disorders among the young. Some of these illnesses have been caused or exacerbated by exposure to commercial chemicals and pollutants. There is little doubt, for example, that tobacco, lead, mercury, radionuclides, solvents, vehicle exhaust, combustion by-products, dioxins, PCBs and many pesticides have caused extensive human illness. Significantly, these chemicals were once thought to be safe at doses now known to be hazardous; as with other substances, the perception of danger grew as governments tested chemicals more thoroughly.

Three trends help to explain the growing chemical burden on the environments and human health: population growth, longevity, and economic expansion. . . .

The United States arguably has the most extensive body of environmental law and regulation in the world. . . . Between 1970 and 1996 several dozen major federal statues and tens of thousands of regulations were adopted. Congress intended these regulation to limit emissions of hazardous chemicals and their residues in surface and ground water, food, soils, consumer products, the air, and oceans.

Legislators may have had high aspirations, but they were naive to assume that the government can control the global economic forces driving the chemical revolution we are experiencing. Moreover, there has never been a master plan for environmental law; instead Congress has adopted statutes in a piecemeal way, responding to compelling and often surprising stories of environmental contamination, damage, and health loss by adopting new laws to govern hazardous materials. Infamous examples include the periodic Cuyahoga River fires in Ohio in the 19950s and 1960s; the discovery of a school built above a chemical dump at Love Canal in New York in the 1970s; the spraying of PCBs on the back roads of Times Beach in Missouri in the mid 1980s; the Union Carbide disaster in Bhopal [in India] in 1984; the Chernobyl nuclear plant explosion in the Ukrainian Republic in 1987; and the *Exxon Valdez* oil spill in Alaska in 1989. The result of this reactionary, rather than preventive approach is an odd patchwork of poorly coordinated regulations rather than a comprehensive body of law to manage chemicals we all experience in daily life. Equally important, U.S. law has come to depend on technical risk assessments that demand ever more evidence to prove chemical danger, rather than requirements that companies prove chemicals' safety prior to their production and sale.

. . .

One important guardian of the health of the U.S. population, the EPA, has since 1976 been required by the Toxic Substances Control Act (TSCA) to maintain an inventory of potentially toxic substances; but the agency cannot demand premarket testing or regulate production unless it has compelling evidence of significant environmental or health risk. This requirement places the burden on government to conduct the testing needed to justify regulation, an impossibility given the staggering number of untested chemicals and combinations. When this law went into effect, 62,000 chemicals already in commerce were listed but immediately exempted or grandfathered from any data submission requirements. Since that time, 45,000 additional chemicals have been introduced to commerce, yet nearly half of these were reported to the EPA after companies began to sell them. The effect is that among U.S. chemicals produced in highest volumes, 90 percent are exempted from federal review under TSCA. Moreover, in 1980 the EPA found that basic toxicity information was available for only 7 percent of these, while none was available for 43 percent. For chemicals produced at lower volumes, the agency had even less information.

Source: John Wargo, *Green Intelligence: Creating Environments that Protect Human Health* New Haven, CT: Yale University Press, 2009), pp. xi –xv.

Document 171: Christopher B. Leinberger on Walkable Neighborhoods with Public Transportation (2010)

After more than 60 years, the trend of people moving from U.S. cities to the suburbs has begun to reverse, and all 30 of the nation's largest metropolitan areas have started to rebuild. Walkable urban places (walkups) are where the wealthiest and most educated people are now choosing to live and where hundreds of companies are moving and investing.

Walkable, compact neighborhoods with easy access to public transportation are not only environmentally more efficient than car-oriented communities, they also have special appeal for the growing number of very elderly people who cannot or should not drive as well as for young adults who like the sociability of cities and choose not to own cars. New technology that enables on-demand car-sharing and ride access is part of the innovation that is helping to spark urban rejuvenation. But walkup areas around the nation require an infusion of both public and private funding to improve transportation infrastructure in order to continue to thrive.

Christopher Leinberger, a real estate developer and professor at the George Washington School of Business, has studied and written about walkups in Washington, D.C., Atlanta, Boston, Detroit, and Toronto.

Urban-style housing in walkable neighborhoods—including those in the inner suburbs–is what's in demand today. And for a variety of reasons, that demand will intensify in the coming years. Only by serving it can the country kick-start growth in an enormous and essential part of the economy.

Yet the creation of new, attractive urban spaces is slow and difficult, and becomes all but impossible without substantial new infrastructure. Most of all, it relies on good transit options—especially rail links—around which walkable neighborhoods can develop. Rail, biking, and walking infrastructure is the backbone of urban development, and as a country we've for the most part neglected to build it in recent decades, in favor of new roads for new suburbs farther and farther away from metropolitan hubs. To support growth in the next decade, we need to change that dynamic—and nourish our walkable urban spaces and neighborhoods. Complicating matters, in these cash-strapped times we need to find a way to do so on the cheap.

Housing comes in two basic types. The first is the now-classic Ozzie and Harriet-style single-family house on its own large lot, from which nearly every trip is taken by car. The second is similar to what we predominantly built before the Great Depression: small-lot single-family houses, town-houses, and apartments that are within walking distance of most everyday needs and are typically connected by public transit to work, shopping, and entertainment—housing that is built at least five times more densely than that in conventional suburbs.

Ten years ago, conventional large-lot housing in wealthy suburbs was the highest-priced housing per square foot, in nearly all metropolitan areas. Today, housing in walkable neighborhoods is typically the most expensive; the lines crossed in the [first decade of the] 2000s.

Why did this happen? Cities, of course, have experienced a cultural renaissance over the past 15 years. Some suburbs, meanwhile have become less attractive as they've grown more congested and lost open space, betraying suburbia's original promise and pushing new subdivisions farther and farther out into the hinterland.

The increasing costs of driving, meanwhile, have put great pressure on suburban family finances. On average, traditional suburban households spend 24 percent of their income paying for and maintaining their cars; urban households in walkable neighborhoods spend only 12 percent of their income on transportation. The difference amounts to half of what a typical household spends on health care—nationally, $700 billion a year in total.

Two-thirds of all households today consist of singles, childless couples, or empty-nesters, and that proportion will rise over the next 20 years. All of these groups tend to prefer walkable urban housing. Millennials—the rising generation of 20-and 30-somethings—are particularly drawn to urban living, seeing it not only as exciting but as healthy and environmentally friendly.

. . .

In the early 20th century, every town of more than 5,000 people was served by streetcars, even though real household income was one-third what it is today. By 1920, metropolitan Los Angeles had the longest street-railway network in the world. Atlanta's rail system was accessible to nearly all residents. Until 1950, our grandparents and great-grandparents did not need a car to get around, since they could rely upon various forms of rail transit. A hundred years ago, the average household spent only 5 percent of its income on transportation.

How did the country afford that extensive rail system? Real-estate developers, sometimes aided by electric utilities, not only built the systems but paid rent to the cities for the rights-of-way.

These developers included Henry Huntington, who built the Pacific Electric in Los Angeles; Minnesota's Thomas Lowry, who built Twin City Rapid Transit; and Senator Francis Newlands from Nevada, who built Washington, D.C.'s Rock Creek Railway up Connecticut Avenue from Dupont Circle in the 1890s. . . . {Newlands] and other developers of the time understood that *transportation drives development*—and that development has to subsidize transportation.

. . .

How would the private funding of public transit work [today]? Most states already have laws in place that allow local groups of voters to create "special assessment districts," in which neighborhood property owners can vote to fund an upgrade to infrastructure by charging themselves, say, a onetime assessment, or a higher property-tax rate for some number of years. If a majority of the property owners believe they would benefit from the improvement, all property owners in that district are obligated to help pay for it. These districts can vote to fund new transit as well (potentially, the transportation-financing agency could even receive a minority-ownership stake in the district's private property in return for building new transit). In the late 1990s the property owners paid for a quarter of the cost of a new Metrorail station in D.C. using this approach; after the station opened, an office developer told me he believed his investment was being returned manifold.

. . .

The encouragement of additional walkable urban development, which all starts with public transit, would have many benefits. Although building the infrastructure that supports dense development seems expensive, in the long run it's actually much cheaper than conventional suburban infrastructure—at most one-tenth the cost per home. A mile of sewer line costs about the same to build whether it is on the metropolitan fringe or in a densely built inner suburb, but the line serves many more people in the inner suburb. And households in walkable urban areas use considerably less energy, in some instances at least a third less. High-density living even appears to spur faster rates of innovation; in a knowledge economy, ideas come faster and can be developed more quickly when more people can meet and mix easily.

But mot immediately, investment in rail, bike, and walking infrastructure, laying the groundwork for developing the kind of housing that is now in demand, is essential if we want to restore the economy to health. In the mid-to-late 20th century, the growth of the suburbs propelled America's economy. Growth of walkable neighborhoods in cities and suburbs and play a similar role in the decades to come, sparking growth in the broader economy—but only if we start preparing today.

Source: Christopher B. Leinberger, "Here Comes the Neighborhood," *The Atlantic*, June 2010, pp. 59-61.

Document 172: Donald Gilliland Reviews Josh Fox's "Gasland" (2010)

Josh Fox's documentary "Gasland," about ruined water wells and flammable water awakened people to the issue of the dangers of the growing use of hydraulic fracturing (fracking) to obtain oil and gas. Fracking, which involves injecting large quantities of liquids under high pressure in order to release oil and gas, has enabled energy companies to extract oil and gas that would otherwise be unobtainable and, in contrast to just a few years earlier, brought the United States close to energy independence. The commercial application of the technique, begun in 1950, made it possible to obtain good flows of oil and gas from shale, tight oil and gas wells, and coal seams, but its opponents point to it as the cause of contaminated surface and underground water and earthquakes.

Tap water isn't supposed to catch fire.

It does in Dimock.

The documentary "Gasland" . . . begins and ends in Dimock, a rural area of Susquehanna County, Pa., where kitchen sinks began to spit methane and catch fire after Cabot Oil & Gas Co. started drilling wells nearby.

Josh Fox, the director of "Gasland," chronicles his search to discover what gas drilling in the Marcellus Shale might do to his beloved Delaware River watershed should he and his neighbors sign the leases they received in the mail. That search takes him first to Dimock and then across the United States, where he meets people struggling with unexpected consequences of gas drilling in multiple states. The film won a prize for documentaries at this year's Sundance Film Festival.

The movie is not perfect (more on that in a moment), but the people it profiles are refreshingly real.

One homeowner clearly enjoys the thrill of igniting the water coming out of his tap: he holds a lighter to the faucet, there's a sudden "whump" of blue flame, and he jumps back, brushing his arm. He laughs and says, "I smell hair!"

A young rancher living in a smog of petrol fumes emanating from the wells around his home worries about the health of his cattle and the quality of the meat he's sending to American tables.

One burly old cowboy whose water went bad growls that the gas company's word isn't worth spit.

"Gasland" is an activist film, but its primary subjects aren't activists. They're real people.

And while it does not aspire to the objectivity of a National Geographic documentary, it also sidesteps the Michael Moore style. Largely absent are the guerrilla editing and snarky narration that have become the trademark of Moore's films. Instead, Fox showcases his subjects, lets their personalities — both good and bad — shine through, and he lets them explain their own problems.

Their insights and frustrations should give Pennsylvanians plenty to ponder.

That said, "Gasland" presents a carefully crafted point of view. Not everything in the film's narration is precisely accurate. Not all of its subjects are completely credible. Some major components of the story are missing.

At no point does Fox examine the voracious American appetite for energy that drives natural gas drilling, nor does he attempt to provoke in the viewer any sense of responsibility for what is shown.

Here, in the interest of full-disclosure, I should note that I grew up living over one of the largest natural gas storage fields in North America and only about 600 yards from one of Dominion Transmission's big compressor stations.

I know what an emergency blow-down feels like at 4 a.m.: One goes bolt upright from sound sleep because the roar sounds like a jet fighter is taking off from your front yard, windows rattling, apocalypse approaching, as all of the gas in the station suddenly blows into the sky to release pressure and prevent an explosion. But in my neck of the woods, the benefits of the industry generally outweigh the drawbacks. My mother retired as an engineer after 20 years of working at the station.

"Gasland" makes gas industry lobbyists apoplectic, and they have "debunked" the film on at least two websites. But these folk are no strangers to selective presentation themselves.

The industry issues a weekly Marcellus newsletter that rips quotes from news stories to make it appear as if outside Harrisburg there's nothing but a cheering section for Marcellus development.

The issue is complicated, and the truth is neither as benign as the lobbyists' vision, nor as apocalyptic as Fox's.

One of the greatest drawbacks of "Gasland" is the film implies that the problems people encounter with their water are the result of the fracking process.

Essentially, Marcellus drilling is a three-step procedure: gas companies drill a very deep hole, then they pump millions of gallons of water, sand and chemicals into the hole to shatter or "fracture" the shale which releases the gas, then they remove the gas over the course of years. Things can go wrong at every stage.

The mantra of the gas industry is there has never been a proven instance of well water contamination caused by the fracking process, which so far remains true.

Most of the problems documented in "Gasland" — including in Dimock — resulted from the drilling, not the fracking procedure. But that does not mean fracking fluids pose no threat to our water supplies. They contain some chemicals that are harmful even in very tiny amounts. The fluid that comes back up out of the ground is saturated with salts, is sometimes radioactive and often contains harmful heavy metals like arsenic.

Carl Kirby, a geologist at Bucknell who does not appear in the film, says the prospect of fracking fluids migrating up through thousands of feet of rock to contaminate water wells is "unlikely but not impossible."

The history of what's gone wrong thus far in Pennsylvania suggests accident and human error pose as much risk as the fracking process, an angle Fox does not explore.

Several weeks ago, a truck full of fracking brine overturned at an intersection about eight miles from my family home. The spill was contained by local volunteer firemen, county emergency responders and the drilling company, and it did not contaminate the small tributary of the Allegheny headwaters nearby, but …

The issue of water contamination is a serious one given the scale of Marcellus development projected for Pennsylvania.

Fox does an excellent job of reminding us how important and fragile this resource really is. And he tells a very good story.

The film's not perfect, but it's definitely worth watching.

Source: www. Pennlive.com/midstate/index.sst/2010/06/ gasland review documentary.

DOCUMENT 173: Barack Obama Recommends a National Policy for Stewardship of the Ocean, Our Coasts, and the Great Lakes (2010)

On June 12, 2009, President Barack Obama created an Inter-agency Ocean Policy Task Force and charged it with "developing recommendations to enhance our ability to maintain healthy, resilient, and sustainable ocean, coasts, and Great Lakes resources for the benefit of present and future generations." The task force, in addition to setting the first U.S. ocean stewardship policy, also recommended a strengthened governance structure to coordinate this policy, developed an implementation strategy, and created "a framework for effective coastal and marine spatial planning that establishes a comprehensive, integrated, ecosystem-based approach to address conservation, economic activity, use conflict, and sustainable use of ocean, coastal, and Great Lakes resources."

Befitting a president born in Hawaii, Obama protected more of the ocean than any other U.S. president. In expanding the Paphanaumokukea Marine National Monument, created by George W. Bush, he set aside the largest marine sanctuary, indeed the largest public park, anywhere in the world.

Many conservatives consider the task force's recommendations a stark example of federal government overreach, and the Trump administration would like to open up several protected areas to fishing and drilling.

The Deepwater Horizon–BP oil spill in the Gulf of Mexico and resulting environmental crisis is a stark reminder of how vulnerable our marine environments are, and how much communities and our Nation rely on healthy and resilient ocean and coastal ecosystems. The ocean, our coasts, and the Great Lakes impact the lives of all Americans, whether we live and work in the country's heartland or along its shores. America's rich and productive coastal regions and waters support tens of millions of jobs and contribute trillions of dollars to the national economy each year. They also host a growing number of important activities, including, recreation, science, commerce, transportation, energy development, and national security and they provide a wealth of natural resources and ecological benefits.

Nearly half of the country's population lives in coastal counties, and millions of visitors enjoy our Nation's seashores each year. The ocean, our coasts, and the Great Lakes are vital places for recreation, including boating, fishing, swimming, nature watching, and diving. These activities not only help fuel our economy, but also are critical to the social and cultural fabric of our country. In addition, coastal ecosystems provide essential ecological services. Barrier islands, coral reefs, mangroves, and coastal wetlands help to protect our coastal communities from damaging floods and storms. Coastal wetlands shelter recreational and commercial fish species, provide critical habitat for migratory birds and mammals, and serve as a natural filter to help keep our waters clean.

Despite the critical importance of these areas to our health and well-being, the ocean, coasts and Great Lakes face a wide range of threats from human activities. Overfishing, pollution, coastal development and the impacts of climate change are altering ecosystems, reducing biological diversity, and placing more stress on wildlife and natural resources, as well as on people and coastal communities. Compounding these threats, human uses of the ocean, coasts, and Great Lakes are expanding at a rate that challenges our ability to plan and manage significant and often competing demands. Demands for energy development, shipping, aquaculture, emerging security requirements and other new and existing uses are expected to grow. Overlapping uses and differing views about which activities should occur where can generate conflicts and misunderstandings. As we work to accommodate these multiple uses, we must also ensure continued public access for recreation and other pursuits, and sustain and preserve the abundant marine resources and healthy ecosystems that are critical to the well-being and prosperity of our Nation.

The challenges we face in the stewardship of the ocean, our coasts, and the Great Lakes lie not only within the ecosystems themselves, but also in the laws, authorities, and governance structures intended to manage our use and conservation of them. United States governance and management of these areas span hundreds of domestic policies, laws, and regulations covering international, Federal, State, tribal, and local interests. Challenges and gaps arise from the complexity and structure of this regime.

The time has come for a comprehensive national policy for the stewardship of the ocean, our coasts, and the Great Lakes. Today, as never before, we better comprehend the links among land, air, fresh water, ocean, ice, and human activities. Advances in science and technology provide better and timelier information to guide decision-making. By applying the principles of eco-system-based management (which integrates ecological, social, economic, commerce, health, and security goals, and which recognizes both that humans are key components of ecosystems and also that healthy ecosystems are essential to human welfare) and of adaptive management (which calls for routine reassessment of management actions to allow for better informed and improved future decisions) in a coordinated and collaborative approach, the Nation will more effectively address the challenges facing the ocean, our coasts, and the Great Lakes and ensure their continued health for this and future generations.

Source: "Final Recommendations of the Interagency Ocean Policy Task Force" (July 19, 2010)pp.1-2, 4. whitehouse.gov/files/OPTF/FinalRecs.

Document 174: The National Congress of American Indians and Bill McKibben et al. Oppose the Keystone XL Pipeline (2011)

The Keystone Pipeline System, the first three sections of which began operating in 2010, delivers Canadian crude oil to U.S. Midwest markets, to Cushing, Oklahoma, and to the Gulf Coast. Although near completion, Phase IV, the Keystone XL Pipeline, designed to carry oil from the tar sands of Alberta to Texas refineries, was opposed with protests by environmentalists, Nebraska landowners, and native rights activists, and a bill to approve its completion was vetoed by Barack Obama in 2016. Phase V, the Dakota Access Pipeline, ran into opposition in 2016. In one of his first actions as president, Donald Trump gave a go-ahead for the completion of both sections of the pipeline. Objection to the Keystone Pipeline stems from concerns that pipeline leaks could cause contamination of major drinking water sources. However, the transport of oil and gas by rail and sea probably pose a greater risk than pipeline transport..

Native American opposition was encouraged by an increasingly vocal movement of indigenous peoples to protect their lands and culture. The mobilization of protesters was coordinated by Bill McKibben, the author of The End of Nature, *and his climate change action organization 350.org. It started with a letter calling for civil disobedience that was signed by Maude Barlow, Wendell Berry, Tom Goldtooth, Danny Glover, James Hansen (see Document 137), Wes Jackson, Naomi Klein (see Document 176), McKibben, George Poitras, David Suzuki and Gus Speth and appeared in both* The Nation *and grist.org (an online environmental magazine). A similar letter calling for protests against the Dakota Access Pipeline appeared in 2016.*

350.org/1Sky.org,was founded in 2007 by McKibben and seven students at Middlebury College as a web platform to support collaborative campaigns aimed at bringing diverse organizations together in support of national and international action to deal with climate change.

A. National Congress of American Indians Resolution Opposing Keystone XL Pipeline

WHEREAS, we, the members of the National Congress of American Indians of the United States, invoking the divine blessing of the Creator upon our efforts and purposes, in order to preserve for ourselves and our descendants the inherent sovereign rights of our Indian nations, rights secured under Indian treaties and agreements with the United States, and all other rights and benefits to which we are entitled under the laws and Constitution of the United States, to enlighten the public toward a better understanding of the Indian people, to preserve Indian cultural values, and otherwise promote the health, safety and welfare of the Indian people, do hereby establish and submit the following resolution; and

WHEREAS, the National Congress of American Indians (NCAI) was established in 1944 and is the oldest and largest national organization of American Indian and Alaska Native tribal governments; and

WHEREAS, a major oil transmission pipeline is planned to extend from northern Alberta, Canada, from areas that have sand mixed with tar and oil, called "tar sands," to refineries in the United States; and

WHEREAS, the route of the pipeline, called Keystone XL because it is the second oil transmission pipeline to be constructed by the same company that built the first Keystone pipeline, crosses through Indian country in northern Alberta, Saskatchewan, Montana, North Dakota, South Dakota and Nebraska, near and potentially over, many culturally significant areas for Tribal Nations within those provinces and states; and

WHEREAS, based on the relatively poor environmental record of the first Keystone pipeline, which includes numerous spills, U.S. regulators shut the pipeline down in late May, 2011, and, therefore, based on the record of the first Keystone pipeline, and other factors, it is probable that further environmental disasters will occur in Indian country if the new pipeline is allowed to be constructed; and

WHEREAS, the First Nations of Canada, representing the vast majority of First Nations impacted by "tar sands" development, have unanimously passed resolutions supporting a moratorium on new "tar sands" development and expansion until a "cumulative effects management system" is in place, and are also in opposition to the pipeline; and

WHEREAS, many U.S. Tribal Nations are also in opposition to the Keystone XL pipeline because it would threaten, among other things, water aquifers, water ways, cultural sites, agricultural lands, animal life, public drinking water sources and other resources vital to the peoples of the region in which the pipeline is proposed to be constructed; and

WHEREAS, Indian tribes including the Affiliated Tribes of Northwest Indians are also in opposition to the Exxon-Imperial "Heavy Haul" proposal to transport "tar sands" equipment through the Nez Perce Reservation and across scenic highways, and several Indian tribes have joined in litigation to stop this proposal; and

WHEREAS, the pipeline is unnecessary as a number of other pipelines are not at full capacity to carry oil from Canada to refineries in the U.S., and the oil is also not likely to end up on the U.S. market but will be exported to foreign countries; and

WHEREAS, Tribal Nations and First Nations within Indian country near the route of the proposed pipeline have already stated their opposition to the proposed route of the pipeline, and because of earlier opposition from both Tribes and environmental groups, a supplemental environmental impact statement has been required by the United States Environmental Protection Agency from the proposed operators of the pipeline, a draft of which is now available for public comment; and

WHEREAS, since the pipeline is designed to cross the U.S.-Canadian border, the United States Department of State is the lead U.S. agency in evaluating whether the pipeline should be allowed to be constructed in the U.S.; and

WHEREAS, the First Nations of Canada and Tribal Nations within the U.S. have a long history of working to ensure protection of their environment, and the Keystone XL pipeline poses grave dangers if it is constructed.

NOW THEREFORE BE IT RESOLVED, that the NCAI does hereby oppose the Keystone XL pipeline and the Exxon-Imperial Heavy Haul proposal and their negative impacts on cultural sites and the environment in those portions of Indian country over and through which it is proposed to be constructed, and agrees to file comments regarding this opposition to the Keystone XL pipeline with the Secretary of State as soon as possible; and

BE IT FURTHER RESOLVED, that the NCAI hereby urges all affected Tribal Nations to submit comments to the U.S. Department of State regarding the Keystone XL project; and

BE IT FURTHER RESOLVED, that the NCAI hereby expresses its solidarity with Canadian First Nations in their efforts to protect their communities, aboriginal land and treaty rights, and their request for a moratorium and better management practices on expanded "tar sands" development and opposition to the Keystone XL pipeline; and

BE IT FURTHER RESOLVED, that the United States is urged to reduce its reliance on the world's dirtiest and most environmentally destructive form of oil – the "tar sands" – that threatens Indian country in both Canada and the United States and the way of life of thousands of citizens of First Nations in Canada and American Indians in the U.S., and requests the U.S. government to take aggressive measures to work towards sustainable energy solutions that include clean alternative energy and improving energy efficiency; and

BE IT FINALLY RESOLVED, that this resolution shall be the policy of NCAI until it is withdrawn or modified by subsequent resolution.

B. Letter Calling for Civil Disobedience Against Keystone XL

Dear Friends,

This will be a slightly longer letter than common for the internet age—it's serious stuff.

The short version is we want you to consider doing something hard: coming to Washington in the hottest and stickiest weeks of the summer and engaging in civil disobedience that will likely get you arrested.

The full version goes like this:

As you know, the planet is steadily warming: 2010 was the warmest year on record, and we've seen the resulting chaos in almost every corner of the earth.

And as you also know, our democracy is increasingly controlled by special interests interested only in their short-term profit.

These two trends collide this summer in Washington, where the State Department and the White House have to decide whether to grant a certificate of 'national interest' to some of the biggest fossil fuel players on earth. These corporations want to build the so-called 'Keystone XL Pipeline' from Canada's tar sands to Texas refineries.

To call this project a horror is serious understatement. The tar sands have wrecked huge parts of Alberta, disrupting ways of life in indigenous communities—First Nations communities in Canada, and tribes along the pipeline route in the U.S. have demanded the destruction cease. The pipeline crosses crucial areas like the Oglalla Aquifer where a spill would be disastrous—and though the pipeline companies insist they are using 'state of the art' technologies that should leak only once every 7 years, the precursor pipeline and its pumping stations have leaked a dozen times in the past year. These local impacts alone would be cause enough to block such a plan. But the Keystone Pipeline would also be a fifteen hundred mile fuse to the biggest carbon bomb on the continent, a way to make it easier and faster to trigger the final overheating of our planet, the one place to which we are all indigenous.

How much carbon lies in the recoverable tar sands of Alberta? A recent calculation from some of our foremost scientists puts the figure at about 200 parts per million. Even with the new pipeline they won't be able to burn that much overnight—but each development like this makes it easier to get more oil out. As the climatologist Jim Hansen (one of the signatories to this letter) explained, if we have any chance of getting back to a stable climate "the principal requirement is that coal emissions must be phased out by 2030 and unconventional fossil fuels, such as tar sands, must be left in the ground." In other words, he added, "if the tar sands are thrown into the mix it is essentially game over." The Keystone pipeline is an essential part of the game. "Unless we get increased market access, like with Keystone XL, we're going to be stuck," said Ralph Glass, an economist and vice-president at AJM Petroleum Consultants in Calgary, told a Canadian newspaper last week.

Given all that, you'd suspect that there's no way the Obama administration would ever permit this pipeline. But in the last few months the president has signed pieces of paper opening much of Alaska to oil drilling, and permitting coal-mining on federal land in Wyoming that will produce as much CO2 as 300 power plants operating at full bore.

And Secretary of State [Hillary] Clinton has already said she's 'inclined' to recommend the pipeline go forward. Partly it's because of the political commotion over high gas prices, though more tar sands oil would do nothing to change that picture. But it's also because of intense pressure from industry. TransCanada Pipeline, the company behind Keystone, has hired as its chief lobbyist for the project a man named Paul Elliott, who served as deputy national director of Clinton's presidential campaign. Meanwhile, the US Chamber of Commerce—a bigger funder of political campaigns than the RNC and DNC combined—has demanded that the administration "move quickly to approve the Keystone XL pipeline," which is not so surprising—they've also told the U.S. EPA that if the planet warms that will be okay because humans can 'adapt their physiology' to cope. The Koch Brothers, needless to say, are also backing the plan, and may reap huge profits from it.

So we're pretty sure that without serious pressure the Keystone Pipeline will get its permit from Washington. A wonderful coalition of environmental groups has built a strong campaign across the continent—from Cree and Dene indigenous leaders to Nebraska farmers, they've spoken out strongly against the destruction of their land. We need to join them, and to say even if our own homes won't be crossed by this pipeline, our joint home—the earth—will be wrecked by the carbon that pours down it.

And we need to say something else, too: it's time to stop letting corporate power make the most important decisions our planet faces.

We don't have the money to compete with those corporations, but we do have our bodies, and beginning in mid August many of us will use them. We will, each day through Labor Day, march on the White House, risking arrest with our trespass. We will do it in dignified fashion, demonstrating that in this case we are the conservatives, and that our foes—who would change the composition of the atmosphere are dangerous radicals. Come dressed as if for a business meeting—this is, in fact, serious business. . . .

And one more thing: we don't want college kids to be the only cannon fodder in this fight. They've led the way so far on climate change. . . . Now it's time for people who've spent their lives pouring carbon into the atmosphere (and whose careers won't be as damaged by an arrest record) to step up too. Most of us signing this letter are veterans of this work, and we think it's past time for elders to behave like elders. One thing we don't want is a smash up: if you can't control your passions, this action is not for you.

This won't be a one-shot day of action. We plan for it to continue for several weeks, to the date in September when by law the administration can either grant or deny the permit for the pipeline. . . .

Winning this battle won't save the climate. But losing it will mean the chances of runaway climate change go way up—that we'll endure an endless future of the floods and droughts we've seen this year. And we're fighting for the political future too—for the premise that we should make decisions based on science and reason, not political connection. You have to start somewhere, and this is where we choose to begin.

If you think you might want to be a part of this action, we need you to sign up here. As plans solidify in the next few weeks we'll be in touch with you to arrange nonviolence training; our colleagues at a variety of environmental and democracy campaigns will be coordinating the actual arrangements.

We know we're asking a lot. You should think long and hard on it, and pray if you're the praying type. But to us, it's as much privilege as burden to get to join this fight in the most serious possible way. We hope you'll join us.

p.s.—Please pass this letter on to anyone else you think might be interested. We realize that what we're asking isn't easy, and we're very grateful that you're willing even to consider it.

Source: A. The National Congress of American Indians Resolution #MKE-11-030 (Opposition to Construction of the Keystone XL Pipeline and Urging the U.S. to Reduce Reliance on Oil from Tar Sands and Instead, to Work towards Cleaner, Sustainable Energy Solutions) adopted by the General Assembly at the 2011 Mid-Year Session of the National Congress of American Indians, held at the Frontier Airlines Center in Milwaukee, WI on June 13-16, 2011. B. https://www.thenation.com/article/bill-mckibben-naomi-klein-call-civil-disobedience-tar-sands/ June 22, 2011.

Document 175: Daniel Yergin on Global Energy Demand (2013)

Daniel Yergin, the author of The Quest: Energy, Security, and the Remaking of the Modern World, *and one of the most influential experts on energy in the world, predicts tremendous growth in the demand for energy during coming decades. To meet these needs and to prevent environmental degradation, innovation and energy efficiency will be required. Because the lead time for developing and bringing new energy resources on line can be ten or more years, if the United States lags in the development of non-fossil-fuel energy sources, the gap will quickly be filled elsewhere, perhaps in China.*

The harnessing of energy is what makes possible the world as we know it. The bounty can be measured in terms of virtually everything we do in the course of a day. But can we bet on that for the future?

The growth in world energy demand in the coming decades will be very large, an increase of as much as 35 to 40 percent by 2030. Can this need be met? This increase alone will be greater than all the energy that the world consumed in 1970. Underpinning it all is a fundamental shift in global energy demand, which reflects big changes in the world economy.

At the start of the 21st century, "developed" countries still represented two-thirds of total oil demand. By the end of the decade the split was 50-50 and the shift continues to this day. In terms of oil, North America, Europe and Japan have already reached peak demand. Because of demographics, increased efficiency and substitution, their petroleum consumption will be flat or declining.

The story will be entirely different in emerging markets owing to what I call the "globalization of demand." China already consumes more total energy than the United States. The same will be true of oil perhaps by the end of the decade, as China becomes more motorized. This year, 20 million new cars will be sold in China, compared to about 15 million in the United States. Some think that number could grow to 30 million.

Even with much greater energy efficiency, rising incomes and standards of living will mean much greater requirement for energy. What kind of energy mix would make this possible without crisis and confrontation? The answers to these questions will be critical to the future.

Innovation will be critical. Fortunately, innovation is a constant feature of the energy system. Solar and wind, which have become so prominent, really had their origins as innovations in the 1970s and 1980s.

The biggest innovation so far in the 21st century is shale gas and the development of "tight oil" that has come with it. This has now reached such a scale that it can be called the "unconventional revolution in oil and natural gas."

Half a decade ago, the United States was expected to be a major importer of natural gas. Now it is so well-supplied that it will export natural gas. U.S. oil production is up almost 45 percent since 2008, and in fact the fastest-growing source of new oil development in the entire world is the United States. This is not what was even imagined a few years ago.

This revolution is having a major economic impact. It currently supports 1.7 million jobs—a number that could go to 3 million or more by the end of the decade. It is happening so fast that thinking still has to catch up. A key question for the future is when this revolution will spread beyond North America. One thing that is clear is that natural gas will assume a bigger role in the world's overall energy mix.

The interaction of environmental concerns with energy will continue to shape the energy marketplace. The biggest question is climate change and carbon. Over 80 percent of world energy is supplied by carbon-based fuels—oil, natural gas and coal. About 75 to 80 percent of world energy is generally expected to be carbon based two decades from now.

Yet the growing importance of the climate change question ensures that this ratio will be strongly challenged both politically and technologically as people strive to decarbonize.

A move away from carbon-based fuels has already begun, but we are in the early stage of a transition—or at least a remixing of the energy mix. Wind and solar are growing rapidly, but they are still a very small part of the overall energy mix.

The two biggest sources of carbon-free electricity today are nuclear and hydropower. Nuclear is growing in some parts of the world, but in others it is stymied. While China is building up its nuclear electricity very fast, Germany intends to shut down all of its nuclear by 2022.

The pace of technological advance is not the only factor affecting the speed of any transition. Another factor is the law of long lead times.

The energy system is large and complex, with an enormous amount of embedded capital. It does not turn over with anything like the speed of mobile phones. A power plant may have a 60-year life span or even more. A major new oil field may require a decade or more between exploration and first production.

By the early 2030s, the world will be using a good deal more energy. But the reason that the mix will not be too different is [the] rapid growth of demand in developing countries, where coal has such a big role.

The law of long lead times still remains. It is really after 2030 that the energy system could start to look quite different as the cumulative effect of innovation and technological advance makes its full impact felt.

Energy efficiency remains a top priority for a growing world economy. Remarkable results have already been achieved, but technologies and tools not available in earlier decades are now at hand.

The real advances will be embodied in behavior and value, but especially in investment—new processes, new factories, new buildings, new vehicles. There are many obstacles, ranging from financing to the fact that efficiency usually comes without the opportunity for good "photo ops." There is "no ribbon to cut."

The challenges of meeting rising energy needs in the decades ahead, of assuring that the resources are available on a sustainable basis to support a growing world, may seem daunting; and, indeed, when one considers the scale, they truly are.

Meeting them requires, among other things, the responsible and efficient use of energy, sound judgment, consistent investment, statesmanship, collaboration, long-term thinking and the thoughtful integration of environmental considerations into energy strategies.

But what provides for reasoned confidence is the increasing availability of what may be the most important resource of all—human creativity. A famous geologist once said, "Oil is found in the minds of men."

We can amend that to say that the energy solutions for the 21st century will be found in the minds of people around the world. And that resource base is growing.

Source: https://danietlyergin.com/inside-the-mind-of-global-energy-demand/cnbc 06.03.2013.

Document 176: Naomi Klein on Capitalism versus the Climate (2014)

The Canadian writer, documentary-maker, and social and environmental activist Naomi Klein is a member of the board of 350.org, and she was one of the organizers of the protest against the Keystone XL Pipeline [see Document 174B]. She contends that civilization is in danger of collapse unless immediate action is taken to drastically decrease fossil fuel use, but posits that corporate globalism and free-market capitalism stand in the way of meaningful action.

When historians look back on the past quarter century of international negotiations, two defining processes will stand out. There will be the climate process: struggling, sputtering, failing utterly to achieve its goals. And there will be the corporate globalization process, zooming from victory to victory: from the first free trade deal to the creation of the World Trade Organization to the mass privatization of the former Soviet economies to the transformation of large parts of Asia into sprawling free-trade zones to the "structural adjusting" of Africa. There were setbacks to that process, to be sure—for example, popular pushback that stalled trade rounds and free trade deals. But what remained successful were the ideological underpinnings of the entire project, which was never really about trading goods across borders—selling French wine in Brazil, for instance, or U.S. software in China. It was always about using these sweeping deals, as well as a range of other tools, to lock in a global policy framework that provided maximum freedom to multinational corporations to produce their goods as cheaply as possible and sell them with as few regulations as possible—while paying as little in taxes as possible. Granting this corporate wishlist, we were told, would fuel economic growth, which would trickle down to the rest of us, eventually. The trade deals mattered only in so far as they stood in for, and plainly articulated, this far broader agenda.

The three policy pillars of this new era are familiar to us all: privatization of the public sphere, deregulation of the corporate sector, and lower corporate taxation, paid for with cuts to public spending. Much has been written about the real-world costs of these policies—the instability of financial markets, the excesses of the super-rich, and the desperation of the increasingly disposable poor, as well as the failing state of public infrastructure and services. Very little, however, has been written about how market fundamentalism has, from the very first moments, systematically sabotaged our collective response to climate change, a threat that came knocking just as this ideology was reaching its zenith.

The core problem was that the stranglehold that market logic secured over public life in this period made the most direct and obvious climate responses seem politically heretical. How, for instance, could societies invest massively in zero-carbon public services and infrastructure at a time when the public sphere was being systematically dismantled and auctioned off? How could governments heavily regulate, tax, and penalize fossil fuel companies when all such measures were being dismissed as relics of "command and control" communism? And how could the renewable energy sector receive the supports and protections it needed to replace fossil fuels when "protectionism" had been made a dirty word?

A different kind of climate movement would have tried to challenge the extreme ideology that was blocking so much sensible action, joining the other sectors to show how unfettered corporate power posed a grave threat to the habitability of the planet. Instead, large parts of the climate movement wasted precious decades attempting to make the square peg of the climate crisis fit into the round hole of deregulated capitalism, forever touting ways for the problem to be solved by the market itself. (Though it was only years into this project that I discovered the depths of collusion between big polluters and Big Green.)

But blocking strong climate action wasn't the only way that the triumph of market fundamentalism acted to deepen the crisis in this period. Even more directly, the policies that so successfully freed multinational corporations from virtually all constraints also contributed significantly to the underlying cause of global warming—rising greenhouse gas emissions. The numbers are striking: in the 1990s, as the market integration project ramped up, global emissions were going up an average of 1 percent a year; by the 2000s, with "emerging markets" like China now fully integrated into the world economy, emissions growth had sped up disastrously, with the annual rate of increase reaching 3.4 percent a year for much of the decade. That rapid growth rate continues to this day, interrupted only briefly in 2009 by the world financial crisis.

With hindsight, it's hard to see how it could have turned out otherwise. The twin signatures of this era have been the mass export of products across vast distances (relentlessly burning carbon all the way) and the import of a uniquely wasteful model of production, consumption, and agriculture to every corner of the world (also based on the profligate burning of fossil fuels). Put differently, the liberation of world markets, a process powered by the liberation of unprecedented amounts of fossil fuels from the earth, has dramatically sped up the same process that is liberating Arctic ice from existence.

As a result, we now find ourselves in a very difficult and slightly ironic position. Because of those decades of hardcore emitting exactly when we were supposed to be cutting back, the things we must do to avoid catastrophic warming are no longer just in conflict with the particular strain of deregulated capitalism that triumphed in the 1980s. They are now in conflict with the fundamental imperative at the heart of our economic model: grow or die.

Once carbon has been emitted into the atmosphere, it sticks around for hundreds of years, some of it even longer, trapping heat. The effects are cumulative, growing more severe with time. And according to emissions specialists like the Tyndall Centre's Kevin Anderson (as well as others), so much carbon has been allowed to accumulate in the atmosphere over the past two decades that now our only hope of keeping warming below the internationally agreed-upon target of 2 degrees Celsius is for wealthy countries to cut their emissions by somewhere in the neighborhood of 8-10 percent a year. The "free" market simply cannot accomplish this task. Indeed, this level of emission reduction has happened only in the context of economic collapse or deep depressions.

. . . [O]ur economic system and our planetary system are now at war. Or, more accurately, our economy is at war with many forms of life on earth, including human life. What the climate needs to avoid collapse is a contraction in humanity's use of resources; what our economic model demands to avoid collapse is unfettered expansion. Only one of these sets of rules can be changed, and it's not the laws of nature.

Fortunately, it is eminently possible to transform our economy so that it is less resource-intensive, and to do it in ways that are equitable, with the most vulnerable protected and the most responsible bearing the bulk of the burden. Low-carbon sectors of our economies can be encouraged to expand and create jobs, while high-carbon sectors are encouraged to contract. The problem, however, is that this scale of economic planning and management is entirely outside the boundaries of our reigning ideology. The only kind of contraction our current system can manage is a brutal crash, in which the most vulnerable will suffer most of all.

So we are left with a stark choice: allow climate disruption to change everything about our world, or change pretty much everything about our economy to avoid that fate. But we need to be very clear: because of our decades of collective denial, no gradual, incremental options are now available to us. Gentle tweaks to the status quo stopped being a climate option when we supersized the American Dream in the 1990s, and then proceeded to take it global.

Source: Naomi Klein, *This Changes Everything: Capitalism vs. the Climate* (New York: Simon & Schuster, 2014), pp. 19-21.

Document 177: Gil Gullickson on Agriculture and Climate Change (2014)

While farmers are concerned about rainfall, drought, and heatwaves and have begun to adopt new, environmentally friendly farming techniques such as no-till agriculture to conserve soil and water, many are politically very conservative. Consequently, the magazine Successful Farming, *read by more than a million farmers and ranchers, avoided using the divisive term "climate change" until 2014, when the magazine's crop technology editor," Gil Gullickson decided it was time come to terms with reality. This article produced a good bit of negative feedback from readers caught up in the dialectics of contentious politics.*

Climate change isn't a liberal conspiracy, it's a reality

I know what you're thinking: Climate change is just some figment of Al Gore's imagination adopted by liberal tree huggers who want to tank the U.S. economy.

Well, maybe. After all, 2014 weather was a growing season dream in many areas. Still, think back over some rough weather you've endured in recent years and ask yourself these questions:

• **Are springs getting wetter?** They sure are in the Corn Belt. Jerry Hatfield, director of the USDA-ARS National Laboratory for Agriculture and the Environment at Ames, Iowa, examined central Iowa spring precipitation over two time frames. Workable field days in April through mid-May decreased 3.5 days in 1995 to 2010, compared to the same time frame from 1979 to 1994.

"Fewer workable field days puts tremendous stress on producers," he says.

• **Are droughts increasing in severity?** They sure are in the southern Great Plains and U.S. Southwest. For example, Oklahoma historically receives more precipitation in the spring and fall. More arid conditions normally prevail in winter and summer. This pattern helps germinate winter wheat in the fall and launch it after it breaks dormancy in early spring.

No more. "We are losing some reliability of our early-season precipitation that drives wheat-based cropping," says Jean Steiner, director of the USDA-ARS Grazinglands Research Laboratory in El Reno, Oklahoma. Late-season freezes have also decimated drought-stressed plants in recent years. "Whether you think this is climate change or just bad weather, you still have to adapt to it," says Clay Pope, a Loyal, Oklahoma, farmer. "Some producers don't believe in climate change, but they do believe in drought," he says.

• **Are rainstorms increasing in intensity?** Yes, particularly in the central United States. From 1900 to 1960 in Des Moines, Iowa, just two years had more than eight days when more than 1.25 inches of rain fell. From 1960 through 2013, seven years had more than eight days hitting the 1.25-inch threshold. More spring rainfall and rainfall intensity fuel other maladies.

"Soils become more anaerobic, so seedling diseases become more prevalent," Hatfield says. "You also get more soil erosion with all the run-off from the field."

When droughts end, they're ending with a bang. "Southern Blaine County (in northwestern Oklahoma) received more than 12 inches of rain in 32 days this year," says Jeanne Schneider, a research meteorologist who heads USDA's Southern Plains Regional Climate Hub in El Reno, Oklahoma. "This is more than one-third of the average annual total that fell in a month."

WHAT'S GOING ON?

Droughts and floods have occurred since man shifted from hunting and gathering to farming over 12,000 years ago. "It's not that we are seeing things that have not happened before," says Schneider. "It's just that they are happening more often. This increased variability is the new normal."

Fueled by more than 10,000 peer-reviewed studies, 97% of climate scientists concur that man-made climate change is occurring. This is backed by a final draft of the United Nations' Intergovernmental Panel on Climate Change released earlier this summer. It states continued emission of greenhouse gases like carbon dioxide will cause further warming and changes in all climate-system components.

Mention that to many farmers and farm groups, though, and shaking heads and rolling eyes result. Reality dictates otherwise. "In our area, I just think climate change is one of the most important factors impacting agriculture," says Don Halcomb, who farms near Adairville, Kentucky, with wife Meredith, son John and his wife Sarah, and son Sam and his wife, Stephanie.

He says efforts like the campaigns that killed cap-and-trade legislation several years ago cost agriculture. Under this legislation, farmers would have been paid for sequestering carbon through methods like no-till. This is one way to reduce gases like carbon dioxide that fuel greenhouse gases.

"The cap-and-trade opponents complain it will cost us in the short run," he says. "In 2011, when drought impacted Texas, it caused a $5 billion loss in agricultural production in Texas alone. Cargill had to close a slaughter plant (in 2013) due to lack of cattle. There is a cost to addressing climate change, but not addressing it also has a cost."

RISKY BUSINESS

Meanwhile, the executives who run agricultural companies are taking climate change seriously.

Last fall, Greg Page, Cargill's executive chairman, joined former New York City mayor Michael Bloomberg, former U.S. Treasury Secretary Hank Paulson, and former senior managing member of Farallon Capital Management Tom Steyer to issue a report called *Risky Business: Our Nation's Economy at Risk Due to Climate Change.*

The report found that without adaptation, yield dips of more than 10% might occur in some Midwestern and Southern counties over the next five to 25 years.

"Several years ago, we commissioned a group of our scientists to look at climate change, to develop models, and to talk to other scientists about what we needed to do for the future," says Robb Fraley, Monsanto's executive vice president and chief technology officer.

"They found even small 1°F. to 2°F. changes on a microclimate level can prompt an insect to hatch or a disease to infest a field," he says.

"So, we put more effort into breeding for disease and breeding for insect traits," says Fraley.

"We also are looking at soil microbes to alleviate plant stress, weather-related nutritional problems, and new ways to protect seeds from fungal diseases and insects. We want farmers to have the tools to mitigate changes in weather and environment."

Source: Gil Gullickson, "@#$*% Weather! No, it's @#$*% climate change!" *Successful Farming*, Oct. 2014, pp. 35-36.

Document 178: John R. Gillis on the Sand Crisis (2014)

The world is running out of the beach-quality sand we need to build our cities. An essential ingredient in concrete, glass, and silicon, this sand is almost as crucial for modern life as clean water and plentiful energy. In parts of Asia and Africa widespread illegal sand-mining supplies a huge black market.

John Gillis, the author of The Human Shore: Seacoasts in History, *notes that some of this precious beach-quality sand is being used to restore our shorelines—an oft-times questionable and wasteful use of a precious commodity.*

To those of us who visit beaches only in summer, they seem as permanent a part of our natural heritage as the Rocky Mountains and the Great Lakes. But shore dwellers know differently. Beaches are the most transitory of landscapes, and sand beaches the most vulnerable of all. During big storms, especially in winter, they can simply vanish, only to magically reappear in time for the summer season.

It could once be said that "a beach is a place where sand stops to rest for a moment before resuming its journey to somewhere else," as the naturalist D. W. Bennett wrote in the book "Living With the New Jersey Shore." Sand moved along the shore and from beach to sea bottom and back again, forming shorelines and barrier islands that until recently were able to repair themselves on a regular basis, producing the illusion of permanence.

Today, however, 75 to 90 percent of the world's natural sand beaches are disappearing, due partly to rising sea levels and increased storm action, but also to massive erosion caused by the human development of shores. Many low-lying barrier islands are already submerged.

Yet the extent of this global crisis is obscured because so-called beach nourishment projects attempt to hold sand in place and repair the damage by the time summer people return, creating the illusion of an eternal shore.

Before next summer, endless lines of dump trucks will have filled in bare spots and restored dunes. Virginia Beach alone has been restored more than 50 times. In recent decades, East Coast barrier islands have used 23 million loads of sand, much of it mined inland and the rest dredged from coastal waters — a practice that disturbs the sea bottom, creating turbidity that kills coral beds and damages spawning grounds, which hurts inshore fisheries.

The sand and gravel business is now growing faster than the economy as a whole. In the United States, the market for mined sand has become a billion-dollar annual business, growing at 10 percent a year since 2008. Interior mining operations use huge machines working in open pits to dig down under the earth's surface to get sand left behind by ancient glaciers. But as demand has risen — and the damming of rivers has held back the flow of sand from mountainous interiors — natural sources of sand have been shrinking.

One might think that desert sand would be a ready substitute, but its grains are finer and smoother; they don't adhere to rougher sand grains, and tend to blow away. As a result, the desert state of Dubai brings sand for its beaches all the way from Australia.

And now there is a global beach-quality sand shortage, caused by the industries that have come to rely on it. Sand is vital to the manufacturing of abrasives, glass, plastics, microchips and even toothpaste, and, most recently, to the process of hydraulic fracturing. The quality of silicate sand found in the northern Midwest has produced what is being called a "sand rush" there, more than doubling regional sand pit mining since 2009.

But the greatest industrial consumer of all is the concrete industry. Sand from Port Washington on Long Island — 140 million cubic yards of it — built the tunnels and sidewalks of Manhattan from the 1880s onward. Concrete still takes 80 percent of all that mining can deliver. Apart from water and air, sand is the natural element most in demand around the world, a situation that puts the preservation of beaches and their flora and fauna in great danger. Today, a branch of Cemex, one of the world's largest cement suppliers, is still busy on the shores of Monterey Bay in California, where its operations endanger several protected species.

The huge sand mining operations emerging worldwide, many of them illegal, are happening out of sight and out of mind, as far as the developed world is concerned. But in India, where the government has stepped in to limit sand mining along its shores, illegal mining operations by what is now referred to as the "sand mafia" defy these regulations. In Sierra Leone, poor villagers are encouraged to sell off their sand to illegal operations, ruining their own shores for fishing. Some Indonesian sand islands have been devastated by sand mining.

It is time for us to understand where sand comes from and where it is going. Sand was once locked up in mountains and it took eons of erosion before it was released into rivers and made its way to the sea. As Rachel Carson wrote in 1958, "in every curving beach, in every grain of sand, there is a story of the earth." Now those grains are sequestered yet again — often in the very concrete sea walls that contribute to beach erosion.

We need to stop taking sand for granted and think of it as an endangered natural resource. Glass and concrete can be recycled back into sand, but there will never be enough to meet the demand of every resort. So we need better conservation plans for shore and coastal areas. Beach replenishment — the mining and trucking and dredging of sand to meet tourist expectations — must be evaluated on a case-by-case basis, with environmental considerations taking top priority. Only this will ensure that the story of the earth will still have subsequent chapters told in grains of sand.

Source: www.nytimes/2014/11/05/opinion/why-sand-is-disappearing.

Document 179: Ben Minteer on Extinct Species and De-extinction

In the future it may be possible to re-engineer extinct species and let them loose in the wild. Conservationists and preservationists, however, make the case that not only does the extinction of a species affect the ecosystem within which it once lived, so that it can never really be reintroduced into its former habitat, but also that such technological intervention interferes with human respect for nature. Emerging technologies will have enormous impact on how humans interact with nature, and we need to be cautious before unleashing some of these technologies, especially biotechnologies.

Ben Minteer, an environmental ethicist at Arizona State University, focuses on the relationships between humans, other species, and wildlands in a rapidly changing world.

For a species that's been dead for a century, the passenger pigeon is having a pretty good year. A flurry of new books, features, and a major documentary has been roughly timed to commemorate the death of "Martha," the last surviving member of the species that drew her final breath in the Cincinnati Zoo on Sept. 1, 1914. It's a kind of national elegy for a bird that no one alive today remembers ever seeing, certainly not in the wild, where it was last spotted around the time shovels first broke ground on the New York subway system.

The bird was a cheap and easily procured source of meat in the 18th and 19th centuries due to its astonishing abundance (once numbering in the billions) and its unfortunate tendency to travel in massive flocks. Its fate was sealed by the 1850s with the expansion of the railroad and telegraph, which fueled an insatiable commercial appetite and profitable pigeon market by providing easy transport and rapid communication about the location of flocks. There were precious few attempts to save the species in that pre–Endangered Species Act era, and none that made a difference.

Less than 20 years following Martha's quiet demise in Cincinnati, the sole surviving heath hen (a close relative of the Greater Prairie-chicken) made its last appearance in southeastern Massachusetts. Nicknamed "Booming Ben" for the bird's distinctive vocalizations during its extravagant mating ritual, he was a relic of a population that was once common from New England to northern Virginia. Like the passenger pigeon, the heath hen was a plentiful and convenient source of protein (a "poor man's turkey") in the 18th and early 19th centuries. By the 1870s, however, the species had been hunted completely off the mainland. Only a few decades later there were fewer than 100 left, all of them hunkered down in a single flock residing in Martha's Vineyard. Not a bad place to convalesce, unless you're a small, genetically isolated, nonmigratory bird population.

Unlike the passenger pigeon, the heath hen had a few efforts to save it, including banning hunting and creating a sanctuary in the Vineyard in the early 1900s. But the die had been cast. Like Martha before him, Booming Ben—and the heath hen along with him—vanished into the evolutionary ether, most likely sometime in the spring of 1932.

Although the public was slow to rally to the conservation cause in the early 20th century, not everyone greeted these losses with resignation. One of the strongest voices agitating for wildlife protection during these years was William T. Hornaday, the rabble-rousing wildlife crusader and founding director of the Bronx Zoo. Hornaday challenged the complacency of an American public unwilling to acknowledge the destructive game it was playing with its wild animals. In his conservationist manifesto, *Our Vanishing Wildlife* (1913), he tried to convey a sense of the biological stakes when a species was pushed to the brink of extinction.

"Let no one think for a moment," he warned, "that any vanishing species can at any time be brought back; for that would be a grave error. . . . The heath hen could not be brought back, neither could the passenger pigeon."

What a difference a century makes.

It's doubtful that even in his wildest dreams Hornaday would've envisioned that someday scientists and their allies would seriously be contemplating bringing long-extinct species—including the passenger pigeon and the heath hen—back from the dead.

Called "de-extinction," the proposal taps into a range of established and still emerging techniques in cloning and genetic engineering, including the ability to rapidly sequence ancient DNA from preserved tissues of extinct animals to allow scientists to create approximations of lost species by "editing" the genomes of closely related (living) species. So, for example, the genome of a contemporary band-tailed pigeon could be altered to more closely resemble that of a passenger pigeon, and a population of the new birds could theoretically be bred and released into the wild.

The techno-environmentalist Stewart Brand is one of the driving forces behind the idea, which over the past 18 months has drawn considerable media attention and scrutiny. Brand's Long Now Foundation is supporting scientific efforts to re-create the passenger pigeon—and exploring possibilities for the heath hen—within its "Revive & Restore" project, which has its sights on a range of candidates for resurrection, from the Tasmanian tiger to the woolly mammoth.

The de-extinction proposal has been met with no shortage of criticism, ranging from concerns about the misallocation of limited conservation dollars to a "vanity project," to worries that the newly engineered species will wreak havoc when released into the environment, especially since we may no longer have the space to accommodate them. Fears have been raised that de-extinction will also lead to the relaxation of public commitment to conservation and to averting future species extinctions.

But Brand argues that de-extinction offers something vital to conservationists today: an alternative narrative unburdened by the hand-wringing over extinction and ecological loss. . . . I respect Brand's long and impressive career as a tech-friendly enviro-maverick, but I think he's wrong about this. De-extinction isn't really a conservation strategy, and it doesn't reflect a sound conservation ethic. In fact, I believe pursuing it will seriously undercut an important source of the value we attach to wild species. Even worse, it could undermine the moral lessons of extinction at a critical time in our environmental history.

Although a revived passenger pigeon, heath hen, or mammoth (setting aside the question of whether an engineered genome does an extinct species make) may have aesthetic, scientific, and even economic value to society, it obviously won't share the natural history of the lost species. The evolutionary toil and historical richness of the forerunner species, including their co-evolution with other species over time, has been lost, replaced by a tale of technological manipulations in a 21st-century genetics lab.

In other words, the backstory is wrong, at least from a conservation perspective. A living species' natural history is only one reason why we value them, but it's a profoundly important one to conservationists (or at least it should be). In part, this is because our understanding of an unengineered species' natural history encourages the adoption of an attitude of humility toward them. As the conservationist-philosopher Aldo Leopold reminds us, "Men are only fellow-voyagers with other creatures in the odyssey of evolution."

. . .

An even deeper cause for concern about species revival, though, is the well-meaning but still misguided attempt to erase the moral narrative of extinction. As Brand puts it in his **defense of the resurrection of the passenger pigeon**, "How fine it would be to reverse the founding human mistake that inspired modern conservation."

If only it were that easy.

But we can't reverse the "founding human mistake" by simply bringing back a few, or even a few scores of lost species (as difficult as that would be to pull off). That's because wiping out the passenger pigeon, the heath hen, the Tasmanian tiger, and so on, as regrettable as these events were, wasn't the *real* mistake. It was only the indicator of a deeper moral and cultural malady.

Source: www.Slate.com/Dec. 2014/Ben Minteer, "Extinct Species Should Stay Extinct: Why We Shouldn't Depend upon Technology to Turn Back the Clock."

Document 180: The Ecomodernist Manifesto (2015)

"An Ecomodernist Manifesto" is the work of 18 environmental activists, researchers, and philanthropists, most of them associated with the Breakthrough Institute, including Ted Nordhaus and Michael Shellenberger (see Document 156), Stewart Brand (see Document 179), and Mark Sagoff -(see Document 125). The tract is pro technology, urbanization and urbanism, aquaculture, industrial agriculture, desalinization, and nuclear energy. It puts forward the idea that humans need to embrace their impact on the environment and employ all the means in their power to enable a more equitable division of the benefits of the modern world.

1

To say that the Earth is a human planet becomes truer every day. Humans are made from the Earth, and the Earth is remade by human hands. Many earth scientists express this by stating that the Earth has entered a new geological epoch: the Anthropocene, the Age of Humans.

As scholars, scientists, campaigners, and citizens, we write with the conviction that knowledge and technology, applied with wisdom, might allow for a good, or even great, Anthropocene. A good Anthropocene demands that humans use their growing social, economic, and technological powers to make life better for people, stabilize the climate, and protect the natural world.

In this, we affirm one long-standing environmental ideal, that humanity must shrink its impacts on the environment to make more room for nature, while we reject another, that human societies must harmonize with nature to avoid economic and ecological collapse.

These two ideals can no longer be reconciled. Natural systems will not, as a general rule, be protected or enhanced by the expansion of humankind's dependence upon them for sustenance and well-being.

Intensifying many human activities — particularly farming, energy extraction, forestry, and settlement — so that they use less land and interfere less with the natural world is the key to decoupling human development from environmental impacts. These socioeconomic and technological processes are central to economic modernization and environmental protection. Together they allow people to mitigate climate change, to spare nature, and to alleviate global poverty.

Although we have to date written separately, our views are increasingly discussed as a whole. We call ourselves ecopragmatists and ecomodernists. . . .

Humanity has flourished over the past two centuries. Average life expectancy has increased from 30 to 70 years, resulting in a large and growing population able to live in many different environments. Humanity has made extraordinary progress in reducing the incidence and impacts of infectious diseases, and it has become more resilient to extreme weather and other natural disasters.

Violence in all forms has declined significantly and is probably at the lowest per capita level ever experienced by the human species, the horrors of the 20th century and present-day terrorism notwithstanding. Globally, human beings have moved from autocratic government toward liberal democracy characterized by the rule of law and increased freedom.

Personal, economic, and political liberties have spread worldwide and are today largely accepted as universal values. Modernization liberates women from traditional gender roles, increasing their control of their fertility. Historically large numbers of humans — both in percentage and in absolute terms — are free from insecurity, penury, and servitude.

At the same time, human flourishing has taken a serious toll on natural, nonhuman environments and wildlife. Humans use about half of the planet's ice-free land, mostly for pasture, crops, and production forestry. Of the land once covered by forests, 20 percent has been converted to human use. Populations of many mammals, amphibians, and birds have declined by more than 50 percent in the past 40 years alone. More than 100 species from those groups went extinct in the 20th century, and about 785 since 1500. As we write, only four northern white rhinos are confirmed to exist.

Given that humans are completely dependent on the living biosphere, how is it possible that people are doing so much damage to natural systems without doing more harm to themselves?

The role that technology plays in reducing humanity's dependence on nature explains this paradox. Human technologies, from those that first enabled agriculture to replace hunting and gathering, to those that drive today's globalized economy, have made humans less reliant upon the many ecosystems that once provided their only sustenance, even as those same ecosystems have often been less deeply damaged.

Despite frequent assertions starting in the 1970s of fundamental "limits to growth," there is still remarkably little evidence that human population and economic expansion will outstrip the capacity to grow food or procure critical material resources in the foreseeable future.

. . .

2

Even as human environmental impacts continue to grow in the aggregate, a range of long-term trends are today driving significant decoupling of human well-being from environmental impacts. Decoupling occurs in both relative and absolute terms. *Relative* decoupling means that human environmental impacts rise at a slower rate than overall economic growth. Thus, for each unit of economic output, less environmental impact (e.g., deforestation, defaunation, pollution) results. Overall impacts may still increase, just at a slower rate than would otherwise be the case. *Absolute* decoupling occurs when total environmental impacts — impacts in the aggregate — peak and begin to decline, even as the economy continues to grow.

Decoupling can be driven by both technological and demographic trends and usually results from a combination of the two. The growth rate of the human population has already peaked. Today's population growth rate is one percent per year, down from its high point of 2.1 percent in the 1970s. Fertility rates in countries containing more than half of the global population are now below replacement level. Population growth today is primarily driven by longer life spans and lower infant mortality, not by rising fertility. Given current trends, it is very possible that the size of the human population will peak this century and then start to decline.

Trends in population are inextricably linked to other demographic and economic dynamics. For the first time in human history, over half the global population lives in cities. By 2050, 70 percent are expected to dwell in cities, a number that could rise to 80 percent or more by the century's end. Cities are characterized by both dense populations and low fertility rates.

Cities occupy just one to three percent of the Earth's surface and yet are home to nearly four billion people. As such, cities both drive and symbolize the decoupling of humanity from nature, performing far better than rural economies in providing efficiently for material needs while reducing environmental impacts.

The growth of cities along with the economic and ecological benefits that come with them are inseparable from improvements in agricultural productivity. As agriculture has become more land and labor efficient, rural populations have left the countryside for the cities. Roughly half the US population worked the land in 1880. Today, less than 2 percent does. Cities occupy just one to three percent of the Earth's surface and yet are home to nearly four billion people.

As human lives have been liberated from hard agricultural labor, enormous human resources have been freed up for other endeavors. Cities, as people know them today, could not exist without radical changes in farming. In contrast, modernization is not possible in a subsistence agrarian economy.

These improvements have resulted not only in lower labor requirements per unit of agricultural output but also in lower land requirements. This is not a new trend: rising harvest yields have for millennia reduced the amount of land required to feed the average person. The average per-capita use of land today is vastly lower than it was 5,000 years ago, despite the fact that modern people enjoy a far richer diet. Thanks to technological improvements in agriculture, during the half-century starting in the mid-1960s, the amount of land required for growing crops and animal feed for the average person declined by one-half.

Agricultural intensification, along with the move away from the use of wood as fuel, has allowed many parts of the world to experience net reforestation. About 80 percent of New England is today forested, compared with about 50 percent at the end of the 19th century. Over the past 20 years, the amount of land dedicated to production forest worldwide declined by 50 million hectares, an area the size of France. The "forest transition" from net deforestation to net reforestation seems to be as resilient a feature of development as the demographic transition that reduces human birth rates as poverty declines.

Human use of many other resources is similarly peaking. The amount of water needed for the average diet has declined by nearly 25 percent over the past half-century. Nitrogen pollution continues to cause eutrophication and large dead zones in places like the Gulf of Mexico. While the total amount of nitrogen pollution is rising, the amount used per unit of production has declined significantly in developed nations.

Indeed, in contradiction to the often-expressed fear of infinite growth colliding with a finite planet, demand for many material goods may be saturating as societies grow wealthier. Meat consumption, for instance, has peaked in many wealthy nations and has shifted away from beef toward protein sources that are less land intensive. As demand for material goods is met, developed economies see higher levels of spending directed to materially less-intensive service and knowledge sectors, which account for an increasing share of economic activity. This dynamic might be even more pronounced in today's developing economies, which may benefit from being late adopters of resource-efficient technologies. Taken together, these trends mean that the total human impact on the environment, including land-use change, overexploitation, and pollution, can peak and decline this century. By understanding and promoting these emergent processes, humans have the opportunity to re-wild and re-green the Earth — even as developing countries achieve modern living standards, and material poverty ends.

Source: Static1.squarespace.com/An+Ecomodernist+Manifesto/pdf

Document 181: The Union of Concerned Scientists Exposes Climate Deception (2015)

The Union of Concerned Scientists (UCS), founded in in 1968 by faculty members of the Massachusetts Institute of Technology, is committed to developing and implementing innovative, practical, science-based solutions to a variety of planetary problems, from global warming to sustainable ways to feed, power, and transport people. Taking a cue from the playbook of the fight against the big tobacco companies, UCS collected internal documents from fossil fuel companies and trade associations and published them in a report called "The Climate Deception Dossiers." The documents, which were organized into seven dossiers, one of which is presented here, provide clear evidence that fossil fuel companies, despite knowing that the human impact on global warming "cannot be denied," have been encouraging skepticism about climate change and spreading questionable information about climate science.

Internal documents from the major fossil fuel companies— including BP, Chevron, ConocoPhillips, ExxonMobil, Peabody Energy, and Shell—reveal an irrefutable story: for nearly three decades, as the scientific evidence concerning climate change became overwhelmingly clear, these companies and their allies developed or participated in campaigns to deliberately sow confusion and block action to address global warming.

This report presents the most complete and up-to-date collection yet available of this deception campaign through seven dossiers—collections containing some 85 internal company and trade association documents that have either been leaked to the public, come to light through lawsuits, or been disclosed through Freedom of Information Act (FOIA) requests. The evidence demonstrates that the world's largest fossil fuel companies knew the reality about the harm their products were causing since 1988; their own scientists warned 20 years ago in an internal memo that human caused global warming "cannot be denied." And yet the deception campaign continued, with documents revealing secret funding of purportedly independent scientists, internal strategy memos outlining intentional misinformation campaigns, and even evidence of the use of forged letters to members of Congress.

During this same time period since 1988— after major fossil fuel companies indisputably knew about the harm their products were causing to people and the planet—more than half of all industrial carbon emissions have been released into the atmosphere.

Deception Dossier 2: American Petroleum Institute's "Roadmap" Memo

Among the most revelatory documents to have emerged about the fossil fuel companies' campaign of deception is an internal strategy document written in 1998, a roadmap memo outlining the fossil fuel industry's plan to use scientists as spokespersons for the industry's views [see Fig.1]. The memo was written by a team convened by the API [American Petroleum Institute], the country's largest oil trade association whose member companies include BP, ConocoPhillips, Chevron, ExxonMobil, and Shell. The innocuously titled "Global Climate Science Communications Plan," written with the direct involvement of fossil fuel companies including ExxonMobil (then Exxon) and Chevron, details a plan for dealing with climate change that explicitly aimed to confuse and misinform the public.

Articulating an Accurate Understanding of Climate Science

The API's Global Climate Science Communications Team consisted of representatives from the fossil fuel industry, trade associations, and public relations firms. At the time, the team's attention was focused on derailing the Kyoto Protocol—the international agreement committing participating countries to binding emissions reductions—that had been adopted by the Parties to the United Nations Framework

Convention on Climate Change in December 1997. In response to this development, and to stave off approval of the treaty by the U.S. Senate and other climate action in the United States, the API team's 1998 memo mapped out a multifaceted deception strategy for the fossil fuel industry that continues to this day—outlining plans to reach the media, the public, and policy makers with a message emphasizing "uncertainties" in climate science.

According to the memo [see Fig.1], "victory" would be achieved for the campaign when "average citizens" and the media were convinced of "uncertainties" in climate science despite overwhelming evidence of the impact of human-caused global warming and nearly unanimous agreement about it in the scientific community.

The timing of this document—1998—is important to note, as an earlier internal memo from 1995 shows that Mobil's own climate scientist had informed the industry that global warming was undeniable. . . . Thus, this memo cannot be interpreted as a legitimate call for "balance" in the understanding of climate change.

In fact, the words eerily echo the strategy developed and implemented by the large tobacco companies to deceive the public about the hazards of smoking and to forestall governmental controls on tobacco consumption. As an infamous internal memo from the Brown and Williamson tobacco company put it: "Doubt is our product, since it is the best means of competing with the 'body of fact' that exists in the minds of the general public."

The fossil fuel companies, mimicking the tobacco companies, adopted a strategy that sought to "manufacture uncertainty" about global warming even in the face of overwhelming scientific evidence that it is human-caused, is accelerating at an alarming rate, and poses myriad public health and environmental dangers. The fossil fuel industry not only took a page from the tobacco playbook in its efforts to defeat action on climate change, it even drew upon a number of the key players who had contributed

to the tobacco industry's deception campaign and a remarkably similar network of public relations firms and nonprofit "front groups," some of whom continue to actively sow disinformation about global warming today.

Identifying, Recruiting, and Training Undercover Scientists

Given that scientists are a trusted source of information for policy makers and the public, it is not surprising that the API roadmap memo calls for cultivating and deploying them. Importantly, the API's communication team realized that scientists seen as spokespeople for the fossil fuel industry would lack credibility. They aimed to "identify, recruit and train a team of five independent scientists to participate in media outreach," and their deception depended on ensuring that these scientists' financial ties to the fossil fuel industry remained hidden from the public—precisely the arrangement they ultimately made with Dr. Wei-Hock Soon. . . . According to the leaked memo, "These will be individuals who do not have a long history of visibility and/or participation in the climate change debate. Rather, this team will consist of new faces who will add their voices to those recognized scientists who are already vocal."

While the funding of the hand-selected scientists was to remain secret, their intended mission was clear: Exxon, Chevron, and the other fossil fuel industry representatives needed these scientists to produce "peer-reviewed papers that undercut the 'conventional wisdom' on climate science." They intended to fund and train the scientists to get their crafted message of uncertainty out to print, radio, and TV journalists.

Targeting Teachers and Students

Another section of the API roadmap memo outlines a plan to target the National Science Teachers Association. Exxon, Chevron, and the other Global Climate Science Communications Team members recognized that the tide might turn against fossil fuels unless they could reach the next generation. So, under the guise of "present[ing] a credible, balanced picture of climate science," they opted to push out materials for teachers and their students that directly countered the scientific evidence. As the memo explains, their assumption was that emphasizing "uncertainties in climate science will begin to erect a barrier against further efforts to impose Kyoto-like measures in the future." The leaked memo also outlines a tactic of working through grassroots organizations to promote debate about climate science on campuses and in communities during the period mid-August through October 1998. In the years since this memo, many of the activities outlined in the memo have been carried out, as evidenced by the API's online curriculum for elementary schools that presents nonrenewable energy sources such as oil, natural gas, and coal, as "more reliable, affordable, and convenient to use than most renewable energy resources."

Fossil Fuel Company Involvement: Direct and Indirect

Fossil fuel companies contributed to the campaign indirectly, through their membership in and funding of the API, and directly, through the participation of their own employees. Joseph Walker of the API facilitated the process, and the largest fossil fuel companies were implicated in this memo. BP, ConocoPhillips, and Shell were members of the API at the time. Along with ExxonMobil and Chevron, all these firms remain API members today. Exxon and Chevron contributed directly to the development of the plan through their representatives Randy [Arthur G.] Randol and Sharon Kneiss, respectively. Exxon, Chevron, and Occidental Petroleum also exerted influence through a team member, Steve Milloy, who was the executive director of a front group, called The Advancement of Sound Science Coalition, funded by these companies. (Milloy had previously aided tobacco firms with their deception campaign.) BP and Shell, among other fossil fuel companies, indirectly supported this deception campaign via their API memberships. It is noteworthy that these companies began to publicly acknowledge the threat of climate change around this time. Shell, for example, publicly acknowledged in its 1998 corporate sustainability report that rising global temperatures were "possibly due in part to greenhouse gas emissions caused by human activity." The report also noted that "human activities, especially the use of fossil fuels, may be influencing the climate, according to many scientists, including those who make up the Intergovernmental Panel on Climate Change." Despite such comments, however, fossil fuel companies' broader campaign to sow confusion continued.

Funding the Campaign

The fossil fuel companies knew that a disinformation campaign of the scope they intended would not be cheap. The Global Climate Science Communications Team estimated the budget for the program at $5,900,000, which included a national media program and national outreach as well as a data center. The roadmap identified an array of fossil fuel industry trade associations and front groups, fossil fuel companies, and free-market think tanks to underwrite and execute the plan, including:

- The American Petroleum Institute and its members
- The Business Round Table and its members
- The Edison Electric Institute and its members
- The Independent Petroleum Association of America and its members
- The National Mining Association and its members
- The American Legislative Exchange Council
- Committee for a Constructive Tomorrow
- The Competitive Enterprise Institute
- Frontiers of Freedom
- The Marshall Institute

Global Climate Science Communications

Action Plan

Project Goal

A majority of the American public, including industry leadership, recognizes that significant uncertainties exist in climate science, and therefore raises questions among those (e.g. Congress) who chart the future U.S. course on global climate change.

Progress will be measured toward the goal. A measurement of the public's perspective on climate science will be taken before the plan is launched, and the same measurement will be taken at one or more as-yet-to-be-determined intervals as the plan is implemented.

Victory Will Be Achieved When

- Average citizens "understand" (recognize) uncertainties in climate science; recognition of uncertainties becomes part of the "conventional wisdom"

- Media "understands" (recognizes) uncertainties in climate science

- Media coverage reflects balance on climate science and recognition of the validity of viewpoints that challenge the "conventional wisdom"

- Industry senior leadership understands uncertainties in climate science, making them stronger ambassadors to those who shape climate policy

- Those promoting the Kyoto treaty on the basis of extant science appear to be out of touch with reality

Current Reality

Unless "climate change" becomes a non-issue, meaning that the Kyoto proposal is defeated and there are no further initiatives to thwart the threat of climate change, there may be no moment when we can declare victory for our efforts. It will be necessary to establish measurements for the science effort to track progress toward achieving the goal and strategic success.

Fig. 1. The American Petroleum Institute's 1998 Memo Presents a Roadmap for Climate Deception: Above is one page of a nine-page strategy memo written in 1998 by a team convened by the American Petroleum Institute (API), the country's largest oil trade association whose member companies include BP, Chevron, ConocoPhillips, ExxonMobil, and Shell Oil among others. The memo, leaked that same year to the *New York Times*, outlines a multifaceted deception strategy for the fossil fuel industry, including a plan akin to that used by the tobacco industry to "identify, recruit, and train" a team of five seemingly independent scientists to confuse the public by accentuating "uncertainties" in climate science where few if any existed. The complete API "roadmap" memo is available online at www.ucsusa.org/ decadesofdeception.

The API Today: Still Fueling Uncertainty
The trade association continues its misinformation efforts today. For instance, since October 2002, the API has carried out its plan to distribute curriculum materials that question the established science through the National Science Teachers Association by maintaining the website Classroom Energy!, which offers lesson plans and materials for teachers of kindergarten through high school. Additionally, the API funded now well-known contrarian scientists such as Wei-Hock Soon, whose work sought to discredit the scientific evidence of human-caused climate change. In 2009, the API attempted to undermine the American Clean Energy and Security Act of 2009— often known as the Waxman-Markey climate bill and a key federal attempt to regulate carbon emissions—by mobilizing front groups to hold staged "energy citizens" rallies in roughly 20 states, rallies designed to suggest that there was significant public opposition to regulating carbon emissions where little actually existed. An API memo leaked to Greenpeace reveals that API urged fossil fuel company executives, including from BP, Chevron, ExxonMobil, and Shell, to send their employees to the staged rallies.

More recently, in 2011, the API protested the EPA's decision to regulate carbon pollution under the Clean Air Act, joining a coalition of industry groups to file a lawsuit challenging the EPA's authority to regulate global warming emissions. The API's lawsuit challenged the EPA on the grounds of the very doubts about climate science the trade group had worked for years to manufacture, stating that the "EPA professes to be 90–99% certain that anthropogenic emissions are mostly responsible for 'unusually high current planetary temperatures,' but the record does not remotely support this level of certainty."

Source: Union of Concerned Scientists, *The Climate Deception Dossiers: Internal Fossil Fuel Industry Memos Reveal Decades of Corporate Disinformation*, July 2015, pp. 48, 9-12, and 38.

Document 182: The EPA'S Clean Power Plan (2015)

In August 2015, Gina McCarthy, the EPA administrator in the Obama administration published "Carbon Pollution Emission Guidelines for Existing Stationary Sources: Electric Utility Generating Units," usually referred to as The Clean Power Plan, establishing the first nationwide limits on pollution from power plant smokestacks. The guidelines, which aimed to cut carbon pollution from the power sector by 32% below 2005 levels by 2030, formed the basis for the U.S. position in its negotiations on the Paris Climate Accords of 2015, from which President Trump withdrew shortly after he was inaugurated in 2018. Although Trump's EPA administrator, Scott Pruitt, would like to eliminate the Clean Power Plan, nineteen states have already publicly pledged to work toward compliance with the plan.

SUMMARY: In this action, the Environmental Protection Agency (EPA) is establishing final emission guidelines for states to follow in developing plans to reduce greenhouse gas (GHG) emissions from existing fossil fuel-fired electric generating units (EGUs). Specifically, the EPA is establishing: 1) carbon dioxide (CO2) emission performance rates representing the best system of emission reduction (BSER) for two subcategories of existing fossil fuel-fired EGUs – fossil fuel-fired electric utility steam generating units and stationary combustion turbines, 2) state-specific CO2 goals reflecting the CO2 emission performance rates, and 3) guidelines for the development, submittal and implementation of state plans that establish emission standards or other measures to implement the CO2 emission performance rates, which may be accomplished by meeting the state goals. This final rule will continue progress already underway in the U.S.

to reduce CO2 emissions from the utility power sector.

A. Executive Summary

1. Introduction

This final rule is a significant step forward in reducing greenhouse gas (GHG) emissions in the U.S. In this action, the EPA is establishing for the first time GHG emission guidelines for existing power plants. These final emission guidelines, which rely in large part on already clearly emerging growth in clean energy innovation, development and deployment, will lead to significant carbon dioxide (CO2) emission reductions from the utility power sector that will help protect human health and the environment from the impacts of climate change. This rule establishes, at the same time, the foundation for longer term GHG emission reduction strategies necessary to address climate change and, in so doing, confirms the international leadership of the U.S. in the global effort to address climate change. In this final rule, we have taken care to ensure that achievement of the required emission reductions will not compromise the reliability of our electric system, or the affordability of electricity for consumers. This final rule is the result of unprecedented outreach and engagement with states, tribes, utilities, and other stakeholders, with stakeholders providing more than 4.3 million comments on the proposed rule. In this final rule, we have addressed the comments and concerns of states and other stakeholders while staying consistent with the law. As a result, we have followed through on our commitment to issue a plan that is fair, flexible and relies on the accelerating transition to cleaner power generation that is already well underway in the utility power sector. Under the authority of Clean Air Act (CAA) section 111(d), the EPA is establishing CO2 emission guidelines for existing fossil fuel-fired electric generating units (EGUs) – the Clean Power Plan. These final guidelines, when fully implemented, will achieve significant reductions in CO2 emissions by 2030, while offering states and utilities substantial flexibility and latitude in achieving these reductions. In this final rule, the EPA is establishing a CO2 emission performance rate for each of two subcategories of fossil fuel-fired EGUs – fossil fuel-fired electric steam generating units and stationary combustion turbines – that expresses the "best system of emissions reduction… adequately demonstrated" (BSER) for CO2 from the power sector.

2. Purpose of this rule

The purpose of this rule is to protect human health and the environment by reducing CO2 emissions from fossil fuel-fired power plants in the U.S. These plants are by far the largest domestic stationary source of emissions of CO2, the most prevalent of the group of air pollutant GHGs that the EPA has determined endangers public health and welfare through its contribution to climate change. This rule establishes for the first time emission guidelines for existing power plants. These guidelines will lead to significant reductions in CO2 emissions, result in cleaner generation from the existing power plant fleet, and support continued investments by the industry in cleaner power generation to ensure reliable, affordable electricity now and into the future. Concurrent with this action, the EPA is also issuing a final rule that establishes CO2 emission standards of performance for new, modified, and reconstructed power plants. Together, these rules will reduce CO2 emissions by a substantial amount while ensuring that the utility power sector in the U.S. can continue to supply reliable and affordable electricity to all Americans using a diverse fuel supply. As with past EPA rules addressing air pollution from the utility power sector, these guidelines have been designed with a clear recognition of the unique features of this sector. Specifically, the agency recognizes that utilities provide an essential public service and are regulated and managed in ways unlike any other industrial activity. In providing assurances that the emission reductions required by this rule can be achieved without compromising continued reliable, affordable electricity, this final rule fully accounts for the critical service utilities provide. As with past rules under CAA section 111, this rule relies on proven technologies and measures to set achievable emission performance rates that will lead to cost-effective pollutant emission reductions, in this case CO_2 emission reductions at power plants, across the country. In fact, the emission guidelines reflect strategies, technologies and approaches already in widespread use by power companies and states.

Source: www.gpo.gov/ "Rules and Regulations," *Federal Register,* Vol. 80, No. 205 Washington D.C. GPO (October 23, 2015), pp. 64662-64.

Document 183: Richard Manning on Agriculture Policy and Undrinkable Water (2016)

Federal farm subsidies are intertwined with government policies on a broad range of issues from energy and biofuels to land use and water pollution. Subsidies encourage farmers to grow enormous amounts of corn for making biofuels as well as corn syrup and soybeans for the production of soybean oil, a staple element of packaged foods.

William Stowe's office sits near the confluence of the Raccoon and Des Moines Rivers, which were laid down by the Des Moines Lobe of the Wisconsin glaciation more than 12,000 years ago. The office was built there to superintend the piping and delivery of river water to half a million customers of the Des Moines Water Works. Stowe is the head of the organization. He trained as both an engineer and a lawyer, and lately has needed the latter set of skills. His utility has sued the county operators of drainage districts in rural Iowa in a case that is pending in federal court. Environmentalists nationwide view the case as a bellwether; it may well produce the legal precedent they need to solve a plague of continental scale. Many Iowans view the dispute as a battle between the city and the country; they see Stowe as a pariah.

"We have had death threats," he says. "We're the 'radicals.' We're the 'revolutionaries' who are declaring war on rural Iowa. In reality we are protecting public health, and we're protecting the economic viability of our consumers."

The problem is simple enough. Rain falls on Iowa pure and clean, but it arrives at Stowe's intake pipes a few hours later sufficiently polluted to violate federal standards for drinking water. Farmers have been raising corn and hogs in Iowa, and the people of Des Moines have been drinking river water, ever since the Civil War, but only in the past decade or two have the nitrogen fertilizers from industrial agriculture rendered that water undrinkable.

Under the current reading of the relevant federal law [*see* Document 116], pollution from a factory pipe is called "point source" and is regulated. If a factory or municipal sewage-treatment plant sends concentrated nitrates and phosphorus down a discharge pipe to a river, the feds will put a stop to it. Runoff from a farm's field, "nonpoint source," is not regulated at all.

Nationwide, any river or stream that wends through farm country suffers pollution to the point of death, but in the Upper Midwest, the plague is nearly total. Agricultural fertilizers traveling from the Corn Belt down the Mississippi River have killed a Connecticut-size stretch of the Gulf of Mexico that is now called the Dead Zone. Iowa occupies less than 5 percent of the land in the Mississippi basin, but it contributes 25 percent of the nitrate pollution responsible for the Dead Zone, almost all of which is attributable to farming.

In August 2014, Corn Belt fertilizer pollution led to a toxic algal bloom that poisoned the water supply of Toledo. John Kasich, Ohio's governor then and now, alleged by some to be the thoughtful conservative among the [2016] Republican presidential candidates, responded to the contamination of a large city by calling out the National Guard to distribute bottled water. Later he signed a palliative bill, endorsed by Big Ag, that did nothing to sully his business-friendly reputation or to limit the phosphates and nitrates responsible for Toledo's problem. None of this is mentioned prominently in his campaign in Iowa.

At least a third of Iowa's farmland is under-laid with drainage pipes, like the veins of a hand. The same is true in much of Kasich's Ohio, as well as in Indiana, Illinois, Minnesota, and parts of Wisconsin and Michigan. Again like veins, the networks gather fluid in bigger and bigger pipes that finally pinch together before discharging into rivers. The Environmental Protection Agency says that farm pollution is not pollution because it doesn't come out of a pipe, but in Iowa, farm pollution does come out of pipes. Nonetheless, paper is waved over the water, a box is checked, and the toxic runoff is transubstantiated.

These days a fair amount of the nitrates are derived not so much directly from chemical fertilizers as from hog manure. There are about 21 million hogs in Iowa, and almost all of them live in hog factories. Each hog produces the waste of about 2.5 people, meaning Iowa bears the shit equivalent, from hogs alone, of about 45 million people, some fifteen times its human population. But Iowa also has 52 million laying chickens, 50 million of which are in concentrated animal-feeding operations (CAFOs) that hold more than 100,000 birds. These birds likewise produce more manure than all the people in the state. Almost none of it passes through a sewage-treatment plant or even a septic tank before making its way through drainage pipes to the public waterways and drinking water.

It is technically possible to remove nitrates from water, and this past year the Des Moines Water Works has been attempting to do that,

at a cost of more than a million dollars. But the level and persistence of the pollution have repeatedly overwhelmed the equipment. Absent cleaner intake water, the Water Works will face up to a $180 million bill to upgrade its equipment, but this amount vastly understates the cost of the problem. There are 260 cities and towns in Iowa that face similar problems with their water supplies, and removing the nutrients from drinking-water intakes does nothing for the life of the rivers themselves.

There's another way to fix the problem. It involves simple measures such as running farm-field drainage pipes into restored wetlands and permanent pastures instead of rivers. Ten acres of wetland can treat the runoff from 1,000 acres of hard-farmed corn. By timing their applications, farmers might also apply less fertilizer while still ensuring their yields. These measures do not mean growing less food, though they might require some different crops, maybe even raising a few cattle on grass. Scientists from the state's agricultural department and Iowa State University have penciled out and tested a program of such low-tech solutions. If 40 percent of the cropland claimed by corn were planted with other crops and permanent pasture, the whole litany of problems caused by industrial agriculture — certainly the nitrate pollution of drinking water — would begin to evaporate. There are no technological or financial hurdles to implementing this program, but there is a political obstacle: the federal government would have to stop subsidizing the growing of corn. Between 1995 and 2012, those subsidies amounted to $84 billion.

At this point we would do well to remember that the time-honored mark of a developing country is that its tap water is undrinkable. Today, "Don't drink the water" is sound advice in much of Iowa. Ironically, the American right wing has become especially fond of charging that the policies, real and imagined, of the Obama Administration have reduced the nation to the status of a banana republic. This complaint is especially prominent in discussions of immigration. Nationally, the chief fire-breather on this matter has been Steve King, the Republican congressman from Iowa's Fourth District. He says that those favoring immigration reform "advocate for the destruction of rule of law and for anarchy and the descending down into Third World status." His district happens to contain some of the state's heaviest concentrations of hog factories, slaughterhouses, and restaurants where it is possible to find decent carne asada.

. . .

Virtually all of the corn that doesn't go to ethanol is eventually consumed by humans, but it usually gets to our plates by a circuitous route. One way or another it is processed. About 12 percent is funneled into industrial refineries that crack corn into its elements: starches and sugars— especially in the form of high-fructose corn syrup, the basis of the high-energy diet that makes so many people sick and fat.

It ought to be harder than it is to account for the American diet. There are, after all, thousands of edible domesticated plants, dozens of animals, and endless ways to raise, combine, and create food. The big picture, however, is depressingly easy to paint. American agriculture is corn, soybeans, wheat, and hay— four crops that account for 85 percent of the nation's farmable land. In Iowa, corn and soybeans cover 23 million of the state's 24 million acres of cropland.

Source: From harpers.org/archive/2016/Richard Manning, "The Trouble with Iowa," Harper's, Feb. 2016.

Document 184: Elizabeth Kolbert on Global Warming (2016)

Although people still debate the rate of climate change, there is no question that icebergs and glaciers are melting, seas are rising, and the ocean is becoming increasingly acidified. Builders and city planners in coastal areas around the world are increasingly focused on the need for resilient designs capable of withstanding flooding, storm surges, and tsunamis. The nature writer Elisabeth Kolbert notes that while people in places like New York and Miami are worried about the effects of global warming, those in northern climes like Greenland and Siberia may look forward to unfrozen waterways and longer growing seasons.

The town of Ilulissat [in Greenland] sits three hundred and fifty miles north of Nuuk, above the Arctic Circle. It's home to one of Greenland's richest archeological sites—a stretch of springy tundra that was inhabited first by the Saqqaq, then by the Dorset, and finally by the Inuit. Near the abandoned settlement is a bare stone ledge overhanging a fjord. Elderly Greenlanders used to jump from the ledge to avoid becoming a burden to their families, or so the story goes.

. . .

The suicide ledge is a good place to go to feel small—presumably that's why it was chosen. Standing at its edge, I could imagine how the Saqqaq and the Dorset were awed by the inhuman beauty. But today even sublimity has been superseded.

The city of ice is the product of the Jakobshavn ice stream. Like the negis [north-east Greenland ice stream], the Jakobshavn originates in central Greenland, only it flows in the opposite direction and into a long fjord. Where the ice meets the water, there's a calving front, and it's here that the ice arches and ice castles take form. These float down the fjord toward Ilulissat. (The town's name is Greenlandic for "icebergs.") They would continue on out to sea, except that they're blocked by a submarine ridge—a moraine—composed of rocky debris left behind when the ice sheet shrank at the end of the last ice age. The biggest icebergs become lodged on the moraine and the smaller ones crowd in behind, as in a monumental traffic jam. The very largest, which weigh upward of a hundred million tons, can hang around for years before slimming down enough to float free. (It is believed that one of these liberated giants from Ilulissat was the iceberg that sank the Titanic.)

Eight thousand years ago, the Jakobshavn filled the fjord completely, all the way to the moraine. By the mid-nineteenth century, when the first observations were recorded, the position of the calving front had shifted inland by about ten miles. Over the next hundred and fifty years, the front's position shifted again, by another twelve miles.

Then, suddenly, in the late nineteen-nineties, the Jakobshavn's stately retreat turned into a rout. Between 2001 and 2006, the calving front withdrew nine miles. Just in the past fifteen years, it has given up more ground than it did in the previous century. The fjord extends for at least another forty miles and deepens as it moves inland. At this point, there doesn't seem to be anything to prevent the calving front from withdrawing the entire way.

"It appears now that the retreat cannot be stopped," David Holland, a professor at N.Y.U. who studies the Jakobshavn using seals equipped with electronic sensors, told me. (When the seals surface after a dive, the sensors transmit data about conditions in the fjord.)

Meanwhile, as the calving front has receded, the ice stream has sped up. This appears to be the result of yet another feedback loop. Since the nineties, the Jakobshavn has nearly tripled its pace. In the summer of 2012, it set what's believed to be an ice-stream record, by flowing at the distinctly unglacial rate of a hundred and fifty feet per day, or more than six feet an hour. The Jakobshavn's catchment area is smaller than the negis's; still, there's enough ice in it to raise global sea levels by two feet.

A lot of Ilulissat is given over to dogs. They have their own neighborhoods—large expanses of dust and rock, where they live chained up around industrial-size vats of water. . . .

. . . As recently as 1995, Ilulissat, a town of some forty-six hundred people, was home to more than eight thousand dogs. In the past twenty years, the canine population has crashed. Now there are only about two thousand dogs. This, too, is an index of global warming.

Ole Dorph, Ilulissat's mayor, works out of a corner office in the town's surprisingly sprawling city hall. He's sixty-one, with a craggy face and rectangular glasses. Dorph grew up in Ilulissat, and he told me that, when he was a child, every year the town was iced in from November to April. During those months, residents used their dog sleds to go fishing and seal hunting. . . .

Since no supply ships could get into Ilulissat's harbor, for six months a year residents had to live off whatever provisions the stores had laid in, plus whatever they caught. When the ice broke up in the spring, and the first ship arrived, "everyone was very happy," Dorph recalled. "We could buy new apples." To announce the boat's approach, the town would "shoot off a cannon three times—*bang, bang, bang.*"

Then, in the nineties, the bay started to freeze later and later, until, finally, it didn't freeze at all. "The last time we had ice we could use was in 1997," Dorph told me.

The loss of ice cover from Disko Bay is part of the general decline in Arctic sea ice—a decline that's been so precipitous it now seems likely there will be open water at the North Pole in summer within the next few decades. Since sea ice reflects the sun's radiation and open water absorbs it, the loss has enormous implications for the planet as a whole. (Sea ice doesn't contribute to sea-level rise, because it floats, displacing an equivalent amount of water.) Locally, in Ilulissat, the most obvious impact has been on transportation. Once the bay stopped freezing, supply ships could arrive in January, and sleds became obsolete. Dogs no longer seemed worth the seal meat it took to feed them. Many were euthanized. Those which remain are used mostly for sport.

Dorph told me that people in Ilulissat were "sad because our dogs are going down," but that this unhappiness was more or less balanced by the benefits of open water. Ilulissat's major source of income is halibut, and its small harbor, which sits on the opposite side of town from the fjord, is crowded with fishing boats.

"The fishermen, they can take their boats out in winter," Dorph said. "They feel it's O.K. The price of fish is going up, so the fishermen, they have good days." I was reminded of what I'd heard in Nuuk—that climate change, while regrettable in many ways, was, for Greenlanders, filled with economic promise. . . .

One evening while I was staying in Ilulissat, I hired a boat to go up the coast. . . .

About ten miles north of Ilulissat, we passed the tiny town of Oqaatsut, a collection of bright-painted houses hugging the rocks. (Oqaatsut is Greenlandic for "cormorants.") From the boat not a soul was visible, but when I looked it up later in the phone book—there's one edition of the white pages for all of Greenland, and it's about an eighth of an inch thick—I found that Oqaatsut had eighteen listed numbers. We motored on, dodging refrigerator-size blocks of floating ice as well as several massive icebergs that had broken free from the moraine. Beyond Oqaatsut, the coast rose up. A thin waterfall hundreds of feet high twisted off the rocks. Almost anywhere else in the world, the falls would have been a major tourist attraction; in the great emptiness of west-central Greenland, it didn't even have a name.

Finally, after about three hours, we came within sight of our destination, a rock-strewn cove. It also had no name; its coördinates— 69.868245N by 50.317827W—had been sent to me by Eric Rignot, a glaciologist from the University of California, Irvine. The cove was shallow, so we paddled ashore in a rubber dinghy, pushing ice chunks out of the way with the oars.

Rignot, who grew up in France, studies both Greenland's ice sheet and Antarctica's. Two years ago, he published a paper arguing that a key section of the West Antarctic ice sheet, the Amundsen Sea sector, had gone into "irreversible retreat." The Amundsen Sea sector contains more than two hundred thousand cubic miles of ice, meaning that, if Rignot's analysis is correct, it will, inevitably, raise global sea levels by four feet.

. . . Rignot and three of his students had set up camp on a steep hill just beyond the beach—a cluster of pup tents facing a glacier-filled fjord. In the slanted sunlight—it was about 9 p.m.— the glacier, known as Kangilernata, seemed to be glowing. Its calving front, a hundred-and-thirty-foot vertical wall of ice, appeared upside down in the milky-blue waters of the fjord. Behind it, ice stretched to the horizon. Again, I was hit, and vaguely sickened, by Greenland's inhuman scale. . . .

Kangilernata is what's known as a marine-terminating glacier. So is Jakobshavn, and so, too, are most of the glaciers in West Antarctica. This means that they have one foot in the water and, as the world warms, are melting from the bottom as well as from the top. NASA is so concerned about this effect that it has launched a research project called, suggestively, Oceans Melting Greenland, or OMG. (Rignot is one of the principal investigators on the project.)

At Kangilernata, the team was measuring the water temperatures at the base of the calving front every other day. This involved taking a Zodiac into the fjord, dangling some instruments over the side, and hoping the boat wouldn't be swamped by falling ice.

"What concerns me the most is that this is the kind of experiment we can only do once," Rignot said. "A lot of people don't realize that. If we start opening the floodgates on some of these glaciers, even if we stop our emissions, even if we go back to a better climate, the damage is going to be done. There's no red button to stop this."

I first visited the Greenland ice sheet in the summer of 2001. At that time, vivid illustrations of climate change were hard to come by.

Now they're everywhere—in the flooded streets of Florida and South Carolina, in the beetle-infested forests of Colorado and Montana, in the too warm waters of the Mid-Atlantic and the Great Lakes and the Gulf of Mexico, in the mounds of dead mussels that washed up this summer on the coast of Long Island and the piles of dead fish that coated the banks of the Yellowstone River.

But the problem with global warming—and the reason it continues to resist illustration, even as the streets flood and the forests die and the mussels rot on the shores—is that experience is an inadequate guide to what's going on. The climate operates on a time delay. When carbon dioxide is added to the atmosphere, it takes decades—in a technical sense, millennia—for the earth to equilibrate. This summer's fish kill was a product of warming that had become inevitable twenty or thirty years ago, and the warming

that's being locked in today won't be fully felt until today's toddlers reach middle age. In effect, we are living in the climate of the past, but already we've determined the climate's future.

Global warming's back-loaded temporality makes all the warnings—from scientists, government agencies, and, especially, journalists—seem hysterical, Cassandra-like—*Otototototoi!*—even when they are understated. Once feedbacks take over, the climate can change quickly, and it can change radically. At the end of the last ice age, during an event known as meltwater pulse 1A, sea levels rose at the rate of more than a foot a decade. It's likely that the "floodgates" are already open, and that large sections of Greenland and Antarctica are fated to melt. It's just the ice in front of us that's still frozen.

Source: www.newyorker.com/magazine/2016/10/24 Greenland-Is-Melting, by Elizabeth Kolbert.

Document 185: The G20 Responds to the U.S. Withdrawal from the Paris Accords (2017)

The Paris Agreement, adopted on December 12, 2015, at a session of the Conference of the Parties to the United Nations Framework Convention on Climate Change (UNFCCC) created a global plan of action designed to prevent disastrous climate change. In late 2016 the United States, under President Obama, became a party to the agreement, but just a few months later Donald Trump withdrew the United States from it. In July 2017 the G20 (a group made up of the 20 leading economies in the world) reacted to Trump's action by developing a blueprint outlining how their nations could reach the pact's goals, declaring that the agreement is irreversible, and leaving the United States visibly isolated.

Economic growth, sustainable development and prosperity are at the heart of G20 cooperation. They rely on universal access to affordable, reliable, sustainable energy sources and clean technologies. The leaders of G20 members will continually develop their economies and energy systems to better reflect the evolution of the global energy and environmental landscape. To facilitate the implementation of UNFCCC, the Paris Agreement and the 2030 Agenda for Sustainable Development, we will strive to move forward in a coherent and mutually supportive

manner that will provide us with significant opportunities for modernising our economies, enhancing competitiveness, stimulating employment and growth and ensuring socio-economic benefits of increased energy access. In addition, and in view of the increasing impacts of climate change, we will strive to increase the resilience of our communities and economies.

Our action will be guided by the Sustainable Development Goals (SDGs) and the Paris Agreement's aim to strengthen the global response to the threat of climate change, in the context of sustainable development and efforts to eradicate poverty, including by holding the increase in the global average temperature to well below 2°C above pre-industrial levels and to pursue efforts to limit the temperature increase to 1.5°C above pre-industrial levels; by increasing the ability to adapt to the adverse impacts of climate change and foster climate resilience; and by making finance flows consistent with a pathway towards low greenhouse gas emissions and climate resilient development. Our actions pursuant to the implementation of the Paris Agreement will reflect equity and the principle of common but differentiated responsibilities and respective capabilities, in the light of different national circumstances.

We emphasise the urgency and priority of accelerating the implementation of pre-2020 commitments and actions, in particular, for parties to the Kyoto Protocol, the ratification of the Doha Amendment.

We share the common understanding of the energy system as the backbone of our economies. Diverse energy systems rely on affordable, secure and sustainable energy sources and clean technologies such as energy efficiency, renewable energy, natural gas and nuclear power for those countries that opt to use it, and advanced and cleaner fossil fuel technologies, employed in a sustainable manner. Such energy systems can contribute greatly to achieving energy services for all at affordable prices and prosperity for future generations. We recognise that our actions contribute substantially to global greenhouse gas emission reductions, global energy developments and global prosperity, leaving no one behind.

Source: www.g20.org/2017-G20-Hamburg-climate-and-energy-action-plan -for-growth, pp.2-3.

Appendix I: Significant Dates in American Environmental History

The following list includes important events in environmental history as well as precedent-setting state and federal legislation. It also includes significant bilateral and multilateral treaties, declarations, protocols, and conventions to which the United States is a party, some of which have not been ratified by the U.S. Senate. The dates for the treaties and conventions are those when the agreements were opened for signature.

1626	Plymouth Colony passes ordinance regulating cutting and selling of timber.
1637	Plymouth Colony passes ordinance regulating herring run.
1639	Newport, Rhode Island, prohibits deer hunting for six months of the year.
1681	William Penn, proprietor of Pennsylvania, requires that one acre of land be left forested for every five acres of land cleared.
1691	Charter renewal for Massachusetts Bay Colony establishes Broad Arrow Policy, setting aside large trees suitable for ship masts by marking them with a "broad arrow."
1743	American Philosophical Society formed to promote useful knowledge and encourage scientific agriculture.
1790	First U.S. Census: population 3,929,627, with over 90% engaged in agriculture.
1804-1806	Lewis and Clark expedition undertakes first federal survey of nation's resources.
1807	Lead Mine Leasing Act establishes policy of leasing mineral rights; repealed in 1847.
1817	Forest Preserve Act establishes first federal forest.
1818	Bird Protection Law, Commonwealth of Massachusetts

1828   First attempt at federal forest management undertaken with live oaks on Santa Rosa Island, Florida; now Naval Live Oaks Reservation, part of Gulf Islands National Seashore.

1832   George Catlin proposes a national park.

1841   Preemption Act allows settlers to squat on public lands and, if the land is put up for sale, to have first right of purchase at $1.25 per acre.

1844   William Cullen Bryant proposes a great municipal park.

            New York Sportsman's Club, first sportsmen's club founded to protect and preserve game for hunting.

1848   Gold discovered at Sutter's Mill, California; marks the beginning of the California gold rush.

            American Association for the Advancement of Science founded.

1849   U.S. Department of the Interior established and given authority to administer public lands.

1850   Swamp and Overflow Act (Swamplands Act) deeds to the individual states swamp and overflow lands within their boundaries and encourages the building of levees on and draining of these lands.

1859   Edwin Drake drills first oil well in Titusville, Pennsylvania.

1862   Homestead Act gives settlers free land on the condition that they inhabit it and cultivate it.

1864   Act Granting Yo-semite to California on condition that California set aside the valley "for public use, resort and recreation" creates first state park.

            George Perkins Marsh publishes *Man and Nature*.

1865   Work begins on Central Park in New York City, the nation's first "rural" city park.

1866   General Mining Act establishes that public mineral lands should be free and open to exploration and occupation.

1869   John Wesley Powell descends the Colorado River and travels through the Grand Canyon.

1870   Timber and Stone Act permits sale of uncultivable public lands containing timber and stone but not minerals.

1871   U.S. Fish Commission established.

1872   Act to Set Apart Land near the Head-Waters of the Yellowstone River as a Public Park creates first U.S. national park, Yellowstone, which was also the first national park in the world.

            Mining Act allows private acquisition and exploration of public lands containing mineral deposits.

April 10 designated as Arbor Day as a result of a campaign spearheaded by J. Sterling Morton.

1873 Timber Culture Act gives land to individuals who agree to plant trees on a portion of it.

1875 American Forestry Association, the first nonprofit U.S. conservation organization, founded to promote forestry.

1876 Franklin B. Hough appointed special agent in Department of Agriculture to study forest conditions.

Appalachian Mountain Club founded.

1877 Desert Land Act allows individuals to purchase federal lands cheaply on the condition that they begin irrigating the land within three years of date of purchase.

1878 Free Timber Act (Timber Cutting Act) sets rules for the acquisition of timber from federal public lands.

1879 U.S. Geological Survey established.

National Board of Health formed.

1881 Division of Forestry created within the Department of Agriculture for the purpose of fact finding.

1882 Thomas Edison builds first central electric power station. American Forestry Congress organized.

1885 Act Establishing the Adirondack Forest Preserve (now called Adirondack State Park) in New York State.

Niagara Reservation created to protect Niagara Falls through the cooperative effort of New York State and the Canadian province of Ontario.

The Division of Economic Ornithology and Mammology (predecessor of the U.S. Biological Survey) established within the Department of Agriculture.

1886 Audubon Society founded by George Bird Grinnell.

Mission of the Division of Forestry is expanded and Bernhard E. Fernow is named division director.

1887 Boone and Crockett Club founded.

1891 Forest Reserve Act/Repeal of Timber Culture Acts authorizes President Benjamin Harrison to set aside 13 million acres in public domain as forest reserves (later to become national forests).

Animal Inspection Act.

Yosemite National Park established.

National Irrigation Congress organized.

1892	Sierra Club organized by John Muir.

1894   Carey Act distributes federal lands to various states on condition that they irrigate the land.

Controversial clause declaring Adirondack Park "forever wild" added to New York State Constitution

1895   American Scenic and Historic Preservation Society founded.

1896   Hawaiian koa finch becomes extinct.

1897   Forest Management Act defines purpose of forest reserves; amended in 1960 by Multiple Use Act.

1898   Cornell University offers first college-level course in forestry.

Gifford Pinchot becomes head of the Division of Forestry in U.S.D.A.

Wildlife Conservation International formed.

1899   Rivers and Harbors Appropriations Act bans discharge of wastes into navigable rivers and harbors without permission from U.S. Army Corps of Engineers; first federal antipollution law.

1900   Lacey Act forbids interstate shipment of game killed in violation of state laws.

William Orton breeds disease-resistant strains of cotton.

Society of American Foresters organized.

1902   Reclamation Act (Newlands Act) launches a federal land reclamation program, and mandates establishment of Reclamation Service (now Bureau of Reclamation) within the Department of the Interior.

1905   Transfer Act puts 86 million acres under domain of Forest Service.

National Audubon Society formed.

Responsibility for forest reserves transferred from the Department of the Interior to the Department of Agriculture's new Forest Service headed by Gifford Pinchot.

Pelican Island, Florida, set aside by President Theodore Roosevelt, with the goal of protecting brown pelican nesting sites, as first national wildlife refuge.

1906   Pure Food and Drug Act attempts to prevent adulteration and mislabeling of foods and drugs.

Antiquities Act allows areas of scientific or historical interest on federal land to be set aside as national monuments.

Meat Inspection Act requires inspection of meat-packing plants to eliminate unsanitary conditions; amended 1967 by Wholesome Meat Act.

1907   Inland Waterways Commission established.

Forest Reserve Act repealed.

1908	Grand Canyon named a national monument.
	Governors' Conference on Conservation convened by Theodore Roosevelt.
	National Conservation Commission appointed to inventory the nation's natural resources.
1909	North American Conservation Conference convened by Theodore Roosevelt.
	First national Conference on City Planning and Congestion.
	National Conservation Association formed as private organization, replacing National Conservation Commission.
	Boundary Waters Treaty between the United States and Canada addresses diversion of water from Lake Erie.
1909-1910	Controversy between Richard Ballinger and Gifford Pinchot disrupts federal conservation activities.
1910	Insecticide Act prohibits interstate transport of mislabeled and adulterated insecticides.
	Bureau of Mines established within the Department of the Interior.
1911	Weeks Act creates numerous national forests in the East.
	American Game Protective and Propagation Association established.
1913	Weeks-McClean Migratory Bird Act puts migratory birds under federal protection; first U.S. law to regulate hunting of migratory birds; replaced by 1918 Migratory Bird Treaty Act.
	Hetch Hetchy Valley in Yosemite National Park given to San Francisco for building a reservoir, ending John Muirled campaign to preserve the valley.
1914	Drinking Water Standards Act.
	Last passenger pigeon dies.
1915	Ecological Society of America founded.
1916	National Parks Service Act establishes National Parks Service to manage national parks.
	Migratory Bird Treaty between the United States and Great Britain (for Canada).
1918	Federal Migratory Bird Treaty Act implements 1916 U.S.-Canada treaty restricting the hunting of migratory birds.
	Last Carolina parakeet dies.
	Save-the-Redwoods League established.
1919	National Parks and Conservation Association established.
1920	Federal Power Commission established and Federal Water Power Act authorizes the Commission to issue licenses for developing hydropower on federal lands.

Mineral Leasing Act establishes regulations for mining on federal lands.

1922   Izaak Walton League of America founded.

Pennsylvania Coal Company v. Mahon et al. raises issue of the right of government to restrict use of private land without compensation to owners.

1924   Clarke-McNary Act extends power of federal government to purchase lands for national forest system and makes provision for private, state, and federal cooperation in forest management.

Oil Pollution Act prohibits dumping of oil in navigable waters except in dire emergencies.

Teapot Dome scandal.

Gila National Forest, New Mexico, designated as the first extensive wilderness area by the Forest Service.

1926   *Village of Euclid v. Ambler Realty Co.* establishes that local governments may enact zoning laws that limit the right to use private property.

1928   Boulder Canyon Project (Hoover Dam) authorized, with the goal of expanding flood control, irrigation, and electrification in western state.

Food, Drug, and Insecticide Administration created by Congress.

1933   Civilian Conservation Corps established.

Tennessee Valley Authority created.

Natural Resources Planning Board created.

Soil Erosion Service established as emergency measure.

1934   Taylor Grazing Act regulates grazing on federal lands.

1935   Soil Conservation and Domestic Allotment Act increases federal involvement in erosion control and mandates establishment of Soil Conservation Service (now Natural Resources and Conservation Service) within the Department of Agriculture.

General Wildlife Federation organized. Name changed to Wilderness Society the following year.

1936   Omnibus Flood Control Act.

National Wildlife Federation founded.

1937   Ducks Unlimited founded.

Pittman-Robertson Act promotes wildlife restoration.

1938   Food, Drug, and Cosmetics Act extends federal authority over misbranded foods, drugs, and cosmetics; amended 1958.

1940   U.S. Fish and Wildlife Service created.

Convention on Nature Protection and Wildlife Preservation in the Western Hemisphere.

1942 DDT introduced into United States.

1944 Soil Conservation Society of America founded.

1945 United States drops atomic bomb on Hiroshima, Japan.

1946 Federal Lands Management Act establishes U.S. Bureau of Land Management to consolidate administration of lands in the public domain.

International Convention for the Regulation of Whaling; amended 1956.

Atomic Energy Commission established.

1947 Federal Insecticide, Fungicide, and Rodenticide Act (FIFRA) attempts to protect consumers from fraudulent pesticide products; amended in 1972 to give greater focus to monitoring health and environmental consequences of pesticides.

Conservation Foundation organized.

Defenders of Wildlife organized.

Las Angeles Air Pollution Control District created. First air pollution agency in the United States.

1948 Federal Water Pollution Control Act (FWPA) authorizes Public Health Service to aid states in developing water pollution control programs and planning sewage treatment plants; amended 1972.

Heavy smog in Domorra, Pennsylvania, causes 20 deaths.

1949 First Sierra Club Biennial Wilderness Conference held.

National Trust for Historic Preservation chartered by congress.

Aldo Leopold publishes *A Sand County Almanac*.

1950 New Mexican grizzly bear becomes extinct.

1951 Nature Conservancy established.

1952 President's (Truman's) Materials Policy Commission issues report.

1953 Outer Continental Shelf Lands Act (Submerged Lands Act) asserts that the federal government has authority over the development of mineral resources in the outer continental shelf; amended 1990.

1954 International Convention for the Prevention of Pollution of the Sea by Oil; amended 1969.

1955 Federal Clean Air Act (FCAA) (Air Pollution Control Act) provides aid for state and local air quality control and research programs; amended 1963, 1965, 1970, 1977, 1990.

Resources for the Future formed to study U.S. resource use.

Symposium on Man's Role in Changing the Face of the Earth, inspired by Marsh's *Man and Nature* (published in 1864).

1956   Water Pollution Control Act creates water pollution control programs on interstate waterways.

Proposed Echo Park Dam, planned for construction in Dinosaur National Monument, deleted from Upper Colorado River Storage Project; marks a major victory for wilderness preservation.

M. King Hubbert predicts that U.S. oil production will peak in 1970s.

1957   Poultry Products Inspection Act makes poultry inspection mandatory; amended 1968.

1958   Food Additive Amendment (Delaney Clause) to 1938 Food, Drug, and Cosmetics Act prohibits approval of any additive "found to induce cancer in man or animal."

Outdoor Recreation Resources Review Commission appointed by Congress.

Space Act Creates National Aeronautics and Space Administration (NASA), one of whose priorities is the study of Earth's atmosphere.

Trout Unlimited formed.

Congress allocates funds for environmental health activities in the budget of the Department of Health, Education, and Welfare.

1959   St. Lawrence Seaway opened.

1960   Federal Hazardous Substances Act requires prominent labeling of hazardous workplace and household products and chemicals.

Multiple Use Act defines purposes for which national forests can be used.

1961   World Wildlife Fund-U.S. established.

Antarctic Treaty sets aside the continent for use "for peaceful purposes only" and provides a base for national groups to perform geophysical and biological research and freely exchange research data.

1962   Rachel Carson publishes *Silent Spring*.

White House Conference on Conservation hosted by John F. Kennedy.

1963   Clean Air Act, expanding on Clean Air Act of 1955, authorizes Department of Health, Education, and Welfare to establish clean air criteria; amended 1965.

Dispute between Arizona and California over allocation of Colorado River water.

Bureau of Outdoor Recreation established.

Nuclear Test Ban Treaty among the United States, the United Kingdom, and the Soviet Union.

1964   Land and Water Conservation Fund Act sets aside funding for local, state, and federal acquisition and development of land for parks and other open areas.

Wilderness Act establishes National Wilderness Preservation System, granting protected status to wilderness areas and excluding them from mining and timber cutting.

Surgeon General's Report, Smoking and Health, links smoking to increased mortality and identifies it as a contributing factor in several diseases.

1965   *Scenic Hudson Preservation Conference v. Federal Power Commission* establishes that environmental factors as well as economic factors must be given consideration in the planning of federal construction projects.

Highway Beautification Act bans many types of billboards from highways.

California Land Conservation Act (Williamson Act).

Water Quality Act gives the federal government power to enact water standards if state action is lacking.

Conference on Natural Beauty hosted by Lyndon Johnson.

1966   Clean Water Restoration Act expands and centralizes water pollution programs in Department of Interior; strengthens efforts in sewage treatment and water purification.

National Historic Preservation Act.

Clean Air Act Amendments extend research efforts to reduce vehicle emissions and establishes federal control over Air Quality Act establishes federal program of air pollution control criteria, standards development, and enforcement.

1967   Air Quality Act establishes federal program of air pollution control criteria, standards development, and enforcement.

Wholesale Meat Act expands and updates Meat Inspection Act of 1907.

Environmental Defense Fund established.

1968   Wild and Scenic Rivers Act identifies areas of scenic beauty for the purpose of setting them aside for recreation and preservation.

Aircraft Noise Abatement Act is the first federal effort to deal with health hazards of noise pollution.

National Trails System Act creates a national network of scenic, historic, and recreation trails; amended 2009.

Wholesome Poultry Products Act makes poultry inspection similar to updated meat inspection program.

California Air Resources Board created.

1969   National Environmental Policy Act (NEPA) creates the Council on Environmental Quality; requires environmental impact statements before major federal actions.

Oil spill near Santa Barbara, California.

Union of Concerned Scientists founded.

1970   Resource Recovery Act shifts focus of waste disposal from solid waste disposal to control, recovery, and recycling.

Occupational Safety and Health Act (OSHA) establishes federal program to set standards for and enforce workplace safety and health.

Clean Air Act Amendments; further amendments 1977, 1990.

Environmental Education Act ensures that teachers receive supplemental education in environmental issues; amended 1974.

National Oceanic and Atmospheric Administration established.

Environmental Protection Agency established.

Natural Resources Defense Council founded.

League of Conservation Voters formed

First Earth Day celebrated on April 22.

1971   Greenpeace founded.

International Convention on Wetlands of International Importance, Especially as Waterfowl Habitat (Ramsar Convention); protocol added in 1982.

1972   Federal Water Pollution Control Act Amendments (popularly known as the Clean Water Act [CWA]) forbids discharge of pollutants into navigable waters; further amendments 1977, 1987.

Marine Mammal Protection Act aims to protect and conserve marine mammals and to encourage international research; amended 1988.

Environmental Pesticide Control Act.

Coastal Zone Management Act.

Marine Protection, Research, and Sanctuaries Act (Ocean Dumping Act); amended 1977, 1988.

Federal Environmental Pesticide Control Act expands product registration, labeling, and environmental protection and expands monitoring of pesticide residues in food and water.

Noise Control Act.

Sierra Club v. Morton raises the issue of the rights of nature in a court of law.

Oregon passes first state bottle recycling law. Environmental Protection Agency bans interstate sales of DDT.

Great Lakes Water Quality Agreement between the United States and Canada; revised 1978; amended 1987.

United Nations Conference on the Human Environment held in Stockholm; marks the beginning of the United Nation Environmental Programme (UNEP) and of a global approach to environmental problems.

Convention on the Prevention of Marine Pollution by Dumping of Waste and Other Matter [London Dumping Convention (LDC)].

Convention on Biological Weapons bans germ warfare.

1973   Endangered Species Act; amended 1988.

Oil embargo by the Organization of Petroleum Exporting Countries.

International Convention for the Prevention of Pollution from Ships (MARPOL); annexes added 1978; amended 1985.

Convention on International Trade in Endangered Species of Wild Flora and Fauna (CITIES); amended 1979.

1974   Safe Drinking Water Act (SDWA) requires the Environmental Protection Agency to set national drinking water standards; amended 1986.

Energy Policy and Conservation Act establishes program to regulate auto fuel economy and set corporate average fuel economy (CAFE) standards for cars and light trucks; requires doubling of new passenger car efficiency to 27.5 miles/gal. by 1985; creates strategic petroleum reserves.

World Watch Institute founded.

1976   Toxic Substances Control Act (TSCA) authorizes EPA regulation of PCBs, asbestos, lead, and other toxic substances.

Resource Conservation and Recovery Act sets rules for disposal of solid waste and hazardous waste.

Fisheries Conservation and Management Act extends U.S. jurisdiction over marine fisheries resources to within 200 miles of coast and establishes regional fisheries councils made up of fishermen to regulate fishing activity.

Federal Land Policy and Management Act regulates lands adjacent to federal lands.

1977   Surface Mining Control and Reclamation Act (Strip-Mining Act).

Department of Energy formed.

1978   Outer Continental Shelf Lands Act imposes liability for oil pollution caused by offshore operations.

Chlorofluorocarbons banned from use in spray cans.

Community of Love Canal, near Niagara, New York, evacuated because of presence of toxic wastes.

California introduces first building code requiring energy efficiency.

1979   Toxic chemical dumping practices of the Hooker-Occidental Chemicals Plant in Lathrop, California, become a public issue.

Partial meltdown of nuclear reactor at Three Mile Island, near Harrisburg, Pennsylvania.

International Convention on Long-Range Transboundary Air Pollution (LRTAP) (Geneva Convention).

1980   Comprehensive Environmental Response, Compensation, and Liability Act (CERCLA) (Superfund Act) deals with the release of hazardous substances caused by spills or from abandoned dump sites and provides funds for cleanup of dump sites.

Energy Security Act, comprising seven acts: U.S. Synthetic Fuels Corporation Act, Biomass Energy and Alcohol Fuels Act, Renewable Energy Resources Act, Solar Energy and Energy Conservation Act, Solar Energy and Conservation Bank Act, Geothermal Energy Act, Ocean Thermal Energy Conversion Act.

Alaska National Interests Lands Act adds 103 million acres of park refuge and wilderness areas to U.S. protected land holdings.

Act to Prevent Pollution from Ships.

National Acid Precipitation Program begun.

Agency for Toxic Substances and Disease Registry established within the Public Health Service.

U.S.-Canada Memorandum of Intent on Transboundary Air Pollution.

1981   Coastal Barrier Resources Act.

1982   World Resources Institute established, with headquarters in Washington, D.C.

United Nations Convention on the Law of the Sea (UNCLOS) governing ocean use and the exploitation of ocean resources. Not ratified by U.S. Senate.

1983   Iowa Enacts nation's first renewable energy standard (RES).

1984   Resource Conservation and Recovery Act (RCRA) attempts to make provision for the safe treatment and disposal of hazardous waste. It is the major federal law regulating solid waste disposal by municipalities.

Toxic gas from a plant owned by Union Carbide, an American company, kills more than 2,000 people in Bhopal, India.

1985   Swampbuster Provision of the Food Security Act (Farm Bill) discourages farmers from using converted wetlands for food production.

Federal Conservation Reserve Program established to remove environmentally sensitive farmland from agricultural production.

United Nations Conference on Ozone Depletion held in Vienna.

Society for Conservation Biology founded.

Vienna Convention on Ozone Protection.

1986   Air Resources Board established in California.

Ronald Reagan reduces CAFE standard to 21-miles/gal.

1987   Water Quality Control Act.

Marine Plastic Pollution Research and Control Act (Annex V of International Convention for the Prevention of Pollution from Ships) prohibits dumping of plastics at sea.

Montreal Protocol on Substances That Deplete the Ozone.

1988   Ocean Dumping Ban Act (Title I of 1972 Marine Protection, Research and Sanctuaries Act) bans dumping of industrial waste and sewage sludge into ocean.

James Hansen's Senate testimony on global warming sparks controversy on the issue.

1989   *Exxon Valdez* oil spill leaks 35,000 tons of oil into Prince William Sound in Alaska.

Basel Convention on the Control of Transboundary Movements of Hazardous Wastes and Their Disposal. Not ratified by U.S. Senate.

1990   Oil Pollution Control Act defines liability for oil spills.

Clean Air Act Amendments.

1991   United Nations moratorium on large drift nets (General Assembly action).

1992   United Nations Framework Convention on Climate Change; Kyoto Protocol added in 1997.

United Nations Conference on Environment and Development held in Rio de Janeiro; it is the first "earth summit."

International Convention on Biological Diversity. Not ratified by U.S. Senate.

1993   Chemical Weapons Treaty.

U.S. Green Building Council founded.

1994   California Desert Protection Act.

1996   Sustainable Fisheries Act requires the nation's eight regional fishing councils to adopt plans for fishery restoration and impose quotas where necessary.

Antarctica Environmental Protection Act prohibits mining in Antarctica for at least fifty more years.

Comprehensive Nuclear Test Ban Treaty (CTBT).

1997	Kyoto Protocol on Climate Change, resulting from United Nations Conference on Global Change. Not ratified by U.S. Senate.
1998	Nick Steinberg develops hydraulic fracturing (fracking) technique for releasing oil from shale..
1999	Invasive Species Council established; brings together departments of Interior, Transportation, Agriculture, Commerce, and Defense and EPA to prevent and control invasive species.
	Seven species of Pacific salmon added to endangered species list, the largest regional group of species ever added to list simultaneously.
	Appeals court rules, in *American Trucking Association* v. *Environmental Protection Agency,* that standards for permissible levels of ozone and fine soot set by the EPA in 1997 are invalid because in setting those standards the EPA exceeded the powers granted to it under the Clean Air Act.
2000	Human genome sequence draft announced.
	U.S. Green Building Council establishes its Leadership in Energy and Environmental Design (LEED) Green Building Rating System.
2001	*Solid Waste Agency of Northern Cook County* v. *U.S. Army Corps of Engineers* determines that some types of wetlands previously viewed as covered by the Clean Water Act are excluded.
	58.5 million acres of national forest (one-third of nation's forest land) protected from new road building and commercial logging by executive order promulgated by Bill Clinton.
	Stockholm Convention on Persistent Organic Pollutants (POPs) phases out 12 long-lived pesticides and other chemicals, including DDT, PCBs, and dioxins. Not ratified by U.S. Senate.
2004	Mendocino County, California, bans genetically modified organisms from farms.
	Google Earth makes satellite imagery of the Earth available to public and provides bird's-eye view of nation's wildlands.
2005	Energy Policy Act provides tax incentives and loan guarantees for energy production of various types, including biofuels, and exempts oil and gas producers from certain provision of Safe Drinking Water Act of 1974/1986.
	Great Lakes–St. Lawrence River Basin Sustainable Water Resources Agreement restricts extraction of water from Great Lakes.
	National forest road-building ban (the Roadless Rule) of 2001 rescinded.
	Hurricane Katrina devastates coasts of Louisiana and Mississippi.
2006	Northwestern Hawaiian Islands National Monument, largest marine sanctuary in the world, is created.

2007   In *Massachusetts et al. v. Environmental Protection Agency et al.* Supreme Court rules that EPA must regulate carbon dioxide levels.

Energy Independence and Security Act amends EPA program and gives more authority to Department of Transportation to set rules.

CAFE standard raised to 35 mi/gal by 2020.

Arctic Sea ice reaches an all-time low.

350.org web platform starts operation as outgrowth of Step It Up campaign to demand action from Congress on climate change.

2008   California Green Building Standards Code published; first statewide green building standards.

2009   In *California et al. v. U.S. Department of Agriculture,* appeals court reinstates the Roadless Rule on 40 million acres of national forest.

U.S. Court of Appeals upholds 2006 decision in U.S. vs. Philip Morris that found the tobacco companies liable for having "engaged in and executed . . . a massive 50-year scheme to defraud the public, including consumers of cigarettes," and sets in motion the establishment of widespread smoking bans.

Omnibus Public Lands Management Act adds more than 2 million acres of wilderness to National Wilderness Preservation System.

2010   Deepwater Horizon-British Petroleum oil rig explosion in Gulf of Mexico results in largest oil spill in U.S. history.

Great Lakes Restoration Initiative launched to protect and restore the largest surface freshwater system in the world.

2011   Protests against Keystone XL Pipeline begin.

Fukishima Daichi Nuclear Reactor disaster results from earthquake.

2014   Huge chemical spill in Nitro, West Virginia.

Flint, Michigan, drinking water crisis begins, potentially exposing more than 100,000 residents to high levels of lead.

Hurricane Sandy, the second costliest hurricane in U.S. history, causes major damage in New York City.

2015   Paris Accords: U.S. agrees to reduce CO2 emissions by 26-28 percent below 2005 levels by 2025.

Hawaii enacts nation's first 100 percent RES goal (100 percent of state's energy will be renewable by 2025).

Clean Power Plan to combat anthropogenic climate change unveiled by EPA.

2016   EPA imposes new fuel economy standards on 18-wheelers, buses, delivery trucks and other heavy duty vehicles (which make up 5 percent of vehicles of vehicles on road but account for 20 percent of CO_2 emissions).

Catastrophic flooding in Louisiana.

Kigali Amendment to the Montreal Protocol aims to phase down the use of hydro-fluorocarbons (HFCs).

Dakota Access Pipeline protests begin.

2017   President Donald Trump approves completion of Keystone XL and Dakota Access Pipelines.

President Donald Trump withdraws from Paris Accords.

Appendix II: Major Conservation and Environmental Organizations

There are thousands of international, national, regional, statewide, and local environmental organizations. Some focus on a single issue in a particular area, such as land conservancy in just one part of a county, while others have a very broad scope of interest. Following is a brief list of some of the most influential national environmental organizations.

Appalachian Mountain Club

Founded 1876, the Appalachian Mountain Club promotes outdoors activities, including hiking, biking, camping, and canoeing, maintains trails, and advocates for conservation in the eastern United States, from Maine to the District of Columbia.

Clean Water Network
cwnheadquarters@cleanwaternetwork.org
www.cleanwaternetwork.org

Clean Water Network is a coalition of public interest organizations that works to encourage the implementation and strengthening of federal clean water and wetlands policy and law.

Defenders of Wildlife
defenders@mail.defenders.org
www.defenders.org

Defenders of Wildlife works to protect native wild animals and plants and their habitats.

Earth First!
greg7@earthfirst.org
www.earthfirst.org

Earth First! is a radical advocacy organization that uses a wide range of techniques from legal action to civil disobedience to protect the environment. Philosophically, it is aligned with the Deep Ecology Movement and has a biocentric view of the world.

Earthjustice Legal Defense Fund
info@earthjustice.org
www.earthjustice.org

The Earthjustice Legal Defense Fund is a public interest law firm that provides free legal representation to citizen groups working to protect wildlife, natural resources, and special places and to ensure the enforcement of environmental laws.

Environmental Defense Fund
www.edf.org

The Environmental Defense Fund strives to develop solutions to environmental problems based on sound science, economics, and the law. Its activities focus on land, water, and wildlife, global warming, oceans, and health.

Friends of the Earth

Friends of the Earth is an advocacy organization that lobbies for legislative change to further environmental justice.

Greenpeace U.S.A.

Greenpeace is a campaigning organization that uses peaceful protests to expose global environmental problems.

League of Conservation Voters
feedback@lcv.org
www.lcv.org

League of Conservation Voters works to find sound environmental policy solutions and to elect candidates who support such policies.

National Audubon Society
www.audubon.org

Founded in 1905, the National Audubon Society is a conglomerate of local chapters, state offices, and Audubon centers working to protect natural ecosystems with a special emphasis on birds. Formed from Audubon Society, which was founded in 1886.

National Coalition for Marine Conservation
www.savethefish.org

The National Coalition for Marine Conservation is the oldest American advocacy group devoted to promoting sustainable recreational and commercial fisheries in our oceans.

National Parks Conservation Association
npca@npca.org
www.npca.org

The National Parks Conservation Association watches over the nation's parks, working to protect and enhance them.

National Wildlife Federation
www.nwf.org

Founded in 1935, the National Wildlife Federation, through affiliates across the country, works to protect wildlife and wildlife habitats.

National Resources Defense Council
nrdcinfo@nrdc.org
www.nrdc.org

The National Resources Defense Council works to safeguard the natural systems on which the Earth's people, plants, and animals depend; to restore the integrity of air, land and water; and to defend endangered natural places.

The Nature Conservancy
www.nature.org

The Nature Conservancy protects sensitive land, rivers, and ocean sites through land purchase and environmental easements.

Oceana
info@oceana.org
www.oceana.org

Oceana focuses on ocean conservation and works to restore the oceans to their former levels of abundance.

People for the Ethical Treatment of Animals
www.peta.org

Peta is the largest animal rights organization in the world.

Rainforest Action Network
www.ran.org

Rainforest Action Network works for the protection of forests and challenges businesses whose profits come at the expense of the natural systems that support life.

Sierra Club
information@sierraclub.org
www.sierraclub.org

The Sierra Club protects wild places and natural communities.

350.org

Founded in 2008, 350.org promotes awareness of climate change and organizes mass public actions on issues such as fossil fuel divestment and oil pipelines.

Union of Concerned Scientists
www.ucsusa.org

The Union of Concerned Scientists is a science-based organization that combines independent research with citizen action. It aims to promote a safer, healthier environment by encouraging changes in government and corporate policy and environmentally friendly consumer choices.

The Wilderness Society
www.wilderness.org

The Wilderness Society focuses its efforts on protecting our nation's public lands, giving special attention to designated wilderness areas.

World Wildlife Fund—U.S.
Founded in 1961, the World Wildlife Fund.

Glossary

acid rain water in the atmosphere that, having picked up acids or acid-forming compounds (such as carbon dioxide) from the air, falls to the earth in the form of rain, snow, or sleet.

ambient temperature temperature of the air in the surrounding space.

anthropocentrism belief that human beings are the most important entities in the universe.

aquaculture the propagation and raising of aquatic species, including shellfish and fish, in a human-controlled environment.

barrier island ocean island that lies roughly parallel to the coast and acts as a protective barrier for the mainland against the ravages of the ocean.

biocentrism belief that all living things have an equal right to flourish and enjoy the benefits of their common environment.

biodegradable capable of being broken down into innocuous natural products through the action of living organisms.

biodiversity variation of the genetic material within a single species, of the totality of species within all taxonomic groupings, and of the landscapes and ecosystems within which these varied species exist.

biofuel liquid fuel that is synthesized by fermenting sugar or grain (such as corn).

biomass energy energy produced using plant materials and animal waste as a source of fuel.

biosphere the segment of the earth where life is found.

biota the totality of the flora and fauna found in a given area.

bison American species of buffalo.

brownfield land, usually a former industrial site, whose reuse, redevelopment, or expansion may be complicated by the presence of hazardous materials or contaminants.

cap and trade system of setting limits on power plant emissions and permitting companies whose emissions are below the set allowance to sell the excess emissions to other power plants.

carbon sink forest, deep ocean, or geological reservoir where carbon dioxide can be absorbed or sequestered away from the atmosphere.

channelization the deepening and straightening of streams and rivers to alter their flow and control flooding.

chlorofluorocarbons (CFCs) organic compounds, such as Freons, that contain chlorine, fluorine, and carbon atoms and, if they are gases, cause a depletion of atmospheric ozone when they are released into the air.

clear-cutting cutting all the trees within a segment of a forest.

climate change change in temperature or weather patterns (such as amount of rainfall) induced by human activity.

climatology study of weather conditions over a long period of time.

commons resources that do not belong to any individual or nation, such as clean air, migratory birds, and noncoastal ocean resources, as well as property held in common by a community or nation, such as park land, communal grazing lands, and community dump sites.

conservation natural resource management to prevent resource destruction, exploitation, and neglect.

DDT dichlorodiphenyltrichloroethane, a chlorinated hydrocarbon (hydrogen-carbon compound) once widely used as a pesticide.

desalination removal of dissolved salts from brackish or salty water to make the water usable for drinking or agriculture.

dioxin any of several synthetic heterocyclic hydrocarbon compounds that are very toxic and have frequently been used in making herbicides (weed killers).

drift net large fishing net designed to drift near the surface of the water and used by fishermen to trap fish or other marine animals.

ecology the study of the relationships among living things and between living things and their nonliving environment.

ecosphere segment of the universe inhabited by living things and where there is interaction among living things and between organisms and nonliving things.

ecosystem ecological community of organisms and their environment that functions as a unit.

endangered species species of wild flora or fauna whose numbers have been so reduced that it is in danger of becoming extinct.

energy usable power (such as heat or electricity) or the resources to produce usable power (such as coal, water, or sunlight).

entropy the increasing degradation of a society or system.

environment totality of biotic, chemical, and physical elements (including air, climate, living things, and nonliving things) that affect an organism or a community.

environmentalism advocacy of the conservation and maintenance of the natural environment and the limitation or reversal of human impact on it.

environmental justice environmental actions based on ethical, moral, and spiritual factors rather than on economic interest or personal preference.

estuary passageway at the lower part of a river where the sea tide meets the river.

ethanol ethyl alcohol made from corn, sugarcane or other plant material that can be used as a renewable fuel.

ethic value system that defines what is good and bad behavior and sets forth moral duties and obligations.

eutrophication process by which a body of water becomes very rich in dissolved nutrients (such as phosphates) either naturally or through pollution that promotes the growth of algae and other plant life that deplete the dissolved oxygen.

extractivism practice of trying to extract as much of a marketable natural resource as possible.

food chain the order of predation of organisms in which each uses the next, usually lower, member as a source of food.

food web the totality of interconnecting food chains in an ecosystem.

fossil fuels coal, natural gas, petroleum, and other natural hydrocarbon resources used as fuel.

fracking See **hydraulic fracturing.**

fuel economy standard set mileage per gallon of fuel required for cars and light trucks.

global warming climate change marked by a worldwide increase in average temperature.

greenhouse effect warming of the lower layers of the atmosphere and of the earth's surface as a result of the increase of carbon dioxide and other heat-trapping gases in the atmosphere.

greenhouse gases carbon dioxide, methane, and other gases that allow the sun's radiant energy to penetrate the earth's atmosphere and then prevent the resultant heat from escaping.

green movements wide-ranging social and political activities that focus on ecological issues.

Green Revolution the development and introduction of new varieties of grains, primarily wheat and rice, that were able to dramatically increase the per acre yield of these crops.

habitat place where an organism or group of organisms lives.

hybrid a plant or animal that is the offspring of parents of two different, but interbreedable, varieties, species, or genera.

hydraulic facturing (fracking) a drilling process that uses a mixture of water, sand, and chemicals injected deep into the earth at high pressure to blast through underground rock in order to extract natural gas and oil.

hydroelectric power electric power generated using flowing water as the source of energy.

insecticide any chemical used to destroy insects.

invasive species plant or animal introduced into an ecosystem where it multiplies rapidly and eventually reduces or replaces native specie populations.

landfill trash and garbage disposed of by dumping it on low-lying ground or burying it between layers of earth.

land reclamation the process of making wetlands and arid land suitable for human uses, including agriculture and the construction of buildings.

locavore someone who consumes primarily locally grown and prepared foods.

microenvironment the total ecosystem of a small area, such as a pond, a forest, or a field.

miner's canary bird or other living thing whose activity can be used to monitor the presence of an environmental hazard.

monoculture farming, including tree farming, that involves raising only one crop or one species of plant over a wide area.

moraine accumulated stone and earth that are carried and deposited by a glacier.

natural resource any material, either organic or inorganic, that is found in nature and is of use to humans.

natural selection the natural process by which those individuals or groups best suited to an environment survive and reproduce and those least able to adapt are eliminated.

organic farming farming that does not use synthetic pesticides or inorganic, manmade fertilizers.

organism any living thing, from a microbe to a tree to a human being.

ozone depletion destruction of the gaseous shield (ozone layer) that protects the earth from harmful radiation.

pollution the contamination of the air, land, or water with undesirable amounts of materials, such as wastes.

pcb (polychlorinated byphenal) organic chemical once widely used as a dielectric or coolant fluid

ppmv (parts per million by volume) a way of expressing the amount of a pollutant gas in a million volumes of air.

predation the killing and consuming of animals of other species as a primary means of obtaining food.

recycling processing materials for reuse.

renewable energy standard (RES) amount of energy required to be generated from renewable sources such as wind or solar.

renewable resources energy sources, such as wind and sun, that are not depleted as a result of use and living resources, such as plants and animals, that can be regenerated.

restoration ecology attempts to restore ecosystems to a natural state by eliminating introduced species and replacing them with species that at one time flourished in the region and by eliminating dams and other man-made structures.

runoff the portion of precipitation that drains off the surface rather than soaking into the ground.

shale fine-grained sedimentary rock that may contain rich deposits of petroleum or gas.

smog a heavy, dark fog that is the result of sunlight causing nitrogen oxides in the atmosphere to react photochemically with hydrocarbons and methane produced by vehicle, power plant, and factory emissions and fumes from volatile solvents.

slow food movement movement begun in Italy in 1986 by Carlo Petrini to preserve traditional and regional cuisine and promote locally grown and prepared foods.

strip mining mining in which power shovels, bulldozers, and other large machinery is used to remove huge chunks of the surface land.

surface water bodies of water, such as lakes, rivers, ponds and oceans, that are on the surface of the earth, as opposed to groundwater, which lies below the surface.

sustainable development economic development, ranging from farming to industrial activity, that encourages the conservation, maintenance, and renewal of natural resources.

synfuel (synthetic fuel) a gaseous or liquid fuel that is synthesized from a fossil fuel that is solid (such as coal) or part of a solid (such as oil shale or tar sands) or from the fermentation of sugar or grain.

tar sands naturally occurring combination of clay, sand, water, and bitumen (viscous oil) that can be mined. Also known as oil sands.

watershed region where numerous underground springs, small streams, and other small water courses deliver water to major rivers or large bodies of water, such as lakes and reservoirs.

wetlands swamps, marshes, bogs, tidal flats, permafrost, and other areas characterized by fluctuating levels of water and an abundance of plants such as spartina that require a great deal of water.

wilderness an area that, together with the living things on it, has been fundamentally undisturbed by human activity.

wildlife nonhuman living things that have not been domesticated.

Notes

Introduction

1. See Jane Lubchenko, "Entering the Century of the Environment: A New Social Contract for Science," *Science* 279 (January 23, 1998): 492.

2. *Critias by Plato; Translated by Benjamin Jowett; http://classics.mit.edu/Plato/criti*ias.html

3. Robert Famighetti, ed., *World Almanac and Book of Facts,* 1999 (Mahwah, NJ: Primedia, 1998), p. 590. Other sources estimate that the world population reached one billion between 1775 and 1800.

4. www.un.org/en/development/desa/population.

5. www.census.gov/population/population profile.

6. www.eia.gov/International energy consumption, updated Feb. 16, 2017.

7. www.eia.doe.gov/U.S. Energy Consumption by Energy Source.

8. www.ncdc.noaa.gov/oa/climate/globalwarming.

9. See, for example, Madeline Bodin, "Freeing the River," *Nature Conservancy,* Summer 2010, pp. 33-41.

10. Richard Kerr, "Ocean Acidification Unprecedented, Unsettling," *Science,* Vol. 328 (June 18, 2010): 1500-1.

11. Jocelyn C. Zuckerman, "Oil Barrens," *Audubon Magazine,* Fall 2016, pp. 24-31.

Part I

1. Most estimates for the first human migration across the Bering Strait range from about 11,000 to 14,000 years ago (from which time there is actual evidence of human settlement in both North and

South America). There is also some questionable evidence of humans living in South America as early as 50,000 years ago, but how these people came to the Americas is unknown.

2. At the time of the Lewis and Clark Expedition, it was estimated that the Indian population of the West was about 225,000 and that of the Great Plains was about 150,000. It seems reasonable to assume that, as a result of disease and warfare, the population had decreased by about one-third since the first contact between Europeans and Native Americans.

3. See Yoshiro Matsuoka et al., "A Single Domestication for Maize Shown by Multiclocus Microsatellite Genotyping," Proceedings of the National Academy of Sciences, Vol. 99, No. 9 (April 30, 2002), pp. 6080-84.

4. See St. Francis of Assisi, "The Song of Brother Sun and of All Creatures," in *St. Francis of Assisi: His Life and Writing as Recorded by His Contemporaries,* trans. Leo Sherley-Price (New York: Harper, 1960), pp. 161-62.

5. Thomas A. Bailey and David M. Kennedy, *The American Pageant,* 8th ed., Vol. 1, (Lexington, MA: Heath, 1987), p. 7. One of the earliest evaluations of the environmental impact of the European exploration and colonization of the Americas is to be found in Alfred W. Crosby, Jr., *The Columbian Exchange: Biological and Cultural Consequences of 1492* (Westport, CT: Greenwood Press, 1972).

6. "These old lands" was land that had been used by the Indians. It is believed that Squanto, who had been taken to England some years earlier and then returned to America on the ship with Smith and the Pilgrims, had learned about using fish for fertilizer during his stay in England.

7. Quoted in Marine Protection, Research, and Sanctuaries Act of 1972, P.L. 92-532, in *United States Statutes at Large,* Vol. 86 (Washington, D.C.: Government Printing Office, 1973), p. 4236.

8. John Reinhold Forster, Preface to Peter Kalm, *Travels into North America,* trans. by John Reinhold Forster, Vol. 1 (Warrington, England: William Eyres, 1772), pp. v-vi.

9. *Beowulf,* trans. Howell D. Chickering, Jr. (Garden City, NY: Anchor/Doubleday, 1977), p. 55.

10. www.AmPhilSoc.Org.

Part II

1. Richard A. Bartlett, *The New Country: A Social History of the American Frontier, 1776-1890* (New York: Oxford University Press, 1974), p. 239 states that John Quincy Adams "was the first President to manifest any real interest in conservation and was ahead of his time in comprehension of the problem." Actually, as a thrifty, prudent New Englander and former secretary of state, Adams understood shipbuilding prerogatives and was simply being realistic about the needs of the navy and the New England fishing industry. He considered it foolish to waste or to permit any other nation to usurp the United States' natural resources.

Part III

1. M. King Hubbert, "Nuclear Energy and the Fossil Fuels" Shell Development Company Publication No. 95 (Houston: Shell Development Company, Exploration and Production Research Division, 1956), p. 5.

2. J .J. Cosgrove, *History of Sanitation* (Pittsburgh: Standard Sanitary Manufacturing Co., 1909), p. 87.

3. See "Croton Aqueduct" and "Water," in Kenneth T. Jackson, ed., *The Encyclopedia of New York City* (New Haven, CT: Yale University Press, 1995), pp. 300-301, 1244-45.

4. Cosgrove, *History of Sanitation*, p. 88.

5. Haeckel, *Generelle Morphologie de Organismen*, trans. and quoted in Council of Learned Societies, *Dictionary of Scientific Biography*, Vol. 6 (New York: Scribner's, 1972), p. 8.

6. See Mark H. Brown, *The Plainsmen of the Yellowstone: A History of the Yellowstone Basin* (New York: Putnam's, 1961), pp. 188-94.

7. Now Section 1 of Article XIV 0f the New York State Constitution.

Part IV

1. U.S. Bureau of the Census, *Historical Statistics of the United States* (Washington, D.C.: Government Printing Office, 1975). The 1850 figures actually apply just to Massachusetts, the only state for which figures are available.

2. Foreword to Frederick J. Turner, *The Frontier in American History* (N.P.: Readex, 1966), p. v.

3. Gifford Pinchot, *The Adironack Spruce* (New York: The Critic, 1898), p. 110.

Part V

1. George Bird Grinnell and Charles Sheldon, eds., *Hunting and Conservation* (New Haven, CT: Yale University Press, 1925), p. vii.

2. Henry Beston, *The Outermost House* (New York: Henry Holt, 1992), p. 10.

3. U.S. Fish & Wildlife Service, "Birding in the United States: A Demographic and Economic Analysis," Addendum to *2011 National Survey of Fishing, Hunting and Wildlife-Associated Recreation*, Report 2011-1 (Arlington, VA: U.S. Fish & Wildlife Service, Division of Economics, December 2013), p. 4.

4. See, for example, the work of one of their chief researchers, Harold Barnett: Harold Barnett and Chandler Morse, *Scarcity and Growth: The Economics of Natural Resource Availability* (Baltimore: Johns Hopkins University Press, 1963). The Galbraith selection, Document 94, comes from another publication prepared by Resources for the Future.

5. See, for example, Donella H. Meadows et al., *The Limits to Growth: A Report for the Club of Rome's Project on the Predicament of Mankind* (New York: Universe Books, 1972).

6. See, for example, Colin A. Campbell and J.H. Laherre, "The End of Cheap Oil," *Scientific American*, March 1998, pp. 78-83, and Kenneth S. Deffeyes, *Hubbert's Peak: The Impending World Oil Shortage* (Princeton, NJ: Princeton University Press, 2001).

Part VI

1. Edwin Dale, Jr., "The Economics of Pollution," *New York Times Magazine*, April 19, 1970, pp. 27-29, 40, 42, 44, 46.

2. Lynn White, Jr., "The Historical Roots of Our Environmental Crisis," *Science* 155, no. 3767 (March 10, 1967): 1206.

3. After more than $100 million had been spent and the project was in its final stages, the Supreme Court ruled that the dam could not be completed because the operation of the dam would destroy the only known habitat of the snail darter. See *Tennessee Valley Authority v. Hill,* in *United States Reports, 1978,*Vol. 437 (Washington, D.C.: Government Printing Office, 1980), pp. 153-213.

4. John H. Cushman, Jr., with Evelyn Nieves, "In Colorado Resort Fires, Culprits Defy Easy Labels," *New York Times,* October 24, 1998, p. A11.

5. Daniel P. Beard, "Dams Aren't Forever," *New York Times,* October 6, 1997, p. A19.

Part VII

1. Quoted in Bill Hosakawa, "It Takes a Lot of Energy to Keep Up with Interior's Jim Watt," *Denver Post,* March 1, 1981, quoted in Lou Cannon, *Reagan* (New York: Putnam's 1982), p. 359.

2. Gary Lucier, Susan Pollack, and Agnes Perez, "Import Penetration in the U.S. Fruit and Vegetable Industry," *Vegetables and Specialties,* VGS-273 (Washington, D.C.: Economic Research Service/ USDA, November 1997), p. 16.

3. Mark Holt and Carl E. Behrens, "Nuclear Energy in the United States," Congressional Research Service, updated July 23, 2003, www.policyalmanac.org/environment/archive/nuclear_energy.

4. See Jane Lubchenko,"Entering the Century of the Environment: A New Social Contract for Science," *Science* 279 (January 23, 1998): 493.

5. Mark Sagoff, "Do We Consume Too Much?," *Atlantic Monthly,* June 1977, p. 16.

6. World Commission on Environment and Development, *Our Common Future* (New York: Oxford University Press, 1987); and *Agenda 21 Earth Summit: The United Nations Programme of Action from Rio* (New York: United Nations, 1992).

7. Arne Naess, "The Shallow and the Deep, Long-Range Ecology Movements," in George Sessions, ed., *Deep Ecology for the Twenty-first Century: Readings in the Philosophy of the New Environmentalism* (Boston: Shambala, 1995), p. 151.

8. U.S. Army Corps of Engineers, Report summarizing work done on the Kissimmee River, June 2010.

9. Edward O. Wilson, "Integrated Science and the Coming Century of the Environment," *Science* 279 (March 27, 1996): 2049.

10. Moustafa Tolba, "The Ozone Agreement—and Beyond," *Environmental Conservation* 14, no. 4 (1967): 287-90, quoted in Robert F. Fleagle, *Global Environmental Change: Interactions of Science, Policy and Politics in the United States* (Westport, CT: Praeger, 1994), p. 185.

11. U.S. Department of Health and Human Services, *Report on Black and Minority Health* (Washington, D.C.: U.S. Department of Health and Human Services, 1985), named for Health and Human Services secretary Margaret Heckler.

12. By 2005 nearly all of the approximately one thousand commercially produced EV-1's had been taken back from the people who had leased them, and had been crushed and shredded. A few survive in museums but have no ability to move. See the DVD *Who Killed the Electric Car* (Sony Pictures Classic Release, Electric Entertainment, 2006), written and directed by Chris Paine, and produced by Jessie Dexter.

13. Intergovernmental Panel on Climate Change, Working Group I, *Climate Change: The IPCC Scientific Assessment,* ed. J. T. Houghton, G. J. Jenkins, and J. J. Ephraums (Cambridge: Cambridge University Press, 1990).

14. Bill McKibben, "The Earth Does a Slow Burn," *New York Times,* May 3, 1997, p. 23

15. See, for example, the discussion in Theo Colborn, Dianne Dumanoski, and John Peterson Myers, *Our Stolen Future* (New York: Dutton, 1996), pp. 122-30, of Ana Soto and Carlos Sonnenschein's discovery of "hormone-disrupting chemicals where you would least expect them—in ubiquitous products considered benign and inert."

Part VIII

1. Frederic C. Rich, *Getting to Green: Saving Nature: A Bipartisan Solution* (New York: W.W. Norton, 2016), p. 55.

2. Mark Potok and Ryan Lenz, "Line in the Sand," *The Intelligence Report of the Southern Poverty Law Center* (June 13, 2016).

3. Sophia Huang and Kuo Huang, "Increased U.S. Imports of Fresh Fruits and Vegetables" (USDA, September 2007), p. 10. www.ers.usda.gov.

4. Lester Brown, "Why Ethanol Production Will Drive World Food Prices Even Higher in 2008," Earth Policy Institute, 2008. www.earthpolicy.org.

5. American Academy of Environmental Medicine, "Genetically ModifiedFoods" position paper, May 8, 2009, www.aaemonline.org/gmopost.html

6. Jeff Biggers, *Reckoning at Eagle Creek: The Secret Legacy of Coal in the Heartland* (New York: Nation Books/Perseus, 2010), p. 220.

7. Bill McKibben, *Eaarth: Making a Life on a Tough New Planet* (New York: Holt/Times Books, 2010), p. 177, 175.

8. www.thesolutionsproject.org/50 states.

Further Readings

Albright, Horace M. (as told to Robert Cahn). *The Birth of the National Park Service*. Salt Lake City: Howe Brothers, 1985.

Ambrose, Stephen E. *Undaunted Courage: Meriwether Lewis, Thomas Jefferson, and the Opening of the American West*. New York: Simon and Schuster, 1996.

Appleman, Philip, ed. *Thomas Robert Malthus: An Essay on the Principle of Population: Text, Sources, and Background, Criticism*. New York: W. W. Norton, 1976.

Bailey, Richard. *The End of Doom: Environmental Renewal in the Twenty-First Century*. New York: Thomas Dunn/St. Martin's Press, 2015.

Barnes, Peter. *Who Owns the Sky: Our Common Assets and the Future of Capitalism*. Washington, DC: Island Press, 2001.

Bartlett, Richard A. *The New Country: A Social History of the American Frontier, 1776-1890*. New York: Oxford University Press, 1974.

Beegel, Susan F., Susan Shillinglaw, and William N. Tiffney, Jr., eds. *Steinbeck and the Environment*. Tuscaloosa: University of Alabama Press, 1997.

Benedick, Richard. *Ozone Diplomacy: New Directions in Safeguarding the Planet*. Cambridge, MA: Harvard University Press, 1991.

Berry, Thomas. *The Dream of Earth*. San Francisco: Sierra Club Books, 1988.

Berry, Wendell. *Home Economics: Fourteen Essays*. San Francisco: North Point Press, 1987.

Billington, Ray Allan. *Land of Savagery, Land of Promise*. New York: W. W. Norton, 1986.

Blake, Nelson M. *Land into Water—Water into Land: A History of Water Management in Florida*. Tallahassee: University Presses of Florida, 1980.

Bowen, Mark. *Censoring Science: Inside the Political Attack on James Hansen and the Truth of Global Warming*. New York: Dutton, 2008.

Boyle, Robert H. *The Hudson River: A Natural and Unnatural History.* New York: W. W. Norton, 1979.

Brinkley, Douglas. *The Wilderness Warrior: Theodore Roosevelt and the Crusade for America.* New York: Harper/HarperCollins, 2009.

Brown, Harrison. *The Human Future Revisited: The World Predicament and Possible Solutions.* New York: W. W. Norton, 1978.

Brown, Lester R. *Plan B 4.0: Mobilizing to Save Civilization.* New York: W. W. Norton, 2009.

—*Who Will Feed China?* New York: W. W. Norton, 1995.

Buchanan, James M. *The Limits of Liberty: Between Anarchy and Leviathan.* Chicago: University of Chicago Press, 1975.

Burdick, Alan. *Out of Eden: An Odyssey of Ecological Invasion.* New York: Farrar Straus and Giroux, 2005.

Cahn, Robert. *Footprints on the Planet: A Search for an Environmental Ethic.* New York: Universe Books, 1978.

Caldecott, Helen. *Nuclear Power Is Not the Answer.* New York: New Press, 2006.

Carter, Luther K. *The Florida Experience: Land and Water Policy in a Growth State.* Baltimore: Johns Hopkins University Press, 1974.

Cohen, Michael P. *History of the Sierra Club, 1892-1970.* San Francisco: Sierra Club Books, 1988.

Colborn, Theo, Dianne Dumanoski, and John Peterson Myers, *Our Stolen Future.* New York: Dutton, 1996.

Coyle, David Cushman. *Conservation: An American Story of Conflict and Accomplishment.* New Brunswick, NJ: Rutgers University Press, 1957.

Cronon, William. *Nature's Metropolis: Chicago and the Great West.* New York: W. W. Norton, 1991.

—*Changes in the Land: Indians, Colonists and the Ecology of New England.* New York: Hill and Wang, 1983.

Crosby, Alfred S., Jr. *The Columbian Exchange: Biological and Cultural Consequences of 1492.* Westport, CT: Greenwood Press, 1972.

—*Ecological Imperialism: The Biological Expansion of Europe.* New York: Cambridge University Press, 1986,

Daily, Gretchen C., ed. *Nature's Services: Society's Dependence on Natural Ecosystems.* Washington, DC: Island Press, 1997.,

—and Katherine Ellison. *The New Economy of Nature: The Quest to Make Conservation Profitable.* Washington, DC: Island Press/Shearwater, 2002

Dale, Edwin, Jr. "The Economics of Pollution." *New York Times Magazine,* April 19, 1970, pp. 27-28, 40-46.

Daly, Herman. *Toward a Steady State Economy.* San Francisco: W. H. Freeman, 1973.

Darling, Jay N. *John Muir and His Legacy.* Boston: Little, Brown, 1981. Dean, Cornelia. *Against the Tide: The Battle for America's Beaches.* New York: Columbia University Press, 1999.

De Bry, Theodore. *Discovering the New World.* Ed. by Michael Alexander. New York: Harper and Row, 1976.

Deffeyes, Kenneth S. *Hubbert's Peak: The Impending World Oil Shortage.* Princeton: Princeton University Press, 2001.

de Steiguer, J .E. *Age of Environmentalism.* New York: McGraw-Hill, 1997.

Devall, Bill, and George Sessions. *Deep Ecology: Living as if Nature Mattered.* Salt Lake City: Gibbs Smith, 1985.

Diamond. Jared. *Collapse: How Societies Choose to Fall or Succeed.* New York: Viking/Penguin, 2005.

Dowie, Mark. *Losing Ground: American Environmentalism at the Close of the Twentieth Century.* Cambridge, MA: MIT Press, 1995.

Duncan, Dayton, and Ken Burns. *Lewis and Clark: The Journey of the Corps of Discovery.* New York: Knopf, 1997.

Dunlop, Riley, and Angela Mertig, eds. *American Environmentalism: The U.S. Environmental Movement 1970-1990.* Philadelphia: Taylor and Francis, 1992.

Engle, J. Ronald. *Sacred Sands: The Search for Community.* Middletown, CT: Wesleyan University Press, 1983.

Esterbrook. Gregg. *A Moment on Earth: The Coming of Age of Environmental Optimism.* Penguin, 1995.

Farrington, S. Kip, Jr. *The Ducks Came Back: The Story of Ducks Unlimited.* New York: Coward-McCann, 1945.

Fitzgerald, Joan. *Emerald Cities: Urban Sustainability and Economic Development.* New York: Oxford University Press, 2010.

Fleagle, Robert G. *Global Environmental Change: Interactions of Science, Policy, and Politics in the United States.* Westport, CT: Praeger, 1994.

Fox, Stephen R. *John Muir and His Legacy: The American Conservation Movement.* Boston: Little, Brown, 1981.

Franck, Irene, and David Brownstone. *The Green Encyclopedia.* New York: Prentice-Hall, 1992.

Friedman, Thomas. *Hot, Flat and Crowded: Why We Need a Green Revolution—and How It Can Renew America.* New York: Farrar, Straus and Giroux, 2008.

Fücks, Ralf. *Green Growth, Smart Growth: A New Approach to Economics, Innovation and the Environment.* Trans. From German by Rachel Harmon. New York: Athaneum, 2015.

Garrett, Laurie. *The Coming Plague: Newly Emerging Diseases in a World Out of Balance.* New York: Farrar, Straus and Giroux, 1994.

Geller, Lawrence D., ed. *Pilgrims in Eden: Conservation Policies at New Plymouth*. Wakefield, MA: Pride Publications, 1974.

Glickson, Artur. *The Ecological Basis of Planning*. Ed. by Lewis Mumford. The Hague: Nijhoff, 1971.

Goldberg, Paul. *Four Fish: The Future of the Last Wild Food*. New York: Penguin Press, 2010.

Goodstein, David. *Out of Gas: The End of the Age of Oil*. New York: W. W. Norton, 2004.

Gottlieb, Allan. *The Wise Use Agenda*. Bellevue, WA: Free Enterprise, 1989.

Gottlieb, Robert. *Forcing the Spring: The Transformation of the American Environmental Movement*. Washington, DC: Island Press, 1993.

—. *Reinventing Los Angeles: Nature and Community in the Global City*. Cambridge, MA: MIT Press, 2007.

Graham, Frank, Jr. *The Audubon Ark*. Austin: University of Texas Press, 1992.

Grinnell, George Bird. *The Passing of the Great West: Selected Papers of*

George Bird Grinnell. Ed. by John F. Reiger. New York: Winchester, 1972.

Grossman, Elizabeth. *High Tech Trash: Digital Devices, Hidden Toxics, and Human Health*. Washington, DC: Island Press/Shearwater Books, 2006.

Hawken, Paul. *The Ecology of Commerce: A Declaration of Sustainability*. New York: HarperCollins, 1993.

—Amory Lovins and L. Hunter Lovins. *Natural Capitalism: Creating the Next Industrial Revolution*. Boston: Little Brown, 1999.

Hays, Samuel P. *Beauty, Health, and Permanence: Environmental Politics in the United States, 1958-1985*. New York: Cambridge University Press, 1987.

Heinberg, Richard. *The Party's Over: Oil, War and the Fate of Industrial Societies*. Gabriel Island, BC, Canada: New Society, 2003.

Helvarg, David. *The War Against the Greens: The "Wise-Use" Movement, the New Right and Anti-environmental Violence*. San Francisco: Sierra Club Books, 1994.

Hofrichter, Richard, ed. *Reclaiming the Environmental Debate: The Politics of Health in a Toxic Culture*. Cambridge, MA: MIT Press, 2000.

Hunter, J. Robert. *Simple Things Won't Save the Earth*. Austin: University of Texas Press, 1997.

Kamen, David. *Song of the Dodo*. New York: Scribner's, 1996.

Keeble, John. *Out of the Channel: The Exxon Valdez Oil Spill in Prince William Sound*. New York: HarperCollins, 1991.

Kolbert, Elizabeth. *Field Notes from a Catastrophe*. New York: Bloomsbury, 2007.

Kaufman, Wallace. *No Turning Back: Dismantling the Fantasies of Environmental Thinking*. New York: Basic Books. 1994.

Kirby, David. *Animal Factory: The Looming Threat of Industrial Pig, Dairy, and Poultry Farms to Humans and the Environment.* New York: St. Martin's Press, 2010.

Lappe, Anna. *Diet for a Hot Planet: The Climate Crisis at the End of Your Fork and What You Can Do About It.* New York: Bloomsbury, 2010.

Lappe, Frances Moor. *Diet for a Small Planet.* New York: Random House/Ballantine, 1992.

Lear, Linda. *Rachel Carson: Witness for Nature.* New York: Holt, 1997. Leiss, William. *The Domination of Nature.* New York: Braziller, 1972. Levine, Adeline Gordon. *Love Canal: Science, Politics, and People.*

Lexington, MA: Lexington Books, 1982.

Linton, Ron. *Terracide.* Boston: Little, Brown, 1970.

List, Peter C. *Radical Environmentalism: Philosophy and Tactics.* Belmont, CA: Wadsworth. 1993.

Lopez, Barry. *Of Wolves and Men.* New York: Macmillan, 1978. McDonough, William, and Michael Braungart. *Cradle to Cradle: Remaking the Way We Make Things.* New York: North Point Press, 2002.

McHenry, Robert, and Charles Van Doren, eds. *A Documentary History of Conservation in America.* New York: Praeger, 1972.

McKibbon, Bill. *Eaarth: Making a Life on a Tough New Planet.* New York: Henry Holt/Times Books, 2010.

The End of Nature. New York: Anchor/Doubleday, 1989.

McPhee, John. *The Control of Nature.* New York: Farrar Straus Giroux, 1989.

Encounters with the Archdruid. New York: Noonday Press, 1971. Margolis, Howard. *Dealing with Risk: Why the Public and the Experts Disagree on Environmental Issues.* Chicago: University of Chicago Press, 1990.

Marx, Leo. *The Machine in the Garden: Technology and the Pastoral Idea in America.* New York: Oxford University Press, 1964.

Mazur, Laurie Ann, ed. *Beyond the Numbers: A Reader on Population, Consumption, and the Environment.* Washington, DC: Island Press, 1994.

Merchant, Carolyn. *Major Problems in American Environmental History.* Lexington, MA: Heath, 1993.

Miller, Henry. *The Frankenfood Myth: How Protest and Politics Threaten the Biotech Revolution.* Westport, CT: Praeger. 2004.

Morgan, Arthur E. *Dams and Other Disasters: A Century of the Army Corps of Engineers in Civil Work.* Boston: Porter Sargent, 1971.

Muir, John. *Our National Parks.* New York: AMS Press, 1970. Reprint of 1901 ed.

Nash, Roderick Frazier. *The Rights of Nature.* Madison: University of Wisconsin Press, 1989.

Wilderness and the American Mind, 3rd ed. New Haven: Yale University Press, 1982., ed. *Readings in the History of Conservation.* Reading, MA: Addison-Wesley, 1968.

Olmsted, Frederick Law, Jr., and Theodora Kimball, eds. *Frederick Law Olmsted: Landscape Architect, 1822-1903*. Bronx, NY: Benjamin Blom, 1970. Reprint of *Forty Years of Landscape Architecture: Being the Professional Papers of Frederick Law Olmsted, Senior* (1928).

Paul, Bill. *Future Energy: How the New Oil Industry Will Change People, Politics and Portfolios*. Hoboken, N.J.: John Wiley, 2007.

Petulla, Joseph M. *American Environmental History*, 2nd ed. Columbus, OH: Merrill, 1988.

Pielke, Roger, Jr. *The Climate Fix: What Scientists and Politicians Won't Tell you About Global Warming*. New York: Basic Books, 2010.

Pilkey, Orrin H. and Linda Pilkey. *Useless Arithmetic. Why Environmental Scientists Can't Predict the Future*. New York: Columbia University Press, 2007.

Platt, Rutherford H. *Land Use and Society: Geography, Law, and Public Policy*. Washington DC: Island Press, 1996.

Pollan, Michael. *The Omnivores Dilemma: The Secrets Behind What You Eat*. New York: Dial Press, 2009.

Pooley, Eric. *The Climate War: True Believers, Power Brokers, and the fight to Save the Earth*. New York: Hyperion, 2010.

Powell, John Wesley. *Selected Prose of John Wesley Powell*. Ed. by George Crossette. Boston: Godine, 1970.

Reich, Charles A. *The Greening of America: How the Youth Revolution Is Trying to Make America Livable*. New York: Random House, 1970.

Reiger, John F. *American Sportsmen and the Origins of Conservation*. New York: Winchester Press, 1975.

Repetto, Robert. *Wasting Assets: The Need for Natural Resources Accounting*. Washington, DC: World Resources Institute, 1989.

Rhodes, Richard. *The Making of the Atomic Bomb*. New York: Simon and Schuster, 1986.

Rich, Frederic C. *Getting to Green: Saving Nature: A Bipartisan Solution*. New York: W.W. Norton, 2016.

Roberts, Paul. *The End of Food*. New York: Houghton Mifflin, 2008. Rogers, Heather. *Gone Tomorrow: The Hidden Life of Garbage*. New York: New Press, 2005.

—. Green *Gone Wrong: How Our Economy Is Undermining the Environmental Revolution*. New York: Scribner, 2010.

Rogers, Marion Lane, ed. *Acorn Days: The Environmental Defense Fund and How It Grew*. New York: Environmental Defense Fund, 1990.

Roosevelt, Franklin D. *Franklin D. Roosevelt and Conservation, 1911-1945*. Ed. by Edgar B. Nixon. 2 vols. Hyde Park, NY: FDR Library, 1957.

Roosevelt, Theodore. *An Autobiography.* New York: Macmillan, 1914. Royte, Elizabeth. *Bottlemania: Big Business, Local Springs, and the Battle Over America's Drinking Water* .New York: Bloomsbury, 2009.

—*Garbage Land: On the Secret Trail of Trash.* New York: Little, Brown/Back Bay Books, 2005.

Rubin, Charles T. *The Green Crusade: Rethinking the Roots of Environmentalism.* New York: Free Press, 1994.

Rybczynski, Witold. *A Clearing in the Distance: Frederick Law Olmsted and America in the Nineteenth Century.* New York: Scribner's, 1999.

Safina, Carl. *Song for the Blue Ocean: Encounters along the World's Coasts and beneath the Sea.* New York: Holt, 1997.

Sagoff, Mark. "Do We Consume Too Much," *Atlantic Monthly,* June 1997, pp. 80-96.

Sale, Kirkpatrick. *The Green Revolution: The American Environmental Movement, 1962-1992.* New York: Hill and Wang, 1993.

Sanger, Marjory Bartlett. *Billy Bartram and His Green World: An Interpretive Biography.* New York: Farrar, Straus and Giroux, 1972. Schneider, Paul. *The Adirondacks.* New York: Henry Holt, 1997.

Sessions, George, ed. *Deep Ecology for the Twenty-First Century: Readings on the Philosophy of the New Environmentalism.* Boston: Shambala, 1995.

Shabecoff, Philip. *A Fierce Green Fire: The American Environmental Movement.* New York: Hill and Wang, 1993.

Shanks, Bernard. *This Land Is Your Land: The Struggle to Save America's Public Lands.* San Francisco: Sierra Club, 1982.

Shutkin, William A. *The Land That Could Be: Environmentalism and Democracy in the Twenty-First Century.* Cambridge, MA: MIT Press, 2000.

Simpson, R. David, Michael A. Toman, and Robert U. Ayres, eds.

Scarcity and Growth Revisited: Natural Resources and the Environment in the New Millennium. Washington, DC: Resources for the Future, 2005.

Sitarz, Dan, ed. *Sustainable America. America's Environment, Economy and Society in the 21st Century.* Carbondale, IL: Earth Press, 1998.

Speth, James. *Red Sky at Morning: America and the Crisis of the Global Environment.* New Haven, CT: Yale University Press, 2008.

Strong, Douglas H. *Dreamers and Defenders: American Conservationists.* Lincoln: University of Nebraska Press, 1971.

Strasser, Susan. *Waste and Want: A Social History of Trash.* New York: Holt/Metropolitan Books, 1999.

Thorne-Miller, Boyce, and John Catena. *The Living Ocean: Understanding and Protecting Marine Biodiversity.* Washington, DC: Island Press, 1991.

Tidwell, Mike. *The Ravaging Tide: Strange Weather, Future Katrinas, and the Coming Death of America's Coastal Cities.* New York: Free Press, 2006.

Tobey, Ronald C. *Saving the Prairies: The Life Cycle of the Founding School of American Plant Ecology, 1895-1955.* Berkeley: University of California Press, 1981.

Tokar, Brian. *The Green Alternative: Creating an Ecological Future.* San Pedro, CA: Miles, 1987.

U.S. Department of Health, Education and Welfare, *Health in America: 1776-1976.* Publication no. HRA 76-616. Washington, DC: Government Printing Office, 1976.

Ward, Barbara, and Rene Dubos. *Only One Earth: The Care and Maintenance of a Small Planet.* New York: W. W. Norton, 1972.

Warren, Louis S. *The Hunter's Game: Poachers and Conservationists in Twentieth-Century America.* New Haven, CT: Yale University Press, 1997.

Watkins, T. H. "Untrammeled by Man: The Making of the Wilderness Act of 1964." *Audubon,* November 1984, pp. 74-90.

Wilson, Edward O. *The Diversity of Life.* Cambridge, MA: Belknap Press, 1992.

—*The Future of Life.* New York: Knopf, 2002.

—*Naturalist.* New York: Warner Books, 1994.

World Commission on Environment and Development. *Our Common Future.* New York: Oxford University Press, 1987.

World Watch Institute. *State of the World 2010: Transforming Cultures from Consumerism to Sustainability.* New York: W.W. Norton, 2010.

Worster, Donald. *Nature's Economy: A History of Ecological Ideas.* New York: Cambridge University Press, 1977.

—*The Wealth of Nature: Environmental History and the Ecological Imagination.* Oxford: Oxford University Press, 1993.

Yergin, Daniel. *The Quest: Energy, Security, and the Remaking of the Modern World.* New York: Penguin Press, 2011

—*The Prize: The Epic Quest for Oil, Money and Power.* New York: Simon and Schuster, 1991.

Yudelson, Jerry. *The Green Building Revolution.* Washington, DC: Island Press, 2008.

Copyright Acknowledgments

Document 88: A SAND COUNTY ALMANAC: AND SKETCHES HERE AND THERE, SPECIAL COMMEMORATIVE EDITION by Aldo Leopold. Copyright 1949, 1977 by Oxford University Press, Inc. Used by permission of Oxford University Press, Inc.

Document 94: M. King Hubbert, "Nuclear Energy and the Fossil Fuels," in American Petroleum Institute Drilling and Petroleum Practice, *Proceedings of the Spring Meeting*, San Antonio, TX, 1956, abstract, p. 7, and Shell Development Company Publication No. 95 (Houston, TX: Shell Development Company, Exploration and Production Research Division, 1956), pp. 23-24, 26-27. Reprinted by permission.

Document 95: John Kenneth Galbraith, *"How Much Should a Country Consume?"* in Henry Jarrett, ed., *Perspectives on Conservation: Essays on America's Natural Resources*, pp. 98-99, © 1958. The Johns Hopkins University Press. Reprinted by permission.

Document 96: David Brower, *For Earth's Sake* (Salt Lake City: Peregrine Smith, 1990), courtesy of David Brower.

Document 98: Lorus J. Milne, PhD., and Margery Milne, Ph.D., *The Balance of Nature* (New York: Knopf, 1961), courtesy of Margery Milne, Ph.D.

Document 99: Lewis Herber (Murray Bookchin), *Our Synthetic Environment* (New York: Knopf, 1962), courtesy of Murray Bookchin.

Document 100: "A Fable for Tomorrow," SILENT SPRING by Rachel Carson. Copyright © 1962 by Rachel L. Carson. Copyright © renewed 1990 by Roger Christie. Reprinted by permission of Houghton Mifflin Company and Frances Collin, Trustee. All rights reserved.

Document 101: Stewart L. Udall, *The Quiet Crisis* (New York: Holt, Rinehart and Winston, 1963), courtesy of Stewart L. Udall.

Document 105: Kenneth E. Boulding, "The Economics of the Coming Spaceship Earth," in Henry Jarrett, ed., *Environmental Quality in a Growing Economy*, pp. 9-10, © 1966. The Johns Hopkins University Press. Reprinted by permission.

Document 106: Lynn White, Jr., "The Historical Roots of Our Environmental Crisis," *Science* 155, no. 3767 (March 10, 1967): 1206, 1207. Reprinted by permission.

Document 107: Paul R. Ehrlich, *The Population Bomb*, rev. ed. (Rivercity, MA: Rivercity Press, 1975; Ballantine Books, 1968), courtesy of Random House, Inc.

Document 108: Garrett Hardin, "The Tragedy of the Commons," *Science* 162, no. 1243 (December 13, 1968): 88, 89, 92. Reprinted by permission.

Document 109: John and Mildred Teal, *The Life and Death of a Salt Marsh* (New York: Ballantine Books, 1971), courtesy of John and Mildred Teal.

Document 110: Ian McHarg, *Design with Nature*, © 1969 by Ian McHarg. Reprinted by permission of John Wiley & Sons, Inc.

Document 114: Dennis Puleston, "Defending the Environment: A Case History," *Brookhaven Lecture Series*, No. 104, September 15, 1971, courtesy of Dennis Puleston.

Document 115: THE CLOSING CIRCLE by Barry Commoner. Copyright © 1971 by Barry Commoner. Reprinted by permission of Alfred A. Knopf, Inc. and Frances Collin, Literary Agent.

Document 138: Dixy Lee Ray with Lou Guzzo, *Trashing the Planet: How Science Can Help Us Deal with Acid Rain, Depletion of the Ozone, and Nuclear Waste (Among Other Things)* (New York: Regnery Publishing, Inc., 1990). Reprinted by permission of Regnery Publishing, Inc.

Document 140: Roger B. Smith, "Industry and the Environment: New Directions for the 90s," address to the National Press Club, Washington, D.C., April 18, 1990. GM Business Research Library, Detroit, MI. Reprinted by permission.

Document 142: John P. Holdren, "Energy in Transition," *Scientific American* 263, no. 3 (September 1990): 157, courtesy of *Scientific American.*.

Document 143: Barry Lopez, *The Rediscovery of North America* (New York: Vintage Books/Random House, 1992). Reprinted by permission of SLL/Sterling Lord Literistics, Inc. Copyright by Barry Hols-hun Lopez 1992.

Document 146: Donella H. Meadows, "Seeing the Population Issue Whole," *The Economist,* June 1993, in Laurie Ann Mazur, ed., *Beyond the Numbers* (Washington, D.C.: Island Press, 1994), pp. 24-32. Reprinted by permission of Island Press.

Document 147: Carl Safina, "The World's Imperiled Fish," *Scientific American* 273 (November 1995): 48-49. Printed by permission of *Scientific American.*

Document 148: Edward Tenner, *Why Things Bite Back: Technology and the Revenge of Unintended Consequences* (New York: Knopf, 1996), pp. 24-25, 72. Reprinted by permission.

Document 149: The Business Roundtable Environmental Task Force, *The Kyoto Protocol: A Gap Analysis* (June 1998), courtesy of The Business Roundtable.

Document 150: From THE BIOTECH CENTURY by Jeremy Rifkin. copyright © 1998 by Jeremy Rifkin. Used by permission of Jeremy P. Tarcher, an imprint of Penguin Group (USA) Inc.

Document 151: Norman Borlaug, "Ending World Hunger: The Promise of Biotechnology and the Threat of Antiscience," *Plant Physiology*, Vol. 124 (October 2000), pp. 487-490. Reprinted by permission of *Plant Physiology.*

Document 153: Bjorn Lomborg: *The Skeptical Environmentalist: Measuring the Real State of the World* (New York: Cambridge University Press), pp. 3. 348-50. Reprinted by permission.

Document 154: Charles W. Schmidt, "E-Junk Explosion," *Environmental Health Perspectives*, Vol. 110, No. 4 (April 2002), pp. 185-92. Reprinted by permssion.

Document 156: Michael Schallenberger and Ted Nordhaus, "The Death of Environmentalism: Global Warming in a Post-Environmental World." www.Breakthrough.org./pdf. Reprinted by permission of The Breakthrough Institute.

Document 157: Bruce Babbitt, *Cities in the Wilderness* (Washington, D.C.: Island Press, 2005), pp. 5-10. Reprinted by permission of Island Press.

Document 158: Myron Ebell, "An Update on Endangered Species Act Reform," in American Legislative Exchange Council, *Issues Analysis*, April 2005. www.cei.org/pdf. Reprinted by permission.

Document 160: Al Gore, *An Inconvenient Truth* (Emmaus, PA: Rodale, 2006), pp. 285-287. Reprinted by permission of Rodale Books.

Document 162: Jeff Biggers, *Washington Post*, March 2, 2008, p. B2. Reprinted by permission.

Document 164: Jared Diamond, "What's Your Consumption Rate?," *New York Times*, June 2, 2008, Section A, op ed page. www.nytimes.com/jared diamond what's your consumption rate. Reprinted by permission of *The New York Times*.

Document 165: Christine MacDonald, Green, Inc.: *An environmental Insider Reveals How a Good Cause Has Gone Bad* (Guilford, CT: Lyons Press, 2008), pp. 54-56. Reprinted by permission.

Document 166A: S. Richard Fedrizzi, Foreword to Jerry Yudelson, *The Green Building Revolution* (Washington, D.C.: Island Press, 2008), p. xv. Reprinted by permission of Island Press.

Document 168: Mark Bittman, *Food Matters: A Guide to Conscious Eating with More than 75 Recipes* (New York: Simon & Schuster, 2009), pp. 16-17. Reprinted by permission.

Document 169: Mark Z Jacobson and Mark A. Delucchi, "A Path to Sustainable Energy by 2030," *Scientific American,* Nov. 2009, pp 58-65. Reprinted by permission of *Scientific American*.

Document 170: John Wargo, Green Intelligence: Creating Environments that Protect Human Health New Haven, CT: Yale University Press, 2009), pp. xi–xv. Reprinted by permission of Yale University Press.

Document 171: Christopher B. Leinberger, "Here Comes the Neighborhood," The Atlantic, June 2010, pp. 59-61. Reprinted by permission of *The Atlantic Monthly*.

Document 172: www. Pennlive.com/midstate/index.sst/2010/06/gasland review documentary. Reprinted by permission.

Document 174A: The National Congress of American Indians Resolution #MKE-11-030 (Opposition to Construction of the Keystone XL Pipeline and Urging the U.S. to Reduce Reliance on Oil from Tar Sands and Instead, to Work towards Cleaner, Sustainable Energy Solutions) adopted by the General Assembly at the 2011 Mid-Year Session of the National Congress of American Indians, June 13-16, 2011. Reprinted by permission of Erin M. Weldon at NCAI.

Document 174B: https://www.thenation.com/article/bill-mckibben-naomi-klein-call-civil-disobedience-tar-sands/June 22, 2011. Reprinted by permission of *The Nation*.

Document 175: https://danietlyergin.com/inside-the-mind-of-global-energy-demand/cnbc 06.03.2013. Reprinted by permission of CNBC.

Document 176: Naomi Klein, *This Changes Everything: Capitalism vs. the Climate* (New York: Simon & Schuster, 2014), pp. 19-21. Reprinted by permission.

Document 177: Gil Gullickson, "@#$*% Weather! No, it's @#$*% climate change!" *Successful Farming,* Oct. 2014, pp. 35-36. Reprinted by permission of *Successful Farming*.

Document 178: www.nytimes/2014/11/05/opinion/why-sand-is-disappearing. Reprinted by permission of *The New York Times*.

Document 179: www.Slate.com/Dec. 2014/Ben Minteer, "Extinct Species Should Stay Extinct: Why We Shouldn't Depend upon Technology to Turn Back the Clock." Reprinted by permission of *Slate*.

Document 180: Static1.squarespace.com/An+Ecomodernist+Manifesto/pdf. Reprinted by permission.

Document 181: Union of Concerned Scientists, *The Climate Deception Dossiers: Internal Fossil Fuel Industry Memos Reveal Decades of Corporate Disinformation,* July 2015, pp. 48, 9-12, and 38. Reprinted by permission of Union of Concerned Scientists.

Document 182: From harpers.org/archive/2016/Richard Manning, "The Trouble with Iowa," Harper's, Feb. 2016. Reprinted by permission of *Harper's Magazine.*

Document 183: www.newyorker.com/magazine/2016/10/24/Greenland-Is-Melting, by Elizabeth Kolbert. Reprinted by permission of *The New Yorker.*

Index

E

N

O

S

V

W